Sophia Studies in Cross-cultural Philosophy of Traditions and Cultures

Volume 35

The Sophia Studies in Cross-cultural Philosophy of Traditions and Cultures focuses on the broader aspects of philosophy and traditional intellectual patterns of religion and cultures. The series encompasses global traditions, and critical treatments that draw from cognate disciplines, inclusive of feminist, postmodern, and postcolonial approaches. By global traditions we mean religions and cultures that go from Asia to the Middle East to Africa and the Americas, including indigenous traditions in places such as Oceania. Of course this does not leave out good and suitable work in Western traditions where the analytical or conceptual treatment engages Continental (European) or Cross-cultural traditions in addition to the Judeo-Christian tradition. The book series invites innovative scholarship that takes up newer challenges and makes original contributions to the field of knowledge in areas that have hitherto not received such dedicated treatment. For example, rather than rehearsing the same old Ontological Argument in the conventional way, the series would be interested in innovative ways of conceiving the erstwhile concerns while also bringing new sets of questions and responses, methodologically also from more imaginative and critical sources of thinking. Work going on in the forefront of the frontiers of science and religion beaconing a well-nuanced philosophical response that may even extend its boundaries beyond the confines of this debate in the West – e.g. from the perspective of the 'Third World' and the impact of this interface (or clash) on other cultures, their economy, sociality, and ecological challenges facing them – will be highly valued by readers of this series. All books to be published in this Series will be fully peer-reviewed before final acceptance.

Ralf Müller • George Wrisley

Editors

Dōgen's Texts

Manifesting Religion and/as Philosophy?

 Springer

Editors
Ralf Müller
Department of Philosophy
University College Cork
Cork, Ireland

George Wrisley
History, Anthropology, & Philosophy
University of North Georgia
Gainesville, GA, USA

Editor-in-Chief
Purushottama Bilimoria

ISSN 2211-1107   ISSN 2211-1115 (electronic)
Sophia Studies in Cross-cultural Philosophy of Traditions and Cultures
ISBN 978-3-031-42245-4   ISBN 978-3-031-42246-1 (eBook)
https://doi.org/10.1007/978-3-031-42246-1

I dedicate this anthology to
Ullrich Thiemann
my philosophy teacher at school and my
friend ever since then in 1990,
and Arifuku Kōgaku
my host and guide to reading Dōgen during
my first stay at Kyōto University in 1999.

Ralf Müller

And I dedicate it to
Hee-Jin Kim, Steven Heine, and Roger
T. Ames, all of whom made Dōgen a living
and ongoing possibility.

George Wrisley

Forewords: Dōgen 2.0

This is a book of Dōgen 2.0. Then what is Dōgen 2.0? Or who is Dōgen 2.0? Dōgen and his works, especially *Shōbōgenzō*, or Treasury of the True Dharma Eye, were first presented to Western scholars as a philosopher and his philosophical texts. Since then, he and his works have been discussed as one of the most prominent examples of premodern Japanese philosophy. Dōgen as philosopher, and his writings as philosophical texts. This is Dōgen 1.0.

The era of Dōgen 1.0 has produced remarkable philosophical interpretations of him and his texts in Western languages. Works of Garfield, Kasulis, Stambaugh, Heine, Olson, Raud, Müller, Davis, and Kopf are among them. In this period, the legitimacy of treating Dōgen as a philosopher, reading *Shōbōgenzō* as a philosophical text, and comparing it with other philosophical theories, or simply put, studying Dōgen as part of the study of Japanese *philosophy*, was considered unproblematic.

In recent years, however, such a Dōgen 1.0 has come under criticism: Dōgen specialists such as Kim, Steineck, and van der Braak have, in their own ways, begun to object to the idea that Dōgen was a "philosopher" in today's sense, that his texts were philosophical texts, and that philosophical interpretations could be given of them. (Van der Braak's chapter in this book provides a nice summary of what I have been writing.)

We do not take issue here with the rightness or wrongness of their criticisms. However, at the very least, these criticisms made it no longer self-evident that Dōgen can be treated as a philosopher and that his texts can be interpreted philosophically. Shortly, they made Dōgen 1.0 problematic.

Now new "in the first place" type of questions have emerged. Who was Dōgen in the first place? And how should we read his texts in the first place? These are more meta- or methodologically oriented questions than those in the Dōgen 1.0 era. The latter question also connects to the question, "How has Dōgen been read so far?" This question is not merely a retrospective one, but also pertains to the here and now question, "How should I read Dōgen now?"

Of course, the fact that the legitimacy of a philosophical reading has become problematic does not mean that it has become forbidden or dismissed as meaningless. It means that we are now forced to be aware of the non-self-evidence of the legitimacy of our philosophical approach to Dōgen's texts. We can no longer naively assume that the outcome of a philosophical reading matches the intentions of Dōgen himself, or the only correct interpretation of his texts.

But on the other hand, no privileged and self-evident alternative to the philosophical approach has appeared. For now, the identity of Dōgen itself has come under question. If Dōgen was not a "philosopher" in today's sense, then who was he? Was he a "religious figure" in today's sense? Or was he someone else who is neither a "philosopher" nor a "religious person" in today's sense? If so, what kind of someone else was he? Any answers to these questions are now no longer self-evident but are matters to be carefully discussed and subjected to critical examination.

No, the situation must, in fact, be more complex. For, as is the case with all human identities, Dōgen's identity may not have been so simple that it can be summarized in a single word. The same can be said of his texts. They may not allow for a unique characterization, whether of philosophy, religion, or a third category.

The upshot is that now the legitimacy of not only philosophical approaches to Dōgen and his texts, but all approaches have come to be no longer self-evident. There can no longer be, in principle, any self-evident and privileged approach, philosophical or otherwise.

This is the age of Dōgen 2.0. Dōgen 1.0 was the philosopher. Dōgen 2.0 has become a giant question mark. Dōgen as a question mark, the text of Dōgen as a question mark. This is exactly what Dōgen 2.0 is.

This book confronts squarely Dōgen as a question mark. On the one hand, it asks who Dōgen is, and on the other hand, it attempts to read his texts from various approaches and to reactivate them in the present intellectual milieu. In this sense, this book is clearly a landmark book that marks the beginning of the Dōgen 2.0 era.

Let us remember. "Who is Dōgen?" "How should we read his texts?" Is it possible to give a philosophical interpretation of those texts? Those methodological issues that mark the Dōgen 2.0 era had been actually already been taken by the first philosophical readers at the very beginning of the modern philosophical interpretation of Dōgen.

For example, Tetsurō Watsuji, a pioneer of the philosophical reading, began his "Dōgen: A Sramana" with a long and somewhat justificatory argument about the validity of his reading Dōgen philosophically. Hajime Tanabe, who followed Watsuji's initiative, also raised similar issues. Interestingly, both of them discussed the validity of their philosophical readings by taking up Dōgen's concept of "Dōtoku (perfect expression)". (Ralf Müller also provides an insightful discussion of "Dōtoku" in this book.) Watsuji and Tanabe used the concept of "Dōtoku" to justify their own philosophical readings of Dōgen's texts. However, there are also subtle differences lying between them that reflect the differences in their respective philosophical personalities. Watsuji acknowledged the residue of "irrational" and "religious" aspects in Dōgen's texts that cannot be reduced to philosophy, whereas

Tanabe held that everything in those texts can be rephrased into philosophy – which is, in fact, a projection of Tanabe's own philosophy.

In any case, the methodological question of "Who is Dōgen?", broadly construed, was a question that was raised at the starting point of the Dōgen interpretations given by academic researchers, as distinct from the interpretation of the patriarch by his sect members. In the sense of returning to the origin of academic Dōgen interpretation, Dōgen 2.0 is not merely an upgrade of Dōgen 1.0, but also an initialization of Dōgen 1.0, an attempt to return to the original point of Dōgen 0.0.

In the age of Dōgen 1.0, Dōgen was a mirror reflecting the face of the philosophical interpreter. As both Watsuji and Tanabe recognized, philosophical readers reflected their own philosophical faces in the mirror of Dōgen as a philosopher. And yet, in the era of Dōgen 2.0, when such self-projection has come under criticism, the situation has not fundamentally changed.

Even in the era of Dōgen 1.0, people were aware that the face reflected in the mirror was a self-projection of the viewer. However, the mirror itself, that is, Dōgen 1.0 as a philosopher, was not a product of self-projection, but was considered to exist strictly independent of the act of "looking in the mirror." In contrast, it is with the Dōgen 2.0 era that people begin to realize that the mirror itself, i.e., Dōgen, was also nothing more than a product of self-projection. Still, we cannot stop looking in the mirror. We can only continue to produce both the mirror and the face in the mirror at the same time through self-projection. Dōgen 2.0 as a giant question mark also continues to be a mirror reflecting our image.

Dōgen said, "Don't look in the mirror; rather, polish the mirror." He continued, "Polish the mirror, not to make it clean, but to polish yourself". Dōgen was trying to say that the mirror, or the true self or Buddhahood itself, is a product of one's practice, or rather, nothing but the act of practice itself. This could also be interpreted to mean that the mirror of Dōgen itself is the product of the act of interpretation, or rather, the act of interpretation itself. Needless to say, such an interpretation is also nothing but a self-projection of myself, the writer of this Foreword.

In the age of Dōgen 2.0, when not only the image in the mirror but also the mirror itself has become an object of interpretation, Dogen's interpretation will become even more diverse than before. This is clearly exemplified by this anthology. The diversity shown in this book is not limited to the diversity of approaches to and interpretations of Dōgen. The diversity of the philosophical and cultural backgrounds of the contributors of this anthology is also remarkable.

Dōgen also wrote, "[when] an Indian looks [in a mirror], the Indian appears [in it], then a Chinese looks, the Chinese appears" and "a Korean looks, the Korean appears, then a Japanese looks, the Japanese appears". By making this remark, he was already welcoming the diversity, transculturality, and pan-culturality of the people who participate in the joint activity of looking into or polishing the mirror or to realize the Buddha way. The transculturality and pan-culturality of the polishing collaboration of Dōgen as a mirror in this book is an extension of a similar spirit in

Dōgen. Watsuji, the founder of the modern philosophical interpretation mentioned above, also spoke of the possibility of the "globalization" of Dōgen. This book certainly pushes Dōgen's globalization a step further. The editors are to be congratulated for their labor in bringing together such a diverse array of contributors and furthering Dōgen's globalization.

Kyoto University   Yasuo Deguchi
Kyoto, Japan

Preface

The thirteenth-century Japanese Zen Master Eihei Dōgen founded a new school of Japanese Zen Buddhism (Sōtō Zen), when he returned from China and began expounding a unique form of the Chan Cáodòng School's form of Buddhism. This form is to be compared with the Rinzai and Ōbaku schools of Japanese Zen. Dōgen's Sōtō Zen is currently the largest of the three in Japan and has spread around the world, along with other forms of Buddhism and non-western religions. However, as with many cultural imports, it has taken some time for Buddhism in general to become the cultural force it has become in the west; that said, its influential presence continues to grow and spread, particularly in the academy.

Yet, again, despite the west's long engagement with non-western traditions, especially those from Asia, the scope and purview of Zen, and Dōgen's work in particular, has been and still is debated. English-speaking scholars *from a variety of disciplines*, for example, have weighed in on Dōgen's status since at least the 1970s with Hee-Jin Kim's seminal *Dōgen Kigen: Mystical Realist*[1] and in the 1980s with Steven Heine's important *Existential and Ontological Dimensions of Time In Heidegger and Dōgen*,[2] and William R. LaFleur's edited volume *Dōgen Studies*[3] standing out, as the latter brought together people such as Masao Abe, Thomas Kasulis, Hee-Jin Kim, Carl Bielefeldt, and John C. Maraldo. In this latter volume, the contributors focus on Dōgen's place in the academy, particularly his status as a philosopher. Nevertheless, despite works since then continuing to sporadically probe the question of Dōgen's status as Zen Master and/or philosopher, there is much still unsettled and more still to be said.

That there is still much to do is in no small part due to the nature of Dōgen's genius, as expressed in his writings and in the details of his vision of Zen practice. A vision whose rigor, complexity, subtlety, and creativeness are awe-inspiring.

---

[1] Reissued as Hee-Jin Kim, *Eihei Dōgen: Mystical Realist* (Somerville: Wisdom Publications, 2004).

[2] See Steven Heine *Existential and Ontological Dimensions of Time in Heidegger and Dōgen*, (Albany: SUNY Press, 1985).

[3] William R. LaFleur, ed., *Dōgen Studies* (Honolulu: University of Hawai'I Press, 1985).

Moreover, we would do well to keep in mind that the status of Buddhism itself in the west is still "in the making," to borrow a phrase Maraldo applies to philosophy.[4]

In this context, we find a good number of scholars happy to call Dōgen's work philosophical if not also claiming Dōgen is a philosopher in the full honorific sense. However, that is, of course, not to say that all such specialists agree that Dōgen is a philosopher – Raji Steineck's chapter in this volume is a case in point. As are the several chapters that find the choice *either philosopher or religious thinker* inadequate.

While the challenges of adjudicating the philosophical nature of a thirteenth-century Japanese Zen Master's texts and Zen are many, two issues in particular provide reason for care. First, "philosophy" and "religion" are Western categories. And we are far from being able to say without controversy that we can coherently analyse non-Western traditions like Buddhism based on these categories. A *possible* alternative is to view Buddhism, especially Dōgen's, as a hybrid form that is slippery to hold when using attributions such as "religion" and "philosophy." Secondly, the process of developing a system of categorisation from within and across the Buddhist tradition(s) that could be used to compare with, and to modify, Western taxonomies is only beginning.

Thus, there are a variety of complicating, if not confounding, factors to keep in mind when pursuing the question of Dōgen vis-à-vis philosophy and religion. Keeping these in mind could well be called a necessary prerequisite for working with Dōgen in Western scholarship. Often, however, these are not fully considered, and simple identities are claimed on Dōgen's behalf. Looking at the diversity of the contributions gathered here, we are convinced that the readers of this anthology will get both: a sense of identity and difference.

Against this background, our anthology shows that discussions between experts from different backgrounds are ongoing and fruitful. These interdisciplinary discussions are as fruitful as they are because primary sources from Dōgen and other Buddhists as well as secondary sources on almost all aspects of Buddhist teaching are abundant and available in multiple translations. Therefore, we hope that this volume will be of particular interest to experts in the fields of Philosophy, Religious studies, Buddhist studies, and Japanese studies, hoping it may serve as a springboard for further investigation in either, and all, direction(s). For doctoral students in these fields, the contributions provide both a case study and an opportunity to pursue the various ramifications of several central questions in comparative philosophy.

Cork, Ireland   Ralf Müller
Gainesville, GA, USA   George Wrisley

---

[4] See John Maraldo, "Defining Philosophy in the Making," in *Japanese Philosophy Abroad*, ed. James W. Heisig (Nagoya: Nanzan Institute for Religion and Culture, 2004).

Bibliography

Heine, Steven. *Existential and Ontological Dimensions of Time in Heidegger and Dōgen*. Albany: SUNY Press, 1985.

Kim, Hee-Jin. *Eihei Dōgen: Mystical Realist*. Somerville: Wisdom Publications, 2004.

LaFleur, William R., ed. *Dōgen Studies*. Honolulu: University of Hawai'I Press, 1985.

Maraldo, John. "Defining Philosophy in the Making," in *Japanese Philosophy Abroad*, ed. James W. Heisig. Nagoya: Nanzan Institute for Religion and Culture, 2004.

Acknowledgements

In my 2007 acknowledgements for my dissertation, I, George Wrisley, thanked my parents, writing, "I am grateful to my parents who neither flinched twelve years ago when I said I wanted to get a BA in philosophy, nor nine years ago when I said I wanted to get an MA, nor still six years ago when I said I wanted to get a PhD. They have always been steadfast in their love and support – I would not be who or where I am if it was not for them. They have made everything possible." It is now 14 years later, and I feel no less grateful to my parents, Linda and Allen Wrisley.

It was in January 2020, Steven Heine, Ralf Müller, and I presented at the Eastern APA's Society for Asian and Comparative Philosophy session. The first move in the series of moves leading to this co-edited volume on Dōgen and philosophy. A move that occurred a week after my mom's diagnosis of late-stage ovarian cancer, to which she would succumb in November, 2020. In the aftermath of her death, my dad developed a Covid-19 infection, leading to his death in January 2021. Thus, this book, from my perspective, is an accomplishment that resisted the bleakness of the Covid pandemic and my parents' deaths. Seeing now even more profoundly all they did to make this life of philosophy, study and teaching, possible, I once again wish to express the bottomless gratitude I have for this life and the relationship we had.

To my wife and "co-conspirator" in grappling with this often all-too-heavy life, Samantha Pinson Wrisley, a fellow philosopher and academic, I owe gratitude in a most profound sense, one that comes from a decade of mutual love and support through some of the most difficult years of our lives. I am grateful for the privilege of such a relationship and for the reciprocal love and respect found therein.

I am profoundly grateful to Steven Heine for his help and encouragement over the years since emailing him in 2013 to ask for his suggestions about learning how to read Dōgen's Japanese. Ever since, he has not hesitated to invite me to participate in conferences and workshops, nor has he flinched in the face of the many emails filled with questions that I've sent him over the years. As many others have noted, he is extra-ordinarily gracious with his time and support.

Since meeting Ralf Müller in January of 2020, I have been engaged in one Dōgen conference or workshop after the other, and soon after first meeting, we jumped at the opportunity to co-edit this volume. In this latter context, Ralf Müller has been extremely helpful and a source of encouragement and guidance.

I also want to thank Jeff Pardue who has been Chair of my department at the University of North Georgia since I changed campuses in 2017. He, along with the department and university more generally, have always been ready to do what was possible, and needed, to allow for my scholarship and travel. I have been fortunate to have their confidence and backing.

I am grateful to Roger T. Ames for his invitation in the fall of 2011 to join the 2012 University of Tokyo-University of Hawaii Summer Residential Institute in Comparative Philosophy, which led to my ongoing friendship with Rika Dunlap (a Dōgen scholar) and my presenting a paper on Dōgen and Wittgenstein at the University of Tokyo in December 2012. Professor Ames was always encouraging and supportive.

And I am grateful for the friendship and support of Rika Dunlap, whom I met at the 2012 Institute in Comparative Philosophy, and who has been an invaluable dialogue partner, discussing and exchanging ideas about, and papers on, Dōgen.

And to my close friend, Kristen Basinger, I am so very, very grateful for her support, encouragement, affirmation, and general cheering on; I and my mental health have benefited more than I can say.

I wish to thank the other contributors to this volume, and those of them especially who contributed to the Dōgen workshop in January 2021 that was so important to this volume coming together the way it did.

Lastly, I would like to thank Christopher Coughlin and the rest of the team of folks at Springer who made this volume possible, seeing it through and supporting it to the end.

There are likely to be those I have not named but who have formed part of the entwined vines of the conditions making my successes and opportunities possible. Thank you.

On my side, I, Ralf Müller, would like to thank my co-editor George Wrisley for his ongoing commitment to this book project, and his "yes" to editing "in spite of everything" (Viktor Frankl). Given all the challenges, impediments, and hindrances in our lives and over the past two or three years, we might wonder how and why we should engage in compiling words, pages, and books. While piles of books can appear as tombstones in a study left behind, to me, they are both nodes of living and condensed forms of life.

Hence, I am grateful to all our contributors who have invested their time to provide us with their viewpoints and rich ideas: Adam Loughnane, Aldo Tollini, Andrei Van der Braak, Eitan Bolokan, Felipe Cuervo, Laura Specker, Laurentiu Andrei, Raji Steineck, Rein Raud, Russell Guilbault, Steve Heine, Zuzana Kubovčáková.

I would also like to express my gratitude towards Steve Heine for his benevolent spirit, without which this book would not have come into existence. Among other things, he introduced me to Christopher Coughlin of Springer Publishing House. Christopher Coughlin, Sowmya Thodur, and more colleagues in India and worldwide worked carefully to have this book published.

Finally, I would like to thank all my family and friends that keep me in good company.

Let's hope peace in the Ukraine and elsewhere prevails long before we can open the cover of this printed book once it will be shipped to our desks from abroad.

Introduction: "Dōgen's Texts: Religion and/as Philosophy?"

Language has magical powers. We see this understanding reflected in most ancient cultures. Words can create things, bring them into existence. This is as true in the East as in the West. In *Genesis*, we read that God, in creating light, says: "Let there be light." With God being the only conscious entity, language use here is not dialogical. Instead, the case suggests that language has a performative and creative power. The opening of John's Gospel also points to the divinity, timelessness, and creative power of the word. Indeed, the Gospel tells us that the Word is God. Sources from India and China read in similar ways. The *beginning* of the cosmos is the Nameless, as stated in the Dao De Jing, but the Named is responsible for the universe's diversity. This layer of language is not lost in philosophical reflection. In the West, however, it holds only a secondary position.

In the forthcoming pages of the initial section (I. Thematic Foundation: Language in Philosophy) of this introduction, the theme of language in philosophy is addressed and the importance of this theme for Dōgen is expounded upon. This lays the groundwork for our collection of essays, which is summarised in the subsequent section (II. Book Overview: The Emergence of Dōgen as Philosopher). I will focus on a core theme that is presupposed by most contributions in this anthology, omitting broad definitions of philosophy and religion. Additionally, I will narrow my focus to Dōgen and the Zen tradition instead of attempting to provide an overview that covers Buddhism and world philosophy as a whole.

In the first section, I will proceed as follows: I begin by comparing the theme of language in the works of Dōgen and Plato. Then, I delve into the significance of language in Dōgen's reception in Japan. Finally, I demonstrate how Dōgen evolved into a philosopher in modern Japan. The emergence of Dōgen as a philosopher had led to ambiguities in his reception, providing scope for further investigation. On this basis, we can explore the full extent of our anthology and show how the ambiguity addressed in the various contributions remains a task to be tackled today. Even if most of the following papers support a philosophical reading of Dōgen, other voices are present such as André van der Braak's or Raji Steineck's.

I. Thematic Foundation: Language in Philosophy

In the early stages of development, almost all philosophical traditions deal with the nature of language. Language functions as the medium for philosophical expression. And any intellectual inquiry assumes, at a minimum, a rudimentary theory of the relationship between words and non-linguistic actuality. If not, such inquiry cannot truly be philosophical and will instead linger in a naïve position towards the world. However, different traditions reveal different basic options that have, in turn, been assessed in manifold ways. Nevertheless, any stance adopted concerning this connection has far-reaching consequences. A preliminary theory of language should be coherent and reflect some aspects of everyday language use.

1. Language East and West

Plato's *Cratylus* sets out one of the most seminal philosophies of language in the West. The dialogue profoundly delves into the essence and characteristics of language. Today, such a philosophical discussion would involve an analysis of words, meaning, and reference. What renders Cratylus a modern discussion is its focus on the relationship between names and their referents. The ancient dialogue's interlocutors also inquire about language's origin. Comprehending the relationship between a name and its meaning requires understanding its genesis, according to the dialogue. This also involves the religious dimension of language. Plato has Socrates play the role of an oracle here.

The transcendence of the primitive religious conception of language is also highlighted by Socrates' treatment of the thesis that the first naming is of divine origin. He mentions this thesis twice, once in conversation with Hermogenes (425d), and once with Cratylus (472c). In neither situation does he deny a divine origin or speak out against it. The religious view is less significant as its language origin is considered irrelevant, not false. Accordingly, Socrates points out that the thesis does not help him answer the questions he is concerned with. So Socrates can indeed be an oracle. He has – also – the potential to be a philosopher. In short, Plato has Socrates bracket the ancient religious view. It simply does not belong in the realm of philosophy. The divine, symbolic, evocative, and participatory aspects of language were left to religion. Philosophy's primary focus is reference, the correct naming of things. The approach taken by the Zen Buddhist Dōgen differs from this.

Considering the enormous conceptual and cultural distance, the comparison of the Zen Buddhist Dōgen with the Athenian philosopher Plato may seem far-fetched, for there is more than just a time gap of over 1500 years that underlines the difference between the two thinkers. Yet there are some similarities: Both are outstanding literary figures who developed their respective genres ingeniously within their own traditions. Both value poetic expression from an aesthetic point of view. They even see this poetic expression as indispensable to the path of knowledge. Yet both deny the value of literature and pursue goals that are predominantly non-literary. They even warn that literature can be dangerous. The similarities between Plato and Dōgen are not limited to their apparent ambivalence towards the written word. With regard to language, they deal with the same fundamental questions and, in some cases, resolve them in similar ways.

Concerning the nature of insight, however, they disagree. The question is how to achieve insight or understanding. For the Zen Buddhist, it requires meditation. The knower must devote special attention and sensitivity to the details of daily life. For the Greek philosopher, on the other hand, discernment requires refraining from everyday tasks and details. Instead, the focus is on intellectual dialogue and the contemplation of abstract concepts. Yet the starting point is again common to them: scepticism about the phenomenal world and the precision of natural language. Both warn against being deceived by appearances, even if they do so for partly different reasons. Natural language is a central part of that same phenomenal reality that calls for scepticism. Therefore, how do perceptual illusions weaken natural language? How do they entice individuals with insufficient insight to accept words at face value? Would the relation to language's origin help reserve different access to the original issue?

Dōgen's modernisation is controversial: The Zen master and founder of the Sōtō school in medieval Japan remains the most widely read pre-modern Japanese author in modern philosophy since the Meiji period. At the same time, however, his philosophical reception has been most severely criticised by his own denomination, the scholars of the Sōtō Zen community. Looking at Dōgen's texts, do they manifest philosophy *and* religion? Or philosophy *as* religion? Or rather, a philosophy *of* religion?

Controversy surrounding Dōgen's philosophical reception arose when non-denominational intellectuals alleged to have forged ahead with a genuine doctrine that could stand independently of the practice of "sitting only" (j. *shikan taza*), which was taught by the Sōtō school as the core of Dōgen's Zen. However, the resultant predominance of a "practical" interpretation of Dōgen tends to obfuscate the significance and linguistic complexity of Dōgen's writings.

2. The Appropriation of Dōgen in Modern Japan

In 1896, the miscellany *A Short Biography of the Great Teacher Jōyō* appeared in Japan in an issue of the world's first journal for the philosophy of East Asia.[1] This miscellany is the earliest article dedicated to the Zen Buddhist Dōgen (1200–1253)[2]

---

[1] The short text is not signed by name but quotes the Zen master Morita Goyū (1834–1915), the 64th head of the Eihei temple; cf. Anonymous, Jōyō Daishi no shoden [A Short Biography of Jōyō Daishi], in: *Tōyō Tetsugaku* 3/4 (1896): 205–206.

[2] Dōgen or with honorific Eihei Dōgen, as Bielefeldt notes (in the corresponding entry in Mircea Eliade (ed.), *The Encyclopedia of Religion*, vol. 2, 1995). The journal article cited above uses the posthumous (in the Meiji period) title Great Teacher Jōyō (j. Jōyō Daishi).

in a philosophical periodical. Nonetheless, it omits his writings' speculative, if not metaphysical, content. The article testifies to the lack of familiarity with Dōgen that prevailed in the Japanese intellectual world at the time, but also to a burgeoning curiosity and interest among non-confessional readers in Japan. Above all, the article indicates the introspection of an Asian intellectual tradition that looks beyond Europe, discovering origins of philosophy not only in India or China, but also in Japan. Subsequently, through the confrontation with Western philosophy and the reconstruction of autochthonous traditions, the foundation is established for a modern philosophical position that cannot be reduced to an extension of the Greco-Roman tradition or an imitation of Western modernity.

2.1 Dōgen as a Source of Philosophy

Historically, Western thought has displayed a strong interest in Oriental philology, as manifested in Germany, for example, in the translations of August Wilhelm Schlegel in the nineteenth century and the philosophical-historical treatises of Paul Deussen at the turn of the twentieth century; not to mention foundational works by other authors such as Abraham Hyacinthe Anquetil-Duperron (1731–1805) or Eugène Burnouf (1801–1852) in France, and William Dwight Whitney (1827–1894) in the United States. At the beginning of the twenty-first century, however, it remains a challenge to approach non-Western traditions *as* philosophy. This is the case with the writings of Dōgen, as is documented in the programmatic titles and meticulous commentaries of recent publications.[3] Such Western difficulties can be contrasted with the Japanese side, as exemplified by the Japanese philosopher Tanabe Hajime (1889–1862), who confronts the task head-on.

In contrast to the Western reluctance to approach non-European resources, which nowadays impacts the self-understanding of philosophy, Tanabe, as early as the year 1937, sought to reconstruct the thought of the medieval monk as the completion of a Buddhist dialectic and as the forerunner of postmodernism that surpasses the Western "ontology of being." Tanabe turns the scepticism of language prevalent in Zen into the foundation of a philosophical reading of the *Shōbōgenzō*, Dōgen's

---

[3] Cf. for example Steineck et al. (eds.), *Dōgen als Philosoph* (Wiesbaden: Harrassowitz 2002) where controversial approaches are discussed and tried out. Nakimovitch, in his *Dōgen et les paradoxes de la Bouddhéité* (Genève: Droz 1999), offers the most detailed commentary on the "Busshō" fascicle in a European language and shows what philological and hermeneutical efforts are necessary to enable a philosophically fruitful interpretation. There are, obviously, many secondary works to name that treat Dōgen in a nuanced way such as Kim's *Eihei Dōgen: Mystical Realist* (Boston: Wisdom Publications, 2004), and his *Dōgen on Meditation and Thinking: A Reflection on His View of Zen* (Albany, NY: SUNY Press, 2007), Steven Heine's *Existential and Ontological Dimensions of Time in Heidegger and Dōgen* (Albany, NY: SUNY Press, 1985), William R. LaFleur (ed.) *Dōgen Studies* (Honolulu: University of Hawaii Press 1985), and others. Most of these stake out room for Dōgen, the philosopher, in various ways, while the fruitful challenge Dōgen poses to philosophy is not widely discussed. It seems most of his readers stick to the option to either include or exclude Dōgen from philosophy.

main theoretical work. Tanabe further elaborates on his interpretation of Dōgen and the latter's concept of the perfect expression of truth (j. *dōtoku* 道得). Tanabe sums up Dōgen's thinking on language thus: "The entanglements [of language] are at the same time the perfect expression [of truth]."[4]

While the present anthology asks to what extent Dōgen's texts can at least also, or perhaps even excellently, be regarded as philosophy, many of the collected contributions give an implicit or explicit answer in their own way as to whether and in what sense "entanglements are at the same time perfect expressions." For Tanabe, the interpretation of this relationship (between entanglements and perfect expressions) is the central basic condition for reading the written work of a Zen Buddhist as philosophy, partly with and partly against tradition. Contrary to the widespread attitude that a mystically interpreted tradition (such as Zen Buddhism) rejects language, Tanabe sees in Dōgen's formulation an affirmative attitude towards language; affirmative, in fact, insofar as language is able to represent, if not partially constitute, the means, medium, and expression of the Buddhist path. In this way, there is a necessary and sufficient overlap with philosophy, which can also be understood as a path and form of life, and which also makes existential use of language and realises itself primarily in it.

Against this background, the anthology is concerned with the possibilities and limits of interpreting Dōgen's texts in their theoretical or speculative content, rather than as a propaedeutic introduction or practical instruction for monastic life. The initial question "whether Dōgen's texts manifest religion and/as philosophy?" aims at the discursive content of the texts, at the form of the text as an end in itself on the path of Buddhist practice. This question is not only of interest from a global philosophical or Dōgenian perspective, since the discussion on/of/with Dōgen renews a confrontation between philosophy and Buddhism in general, which is reminiscent of Arthur Schopenhauer (1788–1860). While many people were working on Buddhism, Schopenhauer was among the few philosophers to discuss it in the context of *philosophy*.

2.2 "De-linguification" of Zen?

Zen Buddhism has been seen as a religion that is compatible with the modern hard sciences. At the same time, Zen represents a religious practice that is based on an originally mystical and rationally irreconcilable dimension. Indeed, the Zen tradition radically renounces written tradition and uses the spoken word primarily to undermine and withdraw the power of language. How, then, could speech or script be the "perfect expression of truth"? Why should Buddhism rely on texts? And how could philosophy depend on practice in order to attain knowledge? When confronted with Buddhism, there arises the question of whether and how philosophy emerged from the detachment of myth and religion or whether it can also exist in a

---

[4]THZ 8: 17; j. *kattō ha sunawachi dōtoku nari* 葛藤は即ち道得なり.

quasi-hybrid form, as it seems to be with parts of the Buddhist tradition. Can Buddhism offer a definitive method for attaining a rational perspective on the world?

We know of quietly meditating monks and enigmatic masters; in Zen, people are silent; they speak only to fall silent again. According to Jens Schlieter, Zen Buddhism marks the culmination of Indo-Chinese language thinking, which displays a proclivity towards "de-linguification."[5] As per this view, the texts of a Zen Buddhist could not say anything significant as the essence of Zen lies in the experience of enlightenment achieved solely through religious practice. And even if this experience found adequate expression in language as an articulated experience, only an enlightened individual could measure it and understand it in its depth. All this seems reason enough to deny the *Shōbōgenzō* the label of philosophy and not attribute any intrinsic relevance to the use of language.

However, Tanabe's approach to Dōgen, which involves a philosophical reconstruction of his work from the monk's reflections on language, places the *Shōbōgenzō* diametrically opposite to the attitude to Zen just described. Tanabe's approach – largely unknown in the West and little discussed in Japan – appears like the precursor of the post-war period in which the importance of language and writing in the *Shōbōgenzō* is emphasised even more clearly, especially by Japanese thinkers who have dealt with the diversity of Buddhist scriptures and with the different traditions of East Asia from Buddhism to Hinduism and Taoism.[6] Recognising the significance

---

[5] Schlieter, *Versprachlichung – Entsprachlichung: Untersuchungen zum philosophischen Stellenwert der Sprache im europäischen und buddhistischen Denken* (Köln: edition chōra 2000). He appropriates the term "Entsprachlichung," in order to use it (correlative to "Versprachlichung," i.e., to render into language) as a designation for a very reflexive relationship to language in Buddhism: In the Buddhist tradition, "training through concentration and meditation is explicitly described as a withdrawal of linguistic thinking, i.e., as an attempt to break through the categorically mediated one-to-one opposition of language and world, subject and object, experiencer and experienced, or thinker and thought. [...] Accordingly, we should speak of 'correspondence' where the withdrawal of language is visible, but at the same time accompanied by corresponding discussions about the structure and effect of language" (Ibid., 14–15). The fact that Buddhist thought is about a movement towards a limit, but by no means about a total standstill of verbal articulation, becomes clear from the complementarity: "'De-linguification' obviously presupposes 'linguification'" (Ibid., 15).

[6] As an example, in his book *Toward a Philosophy of Zen Buddhism* (Teheran: Imperial Iranian Academy of Philosophy 1977), Izutsu Toshihiko states: "[Dōgen's] major work Shōbōgenzō is a record of deep reflection on matters pertaining to Man and the world from the Zen point of view. Besides, it is perhaps the most philosophical work ever written by a Zen master, whether in China or Japan" (Ibid., 58, fn 3). – In contrast to Tanabe, freed from the claim to establish a Japanese philosophy, the importance of Dōgen's works is emphasised here and elsewhere not only within the canon of Buddhist and Zen Buddhist writings of China as well as Japan, but beyond that, their position in contemporary global thought is also inquired into. The uniqueness of the Shōbōgenzō begins at the level of linguistic expression in idiosyncratic Japanese but continues through philosophical reflection in general to language reflection as such. It is the coining of the term "perfect expression" (*dōtoku*) that marks language reflection and forces the remarks to be taken seriously as theoretical reflections. The subsequent question of the positive position of language in Zen is taken up by Japanese authors, each with a different emphasis. For example, in a conversation between Karaki Junzō and two other scholars of Japanese intellectual history: "The character *dō* (way) of the words *dōtoku* [perfect expression] and *dōjaku* [uttering] [in Dōgen's *Shōbōgenzō*] is

of Dōgen in this context contrasts greatly with considering his work as a representation of a once flourishing religious tradition (i.e. Buddhism) now in a state of attrition, as was the perception at the start of the 20th century in Europe.[7]

3. Language in the Works of Dōgen

Reviewing Dōgen's language thinking in depth and detail, as undertaken in this volume's appendix essay, "Two Types of Language in Dōgen's *Shōbōgenzō*," reinforces the approach taken by most, if not all of the contributing authors in our anthology: reading Dōgen's texts as philosophy. While all of the contributors agree that the *Shōbōgenzō* serves both as a religious *and* philosophical text, some authors question the idea of manifesting a religious writing *as* a philosophical text. At present, it is difficult to reach a definitive conclusion the extent Dōgen's influence on philosophy. This is because both his factual impact and the need to reexamine Western categorization, which is based on Graeco-Roman concepts such as "religion" and "philosophy", remain to be determined.

What is the underlying understanding of text and language behind the statement that "the entanglements [of language] are at the same time the perfect expression [of truth],"[8] and what critique of language does this understanding encompass? In the *Shōbōgenzō*, what does Dōgen explain and what does he consider articulated? How does the spoken or written word relate to what is inarticulate or inarticulable? What remains unsaid in linguistic expression? Does perfect expression pertain to a prelinguistic realm accessible only to the Zen master in mystical immersion? Is the purpose to point towards the ineffable?

As a first step towards addressing such questions, let us expand our scope to examine Dōgen's perspective on language in works other than the *Shōbōgenzō*, and how he situates himself within the Zen tradition. We will demonstrate the centrality of language, including the Japanese vernacular, to Dōgen's intellectual pursuits. This is evident even before introducing a crucial language difference that relates to the traditional distinction of the two truths in Buddhism.

---

used with the meaning of 'to say.' It is as though there were a passion to speak in words of that which transcends words. This is my feeling. Yet if one were to fall back into the Zen saying, 'not relying on words or letters,' and let it all go, then one could have an end of it. I feel that the special character of Dōgen's Zen lies in these words, *dōtoku* and *dōjaku*. It seems to me that if 'doing only zazen' were the point, then without writing ninety-five fascicles, 'Do zazen' would have been enough. In spite of this there is a determination to explain completely and logically why it is necessary to do zazen. Isn't Shōbōgenzō a book of great singularity?" See Karaki et al., "Japanese Zen. A Symposium," in *Eastern Buddhist* 10/2 (1977): 80–81; KZ IV: 376)

[7] See Heiler, *Die buddhistische Versenkung: Eine religionsgeschichtliche Untersuchung* (München: Reinhardt 1918).

[8] See fn. 4.

3.1 Dōgen and the Tradition

As a Zen Buddhist, Dōgen's place in his tradition is ambiguous. The Zen tradition is rich in writings, and known for its elaborate practice of textual "riddles" – called *kōans* – which seem to indicate a positive attitude to language *ad absurdum*. Nevertheless, inherent in Dōgen is a critique of *kōan* practice and the traditional self-conception of a "a special tradition [of teaching] outside scholasticism, independent of characters" (j. *furyū monji, kyōge betsuden*).[9] This motto refers to the founding myth of the Zen school with its vivid imagery, according to which only one disciple from an infinite crowd of followers understood the actual message of the awakened one during a sermon by the Buddha on Vulture Peak: The (seemingly) wordless understanding between them is symbolised in Mahākaśyapa's smile when he sees the Buddha hold up a flower and twirl it between his thumb and forefinger. It is the mutual acknowledgement in the silent gesture that seems to point to an intuitive and entirely language-free moment of experience. The mutual acknowledgement also appears to confirm that the critique of language in Zen presupposes the ineffable.[10]

However, in the Mahāyāna Buddhist Indian texts, some statements challenge the negative attitude towards language.[11] Chinese Zen demonstrates further complexity as a continuous narrative emerges from the aforementioned founding myth of the Buddha's teachings: the narrative of a special transmission of the Buddhist teaching outside the scriptures. And a specific language practice evolved: In *kōans*, the narrative of the language-independent transmission becomes a practical question in which the primal scene of Vulture Peak is actualised. The myth also prompts a reflection on language in the medium of language itself as is evident from various *kōan* texts. In this line, Dōgen as the founder of the Japanese tradition of Sōtō Zen demonstrates how a single expression can initiate a reinterpretation of the tradition. He attains enlightenment at the instant when his master, who, despite his old age, practices *zazen* with his students until late at night, scolds a monk for dozing off.

---

[9] This thesis is already attributed to Bodhidharma, the Chinese founder of Zen, although the oldest textual evidence of this idea is found centuries later. See Döll, *Im Osten des Meeres: chinesische Emigrantenmönche und die frühen Institutionen des japanischen Zen-Buddhismus* (Stuttgart: Steiner 2010), 20.

[10] In this way, the school of Zen radically follows on from the well-known silence of the Buddha, which, especially in the Western interpretation of Mahāyāna Buddhism, establishes an ideology in which an entirely "different" way of thinking is projected onto the "smiling East." The different interpretations of the Buddha's silence are summarised in Schlieter, *Versprachlichung – Entsprachlichung: Untersuchungen zum philosophischen Stellenwert der Sprache im europäischen und buddhistischen Denken* (Köln: edition chōra 2000).

[11] Cf. the reference to the criticism of the silence of Vimalakirti in Hori "Kōan and Kenshō in the Rinzai Zen Curriculum" in *The Kōan: texts and contexts in Zen Buddhism*. Ed. by St. Heine and D. S. Wright (New York: Oxford University Press 2000), 297. He refers to two passages from the *Vimalakirti Sutra* which he parallels, although one refers to the "thundering silence" of the wise Vimalakirti, while the argument for linguistic articulation is directed against Sariputra, who says nothing out of nescience. On the *Vimalakirti Sutra* see Thurman, *The holy teaching of Vimalakirti: a Mahayana scripture* (Delhi: Motilal Banarsidass Publications 1991), especially 59 and 77.

Dōgen devises a term for this very moment in his master's spontaneous utterance: "casting off of body and heart" (j. *shinjin datsuraku*).[12] As a means of expressing his enlightenment experience, the phrase serves Dōgen in two ways: on the one hand, he founds his teaching of "sitting only" (j. *shikan taza*), i.e., the strict practice of *zazen*, on it, but at the same time he begins to appropriate instantaneous immersion as a specific experience. Dōgen's writings reflect both the process and outcome of this development.

3.2 A Positive Attitude Towards Language

Dōgen reflects on the early stages of his path against this backdrop of having given voice to something that is only realised in connection with practice. Initially, his understanding of the Zen tradition remained superficial, which is why he writes at the very beginning of the "Notes" about his motive for going to China: "He [Dōgen] wandered in vain through the territory of names and forms [*myōsō*]" (DZZ 7: 2).

In this context, the term "names and forms" pertains to Zen's sceptical attitude towards language. To wander in vain through the territory of names and forms means to delve into theoretical discussions that appear useless, particularly when they are decoupled from the practical concerns of the religious path. Zen distrusts language to mediate reality on the practitioner's path to nirvana, given that it understands language as not correlating with the experience of reality. For Dōgen, however, this does not mean rejecting language altogether. Rather, we ought to reflect on its form and make appropriate and, to a large extent, rational use of it. Hence, Dōgen succeeds in penetrating the "true meaning" of Zen teachings when, in going to China, he learns about a new interpretation of the Buddha's practice.

In China, he meets – according to tradition – a master who not only distinguishes himself as a personality and demonstrates exceptional discipline in the practice of *zazen* despite his old age. Furthermore, the master coins an inventive term for enlightenment based on meditation – the core of Buddhist teaching from the Zen point of view. Although Dōgen discovers the answer to his question during enlightenment, he cannot avoid confronting tradition, which is incomplete in both theory and practice: Dōgen's practice of *zazen* and his intellectual engagement with the tradition continued until the end of his life. Therefore, Dōgen interweaves the theory and practice of Zen meditation in a relationship of mutual fertilisation.

One of the most important achievements of his intellectual engagement with the Zen tradition is Dōgen's *Shōbōgenzō*. For the present context, it is important to note how in this oeuvre, Dōgen criticises the patriarchs' stories, commentaries, and

---

[12] On the transmission history of this expression and its possible misunderstandings due to phonetic similarity with other words on the one hand, and Dōgen's lack of knowledge of the Chinese language on the other, see Nakamura, *Ways of thinking of eastern peoples: India-China-Tibet-Japan* (Honolulu, Hawaii: East-West Center Press 1966), 242 and 348; and Heine, "Dōgen Casts Off 'What.' An Analysis of *Shinjin Datsuraku*" in: *Journal of International Association of Buddhist Studies* 9/1 (1986): 53–70.

discourses when discussing quasi-metaphysical statements. In his interpretations, Dōgen de- and reconstructs these statements, most vividly in the fascicle "Buddha Nature" ("Busshō"). The text of the *Shōbōgenzō* remains unfinished. This is not necessarily a shortcoming since it needs to be considered vis-à-vis the hermeneutic process of continuous unfolding and deepening.

The *Shōbōgenzō* should be approached as a text comprised of the ideas and realizations of an enlightened individual. As a result, it can only be written in the quasi-monological context of the Zen master. This is reflective of Dōgen's own status as the founder of a school upon his return to Japan from China. Indeed, his new understanding of tradition, which he elaborates on and develops in the *Shōbōgenzō*, was only attainable through and in the direct face-to-face engagement with his master. A new path was founded on a dialogical relationship, to put it differently. In his quest for an authentic master, Dōgen locates Nyojō[13] who proves to be skillful and generous in imparting eloquent and unreserved instruction to his dedicated pupil.

Through Nyojo's strictness in practice and openness in conversation, Dōgen is encouraged and inspired to cultivate his critical spirit: Even though respect for the master and his insights is demanded, in *Hōkyōki*,[14] as elsewhere, the importance of conversation, dispute, criticism, and self-criticism between master and student is frequently highlighted – not merely following in silence, submission, or experiencing mystical unity.

3.3 Dōgen's Critique of the Speechless Zen Tradition

At the outset of Dōgen's critique of the Zen tradition, we find theoretical questioning, in contrast to mere meditative absorption, alongside discourse that is intellectual rather than imparting cryptic teachings. The reason for this is that this critique tends to dismantle verbal and written forms. Yet, at the same time, it offers a new and original use of language. Dōgen relates to both the new language practice of *kōan* dialogue and language scepticism when he problematises the concept of a separate transmission. He poses a query that encompasses the significance of the sutras in the transmission of the Buddha's teaching and truth: "In all points of the compass, people today praise [the Zen teaching] as a special tradition outside scholasticism and consider [it] the reason why [the first] patriarch came from the West [India]. What does this mean?" (DZZ 7:4).

According to *Hōkyōki*, Nyojō already establishes a critique of the Zen tradition by rejecting the notion of its exclusivity. Therefore, Dōgen's teacher answers the aforementioned question in the following manner:

---

[13] Tiantong Rujing 天童如淨 (1162–1227), a Chinese Chan monk, dharma heir to Zuan Zhijian 足庵智鑑 in the Caodong 曹洞宗 lineage; often referred to simply as Rujing 如淨.

[14] The *Hōkyōki* 寶慶記, one fascicle, written by Dōgen. A record made by while he was studying in China with Rujing 如淨 (a Caodong 曹洞 master of the Southern Sung).

Why should the great path [of Buddha] have anything to do with inside and outside? That one nevertheless praises [the teaching] as a special tradition outside scholasticism only means that the [first] patriarch [of the Zen tradition] – apart from the tradition of Kashaya Matanga and others – came from the West, that he went directly to China, that he transmitted the Way [of the Buddha] and that he granted [us] the practice [of meditation]. That is why we speak of the particular transmission outside of scholasticism. [But] two teachings of the Buddha cannot exist in the world. (DZZ 7: 4)

Ambivalences arise regarding the Zen tradition on two levels: Firstly, there is the issue of Zen's detachment from the overarching tradition of Buddhism as originally founded by Buddha. Secondly, the question arises as to whether the Zen school can establish its own form of tradition: beyond the authoritative texts of the tradition such as discourses, sutras, and commentaries as laid down in the Tripitaka. Yet this is precisely what Nyojō denies: the practice of meditation in no way justifies a splitting off of a quasi-esoteric lineage and, from this perspective, does not even justify a school name. Thereby, Dōgen retracts the mentioned instruction of Mahākaśyapa by the Buddha in its meaning: The encounter between Buddha and his first follower is reinterpreted within the tradition into the practice of direct instruction between master and disciple in the *kōan* exercise. This practice, which is still carried out today, manifests as a confrontation with paradoxical statements, especially following Rinzai[15] Zen. Dōgen recalls and criticises this practice, preferring a more discursive exchange:

In all directions today, the ancients of the past and present speak of "that which is heard, yet not heard, seen, yet not seen: without any question, here and now, it is the way of the Buddhas and patriarchs." With this [attitude] they raise their fist or flyswatter, utter a shout or beat with a stick; they do not allow their disciples to consider anything in a differentiated way [...]. (DZZ 7: 4)

Dōgen critiques mere scribes (j. *kyōka*) and distances himself from them (cf. DZZ 7: 24). Although he rejects the concept of an "esoteric" tradition, he still engages in *zazen* practice and does not solely pursue scriptural study. He devotes himself to both aspects of Buddhism and does not acknowledge a hierarchy between theory and practice, or differentiate between "complete" and "incomplete" sutras, even if some are written in short form, and others in long form. Regarding the Buddha's discourses, all forms of expression are appropriate. Thus, in dialogue with his mentor, Dōgen discusses the correlation between speech and silence. Ultimately, a unity of articulation and gesture is assumed when it is said: "Sacred silence like sacred teaching, both are the Buddha's business" (DZZ 7: 22). This statement not only neutralises the paradoxical expression but also subverts silence as a privileged mode of communication in the Zen interpretive context.

A positive appreciation of language, which can also be linked to a metaphysical justification of a "concrete monism," is found in a text that Dōgen only wrote in the year 1237 but which reflects an early encounter from his time in China. In his work, Dōgen addresses the importance of language. In *Tenzo kyōkun (Instructions for the*

---

[15] Linji 臨濟, a reference to the Chinese Chan master Linji Yixuan 臨濟義玄 (d. 866-7) and to the tradition of Buddhism that formed based on his teachings, the Linji zong 臨濟宗.

Chief Cook), which primarily sets out rules for the monastery's cook, he recounts a conversation with a monk who, despite his advanced age – and his being in an exalted position – is in charge of the kitchen. This dialogue reveals that "theory" and "practice" are not contradictory, but mutually supportive:

> "Revered master," I asked, "why do you not practice *zazen* in your old age, and why do you not read the *kōan* cases of the ancients, but toil away at this chief cook's office? What is so valuable about preparing meals for the monks?" Then the chief cook laughed aloud. "You good man from abroad! You do not know what the Buddha Way practice is. Nor have you yet grasped words!" [After months they meet again and the chief cook continues:] "Whoever wants to learn words must first recognise their principle. And whoever wants to strive for the Buddha Way practice must first know about its principle." So I asked, "What are 'words'?" "One, two, three, four, five." "And what is the 'Buddha Way practice'?" "All things in the world are unconcealed." [Finally, Dōgen states:] Now I understood that that kitchen master was truly a man of the Buddha Way. The words I had seen so far were one, two, three, four, five, and the ones I saw now [after realising their nature] were six, seven, eight, nine, ten. When the monks practising the Buddha Way see from here what is there and from there what is here, and thus cultivate [the Way] intensively, they will understand that pure Zen is based on words. (DZZ 6:14, 16)[16]

Indeed, the chief cook speaks of comprehending the respective principles of words and practice. While such principles cannot be reduced to the designative aspect of an abstract statement and the path of understanding cannot be reduced to the study of specific texts alone, both practical experience and linguistic context are crucial. Dōgen's statement that "pure Zen is based on words" can also be interpreted in the Sino-Japanese original to suggest that Zen is "above" and words are "below." Nevertheless, it appears appropriate to view this statement as not establishing a rigid justificatory or favouring of one over the other – both Zen and words are inter-related in a powerful sense. Likewise, when counting numbers, they are neither "ordinary" words nor statements of identity. Numbers and their counting are subject to interpretation based on the situation and context. Consequently, an important implication of Dōgen's conversation with the chief cook is that despite the potential hazards, constraints, and drawbacks of language, there exists a vital correlation between the pursuit and enactment of salvation and the use of language (words).

3.4 Dōgen's Linguistic Articulation of Meditation

From this perspective, it becomes clear that Dōgen may prioritize the practice of *zazen* for strategic reasons, but never in principle. Upon returning to Japan, Dōgen goes from being a student searching for answers to his great doubt regarding original enlightenment and the need to practice to the time of instructing his own students; thus, he must strive for a form of authentic meditation. In the writing *Fukan zazen gi* (*Explanations for the General Promotion of Zazen*), he emphasises meditation and reliance on one's own effort and experience. As previously indicated, the

---

[16] It is translated here *monji jō no ichimi zen* (DZZ 6: 16) as "on the words," not as "above the words."

scripture primarily serves as a tool for physical instruction and, can also be used – in its brevity and style – for recitation or be put away. Like a self-exhortation not to be captivated by "names and forms," he writes: "So, refrain from seeking explanations and chasing words! Learn to let the light turn back and shine on your own nature" (DZZ 5:4)! However, it's important to note that this proverb does not necessarily align with traditional Zen teachings.

Dōgen's unconventional way of teaching becomes particularly evident when one reads in *Shōbōgenzō zuimonki* (*Records of what I heard about the Shōbōgenzō*) – written by his next disciple Ejō in the period 1235–1238 – how pragmatically Dōgen spoke about subjects such as the Chinese language, poetry and literature, sutras and analects, teaching and the master-student relationship, debates that go astray, defamation and insult, the appropriate and ethically right form of speaking, and criticism and self-criticism. For him, the student's effort towards independent understanding is crucial. Of course, he stresses that "literature and poetry are meaningless" (DZZ 7:72). And "even the words [j. *gongo*] of the Buddhas and patriarchs should not be loved and studied in excess" (ibid.). Nonetheless, this is not directed against language at such, since Dōgen, on the other hand, urges his students to strive to articulate what they understand:

> Again, [Dōgen] states: One who studies the Way should not read the writings of the book scholars, nor even extra-canonical texts. Read the records of the words [of the ancient masters] that one has to read. Put the other [texts] aside for a while. Today's Zen monks love to hastily and carelessly compose verses or doctrinal discourses [j. *hōgo*]. This is wrong. Write down what you think in your heart, even if you do not write verses; write down the true teaching, even if you are not capable of beautiful literature. [...] But even if you read the Sacred Scriptures, if you gradually understand the principle you find in the sentences, [...] you first see in the sentences what kind of couplets and what kind of intonation they are, and inwardly weigh whether they are good or bad, and only later pay attention to the meaning. [...] Leave the language and the style of writing to themselves – if you write down the principle as you think of it, in all its details, if one is looking for the principle, it is important for the sake of the path, even if later generations give nothing to your style. (DZZ 7: 90–93)

Here, too, an inclination towards rational insight is particularly evident. It is not subject to stylistic aesthetics, as neither metaphor nor other rhetorical devices determine the criterion for comprehension. Dōgen emphasises the affirmative use of everyday language. However, as demonstrated in the following, his consideration of language soon reaches far beyond its appreciation and defence against aesthetic criteria. This is evident in the author's use of phrases such as "so to speak" (j. *iwayuru*), "that means" or "it says" (j. *to iu* or *to wa* and others), which reflect a self-reflexive distance from language. This is also visible through direct word explanations or substitutions of Sino-Japanese expressions with those of spoken Japanese, sometimes casually, sometimes deliberately. Finally, the use of theory-related terminology such as "meaning," "expression," or "metaphor" demonstrates a thorough grasp of the semantic aspect of linguistic signs.

II. Book Outline: The Emergence of Dōgen as Philosopher

Indeed, perhaps more than any other example, the emergence of the *Shōbōgenzō* as a philosophical text is representative of the history of how the creation of "Japanese philosophy" in the modern era has occurred alongside conflict with – or displacement of – the pre-modern confessional approach. For this reason, Dōgen studies in Meiji period Japan can be understood as a passage in which the image projected onto Dōgen changed and multiplied greatly. What exactly happened to Dōgen scholarship during this period remains to be clarified historically and systematically. The same applies to the presentation and discussion of the conditions before the Meiji era and the ensuing changes. Our anthology aims at a core problem that became critical in the Meiji period, in which the philosophical appropriation of Dōgen acted as a catalyst inside and outside the monastery: how should we deal with Dōgen's texts?

This question is not limited to apparent oppositions between pre-modern confessional authority and modern academic discourse, religion and philosophy, or commentary and criticism. The emergence of modern denominational studies (j. *shūgaku*) based on practitioners' self-criticism, or the convergence of philosophical discourse on Dōgen with denominational commentary literature, are examples that undermine such apparent oppositions and show that the issues involved are more complex. As for contemporary Dōgen studies, most of the entanglements stem from a number of different factions among those who were receptive towards Dōgen's writings before, during, or after the Meiji era. These factions include: the Zennists (j. *zenjōka*), who emphasise practice; the Genzōnians (j. *genzōka*), who emphasise the reading of Dōgen texts; the lay movement, which opens both the texts and the practice to people in modern society; and the Genzō scholars (j. *genzō kenkyūka*), who search for the authenticity and truth of Dōgen's writings.

This anthology's collected contributions help clarify, subvert, and/or revise common notions of Dōgen in monasticism, confessional studies, or modern academic philosophy. The aim is to bring into play the various discourses on Dōgen and to discuss their relationship across periods and factions in modernity and pre-modernity. The challenge is to set hermeneutical reading standards and propose new, original, and critical interpretations of his texts. The performative dimension of language and silence circumscribes the framework within which we can place all three topics: the text, the practice, and time as a matter of both religious and philosophical thought. We will give each of these topics its dedicated part. In the first part, on text, the central level of philosophising becomes the subject. In the second part, on practice, we will discuss the text regarding its performativity, which seems closer to religion as an essential category for treating Dōgen. In the third part, we show how the relationship between text and performativity depends on another issue central to religion and the practice of philosophy: time.

Part I: Texts

In chapter "Philosopher, Religious Thinker or Contemplative Practitioner? Making Sense of Dōgen beyond Zen Modernism," André van der Braak (Vrije Universiteit Amsterdam) argues for reading Dōgen as a kind of theologian (or dharmalogian), i.e., as a contemplative practitioner. Van der Braak holds that neither approach alone, Zen master or Philosopher, does full justice to the kinds of texts Dōgen produced in the context of spreading the authentic Dharma on his return from China and having received Dharma transmission from Rujing.

Van der Braak reflects on the different approaches to understanding Dōgen's work. For his own, he uses the philosophical hermeneutics of the German philosopher Hans-Georg Gadamer (1900–2002). According to van der Braak, for Gadamer, understanding is possible through a merging of horizons, one's own with that which one aims to understand. Regarding Dōgen, a central claim of Gadamer's approach to understanding is that it is impossible to understand Dōgen "as he really is" or to understand what he wrote "as he really meant it" – Dōgen's authorial intention is necessarily inaccessible. Since we do not have Dōgen before us, the only access we do have, even using his texts and studying the practices handed down in the Sōtō Zen tradition, is by way of imaginatively reconstructing him. Making sense of Dōgen is always imagining Dōgen. Such imaginings are created even before we encounter one of his texts. They are formed according to our subconscious pre-understandings (*Vorverstehen*): understanding him *as* a philosopher, *as* a religious thinker, *as* a prophet, or *as* a miracle worker. This pre-understanding, then, continues to colour our imagination, even if we read Dōgen with an open mind.

Given this hermeneutical approach, van der Braak presents the various arguments that have been brought forward in the Western Zen modernist literature on Dōgen for reading him as a philosopher, or as a religious thinker. He concludes that neither of these approaches do Dōgen justice. Dōgen's repeated impatience with, and even disdain for, non-Buddhist approaches make it difficult to defend approaching him as a philosopher engaged in an impartial non-dogmatic quest for truth. For Dōgen, the Buddhist way is of prime importance. On the other hand, Dōgen is doing more than just expounding the truth of the Buddhist Way (as a Buddhist religious practitioner would do). He is clearly endeavouring to express truth, albeit within the contours of the Buddhist Way.

Thus, van der Braak argues that we should read Dōgen as a Buddhist theologian (or dharmalogian). Just as Christian theologians try to make sense of God, as a Buddhist theologian, Dōgen tries to make sense of the Buddha Way. While van der Braak acknowledges that the label "theologian" might not be very popular these days (and perhaps the label might also be a stretch in a Buddhist context), exploring this "third way" of reading Dōgen allows us to escape the dualist dilemma of reading Dōgen as a philosopher *or* as a religious thinker. In terms of philosophical hermeneutics, this might be a productive *Vorverstehen* that might also offer resources to escape the particular merging of horizons that have been characteristic of Zen modernism.

In chapter "Going Out to Sea: Dōgen's Ongoing Emphasis on the Creative Ambiguity of Horizons," Steven Heine (Florida International University) provides another "third way" for thinking about Dōgen's status vis-à-vis philosophy and Zen. According to Heine, we need to move beyond the either/or of Dōgen's dual roles as a sectarian trailblazer *or* an autonomous philosopher. This is particularly the case, Heine thinks, given that the debate regarding Dōgen in relation to religion and philosophy has begun to appear artificial and unproductive where it stands.

A central aspect of Heine's approach is to critically examine interpretations by important premodern and modern sources of a difficult but pregnant passage from Dōgen's "Genjōkōan" 現成公案 fascicle. Originally written as an epistle to a lay disciple, "Genjōkōan" is the first fascicle in several traditional editions of Dōgen's masterwork, the *Shōbōgenzō* 正法眼蔵 (*The Treasury of the True Dharma Eye*). The passage in question deals with the way perspectives shift dramatically "when riding a boat out to sea, where mountains can no longer be seen (*yamanaki kaichū* 山なき海中)." According to Heine, this passage is vitally important because of the issues it raises concerning Dōgen's approach to multi-perspectivism, issues that are usually construed in absolutist and relativist terms.

The analogy of sailing past the horizon, where no trace of land is visible and one feels temporarily encircled by the ocean with no other frame of reference available, helps to reveal the innate partiality of human perception, particularly in connection to the Zen goal of awakening to a holistic standpoint that is devoid of divisibility but incorporates an array of standpoints. The image of the moving boat reflects Dōgen's intricate approach to expressing what Heine refers to as "creative ambiguity" (*sōzōtekina aimaisa* 創造的な曖昧さ) concerning the way delusions, which reflect an incomplete and inconclusive level of understanding, invariably shape the quest to attain and disclose the meaning of authentic realisation. This notion refers to a series of misapprehensions in that we tend to commit "mistakes compounded on mistakes" (*shōshaku jushaku* 將錯就錯), a term Dōgen mentions in several fascicles.

According to Heine, these blunders can paradoxically lead to a state of turning an error into one's advantage by making the *right* mistake, which is how the double-edged idiom is often interpreted. The standpoint of creative ambiguity, therefore, refuses to close off options and because it acknowledges limitations that can lead to deficiency and duplicity, it remains open to endless possibilities that are often imaginative and inventive means of disclosing truth not disconnected from untruth. That is, one can either add error to error until a standpoint is hopelessly counterproductive or use an error to enhance understanding, like the act of sharpening a sword.

Whereas the commentators whose work Heine examines were primarily premodern and modern, in chapter "Dōgen's Texts Expounded by the Kyoto School – Religious Commentary or Philosophical Interpretation?," Ralf Müller (Cork University College, Ireland) focuses more closely on modern commentators close to or from the Kyoto school. According to Müller, there have been two approaches within the so-called Kyoto school regarding Dōgen's work. Initially, there were philosophically ambitious interpretations, such as those by Watsuji Tetsurō and Tanabe Hajime. They were ambitious insofar as they attempted to bridge the gap between philosophy and religion. However, from the 1940s onwards, these seminal works tended to recede into the background since they were criticised for assimilating a medieval monk into modern secular thought. Müller discusses the second approach that was put forward by thinkers such as Nishida Kitarō (1870–1945), Nishitani Keiji (1900–1990), and Ueda Shizuteru (1926–2019). They furthered the questioning of religion and philosophy by developing a specific style of reading Dōgen.

Interestingly and analogously to how van der Braak and Heine in their own ways disclaim the felicitousness of either/or approaches to the status of Dōgen and his Zen/texts, so, too, Müller claims that these Kyoto School philosophers' readings of Dōgen lie beyond the limitations of the denominational approach, on the one hand, and the philosophical approach of Watsuji and Tanabe, on the other hand. The question for Müller, then, is whether they create a method that is neither exclusively religious commentary nor philosophical interpretation. Moreover, can such a position be methodologically delineated?

In chapter "Dōgen's Interpretive Charity: The Hermeneutical Significance of "Genjōkōan"," Eitan Bolokan (Tel Aviv University) argues that one of Dōgen's most renowned essays, the "Genjōkōan" of 1233, can be read as an exposition of interpretive sensibilities. By drawing a comparison between the function of the principle of the "dharma position" (*hō'i* 法位) and that of interpretive charity as formulated in the Judaic tradition, he maintains that the "Genjōkōan" fascicle initiates the reader into Dōgen's dialectical interpretive perspective. As Dōgen elaborated on this theme throughout his life, he strived to creatively pacify the lasting tensions between authority and interpretation, textual closure and hermeneutical openness. Thus, Bolokan proposes that examining the dialectics of the "dharma position" as expressed in pivotal passages of the "Genjōkōan," may deepen our appreciation of the hermeneutical value of other cardinal notions in Dōgen's thought.

In the first section of the chapter, Bolokan seeks to illuminate what he calls "The Interpretive Temperament of Zen." Following the work of Okajima Shūryū, he here elucidates sectarian methodologies such as *sankyū* (参究), which he proposes to translate as "participative investigation," and *kenkyū* (研究), often translated simply as "research," to locate Dōgen's philosophy in the context of Zen as an interpretive tradition. In the second section of the chapter, Bolokan follows Moshe Halbertal's seminal work on canon, meaning, and authority in the history of the Jewish textual tradition, to introduce the hermeneutical framework of "interpretive charity." This analysis continues into the third and fourth sections of the chapter, where he follows the works by Ishii Seijun, Tachikawa Musashi, and Itō Shūken, among others, to clarify the resemblance between "interpretive charity" to Dōgen's usage of the "the dharma position" as articulated in "Genjōkōan." By retranslating selected passages of the essay, he seeks to demonstrate the "charitable" nature of the dialectics of the "dharma position" as an interpretive framework.

In the final chapter of Part I, "Traces of the Brush: Examination of Dōgen's Thought Through his Language," Zuzana Kubovčáková (Masaryk University, Brno) begins by situating her discussion of Dōgen's creative and brilliant uses of language in relation to the issue of the self-defining motto of the Chan/Zen schools as a tradition "nondependent upon words and letters" (*furyū monji* 不立文字), "transmitted outside established Buddhist scriptures" (*kyōge betsuden* 教外別傳). As she emphasises, given Dōgen's end of spreading the authentic Dharma, this motto presents a straightforward ambiguity for such a principal matter as the spread of a school of thought itself. For, on the one hand, there is the issue of transmission of recognised written doctrines and texts, as well as understanding and confirmation of a tradition, which usually only occurs through the medium of language. At the same time, however, there is the danger of words giving rise to delusion and misunderstanding rather than acting as vehicles for awakening.

Having situated Dōgen in the complex social and religious context in which he lived, Kubovčáková shifts to an analysis of Dōgen's linguistic strategies. As she remarks, several scholars have already analysed Dōgen's idiosyncratic expressions. For example, in the editor's introduction to the *Treasury of the True Dharma Eye* and under a suitable heading "Decoding the Zen Paradox," Kazuaki Tanahashi presents 13 examples of Dōgen's unique rhetoric. Heine elaborates on Dōgen's "Distinctive Discursive Style," suggesting almost a dozen paradoxical maxims. And in his well-known, "The Reason of Words and Letters," Hee-Jin Kim offers a thorough classification of the master's linguistic methods. And Rein Raud's analysis concentrates on grammatical relationships within compounds.[17]

Inspired by these respected scholars, Kubovčáková takes up the task of laying out her own views of Dōgen's linguistic creativity – not in an attempt to substitute or overshadow the previous contributions. Rather, she seeks to offer a further examination of Dōgen's language and a reflection of his approach to words and expressions. She does this by making use of Kim's dual categories of activity (*gyōji*) and expression (*dōtoku*) as the main avenues that Dōgen employed to teach and express his Zen, a Zen in which there is an underlying nonseparation between the master's language, practice, and philosophy. For Kubovčáková, his thought is firmly rooted in language, wordplay, and original rhetorical devices – albeit, paradoxically, equally in silence – and any separation between Dōgen's thought and Dōgen's language is arbitrary and reflecting a mind of duality. As she sees it, his language is, indeed, a testament to his radical and masterful thought, and Dōgen employs words, as possible vehicles to enlightenment.

Part II: Practice

While the first three papers in Part I challenged the idea that we should think of Dōgen's texts as either philosophical or not, suggesting different third ways for reading and categorising Dōgen, Part II examines key components of the idea that

---

[17] See Tanahashi (ed.), *Treasury of the True Dharma Eye. Zen Master Dōgen's Shobo Genzo* (Boulder: Shambhala, 2012), xxx–xxxi; Heine, *Readings of Dōgen's 'Treasury of the True Dharma Eye'* (New York: Columbia UP 2020), 6; Kim, "The Reason of Words and Letters," in *Dōgen Studies*, ed. by W.R. LaFleur, 61; Raud, "Inside the Concept: Rethinking Dōgen's Language," in *Asian Philosophy* 21/2 (2011): 132.

the practice of Dōgen's Zen or, at least, Dōgen's *own* practice of it, which included his writings, entails or is the doing of philosophy in some form. We begin Part II, however, by considering the fully embodied religiosity of Dōgen's pursuit, practice, and teaching of the authentic Dharma.

Thus, in chapter "Dōgen and the Buddhist Way," Aldo Tollini (Ca' Foscari University of Venice) focuses on *butsudō* (仏道), i.e., the "Buddha's Way" as Dōgen conceived it. As Tollini informs us, it is with Dōgen that the "Buddha's Way" began to be used in Japan in a consistent and specific way to mean that Buddhism is a path that leads, or can lead, whoever undertakes it, to spiritual realisation, i.e., to enlightenment or *satori*. For Dōgen, the identity of practice and enlightenment (*shushō ichinyo*) is revealed in the practitioner's behaviour: though we are originally enlightened, we must nevertheless strive to actualise our true nature by means of a continued effort in practice. This implies always being in practice, manifesting one's buddhahood at all times. Therefore, Tollini argues, every action must be the result of the perfection of one's buddhahood.

Indeed, Dōgen uses the word *igi* (威儀) to mean a correct (or dignified) behaviour in any daily activity. *Igi*, in its most genuine and authentic meaning, is the manifestation and actualisation of one's Buddha nature having cast off all attachments. Pure and uncontaminated practice is, in Dōgen's Buddha's Way, impersonal, or action without production of karmic traces. For this reason, Dōgen's Buddhism is a Way: a path of self-improvement to manifest Buddha nature in all aspects, both external and internal, and physical, mental, and moral.

One aspect of Dōgen's Zen that Tollini emphasises is that in the first half of the thirteenth century, Dōgen was a spiritual master who not only gave a new impulse to Japanese Buddhism, but also inaugurated a new vision of spirituality. He did this by placing the individual at the centre of religious activity, insisting on the concept of personal effort, practice, and the achievement of *satori* open to all, without distinction between people of high and low rank, intelligent, or stupid. In this sense, Dōgen's teachings represent a fracture with the teachings of the previous schools in Japan, especially Tendai and Shingon, and inaugurates a new vision of the Buddha's Way unprecedented up to his time.

Thus, Tollini argues for an understanding of Dōgen's Zen that is centred on Zazen as a practice that one continues to engage off the cushion, as one continuously reinvigorates practice-enlightenment in all one does, with everyone one meets. And this is not something that only occurs in the monastery. It is a path that is open to be practiced by all.

Tollini's chapter pushes us to consider the question of awakening in relation to activities that go, or seem to go, beyond "just sitting." This is particularly true given Tollini's emphasis on the universal availability and applicability of Dōgen's Zen to life beyond the monastery. In the next chapter, we will continue to explore related themes regarding the nature and scope of practice.

We might wonder whether the picture of Dōgen's intense religiosity, as painted by Tollini, excludes identifying Dōgen as a philosopher, or even his doing philosophy. Three of the next four chapters will argue that it does not.

In chapter "Do Not Lose the Rice: Dōgen Through the Eyes of Contemporary Western Zen Women," Laura Specker Sullivan (Fordham University) seeks to elaborate on neglected aspects of Dōgen's Zen. She takes up observations by Gesshin Claire Greenwood, a Soto Zen nun from the United States who ordained in Japan. She describes an interaction with a Japanese nun that a fellow Australian nun later summarises with the phrase, "just do your work, concentrate on that and nothing more, enlightenment is a male fantasy" (Greenwood, p. 74).

We are told that, later, Greenwood uses this interaction as an opportunity to reflect on Buddhist practice and gender through sifting rice, an activity that Dōgen focuses on in the *Tenzo Kyōkun*. The latter text prompts one to wonder about the limits of "Zazen only," since it focuses on the monastery duties of the head cook who does not get much time to do Zazen, and must, therefore, put themselves completely into the activities of planning and feeding the monks and guests. For Dōgen, this is a particularly important moment since it allows him to directly address the idea of awakened discrimination, as one must enact enlightenment while not only sifting rice but planning meals and determining how much is to be cooked given the number of guests and supplies at hand.

With the *Tenzo Kyōkun* as a kind of model, Specker Sullivan describes how contemporary Western Zen women and their allies have understood Dōgen's texts as a tool of personal and social transformation through examination of work by Zen practitioners. In particular, she posits that Zen women have expressed the practical nature of Dōgen's philosophy for contemporary non-monastics, showing how to de-centre oneself through full participation in the activity of the world. This contrasts with self-centred preoccupation with individual enlightenment or spiritual attainment on the cushion alone. Paradoxically, it is the fact that women have often been confined to social roles that prevent their separation from the minutiae of everyday life that allows them to embody Dōgen's dictum to "forget the self and be actualised by myriad things."

In chapter "Philosophy, Not-Philosophy,*Non-Philosophy*: Dōgen's*Religio-Philosophical*Zen," George Wrisley (University of North Georgia) starts by assuming that the normative conception of Zen that Dōgen expounded and practiced constitutes at its heart a *religio-philosophical practice*. Dōgen's zazen-only form of practice is not confined to a strictly seated zazen; it occurs off the cushion, as well. However, whether seated or not, one of the central aspects of Dōgen's Zen is the transformation of apparent dualities into non-dual dualities. Since this activity implicates more than experience, e.g., valuations, desires, goals, actions, reactions, etc., i.e., the entire psycho-physical existence of the practitioner, it is itself philosophical in the demands it makes on practitioners, especially their ability to "weigh emptiness," a phrase Dōgen only uses once or twice in his *Shōbōgenzō* fascicle, "Expressing a Dream in a Dream" and nowhere else.

Yet, following Hee-Jin Kim's treatment of it, weighing emptiness is vital to the dynamicity of practice-realization in the world. This is because weighing emptiness is a way to describe the transformation and engagement with a non-dual duality in the world. While not denying the idea of "equality in emptiness," it insists that differences must be taken into consideration in realizing the fairness, reasonableness, and justness of the practitioner acting in the world.

As a part of the religio-philosophical practice of transforming apparent dualities into non-dual dualities, weighing emptiness is a further philosophical aspect of practice-realization. And it can be further paired with the non-dual non-thinking, which is the mode of existence whereby the practitioner is present and effective in their seated and active forms of zazen. In the latter, it helps mediate the ever changing complexities of balancing thinking and not-thinking as the lived situation demands, all to enact practice-realization.

Thus, Wrisley expounds the manner in which grappling with non-dual duality, weighing emptiness, and non-thinking should be seen as loci of Dōgen's *religio-philosophical* activities. The extent to which someone can engage the philosophical dimensions will depend on the person, their motivations, and that of their teachers. Yet, the more deeply one can penetrate the various issues, ideas, and concepts at stake, the deeper one's practice-realization.

In chapter "Flowers of Dim-Sightedness: Dōgen's Mystical 'Negative Ocularcentrism'," Adam Loughnane (University College Cork) seeks to establish a framework for interpreting Dōgen's appeals to vision in view of addressing Kim's ascription of "mystical realist" to Dōgen. Kim emphasises the "realisational" dynamic that actualises (rather than relativises or transcends) visual polarities of light and darkness, visibility and invisibility, clarity and opacity.

Loughnane explores the limits of such realisation by considering Dōgen's notion of "obstruction" (罣礙 *keige*). The central question is: can a negatively ocularcentric mysticism be realist if a dynamic obstruction remains as a constitutive aspect of visual activity and expression? Further, Loughnane proposes expanding Dōgen's thought on vision by reading it through his notion of obstruction – specifically the logic of time as "obstruction obstructing obstruction" (礙は礙を罣礙するなり、これ時なり) – to distance his thought from both the positivism of ocularcentrism and realism of mysticism. Despite the dangers some have articulated regarding the hegemony of the visual (David McMahan and D.M. Levin), Loughnane seeks to cast Dōgen's philosophy as a "negative ocularcentrism." The claim he develops is that the dangers of visual dominion reside not in the philosophical prioritisation of vision to the neglect of other perceptual modalities, but specifically in the latent positivism visual metaphor tends towards.

In chapter "Dōgen as Philosopher, Metaphysician, and Metaethicist", Russell Guilbault (University of Chicago) completes Part II on practice with "Dōgen as Philosopher, Metaphysician, and Metaethicist." As Guilbault points out, philosophers interested in mining the Buddhist tradition for insights have long been drawn to Dōgen, and in particular to his *Shōbōgenzō*. He directly engages with the writings of Raji Steineck who has challenged the practice of taking Dōgen as a philosophical interlocutor, suggesting that Dōgen's language and methodology tell against reading Dōgen as a philosophical figure. Guilbault defends this practice, arguing that Dōgen's mystical and paradoxical language can generally be cut through, yielding straightforward assertions of determinate philosophical views. As a proof of concept, he offers philosophical readings of Dōgen on two issues. First, he argues that

Dōgen's intervention in the Japanese Buddhist discourse on "Buddha nature" (*busshō* 佛性) expresses an overarching metaphysical position that unifies the *Shōbōgenzō*. He then argues that Dōgen recognises and attempts to solve a meta-ethical problem raised by Dōgen's understanding of Buddha nature. Along the way, he shows how careful attention to Dōgen's position in the intellectual history of the Buddhist tradition can illuminate how he builds on the philosophical legwork of his forebears.

Part III: Time

In our final part, we turn to discussions of how to understand Dōgen's relationship to philosophy by way of examining different aspects of what is so often taken to be one of Dōgen's most philosophical fascicles from the *Shōbōgenzō*, namely, "Uji" or "Being/Existence-Time." Our first chapter in Part III pushes back hardest of all the chapters collected in this volume against the idea of Dōgen's being a philosopher writing philosophy texts.

In chapter "From Uji to Being-time (and Back): Translating Dōgen into Philosophy," Raji Steineck (Zurich University) argues that the declared aim of Dōgen's writings, which were often edited versions of ritualised verbal teachings, was to guide disciples on the Buddha Way – a practical path to salvation that was clearly defined and delimited by an authoritative tradition. Dōgen, therefore, tried to preclude rather than foster the open-ended discussion of fundamental problems of human life that is otherwise usually associated with the concept of philosophy. Hence, Dōgen speaks a language of persuasion that is guided by aims and rules of discourse different from those of philosophy. This, or so Steineck argues, is an aspect that is often lost when Dōgen's thoughts are transferred into philosophical debates. The result is, in many instances, a rather facile alignment with the recipient's own preconceptions.

To substantiate his hypothesis, Steineck starts from factual observations concerning the modern philosophical reception of Dōgen's teachings on time in Japan and the Anglophone world, focusing on the semantic shifts occurring in interpretations by prominent authors such as Tanabe Hajime, Ōmori Shōzō, Rein Raud, and others. He then turns to the theory of translation to analyse the seminal factors at play in this observed process of transformative reception. Finally, he reflects on how conceiving of the transfer of Dōgen's thought into philosophical discourse as a process of translation can help to build interpretations that are both hermeneutically sound and philosophically interesting.

In chapter "Thinking the Now: Binary and Holistic Concepts in Dōgen's Philosophy of Time," Rein Raud (Tallinn University) stands in clear opposition to Steineck's main positions. The chapter contributes to the debate on Dōgen's theory of time by discussing the key concepts of the "Uji" fascicle of the *Shōbōgenzō* in a broader context, comparing them with other cases of usage in the entire work, their

provenance in the tradition of Zen thought, as well as with their possible translational equivalents and their connotations in the Western tradition. The chapter provides further argument for the claim that a presentist reading of the fascicle (as well
as other related passages in Dōgen's work) leaves the least of the cryptic passages
unexplained. It does this while blending seamlessly with Dōgen's other claims
about reality, language, our ways to understand them, and praxis, or the mode of
behaviour that allows human beings to transcend the limitations of their firsthand
experience of the world.

Raud begins, however, by touching on the much-discussed issue of Dōgen's relationship with philosophy, and argues that it is incorrect to exclude non-Western
thinkers and texts from the domain of philosophy because of particular features that
certain canonically recognised Western thinkers and texts also possess. The issue is
important, because it legitimates a register of reading of texts such as Dōgen's in a
way that places them in dialogue with ideas that they have historically had no connection with. And it also enables us to use them in contexts for which they have no
historical relevance – something that treating them solely as subject matter for the
history of ideas would not let us do.

In chapter "On Flowing While Being: The (Mereo)Logical Structure of Dōgen's
Conception of Time," Felipe Cuervo (Los Andes University), in part a critic of
Raud, continues the interconnected discussion. As Cuervo writes, quite often, the
hermeneutical challenges associated with reading Dōgen in the West are summarised as one question: should we read him as a philosopher? The purpose of
Cuervo's chapter is to argue for a more precise position: He demonstrates that reading Dōgen through the lens of contemporary logic can help dispel obscurities and
solve interpretative dilemmas. He argues in favour of this hermeneutic technique
performatively by showing its advantages when faced with one of the most difficult
sides of Dōgen's writings, his ideas on time, mostly, though not limited to, the manner in which they are expressed in the "Uji" fascicle. Cuervo discusses the most
commonly quoted passages from Dōgen's writings concerning time and argues that,
instead of there being one paradox, there are two distinct paradoxical issues. The
first concerns the ontological imbrication of distinct times, and the second, the fact
that Dōgen at times seems to emphasise the ontological priority of temporal instants
and, at other times, the ontological priority of time as a continuous flow. He then
critiques the metaphysical interpretations of Dirck Vorenkamp and Raud, and points
out several of what he takes to be their shortcomings, mostly due to their not having
sufficiently differentiated both aspects of the problem.

In our final chapter, "A Philosophical Endeavour: The Practice of Time in Dōgen
and Marcus Aurelius," Laurentiu Andrei (University Clermont-Auvergne) recounts
the basic issue of Dōgen's relationship to philosophy in the following way: The
Buddhist monk Dōgen (1200–1253), a major religious figure of his time, was also
considered as one of the first philosophers in Japan. Meiji intellectuals paved the
way to a philosophical reading of Dōgen's texts. However, other voices questioned
whether this is a proper approach to Dōgen and his texts. Was Dōgen really engaged
in a philosophical endeavour or was he instead oriented to an extra-philosophical
scope? In order to tackle this question, he proposes to consider Dōgen's case as

pertaining to a larger issue present in Buddhist Studies: the problem of a tenacious refusal to qualify as "philosophical" certain texts within the Buddhist canon.

Nevertheless, several attempts were made to parallel Buddhist texts and philosophical texts from the Hellenistic period, notably those of the Stoic school. Andrei's argument is consistent with this kind of comparative approach and probes a paradigmatic example of spiritual training – that he calls *the practice of time* – focused on the ideas of impermanence (*mujō* 無常) and change (μεταβολή), such as they appear in some of Dōgen's writings and in the *Meditations* of the Roman emperor Marcus Aurelius (121–180). For Laurentiu, this comparative asceticism shows how similarities in their practices of time allow us to consider their respective endeavours as philosophical.

Ralf Müller

References

DZZ = *Dōgen Zenji zenshū* [Zen mNaaster Dōgen's Complete Works]. 7 vols. Ed. by Sasaki Kakuzen et al., Shunjūsha, 1988–1993.

THZ = *Tanabe Hajime zenshū* [Tanabe Hajime's Complete Works]. 15 vols. Ed. by Nishitani Keiji et al., Chikuma Shobō, 1963–1964.

ZGDJ = *Zengaku daijiten* [Great Dictionary of Zen Studies]. Daishūkan Shoten, 1985.

RICCI = *Grand dictionnaire Ricci de la langue chinoise*. 8 vols. Paris: Desclée de Brouwer.

Anonymous. "Jōyō Daishi no shoden" [A Short Biography of Jōyō Daishi]. In: *Tōyō Tetsugaku* 3 (4), (1896): 205–206.

Bielefeldt, Carl. "Dōgen" in: vol. 2 of *The Encyclopedia of Religion*. 8 vols. Ed. by Mircea Eliade. New York: Simon & Schuster Macmillan, 1995.

Döll, Steffen. *Im Osten des Meeres: chinesische Emigrantenmönche und die frühen Institutionen des japanischen Zen-Buddhismus*. Stuttgart: Steiner, 2010.

Heiler, Friedrich. *Die buddhistische Versenkung: Eine religionsgeschichtliche Untersuchung*, München: Reinhardt, 1918.

Heine, Steven. *Existential and Ontological Dimensions of Time in Heidegger and Dōgen*. Albany: SUNY Press, 1985.

Heine, Steven. "Dōgen Casts Off 'What.' An Analysis of *Shinjin Datsuraku*". In: *Journal of International Association of Buddhist Studies* 9 (1), (1986): 53–70.

Heine, Steven. *Readings of Dōgen's 'Treasury of the True Dharma Eye'*. New York: Columbia UP, 2020.

Hori, G. Victor Sōgen. "Kōan and Kenshō in the Rinzai Zen Curriculum." In: *The Kōan: texts and contexts in Zen Buddhism*. Ed. by Steven Heine and Dale S. Wright. 280–315. New York: Oxford University Press, 2000.

Izutsu, Toshihiko. *Toward a Philosophy of Zen Buddhism*. Teheran: Imperial Iranian Academy of Philosophy, 1977.

Karaki Junzō/Haga Kōshirō/Osaka Kōryū. "Japanese Zen. A Symposium." In: *Eastern Buddhist* 10 (2), (1977): 76–101.

Katō Shūkō. *Shōbōgenzō yōgo sakuin* (An Index on Core Terms of the *Shōbōgenzō*). 2 vols., 1987.

Kim, Hee-Jin. *Eihei Dōgen: Mystical Realist*. Boston: Wisdom Publications, 2004.

Kim, Hee-Jin. *Dōgen on Meditation and Thinking: A Reflection on His View of Zen*. Albany, NY: SUNY Press, 2007.

Kim, Hee-Jin."'The Reason of Words and Letters.'" In *Dōgen Studies*. Ed. by W.R. LaFleur. 54–82. Honolulu: University of Hawaii Press, 1985.

LaFleur, William R., ed. *Dōgen Studies*. Honolulu: University of Hawaii Press, 1985.

Nakamura, Hajime. *Ways of thinking of eastern peoples: India-China-Tibet-Japan.* Honolulu, Hawaii: East-West Center Press, 1966.

Nakamura Hajime. *Iwanami bukkyō jiten* [Iwanami Dictionary of Buddhism], Iwanami, 1995.

Nakimovitch, Pierre. *Dōgen et les paradoxes de la Bouddhéité.* Genève: Droz, 1999.

Raud, Rein. "Inside the Concept: Rethinking Dōgen's Language." In *Asian Philosophy* 21/2 (2011): 123–137.

Schlieter, Jens-Uwe. *Versprachlichung – Entsprachlichung: Untersuchungen zum philosophischen Stellenwert der Sprache im europäischen und buddhistischen Denken.* Köln: edition chōra, 2000.

Steineck, Christian/ Rappe, Guido/ Arifuku Kōgaku, eds. *Dōgen als Philosoph.* Wiesbaden: Harrassowitz, 2002.

Tanahashi, Kazuaki, ed. *Treasury of the True Dharma Eye. Zen Master Dōgen's Shobo Genzo.* Boulder: Shambhala, 2012.

Thurman, Robert A. F. *The Holy Teaching of Vimalakirti: A Mahayana Scripture.* Delhi: Motilal Banarsidass Publications, 1991.

Contents

About the Authors

Laurentiu Andrei (Ph.D.) is an affiliated researcher at the *Philosophies et Rationalités* Research Center of the *Université Clermont-Auvergne*, specialised in comparative and trans-cultural philosophy, Japanese Zen Buddhism, and Hellenistic philosophy. He taught for several years at the *Université Paris 1 Panthéon-Sorbonne* and teaches now philosophy in the *Académie de Nantes*.

Eitan Bolokan (Ph.D.) is a lecturer at the Department of East Asian Studies of Tel Aviv University. A graduate of the University's School of Philosophy, Dr. Bolokan has also studied at the faculty of Buddhist Studies of Komazawa University in Tokyo. His research interests include Comparative Religion, mainly Buddhist and Jewish thought, comparative ethics, and hermeneutics. Dr. Bolokan's works were published in journals such as *Philosophy East and West*, *Contemporary Buddhism*, *Japanese Studies Review*, and *Asian Philosophy*. His collection of Hebrew translations of Dōgen's essays is due to be published next year by The Hebrew University Magnes Press.

André van der Braak (Ph.D.) works at the Faculty of Religion and Theology of the Vrije Universiteit Amsterdam since 2012, first as a professor of Buddhist Philosophy in Dialogue with other World Views, and since 2021 as a professor of Comparative Philosophy of Religion. He published various articles on Dōgen, and two monographs on Zen and the West: *Nietzsche and Zen: Self-Overcoming without a Self* (Lanham, MD: Lexington, 2011) and *Reimagining Zen in a Secular Age: Charles Taylor and Zen Buddhism in the West* (Leiden: Brill Publishing, 2020). He is also an authorized Zen teacher since 2013, and teaches various Zen retreats in the Netherlands.

Felipe Cuervo Restrepo is a Colombian philosopher who is currently finishing his Ph.D. in Philosophy at Los Andes University (Bogotá, Colombia) with a thesis on the ontology and perception of temporal entities (occurrents). His previous studies include an undergraduate degree in Philosophy from the National University of Colombia (Bogotá, Colombia) and a Master's degree in Semiotics from Tartu

University (Tartu, Estonia). Besides the metaphysics of time (from both an Analytical and Continental perspective), his current interests include the history of Analytic Philosophy, the history of German Idealism, and Japanese Philosophy (specially Dōgen and the Kyōto School). Currently, he works as an assistant professor of Philosophy at El Bosque University (Bogotá, Colombia).

Audrey Guilbault   is a Ph.D. student in the Department of Philosophy and the Divinity School at the University of Chicago. Her work focuses on Buddhist philosophy, spanning across both classical India and East Asia, with a particular emphasis on Buddhist approaches to ethics and practical reasoning, and their metaphysical and epistemological underpinnings.

Steven Heine   (Ph.D.), professor of Religious Studies and History and founding director of Asian Studies at Florida International University, has published three dozen monographs and edited volumes on the history of Zen thought in China and Japan, including the implications for both medieval modern East Asian societies. A recipient of Japan's prestigious award, the Order of the Rising Sun, Heine's particular emphasis is on the life and works of Zen master Dōgen, as in the following books: *Dōgen and the Kōan Tradition*, *The Zen Poetry of Dōgen*, *Did Dōgen Go to China?*, *Dōgen: Textual and Historical Studies*, *Dōgen and Sōtō Zen*, *Readings in Dōgen's Treasury of the True Dharma Eye*, and *Dogen: Japan's Original Zen Teacher*.

Zuzana Kubovčáková   (Ph.D.) is an assistant professor in the Department of Japanese Studies at Masaryk University in Brno, Czech Republic, and earned her MAs from the Department of Language and Cultures of East Asia at Comenius University in Bratislava, Slovakia, and SOAS, University of London, concentrating on the earliest history of Zen schools in Japan. After receiving scholarship of the Japanese Ministry of Education (*Monbukagakushō*) at Ōsaka University of Foreign Studies (*Ōsaka gaikokugo daigaku*), she pursued her Ph.D. at the Department for the Study of Religions, Masaryk University in Brno, Czech Republic. Head of the Department of Japanese Studies at Masaryk University between 2013 and 2017, Dr. Kubovčáková left the position between 2017 and 2018 to teach as a Numata Visiting Professor in Buddhist Studies at Institute for South Asia, Tibet and Buddhist Studies, University of Vienna, Austria, and at the Center for Japanese Studies, Nanzan University in Nagoya, Japan. Her research interests include study and translation of the *Shōbōgenzō* and Dōgen thought, as well as recent history of the Sōtō school in central Europe.

Adam Loughnane   (Ph.D.) is a lecturer (associate professor) in Philosophy at University College Cork, Co-Director of the Irish Institute of Japanese Studies, and Associate Editor at the *European Journal of Japanese Philosophy* and Editor of the *Journal of Aesthetics and Phenomenology*. His research and teaching center on the phenomenological and aesthetic traditions of Europe and Asia. Focusing mostly on French and Japanese philosophies, Adam explores themes such as non-duality, non-theistic conceptions of faith, phenomenological accounts of motion, perception, and expression, as well as intercultural philosophical methodology. He has recently completed a monograph entitled *Nishida and Merleau-Ponty: Artistic Expression as Motor-Perceptual faith* (SUNY 2019), is presently working on an introduction to Japanese philosophy, *Phenomenology of Tea* (Bloomsbury, 2023), and co-editing a forthcoming volume *Tetsugaku Companion to Ueda Shizuteru: Languge, Experience, and Zen*, (Springer, 2022). His work in intercultural philosophy and aesthetics has been published in *Philosophy East and West, The European Journal of Japanese Philosophy, Performance Philosophy, Polylog*, and the *Stanford Encyclopedia of Philosophy*.

Ralf Müller (Ph.D.) has been a visiting scholar at the Department of Philosophy, University College Cork since April 2022 and was a research assistant at the Institute of Philosophy, University of Hildesheim for many years. His fields of work include Philosophy of language and culture, especially based on the works of Ernst Cassirer and Wilhelm von Humboldt. His interests include regional philosophies, including pre-modern Buddhist and modern Japanese philosophy. After research stays in Switzerland, Japan, and the USA, he is working on a concept of intercultural philosophy as "philosophy in and as translation." His selected publications are "The Philosophical Reception of Japanese Buddhism After 1868", in: *Dao Companion to Japanese Buddhist Philosophy*, Dordrecht 2019.He is also a co-editor of *Überlieferung und Übersetzung von Philosophie* (AZP-Beihefte, in preparation) and *The Cross-Cultural Question of the Human: Inviting Nishida Kitarō to the Davos Disputations* (in preparation). Homepage: www.ralfmueller.eu

Rein Raud (Ph.D.) is a professor of Asian and Cultural Studies at the School of Humanities, Tallinn University. He has published widely on various subjects in philosophy and cultural theory (*Being in Flux*, Polity 2021, *Meaning in Action*, Polity 2016, *Practices of Selfhood*, co-written with Zygmunt Bauman, Polity 2015) as well as Asian thought (*Asian Worldviews: Religions, Philosophies, Political Theories*, Wiley-Blackwell 2021). Dōgen's thought has been one of his main topics of focus, and he has published a series of articles about it in journals such as *Philosophy East and West, Asian Philosophy*, and *Religions* and edited volumes published by Hawai'i and Tokyo University Presses.

Raji C. Steineck (Ph.D.) is a professor of Japanology at the University of Zurich (Switzerland), visiting professor at Yamaguchi University's Research Institute for Time Studies, and president of the International Society for the Study of Time (ISST). He obtained his Ph.D. in Philosophy and the Ph.D. habil in Japanology at Bonn University (Germany), and has held temporary or visiting positions at Frankfurt University, Adam Mickiewicz University (Poznań, Poland), Dōshisha University (Kyōto), Kyōto University, and Tōkyō University. His research interests are the philosophy and critical study of symbolic forms, Japanese philosophy and intellectual history, and the study of time. He has published translations of several of Dōgen's works into German, observations on ritual, ethics, and time in Dōgen's teaching, and reflections on conceptual issues in Dōgen studies. He is currently preparing a monograph exploring the expressive, practical, theoretical, and spiritual aspects of time in Dōgen.

Laura Specker Sullivan (Ph.D.) is a specialist in Japanese philosophy and bio-ethics. She is an assistant professor of Philosophy at Fordham University. She is the former director of Ethics at the Medical University of South Carolina and was an assistant professor of Philosophy at the College of Charleston. She has held fellow-ships at the Center for Bioethics at Harvard Medical School, the Center for Sensorimotor Neural Engineering at the University of Washington, Neuroethics Canada at the University of British Columbia, and the Kokoro Research Center at Kyoto University. Her Ph.D. in philosophy is from the University of Hawaii with a graduate certificate in Japanese Studies. She is currently the category leader for philosophy/history for the American Society for Bioethics and Humanities and a member of the program and nominating committees for the International Neuroethics Society. Her work has appeared in *Asian Philosophy,* the *Journal of Japanese Philosophy,* the *Kennedy Institute of Ethics Journal*, *Bioethics, Social Science and Medicine, Ethical Theory and Moral Practice*, and the *International Journal of Philosophical Studies.*

Aldo Tollini (Ph.D.) is a former professor at Ca' Foscari University of Venice, Italy, where he taught for many years Japanese Classic Language.His work has mainly focused on the translation of medieval Buddhist texts, particularly those of the Japanese master Dōgen (1200–1253). In addition, he has been interested in and published on topics concerning medieval Japanese culture and the influence of Zen Buddhism.Currently, his field of research focuses on medieval Zen Buddhism – mainly from the Kamakura and Muromachi periods – and its cultural and artistic environment with an approach based on the translation of original texts.

George Wrisley (Ph.D.) is a professor of Philosophy at the University of North Georgia (Gainesville). He earned his Ph.D. in Philosophy at the University of Iowa, specializing in the Philosophy of Language and Metaphysics. At Georgia State University, he earned an M.A. in Philosophy, specializing in Wittgenstein. He has since gone on to focus his research on metaphilosophy, and his long-standing inter-ests in Nietzsche, Buddhism, and Zen, particularly Dōgen's Sōtō Zen; one interest has been to bring Nietzsche's work on suffering and a passionate affirmation of life into conversation with Dōgen's Zen. His publications include, "Wherefore the Failure of Private Ostension?" in the *Australasian Journal of Philosophy (2011)*; "The Nietzschean Bodhisattva—Passionately Navigating Indeterminacy" in *The Significance of Indeterminacy: Perspectives from Asian and Continental Philosophy* (Eds. Robert H. Scott and Gregory S. Moss, Routledge, 2020); "The Role of Compassion in Actualizing Dōgen's Zen." *Japan Studies Review*. Volume XXIV. 2020; and the forthcoming, "Revitalizing the Familiar: A Practical Application of Dōgen's Transformative Zen" in *Introduction to Buddhist East Asia: An Interdisciplinary Resource*. Eds. Robert H. Scott and James McRae. SUNY Press.

Philosopher, Religious Thinker or Contemplative Practitioner? Making Sense of Dōgen Beyond Zen Modernism

André van der Braak

In the philosophical reception of Dōgen's work in the West over the past century, various Zen modernist imaginings of the nature of his work have been presented. Can Dōgen best be interpreted as a philosopher? Or can he best be interpreted as a Buddhist religious thinker? In this article I want to reflect on such approaches to understanding Dōgen's work. I will be following the approach of the German philosopher Hans-Georg Gadamer (1900–2002) called philosophical hermeneutics.[1] According to Gadamer, understanding is possible through a merging of the horizon of that which one aims to understand with one's own horizon. Central in Gadamer's approach to understanding is the impossibility of understanding Dōgen "as he really is" or understanding what he wrote "as he really meant it" (gaining access to his authorial intention). We do not have immediate access to Dōgen. Making sense of Dōgen is always imagining Dōgen, according to our subconscious pre-understandings (*Vorverstehen*): understanding him *as* a philosopher, *a*s a religious thinker, *as* a prophet, or *as* a miracle worker.

This article will present the various arguments that have been brought forward in the Western Zen modernist literature on Dōgen for reading him as a philosopher, or as a religious thinker. My conclusion will be that both of these approaches to Dōgen, as long as they are defined within a Western modernist context, do not do his work justice. Dōgen's repeated impatience with, and even disdain for, non-Buddhist approaches make it difficult to defend approaching him as a philosopher engaged in an impartial non-dogmatic quest for truth. For Dōgen, the Buddhist way is of prime importance. On the other hand, Dōgen is doing more than just expounding the truth

---

[1] Gadamer, *Philosophical Hermeneutics* (Berkeley: University of California Press, 1976).

A. van der Braak (✉)
Vrije Universiteit Amsterdam, Amsterdam, Netherlands
e-mail: a.vander.braak@vu.nl

© The Author(s), under exclusive license to Springer Nature Switzerland AG 2023
R. Müller, G. Wrisley (eds.), *Dōgen's Texts*, Sophia Studies in Cross-cultural Philosophy of Traditions and Cultures 35,
https://doi.org/10.1007/978-3-031-42246-1_1

of the Buddhist Way (as a Buddhist religious thinker would do). He is clearly endeavoring to enact truth, albeit within the contours of the Buddhist Way.[2]

My argument in this article will be to read Dōgen in a third way, beyond either philosophy or religion in the orthodox sense. Both "philosophy" and "religion" are notions that rest on certain *Vorverstehens* that turn out to be dependent on contingent historical and social developments in Western Europe. Therefore, it is important to escape the dualist dilemma of reading Dōgen as either a philosopher or as a religious thinker. Such a third way is defended by Monika Kirloskar-Steinbach and Leah Kalmanson in their new book *A Practical Guide to World Philosophies*.[3] In terms of philosophical hermeneutics, this might be a productive *Vorverstehen* that might also offer resources to escape the particular mergings of horizons that have been characteristic of Zen modernism. I discuss the recent translation and commentary of Dōgen's *Shushōgi, Engaging Dōgen's Zen*, as an example of such a new religio-philosophical approach to Dōgen.[4] In the discussion section, I will briefly explore using the hermeneutical label of "contemplative practitioner" as a third approach to Dōgen's thought and practice.

1   Making Sense of Dōgen

Why is it important to be explicit about how we make sense of Dōgen? An important point of cross-cultural philosophical hermeneutics is that our categories co-determine our understanding. Philosophical hermeneutics questions the possibility of reaching "objective" meanings by eliminating preconceptions. Rather, it strives to make those preconceptions explicit, in order to make constructive cross-cultural dialogue possible. Becoming aware of Western preconceptions about what a "philosopher" is, or what a "religious thinker" is, can help us to engage in a constructive dialogue with Dōgen's thought.

Philosophical hermeneutics stresses that interpretation is always contextually and historically determined, and therefore open to change. There is no such thing as a final interpretation of Dōgen. Dōgen's thought, as it is given to us, is always mediated through language, culture and history. We interpret it according to the contextual clues that we manage to gather.

Philosophical hermeneutics reverses the relationship between understanding and interpretation. It is usually assumed that our interpretation of Dōgen's texts leads to an understanding of them. However, from a philosophical hermeneutical approach,

---

[2] For the importance of enactment with regard to Dōgen's view of *zazen*, see Leighton, "Zazen As an Enactment Ritual," in *Zen Ritual: Studies of Zen Buddhist Theory in Practice*, Steven Heine and Dale S. Wright (eds.) (Oxford: Oxford University Press, 2008) 167–184.

[3] Kirloskar-Steinbach and Kalmanson, *A Practical Guide to World Philosophies: Selves, Worlds, and Ways of Knowing* (London: Bloomsbury, 2021).

[4] Wirth, Schroeder, and Davis (eds.). *Engaging Dōgen's Zen: The Philosophy of Practice as Awakening* (Somerville, MA: Wisdom Publications, 2016).

our interpretations of Dōgen's texts are always already shaped by our (explicit or implicit) "pre-understanding" (*Vorverstehen*) of Dōgen. As Heidegger wrote in section 32 of *Being and Time*: "interpretation is grounded existentially in understanding: the latter does not arise from the former. Nor is interpretation the acquiring of information about what is understood; it is rather the working-out of possibilities projected in understanding."[5]

Unless we pre-understand Dōgen already in some way, we could never come to an interpretation of his thought. In our interpretations of Dōgen we come to consciously know what we have understood preconsciously. Interpretation makes our implicit pre-understanding explicit. Dale Wright expressed this as follows: "When we understand something, we understand it "in terms of" something else already familiar and available within our world. [...] interpretations are exercises in connecting one thing to another, a phenomenon to an image in our minds, and that connection to the totality of our understanding."[6]

When we try to understand Dōgen, we always imagine him *as* a philosopher, *as* a religious thinker, *as* a Buddhist, *as* a mystic. There is no way around this. We never arrive at Dōgen "as he really is." The commendable effort to eliminate our preconceptions with regard to Dōgen will never be completed. It is *because* of our preconceptions that we are able to understand Dōgen at all. Only by connecting Dōgen's thought to something else already known to us can it become meaningful to us. Therefore, we must obviously attempt to avoid projection and prejudice, but we do so by critically appraising those. By locating inappropriate projections in certain imaginings of Dōgen, they can be revised or replaced by more appropriate ones.

In the next sections, I will critically appraise imaginings of Dōgen as a philosopher and a religious thinker.

2   Dōgen as a Philosopher

Raji Steineck has critically reviewed the history of Dōgen the philosopher.[7] The imagining of Dōgen as a philosopher started in 1926 with Watsuji Tetsurō (1889–1960) who, in his *Dōgen the Shramanera*, translated Dōgen into the idiom of the European philosophy of his time, bringing him into dialogue with Nietzsche and

---

[5] Heidegger, *Being and Time*, translated by J. Macquarrie and E. Robinson (New York, NY: Harper and Row, 1962).

[6] Wright, *Philosophical Meditations on Zen Buddhism* (Cambridge: Cambridge University Press, 1998).

[7] Steineck, "A Zen Philosopher? – Notes on the Philosophical Reading of Dōgen's Shōbōgenzō," in *Concepts of Philosophy in Asia and the Islamic World*, R.C. Steineck (ed.) (Leiden: Brill, 2018a), 577–606.

Hegel.[8] As Steineck notes: "Watsuji did not deny the Buddhist context of Dōgen's life and work. But he forcefully argued that his writings, as texts, were open to a purely theoretical understanding and interpretation."[9] This work has set the tone for much of the philosophical reception of Dōgen's writings. Members of the Kyoto school further developed the notion of Dōgen as a dialectical philosopher *avant la lettre*.[10]

Modern Dōgen scholarship in the West has taken place, following the division of Hee-Jin Kim[11] in three areas: textual-historical criticism, comparative-philosophical analysis, and methodological-hermeneutical study. Representative works in the comparative-philosophical area of Dōgen scholarship read his work in comparison to Nietzsche, Wittgenstein, Heidegger and Derrida.[12] In such comparisons, he is mostly interpreted as an anti-metaphysical or deconstructivist philosopher, with a focus on such issues as the nonsubstantiality and radical relatedness of all things,

[8] Watsuji, *Shamon Dōgen* [Dōgen the Shramanera, 1926], in *Watsuji Tetsurō Zenshū*, Abe Yoshishige (ed.), volume 4,. (Tōkyō: Iwanami shoten, 1962), 156–246.

[9] Steineck, "A Zen Philosopher? – Notes on the Philosophical Reading of Dōgen's Shōbōgenzō," 577.

[10] See Tanabe, *Shōbōgenzō no tetsugaku shikan* [My view of the Philosophy of the Shōbōgenzō], (Tōkyō: Iwanami shoten, 1939); Nishitani, *Religion and Nothingness* (Berkeley, CA: University of California Press, 1982); Abe, *A Study of Dōgen: his Philosophy and Religion* (Albany, NY: State University of New York Press, 1992).

[11] Kim, *Eihei Dōgen: Mystical Realist* (Boston: Wisdom Publications, 2004), xvi.

[12] Kasulis, *Zen Action/Zen Person* (Honolulu: University Press of Hawaiʻi, 1981); Stambaugh, *Impermanence is Buddha-nature: Dōgen's understanding of temporality* (Honolulu: University of Hawaiʻi Press, 1990); Heine, *Existential and Ontological Dimensions of Time in Heidegger and Dōgen* (Albany, NY: State University of New York Press, 1985); Heine, *Readings of Dōgen's Treasury of the True Dharma Eye* (New York, NY: Columbia University Press, 2020); Olson, *Zen and the Art of Postmodern Philosophy: Two Paths of Liberation from the Representational Mode of Thinking* (Albany, NY: State University of New York Press, 2000); Müller, *Dōgens Sprachdenken: historische und symboltheoretische Perspektiven*, (Freiburg: Alber, 2013); Müller, "Philosophy and the Practice of Reflexivity. On Dōgens Discourse about Buddha-Nature," in *Concepts of Philosophy in Asia and the Islamic World*, R.C. Steineck (ed.) (Leiden: Brill, 2018), 545–576; Raud, "The Existential Moment: Rereading Dōgens Theory of Time," in *Philosophy East and West* 62, no. 2 (2012): 153–173; Raud, "Thinking with Dōgen: Reading Philosophically into and beyond the Textual Surface," in *Whither Japanese Philosophy*, Nakajima Takahiro (ed.) (Tokyo: UTCP, 2013) 27–35; Raud, "Dōgen's Idea of Buddha-Nature," *Asian Philosophy* 28, no. 4 (2015): 332–347; Raud, "Dōgen and the Linguistics of Reality," *Religions* 12, no. 5 (2021): 331; Davis, "The Presencing of Truth: Dōgen's Genjōkōan," in *Buddhist Philosophy: Essential Readings*, W. Edelglass and J. L. Garfield (eds.) (Oxford: Oxford University Press, 2009) 251–259; Davis, "The Philosophy of Zen Master Dōgen: Egoless Perspectivism," in *The Oxford Handbook of World Philosophy* (Oxford: Oxford University Press, 2011) 348–360; Kopf, *Beyond Personal Identity: Dōgen, Nishida and a Phenomenology of No-Self* (Richmond: Curzon Press, 2001).

Dōgen's nonrepresentational view of language and thinking[13] and the self-overcoming of mind and body.[14]

However, as Kim argues, the discovery of Dōgen as a philosophical thinker was strictly a modern phenomenon. It can be said to be a part of the general movement of Zen modernism: a tendency to reimagine classical Chinese and Japanese Zen thinkers in terms that were compatible with the Western discourses of Enlightenment, Romanticism and Protestantism.[15] This was part of a decontextualized presentation of Japanese Zen to the West that focused on the notion of "pure experience," attributed by many scholars to the writings of D.T. Suzuki,[16] that made Zen commensurable with the Western modernist immanent frame as described by Charles Taylor.[17] I have described this process more fully in *Reimagining Zen in a Secular Age*.[18]

Kim is critical of the comparative-philosophical approach to Dōgen. For him, Dōgen's overriding concern is religious and soteriological. He argues that "the comparative-philosophical approach, by and large, tends to lift Dōgen's thought from its religious and historical moorings."[19]

---

[13] See e.g. Kim, *Dōgen on Meditation and Thinking: A Reflection on His View of Zen* (Albany, NY: State University of New York Press, 2007); Müller, *Dōgens Sprachdenken: historische und symboltheoretische Perspektiven*, (Freiburg: Alber, 2013); Raud, "Dōgen and the Linguistics of Reality," *Religions* 12, no. 5 (2021): 331; van der Braak, "Dōgen on Language and Experience," *Religions* 12, no. 3 (2021): 181.

[14] Shaner, *The bodymind experience in Japanese Buddhism: a phenomenological perspective of Kūkai and Dōgen* (Albany, NY: State University of New York Press, 1985); Kopf, *Beyond Personal Identity: Dōgen, Nishida and a Phenomenology of No-Self* (Richmond: Curzon Press, 2001); van der Braak, "Nietzsche and Japanese Buddhism on the Cultivation of the Body: To What Extent does Truth Bear Incorporation?" *Comparative and Continental Philosophy* 1, no. 2 (2009): 223–251.

[15] See McMahan, "Repackaging Zen for the West," in *Westward Dharma: Buddhism Beyond Asia*, C.S. Prebish and M. Baumann (eds.) (Berkeley, CA: University of California Press, 2002), 218–229; McMahan, *The Making of Buddhist Modernism* (Oxford: Oxford University Press, 2008).

[16] See e.g. Suzuki, *An Introduction to Zen Buddhism* (Kyoto: Eastern Buddhist Society, 1934).

[17] Taylor, *A Secular Age* (Boston: Belknap Press, 2007). For critical evaluations of Zen modernism and Suzuki's part in it see Sharf, "Buddhist Modernism and the Rhetoric of Meditative Experience," *Numen* 42, no. 3 (1995a): 228–283; Sharf, "Sanbōkyōdan: Zen and the Way of the New Religions," *Japanese Journal of Religious Studies* 22, no. 3–4 (1995b): 417–458. For a more nuanced view on this process, and Suzuki's role in it, see Hori, "D.T. Suzuki and the Invention of Tradition," *The Eastern Buddhist* 47, no. 2 (2019): 41–81. See also Proudfoot, *Religious Experience* (Berkeley: University of California Press, 1985).

[18] van der Braak, *Reimagining Zen in a Secular Age: Charles Taylor and Zen Buddhism in the West* (Leiden: Brill Publishing, 2020). For a description of the cross pressures between such a modernized presentation of Zen to the West and historical-critical studies, see Heine, "Introduction: Fourth-Wave Studies of Chan/Zen Buddhist Discourse," *Frontiers of History in China* 8, no. 3 (2013): 309–315; Heine, *From Chinese Chan to Japanese Zen. A Remarkable Century of Transmission and Transformation* (Oxford: Oxford University Press, 2018).

[19] Kim, *Eihei Dōgen: Mystical Realist*, xvii.

3   Arguments Against Dōgen as a Philosopher

Kim's criticism are echoed by Steineck, who offers various arguments against reading Dōgen as a philosopher.[20] The assumption behind such an approach is that
Dōgen shares some of the intellectual problems and communicative strategies of
philosophy. Steineck argues that this is problematic. In his article he defends two
propositions: (1) The *Shōbōgenzō* is not a philosophical text[21]; (2) What Dōgen is
doing can be seen as an alternative to philosophy, rather than an alternative form of
philosophy.[22]

1. The *Shōbōgenzō* is a collection of writings that were based on informal sermons
   (*jishu*), similar to, for example, the writings of Meister Eckhart. According to
   Steineck, although the *Shōbōgenzō* is not a philosophical text, it may be meaningful and possible to reconstruct a philosophy of the *Shōbōgenzō*.

Realizing that the *Shōbōgenzō* is doing something other than philosophy, and
acknowledging the need to reconstruct Dōgen's thoughts in order to make them
philosophical, makes for philosophically more astute engagements with his thinking, Steineck argues. For example, the *Genjōkōan* (one of the most discussed fascicles of the *Shōbōgenzō*), can hardly be considered a philosophical writing. Rather
than explaining or arguing doctrinal positions, Dōgen presents his own views here
and encourages his disciples to study them in practice.[23] Like Meister Eckhart in his
sermons, Dōgen presents a quotation from the Canon, and goes on to explore its
meaning. The *Genjōkōan* is not a philosophical essay, but an instruction for contemplative exercise. As another example, the fascicle entitled *Buddha-nature* does not
actually argue a position on Buddha-nature – even though it does negate several
interpretations of it (e.g., that Buddha-nature is like a seed of enlightenment).[24]

Steineck anticipates the objection that one might interpret this as a specific style
of philosophical instruction, to get his disciples to think for themselves. This would
be an alternative style of doing philosophy. However, a passage in Dōgen's *Gakudō
yōjin shū* [Guidelines for Studying the Way] reads that the disciple's mind is a
receptacle meant to hold nothing but the teacher's dharma:

[20] Even though he admits to having done so himself in Steineck, Rappe, and Arifuku (eds.). *Dōgen
als Philosoph* (Wiesbaden: Harrassowitz, 2002).
[21] Tanahashi (ed.), *Treasury of the True Dharma Eye. Zen Master Dōgen's Shobo Genzo* (Boulder:
Shambhala, 2012).
[22] Steineck, "A Zen Philosopher? – Notes on the Philosophical Reading of Dōgen's Shōbōgenzō."
(Leiden:Brill 2018a), 579.
[23] Ibid., 585.
[24] Ibid., 588.

> When you practice with a teacher and inquire about dharma, clear body and mind, still the eyes and ears, and just listen and accept the teaching without mixing in other thoughts. Your body and mind will be one, a receptacle ready to be filled with water.[25]

This does not sound very much like the open-ended practice of philosophy. However, Steineck allows that it could be argued that such a passage might be meant for beginners.[26]

2. In order to determine what it is that Dōgen is doing in his work, if it is not philosophy, Steineck goes on to analyze Dōgen's use of several key terms. The term *ken* (view, opinion) is mostly rejected by Dōgen. A *ken* is typically something one should not have or produce, and should be left behind: "*Ken* are not to be pondered, discussed, analysed, or even refuted."[27] In the *Bendōwa*, non-Buddhist doctrines are rejected simply because they are non-Buddhist tenets. The disciples should not relate the teaching they receive from their master to other ideas. The *Shōbōgenzō* texts do not argue for the legitimacy of the Buddha Way. They "do not embrace or endorse impartial rational comparison and appreciation of different positions as a methodological ideal."[28]

The term *kyō* (teaching) is not used that much. It is mostly used to qualify a given instruction, either positively or negatively.[29] The term *dō* ("way" in the sense of a normative way of life) is used much more often, mostly in the context of the Buddha Way (*butsudō*) as something that can be reached or entered, and that can be matched or mismatched by certain actions, expressions or understandings.[30]

Steineck concludes from this analysis that the *Shōbōgenzō* texts do not practice philosophy, but an alternative to it: they encourage disciples to practice the Buddha Way: "The Buddha Way is a pre-existent way that can be and has to be followed, it is not to be developed further or re-invented. Following the way means to accept the model and standards of the Buddhas and patriarchs."[31] Practicing the Buddha Way runs counter to the practice of philosophy: "Dōgen's normative idea of the 'Buddha Way' runs counter to the kind of open-ended reflection and interpretation that is usually associated with philosophy."[32]

Steineck allows that such an open reading of Dōgen's texts is possible today. However, such a reading would run counter to the kind of reading that Dōgen

---

[25] Tanahashi, *Moon in a Dewdrop: Writings of Zen Master Dōgen* (San Francisco: North Point Press, 1985), 38.

[26] Steineck, "A Zen Philosopher? – Notes on the Philosophical Reading of Dōgen's Shōbōgenzō." (Leiden:Brill 2018a), 590.

[27] Ibid., 592.

[28] Ibid., 593.

[29] Ibid., 594.

[30] Ibid., 597.

[31] Ibid., 597–598.

[32] Ibid., 598.

himself envisioned, he argues. Dōgen's mode of reflection is contemplative, rather than investigative.

For Dōgen, practicing the Buddha Way involved studying the Way by way of body and mind, especially through seated meditation (zazen), rather than practicing philosophy: "to walk Dōgen's Buddha way means to sacrifice some of the defining ideals of philosophy, such as the ideal of an open and critical discussion of fundamental ideas and questions, and the ideal of a community of truth-seekers that transcends the boundaries of denominations and traditions."[33] Therefore, Steineck concludes, Dōgen's work is most productively approached as an alternative to philosophy, rather than as an alternative way of doing philosophy.

4   Dōgen as a Way-Seeking Philosopher

However, approaching Dōgen's work as an alternative way of doing philosophy is exactly what some other authors are arguing for. In his article, Steineck takes great pains to be hermeneutically sensitive to the question of how to define philosophy. He follows Kaufmann in the following definition:

> Philosophical texts attempt to *persuade* their addressees of *thoughts* or *ideas* on certain *essential,* but *contested matters of human interest.* […] In doing so, they provide for some *reasoning* that gives legitimation to these thoughts and ideas, while responding to the challenge that *there is no absolutely authoritative source or method* to settle the matter in question.[34]

As Steineck himself notes, this definition fairly closely resembles notions of philosophy standardly employed in current Western classrooms and philosophical publications. He denies, however, that it is Eurocentric, since it was formed with also non-Western texts in mind, such as the *Shōbōgenzō*.[35]

Perhaps unsurprisingly, other authors do find such a definition of philosophy Eurocentric. David Hall and Roger Ames have called such a Western approach to doing philosophy "Truth-seeking." They contrast this with Chinese approaches to doing philosophy that they call "Way-seeking": "In the West, truth is a knowledge of *what* is real and what represents that reality. For the Chinese, knowledge is not abstract, but concrete; it is not representational, but performative and participatory; it is not discursive, but is, as a knowledge of the way, a kind of know-how."[36]

---

[33] Ibid., 602.

[34] Steineck, "A Zen Philosopher? – Notes on the Philosophical Reading of Dōgen's Shōbōgenzō." (Leiden:Brill 2018a), 582.

[35] Nevertheless, Steineck argues that the *Shōbōgenzō* is not a philosophical text according to this definition.

[36] Hall and Ames, *Thinking from the Han: Self, Truth and Transcendence in Chinese and Western Culture,* (Albany, NY: State University of New York Press, 1998), here: 104.

Therefore, the difference between Truth-seekers and Way-seekers is quite substantial:

> Truth-seekers want finally to get to the bottom line, to establish facts, principles, theories that characterize the way things are. Way-seekers search out those forms of action that promote harmonious social existence. For the Way-seekers, truth is most importantly a quality of persons, not of propositions. Truth as "Way" refers to the genuineness and integrity of a fully functioning person.[37]

In his contribution to the workshop we participated in, "Dōgen's texts: Manifesting philosophy and/as/of religion?" (January 21–23, 2021), George Wrisley argues for engaging Dōgen's work as that of a philosopher doing philosophy. He starts out with the question of the nature of the philosophy (which is itself a philosophical question already). He notes that, just as various Western philosophers have had their own different normative views of what philosophy is, Dōgen had his own normative view on what the Buddha Way is. What counts as philosophy changes throughout time, responsive to the changing conditions of society and culture.

Wrisley construes philosophy as Way-seeking philosophy, responding to the question "how should I live?"[38] He argues that Dōgen's work doesn't offer a final and singular answer to this question, but answers it with an awareness of the changing conditions of life. The way one should live is to respond as best as possible to the changing conditions and situations of life. Such an approach to doing philosophy leaves open the place of argument in philosophy. Giving reasoned arguments in some format is not the only legitimate way to think through possible responses to the problems of life.

Wrisley quotes Dōgen's famous *Bendōwa* response that "A Buddhist should neither argue superiority or inferiority of doctrines, nor settle disputes over depth or shallowness of teachings, but only be mindful of authenticity or inauthenticity of practice."[39] As Kim explains, authenticity of practice refers to the manner and quality of negotiating the Way in different circumstances. To practice, to enact enlightenment, means to negotiate the Way. Such a negotiation is not a means to some end but the end itself. Therefore, not solving philosophical problems is the greatest good, but doing philosophy, i.e., philosophical discussion. Dōgen's practice of philosophy, seen in this way, can be interpreted as a continual probing and penetrating of what it means to authentically negotiate the Way according to changing circumstances. In reading the *Shōbōgenzō*, one must continually figure out the best response to what is being said: its contents provoke philosophical reflection.

---

[37] Ibid., 105.

[38] See George Wrisley, "Dōgen as Philosopher, Dōgen's Philosophical Zen." Presented at the workshop, "Dōgen's texts: Manifesting philosophy and/as/of religion?" January 21–23, 2021.

[39] Quoted in Kim, *Dōgen on Meditation and Thinking: A Reflection on His View of Zen* (Albany, NY: State University of New York Press, 2007), 22.

5 Dōgen as a Religious Thinker

Ironically, although Wrisley references Hee-Jin Kim quite often in his defense of
Dōgen the philosopher, Kim himself is critical of engaging Dōgen as a philosophical thinker. He prefers to engage him through a methodological-hermeneutical
approach. Rather than attempting to ahistoricize or atemporalize Dōgen's thought,
Kim focuses on "how Dōgen *does* his religion, especially his way of appropriating
language and symbols soteriologically."[40] Kim's methodological-hermeneutical
approach focuses on how Dōgen negotiates the Buddha Way.

Does this mean, then, that we should engage Dōgen as a Buddhist, or more generally, a religious thinker? Steineck is reluctant to take this approach, since the term
"religion" has such a problematic status in current thinking.[41] To qualify Dōgen as a
religious thinker would contribute to a taxonomy in which religious and philosophical thought become mutually exclusive.[42] Also, Dōgen differs from other religious
thinkers in his flexibility. According to Kim, Dōgen's ongoing negotiation of the
Way is characterized by his willingness to confront the messiness of negotiating the
way, rather than "the sage who, rooted in an unmediated grasp of the ineffable
ground of existence, spontaneously and perfectly responds to any situation they are
confronted with."[43]

Another difficulty in approaching Dōgen's work as that of a religious thinker is
the complex history of the terms "philosophy" and "religion" in Japanese history. At
the time of Dōgen, there was neither philosophy nor religion in Japan. Dōgen's
work would have been categorized as *buddha-dharma* (Jp. *Buppō*), the teachings of
Śakyamuni Buddha. The term religion only made its entry in Japan in international
trade treaties of the late 1850s, which included clauses requiring Japan to acknowledge "freedom of religion."[44] Eventually, the Japanese word *shūkyō* was agreed on
as a translation of religion. For the translation of the term "philosophy," the Japanese
term *tetsugaku* was coined in 1874 by Nishi Amane (1829–1897). The exact meaning of this new foreign discipline was much debated in Japan. Eventually, through
this term, a transmission of a specific, limited, Eurocentric version of philosophy to
Japan took place. This was a type of philosophy that "perceived itself as a branch of
independent inquiry that had been hugely successful in sundering its ties with

---

[40] Kim, *Eihei Dōgen: Mystical Realist* (Boston: Wisdom Publications, 2004), xviii.

[41] See Steineck, "'Religion' and the Concept of the Buddha Way: A Study of Semantics of the
Religious in Dōgen." *Asiatische Studien/Etudes Asiatiques* 72, no. 1 (2018b): 177–206, for a much
more elaborate discussion.

[42] Steineck, "A Zen Philosopher? – Notes on the Philosophical Reading of Dōgen's Shōbōgenzō."
(Leiden:Brill 2018a), 603.

[43] See George Wrisley, "Dōgen as Philosopher."

[44] Josephson, *The Invention of Religion in Japan* (Chicago: University of Chicago Press, 2012).

ecclesiastical authority in Europe" thanks to "the fierce allegiance of its practitioners to the power of reason."[45]

This self-image of philosophy as being free from religious authority is one of the reasons that Steineck rejects Dōgen as a true philosopher, as we have seen, because Dōgen accepts the "ecclesiastical authority" of Zen patriarchs and ancestors. In my opinion, however, approaching Dōgen as a Buddhist thinker (or theologian, or dharmalogian), in the sense of him not being interested in open-ended exploration but merely concerned with transmitting the Buddha Way, the tradition of Zen patriarchs and ancestors, seems not to do justice to his work.

The French philosopher Paul Ricoeur has famously distinguished between two modes of interpreting religion in religious studies: the hermeneutics of recollection (popular in theology and phenomenology of religion), that assumes that religious practitioners are in touch with something real, and the hermeneutics of suspicion (popular in social scientific approaches to religion), that favors reductionist naturalistic explanations of religion, because it denies that there is a divine reality in religion.[46] Philosopher of religion D.Z. Phillips has argued that the task of the philosopher of religion is not to be for or against religion, but to understand it. Both the hermeneutics of recollection and the hermeneutics of suspicion have certain methodological assumptions that stand in the way of an inquiry into religion. Phillips proposes a hermeneutics of contemplation that attempts to do conceptual justice to religious beliefs and practices without advocating personal acceptance of such beliefs and practices.[47] Perhaps such a hermeneutics of contemplation may be a fruitful approach to Dōgen as a religious thinker.

6 Decolonizing the Practice of Philosophy

Rather than attempting to engage Dōgen through the preformatted categories of philosophy and religion, the engagement with his thought may help to expand our notion of what it means to do philosophy (and what it means to do religion). In their book *A Practical Guide to World Philosophies: Selves, Worlds, and Ways of Knowing*, Monika Kirloskar-Steinbach and Leah Kalmanson offer a reformulation of philosophical methodology beyond the self-aggrandizing parochialism of a "Western" approach to philosophy that represents itself as the only truly universal wisdom. They argue against approaching philosophy as a decontextualized, culturally invariant mode of inquiry; such an approach rests on a Eurocentric faith (Western Europe's self-affirmation as being a unique civilization in human history)

---

[45] Kirloskar-Steinbach and Kalmanson, *A Practical Guide to World Philosophies: Selves, Worlds, and Ways of Knowing* (London: Bloomsbury, 2021), 27.

[46] Ricœur, *Freud and Philosophy: An Essay on Interpretation* (New Haven: Yale University Press, 1970).

[47] Phillips, *Religion and the Hermeneutics of Contemplation* (Cambridge: Cambridge University Press, 2001).

that is not corroborated by practice.[48] There are different ways of understanding philosophical inquiry that have arisen in different parts of the globe. Bret Davis argues that, rather than claiming that some cultures and not others had special access to universal reason, "it could be said that each act of philosophizing enacts a particular approach to universality, and we have no access to universality that bypasses these particular approaches.[...] This is not to say that we are locked into the horizons of these particularities, but we always begin to philosophize from somewhere."[49]

Therefore, a holistic, contextualized methodology is called for in the field of comparative philosophy.[50] Such a methodology, Kirloskar-Steinbach and Kalmanson argue, can be connected to the recent call for epistemic decolonization in philosophy: "Eurocentric approaches to philosophy cannot adequately capture all, or other ways of being, notwithstanding its contrary claims."[51]

The comparative-philosophical engagement with Dōgen has been part of the postwar wider movement of comparative philosophy that began, Kirloskar-Steinbeck and Kalmanson argue, as a laudable venture. However, the last few decades have shown the limited applicability of this approach to our world: "Neither the vision of a monolithic world order nor the binaries emanating from it give us appropriate tools to make sense of our interconnected postcolonial world. Rather our age [...] demands us to conceptualize a decidedly open understanding of philosophy."[52]

Such an open understanding of philosophy with regard to Dōgen's writings has been argued for earlier by Dōgen scholars such as Ohashi & Eberfeld (2006), Kasulis (1985) and Müller.[53] A more recent example of a new approach to Dōgen based upon such an open understanding of philosophy is the collection of essays *Engaging Dōgen's Zen*, edited by three comparative philosophers that are also practitioners of Dōgen's Buddha Way.[54] This essay collection contains a translation and

---

[48] Kirloskar-Steinbach and Kalmanson, *A Practical Guide to World Philosophies: Selves, Worlds, and Ways of Knowing* (London: Bloomsbury, 2021), 63–64.

[49] Davis, "Introduction: What is Japanese Philosophy?" In *The Oxford Handbook of Japanese Philosophy* (New York: Oxford UP, 2020), 53–54.

[50] For a contextualized approach to Dōgen see Heine, *From Chinese Chan to Japanese Zen. A Remarkable Century of Transmission and Transformation* (Oxford: Oxford UP, 2018).

[51] Kirloskar-Steinbach and Kalmanson, *A Practical Guide to World Philosophies: Selves, Worlds, and Ways of Knowing* (London: Bloomsbury, 2021), 82. See also Maraldo, "A Call for an Alternative Notion of Understanding in Interreligious Hermeneutics," In *Interreligious Hermeneutics*, 89–115 (Eugene, OR: Cascade Books, 2010) for a call to expand epistemic approaches to also include embodied epistemologies with regard to the field of interreligious hermeneutics.

[52] Kirloskar-Steinbach and Kalmanson, *A Practical Guide to World Philosophies: Selves, Worlds, and Ways of Knowing* (London: Bloomsbury, 2021), 14.

[53] See their writings in my bibliography. See also Garfield, *Empty Words: Buddhist Philosophy and Cross-Cultural Interpretation* (Oxford: Oxford University Press, 2002) for an extensive discussion of these matters.

[54] See Wirth, Schroeder, and Davis (eds.), *Engaging Dōgen's Zen: The Philosophy of Practice as Awakening.* (Somerville, MA: Wisdom Publications, 2016).

commentary of the *Shushōgi* [The Meaning of Practice-Realization], a primer of Dōgen's work that was first published in Japan in 1890. The *Shushōgi* is a collection of highly selective interwoven passages selected from the *Shōbōgenzō,* addressing such religious topics as "repenting and eliminating bad karma," "receiving precepts and joining the ranks," "making the vow to benefit beings," and "practicing Buddhism and repaying blessings."[55] The fact that zazen is not discussed at all in the *Shushōgi* would make the text completely uninteresting for Zen modernists. Its translation into English in this volume is an indication of the shifting tides with regard to the engagement with Dōgen's work.[56]

7 Discussion

The hermeneutical questions of this essay (should we read Dōgen as a philosopher, a religious thinker, or both?) may seem overly academic and less relevant to the real world. But the opposite is the case. Such hermeneutical decisions have real conse-quences in the real world. Virtually all chairs of Buddhist philosophy are at Religious Studies departments of universities, rather than at philosophy departments. When in 2013 the establishment of my own chair, *Buddhist Philosophy in Dialogue with other World Views,* at the Faculty of Religion and Theology was under discussion at Vrije Universiteit in Amsterdam, the representative of the Philosophy department was unwilling to co-establish the chair at his department. The name of the chair was better changed to "Buddhist spirituality," he remarked, echoing Hegel's famous claim, in his *Lectures on the History of Philosophy*, that "what we call Eastern Philosophy is more properly the religious mode of thought."[57]

As Kirloskar-Steinbach and Kalmanson argue, we need to go beyond Eurocentric categories, perhaps even beyond the very categories of philosophy and religion as well. Perhaps there is a third way to categorize Dōgen beyond philosophy and reli-gion. Recently, the notion of contemplative studies is gaining acceptance, as is evi-denced by the works of Louis Komjathy,[58] and in the recent establishment of the *International Society for Contemplative Research* which focuses on the interdisci-plinary investigation of traditional and modern forms of contemplative and other

---

[55] van der Braak, *Reimagining Zen in a Secular Age: Charles Taylor and Zen Buddhism in the West* (Leiden: Brill Publishing, 2020), 227–235, for a discussion of these topics in the *Shushōgi.*

[56] For another indication of these shifting tides, see Davis, *Zen Pathways: An Introduction to the Philosophy and Practice of Zen Buddhism* (Oxford: Oxford University Press, 2022).

[57] Hegel, *Lectures on the History of Philosophy: Greek Philosophy to Plato* (Lincoln: University of Nebraska Press, 1995), 117. In 2021, the name of the chair was changed to "Comparative Philosophy of Religion," in order to better fit with the structure of the Faculty of Religion and Theology.

[58] See Komjathy (ed.), *Contemplative Literature: A Comprehensive Sourcebook on Meditation and Contemplative Prayer* (Albany, NY: State University of New York Press, 2015); Komjathy, *Introducing Contemplative Studies* (Oxford: Wiley Blackwell, 2018).

mind-body practices in accord with their culture and context.[59] Since Steineck characterized Dōgen's project as contemplative rather than investigative, perhaps the label of "contemplative practitioner" would be hermeneutically fruitful.

However, we do not have to make a choice between these hermeneutical labels. It is my conviction that Dōgen the philosopher can help us to widen our *Vorverstehen* of what philosophy is, what constitutes a philosophical text, and how to do philosophy. Dōgen the religious thinker can expand our ideas of what it means to be religious, and how to do religion. And Dōgen the contemplative practitioner might also open up new horizons for research into Dōgen's thought and practice. All three of these labels can help us to go beyond limiting Zen modernist approaches to Dōgen.

References

Abe, Masao. *A Study of Dōgen: his Philosophy and Religion*. Albany, NY: State University of New York Press, 1992.

van der Braak, André. "Nietzsche and Japanese Buddhism on the Cultivation of the Body: To What Extent does Truth Bear Incorporation?" *Comparative and Continental Philosophy* 1, no. 2 (2009): 223–251.

van der Braak, André. *Reimagining Zen in a Secular Age: Charles Taylor and Zen Buddhism in the West*. Leiden: Brill Publishing, 2020.

van der Braak, André. "Dōgen on Language and Experience." *Religions* 12, no. 3 (2021): 181.

Davis, Bret W. "The Presencing of Truth: Dōgen's Genjōkōan." In William Edelglass and Jay L. Garfield, eds. *Buddhist Philosophy: Essential Readings*, 251–259. Oxford: Oxford University Press, 2009.

Davis, Bret W. "The Philosophy of Zen Master Dōgen: Egoless Perspectivism." In *The Oxford Handbook of World Philosophy*, 348–360. Oxford: Oxford University Press, 2011.

Davis, Bret W. "Introduction: What is Japanese Philosophy?" In *The Oxford Handbook of Japanese Philosophy*, edited by B.W. David, 1–79. New York: Oxford, 2020.

Davis, Bret W. *Zen Pathways: An Introduction to the Philosophy and Practice of Zen Buddhism*. Oxford: Oxford University Press, 2022.

Gadamer, Hans-Georg. *Philosophical Hermeneutics*. Berkeley: University of California Press, 1976.

Garfield, Jay L. *Empty Words: Buddhist Philosophy and Cross-Cultural Interpretation*. Oxford: Oxford University Press, 2002.

Hall, David L., and Roger T. Ames. *Thinking from the Han: Self, Truth and Transcendence in Chinese and Western Culture*. Albany, NY: State University of New York Press, 1998.

Hegel, G.W.F. *Lectures on the History of Philosophy: Greek Philosophy to Plato*, translated by E.S. Haldane. Lincoln: University of Nebraska Press, 1995.

Heidegger, Martin. *Being and Time*, translated by J. Macquarrie and E. Robinson. New York, NY: Harper and Row, 1962.

Heine, Steven. *Existential and Ontological Dimensions of Time in Heidegger and Dōgen*. Albany, NY: State University of New York Press, 1985.

Heine, Steven. "Introduction: Fourth-Wave Studies of Chan/Zen Buddhist Discourse." *Frontiers of History in China* 8, no. 3 (2013): 309–315.

Heine, Steven. *From Chinese Chan to Japanese Zen. A Remarkable Century of Transmission and Transformation*. Oxford: Oxford University Press, 2018.

---

[59] See the ISCR 2022 report.

Heine, Steven. *Readings of Dōgen's Treasury of the True Dharma Eye*. New York, NY: Columbia University Press, 2020.
Hori, G. Victor Sōgen. "D.T. Suzuki and the Invention of Tradition." *The Eastern Buddhist* 47, no. 2 (2019): 41–81.
ISCR 2022. *International Society for Contemplative Research*. https://www.contemplativeresearch.org
Josephson, J.A. *The Invention of Religion in Japan*. Chicago: University of Chicago Press, 2012.
Kasulis, Thomas P. *Zen Action/Zen Person*. Honolulu: University Press of Hawai'i, 1981.
Kasulis, Thomas P. "The Incomparable Philosopher: Dōgen on How to Read the Shōbōgenzō." In William LaFleur, ed., *Dōgen Studies*, 83–98. Honolulu: University of Hawai'i Press, 1985.
Kim, Hee-Jin. *Eihei Dōgen: Mystical Realist*. Boston: Wisdom Publications, 2004.
Kim, Hee-Jin. *Dōgen on Meditation and Thinking: A Reflection on His View of Zen*. Albany, NY: State University of New York Press, 2007.
Kirloskar-Steinbach, Monika, and Kalmanson, Leah. *A Practical Guide to World Philosophies: Selves, Worlds, and Ways of Knowing*. London: Bloomsbury, 2021
Komjathy, Louis, ed. *Contemplative Literature: A Comprehensive Sourcebook on Meditation and Contemplative Prayer*. Albany, NY: State University of New York Press, 2015.
Komjathy, Louis. *Introducing Contemplative Studies*. Oxford: Wiley Blackwell, 2018.
Kopf, Gereon. *Beyond Personal Identity: Dōgen, Nishida and a Phenomenology of No-Self*. Richmond: Curzon Press, 2001.
Leighton, Taigen Dan. "Zazen As an Enactment Ritual." In Steven Heine and Dale S. Wright, eds. *Zen Ritual: Studies of Zen Buddhist Theory in Practice*, 167–184. Oxford: Oxford University Press, 2008.
Maraldo, John C. "A Call for an Alternative Notion of Understanding in Interreligious Hermeneutics." In Catherine Cornille and Christopher Conway, eds. *Interreligious Hermeneutics*, 89–115. Eugene, OR: Cascade Books, 2010.
McMahan, David L. "Repackaging Zen for the West." In Charles S. Prebish and Martin Baumann, eds. *Westward Dharma: Buddhism Beyond Asia.*, 218–229. Berkeley, CA: University of California Press, 2002.
McMahan, David L. *The Making of Buddhist Modernism*. Oxford: Oxford University Press, 2008.
Müller, Ralf. *Dōgens Sprachdenken: historische und symboltheoretische Perspektiven*. Freiburg: Alber, 2013.
Müller, Ralf. "Philosophy and the Practice of Reflexivity. On Dōgens Discourse about Buddha-Nature." In Raji C. Steineck, Ralph Weber, Robert Gassmann, and Elena Lange, eds., *Concepts of Philosophy in Asia and the Islamic World*, Vol. 1: China and Japan, 545-576. Leiden: Brill, 2018.
Nishitani, Keiji. *Religion and Nothingness*. Berkeley, CA: University of California Press, 1982.
Ohashi, Ryosuke, and Rolf Eberfeld. *Shōbōgenzō. Ausgewählte Schriften. Anders Philosophieren aus dem Zen*. Tokyo: Keio University Press, 2006.
Olson, Carl. *Zen and the Art of Postmodern Philosophy: Two Paths of Liberation from the Representational Mode of Thinking*. Albany, NY: State University of New York Press, 2000.
Phillips, D.Z. *Religion and the Hermeneutics of Contemplation*. Cambridge: Cambridge University Press, 2001.
Proudfoot, Wayne. *Religious Experience*. Berkeley: University of California Press, 1985.
Raud, Rein. "The Existential Moment: Rereading Dōgens Theory of Time." *Philosophy East and West* 62, no. 2 (2012): 153–173.
Raud, Rein. "Thinking with Dōgen: Reading Philosophically into and beyond the Textual Surface." In *Whither Japanese Philosophy*, edited by Nakajima Takahiro, 27–35. Tokyo: UTCP, 2013.
Raud, Rein. "Dōgen's Idea of Buddha-Nature." *Asian Philosophy* 28, no. 4 (2015): 332–347.
Raud, Rein. "Dōgen and the Linguistics of Reality." *Religions* 12, no. 5 (2021): 331.
Ricœur, Paul. *Freud and Philosophy: An Essay on Interpretation*, translated by Denis Savage. New Haven: Yale University Press, 1970.

Shaner, David Edward. *The bodymind experience in Japanese Buddhism: a phenomenological perspective of Kūkai and Dōgen*. Albany, NY: State University of New York Press, 1985.

Sharf, Robert H. "Buddhist Modernism and the Rhetoric of Meditative Experience." *Numen* 42, no. 3 (1995a): 228–283.

Sharf, Robert H. "Sanbōkyōdan: Zen and the Way of the New Religions." *Japanese Journal of Religious Studies* 22, no. 3–4 (1995b): 417–458.

Stambaugh, Joan. *Impermanence is Buddha-nature: Dōgen's understanding of temporality*. Honolulu: University of Hawai'i Press, 1990.

Steineck, Christian, Guido Rappe, and Kōgaku Arifuku (eds.). *Dōgen als Philosoph*. Wiesbaden: Harrassowitz, 2002.

Steineck, Raji C. "A Zen Philosopher? – Notes on the Philosophical Reading of Dōgen's Shōbōgenzō." In Raji C. Steineck, ed. *Concepts of Philosophy in Asia and the Islamic World*, 577–606. Leiden: Brill, 2018a.

Steineck, Raji C. "'Religion' and the Concept of the Buddha Way: A Study of Semantics of the Religious in Dōgen." *Asiatische Studien/Etudes Asiatiques* 72, no. 1 (2018b): 177–206.

Suzuki, Daisetz Teitarō. *An Introduction to Zen Buddhism*. Kyoto: Eastern Buddhist Society, 1934.

Tanabe, Hajime. *Shōbōgenzō no tetsugaku shikan* [My view of the Philosophy of the Shōbōgenzō]. Tōkyō: Iwanami shoten, 1939.

Tanahashi, Kazuaki, ed. *Moon in a Dewdrop: Writings of Zen Master Dōgen*. San Francisco: North Point Press, 1985.

Tanahashi, Kazuaki, ed. *Treasury of the True Dharma Eye. Zen Master Dōgen's Shobo Genzo*. Boulder: Shambhala, 2012.

Taylor, Charles. *A Secular Age*. Boston: Belknap Press, 2007.

Watsuji, Tetsurō. *Shamon Dōgen* [Dōgen the Shramanera]. In *Watsuji Tetsurō Zenshū*, edited by Abe Yoshishige, volume 4, 156–246. Tōkyō: Iwanami shoten, 1962.

Wirth, Tetsuzen Jason M., Schroeder, Shudo Brian and Davis, Kanpu Bret W. (eds.). *Engaging Dōgen's Zen: The Philosophy of Practice as Awakening*. Somerville, MA: Wisdom Publications, 2016.

Wright, Dale S. *Philosophical Meditations on Zen Buddhism*. Cambridge: Cambridge University Press, 1998.

Wrisley, George. "Dōgen as Philosopher, Dōgen's Philosophical Zen." Presented at the workshop, "Dōgen's texts: Manifesting philosophy and/as/of religion?" January 21-23, 2021. Available at: https://www.georgewrisley.com/Do%CC%84gen%20as%20Philosopher,%20 Do%CC%84gen%E2%80%99s%20Philosophical%20Zen-Wrisley.pdf

Going Out to Sea: Dōgen's Ongoing Emphasis on the Creative Ambiguity of Horizons

Steven Heine

> *Fare forward, you who think that you are voyaging;*
> *You are not those who saw the harbor*
> *Receding, or those who will disembark.*
> *Here between the hither and farther shore*
> *While time is withdrawn, consider the future*
> *And the past with an equal mind.*

T.S. Eliot from Four Quartets.

1 The Question of Going Out to Sea[1]

What hermeneutic methods should be summoned to interpret critically an intriguing yet endlessly puzzling sentence in the "Genjōkōan" (現成公案) fascicle of Sōtō sect founder Dōgen's (道元, 1200–1253) *Shōbōgenzō* (正法眼蔵), which deals with the way perspectives shift dramatically "when riding a boat out to sea, where mountains can no longer be seen (*yamanaki kaichū* 山なき海中)"?[2] The analogy of

---

[1] Some of this material appears in Steven Heine "'When Mountains Can No Longer Be Seen': A Critical History of Interpretations of an Ambiguous *Shōbōgenzō* Sentence," *Journal of Chan Buddhism*, vol. 2 (2021).

[2] For the full text of *Shōbōgenzō* "Genjōkōan" see *Dōgen Zenji zenshū* 道元禪師全集 [Dōgen's Complete Works], 7 volumes, ed. Kawamura Kōdō 河村孝道, Kagashima Genryū 鏡島元隆, Suzuki Kakuzen 鈴木格禅, Kosaka Kiyū 小坂機融 et al. (Tōkyō: Shunjūsha, 1988–1993) [DZZ]: 1:2–7; SZ 1:3–9; and T no. 2582, 82.23b27–25a19. Citations from this and other passages by Dōgen are from DZZ. For a discussion of some similar themes see also Steven Heine, "What Is on the Other Side? Delusion and Realization in Dōgen's 'Genjōkōan,'" in *Dōgen: Textual and Historical Studies*, ed. Steven Heine (New York: Oxford University Press, 2012).

S. Heine (✉)
Florida International University, Miami, FL, USA
e-mail: heines@fiu.edu

© The Author(s), under exclusive license to Springer Nature Switzerland AG 2023
R. Müller, G. Wrisley (eds.), *Dōgen's Texts*, Sophia Studies in Cross-cultural Philosophy of Traditions and Cultures 35,
https://doi.org/10.1007/978-3-031-42246-1_2

19

sailing past the horizon, so that any trace of land is not visible and one feels tempo-rarily encircled by the ocean with no other frame of reference available, raises key phenomenological issues regarding the innate partiality or insufficiency of human perception in connection to the Zen goal of awakening to a holistic standpoint that is devoid of divisibility but incorporates an array of standpoints.

According to the colophon, "Genjōkōan" was composed in 1233 as an epistle to a layman, Yō Kōshū (楊光秀) from Kyushu, which makes it unique in a text that otherwise includes discourses originally delivered for the sake of monastic practi-tioners.[3] Dōgen continued to edit the fascicle until the year before his death, and it eventually became the opening section of the 75–fascicle and 60–fascicle editions of the *Shōbōgenzō*, while taking third position in the 95–fascicle edition. "Genjōkōan" has often been referred to by commentators as a fascicle that epito-mizes all of the primary themes so that its title could well serve as the name of the entire work. How can the various philological implications and philosophical nuances of the particular passage get sorted out? The first main step is to clarify the hermeneutic context though surveying the history of premodern and modern com-mentaries in light of the overt intentions as well as likely hidden agendas that guide their respective approaches. Many of the medieval and early modern sources, in addition to Meiji era and post–Meiji academic studies as well as *teishō* (提唱)–ori-ented homilies that treat the *Shōbōgenzō*, highlight the significance of Dōgen's rhetoric in illuminating and productive ways that sometimes reinforce but also help uncover and unravel stereotypical interpretations regarding his view of perceptivity.

The image of the moving boat reflects Dōgen's intricate approach to expressing what I refer to as "creative ambiguity" (*sōzōtekina aimaisa* 創造的な曖昧さ) con-cerning the way delusions, which reflect an incomplete and inconclusive level of understanding, invariably shape the quest to attain and disclose the meaning of authentic realization.[4] This term, therefore, refers to a series misapprehensions in that we tend to commit "mistakes compounded on mistakes" (*shōshaku jushaku* 將錯就錯), a term Dōgen mentions in several fascicles. These blunders can paradoxi-cally lead to a state of turning an error into one's advantage by making the right

---

[3] Other exceptions are "Zenki" (全機) and "Kobusshin" (古佛心) which were both presented to Dōgen's samurai patron, Hatano Yoshishige (波多野義重), and his entourage off-site from Dōgen's Kōshōji temple in Kyoto in the early 1240s. "Shōji" (生死) is probably another example but no information is available about its origins.

[4] I am influenced by Ōe Kenzaburo's 大江健三郎 Noble Prize lecture in 1994, *Aimai na Nihon no watakushi* 曖昧な日本の私 [Japan, the Ambiguous, and Myself] (Tokyo: Iwanami shinsho, 1994) in which the term "*aimai na*" (ambiguous) replaces *utsukushii* (beautiful) in Kawabata Yasunari's 川端康成 1968 Nobel lecture, "Utsukushii Nihon no watakushi" from 1968; it is included in Ōe, *Aimai na Nihon no watakushi*, 1–17. Yet Ōe's notion recalls, from a different perspective, Kawabata citation from the traditional *Ryōjin hishō* (梁塵秘抄), "Although the Buddha is always present, because in the soundless dawn he does not appear, it seems like nothing but a dream" (仏は常にいませども，現ならぬぞあわれなる，人の音せぬ暁に，ほのかに夢に見えたもう).

mistake, which is how the double–edged idiom is often interpreted.[5] The standpoint of creative ambiguity therefore refuses to close off options and, because it acknowledges limitations that can lead to deficiency and duplicity, it remains open to ongoing possibilities that are often imaginative and inventive means of disclosing truth not disconnected from untruth. That is, one can either add error to error until a standpoint is hopelessly counterproductive or use an error to enhance understanding, like the act of sharpening a sword. Being fearful of mistakes may lead to injudicious attempts to suppress or eliminate their impact in a way that only makes the situation worse. However, by recognizing the value of mistakes, we discover that uncertainty and conflict constitute an essential stage in developing and refining genuine insight.

2 Reorienting a Stereotypical Debate

A careful analysis of the "Genjōkōan" passage helps reorient an important though misleading area of debate that often preoccupies current reflections on the status of Dōgen's thought yet fails to facilitate an appropriation of a broad range of commentaries. The infelicitous dispute I seek to eclipse involves assessing the value of Dōgen's prolific writings on Buddhist theory and practice in relation to his apparently dual roles as a sectarian trailblazer or an autonomous philosopher. The Kamakura–era Zen teacher, who spent 4 years during the 1220s studying in China before "returning home empty–handed" (*kushū genkyō* 空手還郷), is often regarded in binary fashion that features sharp ideological clashes among participants in the debate who frequently engage in contentious polemics. Discussions of the core polarity are generally attributed to the contrast between two prominent books that gained international attention in the first half of the twentieth century and were written by a denominational and a non–denominational author.

The debate these books foster considers whether Dōgen is primarily seen as a truth–seeker, whose teachings bear contemporary resonances not necessarily linked to the training techniques of a specific Buddhist school by at once epitomizing premodern Japanese thought influenced by Song–dynasty sources and foreshadowing recent developments in epistemology, ethics, environmentalism, existentialism, and cross–cultural linguistics.[6] Was Dōgen an incipient modern philosopher? This view was proposed by Kyoto School thinker Watsuji Tetsurō (和辻哲郎, 1889–1960), who stressed Dōgen's self–determining philosophy in *Shamon Dōgen* (沙門道元)

---

[5] The phrase appears in "Sokushin zebutsu" (即心是佛), "Gyōbutsu iigi" (行佛威儀), "Hakujushi" (柏樹子), and "Daishugyō" (大修行). For an example of its use in the *Biyanlu* that impacted Dōgen's rhetoric, see Thomas Cleary and J.C. Cleary, trans. *Blue Cliff Record*, 3 volumes (Boston: Shambhala, 1977), especially cases 8, 16, 28, 32, 36, 38, 39, 50, 55, 64, 85, 89, 91, 96.

[6] See Taigen Dan Leighton and Shohaku Okumura, trans. *Dogen's Extensive Record: A Translation of the Eihei Kōroku* (Boston: Wisdom, reprint 2010), 1.

published in 1926.[7] Or, it can be asked if Dōgen should be defined as the monk who established the Sōtō sect by transmitting to his native country the lineal tradition based on zazen (坐禅) practice as propagated by his continental mentor Rujing (如淨, 1163–1227). This approach was articulated in *Shūso toshite no Dōgen Zenji* (道元禅師の宗教と現代) published in 1944 by sectarian leader Etō Sokuō (衛藤即応, 1888–1958), who emphasized Dōgen's religious vision inextricably tied to his denominational functions.[8]

This discrepancy continues to influence studies of the *Shōbōgenzō* on both sides of the Pacific.[9] For example, Ralf Müller recently remarked on behalf of the Dōgen-as–philosopher position, "The dispute was caused by the pretensions of non–denominational intellectuals to pave the way for an authentic apprenticeship independent of the practice of 'sitting–only' (J. *shikan taza* 只管打坐), which was taught by the Sōtō school as the core of Dōgen's Zen. However, the predominance of a 'practical' interpretation of Dōgen covers up the linguistic complexities of Dōgen's writings."[10] Müller suggests going beyond a strictly religious standpoint to open the door to a more comprehensive clarification of the complexities of Dōgen's theoretical implications, but he adjusts that assertion by pointing out that, "It seems wrong to maintain that Dōgen was (re–)discovered in modernity by non–denominational intellectuals [such as Watsuji]… Rather, more than a momentary event, the discovery of the modern Dōgen is a process, which spans most of the Meiji–period."

Although this clarifying remark challenges the typical sectarian versus non–sectarian paradigm, it still supports an opposition of binary factors based on the notion that there is a so–called modern Dōgen that is philosophical, even if that trend started a few decades before Watsuji. Müller's approach, therefore, does not necessarily leave room to evaluate how the legacy of voluminous premodern commentaries, mostly but not entirely generated by Sōtō scholar–monks, has greatly influenced nearly all recent Japanese scholarship concerning Dōgen's work, including varying methodologies used in the postwar period both within and outside of the sect.

My aim is to build on Müller's observation that pre–Watsuji discussions are important by arguing that it is crucial to provide a more thorough historical explanation of earlier Sōtō Zen elucidations of Dōgen, beginning with the monumental

---

[7] Watsuji's work, *Shamon Dōgen*, was originally published in Tetsurō Watsuji 和辻哲郎, *Nihon seishinshi kenkyū* 日本精神史研究 [Studies of Japanese Spirituality] (Tōkyō: Iwanami shoten, 1926).

[8] Etō's *Shūso toshite no Dōgen Zenji* has been translated as, *Zen Master Dōgen as Founding Patriarch*. See Sokuō Etō, *Zen Master Dōgen as Founding Patriarch*, trans. Ichimura Shohei (Washington State: North American Institute of Zen and Buddhist Studies, 2001).

[9] See Seijun Ishii 石井清純, "New Trends in Dōgen Studies in Japan," in *Dōgen: Textual and Historical Studies*, ed. Steven Heine (New York: Oxford University Press, 2012); and Kiyotaka Kimura, 木村清孝, *Shōbōgenzō zenbon kaidoku* 正法眼蔵全巻解読 [Comments on the Entire Collection of the *Shōbōgenzō*] (Tōkyō: Kōsei shuppan, 2015), 13–15.

[10] Ralf Müller, "The Philosophical Reception of Japanese Buddhism After 1868," in *The Dao Companion to Japanese Buddhist Philosophy*, ed. Gereon Kopf (Dordrecht: Springer, 2019), 174.

Shōbōgenzō kikigakishō (正法眼蔵聞書抄).[11] This eminent treatise, completed in 1308 after four decades of writing, was the initial substantial prose commentary covering the entire 75–fascicle *Shōbōgenzō*. The collective work is often known by the abbreviated title, the *Goshō* (御鈔). Although lost for several centuries, the *Goshō* was recovered in the early Edo period and cited extensively as authoritative by most of the major Sōtō scholastics of the seventeenth and eighteenth centuries who examined Dōgen's masterwork.[12] This list includes the mainstream faction of Manzan Dōhaku (卍山道白, 1635–1715), Menzan Zuihō (面山瑞方, 1683–1769), and Banjin Dōtan (萬仭道坦, 1698–1775), in addition to several dozen lesser known monk–scholars of the era, many of whose views were challenged by the rival clique of Tenkei Denson (天桂傳尊, 1648–1735) and his followers.

It is clear that the *Goshō*'s detailed interlinear comments explicating nearly every sentence of the *Shōbōgenzō*, along with numerous early modern annotations derived from or related to the Senne–Kyōgō compendium, were crucial in setting the stage for most of the important modern interpretative developments. Viewing the hermeneutic situation in terms of the historical context reveals that the major sectarian voice in the twentieth century was probably not Etō's but that of Nishiari Bokusan (西有穆山, 1821–1910), another Sōtō luminary, in his pioneering three–volume *Shōbōgenzō keiteki* (正法眼蔵啓迪) that was based on a series of lectures he delivered in the first decade of the 1900s.[13] Etō, whose work is remarkable in its own way, was less impactful no doubt because his apologetic method in reacting to Watsuji did not lead to an open–ended investigation of the *Shōbōgenzō*. In discussing "Genjōkōan" and other selections, Nishiari's approach relies but offers an innovative twist on the *Goshō* commentary that, in turn, influenced important members of his lineage, particularly Kurebayashi Kōdō (樽林皓堂1893–1988), who edited the main reprint of the *Shōbōgenzō keiteki* in 1965. Kurebayashi also published posthumously in 1991 a noteworthy monograph, *Genjōkōan wo kataru: ima wo ikiru, Shōbōgenzō kōsan* (現成公案を語る　今を生きる正法眼蔵講讃) based on a set of lectures he had given 20 years earlier.[14] In the aftermath of Kurebayashi's provocative and controversial approach to Dōgen's opening fascicle, which extends some of the implications of Nishiari's argument beyond what might be expected of

---

[11] This text is included in *SZ*, volumes 10–11; the specific "Genjōkōan" passage is discussed in 10.12–14. See also Jinbō Nyoten神保如天 and Andō Bun'ei 安藤文英, eds. *Shōbōgenzō chūkai zensho* 正法眼蔵注解全書 [Complete Commentaries on the *Shōbōgenzō*], 11 volumes (Tōkyō: Shōbōgenzō bussho kankōkai, reprint 1957) for additional commentaries.

[12] See Steven Heine, *Flowers Blooming on a Withered Tree: Giun's Verse Comments on Dōgen's Treasury of the True Dharma Eye* (New York: Oxford University Press, 2020).

[13] See Nishiari, *Shōbōgenzō keiteki*; and Nishiari, *Dōgen's Genjo Koan*, Bokusan Nishiari 西有穆山, *Shōbōgenzō* keiteki 正法眼蔵啓迪 [Edifying Discourses on the *Shōbōgenzō*], 3 volumes, ed. Kurebayashi Kōdō 樽林皓堂 (Tōkyō: Daihōrinkan, reprint 1965) and Bokusan Nishiari, "Commentary on Dogen's Genjo Koan," in *Dogen's Genjo Koan: Three Commentaries*, trans. Sojun Mel Weitsman and Kazuaki Tanahashi (Berkeley: Counterpoint Press, 2011).

[14] See Kōdō Kurebayashi, *Genjōkōan wo kataru: ima wo ikiru Shōbōgenzō kōsan* 現成公案を語る—今を生きる正法眼蔵講讃 [Discussions of "Genjōkōan": Lectures on the *Shōbōgenzō* for Living Today] (Tōkyō: Daihōrinkan, 1992).

a sectarian commentator, several Sōtō scholars representing diverging standpoints have made innovative interpretative contributions, including Yoshizu Yoshihide (吉津宜英, 1944–2014), Matsumoto Shirō (松本史郎, 1950–), and Ishii Seijun (石井清純, 1958–).

By investigating the meaning of the "Genjōkōan" passage in a way that is cognizant of a broad range of *Shōbōgenzō* interpretations stemming from the premodern to Meiji and subsequent reflections by scholars and Zen teachers, whether or not affiliated with the Sōtō sect, the debate about religion versus philosophy starts to appear artificial and unproductive. A careful reading of the relevant sources demonstrates a diverse discourse that cuts across and redefines denominational and conceptual boundaries by emphasizing a more fundamental and revealing question: What is Dōgen's view, regardless of ideological labels, of the relation between perception and reality, or subjectivity and objectivity? That is, how are everyday sensations and impressions linked to knowledge of one's surroundings that can be cultivated through contemplative awareness?

At first, this topic may seem to foster a new polarity because some interpretations maintain that Dōgen endorses the standpoint of absolutism (*zettaishugi* 絶対主義), for want of a better term, as suggested by the *Goshō*'s emphasis on the idea expressed in "Genjōkōan" of the "complete unimpeded penetration of a single dharma" (*ippō gūjin* 一法究盡). Supporters of the notion of undivided truth point to related doctrines in the *Shōbōgenzō*, such as "total activity" (*zenki* 全機), "triple world is mind–only" (*sangai yuishin* 三界唯心), the oneness of "birth–death" (*shoji* 生死), or "the moon" (*tsuki* 都機). The absolutist interpretation, introduced by the *Goshō* commentary that is echoed yet also somewhat revised by Nishiari, suggests that apparent partiality is actually intended to indicate limitless capacity. That is, the image of sailing past the horizon is linked to a sentence that comes a little later in the fascicle, "To obtain one dharma is to penetrate one dharma, and to receive one practice is to cultivate one practice" (*toku ippō tsū ippō nari gū ichigyō shu ichigyō nari* 得一法通一法なり, 遇一行修一行なり).

Other commentators stress the notion of relativism (*sōtaishugi* 相対主義), which is occasionally linked to postmodern theoretical standpoints that sometimes claim Dōgen as a compelling precursor based on the view of the "impossibility of complete unimpeded self–awareness" (*jiko zentai ninshiki dewanai koto* 自己全体認識ではないこと).[15] Proponents of fallibilism highlight the *Shōbōgenzō* doctrines of "impermanence–as–Buddha–nature" (*mujō–busshō* 無常佛性), "disentangling entangled vines" (*kattō* 葛藤), "dreaming within a dream" (*muchū setsumu* 夢中説夢), or "making mistake after mistake."[16] The view that there is a fundamental deficiency or gap in understanding, even for the enlightened, which must be accepted and penetrated instead of dismissed or blocked, is associated with a saying often

---

[15] See Kazuo Morimoto 森本和夫, *Derrida kara Dōgen e: datsu–kochiku to shinjin datsuraku* デリダから道元へ—脱構築と身心脱落 [From Derrida to Dōgen: Deconstruction and Dropping Off Body-Mind] (Tokyo: Fukutake Books, 1989).

[16] See Takushi Odagiri, "Dōgen's Fallibilism: Three Fascicles of *Shōbōgenzō*," *The Journal of Religion* 96, no. 4 (2016).

used in Chinese Chan kōan (公案Ch. gongan) commentaries that refers sarcastically to a "board–carrying fellow (檐板漢)," that is, someone who by indulging a blind spot since they metaphorically lug a plank across their shoulder is unable to be aware of other perspectives beyond any horizon.[17]

However, I will show that the categories of absolutism vis-à-vis relativism do not always constitute one more binary evoking standard oppositions, whereby sectarian orthodoxy would support the absolutist view in contrast to non–sectarian philosophy backing the relativist view since, when the diversity of interpretations is taken into account, the lines of demarcation quickly and even radically change. It becomes apparent, for example, that the strongest proponents of the absolutist view indicating, "one in all, and all in one," are modern secular philosophers such as Akiyama, Tanabe, and Nishitani, who use speculative methodology to provide an ontological foundation for holism, even though they are not wedded to a denominational standpoint. At the same time, the most nuanced exponents of relativism, for whom indefiniteness and indecision must be taken into account, include Kurebayashi, who draws inspiration from Nishiari and several other denominational figures he influenced, even though their view seems to defy the strictures of traditional Sōtō theology (dentō shūgaku (伝統宗学).

3   Unraveling the Debate by Revisiting Textual and Historical Contexts

In order to disentangle and refashion the debate regarding religious as opposed to philosophical interpretations of Dōgen, it is helpful to clarify some of the basic goals of Watsuji Tetsurō and Etō Sokuō that undergird and possibly link their respective views, while also exploring how the "Genjōkōan" passage about perceptions that shift when sailing out to sea provides a basis for new investigations of the meanings and methods of the Shōbōgenzō. The analysis offered here addresses the need to go beyond the framework of the core binary dispute between philosophical and religious approaches through taking into account a wider range of commentaries dealing with Dōgen's masterwork, including premodern and modern in addition to sectarian and non–sectarian sources.

A fundamental observation is that Watsuji and Etō are perhaps not so far apart as they may seem based on an initial reading of their works. Comparing biographies, they crossed paths in that the scholars each spent time during the 1920s studying in Europe, where they gained a sense of the inescapable expectation, whether appreciated or repudiated, that traditional Japanese thought should be presented in light of contemporary Western views and values. Both resisted the impetus to let East Asian Buddhism be subsumed by foreign intellectual classifications or research techniques and, despite absorbing some influences, they instead sought to explicate the

---

[17] See Cleary and Cleary, *Blue Cliff Record*, cases 4, 10, 16.

ultimate basis of native spirituality on its own terms. Furthermore, Watsuji earned his doctorate at Tokyo University and later taught there for many years after lecturing on ethics at Kyoto University.

This position was based on an invitation from famed philosopher Nishida Kitarō (西田幾多郎, 1870–1945), who similarly evoked elements of Dōgen's thought in explicating his notion of "absolute nothingness" (*zettai mu* 絶対無). Also, Etō's book was completed as a doctoral dissertation at Kyoto University and he became professor and president of Komazawa University in Tokyo for a term beginning in 1953. That institution was founded as the Sōtōshū Daigaku in the 1880s as part of a Meiji era initiative to support higher education by transforming a couple of long-standing Edo period Sōtō seminaries, especially Kichioji (吉祥寺) temple (aka. Sendarin 旃檀林), which was known as the site where Menzan and many other teachers had lectured extensively, sometimes for weeks at a time, on the contents of the Shōbōgenzō.[18]

Watsuji's short treatise, consisting of about 70 pages in the original publication, was contained as a section of his *Nihon seishinshi kenkyū* (日本精神史研究), a wide–ranging series of cultural studies seeking to situate Japan on a par with Western intellectual history by showing, for example, that Dōgen could be ranked as a world–class philosopher or that Nara Buddhist temples lived up to ancient Greek models of architecture. It is an exaggeration to say, as many have, that Watsuji single–handedly brought Dōgen's work out of nearly total obscurity, given that several non–sectarian philosophers, especially Inoue Enryō (井上円了, 1858–1919) in 1893 but also including Yamagami Shōfū (山上嘯風) in 1906 and Yodono Yōjun (淀野耀淳) in 1911, all attempted systematic examinations of the *Shōbōgenzō*.[19] However, Watsuji was the first to suggest rather forcefully that denominational considerations of Dōgen's writings should be tossed aside altogether for being terribly uninformed and corrupted by extraneous sociopolitical demands and commercial interests in that religion had become a kind of commodity functioning under the auspices of the state.

According to Watsuji's decidedly anti–sectarian stance, "To enter a Zen temple is to distance oneself from Dōgen. This is because the sect that takes Dōgen as founder is no longer solely concerned with the establishment of the realm of truth but concentrates on building massive halls and pagodas and on the prestige of the position of abbot."[20] Furthermore, Watsuji is anti–hagiographical in calling legend-

---

[18] See David E. Riggs, "The Life of Menzan Zuihō, Founder of Dōgen Zen," *Japan Review* 16 (2004).

[19] See Enryō Inoue 井上圓了, *Zenshū tetsugaku joron* 禅宗哲学序論 [Prolegomenon to a Philosophy of the Zen School] (Tōkyō: Tetsugaku shoin. 1893); Shōfū Yamagami 山上嘯風 "Dōgen zenji no uchūkan" 道元禅師の宇宙観 [Zen Master Dōgen's View of the Universe], *Wayūshi* 和融社 10 (1906); and Yōjun Yodono 淀野耀淳, "Dōgen no shūkyō oyobi tetsugaku" 道元の宗教及び哲学 [Dōgen's Religion and Philosophy] *Tōyō tetsugaku* 東洋哲学18 (1911), 3.1–9, 4.16–29, 5.15–29, 6.16–25, 7.13–23.

[20] Steve Bein, *Purifying Zen: Watsuji Tetsuro's Shamon Dogen*, trans. Steve Bein, Commentary by Steve Bein, (Honolulu: University of Hawai'i Press, 2011), 26.

ary accounts an "insult" to the integrity of Dogen: "The more I appreciate Dōgen's work, the more I cannot help but feel resentment toward senseless biographies. They ignore Dōgen's noble lifestyle of authenticity, focusing instead on all the mundane values and nonsensical miracles piled up to create an artifice of nobility."[21] Therefore, Watsuji embraces the role of being an outsider (*mongekan* 門外漢) and harsh critic of the Sōtō sect, who is thereby able to provide an objective assessment, without bias or misjudgment, of the importance of Dōgen's legacy in light of both Kamakura–era Buddhist developments and current global or comparative philosophical perspectives.

While he was writing his dissertation, Etō spent several years editing a four–volume paperback edition of the 95–fascicle *Shōbōgenzō* published by Iwanami bunko from 1939 to 1943,[22] which was at first acclaimed as the new standard version but was later discredited and eventually taken out of circulation and replaced by the press.[23] For Etō and many others then associated with Sōtō orthodoxy, Dōgen's greatness derived from an untiring commitment to just sitting and the rigors of clerical discipline in a way that defies characterization in terms of any philosophical argot that seems to fill the pages of the *Shōbōgenzō*.

That explains why Dōgen's approach culminates in deceptively commonplace evocations of true suchness (Skr. *tathātā*, Jp. *inmo* 恁麼), as evoked in the *kanbun* sermons of the *Eihei Koroku* (永平廣録), such as "my eyes are horizontal and nose is vertical" (鼻与臍対, 耳対肩) or "every single day the sun rises in the east, and every single night the moon sets in the west (朝朝日東出, 夜夜月落西)."[24] According to Etō, Dōgen's standpoint is based on "personal authentication" rather than abstract speculation or even experiential corroboration, which implies a subtle yet devastating gap between interior awareness and exterior existence.[25] Etō refers to Buddhist sūtras and śāstras as "ladles" dipping into the fountainhead of the Dharma, but maintains that "Dōgen alone discarded all ladles and himself, body and mind together… to actualize the entirety of Śākyamjni's spirituality in the oneness of his body and mind."[26]

Focusing on the conflict between Watsuji and Etō about whether Dōgen's approach lies beyond sectarian boundaries or is situated only within the confines of Sōtō Zen conceals important ideological similarities linking these scholars. The

---

[21] Ibid., 28–29.

[22] See Sokuō Etō衛藤即応, ed. *Shōbōgenzō* 正法眼蔵, 3 volumes (Tōkyō: Iwanami bunko, 1939–1943).

[23] Etō was criticized by a research associate for apparent errors included in the published text and, eventually, the 95-fascicle on which he relied was discredited and replaced in the early 1990s by the 4–volume edition edited in Yaoko Mizuno 水野弥穂, ed. *Shōbōgenzō*正法眼蔵, 4 volumes (Tōkyō: Iwanami bunko, 1990–1993).

[24] *DZZ* 4.22 (entry 6.432), and *DZZ* 3. 34 (entry 1.48).

[25] Etō, *Zen Master Dōgen as Founding Patriarch*, xxiii.

[26] Ibid, 59. Furthermore, "No matter how profound Dōgen's insight may have been, if we view it simply as philosophical thought, we will fail to uncover the fundamental aspect of the Zen master," 19.

main endeavor for both was to revive an interest in the *Shōbōgenzō* that previously, outside of a small circle of specialists familiar with Dōgen's obscure allusions and confounding grammatical constructions crossing Sinitic syntax with vernacular pronunciations, was considered an archaic and impenetrable text primarily read in a drastically compressed abridgement, the *Shushōgi* (修証義), which was created in 1891. The views of Watsuji and Etō are based on being able to read the text with "two eyes," as Nishiari's main follower Kishizawa Ian (岸澤惟安, 1865–1955) was known to say, in order to disclose its essential meaning not limited by the conventions of text–historical studies. Furthermore, Watsuji acknowledges that Dōgen's particular sense of drive and determination is key to his greatness, whereas Etō recognizes that in some passages such as the "Bukkyō" (佛教, Buddhist Teachings) fascicle, Dōgen emphasizes the role of genuine Buddhism without endorsing nomenclature that proclaims the independence of the Zen sect.

More significantly, the scholars share an evaluation that Dōgen's articulation of religious insight is eminently successful and neither one voices a degree of skepticism about his style of argumentation or the conclusions drawn. Indeed, Watsuji's interpretation dealing with Dōgen's "perfect expression of truth (*dōtoku* 道得) amounts to nothing less than a reiteration of the dynamics of perfect expression in Hegelian terms."[27] This is not far from Etō's assessment that is derived from the notion that Dōgen achieves transcendence–through–sublimation (*kōjō* 向上) in a way comparable to the German philosophical notion of *Aufgehoben*. Therefore, the main polarity separating the scholars is not really a matter of religion versus philosophy. Rather, it concerns the question of whether, for Dōgen, truth itself must be accessed through face–to–face (*menju* 面授) transmission directly received from a venerated teacher, such as his Chinese mentor Rujing, as argued by the Manzan lineage and propagated in Etō's orthodoxy.[28] Or is truth instead available to anyone through the universal capacity to disclose the Way, according to the outlook of Tenkei's heterodox faction that is cited briefly by Watsuji, who sees Dōgen "attaining freedom in the midst of a thorny forest" of deceptions?[29]

Probing further, there is yet another level of polarity that becomes evident from construing the intentions of Watsuji and Etō which evokes the parameters of an early modern dispute involving the relation between truth and untruth. This debate took place mainly among Sōtō scholastics but was also influenced by the denunciations of some of the rhetoric used in the *Shōbōgenzō* by the Rinzai monk Mujaku Dōchū (無著道忠, 1653–1745), who agreed with Tenkei's claims that Dōgen often misunderstands and misrepresents Sinitic sources.[30] Therefore, rather than being

---

[27] Müller, "The Philosophical Reception of Japanese Buddhism After 1868," 187.

[28] See William M. Bodiford, "Dharma Transmission in Soto Zen: Manzan Dōhaku's Reform Movement," *Monumenta Nipponica* 46, no. 4 (1991).

[29] Bein, *Purifying Zen*, 17.

[30] See John Jorgensen, "Zen Scholarship: Mujaku Dōchū and His Contemporaries," *Zenbunka kenkyūsho kiyo* 禅分化研究所紀要27 (2004).

hailed as a "genius of misreading"[31] for his interpretative innovations, according to the Tenkei–Mujaku standpoint, Dōgen is sorely in need of a significant amount of editing or rewriting. Disagreements about the function of transmission dovetailed with a parallel debate concerning how to prioritize the various editions of the *Shōbōgenzō*, with Manzan supporting the 75–fascicle version commented on by Senne and Tenkei favoring the 60–fascicle version that was commented on in 1329 by Giun, fifth abbot of Eiheiji, because that edition apparently deleted those controversial sections that displayed Dōgen's problematic treatment of Chinese language and teachers.

Considering these premodern schisms helps make it clear that underlying all of the differences between Watsuji and Etō stands a basic agreement that, since the perfection of truth prevails for Dōgen, there is no imperative to explore the notion that untruth and deception continue to impact perception even within the midst of truth, or vice-versa. Although the development of the standpoint suggesting that the *Shōbōgenzō* is not flawless and should be the subject of textual criticism or in some cases a degree of refutation that might be expected of a non–sectarian commentator, much like Etō's approach Watsuji does not seriously consider the objections that were raised by Tenkei despite the ample component of fallibilism in many examples of Dōgen's discourse. It seems clear that Watsuji and Etō are not really in discord regarding the foundational matter of truth. That is why it is so important that an investigation of whether Dōgen's thought can or should be reevaluated and possibly corrected is evident in the studies of several modern sectarian interpreters, including Kurebayashi and those he influenced, rather than secular philosophers, who remain committed to perfectionism.

The relevance of surveying an array of interpretations of the enigmatic "Genjōkōan" boat analogy in the context of discussing truth in relation to untruth, while tracing the history of the revisionist outlook that has impacted some prominent contemporary commentators, is that this passage offers an important case study of Dōgen's own view of the issue of inadequate perceptivity in relation to the possibility of fully disclosive awareness. He indicates that when traveling out to sea, "all we seem to view is a circle" (*tada maru ni nomi miyu* ただまろにのみみゆ), even though we know better than to accept that sensation. This metaphor, which follows an intriguing chiasmic statement about challenges to attaining spiritual realization because a sense of lack pervades an awareness of the Dharma, highlights the partiality of comprehension while recognizing on some level the unboundedness of perspectives. Are the outlooks of partiality and fullness to stand in one more binary set, or is there a sense of balance and harmony that can be attained?

Let us look more closely at a translation of the "Genjōkōan" paragraph:

When the Dharma has not yet been studied fully with body–mind, it seems adequate; but if the Dharma is amply realized with body–mind, one has a feeling of lack. For example, when riding a boat out to sea, where mountains can no longer be seen, we look around in four directions and all we seem to view is a circle. We do not see any other shapes.

---

[31] Yansheng He 何燕生, *Dōgen to Chūgoku Zen no shisō* 道元と中國禪思想 [Dōgen and Chinese Chan Thought] (Kyoto: Hōzōkan, 2001), viii.

Nevertheless, the great ocean is not round, nor is it square, and the remaining features of the ocean are altogether inexhaustible, so that [to a fish] it is like a palace or [to a deva] it is like a jeweled necklace. But, for that particular moment, all our eyes can take in appears round. (身心に, 法いまだ參飽せざるには, 法すでにたれりとおぼゆ. 法もし身心に充足すれば, ひとかたはたらずとおぼゆるなり. たとへば, 船にのりて山なき海中にいでて四方をみるに, ただまろにのみみゆ. さらにことなる相, みゆることなし. しかあれど, この大海, まろなるにあらず, 方なるにあらず, のこれる海徳, つくすべからざるなり. 宮殿のごとし, 瓔珞のごとし, ただわがまなこのおよぶところ, しばらくまろにみゆるのみなり).[32]

In this and the next paragraph of the fascicle Dōgen maintains that people are riddled by the conundrum that the more they know, the more they realize they do not know. This condition is crucial for the attainment of Zen awakening, if properly cultivated, and is comparable to Confucius' view that, "To know what you know and what you do not know, that is knowing" (知之為知之, 不知為不知, 是知也).

The image of riding a boat out to sea captures the moment one can tell that there are unlimited possibilities for additional perceptions, while understanding we are invariably bound to a partial and thus misleading standpoint. As we are unsure of what the eye is capable of seeing, on some level we realize there are innumerable other shapes besides circles and squares that can be observed by different beings. According to the "the four views of water" (issui shiken 一水四見) in Yogācāra Buddhist literature, which is also evoked the "Sansuikyō" (山水經) fascicle, in addition to the perceptions of fish and deva, humans see water as liquid and hungry ghosts see it as pus and blood.[33] Dōgen further suggests we should realize that the various virtues of oceans and mountains are unlimited, which is true "not only for what surrounds us, since vastness exists right under our feet or even within a single drop of water."

It is also interesting to note several passages related to the question of shifting perspectives caused by the act of sailing that are included in various fascicles. For example, in "Genjōkōan," Dōgen evokes a boat analogy to symbolize the relativity of the movement of the vessel vis-à-vis the shoreline that leads one to ask, even if for just an instant, which object remains steady: "When people ride in a boat, if they turn their eyes and gaze at the shore, they make the mistake of thinking that the shore is moving. But if they fix their eyes more closely on the vessel, they understand that it is the boat advancing."[34] In a similar passage Dōgen says of fish swimming in water and birds flying in the air that "they do not fail to be aware of the limits of their environs, but do not stop overturning each particular location" (頭頭に邊際をつくさずといふことなく處處に踏飜せずといふことなし).[35]

---

[32] ???

[33] DZZ 1.324.

[34] In other texts Dōgen often refers to two Tang Chan masters: the Boatman Monk Chuanzi Decheng (船子德誠, 820–858), who for decades rode in a boat without ever landing; and Xuansha (玄沙, 835–908), who before becoming a monk used a fishing boat.

[35] The verb tōhon (踏飜), rendered here as "overturning," as in tipping over a boat, is used in Chan texts to express an adept's ability "to toss topsy-turvy the great ocean or leap beyond Mount Sumeru" (踏翻大海趯倒須彌).

In a sardonic remark cited in "Shunjū" (春秋), Dōgen comments on a verse by Song Chan master Foxing (佛性, n.d.): "The place where there is no cold or heat is penetrated, / The withered tree blooms once again. / Those who notch the boat to find a sword are laughable / Even so they now occupy a state of cold ashes" (無寒暑處爲君通 / 枯木生華又一重 / 堪笑刻舟求劍者 / 至今猶在冷灰中).[36] Here the phrase, "notch the boat to find the sword" (刻舟求劍), refers to the folly based on a story from the Chinese classic *Chunqiu* (春秋) of a senseless man who dropped his sword from a vessel and marked the spot by marking the side of the boat. On the other hand, in "Zenki" (全機) Dōgen evokes the eminently positive image of poling a boat to represent the completely realized present moment that is at once cut off from and encompassing of past and future events, whereby "I do not exist apart from the boat and the boat functions as a vehicle because I am riding in it. You must make the effort to study such a moment as this." (われふねにのりて, このふねをもふねならしむ. この正當恁麼時を功夫參學すべし).[37]

4   Situating Traditional Commentaries

The primary aim of the *Goshō*, on the other hand, is to anticipate possible objections to some of Dōgen's bewildering assertions and explicate the intentions of the author in light of or by identifying some of his Sinitic sources while critiquing, whether directly or indirectly, the standpoints of rival Zen figures such as Dainichi Nōnin, founder of the Daruma school in the late 1100s, and the Rinzai school émigré monk, Rankei Dōryū (蘭渓道隆, Ch. Lanqi Daolong), who became abbot of Kenchōji temple in 1253. Both Nōnin and Rankei endorsed the suddenness of enlightenment in ways that Dōgen explicitly refuted.[38] A former Tendai monk no doubt accustomed to the subtleties of dialectical reasoning, Senne recognized that Dōgen's persistent use of paradoxes and rhetorical reversals could be misconstrued for lacking clarity or seen as inconsistencies. The *Goshō* often refers to a particular word or phrase "sounding rather odd" or "seeming unclear," and tries to address rather than bypass or suppress those concerns by providing an overall vision of Dōgen's underlying consistency. The authors mainly seek solutions to the enigmas from other passages expressed within the discourse of the *Shōbōgenzō*, instead of looking for answers outside of the masterwork, but they occasionally draw from examples of Tendai thought or Zen records.[39] The lack of objective reasoning in favor of a kind

---

[36] *DZZ* 1.413.

[37] *DZZ* 1.260.

[38] See Naohiro Matsunami松波直弘, *Kamakura ki Zenshū shisōshi no kenkyū* 鎌倉期禅宗思想史の研究 [Studies of the Intellectual History of the Zen School in the Kamakura Era] (Tokyo: Pelikan, 2011).

[39] William M. Bodiford, *Sōtō Zen in Medieval Japan* (Honolulu: University of Hawai'i Press, 1993), 44–48.

of circular logic committed to endorsing Dōgen's standpoint caused the *Goshō* to later become a target of criticism by the Tenkei faction.

Although written separately as coequal comments in that Kyōgō's glosses composed in paragraphs are independent and not necessarily an extension of Senne's explanations, which consist of a series of bulleted remarks, the two sets of annotations are usually treated as a unified work with the comments by Kyōgō appearing first in the modern edition. I will briefly summarize some of the main points in regard to how the *Goshō* portrays the boat analogy as exemplary of the chiasmic sentence about insufficiency by highlighting the relativity of human perceptions while in the end putting forth an absolutist interpretation of Dōgen's thought. The key question is whether and to what extent Senne–Kyōgō address Dōgen's apparent introduction of the notion of fallibilism in a way that opens the door to relativist interpretations articulated by several modern commentators while preserving their emphasis on the perfection of truth.

The *Goshō*'s interpretation of Dōgen's passage dealing with partiality and limitation is based on distinguishing between a false sense of insufficiency, which is bound to delusion, and a true sense, which does not impede Zen realization. The text starts by referring to a an earlier paradoxical sentence in the fascicle, "People, when they first seek the Dharma, assume they are far removed from its environs; the Dharma, once it has been authentically transmitted, is immediately realized by one's true self" (人、はじめて法をもとむるとき、はるかに法の邊際を離却せり；法、すでにおのれに正傳するとき、すみやかに本分人なり). Kyōgō then explains the sailing metaphor in connection with the positive view of insufficiency through commonsense analogies showing that even adepts must learn to try harder because, "If we practice the Way with sincerity, [when cutting a tree], the more one cuts the harder it becomes; and [when climbing a mountain], the more one looks up the higher it appears."

Senne's approach to the question of lack affirms the unity of singularity and particularity symbolized by Dōgen's notion that one drop of water in complete in itself, but he also uses the rhetoric of *via negativa* in noting, "When we are filled with zazen, this means we are killing Buddha," thus evoking an injunction associated with Linji (臨濟, d. 866). He also suggests that, "The triple world is only one mind, for there is nothing outside the mind," and further clarifies that the phrases, "There is nothing (*mu*)" and "outside," actually have the same meaning because we can know the limitless virtues of the sea through the specific form of a square or a circle.

Senne probes the matter of inconsistency by highlighting a seemingly innocuous phrase that appears in the follow–up paragraph of the fascicle: "If we wish to perceive the traits of the myriad phenomena, in addition to seeing the rectangular and the circular, we should realize that there are worlds in the four directions in which the remaining features of the seas and mountains are numerous and unbounded." Senne admits that the phrase "in addition to" (*nokoreru kaitoku* のこれる海徳), which implies "other than" (*hoka ni* ほかに), is unclear and he asks whether it is part of realization to view the sea as a square or a circle while also knowing the features of the ocean beside those characteristics. Or does the phrase mean that to view the sea as a square or a circle is a deluded view? Since "in addition to" being seen as a square or a circle seems incomplete, it sounds like the sea is neither a square nor a circle and, thus, it is only obvious what the seas and mountains are not.

That tentativeness is resolved when Senne connects the idea of being unable to see beyond the horizon while riding a boat to a previous "Genjōkōan" passage, "When we see forms or hear sounds with body and mind, although we understand them intimately, it is not like the reflection in a mirror or like the water and the moon. When one side is illumined, the other side is dark" (身心を舉して色を見取し, 身心を舉して聲を聴取するに, したしく會取すれども, かがみにかげをやどすがごとくにあらず, 水と月とのごとくにあらず. 一方を證するときは, 一方はくらし). According to the *Goshō*, the word *ippō* (一方) translated here as "one side" is understood as having the identical meaning as *ippō* (一法) or "one dharma."

This deliberate conflation seems to represent the kind of philosophical pun Dōgen frequently uses and implies that the passage dealing with seemingly faulty perception at sea also evokes the doctrine of *ippō gūjin*. From the standpoint of that interpretation, there is neither limit nor partiality in human perception in that Dōgen expresses the concept of the oneness of the person and the object, and thereby denies the separate status of either aspect. Moreover, "When one side is illumined, the other side is dark [or: concealed, obscure]" suggests that all things have become aligned with one whole Dharma. because if a person intimately perceives things by engaging the whole body and mind, he or she will realize the meaning of the Dharma–as–truth infusing each and every dharma–as–object. Senne concludes, "'Nothing outside the mind' refers to the mind–ground. This means that the 'triple world is only one mind.' At this time, nothingness is the mind–ground." Therefore, we must know that there are inexhaustible characteristics in either seas or mountains besides a circle or a square, which means that their features are neither one nor more than one.

5 Nishiari and His Predecessors and Followers

Nishiari shows that the standpoint of the *Goshō* is best understood not in isolation but with reference to early modern interpretative disputes. In assessing a representative group of major *Shōbōgenzō* commentaries Nishiari placed them in order of relevance instead of chronology as part of a ranking that helped solidify sectarian perspectives, for better or worse, prior to the initiation of postwar historical examinations of Zen literature in light of current linguistic methods, including the study of colloquial Chinese and ancient Japanese literature. The list of commentaries includes: (1) *Goshō* by Senne and Kyōgō; (2) *Monge* by Menzan and his disciple Fuzan Gentotsu (斧山玄鈯, d. 1789); (3) *Sanchū* (or *Kyakutai ichijisan*) by Honkō; (4) *Shiki* by Zōkai; (5) *Zokugen kogi* by Otsudō; (6) *Naippō* by Roran; and (7) *Benchū* by Tenkei.

Nishiari praises the painstakingly detailed remarks of *Monge*, which demonstrates grandmotherly solicitude by explaining literal connotations for novices, although he feels Menzan allows sermonizing to intrude on interpretations of Dōgen's basic teaching. Zōkai's *Shiki* (私記) receives a similar evaluation. Nishiari admires *Sanchū* (参註) by Honkō as the most thorough annotation that provides an impeccable outline of the *Shōbōgenzō*'s contents which is also helpful with regard to discerning its spiritual significance. Unsurprisingly, Nishiari sharply criticizes *Benchū* (弁註) by Tenkei as extreme, destructive, heretical, and unscrupulous and he indicates that Roran's *Naippō* (那一宝) shows some improvement over the teacher's work but is still deficient, whereas he appreciates Otsudō Kanchū's (乙堂 喚丑, ?–c. 1760) contentious but skillful rebuttal to Tenkei's standpoint in *Zokugen kogi* (続絃講義). Nevertheless, I suggest that Nishiari offers a view that begins to capture Dōgen's standpoint of constructive ambiguity because he was to some extent influenced by Tenkei's skeptical attitude that was in some ways an outgrowth of the modest degree of questioning already found in the *Goshō* of some examples of Dōgen's puzzling phrasings.

As the last great proponent of traditional Sōtō Zen whose discursive techniques, although not philosophical, were suited to a new era of open–ended investigations, Nishiari provides a fresh understanding of the venerated medieval commentary. In amplifying Kyōgō's comments regarding the chiasmic opening sentence of the "Genjōkōan" paragraph about insufficiency or lack Nishiari writes, "The more deeply you study, the more things you find that you don't understand. A scholar said, 'It's a real problem to be an expert.' Usually it's easy to get away with not claiming expertise in a certain field, but an expert cannot do this."[40] That is, a specialist knows better than to utter triumphalist boasts even if this leads to disappointing expectations. Suzuki Shunryū (鈴木俊隆, 1904–1971), who studied the *Shōbōgenzō* with Kishizawa Ian, adds that the famous Japanese author Fumiko Hayashi frequently said, "'This work is not all my ability'… People say she is good, but she says, 'I am not a good writer. I cannot express my feelings yet. There is more I want to express.' 'Something is missing' in this sense… When she says, 'This is exactly what I wanted to say,' she may not be such a good writer."[41]

Perhaps Nishiari's single main contribution to a relativist interpretation of the boat analogy is to underscore the role of the voyage itself in term of the personal or existential implications of Dōgen's travels to China from 1223 to 1227 to conquer his great doubt about original enlightenment thought (*hongaku shisō* 本覺思想). "When Dogen Zenji went to Great Song," the *Keiteki* maintains, "he had an actual experience of crossing the ocean. He comments on this from the viewpoint of practice. This represents a teaching based on his personal sense of memory. When one goes out in the ocean, there is no mountain, land, or anything that obstructs the eyes. Then, does it only look circular?"[42] Uchiyama Kōshō (内山興正, 1912–1998)

---

[40] Nishiari, *Dōgen's Genjo Koan*, 80.

[41] Ibid., 117.

[42] Ibid., 81.

supplements Nishiari's remarks connecting the sailing metaphor to Dōgen's travels: "It must have been scary to cross the ocean in a small boat like a leaf. Once at sea, he could only see the horizon. Actually, there were islands and ports on the other side of the ocean, but they could not be seen." Suzuki further notes, "Dogen had a pretty hard voyage when he went across the ocean to China."

The map in Fig. 1 and the drawing of Dōgen riding a vessel in Fig. 2 are also presented in light of the fact that the original recipient of the "Genjōkōan" missive was likely the boatman from Kyushu who had transported him to and from the mainland.[43] The significance of considering the passage by personalizing the significance of the journey to China is that Nishiari, who was aware that Dōgen did not write an autobiography, highlights how the master served as his own best narrator through offering diverse reflections and ruminations regarding his odyssey that fill the pages of the *Hōkyōki*, the *Shōbōgenzō zuimonki*, the *Tenzokyōkun*, and other works regarding his experiences of continental Chan life. In the opening paragraph of *Hōkyōki*, for example, Dōgen says, "Crossing the sea in a boat for many miles, I entrusted my ephemeral existence to the roaring waves before landing in Song China… and enrolling in Tiantong temple to study with Rujing."[44]

This trip took place while Dōgen was still in a state of delusion before he resolved this doubt through the enlightenment experience (*daigo* 大悟) of dropping off body–mind (*shinjin datsuraku* 身心脱落). We must also take into account the risk of sailing in deep waters in the early thirteenth century. Dōgen embarked with Myōzen (明全, 1184–1225) and two other companions from the port of Hakata in the northwestern region of Kyushu, near where Eisai (栄西, 1141–1215) established Shofukuji as the first Zen temple in Japan when he returned from China in the early 1190s. The group probably reached this harbor after leaving the capital by navigating inland waterways in smaller boats. However, the trip across the Sea of Japan would have felt like a tremendous challenge in that Dogen was cast out into the ocean, where storms and piracy were so common in this era that it is estimated over half of those who ventured to the continent did not return.

Moreover, Nishiari indicates the journey created a dramatic transition with profound theoretical implications from Dogen's previously landlocked outlook to the awakening of a more comprehensive, multi–perspectival approach for understanding the complexity of reality in relation to human perception. There marked an abrupt and irreversible sense of shifting away from a physical connection with the shore to an incomparable feeling of solitude and the inescapability of realizing just how much one cannot possibly know while taking in the seemingly limitless four corners. Therefore, fallibilism implicit in the inseparability of self–deception and self–realization is revealed in a way that can be considered Dōgen's initial major spiritual breakthrough before he disembarked in China, where he would soon be

---

[43] Based on conversations with Frédéric Girard at Komazawa University (May 18, 2019); see Frédéric Girard, "Le bouddhisme médiéval japonais en question," *Bulletin de l'École française d'Extrême-Orient* 87, *Me'langes du Centenaire* 2 (2000).

[44] In traditional accounts, during a threatening storm on his return trip Dōgen encountered a mysterious manifestation of One–Leaf Kannon (一葉の観音), who quieted the waves.

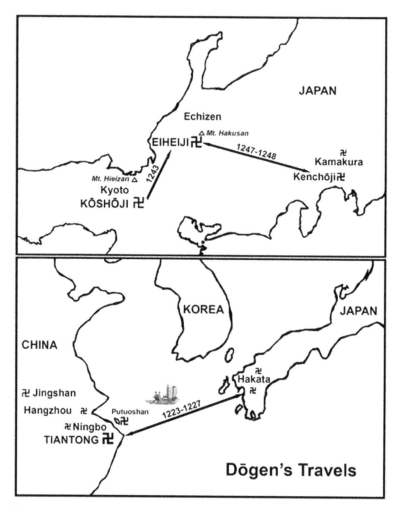

Fig. 1 A map of Dōgen's travels, including the journey to China from 1223 to 1227. (Image created by Maria Sol Echarren with Steven Heine)

told by an anonymous monastery cook that "nothing is concealed in the entire universe" (*henkai fuzōzō* 扁界不會藏).

6 Features of Creative Ambiguity

Extending from the Nishiari- and Kurebayashi–influenced approaches to "Genjōkōan" that are seen in light of a variety of sectarian and non–sectarian interpretations regarding the subjectivity of perceptions in relation to objective reality, I suggest that Dōgen's standpoint of creative ambiguity represents a purposeful

Fig. 2 An illustration of Dōgen looking out from the boat where no land can be seen past the horizon, as highlighted by the commentaries of Nishiari and Uchiyama. (Image created by Maria Sol Echarren with Steven Heine)

reversal of the Buddhist notion of two truths. Conventional truth for Dogen is paradoxically reflected by absolutism, which is evoked as a skillful means for overcoming pessimism or nihilism but is not advocated as either an inconclusive or conclusive standpoint. Much as Shinran (親鸞, 1173–1263) reverses conventional doctrinal hierarchy by asserting that all teachings other than those proclaiming Amida Buddha's vows are provisional, ultimate truth for Dōgen is disclosed as a higher level of insight embracing uncertainty and doubt as appropriate to the level of understanding of advanced practitioners who continually cast aside false assumptions without expecting a closure to that process. Dōgen suggests that perception is necessarily delimited by the boundary of *yamanaki kaichū*, but this border is ever shifting when someone is traveling from land to sea and back, first locating partially with the eyes, then losing sight for a while, and finally observing land once again as each leg of the journey is tentatively completed yet segues into a new initiative.

Bibliography

Primary Sources

Dōgen Zenji zenshū 道元禪師全集 [Dōgen's Complete Works], 7 volumes, edited by Kawamura Kōdō 河村孝道, Kagashima Genryū 鏡島元隆, Suzuki Kakuzen 鈴木格禅, Kosaka Kiyū 小坂機融 et al. Tōkyō: Shunjūsha, 1988–1993. [DZZ]
Sōtōshū zensho 曹洞宗全書 [Sōtō Sect Collection], 18 volumes, edited by Sōtōshu Zensho jōkankōkai. Tōkyō: Sōtōshū shūmuchō, 1970–1973. [SZ]
Taishō shinshū daizōkyō 大正新脩大藏經 [Taishō Tripitaka], 100 volumes, edited by Takakusu Junjirō 高楠順次郎 and Watanabe Kaigyoku 渡邊海旭. Reprint ed. 1962. Tōkyō: Taishō shinshū daizōkyō kankōkai, 1924. [T]

Secondary Sources

Akiyama, Hanji 秋山範二. *Dōgen no kenkyū* 道元の研究 [Studies of Dōgen]. Tōkyō: Iwanami shoten, 1935.
Bein, Steve. *Purifying Zen: Watsuji Tetsuro's Shamon Dogen*. Translated by Steve Bein. Commentary by Steve Bein. Honolulu: University of Hawai'i Press, 2011.
Bodiford, William M. "Dharma Transmission in Soto Zen: Manzan Dōhaku's Reform Movement." *Monumenta Nipponica* 46, no. 4 (1991): 423–451.
Bodiford, William M. *Sōtō Zen in Medieval Japan*. Honolulu: University of Hawai'i Press, 1993.
Bodiford, William M. "Textual Genealogies of Dōgen." In *Dōgen: Textual and Historical Studies*, edited by Steven Heine, 15–41. New York: Oxford University Press, 2012.
Cleary, Thomas and J.C. Cleary, translators. *Blue Cliff Record*, 3 volumes. Boston: Shambhala, 1977.
Etō, Sokuō 衛藤即応, ed. *Shōbōgenzō* 正法眼蔵, 3 volumes. Tōkyō: Iwanami bunko, 1939–1943.
Etō, Sokuō. *Shōbōgenzō jōsetsu*: Bendōwa gikai 正法眼蔵序説—弁道話義解 [Preface to the *Shōbōgenzō*: An Interpretation of "Bendōwa"]. Tōkyō: Iwanami shoten, 1959.
Etō, Sokuō. *Shūso toshite no Dōgen Zenji* 宗祖としての道元禅師 [Dōgen as Founder of a Sect]. Tōkyō: Iwanami shoten, 1944.
Etō, Sokuō. *Zen Master Dōgen as Founding Patriarch*. Translated by Ichimura Shohei. Washington State: North American Institute of Zen and Buddhist Studies, 2001.
Girard, Frédéric. "Le bouddhisme médiéval japonais en question." *Bulletin de l'École française d'Extrême-Orient* 87, *Me'langes du Centenaire* 2 (2000): 645–676.
Hashida, Kunihiko 橋田邦彦. *Shōbōgenzō shakui* 正法眼蔵釋意 [Comments on the *Shōbōgenzō*]. Tōkyō: Sankibō busshorin, 1939.
He, Yansheng 何燕生. *Dōgen to Chūgoku Zen no shisō* 道元と中國禪思想 [Dōgen and Chinese Chan Thought]. Kyoto: Hōzōkan, 2001.
Heine, Steven. "'When Mountains Can No Longer Be Seen': A Critical History of Interpretations of an Ambiguous *Shōbōgenzō* Sentence." *Journal of Chan Buddhism* 2 (2021): 1–38.
Heine, Steven. *Flowers Blooming on a Withered Tree: Giun's Verse Comments on Dōgen's Treasury of the True Dharma Eye*. New York: Oxford University Press, 2020.
Heine, Steven. "What Is on the Other Side? Delusion and Realization in Dōgen's 'Genjōkōan.'" In *Dōgen: Textual and Historical Studies*, edited by Steven Heine, 42–74. New York: Oxford University Press, 2012.
Inoue, Enryō 井上圓了. *Zenshū tetsugaku joron* 禅宗哲学序論 [Prolegomenon to a Philosophy of the Zen School]. Tōkyō: Tetsugaku shoin. 1893.
Ishii, Seijun 石井清純. "New Trends in Dōgen Studies in Japan." In *Dōgen: Textual and Historical Studies*, edited by Steven Heine, 223–236. New York: Oxford University Press, 2012.

Ishii, Seijun. "'Genjōkōan' no imi suru mono: Dōgen Zenji no shisōteki kiban nitsuite" 「現成公案」の意味するもの—道元禅師の思想的基盤について [The Meaning of "Genjōkōan": On the Foundations of Zen Master Dōgen's Thought]. *Komazawa Daigaku Bukkyōgakubu ronshū* 駒澤大學佛教學部論集36 (2004): 97–110.

Jorgensen, John. "Zen Scholarship: Mujaku Dōchū and His Contemporaries." *Zenbunka kenkyūsho kiyō* 禅分化研究所紀要27 (2004): 1–60.

Kimura, Kiyotaka 木村清孝. *Shōbōgenzō zenbon kaidoku* 正法眼蔵全巻解読 [Comments on the Entire Collection of the *Shōbōgenzō*]. Tōkyō: Kōsei shuppan, 2015.

Kurebayashi, Kōdō 榑林皓堂. *Dōgen no honryū* 道元禅の本流 [Mainstream of Dōgen Zen]. Tōkyō: Daihōrinkan, 1970.

Kurebayashi, Kōdō. *Genjōkōan wo kataru: ima wo ikiru Shōbōgenzō kōsan* 現成公案を語る—今を生きる正法眼蔵講讃 [Discussions of "Genjōkōan": Lectures on the *Shōbōgenzō* for Living Today]. Tōkyō: Daihōrinkan, 1992.

Leighton, Taigen Dan, and Shohaku Okumura, translators, *Dogen's Extensive Record: A Translation of the Eihei Kōroku*. Boston: Wisdom, reprint 2010.

Ling, Sam, and Marisa Carrasco. "When sustained attention impairs perception." *Nature Neuroscience* 9, no. 10 (2006): 1243–1245.

Matsumoto, Shirō 松本史朗. *Dōgen shisōron* 道元思想論 [Examination of Dōgen's Thought]. Tōkyō: Daizō shuppan, 2000.

Matsunami, Naohiro 松波直弘. *Kamakura ki Zenshū shisōshi no kenkyū* 鎌倉期禅宗思想史の研究 [Studies of the Intellectual History of the Zen School in the Kamakura Era]. Tokyo: Pelikan, 2011.

Mizuno, Yaoko 水野弥穂, ed. *Shōbōgenzō*正法眼蔵, 4 volumes. Tōkyō: Iwanami bunko, 1990–1993.

Morimoto, Kazuo 森本和夫. *Derrida kara Dōgen e: datsu–kochiku to shinjin datsuraku* デリダから道元へ—脱構築と身心脱落 [From Derrida to Dōgen: Deconstruction and Dropping Off Body-Mind]. Tokyo: Fukutake Books, 1989.

Müller, Ralf. "The Philosophical Reception of Japanese Buddhism After 1868." In *The Dao Companion to Japanese Buddhist Philosophy*, edited by Gereon Kopf, 155-203. Dordrecht: Springer, 2019.

Nishiari, Bokusan. "Commentary on Dogen's Genjo Koan," in *Dogen's Genjo Koan: Three Commentaries*. Translated by Sojun Mel Weitsman and Kazuaki Tanahashi, 5–90. Berkeley: Counterpoint Press, 2011.

Nishiari, Bokusan 西有穆山. *Shōbōgenzō keiteki* 正法眼蔵啓迪 [Edifying Discourses on the *Shōbōgenzō*], 3 volumes, edited by Kurebayashi Kōdō 榑林皓堂. Tōkyō: Daihōrinkan, reprint 1965.

Nishitani, Keiji 西谷啓治. *Shōbōgenzō kōwa* 正法眼蔵講話 [Lectures on the *Shōbōgenzō*], 4 volumes. Tōkyō: Chikuma shobō, 1987–1989.

Nishitani, Keiji. *Nishitani Keiji chosakushū* 著作集 [Collected Works of Nishitani Keiji], 26 volumes. Tōkyō: Sōbunsha 1986–1995.

Nyoten, Jinbō 神保如天, and Andō Bun'ei 安藤文英, eds. *Shōbōgenzō chūkai zensho* 正法眼蔵注解全書 [Complete Commentaries on the *Shōbōgenzō*], 11 volumes. Tōkyō: Shōbōgenzō bussho kankōkai, reprint 1957.

Odagiri, Takushi. "Dōgen's Fallibilism: Three Fascicles of *Shōbōgenzō*," *The Journal of Religion* 96, no. 4 (2016): 467–487.

Ōe, Kenzaburō 大江健三郎. *Aimai na Nihon no watakushi* 曖昧な日本の私 [Japan, the Ambiguous, and Myself]. Tokyo: Iwanami shinsho, 1994.

Riggs, David E. "The Life of Menzan Zuihō, Founder of Dōgen Zen." *Japan Review* 16 (2004): 67–100.

Rutschman-Byler, Jiryu Mark. "Sōtō Zen in Meiji Japan: The Life and Times of Nishiari Bokusan." Master's thesis, University of California–Berkeley, 2014.

Snodgrass, Judith. *Presenting Japanese Buddhism to the West: Orientalism, Occidentalism, and the Columbian Exposition*. Chapel Hill: University of North Carolina Press, 2003.

Tanabe, Hajime 田辺元. *Shōbōgenzō no tetsugaku shikan* 正法眼蔵の哲学私観 [My Philosophical View of the *Shōbōgenzō*]. Tōkyō: Iwanami shoten. 1939.

Watsuji, Tetsurō 和辻哲郎. *Shamon Dōgen* 沙門道元 [Monk Dōgen]. Tōkyō: Iwanami bunko, reprint 1982.

Watsuji, Tetsurō 和辻哲郎. *Nihon seishinshi kenkyū* 日本精神史研究 [Studies of Japanese Spirituality]. Tōkyō: Iwanami shoten, 1926.

Wirth, Jason M., Brian Schroeder, and Bret W. Davis, eds. *Engaging Dōgen's Zen: The Philosophy of Practice as Awakening*. Boston: Wisdom, 2017.

Yamagami, Shōfū 山上嘯風. "Dōgen zenji no uchūkan" 道元禅師の宇宙観 [Zen Master Dōgen's View of the Universe]. *Wayūshi* 和融社 10 (1906): 32–39.

Yasutani, Hakuun 安谷白雲. *Shōbōgenzō sankyū: Genjōkōan* 正法眼蔵参究一現成公案 [Reflections on *Shōbōgenzō* "Genjōkōan"]. Tōkyō: Shunjūsha, 1967.

Yasutani, Hakuun. *Flowers Fall: A Commentary on Zen Master Dōgen's Genjōkōan*. Translated by Paul Jaffe. Boston: Shambhala, 1996.

Yodono, Yōjun 淀野耀淳. "Dōgen no shūkyō oyobi tetsugaku" 道元の宗教及び哲学 [Dōgen's Religion and Philosophy]. *Tōyō tetsugaku* 東洋哲学 18 (1911), 3.1–9, 4.16–29, 5.15–29, 6.16–25, 7.13–23.

Yoshizu, Yoshihide 吉津宜英. "'Ippō wo shōsuru toki wa ippō wa kurashi' no ikku no kaishaku nitsuite" 「一方を証するときは一方はくらしの一句」の解釈について [Comments on the phrase, "When one side is illumined, the other side is dark"]. *Shūgaku kenkyū* 宗学研究 35 (1993): 12–17.

Dōgen's Texts Expounded by the Kyoto School – Religious Commentary or Philosophical Interpretation?

Ralf Müller

There have been two approaches within the so-called Kyoto school regarding the medieval Japanese Zen Buddhist Dōgen's work. Initially, there were philosophically ambitious interpretations, such as those by Watsuji Tetsurō (1889–1960) and Tanabe Hajime (1885–1962). They were ambitious insofar as they attempted to bridge the gap between philosophy and religion. However, from the 1940s onwards, these seminal works tended to recede into the background since they were criticised for assimilating a medieval monk into modern secular thought.

This presentation discusses the second approach that was put forward by thinkers such as Nishida Kitarō (1870–1945), Nishitani Keiji (1900–1990) and Ueda Shizuteru (1926–2019). They furthered the questioning of religion and philosophy by developing a specific style of reading Dōgen. My claim is that their reading lies beyond the limitations of the denominational approach, on the one hand, and the philosophical approach of Watsuji and Tanabe, on the other hand. The question is whether they create a method that is *neither exclusively religious commentary nor philosophical interpretation*. Moreover, can such a position be methodologically delineated?

Two critical aspects of the Nishida-Nishitani-Ueda standpoint come into view. First, many passages in Dōgen's texts appear to the unprepared reader as entirely arbitrary, presenting anecdotes of Zen masters or other exemplary stories without further explanation or logical argumentation. My thesis is that these citations function as a matter of extra-textual allusion, i.e., as a figure of speech in which an object or circumstance from an unrelated context is referred to covertly or indirectly. Second, Dōgen's writings contain quasi-philosophical expressions that Nishida and his successors import into philosophical discourse. By so doing, they can bridge

R. Müller (✉)
Department of Philosophy, University College Cork, Cork, Ireland

© The Author(s), under exclusive license to Springer Nature Switzerland AG 2023
R. Müller, G. Wrisley (eds.), *Dōgen's Texts*, Sophia Studies in Cross-cultural Philosophy of Traditions and Cultures 35,
https://doi.org/10.1007/978-3-031-42246-1_3

rhetorical and philosophical argumentation, or Buddhist religiosity and logical analysis. Dōgen's expressions, thereby, obtain a new meaning derived by linking the original source to modern philosophical interpretations.

1   Intro: Dōgen as Philosopher?

The main thrust of the following argument is based on the idea that Nishida, Nishitani, and Ueda contribute to a change in philosophical discourse by using and partly incorporating the religious writings of Dōgen. How exactly do they achieve this? The crucial question is whether and in which way it is possible to integrate a sacred text into philosophical discourse or how to communicate Dōgen's writings to the philosophically-minded reader. Finding a way to do this will help to undermine a long-held prejudice about Zen Buddhism as an anti-rational enterprise. Indeed, due to Dōgen or, at least, due to research about his perplexing writings, it has become more and more prevalent that the Zen Buddhist tradition is not the radical other of rationality.

While different pathways seem viable, I will discuss how Nishida, Nishitani and Ueda address Dōgen and assess his writings for philosophy. Their approach is critical to point out because, in the first place, some Kyōto school thinkers such as Tanabe and Watsuji and other philosophers set their readings of Dōgen implicitly or explicitly in opposition to denominational scholars. Denominational scholars treat Dōgen, of course, as founder. And the two identities of Dōgen as philosopher and as founder are not readily reconcilable. Being sympathetic with Nishida, Nishitani, and Ueda in various ways, I will discuss their means of approaching Dōgen as philosopher *and* founder.

I have chosen this issue instead of an equally important one that functions as one of their underlying assumptions, namely, that Dōgen *is* a philosopher. This assumption is based on – and biased by – a dichotomy inherited from Western academic discourse posing and opposing such notions as "philosophy" and "religion." In the current account, "philosophy" and "religion" are taken at face value and do not represent clear-cut/mutually-excluding notions. Furthermore, I do not consider this a hindrance: Rather than treating these terms to signify isolated areas of discourse, I believe them to represent poles of a continuous field in which we are to place Dōgen. Hence, what I will talk about in the following is Dōgen as a philosopher *in the making*; borrowing an expression of John Maraldo's.

As indicated above, philosophy and religion will be used as opposite poles. And on a textual level, this opposition can be applied in the following way: According to my understanding, Nishida, Nishitani, and Ueda presuppose access to Dōgen in a way that intimately bridges or mediates what we can call "religious commentary" and "philosophical interpretation." Admittedly, commentaries are not always religious, and interpretations are not necessarily philosophical. However, I treat both textual genres as paradigmatic for one and the other: commentaries represent a textual genre prevalent in the context of religious practice because religion requires a more conservative treatment of tradition, its preservation and devotion. As opposed to this keeping or retaining of the given canon, philosophy is more about transcending the given. Philosophy aims at overcoming what has been transmitted since ancient times. Philosophy is motivated by interpretation and ingenious altering of what there is or has been for too long.

In which way, then, do Nishida and others mediate between these two kinds of textual genres? Formally speaking, they achieve this mediation by integrating particular fragments of Dōgen's texts and leaving them, at the same time, unaltered as religious texts. By integrating Dōgen's text without transferring it – via interpretation – ultimately into philosophical discourse, Nishida achieves a cohabitation of commentary and interpretation. This handling of texts needs, of course, further elaboration and determination.

Since the review of Nishitani's and Ueda's approach in the light of Nishida's would single out the same elements, the present article will mainly focus on Nishida. Given that Nishida's approach consists of short and fragmentary references to Dōgen's texts it is possible to elaborate on Nishida more deeply.

2 Main Part: The Cohabitation of Interpretation and Commentary in the Philosophical Reading

It is not easy to determine when exactly Nishida started to read Dōgen. From his diaries, it is, however, clear that his exegesis in 1939 was a response to his students and colleagues Tanabe and Watsuji. To better understand Nishida's approach, it is critical to understand it in terms of this invocation of his students. However, before delineating Nishida's response, in particular to Tanabe, it is important to see how Dōgen emerged as philosopher.

The philosophical reception of Dōgen started in 1893. The reception comprises several authors before Watsuji who is commonly known as the one who "discovered" Dōgen as philosopher. He published a series of articles on Dōgen in the Taishō period in search for a non-Western tradition of philosophy from within Japan. The same is true for earlier readers of Dōgen such as the well-known Buddhist philosopher Inoue Enryō (1858–1919), the lesser known and early deceased logician Yodono Yōjun who published a series of articles in the journal *Eastern Philosophy* in the last year of the Meiji period, i.e., in 1911, entitled "Dōgen's religion and philosophy." Philosophically-minded articles on Dōgen can also be found outside of academic philosophy, for example, in the editions of the denominational journal *Wayūshi* dedicated to Dōgen's 800th anniversary of his birth and to his 750th anniversary of his death. This development is important to keep in mind to get a better understanding of the divergent approaches to reading Dōgen inside and beyond philosophy. Taking this yet broader perspective allows for the conceptualisation of his works according to the schema of philosophy in contradistinction to religion.

In fact, the philosophical reception can be located within the re-emergence of Dōgen in the modern era across different fields. It is true that Dōgen, the Zen Buddhist, remains the most widely read pre-modern Japanese author in philosophy since the Meiji period until today, but, at the same time, his philosophical reception is most fiercely criticised by his own denomination, i.e., by scholars of the Sōtō Zen community. The dispute was caused by the pretensions of non-denominational intellectuals to pave the way for an authentic apprenticeship independent of the practice of "sitting-only" (j. *shikan taza* 只管打坐) which was taught by the Sōtō school as the core of Dōgen's Zen.

However, the predominance of a "practical" interpretation of Dōgen obscures the linguistic complexities of Dōgen's writings. In particular, only few monks were able to master the *Shōbōgenzō's* peculiar style in which Dōgen draws on grammar and semantics at the margins of both the Japanese and Chinese languages. For this reason, non-denominational scholars challenged or even threatened the sectarian authority of the Sōtō school. And it became evident that more than basic knowledge of the Buddha's teaching and more than training in sitting meditation were required to achieve an understanding of what Dōgen expounds in the *Shōbōgenzō* 正法眼蔵.

The core dispute, based on the opposition of textual and practical study of Dōgen's teaching mentioned above, brings into view various groups. Except for one, all groups maintain the importance of seated meditation, while the importance placed on Dōgen's writings varies greatly. Hence, Dōgen readers can be located either closer to the genre of commentary or closer to the genre of interpretation.

In the case of the so-called "Zennist" group (j. *zenjōka* 禅定家), all emphasis is put on the practical study of meditation. Hence, all of Dōgen's writings are set aside, unless they serve as purely practical guidance for Zazen, or for cloistered life in general. Another group established under the auspices of Morita Gōyu, placed more importance on Dōgen's writings, in particular to the *Shōbōgenzō*. These "Genzōnians" (j. *genzōka* 眼蔵家) as they were known, worked in continuity with traditional commentaries since the Edo period. While they were critical of an abridged version of the *Shōbōgenzō*, which was compiled in the late 1880's (the *Shushōgi*), they strictly adhered to the practice of Zazen, claiming that the 95-chapters of the *Shōbōgenzō* were nothing but footnotes to "sitting only."

As a third group, the laity-movement was strongly promoted by Ōuchi Seiran, the 'Vimalakīrti' of Meiji-Japan. While being a lay person, Ōuchi helped to compile the *Shushōgi* as a kind of catechism. Extracted from the original *Shōbōgenzō* text, this kind of work presupposed great linguistic and buddhological skills on his part. However, guidance for the laity went hand in hand with somewhat limited resources both in practical as well as textual study of Dōgen's teaching, and entailed some 'deviation' from the 'pure' standards of practical and textual study within the monastery.

Finally, the fourth group shifted the standards for understanding Dōgen's Zen to an even greater extent, yet brought these standards further away from the practical and closer to the textual level. One may even say that the so-called Genzō-researchers (j. *genzō kenkyūka* 眼蔵研究家) dug deeper on a textual level than ever before so that the denominational studies (j. *shūgaku* 宗学) of the Sōtō school were heavily indebted to them.[1] But matters of belief and faith were put aside in the case of Genzō-researchers,[2] especially among philosophers such as Watsuji and Tanabe, who considered the concept of truth to be the guiding light.

2.1 Fighting the Assimilation of Zen as Philosophical Text

To discuss Nishida as a turning point in the philosophical reception of Dōgen, it is essential to note that he refers to Dōgen only in passing in his later writings and in letters to his colleagues. He only uses quotes from Dōgen and very few of them; rather than interpreting them in detail, he leaves them as is. And the passages in which he quotes Dōgen are highly redundant. Furthermore, these quotes seem, at the same time, opaque and non-sensical in relation to the passages in which they are used. In other words, leaving out the quotes does not diminish the content of the respective passage in Nishida's text. And – at least at first sight – the quotes do not extend the content of the text in any way that appears important for gaining a better understanding of Dōgen. The question then is what the quotes mean in the passages given. To underline his approach, Nishida does not assimilate Dōgen into his thinking. Instead, it appears more like he is looking for a meeting ground for his own thinking with Dōgen's.

Following this trajectory of Nishida's approach to Dōgen, we will move away from an interpretation that places the philosophical and systematic approach in the foreground as in the case of Watsuji or Tanabe. At the centre will be practice and lived experience; Dōgen's religious thinking will be articulated from a different point of view that avoids simply assimilating it as pure philosophy.

The initial setting from which to discuss Nishida's reading of Dōgen, is the broader frame of his relation to Zen and philosophy: Can it be thought of in terms of unification as some Nishida researches seem to suggest? Some kind of relation is obvious both from what Nishida explicitly states in his published and unpublished works. However, from the 1930s onward, that relation becomes appealing enough to be taken up. It seems right to say that from 1939 onwards, Nishida relates his systematic thinking to concepts, texts and authors of the Buddhist tradition. The question is what this relation consists in. As noted above, and as we will see below, Nishida uses little more than short quotes from Dōgen's original texts. While doing so, he relies on his colleagues who specialised in Buddhology and Buddhist practice to stay informed about Dōgen and to support and affirm his eventual interpretation of Dōgen.

Moreover, it is necessary to differentiate between using quotes of Buddhist texts and using Buddhist words or terms as philosophical concepts. The latter does not happen in the case of Nishida and, hence, marks his approach to Dōgen. This, too,

---

[1] Cf. Wakatsuki 1986: 125–344.

[2] Cf. for an opposing example Oka 1927.

holds true for the Sino-Japanese expression *mu* 無 (nothing/ness) which comes up in the text discussed in the following, even though it cannot straightforwardly be assigned to any particular tradition such as Buddhism or Daoism. In other words, even this ubiquitous and underdetermined expression is not introduced or worked out as a concept by Nishida. Hence, it seems right to interpret Nishida as assuming that there is an intrinsic relation between philosophy and Zen Buddhism, one that is simply conspicuous and not in need of further justification.

The question then is whether we can concur with Nishida's presupposition and, if so, in which way? How does this intrinsic relation occur? This question hardly seems a matter of theory. In fact, we need to take it as a challenge to the text at hand and of Nishida's praxis of philosophy: Is Nishida's approach to and the handling of Dōgen's works born out of an experiential struggle with existence? And are the quotes and anecdotes that Nishida incorporates into his writings themselves expressions of existential experiences? Can we take these snippets as allusions, i.e., as figures of speech that work partly as intertextual and partly as extratextual references?

While others have discussed the issue at hand concerning Nishida's use of quotations from texts usually assumed to be religious, they have not gone into sufficient detail. James W. Heisig's remarks, for example, remain vague. Given the words from, and the various other references to, Buddhist texts scattered throughout Nishida's works, Heisig writes: "It is no more correct to speak of the Kyoto philosophers as representing eastern philosophy than it is to speak of their use of Zen and Pure Land Buddhism as representing Mahayana Buddhism. Let there be no mistake about it: the Kyoto philosophers are eastern and they are Buddhist. But their aim and context is neither eastern nor Buddhist."[3]

Heisig thinks of Buddhist quotes in Nishida's texts as a way of "upholstering" his writings. He is not motivated to attempt to work out the argumentative potential of these quotes or other forms in which Nishida relates his ideas to the Buddhist tradition. Similarly, Gereon Kopf takes them as mere illustrations. John Maraldo is closer to the truth when he uses the term of allusion to address Nishida's use of Buddhist or Zen Buddhist quotes. Nevertheless, he does not differentiate allusion from upholstering and illustration, and he disregards the conceptual potential of this figure of speech.

2.1.1   Critique of Tanabe's Assimilation of Dōgen

It is noteworthy that Nishida (as well as Nishitani and Ueda after him) undertake a reading of a Sōtō Zen Buddhist, although all of them adhere to Rinzai Zen practice. This is remarkable not only for the freedom in which they approach different thinkers of the Zen Buddhist tradition. I think it is also a statement about Dōgen in so far as his writings are the most impressive in the Zen tradition. But this practical

---

[3] NKZ 20: 179, Letter #877, date 11.08.1926; *German in the original.

approach is critical because it determines the way in which Dōgen is read by Nishida. Just to mention one point before going into details: While Tanabe's explanations of Dōgen culminate in an abstract understanding of "genjōkōan," which he interprets as the universalised expression of contradictory reality, Nishida emphasises the "realisational" foundation of Dōgen's teaching: in other words, "religious practice."

Nishida starts from the "Zen meditation of dropping off body and mind"[4] and rephrases the well-known passage from the "Genjōkōan," saying that to learn the Buddha way is to learn the self, to learn the self is to forget the self, and to verify the self by the ten thousand things coming forth.[5] This focus in reading Dōgen helps us understand Nishida's engagement of Buddhism in his writings. He focuses on Buddhist practice rather than speculative matters. Hence, he views Buddhism rather as something that remains in the background and undergirds his work. In fact, in regard to Dōgen and any other Buddhist author, he leaves aside particular terms that could be adopted as theoretical concepts. What then is specific about the way he treats Buddhism in general, and in the present case, in particular, when quoting the expression "dropping off body and mind?"

The specificity can be delineated when seen in the context of Nishida's critique of Tanabe, his student. In particular, his quotes of Dōgen relate to Tanabe appropriation of the Sōtō monk. On September 21st, 1939, he writes a letter to Hisamatsu Shin'ichi (1889–1980). Next to Suzuki Daisetsu (1870–1966), Hisamatsu is one of the essential 'informants' when Nishida has questions about Zen Buddhism. His letter to Hisamatsu dates shortly before he submits his "Philosophical Essays III" to Iwanami. In this letter, he defends his philosophical point of view and suggests how it verbalises his ideas in accordance with Zen-Buddhist forms of expression. And on these grounds, he indicates in which way he feels misunderstood and falsely criticised by Tanabe:

> At the end of my next book that will be published soon, I touch upon the matter of religion. Thereby, I respond to Tanabe and others who maintain that [in my writings] the absolute and the relative dissolve into the other. I say that the absolute must be one (but it isn't, of course, the only one thing). [...] I surely disagree with saying that the absolute and the relative dissolve in one another. What one conceives of as the absolute cannot be thought as such a thing. [...] As I pointed out in my previous manuscript: The absolute must be one in the sense of 'dropping off body and mind is body and mind dropping off' and 'the donkey looks at the well and the well looks at the donkey'; the absolute must be the unity of opposites and so on and so forth.[6]

Here, as in other places, Nishida insists on the momentum of difference in the absolute, even if he clings to the momentum of unity. To Nishida, the absolute exhibits a discontinuous structure: it is self-identical and, yet, it is self-contradictory since the relative does not dissolve into the absolute. Nishida finds this kind of thinking in Dōgen's expression "dropping off body and mind is body and mind dropping off"

---

[4] NKZ 8: 512.
[5] NKZ 8: 513.
[6] NKZ 22: 262–263, Letter #3055.

and, similarly, in other Zen texts. In order to provide evidence for his understanding of Dōgen, Nishida refers back to a passage from a koan collection that he seems to be more familiar with. In fact, he is fighting over who is wrong and who is right in one's understanding of Dōgen – from the point of view of the Rinzai tradition. Tanabe (1939), on his part, worked out his interpretation of Dōgen based on a radical critique of the Rinzai tradition. It is this reading of Dōgen and his critique that Nishida refers to more explicitly in another letter. Three months before the previous letter, he writes from Kyoto on June 13th, 1939:

> That essay of Tanabe's on Dōgen is unacceptable. But what is your opinion? In a certain sense Tanabe's essay remains entirely on the standpoint of understanding [Verstand], is it not? And is this not opposed to Dōgen's viewpoint? Would it be possible to consider Dōgen a successor of the 6th patriarch were he a proponent of Tanabe's view?[7]

2.2   Saving the Performative Text Layer of the Religious Text for Philosophy

What are the characteristics of the way Nishida makes use of Zen quotes? Without identifying the quote, it appears to the reader as sudden, unmotivated, and opaque while for Nishida the quote seems to flow from what he is working out in his argumentation.

Based solely on Nishida's text, this enigma is difficult to overcome. Further, the quotes do not illustrate the argumentation of Nishida because of their partly poetic, partly Buddhist-terminological character. Potentially, they allude to something, but this is so only for someone who is acquainted with Zen. In the case of an allusion, quotes from Zen Buddhist texts might help facilitate the understanding of philosophical concepts. But for someone who is not steeped in Zen practice, an allusion cannot be established. To look at this question from another angle, given that the quotes illustrate particular concepts only partly if at all, one could ask the following: Can we read Nishida's terminological coinages as experimental concepts? Concepts that are based on Nishida's 'original' insight? Concepts that work in a heuristic fashion?

In a formal sense, a term is part of a conceptual system that presumes a precise determination and limitation of one concept against another. In regard to the content of the present quote, however, "dropping off body and mind" seems to gain the character of an allusion to an original insight, which helps to anchor the conceptual coherence of the text and to correct its lack of content. The allusion is a rhetorical figure in which a simple or complex expression refers – directly or indirectly – to another text. This is different from mere intertextuality since the reference is intended by the author and it is fulfilled if and only if the reader acknowledges/

---

[7] NKZ 22: 237–238, Letter #2989.

recognises this reference.[8] Through allusion, the text referred to attains a different, extended, or changed meaning based on being integrated into a new context. This needs further deliberation.

2.2.1 The Example from the Appendix to *The Unity of Opposites*

In the following, I will refer to a small part of a short text that is not even part of an essay in its own right. This underlines the degree of importance Buddhist texts have for a thinker that is famed for his Buddhist background. The quotes from Dōgen are somewhat hidden in the occasional writing, which is appended to a collection of essays including the 1939 *The Unity of Opposites*. The functions of quotations from a Buddhist text in Nishida's essays need to be examined case by case. What I will show in the following cannot be generalised over all the Zen Buddhist quotes that come up in Nishida's writings. It is thus also true that the quotes can work on different levels at the same time depending on context. In the present case the quotes work in at least two ways: as argument – as one would expect in a philosophical text – and as allusion. The latter function, to be more precise, the one of extra-textual allusion is here of greater importance. The aim is to pinpoint the Zen quotes as figures of speech that serve to allude to a particular lived experience based on religious practice. In quoting these texts, the extra-textual reference sets in motion the oscillation between the presence of experience and its representation in the text. Allusion, then, works as evocation.[9]

Nishida writes:

> The mere transcendence is not absolute; mere nothing is not the absolute nothingness. The dropping off body and mind is the body and mind dropping off (The donkey looks at the well, the well looks at the donkey),[10] the absolute must be one, it must be a contradictory self-identity. The absolute must be a force, it does not dissolve into the relative. What we call logic or ethics cannot be abstracted from religion. The true, the good, and the beautiful emerge from the standpoint of unity of opposites. However, it would be wrong to consider religion from this point of view.

There are several things to note about the above quote and its context. Within slightly more than two pages we can find a dozen references. Still, only two of them are indicated by name: one quote is explicitly referencing "Buddha Shakyamuni" and the other Dōgen. Nishida introduces the quotes immediately following an important philosopheme of Nishida's, i.e., the unity of opposites, and he introduces it in parallel with an explanation where he goes on to write: "Thus it must be a religious exercise – Dōgen also speaks of 'sitting in meditation' in which 'body and mind drop off.'" With this quote, the thematic kernel of the passage becomes articulated. At the same time, it underlines the double structure of the allusion: By the

---

[8] See Irwin 2001, 289.

[9] Please refer to the end of this draft for the full translation of the appendix.

[10] Jap. *shinjin datsuraku, datsuraku shinjin* 身心脱落、脱落身心: Records of Rujing, DZZ 7:246.

words "sitting in meditation" (*taza* 打坐) he references a practice, but the expression "dropping off body and mind" (*shinjin datsuraku* 身心脱落) articulates a specific experience which Dōgen had in the practice of meditation. This verbal expression then becomes part of a textual transmission and, only thereby, citable. Placing the expression "dropping off body and mind" at the beginning, it attains an emblematic character and remains a textual anchor until the end of the text for various references that occur throughout.

This given quote is not the only reference to Dōgen's writings. And the emblematic framing of the text by alluding to "dropping off body and mind" is not the only coinage used by Nishida that refers back to Dōgen. Privileging Dōgen by naming him, the remaining Dōgen references form the backbone of the text. In parallel to the initial "sitting in meditation in which body and mind drop off" from Dōgen's diary *Hōkyō-ki*, Nishida refers at a later point to *Nyojo Goroku* in the passage "dropping off body and mind is body and mind dropping off." Immediately after the *Hōkyō-ki* quote, we find another quote, but this time from the guide on doing *zazen*, the *Fukan zazengi*, which reads "to take a step back and let the light shine inwards" (*ekō henshō no taiho* 廻向返照の退步). And finally, there is a quote from "Genjōkōan" that has more than a merely allusive character. It is a quote in which Dōgen puts forth his understanding of the Buddha-way; almost in the form of argumentation. Nishida cites more than the kernel of that passage, and does more than simply allude indirectly to it, but he does all this in a paraphrastic manner, step by step through rephrasings and quotes from other Zen masters, and in this way he adopts for his own text the structure of argumentation inherent to the original passage of the Genjōkōan.

2.2.2 The Structure of Allusion

Before laying out this structure of argumentation as part of the appendix, it is crucial to keep in mind the tension that builds up due to the structure inherent to the philosophical conceptualisation that is opposed to the quote as allusion. This leads to an issue that cannot be solved at this point but must be pointed out. Quotations and concepts build up a tension due to the fact that the quote works as an allusion that references something beyond the text that is an artefact of singularity, whereas the concept is part of a net of concepts, and in the present case a system of philosophical concepts that must be elucidated reciprocally.

Both allusion and concept are hermetically self-contained in regard to their relationality. The tension occurs due to their cohabitation within the same text, their immediate presence to each other. The question then is how is it possible for Nishida to see a relation between the two: What is it that appears to him as a kind of reciprocity? Wherein lies the isomorphy that allows him to take the quote as a reason in argumentation saying "thus Dōgen speaks of…?" And is it possible to think of the transition from quote to concept as a semiotic transformation? Does this transformation follow a rule? Is the quote merely a poetic analogy of a logical form?

Nishida is primarily a philosopher. Therefore, he builds up the tension mentioned above within the horizon of his own philosophical design, by introducing quotations of a philosophical text and not the other way around. An alternative approach would, for example, use philosophical concepts within a koan-dialogue. To the reader of the appendix, it seems clear from the beginning that Nishida's is a philosophical text, since the Zen Buddhist quote occurs only after Nishida has begun the appendix using his own basic concept of the unity of opposites.

He writes:

> As the unity of opposites of integrated one and the individual many, the world is self-contradictory in its coming into being, and as the individuum of this world, our self is self-contradictory in every respect. This is where the beginning and end of the deep question of human life lies. And this is also at the same time the question of the world. We penetrate the root source of this self-contradiction of the self and attain the true life at the standpoint of the unity of opposites. This is religion. This is where there must be an absolute negation. This is what one calls the religious practice within which one forsakes body and life. That does not mean to think through something logically or to act morally. Thus, there must be a religious practice – Dōgen also speaks of 'sitting in meditation,' in which 'body and mind drop off' (he says 'learn to take a step back so that the light turns inwards and radiates').

Interpretation of the Quoted Passage

As the opening of the appendix elucidates, for Nishida it is easy to make the transition from theoretical concepts to a Zen Buddhist quote, i.e., from the conception of reality as the unity of contradictories via a few thetical sentences to a kind of conclusion in the form of an allusion to lived experience. To Nishida, in terms of content, it seems unnecessary or impossible to motivate the relation or an isomorphy between quote and theoretical assumptions. Still, one needs to be aware of the fundamental differences of the gaps between the philosophical concept and the Zen Buddhist quote, even if Nishida does not outline the preceding relations of thetical propositions all of which belong to philosophical discourse.

How can Nishida pass from the unity of contradictions to Dōgen's expression "dropping off body and mind?" Nishida introduces his text with the basic intuition that human life is self-contradictory – due to its finiteness, i.e. due to its being inherently tied to what is called death. Even what we consider as the world that encompasses our existence cannot offer an unbroken unity of life and individual lives because of a reciprocal dependency: The questionability of one's own life is the questionability of the world and vice versa.

Man attains a conversion only by taking a step into religion. This is where, according to Nishida, the contradictoriness of self and world changes fundamentally. Since "we penetrate the root source of this self-contradictoriness of the self and attain true life at the viewpoint of the unity of contradictions. This is religion." Nishida adds a logical form to the standpoint of religion and its path. Thus, one attains, as Nishida puts it, the true life only through passing through the questionability of one's own existence. To pass through this questionability is to entrust oneself to the radical negation of the self. To put it differently, one reaches the religious life not as a sovereign subject, but as a human that cultivates himself in a religious way. "Thus, there must be, a religious practice – Dōgen also speaks of 'sitting in meditation', in which 'body and life drop off.'"

One can comprehend rationally what Nishida thinks of religious practice in his structural analysis. Subject and object, self and world are reciprocally intertwined. Within this intertwining, the practice of sitting meditation manifests itself as a self-negation in the sense of a step back. This step back means that the self that wants to know and to act submits itself to the things rather than subsuming actively the things to the self. It means that the self is recreated by things in an original way and always anew. This kind of elucidation is sufficient without the Dōgen quote. In other words, the elucidation relates to the thetical propositions of Nishida and could affect the quote in order to interpret the expression of "dropping off body and mind" by analogy with Nishida's conception. This would be easy because the given elucidation is put into words in a metalinguistic fashion, i.e., *not* in Nishida's own words and philosophical concepts. A metalinguistic elucidation is hermeneutical and, as such, could be discussed, even criticized or possibly refuted.

It is different in the case in which Nishida's quotation follows his own conceptions. He introduces those quotes and presupposes thereby that expressions such as "dropping off body and mind" or "taking a step back so that the light turns inward and radiates" express something similar or identical to, or exactly that which would be needed to conclude. And again, one needs to ask what could motivate the isomorphy or relation of different kinds in order to make the transition from Nishida's proposition to Dōgen's quote? Structurally, it is the momentum of negation, to be more precise, in Nishida's words, the momentum of "absolute negation," in which it could be verbalised as "dropping off" or as "step back." In terms of content, there is an isomorphy, indeed, only for those readers who are acquainted with the context and quote in a theoretical or practical fashion. Similar to the expression of religious cultivation in the form of sitting meditation, the talk of dropping off catches the specific mode of exercise/practice.

Relation to Illustration and Argumentation

The quote is not illustrative primarily for the following reason. Indeed, Nishida does not bother to work out vivid similarities. But this is not the main point. Rather, nothing appears in the relation between quote and concept that could manifest as the relation of similarity between the two poles of quotation and concept. This is so even if someone who is acquainted with the experience of the dropping off body and mind would know what the quote alludes to. A graphic depiction would likewise remain unintelligible unless one knew what the words were about. Moreover, there would, again, be the question of what the relation would be grounded in, whatever graphic means of expression was used.

The allusive function of the quote can best be motivated by Nishida's own propositions about the relation of religious practice and philosophy. To him, religion is an irreducible fact. It cannot be rationalised or conceptualised. Hence, he writes in a letter to Hisamatsu: "I am entirely of your opinion that religion can't be substanti-ated either philosophically or morally. What is called philosophy of religion is noth-ing more than the conceptual expression of religious experiences."[11]

In the beginning, there is the fact of religious life and lived experience. Only after that is it possible to conceive of it in philosophical terms. The conceptual elucida-tion cannot, however, provide either a causal explanation or a moral, epistemologi-cal or ontological reasoning. Thus, in the appendix – analogously to his previous observations that he communicates to Hisamatsu – Nishida draws the following conclusions: According to him, authentic philosophising is nourished by the same source as religion:

> What we call logic or ethics cannot be separated from religion. The true, the good, and the beautiful [of philosophy] emerge at the viewpoint of the unity of contradictories. It would, however, be wrong to think religion from this point of view.[11]

As indicated before, Nishida takes a stand in opposition to Tanabe, who presents Dōgen's texts as a philosophical elucidation of his own thinking; a strategy built on getting rid of ambivalences inherent to Dōgen's writings that are thus reduced to a particular schema of argumentation. Nishida, on his part, highlighted the momen-tum of practice and, on this basis, he tried to let Dōgen's own thinking come forth in broad, but pregnant strokes using few but crucial quotes; his approach is closer to using calligraphy to sketch the core traits of something that wants to be depicted.

I would maintain that Nishida's reflections on Dōgen take on the form of argu-mentation to the degree that he tries to defy Tanabe's interpretation of Dōgen. This means that he uses Dōgen's name, and disambiguates passages of, and propositions about, the relevant texts. He even illuminates the degree to which Dōgen is inher-ently philosophical. However, a philosophical interpretation of the religious text is not what Nishida aims for of his own accord.

3   Conclusion: The Impact of Nishida's Dōgen on Philosophy

The initial question was whether the Kyoto School – or one faction of it – expounds the texts of Zen Master Dōgen as religious commentary or philosophical interpreta-tion. Nishida and his followers try to enter into this struggle between an approach that would let go of its philosophical claims and adopt the religious discourse as is, on the one hand, and the projection of an intellectual enterprise onto the discourse, on the other hand. Nishida suggests a middle path.

There are two options for a middle path: One would be a kind of text that is nei-ther a religious commentary nor a philosophical interpretation. My understanding of Nishida's approach is that in his writings, both sorts of texts collide fruitfully. Nishida introduces the religious layer of Dōgen's and other Zen Buddhist's writings into his philosophical text. While his attempt remains preliminary, the emerging text

---

[11] NKZ 10: 295–296.

is not definite and has not taken on a final form. It's more like experimentation with accommodating unusual layers of texts into one writing. Nishida temporarily achieves a text that exhibits a mode of cohabitation. His aim is not to entirely integrate and dissolve the borders. But this is also true of Dōgen's own texts as I will point out in the following.

In fact, Nishida and others primarily integrate the performative layer of the text that remains modelled after the ritualised encounter between master and disciple. And the attempt was to delineate this methodologically, i.e., Nishida integrated texts that worked as extra-textual allusions. Nevertheless, it is also true that Dōgen's writings contain quasi-philosophical expressions. Nishida could have made use of these and could have imported these directly into philosophical discourse. But he didn't. The obvious question is, then, how do these two layers appear in Dōgen's own texts.

3.1   Looking Back: Dōgen's Texts as a Model for Philosophy?

Moving back to Dōgen, we can analyse his own readings analogously in two respects: how do the theoretical, if not philosophical discourses relate to the language of koan? Further, how do the koans relate to the religious text as such? As indicated before, Nishida chose the allusive character of koan over theoretical discourse. While the philosophical text opens up to this original level of symbolic expressions, those expressions in themselves lay open a level of immediacy that is generally lost for the canonical text. The question is to which degree Dōgen's texts present a model for or an alternative to philosophical discourse.

The analogy is indeed given because in Dōgen's own texts koans are meant to undermine theoretical discourse at exactly the same point. Just where the theoretical discourse evolves and reaches reasonable conclusions, the reader faces the opaque comments that the koan inserts into the reading, thereby leaving them alone, out in the open, and confronting a seemingly irrational discourse. Or, to put it differently, the rational discourse seems to be derailed and locked in a dead-end. When one looks at Dōgen's writings with greater scrutiny, we see that he follows two strategies: On the one hand, he supports a theoretical discourse that can be reconstructed. But it seems one-sided to cling to this part alone. Hence, the question is how the two layers are related and how koans tend to undermine theoretical discourse.

The question then is to see how does Dōgen himself relate these different forms of language, i.e., idiosyncratic enunciations, the imprinting of the Buddha-seal, and theoretical discourse. Moving on to the "Busshō" fascicle provides an approach to this question. "Busshō's" theoretical discourse returns to themes set out in both *Hōkyōki* and *Bendōwa*, while it proceeds with the reinterpretation of the main notion of "Buddha-nature." An encompassing interpretation of the fascicle is beyond the scope of this paper. Still, existing, even divergent, examinations of Dōgen's reinterpretation suggest it to be coherent and consistent based on most parts of the text.

However, despite the possible coherence and consistency of Dōgen's theoretical discourse, the necessity to piece the discourse together from the "Busshō" fascicle in a discontinuous way leads, no doubt, to the conclusion that Dōgen's writing is far from a treatment of the notion of Buddha-nature in a scholastic fashion; it is not a systematic treatise on this term. The fragmented structure of "Busshō" is partly due to its transmission and redaction, partly due to the repeated alternation of quotation and comment whereby the quotes of esteemed teachers of the tradition are ordered along an ascending timeline.

For a theoretical reconstruction, however, the opaque interjections, and the semantic-syntactic enclosures that can be singled out in the text, present a greater challenge. Precisely the entwining of two different usages of language, theory-formation and theory-contestation, means Dōgen's style in the "Busshō" fascicle is similar to the previous case where Dōgen's question about the essence of Śākyamuni's words invokes a blatant koan-like response – "What it is this that thus comes?" – thus undermining the intelligibility of the text. In fact, as lucidly as Dōgen makes use of categorical distinctions, his vocabulary is equally splendid expressing logical relations, including syllogisms, counterfactual hypotheses, causal relations and the like.

To sum up, it seems unreasonable to infer from the repeated interjection of koan-like phrases, quotes, or passages that Dōgen ultimately wants to overcome language in part or in its entirety. Instead, it seems rather important to acknowledge the ongoing oscillating movement between interjections and theory, whereby the theoretical discourse is irreducible to the same extent as the interjections rely on the theoretical discourse.

3.2   Looking Ahead to Nishitani and Ueda

While it is possible to project the analysis of Nishida's reading back onto Dōgen's own texts, it is also possible to draw forwardly directional lines to Nishida's successors and span a time frame of roughly 50 years. About 25 years after Nishida's critique of Tanabe, Nishitani lectures on Dōgen and discusses his writings in *Religion and Nothingness* (*Shūkyō wa nanika* 宗教は何か).[12] And at the beginning of the 1990s Ueda publishes a careful translation of "Genjōkōan" and other fascicles with extensive commentary. In both cases, the way they are working with Dōgen's text is more extensive and comprehensive and thus requires more scrutiny in analysing the various levels. And the treatment is more complex for another reason: the historical context in which premodern figures become eminent for producing what can be called Japanese philosophy. Therefore, the following remarks present a complex picture in broad strokes. Nevertheless, I think it is possible to discern two different levels: challenging the philosophical discourse on the one hand, and the philosophical practice, on the other.

---

[12] Nishitani 1982.

3.2.1 Altering the Philosophical Discourse

Dōgen's philosophical discourse is what Nishitani is aiming at. Nishitani introduces Dōgen at a point in time where he suggests introducing Buddhist notions or terms into a discourse that is based almost exclusively on Greek and Latin words. Seen from this perspective, the novel use of other languages for terminological purposes becomes apparent.

Within this horizon, he places Dōgen. It would be wrong to say that Nishitani borrows Dōgen's terms, but he places Dōgen more prominently than Nishida had ever done so as to present a new layer into the philosophical text. Dōgen is probably even the most essential source drawn on in this text. In terms of Dōgen, there is, of course, a second important text: Nishitani's lectures on the *Shōbōgenzō* (*Shōbōgenzō kōwa* 正法眼蔵講話), in which he enacts a reading of and introduction to Dōgen's magnum opus.[13] Similar to Nishida, he uses the quote from "Genjōkōan" evocatively and allusively, and simply states that "the problem [of absolute this-worldliness] is also posed by the famous words of Dōgen's 'Genjōkōan.'"[14] Nishitani is then quick to quote Musō Kokushi 夢窓国師 (1275–1351), a Rinzai Master, maintaining that this second quote would express the same as Dōgen's quote.

Without further explanation or interpretation of these quotes through Nishitani, they appear to the lay reader as entirely arbitrary examples. In fact, these quotes are introduced abruptly and discontinuously with the preceding form of discourse. The authority the patriarch's writings induce does not come by way of logical argument. Instead, it is an extra-textual allusion. In other words, this authority comes from an insight based on lived experience accessible only to those familiar with Buddhist practice and texts. Further scrutiny is necessary to determine how these allusions function on a rhetorical and argumentative level. In fact, at the point where the reader is willing to adopt his idea, Nishitani himself questions the entire reasoning leading to the idea.[15]

From the side of the usage in *Religion and Nothingness*, one should add that Nishitani avoids imposing a preconceived "philosophical" meaning onto Dōgen's expression. Instead, he opens up a hermeneutical space between pre-modern expressions and modern philosophical terminology. Nevertheless, these Buddhist writings, in particular Dōgen's, contain quasi-terminological expressions that Nishitani imports into philosophical discourse, and by so doing he bridges rhetoric and philosophical argumentation. Through this shift from a Buddhist to a philosophical text, Dōgen's expressions obtain a new meaning derived from neither their original

---

[13] The lectures were held at the "International Research Institute for Japanese Studies" (Nishinomiya) from 1965–1978, and they first appeared in print in the Christian journal "Kyōdai" from 1966 to 1979. They were finally reissued in four volumes by Chikuma Shobō from 1987 to 1989, and later in 1991 included in Nishitani's collected works as vols. 22 and 23. These lectures cannot be fully considered here, but the author prepared selected translations and commentary (Nishitani 2025).

[14] Ibid.

[15] Nishitani 1982: 107.

source text nor their new target context, i.e., Nishitani's writings. In other words, Nishitani generates new sources of meaning.

3.2.2   Altering the Practice of Philosophy

A later successor of Nishida is Ueda. His being Nishida's successor also becomes apparent from the way Ueda handles Dōgen. This third stage (after Nishida und Nishitani) of navigating between philosophy and religion is more modest in terms of Zen Buddhist thinking colliding with the Western tradition. Ueda puts Dōgen's practical writings at the centre of his interpretation. He is the most cautious in approaching Dōgen from his own systematic enterprise. In practice, he opens up to a collaborative enterprise with the Buddhologist when reading Dōgen. In other words, he provides access to the original but leaves it open for the readers to make of the text what they will in interpretative terms. Ueda goes beyond the philosophical discourse by questioning the very practice of philosophy. It is a new attempt at doing philosophy. In this sense, Ueda is more modest and more radical at the same time.

Ueda furthers this questioning of what religion and philosophy are, by developing a reading of Dōgen beyond the limitations of the denominational approach on the one hand, and the philosophical approach of Watsuji and Tanabe on the other. As in the case of Nishida and Nishitani, he raises the existential theme of meditational practice in the face of death and impermanence. From this position, he asks how to place Dōgen in the field of religion and philosophy, practice and theory, lived experience and linguistic expression.

His careful commentary on fascicles such as the "Genjōkōan" is neither – as in the case of Nishida – framed by his own philosophy, nor – as in the case of Nishitani – based on a philosophical appropriation of Buddhist terms.[16] Moreover, in a critique of Tanabe and Watsuji, he cautions that an interpretation of Dōgen's quasi terminological expression j. *dōtoku*, i.e., "perfect expression of truth," must still consider the relation to practice. The same is true for Dōgen's critique of the 'speechlessness' of the Zen tradition as indicated by the Zen credo j. *furyū monji*, i.e., a transmission of the Buddhist teaching not founded on words and letters (i.e., the scholastic writings of the Buddhist tradition).

As Ueda points out, the *Shōbōgenzō* must be interpreted through the unspoken, which is 'perfectly expressed' in the text.[17] More precisely, it is the outside of the text that speaks in the unspoken, as a non-text, i.e., the relation of the text to its "outside," i.e., zazen, serves as the source of the text itself. This explains Ueda's choice of writings: he presents a translation of the *Fukan zazengi* (and variants), the *Bendōwa*, the *Shōbōgenzō* "Genjōkōan" (and at the end of the commentary the supplemental fascicle "Shōji"). In other words, he places emphasis on the early writings,

---

[16] Ueda 1995.
[17] Cf. Ueda 1995: 173–174.

which are more practical and introductory than the more sophisticated "philosophical" writings such as Busshō.

The rationale is obviously to show how the two poles of Dōgen's thought are connected: his strong adherence to the strict practice of zazen on the one hand, and his remarkable writings that flow from a source of deep religious insight, on the other: "These three [writings] are everlasting documents of the Buddha-Dharma of the right transmission that Dōgen newly established in Japan."[18]

Ueda then sums up the relation between the three writings: *Fukan zazengi* provides the correct principles for the practice of zazen, *Bendōwa* explains why zazen is the right entrance to the Buddha-dharma, and "Genjōkōan" is part of those writings in which "the self-fulfilling samadhi, that is zazen, has become the words in the 'between [*aida*]' of self and other as the self-enlightenment and enlightenment of others for 'the salvation of all living beings [*kuhō gushō*]'".[19] He adds, that the "Genjōkōan" text "sketches the world that opens up on the basis of and, again, through zazen".[20] In short, only in the third text are words of intrinsic value.

Relating Dōgen's writings to the practice of zazen provides the base for Ueda to pursue the question "why was the *Shōbōgenzō* written"[21] at all? In his answer he repeats his critique of both denominational and philosophical readings of Dōgen. Usually, not the practical but only the intellectual aspect of Buddhism is taken into account: Buddhism is a religion of wisdom, and so is Dōgen's teaching of Zen. Hence, Dōgen wrote the *Shōbōgenzō*.

But Ueda reproaches such reasoning on two points: all other schools of the Buddhist tradition left writings behind, and thus an answer to the question needs a more specific determination of Dōgen's particular text.[22] More importantly, though, regarding Shakyamuni Buddha himself, it is not the case that Dōgen chose to abolish meditation practice even after enlightenment or after he began teaching: his teachings remain grounded in zazen as their source. Thus, zazen itself is the practice of a Buddhism of wisdom and complementary to wisdom and writings expressing this wisdom to others.

In Ueda's explanation to the initial question why the *Shōbōgenzō* was written, the relation of wisdom and meditational practice is dialectical: Wisdom is dialectically mediated through zazen as the radical negation of all thought. Or, again, linguistic articulation is thought to be intrinsic to sitting meditation by its very negation of language. Thus, Ueda emphasises the importance of the relation of "text and non-text"[23] from within Dōgen's own writings, as expressed in the "Dōtoku" fascicle.[24] His final answer is as follows:

---

[18] Ueda 1995: 98.
[19] Ueda 1995: 98.
[20] Ueda 1995: 99.
[21] Ueda 1995: 218.
[22] Ueda 1995: 209.
[23] Ueda 1995: 174
[24] Cf. ibid.

The fact of intensive sitting [j. *shikan taza to iu koto* (事)] is the word of intensive sitting [j. *shikan taza to iu koto* (言)], but in between thing and word there is a thorough negation [j. *tettei teki hiteisei*]. In the fashion of this being echoed, this dynamism as such becomes investigated on the plane of original thought [j. *genshisō*] in which intensive sitting comes into existence as already being such a word. There lies the original reason why the SBGZ was written.[25]

Appendix[26]

As the absolutely contradictory self-identity [j. *zettai mujunteki jikodōitsu* 絶対矛盾的自己同一] of the organic one and the distinct/independent manifold, the world is self-contradictory in its coming into being, and the self as the individual/particular of this world is, in every respect, self-contradictory. This is where the beginning and the end of the deep/profound quest/ion of human's life is rooted. And this quest/ion is, at the same time, the quest/ion of the world. At the standpoint of the unity of contradictories, we penetrate the root [j. *kongen* 根] of this self-contradiction of the self and attain true life. This is religion. There must be absolute negation. We call this religious practice in which one renounces body and life.[27] This does not mean immersing oneself logically or acting morally. Therefore, it must rather be – Dōgen talks of sitting in meditation in which body and mind are dropping off[28] – religious practice (he says learn to take a step back and let the light turn inwards and shine/radiate[29]). The standpoint of understanding in relation to objects which comprises representation, perception and discrimination[30] must be rooted differently. The Buddha-way is to learn the self, to learn the self is to forget the self.[31] Even if one speaks of negation, it is impossible to encounter/touch absolute negation through a moral act. This would be the same as looking for one's head with one's head or placing one's head on the head.[32] As it is said, it would be an illusion to confirm things by taking the self to them.[33] Religious practice is not to alter/change something through the mediation of an acting subject; instead, it is the turning/reversal[34] of the subject through the unity of contradictories. Nevertheless, it does not mean attaining

---

[25] Ueda 1995: 222.

[26] The appendix is included in NKZ 8: 512–514.

[27] For the expression *sōshin shitsumyō* 喪身失命 ZGDJ 738d refers to both Records of Línjì case 5 and Dōgen's Eihei Kōroku 9, DZZ 4.

[28] J. *shinjin datsuraku no taza* 身心脱落の打座: Hōkyōki 15, DZZ 7:18.

[29] J. *ekō henshō no taiho* 廻光返照之退歩: Fukan zazengi, DZZ 5:4.

[30] J. *nensōkan teki sokuryō* 念想観的測量: Fukan zazengi, DZZ 5:4; see ZGDJ 1004a.

[31] Genjōkōan, DZZ 1:3.

[32] Nishida puts together two quotes in parallel from Records of Línjì cases 20 and 18.

[33] Genjōkōan, DZZ 1:3.

[34] crisis/metanoia

this turning/reversal at once and intending the whole world without mediation. It is an endless progression in this direction; Shakyamuni Buddha called this "being deeply in the midst of practice [j. *shugyō saichū* 修行最中]." In other words, religious practice does not mean leaving or transcending the world. In religious practice – truly as contradictory self-identity [j. *mujunteki jikodōitsu* 矛盾的自己同一] – one conceives a thing in becoming that thing, one practices a thing in becoming that thing. Enlightenment is things come forward to practice and confirm the self.[35] Science and morality must also be religious practice. The mere transcendence is not absolute; the mere nothingness is not an absolute nothingness. The dropping off body and mind is the body and mind dropping off[36] (the donkey looks at the well, the well looks at the donkey[37]), the absolute must be one, it must be a contradictory self-identity. The absolute must be a force; it does not dissolve into the relative. What we call logic or ethics cannot be abstracted from religion. The true, the good, and the beautiful emerge from the standpoint of unity of contradictories. However, it would be wrong to think/consider religion from this standpoint. Concerning the Buddha dharma, one says that it is without effort, it is just this: ordinary and effortless. That is not to say that to shit, to take a piss, to wear clothes and to eat meals[38] is already enough. However, from the standpoint of the unity of contradictories, we cannot put it in other words. The mind is without form and penetrates all ten directions; is the mind present in the eye, one calls it vision, is it present in the ear, one calls it listening.[39] At this standpoint, the smart and the dumb, the tall and the little, must be one. There all things arise and return to. Everydayness is the root of all things. That is not to say that all things are indifferently/indistinguishably one. What it means is this: When the stranger comes, the stranger appears; when the barbarian comes, the barbarian appears.[40] It must be – contradictorily self-identically – an endless difference as "one is all, all is one."[41] Some say it is impossible to conceive of the many and the one as the same in every respect. However, we are always contradictorily self-identical through our poiesis. What one calls the unity of body and mind[42] must be a contradictory self-identity. From this, our self is never separated. Religious practice is to confirm this unity of body and mind. As it said to learn the self is to forget the self, to forget the self is to be confirmed by the ten thousand things. It must be a being confirmed in the sense of the unity of body and mind. The

---

[35] Ibid.

[36] J. *shinjin datsuraku, datsuraku shinjin* 身心脱落、脱落身心 in Records of Rujing, DZZ 7: 246.

[37] Case 52 from The Book of Serenity. Nishida adds two answers from the dialogue into one expression.

[38] Records of Línjì case 12.

[39] Records of Línjì case 10.

[40] Records of the Transmission of the Lamp case 10.

[41] Cf. Kegon ichijō kyōbun ki 華厳一乗教分記 for j. *issoku issai, issai sokuichi* 一即一切、一切即一.

[42] J. *shinjin ichinyo* 身心一如, Fukanzazengi, DZZ 5; see also The Blue Cliff Record case 60.

same holds for everyday activities. Our self encounters the absolute negation at the root of its coming into being. Where there is no light turned inwards to radiate/ shine, there is no religious quest/ion of religion.

References

DZZ = Dōgen zenji zenshū (The Complete Works of Zen Master Dōgen). 7 vols. Tokyo: Shunjūsha, 1988-1993.
NKZ = Nishida Kitarō zenshū shinpan (The New Edition of the Complete Works of Nishida Kitarō). 24 vols. Tokyo: Iwanami Shoten, 2002–2009.
THZ = Tanabe Hajime zenshū (The Complete Works of Tanabe Hajime). 15 vols. Tokyo: Iwanami Shoten, 1963-1964.
ZGDJ = Zengaku Daijiten (The Great Dictionary of Zen Studies) (2. ed.), Tōkyō: Daishūkan Shoten, 1985.

Sources

The Blue Cliff Record, c. Bìyán Lù 碧巖錄 (j. Hekigan-roku) trans. by Thomas Cleary and J. C. Cleary BDK America, 1998.
The Book of Serenity, c. Cóngróng Lù 從容錄 (j. Shōyō-roku) trans. by Thomas Cleary. Shambhala Publications.
Records of Línjì, c. Línjì Lù 臨済錄 (j. Rinzai-roku) transl. by Burton Watson (as The Zen Teachings of Master Lin-Chi). New York: Columbia University Press, 1999.
Records of the Transmission of the Lamp, c. Jǐngdé Chuándēng Lù 景德傳燈錄 (j. Keitoku Dentō-roku) transl. by Randolph S. Whitfield, Books on Demand, 2015.
Kegon ichijō kyōbun ki 華厳一乗教分記.

Secondary Works

Heisig, James W. (2001), Philosophers of nothingness: an essay on the Kyōto school (Honolulu, Hawaii: University of Hawai'i Press).
Irwin, William (2001), "What Is an Allusion?", in: The Journal of Aesthetics and Art Criticism, 59, 287–97.
Maraldo, John C. (2010), "Nishida Kitarō," in: Stanford Encyclopedia of Philosophy, accessed on May 05 2019.
Müller, Ralf (2009), "Watsuji's Reading of Dōgen's Shōbōgenzō," in: James W. Heisig and Raquel Bouso (eds.), Frontiers of Japanese Philosophy 6, 174–91.
Müller, Ralf (2013). Dōgens Sprachdenken: Historische und symboltheoretische Perspektiven (Welten der Philosophie). Verlag Karl Alber.
Müller, Ralf (2019). "The philosophical reception of Japanese Buddhism after 1868." In G. Kopf (Ed.), Dao Companion to Japanese Buddhist Philosophie.
Nishitani Keiji (1982). Religion and nothingness. Berkeley: Univ. of California Press.
Nishitani Keiji (2025), Lectures on the Shōbōgenzō (Shōbōgenzō kōwa), transl. by Ralf Müller (forthcoming).
Oka Sōtan. (1927). Zen no shinkō (The faith of Zen). Tōkyō: Kōmeisha.

Tanabe Hajime (1939), My personal view about the philosophy of the *Shōbōgenzō* (*Shōbōgenzō* no tetsugaku shikan), in: THZ 5: 443–94.

Tanabe Hajime (2011), "Shōbōgenzō no tetsugaku shikan", transl. by Ralf Müller, in: James W. Heisig, Thomas P. Kasulis und John C. Maraldo (Hg.), Sources of Japanese philosophy.

Ueda, Shizuteru. 1995. Kaisetsu [commentary]. In Daijō butten 23: Dōgen, eds. Shizuteru Ueda and Seizan Yanagida, 93–255. Tōkyō: Chūō kōron sha.

Wakatsuki Shōgo (1986). Dōgen zenji to sono shūhen. Tōkyō: Daitō shuppan.

Dōgen's Interpretive Charity: The Hermeneutical Significance of "Genjōkōan"

Eitan Bolokan

Abbreviations

DZZ   *Dōgen Zenji zenshū* 道元禪師全集 [Dōgen's Complete Works], 7 volumes, edited by Kawamura Kōdō 河村孝道, Kagashima Genryū 鏡島元隆, Suzuki Kakuzen 鈴木格禅, Kosaka Kiyū 小坂機融 et al. Tōkyō: Shunjūsha, 1988–1993.
TTDY Tanahashi, Kazuaki, ed., trans. *Treasury of the True Dharma Eye: Zen Master Dōgen's Shōbō Genzō*, 2 volumes. Boston: Shambhala, 2010.
ZSJT *Zen no shisō jiten* 禅の思想辞典, edited by Tagami Taishū 田上太秀 and Ishii Shūdō 石井修道, Tōkyō: Shoseki, 2008.

The portrait of Dōgen Zenji as the founder (*kaisan*, 開山) of the Sōtō sect of Japanese Zen, as a religious leader (*shūkyōka*, 宗教家), and as a philosopher (*tetsugakusha*, 哲学者), is widely known. Yet it is clear to anyone who has carefully read Dōgen's essays and recorded sermons that his figure is also that of a rigorous, at times even subversive, commentator. Seeing Dōgen as a creative commentator of the tradition may assist in pacifying the somewhat rigid tensions between the categories of religion and philosophy. Therefore, in this study I return to one of Dōgen's earliest essays, the "Genjōkōan", and focus on a key principle that appears in it and which serves as a pivotal exegetical framework – the "dharma position" (*hōi*, 法位).

"Genjōkōan" (現成公案) is widely considered as one of Dōgen Zenji's most pivotal and celebrated essays. Written in 1233 for Yōkū Shū (楊光秀), a lay disciple

E. Bolokan (✉)
Tel Aviv University, Tel Aviv, Israel

© The Author(s), under exclusive license to Springer Nature Switzerland AG 2023
R. Müller, G. Wrisley (eds.), *Dōgen's Texts*, Sophia Studies in Cross-cultural
Philosophy of Traditions and Cultures 35,
https://doi.org/10.1007/978-3-031-42246-1_4

63

from the island of Kyūshū, the essay's poetic imagery, deep religious insights, and philosophical ambiguities have captured the imagination and curiosity of readers throughout the centuries. Numerous commentaries were dedicated to the attempt of elucidating its dynamics of revealment and concealment. Even today, the essay is frequently regarded and celebrated as the crux of the preeminent source of Dōgen's teachings – "The Treasury of the True Dharma Eye" (*Shōbōgenzō*, 正法眼蔵).[1] As such, Akizuki maintains that the "Genjōkōan" is "the vital point of Dōgen's thought" (*Dōgen no shisō no kaname*, 道元の思想の要), and Tanaka claims that the insight of the *Shōbōgenzō* "springs out of the 'Genjōkōan and returns to the 'Genjōkōan'" (*Genjōkōan yori idete Genjōkōan ni kaeru*, 現成公案より出でて現成公案に帰る).[2]

Indeed, the heart of the "Genjōkōan" escapes any easy definition. As the very nature of the text is the interplay between duality and nonduality, practice and realization, revealment and concealment, it would not be an exaggeration to suggest that the essay functions as a *kōan* that illumines the *kōan* which is no other than the ambiguities of reality itself. As Kagamishima maintains:

We should understand that [according to Dōgen] all that is revealed to us is a *kōan*. For Dōgen Zenji, the meaning of *kōan* is not that of ancient cases, but that of the unmovable norm, law or absolute reality. Accordingly, the meaning of "Genjōkōan" is that all that is revealed to us is in itself absolute reality.[3]

In the following I propose to widen the philosophical implications of the "Genjōkōan" by reading it as an essay that uncovers deep notions of Dōgen's interpretive sensibilities. Specifically, I will concentrate on passages which are identified with the principle of "dharma position" and will show that they can be retranslated as an articulation of an interpretive perspective. To clarify and explicate this, I will borrow the framework of interpretive charity as formulated in Judaic traditions.

In doing so, I seek to deepen Maraldo's suggestion that "Dōgen challenges us to see practice as the principle through which the text is to be understood".[4] Only instead of the category of "practice" my inclination is towards that of "principle", as I find that the "dharma position" constitute the theoretical thrust of the "Genjōkōan" and thus can also be understood as an interpretive principle. My approach is also

---

[1] In traditional Sōtō hermeneutics, the essay is considered as one of the three central fascicles of the *Shōbōgenzō*, together with the "Bendōwa" (弁道話) and "Busshō" (仏性). This categorization is known as *"Ben-Gen-Bu"* (弁・現・仏). See Tsunoda Tairyū 角田泰隆, *Dōgen Zenji no shisō teki kenkyū* 道元禅師の思想的研究 (Tōkyō: Shunjūsha, 2015), 13–14.

[2] Akizuki Ryōmin 秋月龍珉, *Dōgen nyūmon* 道元入門 (Tōkyō: Kōdansha Gendaishinsho, 1970), 184; Tanaka Akira, *Shōbōgenzō no tetsugaku* (Tōkyō: Hōzōkan, 1982), 186.

[3] Kagamishima Genryū 鏡島元隆, "Dōgen no shisō," in Kagamishima Genryū and Tamaki Kōshirō (eds.), *Kōza Dōgen 1: Dōgen no shōgai to shisō* 講座道元 1: 道元の生涯と思想 (Tōkyō: Shunjūsha, 1979), 13.

[4] John C. Maraldo, "The Hermeneutics of Practice in Dōgen and Francis of Assisi: An Exercise in Buddhist-Christian Dialogue," *The Eastern Buddhist* 14, no. 2 (1981), 33.

inspired by Heine, who clarified the temporal ground of Dōgen's hermeneutics, showing the hermeneutical dialectics of such pivotal concepts *kyōryaku* (経歴) and *nikon* (而今).[5]

1   The Interpretive Temperament of Zen

Before proceeding to the analysis of Dōgen's interpretive charity as I propose to locate it in the "Genjōkōan", a few words are necessary regarding the complex theme of Buddhist and Zen hermeneutics.

The theme of Buddhist hermeneutics has gained a growing interest in recent decades. Pivotal studies by Maraldo (1986) and Lopez (1992), for example, shed much needed light on the central role and complex nature of what may be defined as Buddhist hermeneutical orientations and interpretive methods. In the field of Dōgen studies we find a similar tendency that aims at clarifying the appropriate interpretive methods (*kaishaku hōhō*, 解釈方法) for elucidating Dōgen's texts and their affinity to the *Mahāyāna* canon and the vast treasury of Chan literature.

In Japan, we may distinguish between two main forms of hermeneutical orientations used by the Sōtō School and Japanese academics, to "harmonize" Dōgen's teachings and their growing number of interpretations. These are the methods of *sankyū* (参究), which I propose to translate here as a "participative investigation", and *kenkyū* (研究) which is often translated simply as "research". Of course, these methodological categories are also found in the interpretive endeavors of other Buddhist and Zen sects, yet in the following I will concentrate on their prominence in the Sōtō School.

According to Tsunonda, the hermeneutical style of *sankyū* is the traditional way through which scholars, mostly monks of the school, orientated their study of Dōgen from around the time of his death up to modern times. Hermeneutics as *sankyū* is understood to be based upon faith (*shin*, 信), and as such it originates from within the tradition and reflects the subjective (*shukanteki*, 主観的) interpretive stance of the traditionalist, whose efforts are shaped by and dedicated to the authority of the tradition.[6] Tagami notes that the origin of *sankyū* is in the intimate audience and

---

[5] In his analysis of "Dōgen's temporality of hermeneutics", Heine maintains that "Just as *kyōryaku* is the foundation of Buddha-nature, it also constitutes the ground which determines the hermeneutic process. [...] The simultaneous interrelatedness of past and present enlightenment experiences demands that the Dharma be perpetually reexplored and renewed through creative expressions of its inexhaustible meanings." See Steven Heine, "Temporality of Hermeneutics in Dōgen's *Shōbōgenzō*," *Philosophy East and West* 33, no. 2 (1983), 145.

[6] According to Tsunoda, *Sankyū* was commonly described by the term *shūjō* (宗乗) or "The Sōtō Vehicle" and is regarded as part of the *dentō-shūgaku* (伝統宗学) or "traditional study of the doctrine" method. See Tsunoda Tairyū, "Shūgaku saikō," *Komazawa tanki daigaku kenkyū kiyō* 27 (1999): 101, note.2.

correspondence (*ekken*, 謁見) between a teacher and a disciple, thus highlighting the authoritative stance of the former, to which the latter is to respond.[7]

After the Meiji restoration of 1868 new trends in Dōgen hermeneutics began to appear in Japan, falling under the broader category of *kenkyū*. The growing popularity of the Sōtō School, the adoption of new methods and perspectives on philology, and ongoing developments within the field of Chan Studies – all had a major impact on the ways by which Dōgen's thought was examined and commented upon. The *kenkyū* approach became widespread through promoting more objective prisms (*kakkanteki*, 客観的), rather than sectarian, and thus seemingly subjective, standpoints.[8]

The *kenkyū* paradigm has continued to develop all throughout the Shōwa period and examined Dōgen's Zen considering the broader frameworks of Buddhist studies (*bukkyōgaku*, 仏教学). This led to the term *kenkyū* being used alongside the traditional *sankyū* when questioning the methodological and hermeneutical approach assumed when engaging Dōgen's Zen.[9]

A recent contribution to the field of Dōgen hermeneutics is a study titled "Dōgen's thought as Dialogical Philosophy" (*Taiwa tetsugaku toshite no Dōgen shisō*, 対話哲学としての道元思想), written by Okajima Shūryū of Aichigakuin University. Okajima's proposes three perspectives that stress the dialogical nature of Zen as an interpretive tradition. The first is "Zen as a religion of questioning" (*toikake no shūkyō toshite no zen*, 問いかけの宗教としての禅).[10] Here, Okajima notes the centrality of the "Beginner's Mind" ideal (*shoshin*, 初心), and argues that the tradition, and especially Dōgen's Zen, strives to lead the practitioner back to this questioning temperament and a sense of wonder. Okajima writes:

Zen is a religion of questioning. A questioning about all there is. It is a questioning that asks for the return to the source of things no matter how many times. It is a questioning that turns us back to wonder about the most fundamental issues, indeed the most essential issues at hand. […] The difficulty is that nowadays, Zen as but a skeleton remains. […] It is overwhelmingly lacking in any sincere questioning thrust. […] If we do not inquire what it is that we must question, this essential questioning will not come alive.[11]

---

[7] Tagami Taishū, entry for "*Sankyū* 参究," in *Zen no shisō jiten* (hereafter ZSJT) 禅の思想辞典, ed. Tagami Taishū 田上太秀 and Ishii Shūdō 石井修道 (Tōkyō: Shoseki, 2008), 223.

[8] Seijun Ishii, "Recent developments in Dōgen Studies," in *Dōgen: Textual and Historical Studies*, ed. Steven Heine (New York: Oxford University Press, 2012), 223–236.

[9] An important work that represents the maturity of the universal *kenkyū* approach was "Zen Master Dōgen as a Founding Father" (*Shūso to shite no Dōgen Zenji*, 宗祖としての道元禅師) by Etō Sokuō 衞藤即應 (1888–1958). Etō's work had a major role in combining the traditional prisms of the *sankyū* method, with the new perspectives of general religious studies (*shūkyōgaku*, 宗教学) thus constituted a crucial juncture in the debut of modern Sōtō academics. See Tsunoda, *Dōgen Zenji no shisō teki kenkyū*, 86 // Tsunoda, "Shūgaku saikō," 86 ((Tsunoda, p. 86.))

[10] Okajima Shūryū 岡島秀隆, *Taiwa tetsugaku toshite no Dōgen shisō* 対話哲学としての道元思想 (Kyoto: Hōzōkan, 2021), 16.

[11] Ibid., 16.

The second interpretive perspective that Okajima proposes is "Zen as a dialogical religion" (*taiwa no shūkyō toshite no zen*, 対話の宗教としての禅). He writes:

We can say that Zen is a dialogical religion. For example, in the scene of the study of ancient traditional *kōan* cases, the dialogical and mutual correspondence of the inner workings of both teacher and disciple are indispensable. [...] Defining [the nature of these] *kōan* dialogues as merely ceremonial is therefore not desirable.[12]

This provides us with a deep insight regarding the interpretive vigor of Zen: formality enables the expression and disclosure of new interpretive perspectives, and these perspectives shed new light on the constant formalities of the tradition. By defining Zen as a dialogical religion, Okajima points to the fact that the interpretive criteria are not to be limited to the authority and formality of the tradition alone.

This leads to the third perspective that Okajima notes, which is "Zen as a religion of creation" (*sōzō no shūkyō no zen*, 創造の宗教の禅). Okajima explains that the very language of Zen, its inclination towards the creative, ambiguous, and dialectical, encourages a terminological widening and an expansion of imagery, ideas, and interpretive notions. This expansion (*kakuchō*, 拡張) of the terminological field is of crucial importance when examining Dōgen's notions of hermeneutics. Thus, questioning vigor, dialogical openness, and the creative expansion of the terminological field are all vital to our elucidation of Zen as an interpretive tradition.[13]

In the following, I will continue developing Okajima's analysis. By borrowing the hermeneutical framework of "interpretive charity" as formulated in Judaic traditions, I will engage Dōgen's "Genjōkōan" and show that the text itself reveals an interpretive methodology that is rooted in the dialectics of the "dharma position".

2   Interpretive Charity

To clarify the interpretive function of the "dharma position" as expressed in the "Genjōkōan", I propose an insightful example taken from the Judaic hermeneutical tradition. In his study of canon, meaning, and authority in the history of Jewish textual tradition, Moshe Halbertal shows that there is a constant movement between openness and closure in the boundaries of the textual canon and the scope of interpreters to determine textual meaning.[14] Halbertal explains:

---

[12] Ibid., 17.

[13] Ibid., 20. For a survey and an analysis of Dōgen's terminological expansion and interpretive creativeness see also Niimoto Toyozō新本豊三, "Dōgen ni okeru butten no tenshaku道元におけ る仏典の転釈," *Zen kenkyūsho kiyō* 12 (1984): 33–49.

[14] Halbertal presents four kinds of canon as texts of special status. The first is a normative canon that is ought to be obeyed and followed. The second is a formative canon that provides a society or a profession with a shared vocabulary. The third is an exemplary canon that serves as paradigmatic example of aesthetic ideals and achievements. In the Jewish tradition, for example, the *Talmud* serves as both normative and formative canon. See Moshe Halbertal, *People of the Book: Canon, Meaning, and Authority* (Cambridge, Mass: Harvard University Press, 1997), 3–4.

Canonization of a text may at times serve to take the authority away from its original meaning, allowing the commentator to choose the meaning that will be deemed authoritative. [...] This phenomenon in the interpretation of a canonical text is an example of what Willard Quine has called "the principle of charity," a topic that promises to broaden our perspective on the subject of canonization. The principle of charity is an interpretative method that would yield an optimally successful text. For example, although a person's words might be read as self-contradictory and thus meaningless, they should not be interpreted in that way. [...] Making use of the principle of charity, the following principle can be stipulated: the degree of canonicity of a text corresponds to the amount of charity it receives in its interpretation. The more canonical a text, the more generous its treatment.[15]

Borrowing Quine's notion of "the principle of charity", Halbertal maintains that the sealing of religious canon does indeed affirm its authority, yet also invokes an ongoing and complex interpretive activity that puts this very authority into question. In this way, the principle of charity is not only a method that yields an optimal elucidation, but an interpretive tendency that "instigates a comprehensive upheaval within the Jewish community".[16] An upheaval that is generous – that is charitable (Heb. *hesed*) – in its flexible and enhanced interpretive inclinations. As Halbertal concludes:

"There is an interesting asymmetrical relation between canonization and hermeneutical openness. The more canonized the text, the broader interpretative possibilities it offers."[17]

Following this analysis by Halbertal, Wolfgang Iser, in his elucidation of the principle of charity in the Judaic tradition, notes the following:

The principle of charity [...] seeks to ensure the meaningfulness of the canonical text in instances where the literal meaning creates an impression of meaninglessness in relation to other texts of the canon; simultaneously, it aims to bring out the plethora of meanings enfolded in the text. Charity therefore entails giving a positive slant to whatever the text says, in order to bring it to full fruition, so that it can be perceived in the light of its inherent perfection.[18]

The analysis by Halbertal and Iser echoes Steiner's assertion that the "determination of the interpretive act is inherently inflationary: it proclaims that 'there is more than meets the eye'".[19]

Indeed, interpretive charity in the Judaic tradition rises *vis-a-vis* the canonicity of the religious text. The generous interpretive treatment, which involves the clarification of meaning and many times the creation of a new one, emerges from the recognition of the interpreter that the text is indeed central to the tradition. Thus, while

---

[15] Ibid., 27–29.

[16] Ibid., 19–20.

[17] Ibid., 44.

[18] Wolfgang Iser, *The Range of Interpretation* (New York: Columbia University Press, 2000), 18.

[19] George Steiner, *After Babel: Aspects of Language and Translation* (Oxford, New York: Oxford University Press, 3rd ed., 1998), 316.

authority certainly commands a restricted reading entwined with a common sense of meaning, it also kindles broad interpretive sensibilities and significance.

We may term this as the subversive nature of the principle of interpretive charity: it is *dependent* on yet not *limited* to authority. It reflects a deep commitment and a lasting sense of the past, yet it is not denying a sense of a future. New meaning is being revealed while engaging past significance. Hence, the charitable exegete functions within the lasting tension between tradition and controversy; textual authority and interpretive creativeness.[20]

As mentioned earlier, Dōgen's "Genjōkōan" is a renowned essay. Considered one of the three central fascicles of the *Shōbōgenzō*, it may be regarded as a canonical text. If we pursue Halbertal's conclusion that the more canonized a text, the broader interpretative possibilities it offers, than the "Genjōkōan" seems to fit the criteria, along with other texts such as the *Fukanzazengi*, and the fascicles "Bendōwa" (弁道話) and "Busshō" (仏性). Each of these nourished, and still nourishes, an abundance of commentaries in traditional circles, academic studies, and popular readership.[21]

At this point, I propose to take Halbertal's definition of interpretive charity a step forward. Not denying the role of its canonicity in igniting an exegetical inspiration, I maintain that the language and imagery of the "Genjōkōan" express an interpretive tendency that is a mode of the principle of charity. This charitable language is rooted in the dialectics of the "dharma position". In this way, the "Genjōkōan" exemplifies how interpretive charity is a principle that emerges from the very thrust of the text, and not only as the outcome of its authoritative canonicity.

Yet before exemplifying the way in which the "dharma position" functions as interpretive charity, we should briefly clarify the origins and meaning of the term.

3   The Meaning of "Dharma Position"

According to Ishii, the central appearance of the term "dharma position" (*hōi*, 法位), which also appears in the variant "abiding/dwelling in a dharma position" (*jūhōi*, 住法位) is found in the following verse from "The Chapter on Skillful Means" (*Hōben gebun*, 方便偈文) of the "Lotus Sūtra of the Wonderful Dharma" (*Myōhō rengekyō*, 妙法蓮華経):

---

[20] Halbertl elucidates three exegetical views of controversy and tradition. The first is the "revival model" of Abraham Ibn Daud (1110–1180) of the tradition of the Geonim. The second is the "cumulative view" of Maimonides (1135–1204). The third is the "constitutive view" of Nachmanides (1194–1270). See Halbertal, *People of the Book*, 54–72.

[21] For a detailed study of the traditional commentaries on the *Honzan* (本山) version of the *Shōbōgenzō* see: Steven Heine and Katarina Ankrum, "Outside of a Small Circle: Sōtō Zen Commentaries on Dōgen's *Shōbōgenzō* and the Formation of the 95-Fascicle *Honzan* Edition," *Japan Studies Review* 21 (2017): 85–127.

"Dharmas abide in their dharma positions as the form of the world constantly abides" (*hō jūhōi sekensō jōjū*, 法住法位世間相常住).[22]

The verse is one of the clearest examples of what Tachikawa defines as the affirmative aspect (*kōtei-teki sokumen*, 肯定的側面) of the philosophy of emptiness. While emptiness can indeed be seen as a form of negation (*hitei*, 否定), Tachikawa claims that it also serves as an affirmative doctrine in East–Asian Buddhist Schools.[23] A concise definition of the affirmative meaning of the term "dharma position" is offered by Nakamura:

Each of the myriad things is entirely real in its particularity both in form as well as in function. Thus, each thing in itself is nothing but the absolute. As such, [dharma position] designates a reality of self-reliance and independent particularity. A particular and unattached existence. Each thing in itself is peacefully abiding in its own dharma position.[24]

According to this affirmative rendering, as all phenomena arise interdependently, each is emptied of any "self–nature", yet this very emptying simultaneously gives rise to and enables all other phenomena. Thus, emptiness is not to be understood only as a subversive force, but as an affirmative vitality that confirms all phenomena in their particular independence (*dokuritsu*, 独立).[25] According to Kurebayashi, Dōgen's thought as a whole clearly expresses this affirmative aspect.[26]

The affirmative meaning of the "dharma position" gained much interpretive treatment throughout the centuries. In his study of the oldest sectarian commentaries of the "Genjōkōan" found in the *Goshō* writings (御抄) of Senne (詮慧, n.d) and Kyōgō (経豪, n.d), Itō shows how the "dharma position" was described in terms of "total

---

[22] Seijūn Ishii, entry for "*hōjū hōi*法住法位, "in ZSJT, p. 437. Dōgen quotes this verse in several fascicles of the *Shōbōgenzō*, such as "Shohō jissō" (諸法実相) and "Immo" (恁麼), and also in his recorded sermons. Tanahashi translates the verse as "things abiding in the world of phenomena, and the everlasting reality of the world". See Tanahashi Kazuaki (ed., trans.), *Treasury of the True Dharma Eye: Zen Master Dōgen's Shōbō Genzō*, (hereafter TTDY), vol. 2 (Boston: Shambhala, 2010), 522. Also, in his translation of the fascicle "Immo" (恁麼 "Thusness"), Tanahashi renders the verse as: "Things abide in their conditions, and there is the aspect of the world as permanent." See TTDY 1: 330.

[23] Tachikawa Musashi立川武蔵, *Kū no shisōshi* 空の思想史 (Tōkyō: Kōdansha Gakujutsubunko, 2004), 6–7.

[24] Nakamura Sōichi 中村宗一, *Shōbōgenzō yōgo jiten* 正法眼蔵用語辞典 (Tōkyō: Seishin Shobō, 1975), 174.

[25] Tachikawa, *Kū no shisōshi*, 54. For a detailed discussion of this affirmative aspect, known as "All things in their True aspect" (*shohō jissō*, 諸法実相) within Tendai circles, see ibid., 271–283. Tachikawa's "affirmative aspect" of emptiness, which confirms (*shō*, 証) all phenomena in their "particular independence," echoes Hee-Jin Kim's distinction between the deconstructive and reconstructive aspects of emptiness. See Hee-Jin Kim, *Dōgen on Meditation and Thinking: A Reflection on His View of Zen* (Albany: State University of New York Press, 2007), 42.

[26] Kurebayashi Kōdō 博林皓堂, *Dōgen Zen no honryū* 道元禅の本流, (Tōkyō: Daihōrikaku, 1980), 136.

exertion" (*gūjin*, 究尽) and "the penetration of one dharma" (*ippō tsū*, 一法通).[27] Notably, these are expression used by Dōgen throughout his writings and sermons.[28]

In his analysis, Itō showed that the "dharma position" came to signify the affinity between the total penetration of a single thing through the wisdom of emptiness and the affirmation of its very particular existence. In the *Goshō* commentaries, this affirmation was rendered as "the independence of the particular" (一法独立, *ippō dokuritsu*).[29] In light of this, "dharma position" functions as the reconstructive principle of Emptiness. It is the affirmation of the particular, all while this same particularity is simultaneously dependent upon all other particularities.

4 "Dharma Position" as Interpretive Charity

The reconstructive meaning of the "dharma position" has profound hermeneutical implications. Specifically, I maintain that it operates as a form of interpretive charity. As noted earlier, in the case of "Genjōkōan", this form of charity is not based necessarily on the authority of the text, but such that springs from its very terminology and expressions.

In light of that, the following is an exercise in a retranslation of five passages from the "Genjōkōan" in which the principle of "dharma position" is expressed, either explicitly or implicitly. Each passage appears both in the original and in translation and followed by a rereading of the original as an interpretive teaching.

The first passage reads as follows:

1. Firewood becomes ash, and does not become firewood again. Yet, do not suppose that the ash is after and the firewood before. Understand that firewood abides in its condition as firewood, which fully includes before and after, while it is independent of before and after. Ash abides in its condition as ash, which fully includes before and after.[30]

---

[27] Itō Shūken 伊藤秀憲, "Ippō wo shōsuru toki wa ippō wa kurashi no ronri 一方を証するときは一方はくらしの論理," *Komazawa daigaku bukkyōgakubu ronshū* 7 (1976): 165–170.

[28] For example, according to Ryōdō Awaya, the term "total exertion" (*gūjin*, 究尽) appears seventy-one times throughout the *Shōbōgenzō*. See in detail Ryōdō Awaya 良道粟谷, "Shōbōgenzō ni okeru gūjin nitsuite: Shōbōgenzō to no hikaku 正法眼蔵における究尽について:正法眼蔵抄との比較," *Shūgaku kenkyū* 28 (1986): 290.

[29] Itō, "Ippō wo shōsuru toki wa ippō wa kurashi no ronri," 172–4.

[30] All translations of the essay are by Tanahashi. See TTDY 1: 30. Original Japanese of the "Genjōkōan" is taken from *Dōgen Zenji zenshū* (hereafter DZZ) 道元禪師全集 [Dōgen's Complete Works], 7 vols., ed. Kawamura Kōdō 河村孝道 et al. (Tōkyō: Shunjūsha, 1988–1993), 1: 2–7: たき木、はひとなる、さらにかへりてたき木となるべきにあらず。しかあるを灰はのち、薪はさきと見取すべからず。しるべし、薪は薪の法位に住して、さきありのちあり。前後ありといへども、前後際断せり。灰は灰の法位にありて、のちありさきあり。

This is one of the most evident appearances of the "dharma position" in the essay. Here, the dialectics of firewood and ash can exemplify the relation between text and its interpretation. Translating the passage in this manner, I propose the following rendering:

A text is interpreted and does not remain the same text. Yet, do not suppose that the interpretation is after and that the text is before. Understand that a text abides in its condition as a text, which fully includes before and after, all while it is independent of before and after. Also, the interpretation abides in its condition as an interpretation, which fully includes before and after.

The following passage is traditionally regarded and interpreted as a description of the soteriological implications of the "dharma position", expressing the nonduality between the relative and the absolute.[31] Dōgen wrote the following:

2. Enlightenment is like the moon reflected on the water. The moon does not get wet, nor is the water broken. Although its light is wide and great, the moon is reflected even in a puddle an inch wide. The whole moon and the entire sky are reflected in dewdrops on the grass, or even in one drop of water.[32]

Considering the above, I propose to render "realization" as "meaning", "moon" as "text", and the various reflection on water as "interpretation". Thus, the passage may be reread as follows:

The meaning of a text is reflected in its various interpretations. The text is not forgotten, nor are the interpretations discarded. Although its significance is wide and great, the meaning of a text is implied even in its most modest of interpretations. Thus, the various meanings of a text are reflected in the wide field of its numerous interpretations, yet also implied by each and every one of them.

The third passage continues the elucidation of nonduality between the relative and the absolute; delusion and awakening. Dōgen writes:

3. Enlightenment does not divide you, just as the moon does not break the water. You cannot hinder enlightenment, just as a drop of water does not hinder the moon in the sky. The depth of the drop is the height of the moon.[33]

---

[31] Throughout my analysis of the dialectics of the dharma position, I use the category of nonduality rather than that of unity. By that I follow Masao Abe's claim that "Monism is not yet free from duality, for it is still opposed to dualism or pluralism. Being beyond duality […] is not monistic but rather non-dualistic." See Masao Abe, *Zen and Western Thought*, ed. William LaFleur (Honolulu: University of Hawai'i Press, 1989), 208. For a study of the prevalence and significance of the *via-negativa* (or *apophatic*) articulations in Dōgen's thought and an elucidation of his usage of the term "not two" (*funi*, 不二) see Eitan Bolokan, "Zen Words of the Unsayable: An Inquiry into Dōgen Zenji's Apophatic Terminology," *Asian Philosophy: An International Journal of the Philosophical Traditions of the East* 30, no. 3 (2020): 195–213.

[32] DZZ 1: 31: 人の、さとりをうる、水に月のやどるがごとし。月ぬれず、水やぶれず。ひろくおほきなるひかりにてあれど、尺寸の水にやどり、全月も弥天も、くさの露にもやどり、一滴の水にもやどる。

[33] Ibid.: さとりの、人をやぶらざること、月の、水をうがたざるがごとし。人の、さとりを罣礙せざること、滴露の、天月を罣礙せざるがごとし。ふかきことは、たかき分量なるべし。

Considering the nonduality expressed in the above, and shifting it to the affinity between the particular text and the various possibilities of interpreting it, I propose the following reading:

Your understanding of a text does not hinder/restrict you from understanding it differently, just as the particularity of a certain text is not discarded by any of its other possible interpretations. The more diversified are the interpretations, the clearer are the significance and complexity of the particular text.

The fourth passage is the famous dialogue between Zen Master Mayu and a disciple at the end of the essay. Dōgen writes:

4. Mayu, Zen master Baoche, was fanning himself. A monk approached and said, "Master, the nature of wind is permanent and there is no place it does not reach. Why, then, do you fan yourself?" "Although you understand that the nature of the wind is permanent," Mayu replied, "you do not understand the meaning of its reaching everywhere." "What is the meaning of its reaching everywhere?" asked the monk again. Mayu just kept fanning himself. The monk bowed deeply.[34]

Exchanging between the figure of the Zen master to that of a great interpreter, and between the concept of the "permanent nature of wind" (風性常住, *fūshō jōjū*) to "the stable meaning of the text", the above dialogue may be rendered as follows:

A great interpreter was writing his interpretation. A student approached and asked, "Master, the meaning of the text is stable and there is no place where it is not known. Why, then, are you interpreting it?" The great interpreter replied: "Although you understand that the meaning of the text is stable, you still do not understand the meaning of its being known everywhere." The student asked: "What is the meaning of its being known everywhere?". The Master kept writing his interpretation.

Immediately after this dialogue, appears the following passage which brings the "Genjōkōan" to its conclusion:

5. The actualization of the buddha-dharma, the vital path of its correct transmission, is like this. If you say that you do not need to fan yourself because the nature of wind is permanent and you can have wind without fanning, you will understand neither permanence nor the nature of wind. The nature of wind is permanent. Because of that, the wind of the buddha's house brings forth the gold of the earth and makes fragrant the cream of the long river.[35]

---

[34] DZZ 1: 32: 麻谷山宝徹禅師、あふぎをつかふちなみに、僧きたりてとふ、風性常住、無處不周なり、なにをもてかさらに和尚あふぎをつかふ。師い云く、なんぢただ風性常住をしれりとも、いまだところとしていたらずといふことなき道理をしらず、と。僧曰く、いかならんかこれ無處不周底の道理。ときに、師、あふぎをつかふのみなり。僧、礼拝す。

[35] DZZ 1: 33: 仏法の証験、正伝の活路、それかくのごとし。常住なればあふぎをつかふべからず、つかはぬをりもかぜをきくべきといふは、常住をもしらず、風性をもしらぬなり。風性は常住なるがゆゑに、仏家の風は、大地の黄金なるを現成せしめ、長河の蘇酪を参熟せり。

Rendering "The actualization of the buddha-dharma" (*buppō no shōken*, 仏法の証験) as "The actualization of meaning" and "the vital path of its correct transmission" (*shōden no karro*, 正伝の活路) as "the vital path of correct interpretation", I propose the following reading:

The actualization of meaning, the vital path of correct interpretation, is like this. If you say that you do not need to interpretate a text because its meaning is stable and known to all, you will understand neither the meaning of its stability nor its other various meanings. Indeed, the meaning of a text is stable. Yet because of that, all the various interpretations bring forth its vital essence and make fragrant the cream of its meaning.

Bringing together all the above retranslations, the following interpretive rendition of the "Genjōkōan" as reflecting a hermeneutical perspective may be formulated:

A text is interpreted and does not remain the same text. Yet do not suppose that the interpretation is after and that the text is before. Understand that a text abides in its condition as a particular text, which fully includes before and after, all while it is independent of before and after. Also, the interpretation abides in its condition as an interpretation, which fully includes before and after.

The meaning of a particular text is reflected in its various interpretations. The text is not forgotten, nor are the interpretations discarded. Although its significance is wide and great, the meaning of a text is implied even in its most modest of interpretations. Thus, the various meanings of a text are reflected in the wide field of its numerous interpretations, yet also implied in each and every one of them.

Your understanding of a text does not hinder/restrict you from understanding it differently, just as the particularity of a certain text is not discarded by any of its other possible interpretations. The more diversified are the interpretations, the clearer are the significance and complexity of the particular text.

A great interpreter was writing his interpretation. A student approached and asked, "Master, the meaning of the text is stable and there is no place where it is not known. Why, then, are you interpreting it?" The great interpreter replied: "Although you understand that the meaning of the text is stable, you still do not understand the meaning of its being known everywhere." The student asked: "What is the meaning of its being known everywhere?". The Master kept writing his interpretation.

The actualization of meaning, the vital path of correct interpretation, is like this. If you say that you do not need to interpretate a text because its meaning is stable and known to all, you will understand neither the meaning of its stability nor its other various meanings. Indeed, the meaning of a text is stable. Yet because of that, all the various interpretations bring forth its vital essence and make fragrant the cream of its meaning.

5 Concluding Remarks

The "Genjōkōan" and its poetic articulations of the "dharma position" is of cardinal importance in Dōgen's thought. The dialectics of duality and nonduality, the affirmation of the relative and the reconstruction of the particular through the insight of emptiness, reflect not only Dōgen's philosophical and poetic tendencies, but his attitude towards actual practice and the religious life.

Nonetheless, I proposed that these practical and ontological implications are not limited to the various concrete forms of Zen life, but also shape the practitioner's intellectual attitude towards the tradition and its teachings. By its very dialectical nature, the principle of "dharma position" enables a charitable interpretation of the tradition and a creative formation of its new expressions. If Zen practice is to be understood according to the tradition's conceptual framework and insights, then so are its hermeneutical sensitivities and interpretive inclinations. In this sense, the way one practices a religious life reflects one's hermeneutical dispositions and interpretive orientation towards the tradition and its authority.

For this reason, I proposed that the principle of the "Dharma position", in its role as an interpretive charity, has enabled Dōgen, as early as in 1233, to voice his own creative style of teaching and articulation, negotiating the path between the textual authority and imagery of the tradition and his own creativeness. Throughout his life, Dōgen continued to express and articulate these complexities in various writings and sermons as, for example, in his pivotal 1243 essay "Entangled Vines" ("kattō", 葛藤).

The figure of Dōgen as a creative interpreter of the tradition lies in the clarification of the manners in which he pacified, or tried to pacify, these various tensions. As such, the "Genjōkōan" reflects interpretive tendencies and inclinations that echo through Dōgen's life, showing that the authority of the Zen master and the religious leader constitutes the creativeness of the Zen philosopher and even more so – the Zen interpreter.

In this way, what may be rendered as the metaphysical framework of the "dharma position", serves as a charitable hermeneutical sensibility that enabled Dōgen to express his insights in such a provocative manner, one that questioned the tradition, all while cherishing its significance and authority. In this sense, Dōgen was so charitable to his own tradition that he was able to comment upon it creatively and honestly. The "Genjōkōan", by the dialectics of the "dharma position", initiates us to this subversive, creative, and charitable interpretive framework. Interpretation (*kaishaku*, 解釈) is thus a vital and useful category when examining the complexities and tensions reflected in Dōgen's portrait as a religious leader and a philosopher and may serve as an intermediate framework for clarifying the manners in which he expressed his unique path.

References

Akizuki, Ryōmin 秋月龍珉. *Dōgen nyūmon* 道元入門. Tōkyō: Kōdansha Gendaishinsho, 1970.
Abe, Masao. *Zen and Western Thought*, edited by William LaFleur. Honolulu: University of Hawaiʻi Press, 1989.
Bolokan, Eitan. "Zen Words of the Unsayable: An Inquiry into Dōgen Zenji's Apophatic Terminology." *Asian Philosophy: An International Journal of the Philosophical Traditions of the East* 30, no. 3 (2020): 195–213.

Halbertal, Moshe. *People of the Book: Canon, Meaning, and Authority*. Cambridge, Mass: Harvard University Press, 1997.

Heine, Steven. "Temporality of Hermeneutics in Dōgen's Shōbōgenzō." *Philosophy East and West* 33, no. 2 (1983): 139–147.

Heine, Steven, and Katarina Ankrum. "Outside of a Small Circle: Sōtō Zen Commentaries on Dōgen's Shōbōgenzō and the Formation of the 95-Fascicle Honzan Edition." *Japan Studies Review* 21 (2017): 85–127.

Iser, Wolfgang. *The Range of Interpretation*. New York: Columbia University Press, 2000.

Ishii, Seijun. "Recent developments in Dōgen Studies." In *Dōgen: Textual and Historical Studies*, edited by Steven Heine, 223–236. New York: Oxford University Press, 2012.

Itō, Shūken 伊藤秀憲. "Ippō wo shōsuru toki wa ippō wa kurashi no ronri 一方を証するときは一方はくらしの論理." *Komazawa daigaku bukkyō gakubu ronshū* 駒沢大学仏教学部論集 7 (1976): 160–174.

Kagamishima, Genryū 鏡島元隆. "Dōgen no shisō." In *Kōza Dōgen 1: Dōgen no shōgai to shisō* 講座道元 1: 道元の生涯と思想, edited by Kagamishima Genryū and Tamaki Kōshirō. Tokyo: Shunjūsha, 1979.

Kim, Hee-Jin. *Dōgen on Meditation and Thinking: A Reflection on His View of Zen*. Albany, NY: State University of New York Press, 2007.

Kurebayashi, Kōdō 栄林皓堂. *Dōgen zen no honryū* 道元禅の本流. Tōkyō: Daihōrinkaku, 1980.

Lopez, Donald. *Buddhist Hermeneutics*. Honolulu: University of Hawai'i Press, The Kuroda Institute, 1992.

Maraldo, John C. "Hermeneutics and Historicity in the Study of Buddhism." *The Eastern Buddhist* 19, no. 1 (1986): 17–43.

Maraldo, John C. "The Hermeneutics of Practice in Dōgen and Francis of Assisi: An Exercise in Buddhist–Christian Dialogue." *The Eastern Buddhist* 14, no. 2 (1981): 22–46.

Nakamura, Sōichi 中村宗一, ed. *Shōbōgenzō yōgo jiten* 正法眼蔵用語辞典. Tōkyō: Seishin Shobō, 1975.

Niimoto, Toyozō 新本豊三. "Dōgen ni okeru butten no tenshaku 道元における仏典の転釈." *Zen kenkyūsho kiyō* 禅研究所紀要 12 (1984): 33–49.

Okajima, Shūryū 岡島秀隆. *Taiwa tetsugaku toshite no Dōgen shisō* 対話哲学としての道元思想. Kyoto: Hōzōkan, 2021.

Ryōdō, Awaya 良道粟谷. "Shōbōgenzō ni okeru gūjin nitsuite: Shōbōgenzō to no hikaku 正法眼蔵における究尽について:正法眼蔵抄との比較." *Shūgaku kenkyū* 宗学研究 28 (1986): 290–306.

Steiner, George. *After Babel: Aspects of Language and Translation*. Oxford, New York: Oxford University Press, 3rd ed., 1998.

Tachikawa, Musashi 立川武蔵. *Kū no shisōshi* 空の思想史. Tōkyō: Kōdansha Gakujutsubunko, 2004.

Tagami, Taishū 田上太秀. Entry for 参究 *Sankyū*. In *Zen no shisō jiten* 禅の思想辞典, edited by Tagami Taishū 田上太秀 and Ishii Shūdō 石井修道, 223. Tōkyō: Shoseki (2008).

Tanaka, Akira 田中晃. *Shōbōgenzō no tetsugaku* 正法眼蔵の哲学. Tōkyō: Hōzōkan, 1982.

Tsunoda, Tairyū 角田泰隆. *Dōgen Zenji no shisō teki kenkyū* 道元禅師の思想的研究. Tōkyō: Shunjūsha, 2015.

Tsunoda, Tairyū. "Shūgaku saikō." *Komazawa tanki daigaku kenkyū kiyō* 27 (1999): 101.

Traces of the Brush: Examination of Dōgen's Thought Through His Language

Zuzana Kubovčáková

The beginning of Zen is attributed to a renowned account of Buddha Shākyamuni's silent transmission to his follower and disciple Mahākāśyapa related in case six of the *Gateless Gate* or *Wumen's Barrier* kōan collection, *Mumonkan* 無門関. Surrounded by his followers and disciples on Vulture Peak, Shākyamuni Buddha was seated, ready to expound his teaching. Instead of a verbally pronounced lecture, however, his audience received a silent sermon of the Buddha lifting a flower in his fingers, blinking his eyes and showing it to the assembly. Everyone remained silent, waiting in blank amazement, only Mahākāśyapa's face broke into a soft smile. That was when the Buddha said, "I possess the treasury of the true dharma eye, the wondrous mind of nirvāna, the true form without form, the subtle dharma gate. It is nondependent upon words and letters, transmitted outside scriptures, and I hereby impart it to Mahākāśyapa."[1] Thus, the characteristic Chan/Zen narrative of silent transmission, also referred to as the story of "holding up a flower and smiling softly" (*nenge mishō* 拈華微笑) was born.

The account introduces a self-defining motto of Chan/Zen schools as a tradition nondependent upon words and letters (*furyū monji* 不立文字), transmitted outside what was considered established Buddhist scriptures (*kyōge betsuden* 教外別傳), a statement that presents a straightforward ambiguity for such a principal matter as the spread of a school of thought itself. On the one hand, there is the issue of transmission of recognized written doctrines and texts essential for the tradition, as well as the school's confirmation and identity, which is generally understood as the most

---

[1] *Taishō shinshū daizōkyō Text Database* 大正新脩大藏經テキストデータベース (hereafter T), 48.293c.

Z. Kubovčáková (✉)
Masaryk University, Brno, Czech Republic

© The Author(s), under exclusive license to Springer Nature Switzerland AG 2023   77
R. Müller, G. Wrisley (eds.), *Dōgen's Texts*, Sophia Studies in Cross-cultural
Philosophy of Traditions and Cultures 35,
https://doi.org/10.1007/978-3-031-42246-1_5

efficient by means of textual exchange and dissemination. At the same time, however, there is the looming danger of words becoming triggers for delusion and misunderstanding rather than vehicles for breakthrough and enlightenment.

The Japanese Zen master Dōgen 道元 (1200–1253) approached this perennial paradox in his own manner, creating an abundant body of writings and resources that have been studied, copied, and edited for centuries since his lifetime.[2] Dōgen was most prolific in producing written sermons both in literary Chinese, as was the custom of his time, as well as in Japanese, which on the contrary was novel and original. His ample literary endeavors form Dōgen's most representative works of the Chinese-style *Extensive Record* (*Eihei kōroku* 永平廣録) and *Treasury of the True Dharma Eye* (*Shōbōgenzō* 正法眼蔵) composed in vernacular Japanese in combination with classical Chinese. Furthermore, Dōgen left behind numerous temple regulations (*shingi* 清規) for a Zen community dedicated to a continuous monastic practice (*gyōji* 行持), in addition to other doctrinal, philosophical, and poetic works. His contribution lies not only in introducing Zen thought and meditation practice of "just sitting" or "mere sitting" (*shikan taza* 只管打坐) to his homeland but also in his profuse literary legacy reflecting a mind that was unique in expressing the dharma as well as deeply concerned with the correct transmission of the ancestral teaching in Japan. Teaching and establishing a tradition that originated with Shākyamuni Buddha, "What Dōgen attempted was not a mere return or recapitulation of Buddha's teachings but a radical reexpression and reenactment of them," writes Hee-Jin Kim in his ground-breaking publication on Dōgen in the western world.[3] In the introduction to *Eihei Dōgen: Mystical Realist*, Kim further states that the master's concern was a "passionate search for liberation through concrete activities and expressions,"[4] noting that the quest and combination of continuous monastic activities (*gyōji*) and expressions (*dōtoku* 道得) were essential to Dōgen's work and thought. This blending of things enacted through body and expressed via language epitomized the description of Dōgen used by William LaFleur in his introduction to a seminal work on the meditation teacher stating that "Dōgen, after all, was a writer in addition to being a Zen master."[5]

Besides being known as one of the founders of the Sōtō school 曹洞宗, a writer, and a thinker, Dōgen is also remembered as a poet, expressing himself in doctrinal texts and contexts as well as in lyrical and metaphorical images. In his collection of Japanese *waka* poems, there is one bearing the name of the aforementioned conundrum of "nondependence upon words and letters," conveying, in poetic terms, the

---

[2] Due to a period of interim when the study of the *Treasury of the True Dharma Eye* produced no written commentaries from 1329 until the middle of the Edo era, especially Western scholars have heretofore assumed that Dōgen's masterwork was given little attention by members of the Sōtō school itself in the medieval times. However, recent research of Heine proves otherwise, see Steven Heine, *Flowers Blooming on a Withered Tree* (New York: Oxford University Press, 2020b).

[3] Hee-Jin Kim, *Eihei Dōgen: Mystical Realist* (Boston: Wisdom Publications, 2004), 54.

[4] Kim, *Eihei Dōgen*, 9.

[5] William LaFleur, "Dōgen in the Academy," in *Dōgen Studies*, ed. William LaFleur (Honolulu: University of Hawai'i Press, 1985), 15.

master's understanding on the apparent contrast between the polarizing bounded-ness by language on the one hand and a freedom of expression on the other.

不立文字	*Furyū monji*	Nondependence Upon Words and Letters[6]
謂いすてし	*Ii sute shi*	What is spoken
其言の葉の	*Sono koto no ha no*	Beyond words
外なれば、	*hoka nare ba*	Does not
筆にも跡を	*Fude ni mo ato wo*	Leave traces
留めざりけり	*Todome zari keri*	Of the brush

This poem is exemplary in how it illustrates Dōgen's view on leaving behind thoughts, teaching, and doctrines as "traces of the brush" in the form of writings, as a note to Shākyamuni's silent sermon. In its mere thirty-one Japanese syllables, Dōgen makes reference to the phrase attributed to the Buddha, albeit in his original way and interpretation, as well as expresses his own understanding of the matter of the silent transmission. His *koto no ha no hoka* 言の葉の外 literally translates as "outside of words," alluding to the above mentioned "outside of scriptures," *kyōge betsuden*, while *fude ni mo ato* 筆にも跡 converts to "traces of the brush," hence the "words and letters" of *monji* used in the title of the poem. Therefore, through the medium of words, Dōgen at once succeeds in both creating a continuation with Shākyamuni himself through his use of expressions that hint at the discourse with Mahākāśyapa, as well as manifesting his own understanding of how words and phrases should be regarded and employed: without dependence and without traces.

There are many mentions in Dōgen's writings that can be traced back to Shākyamuni's silent dharma transmission, some of which I intend to address in this paper. My primary goal lies in the examination of Dōgen's zealous literary activity vis-à-vis the almost orthodox Zen formula of "nondependence on words and letters" and "transmission outside scriptures." I will present instances from the *Treasury* where Dōgen uses such phrases to demonstrate the master's own view relating the issue of transmitting a teaching that is supposed to be nondependent on words via a written medium, as well as the creation of his philosophy with the help of words, language, and expressions. Furthermore, I will examine Dōgen's standpoint toward the question of dependence or nondependence upon words by means of analyzing some of his literary techniques or methods employed in the *Treasury*, which can serve as instances of his creative thought process as well as his idiosyncratic stance toward language as an ultimate – or ultimately delusive – means of expression. My interest lies in exploring Dōgen's own outlook on words, phrases, and expressions, how he approached the double-edged sword of language, what were his "beliefs," attitudes, and approaches regarding verbal expressions, in sum, where does the mas-ter himself stand in the Zen literary arena of "nondependence on words and letters transmitted outside scriptures," and how does language shape Dōgen's thought and the articulation of this thought.

---

[6] *Dōgen Zenji zenshū* (hereafter DZZ) 道元禅師全集, 7 vols., ed. Kawamura Kōdō 河村孝道 et al. (Tōkyō: Shunjūsha, 1989–1995), 7: 159.

1 Treasuries of the True Dharma Eye

The Buddhist teaching originated with Shākyamuni Buddha's meditation under the bodhi tree, yet when referring to his awakening experience, as we are reminded by Yorizumi Mitsuko, a Tōkyō University specialist on Dōgen, "one cannot convey anything about the actual content of the truth of his awakening."[7] Yorizumi is quick to acknowledge the fundamental contrasting relationship between the nature of enlightenment and its subsequent expression, stating that the truth of Buddha's awakening is impossible to disclose precisely because of the view that the essence of the experience transcends ordinary language (*gongo chō'otsu* 言語超越). Also, Yorizumi adds, the reason Shākyamuni Buddha himself hesitated about sharing the matter of his enlightenment experience was due to the difficulty that spreading the dharma necessarily requires surpassing ordinary language and opting for the language of truth and awakening.

Hee-Jin Kim, who has already been mentioned, describes Dōgen's thought as "enormously complex, subtle, and elusive,"[8] while also suggesting that despite the initial conflict between enlightenment and its expression, there was a clear objective behind the master's endeavors: "We can reasonably maintain that Dōgen's intention was not to establish any particular sect or school of Buddhism or Zen but to disseminate what he called 'rightly transmitted Buddha-dharma' (*shōden no buppō* 正傳の佛法), which [...] was the symbol for the spirit of Shākyamuni the Buddha which opened up the mysteries and horizons of Buddha-nature...."[9] To continue in the same vein, elsewhere Kim presents his view relating the purpose behind Dōgen's literary strategy: "The quest here is directed toward the principle of absolute emptiness, which is none other than the truth of Buddha-dharma. That is to say, it has to do with the dialectical relationship between nonduality and duality, between equality and differentiation, between original enlightenment and acquired enlightenment."[10] In the case of Dōgen, however, it is important to add that the pursuit of words and letters also has to do with further dialectical relationship pertaining the interplay between pronouncements and silence, between conveying the principle of the Buddhist teaching clearly and succinctly on the one hand, and the innate unfeasibility of such expression on the other, as the core message of Buddhism is in essence impossible to communicate, describe, or impart by means of words.

Agreeing with Kim, Tsunoda Tairyū, a leading scholar in Dōgen studies, also describes the *Treasury* as a collection of essays that reveal "rightly transmitted Buddha dharma," which represents Dōgen's central work among all his other literary accomplishments.[11] Even though Tsunoda sees Dōgen as a stern figure, he also maintains that one can understand and even come into contact with the personality

[7]Yorizumi Mitsuko 頼住光子, *Shōbōgenzō nyūmon* 正法眼蔵入門 (Tōkyō: Kadokawa bunko, 2016), 64.

[8]Kim, *Eihei Dōgen*, 51.

[9]Kim, *Eihei Dōgen*, 52.

[10]Hee-Jin Kim, "'The Reason of Words and Letters': Dōgen and the Kōan Language," in *Dōgen Studies*, ed. William LaFleur (Honolulu: University of Hawai'i Press, 1985), 54.

of the master himself by none other than his words. "It is very difficult to correctly convey the rightly transmitted teachings of Buddhism through words alone, as words have their limitations. However, Dōgen took it upon himself to attempt this."[12] To attest this, one only needs to look at the title of Dōgen's masterwork, the *Treasury of the True Dharma Eye*, which leads back to Shākyamuni's legendary silent discourse and the words that he thereafter addressed to Mahākāśyapa. When asking what it was that the Buddha imparted to his heir, Tsunoda replies it was the "treasury of the true dharma eye (*shōbōgenzō*), the wondrous mind of nirvāna (*nehan myōshin* 涅槃妙心)," which is none other than "a tentative verbal expression of a teaching that cannot be conveyed by means of language. In fact, it cannot and should not be interpreted by language. If so, it should be described as 'the wondrous heart of nirvāna.'"[13]

Therefore, Dōgen made the first line of Buddha's silent sermon the title of his own collection of lectures in vernacular Japanese in order to epitomize Shākyamuni's teaching itself. To recognize and honor Shākyamuni's message to Mahākāśyapa about dharma that cannot be expressed in words, Dōgen reached for Buddha's enigmatic expression and named his own body of discourses collectively *Treasury of the True Dharma Eye*, thereby strengthening continuity with the tradition and its founder, as well as the lineage of ancient masters. Dōgen's choice of the *Treasury*'s title indicates that despite the impossibility to convey the essence of the teachings, it has to be attempted and communicated, as Shākyamuni's lifting up a flower and Mahākāśyapa's smiling softly demonstrates. The renown Dōgen expert Ōtani Tetsuo asserts that Shākyamuni Buddha chose language as a means to express and transmit the dharma.[14] Similarly, inspired by the ancient masters, their wisdom and relentlessness, and trusting in the power of words, Dōgen also decided to transmit the teaching of the ancestors both in oral and written form. It is known that he was editing and rewriting the many chapters of the *Treasury*, which were supposedly intended to amount to a one-hundred-essay collection, until the year of his demise. Due to his constant revisions of the manuscript, Tsunoda believes Dōgen's objective was to leave behind for his students and disciples, including generations in the distant future, Shākyamuni's transmission of "treasury of the true dharma eye, wondrous heart of nirvāna."[15]

As a matter of fact, the expression "treasury of the true dharma eye," *shōbōgenzō*, besides alluding to the legend of Shākyamuni's silent transmission, carries a further symbolical meaning. *Genzō* 眼蔵, standing for "the eye of the treasury," couples sight (眼) that regards, reflects, and takes in all manner of things, with treasury (蔵)

---

[11] Tsunoda Tairyū 角田泰隆, *Dōgen Shōbōgenzō wo yomu* 道元『正法眼蔵』を読む (Tōkyō: NHK shuppan, 2021), 18.

[12] Tsunoda, *Dōgen Shōbōgenzō wo yomu*, 22.

[13] Tsunoda, *Dōgen Shōbōgenzō wo yomu*, 27–28.

[14] Ōtani Tetsuo 大谷哲夫 (ed.), *Dōgen yomi kaki jiten* 道元読み書き辞典 (Tōkyō: Kashiwa shōbō, 2013), 287.

in which these are stored. Thus are enlinked the two apparent opposites of the perceptions of the outside world on the one hand, and their being stored within an inner treasury of the self on the other. Since *shōbō* 正法 refers to "true dharma," the entire phrase is evocative of all things being reflected and contained within the eye of the treasury as manifestations of the virtue of the supreme dharma. In this way, Dōgen emphasizes the necessity of seeing things clearly and correctly as expressions of the true dharma, and thereby encapsulates the essence of Buddhist teaching.[16]

In truth, the *Treasury* is not Dōgen's only text that bears the title "*Shōbōgenzō*," as he made use of the expression on a number of occasions. The very first time Dōgen turned to this Shākyamuni's phrase was in 1235 when he employed it for the *Three Hundred Kōan Case Collection*, *Shōbōgenzō Sanbyakusoku* 正法眼蔵三百則. This kōan anthology without any prose or poetic commentary composed during the years he spent at Kōshōji temple 興聖寺 south of Kyōto was a compilation of kōan narratives written in Chinese *kanbun* style, which is why it is also called *Shinji Shōbōgenzō* 真字正法眼蔵, or *Chinese Treasury of the True Dharma Eye*. The specification in its title aims to distinguish the Chinese *Shinji* collection from the vernacular *Keji Shōbōgenzō* 仮字正法眼蔵 referring to the *Treasury* composed in native Japanese language in irregular fashion between 1231 and 1253. The third of Dōgen's writings that bears the name of *Shōbōgenzō* is the *Record of Talks* (also known as *Treasury of Miscellaneous Talks* or *Record of Things Heard*), or *Shōbōgenzō Zuimonki* 正法眼蔵随聞記, a six-volume collection of the master's evening sermons also delivered at Kōshōji and recorded by his disciple and editor Ejō 壊奘 (1198–1280), who is therefore sometimes erroneously listed as its author. Nevertheless, the first to use the title *Shōbōgenzō* 正法眼蔵, or *Zhengfa yanzang* in Chinese, for his own body of work was probably the Chinese master Dahui 大慧 (Jp. Dai'e, 1089–1163) of the Linji school for a collection featuring 661 kōans occasionally supplemented with prose comments.[17] Although Dōgen often criticized Dahui, it seems the Sōtō founder's own *Treasury* was intended to propagate the dharma by besides referring to Shākyamuni also demonstrating a link to Chinese kōan anthologies and to highlight the importance of transmission of wisdom by means of referencing the characteristic genre of the meditation school as a symbol of the ultimate means of expression.

2   Dōgen's Intention Behind Words and Letters

Throughout his life, Dōgen remains primarily a teacher and a writer who composes his works for his disciples and followers. In the intimately worded "Bendōwa" 辦道話, translated somewhat diversely as "On the Endeavor of the Way" or "Discerning

---

[15] Tsunoda, *Dōgen Shōbōgenzō wo yomu*, 22.

[16] *Zengaku daijiten* 禅学大辞典 (Tōkyō: Taishūkan shoten, 2020), 580a.

[17] Steven Heine, *Readings of Dōgen's Treasury of the True Dharma Eye* (New York: Oxford University Press, 2020a), 21.

the Way," written in 1231, four years after his return from Song China, Dōgen disclosed that his main goal was to transmit and teach the dharma in Japan to save
sentient beings, and, as his abundant writings attest, he does not seem to thereafter
divert from this determination. In "Bendōwa," which represents his private thoughts
and a concise introduction to the *Treasury*, Dōgen essentially defines his motivation
and goals as follows:

> In 1228, I returned to my home country with the intention of spreading the dharma and sav-
> ing sentient beings. It was as if I was carrying a heavy burden on my shoulders. Nevertheless,
> I have put aside my wish to spread the teaching widely and waited for the opportune
> moment. For a time, I drifted as a cloud and floated like a reed but now I wish to transmit
> the way of ancient sages.
>
> There are perhaps those who, unconcerned with fame and fortune, put the thought of
> enlightenment before everything else and pursue the study of the truth. In vain, they sur-
> round themselves with unfit teachers, needlessly preventing themselves from correct under-
> standing, fruitlessly steeped in self-delusion and endlessly sinking into the realm of
> ignorance. How can they grow the seed of wisdom and find the time for attaining the way?
>
> Given that I am presently drifting as a cloud and floating like a reed, at which mountain
> or river can they drop by [to see me]? Distressed by this, as I recently experienced the style
> and rules of Zen temples of Great Song China and received the profound teaching of my
> master, I hereby record and gather this, to leave it for people studying the way and to make
> known the true dharma of the Buddha house.[18]

This excerpt is valuable for a number of reasons. It reads almost like a diary, a
personal confession disclosing Dōgen's inner train of thought including his fears
and hopes, and clearly indicates the master's dilemmas and aspirations for their
solutions. Despite his initial plan to bide his time and spend his days idly – "drifting
like a cloud and floating like a reed" – he realized his profound intention was to
"spread the dharma and save sentient beings," *guhō gushō* 弘法救衆. Deeply concerned with what has already been mentioned as "rightly transmitted dharma,"
Dōgen sees as a shadow play enacted in front of his eyes all the dangers of a dissemination of the teaching by incapable teachers who were not as fortunate as to
have penetrated into a true understanding of dharma. Acting out of deep concern
and compassion for all beings, he decides to share what he has learned in China and
spread the Zen tradition in Japan. What is of great interest, however, is that in his
determination, Dōgen vows to put his own experience and knowledge to paper, so
that it can be of benefit to "people studying the way." He notes that he plans to
"record and gather," *shirushi atsumete* しるしあつめて, the teaching that was
transmitted to him from his master Tiantong Rujing 天童如淨 (Jp. Tendō Nyōjō,
1163–1228). There is no metaphor or idiosyncrasy about the phrase, unlike on other
occasions; Dōgen unambiguously admits a need for writing down and collecting all
that he has seen, heard, and learned during his stay in China, while simultaneously
acknowledging the importance of such activity. The incentive behind his endeavors
is, simply and essentially, "spreading the dharma and saving sentient beings," "to
make known the true dharma of the Buddha house" among those who "put the
thought of enlightenment before everything else and pursue the study of the truth."

---

[18] DZZ 2: 461.

With Rujing, Dōgen had another dialogue that he recorded in *Hōkyōki* 宝慶記, *Record of the Hōkyō Era*, an account of Dōgen's exchanges with his teacher conducted in the abbot's quarters at Mount Tiantong. In the very first face-to-face conversation with the master that Dōgen notes in *Hōkyōki*, he asks the patriarch about the meaning of transmission outside scriptures:

> On the second day of the seventh month, 1225, Dōgen entered the abbot's quarters and asked: "Nowadays, in many places, people speak about 'transmission outside scriptures.' What is then the meaning of what is called 'Bodhisattva's coming from the west?'"
> Rujing said: "The great way of Buddha ancestors is not concerned with inside or outside. What is called 'transmission outside scriptures' is simply that after Mahākāśyapa's transmission of the tradition, Bodhidharma arrived from the west, reached China, and imparted the teaching of the Way. Therefore, it is called 'transmission outside scriptures.' Yet there are no two Buddha dharmas in the world. Before Bodhidharma came to China, there were only practices but not yet any masters. When Bodhidharma arrived, it was as if the people had acquired a king under whom the entire land, wealth, and people were united."[19]

Despite the fact that the *Record of the Hōkyō Era* may not be an accurate account of Dōgen's stay in Song China and may only have been compiled toward the end of his life, it can nevertheless be read as a reflection of what Dōgen was probably concerned with in the early stages of his training with Rujing or an account of the direction their first dialogues may have taken. As a foreign student, Dōgen reveals the beginnings of his personal encounters with Rujing relating to the then apparently poignant issue of transmission outside scriptures, whereby Chan/Zen was portraying itself. To Dōgen's request for clarification, Rujing replies, there is "no inside or outside" on the "great way of Buddha ancestors," *busso no daidō* 仏祖の大道. As the path is merely the one "great way of Buddha ancestors," Rujing clearly states an absence of differentiation as well as separation. Also, adds the Chinese master, "there are no two Buddha dharmas in the world," albeit without further specification but also sans distinction.

Throughout the *Treasury*, Dōgen proves himself to be not merely a critical scholar but a thinker with a mind that is truly unlimited and nondualistic. While fully accepting and acknowledging the dichotomy of language, he also always returns to the teaching itself, which for him contains the highest truth and wisdom. In the fascicle "Thusness," "Inmo" 恁麼, he reflects:

> In the Lotus Sūtra, it is said: "When those without wisdom doubt, they will be lost forever." Although wisdom is neither being nor nonbeing, there is the being of timeless spring pine and the nonbeing of autumn chrysanthemums. At such time of no wisdom, perfect enlightenment is doubt and all things are doubt. At such time, those without wisdom will be lost forever. Words that one hears and dharmas that one realizes are doubt. There is no self and no place to hide in the entire world. There is no other, just one iron rod ten thousand miles long. Even as leaves scatter from the branches thus, in all Buddha lands of the ten directions, there is only the true dharma of the One Vehicle.[20]

Dōgen is astutely aware that human senses, including one's eyes and ears create confusion and doubt. This causes a state of mind that Dōgen calls "a time of no

---

[19] DZZ 7: 2–5.

wisdom," which makes one feel as if they were "lost forever." It begins with mis-
trusting one's hearing and doubting the perception of the surrounding world with
the six senses and continues with a skepticism that attacks the fundamental matter
of personal identity and surrounding reality; then one has misgivings even about the
existence and individuality of self and others. Yet, much as one feels forlorn and
stranded far from wisdom, Dōgen, deeply rooted in the tradition of ancient sages,
offers direction by returning to the promise entailed in the Buddhist teaching itself,
as "there is only the true dharma of the One Vehicle."

3   Nondependence Outside Scriptures

To provide Dōgen's personal view on the phrases used in Shākyamuni's silent sermon, I attempted to look for the statement of "nondependence upon words and letters," *furyū monji* and "transmitted outside scriptures," *kyōge betsuden* throughout
the *Treasury* itself. It appears, however, that Dōgen did not pay much attention to
the first utterance, as there is no instance of the compound "nondependence upon
words and letters" in the *Treasury* at all. Out of sheer curiosity, I proceeded to look
separately for characters describing "nondependence" and "words and letters."
Interestingly, the first two ideograms indicating "nondependence" appear in only
one essay of the entire *Treasury*, "Entangling Vines," "Kattō" 葛藤, where Dōgen
mentions "no marrow to depend upon."[21] On the other hand, Dōgen is more deliberate with "words and letters" – in a true sense of the expression – as *monji* appears in
the *Treasury* repeatedly, most frequently, namely on five occasions, in the fascicle
"Buddhas' Teaching," "Bukkyō" 佛教, as well as in several other chapters.[22]

Intriguingly, "Buddhas' Teaching," is the sole text in the *Treasury* that makes
mention of the second compound, "transmission outside scriptures," *kyōge betsuden* in its entirety. The expression features repeatedly throughout the essay and as
it clearly reflects Dōgen's personal ideas on the matter in question, I opted for a
somewhat longer excerpt to better illustrate the master's thought:

> A learned person once said:
> "Old sage Shākyamuni, besides expounding the scriptures throughout his lifetime
> authentically transmitted the supreme vehicle of the dharma of one mind to Mahākāśyapa,
> which has since been directly transmitted from master to disciple. Only the teaching is a
> hollow theory affected by the listeners' capacity, while its heart is the truth of essential
> nature. This authentically transmitted one mind is called 'transmission outside scriptures.'

---

[20] DZZ 1: 210.

[21] 髄也不立, read as 髄も也立たず, DZZ 1: 420–421.

[22] Katō Shūkō 加藤宗厚 (ed.), *Shōbōgenzō yōgo sakuin* 正法眼蔵用語索引 (Tōkyō: Risōsha,
1963), vol 1: 2878.

It is not the same as that which is discussed in the Three Vehicles and Twelve Divisions of Teaching.[23] Because it is the supreme vehicle of the one mind, it is called 'pointing directly to human mind, seeing original nature and becoming Buddha.' [...]

And yet, authentically transmitting one mind without authentically transmitting Buddha's teaching means not knowing the Buddha dharma. [It means] not knowing the one mind of Buddha's teaching and not understanding the one mind of Buddha's teaching. When you say the Buddha's teaching is outside the one mind, it is your own mind, not the one mind. When you say one mind is outside the Buddha's teaching, it is your own Buddha's teaching, not the teaching of the Buddha. Even if you inherited erroneous views of 'transmission outside scriptures' and you do not yet know the inside and the outside, the words and the truth do not match. [...]

However, those who speak of 'transmission outside scriptures' do not understand its meaning. Therefore, they believe the erroneous views of 'transmission outside scriptures' and misunderstand the Buddha's teaching. If it was as they say, the Buddha's teaching would have to be called 'transmission outside the mind.' If it was called 'transmission outside the mind,' not a single word or half a verse would be transmitted. If it is not called 'transmission outside the mind,' one should not say 'transmission outside scriptures.'"[24]

In this passage, Dōgen commences with describing the silent sermon, to then arrive at a differentiation between the teaching (kyō 教) being "a hollow theory affected by the listeners' capacity," and the heart (shin 心) representing "the truth of essential nature," which is none other than "the supreme vehicle of the one mind." Here, Dōgen identifies the teaching transmitted from heart to heart and master to disciple to the tradition of "one mind" of Buddhas and ancestors. Nevertheless, Dōgen does not conclude here, he further develops the equation and seemingly contradicts his own words as he claims it is impossible to spread the tradition of one mind (心) without simultaneously transmitting the teaching (教) itself. He distinguishes between the two, yet at the same time affirms their mutual nondifferentiation. Those who do not comprehend this nonduality, Dōgen continues, are mistaken and deluded, misunderstanding the heart of the teaching and speaking from the separation of their minds from "the one mind" of Buddha ancestors. Acknowledging the nontextual identification of the tradition, Dōgen returns to its self-definition: if transmission of mind was more important than transmission of teaching, the school would have to be called transmission outside the mind, writes Dōgen, and not one word or verse of Buddha's teaching would be shared and taught. But people should neither call it this – transmission outside the mind – nor that – transmission outside scriptures – as the appellations are, in the end, mutually exclusive if their usage only rests in their appellations. Dōgen plays with the same words but uses them as forms that he infuses with diverse meanings; he shuffles and combines the different expressions in order to bring attention to the content of the phrases, since if one does not know the essence of the teaching – whether outside the scriptures or outside the mind – "the words and the truth do not match."

---

[23] "Three vehicles and twelve divisions of teaching" refers to the entire Buddhist canon, the sum of all scriptures.
[24] DZZ 1: 381–382.

4   True Form Without Form

Tsunoda summarizes the ever-present Zen conundrum of expression and expressivity by saying: "The true nature of things cannot be fully expressed with words. Words are, after all, always words, and not the truth. Words are one [manner of] expression that describe the truth but cannot encompass it all. This is the basic position of Zen." While acknowledging the underlying dichotomy of Zen and language and the tension between the two, however, Tsunoda regards the issue in an appealing light: "The challenge to express things by means of words is the interesting point of Zen."[25]

This "interesting point" of Dōgen's literary originality is exemplified, in part, by his lexical and grammatical inventiveness and unencumberedness. One aspect of Dōgen's writing – both fascinating and challenging – lies in his approach to quotations from Buddhist manuscripts, Chan transmission of the light records (*dentōroku* 傳登録), or statements of Chinese ancestors featured in various kōan collections. As Kazuaki Tanahashi writes in his introduction to *The Treasury of the True Dharma Eye: Zen Masters Dogen's Shobo Genzo*, "In exploring the deeper meanings of Zen stories, poetry, teachings, and Buddhist sutras, Dogen expands, twists, and manipulates the meanings of the words from the texts he quotes."[26] Dōgen takes an original sentence, a quotation from a sūtra or an utterance of an earlier Chan master, and dissects the line into separate parts that, given the difference between classical Chinese and Japanese in combination with Dōgen's innovative rearrangement or interpretation of the initial phrase, assume a diverse meaning in the latter language. He arrives at an unexpected reading and connotation by breaking down the quoted statement into individual characters – often disregarding the rules of the original language and its customary rendering in traditional Japanese reading of Chinese texts – and by reordering or construing them in such a manner that they ultimately represent a novel idea with unexpected semantic, doctrinal, and philosophical implications.

The Buddha's utterance to Mahākāśyapa seems to have influenced Dōgen beyond "nondependence on words and letters" and "transmission outside scriptures;" not as a similarly formulated saying but as a tendency underlying his *Treasury* essays in regard to the verse of "true form without form," *jissō musō* 實相無相 of the legendary Shākyamuni's expression, which Dōgen repeatedly exhibits throughout his magnum opus. The intricacy, complexity, and entanglements – to borrow the master's own jargon – of Dōgen's language have been concisely commented upon by many. Thomas Kasulis, for example, writes "No other Japanese before or after Dōgen wrote in the language of the *Shōbōgenzō*. It is Dōgen's own language."[27] And

---

[25] Tsunoda Tairyū 角田泰隆, *Zen no susume, Dōgen no kotoba* 禅のすすめ　道元のことば (Tōkyō: Kadokawa bunko, 2018), 170.
[26] Kazuaki Tanahashi (ed.), *Treasury of the True Dharma Eye: Zen Master Dogen's Shobo Genzo* (Boulder, CO: Shambhala, 2012), xxx.

while Kim calls him "a magician or an alchemist of language," Raud believes Dōgen is "probably the most linguistically sophisticated thinker ever to have emerged from Japan."[28]

Dōgen's sophistication and idiosyncrasy, however, the form and manner of his expressiveness, are one of the first "obstacles" scholars encounter when trying to make contact with the personality of the master through his original texts, as Tsunoda suggested. To illustrate the scope of such "obstacles," it seems appropriate to quote another fitting description from Kasulis: "To read the *Shōbōgenzō* carefully is hard work. At first, one may suspect there is a linguistic problem: perhaps one is shaky in medieval Japanese grammar or perhaps one is being confused by the Song Chinese colloquialisms Dōgen sprinkles throughout. On the other hand, the difficulty may be more historical: more study of the intellectual climate of Kamakura period may be required. Then, again, there could be buddhological complexities and one may need more background in the development of Buddhist doctrine or the subtle nuances of Buddhist terminology. The reference works – commentaries, dictionaries, glossaries, histories, grammars – begin to pile up on the desk."[29] This, I believe, describes many a determined reader's encounter with the master-thinker – and master thinker. In Dōgen's own words, however, "Obstructions stand in the way of obstructions, and see obstructions."[30] One therefore needs to clearly see the problem that runs around disguised as an insurmountable obstruction; and rather than having the field of vision or path hindered by further conjectured obstacles, one is to proceed – in time – toward the supposed obstruction itself.

As a result, a number of scholars have already commented on and analyzed Dōgen's idiosyncratic expressions that are both hard to grasp and translate. In the editor's introduction to the *Treasury of the True Dharma Eye* and under a suitable heading "Decoding the Zen Paradox," Tanahashi presents thirteen examples of Dōgen's unique rhetoric; introducing Dōgen's "Distinctive Discursive Style," Heine suggests almost a dozen paradoxical maxims; Kim offers a thorough classification of the master's linguistic methods, while Raud's analysis concentrates on grammatical relationships within compounds.[31] Inspired by these respected scholars, I would like to lay out my own view of Dōgen's linguistic creativity; not in an attempt to substitute or overshadow the previous illuminating contributions but to offer my own examination of Dōgen's language and a reflection of his approach to words and expressions. As stated previously, words, expressions, and language itself can represent the ultimate – or ultimately delusive – path to awakening. In fact, I believe

---

[27] Thomas Kasulis, "The Incomparable Philosopher: Dōgen on How to Read the *Shōbōgenzō*," in *Dōgen Studies*, ed. William LaFleur (Honolulu: University of Hawai'i Press, 1985), 90.

[28] Kim, "'The Reason of Words and Letters,'" 63; Rein Raud, "Inside the Concept: Rethinking Dōgen's Language," *Asian Philosophy* 21, no. 2 (2011): 124.

[29] Kasulis, "The Incomparable Philosopher," 90.

[30] DZZ 1: 246.

[31] Tanahashi, *Treasury of the True Dharma Eye*, xxx–xxxi; Heine, *Readings of Dōgen's Treasury*, 6; Kim, "'The Reason of Words and Letters,'" 61; Raud, "Inside the Concept," 132.

what has been named Dōgen's thought or Dōgen's philosophy is rooted in, and interdependent with, the medium of language itself, demonstrating Dōgen's unparalleled ability to treat words as creative tools to awakening, manifesting a mind of profound wisdom and nonduality that utilizes expressions as devices that can open up a path to that same wisdom and nonduality. Making use of Kim's dual categories of activity (*gyōji*) and expression (*dōtoku*) as the main avenues that Dōgen employed to covey his teaching, it is possible to assume that he viewed language (expression) equally essential and experiential as practice (activity) itself. Thus, there is an underlying nonseparation between the master's language, practice, and philosophy. Dōgen expresses ideas that form the kernel of his teaching by means of verbal expressions and through his boundless inventiveness that is reflected in, but not limited to, his usage of words and phrases. His thought is firmly rooted in language, verbal creativity, and original rhetorical devices – albeit, paradoxically, equally in silence. Moreover, any separation between Dōgen's thought and Dōgen's language is arbitrary and reflecting a mind of duality. His language is, indeed, a testament to his radical and masterful thought, and Dōgen employs words, as I intend to illustrate, as possible vehicles to enlightenment.

Throughout the *Treasury*, Dōgen's genius lies in his devising new forms and expressions, new meanings and connotations, which he achieved in several ways. I have attempted to summarize his methods and approaches under the headings presented below, although in the same breath it is necessary to mention that some examples can be shared among several categories, while others can be seen as subgroups of different headings. Also, the classification is rather tentative, as I am aware that the groupings vary between grammatical, semantic, lexical, syntactic, and rhetorical. I am certain there are other groups that I have not thought of, or yet become aware of, and I therefore assume it would need a great many years (and pages) to offer a definitive systematic arrangement of Dōgen's literary genius. For the time being, therefore, the present categories include techniques that can be summarized as follows:

(a) Reshuffling of Characters
(b) Literal Reading of Characters
(c) Dissecting Expressions into Individual Characters
(d) Attributing Novel Meanings to Conventional Expressions
(e) Tautology
(f) Negative Tautology
(g) Turning Nouns into Verbs
(h) Repeating the Same Expression as Noun and Verb
(i) Experimenting with Homonymous Expressions
(j) Experimenting with Synonymous Expressions

---

[32] Heine, *Readings of Dōgen's Treasury*, 105.

[33] DZZ 1: 57.

[34] Kim, "'The Reason of Words and Letters,'" 62.

(k) Reflecting a Poetic Melodiousness in Successive Expressions
 (l) Reduplicating Characters
(m) Using Negative Expressions

5   In an Attempt to Unravel the Clew

Intrigued by Dōgen's masterful verbal creativity, I would now like to offer in some detail a few passages from the *Treasury* that will serve as examples for the categories listed above. I am aware that there may be further instances that present Dōgen's originality in a better light or that others may find more appropriate, which, ultimately, attests to the master's incomparable inventiveness.

(a) Reshuffling of Characters

Changing the order of characters in an utterance – or, as Heine calls it, "deliberate misreading of the original source"[32] – is almost a trademark of Dōgen's. One of the highlights of Dōgen's phenomenal creativity that falls under this group can be found in the fascicle "The Mind Itself is Buddha," "Sokushin zebutsu" 即心是佛. In it, Dōgen repositions the original four-character phrase "the mind itself is Buddha" of the renown Chan master Mazu 馬祖 (Jp. Baso, 709–788) in four different ways, exhausting thus all possible variations of the characters in the initial statement. In the text itself, Dōgen exhorts: "Thoroughly study the mind itself is Buddha, thoroughly study the mind that is Buddha itself, thoroughly study Buddha itself that is the mind, [and] thoroughly study itself, the mind, which is Buddha. Such thorough study of this 'the mind itself is Buddha' upholds and authentically transmits it to 'the mind itself is Buddha.' Authentically transmitting it thus, it has reached the present."[33] The Chan patriarch's utterance in Dōgen's thorough variation in the sequence of characters brings about a radical alteration in meaning of the pronouncement and attests to Dōgen's creative playfulness vis-à-vis statements of earlier masters.

Another example of Dōgen's ingenuity stemming from a deliberate rearranging of characters in a compound is the word *seppō* 説法, which translates as "expounding the dharma." When the sequence of the characters changes, *seppō* becomes *hōsetsu* 法説, thus shifting from "expounding the dharma" to "dharma's discourse." Kim very lightly describes this as "fanciful, even playful trait in Dōgen's diction."[34]

In various chapters of the *Treasury*, Dōgen's creativity flourishes and he at times reorders characters in compounds with more nuanced grammatical connotations. The earlier variation in meaning that occurred with the change in the sequence of the characters can become further elaborated also indicating a difference in syntactic associations within the phrase. Here, as in other instances, Dōgen disregards the Chinese syntactic rules. In "Buddha Nature," "Busshō" 佛性, Dōgen finds inspiration for his discourse in the figure of the great Indian thinker Nāgārjuna. He

---

[35] DZZ 1: 26–27.

commences this section with the philosopher's poem, to then express his own view on the matter:

> The body manifests in the shape of a full moon,
>   Expressing the bodies of Buddhas.
>   Expounding the dharma has no shape,
>   Discussing it is without sound or color.
>   [...] Now, listen to what Nāgārjuna is expressing with his verse. It says, 'The body manifests in the shape of a full moon, expressing the bodies of Buddhas.' Since the manifested body expresses the bodies of Buddhas, it is in the shape of a full moon. Therefore, you should study everything [that is] long and short, square or round as this manifested body. To be unaware about the body and manifestation is not only to be in the dark about the shape of the full moon but also about the bodies of Buddhas.[35]

In this passage, Dōgen arrives at the semantic interpretation by means of syntactic reordering of the characters from the original verse. While the poem quoting Nāgārjuna says "body manifests," Dōgen turns the noun-verb pair into adjective-noun couplet that he presents as "manifested body," or alternately as two separate nouns in "body and manifestation." By alternating the syntax, Dōgen arrives at a novel semantic representation of the characters, resulting in a hermeneutical innovation.

(b) Literal Reading of Characters

In this subgroup, Dōgen breaks down a given expression into its separate characters which he then reads literally. The original statements that Dōgen thus alters are usually Chinese phrases that he "misreads" in an original manner. For instance, in "Shoaku makusa" 諸悪莫作 – translated variously as "Refrain from Unwholesome Action" or "Refrain from Any Evil"– Dōgen, true to his ingenious view of language, transforms the traditional Nirvāna Sūtra expression *shoaku makusa* 諸悪莫作 that is hence used as the title of the entire fascicle. In the customary manner of reading Chinese texts, the Sino-Japanese transliteration of the original sequence of the characters is read *shoaku tsukuru nakare* 「諸悪作る莫れ」, indicating a negative imperative or prohibition, and translated therefore as "to refrain from unwholesome action" or "to not act in unwholesome or evil manner." Dōgen, however, radically reinterpreted this phrase. By following the original word order and reading the compound in a descriptive or literal manner as *shoaku wa makusa nari* 「諸悪は莫作なり」, he shifted the meaning into "unwholesome action is to be refrained from" or "unwholesome action is not to be performed."[36] In the end, Dōgen uses the same characters that appear in the original statement, yet he reads them in their literal word order, thus turning what has previously been an inhibition into a primarily ethical Buddhist statement emphasizing attentive activity grounded in nonduality.

---

[36] DZZ 1: 346; Yorizumi, *Shōbōgenzō nyūmon*, 68.
[37] DZZ 1: 14.

(c) Dissecting Expressions into Individual Characters

An oft-cited example of Dōgen's creative genius, inspired by the Nirvāna Sūtra, is found in the already mentioned chapter "Buddha Nature." In the opening line, Dōgen quotes a passage of the sūtra that says: "Shākyamuni Buddha said, all beings have Buddha nature," and continues with a semantically profound elaboration of this very first line. He ponders, "What is the essence of Shākyamuni's words 'All beings have Buddha nature?' It is the turning of the wheel of dharma of the expression 'What has thus come?' One also calls them 'sentient beings,' 'living beings,' 'various beings,' 'all beings.' The word for 'all beings' is 'sentient beings' or 'various beings.' That is, 'all beings are Buddha nature.' The entirety of all beings is called 'sentient beings.'"[37] Dōgen has thus, quite fluidly and almost seamlessly, moved from Shākyamuni's original quote of "all beings have Buddha nature" to his own rendering of the line as "all beings are Buddha nature." He was free to exercise such inventiveness due to the meaning of the character u or yu (有) that can be translated both as "to be" and "to have." With an openness to interpretations arising from nonduality, Dōgen thus alternates between metaphorical and literal meanings in a unique and deliberate manner that is characteristic of his teaching and writing style.

(d) Attributing Novel Meanings to Conventional Expressions

Kim claims that "Dōgen resurrects forgotten metaphors, infusing them with new, immediate value; in other cases, he discovers hidden meanings, while in still others, he liberates them from conventional constraints."[38] An apt example in this case is the word mu 夢, a dream, in traditional Buddhist notion referring to something vague, delusory, and unrealistic. This understanding of a dream comes from a verse in the Diamond Sūtra, which identifies nocturnal visions with impermanence and illusion:

> All compounded phenomena
>   Are like stars, shade, lamp, illusion,
>   Like dew, bubbles, dreams, lightning, clouds.
>   Thus they should be regarded.[39]

Dōgen distances himself from a dualistic view of words and true reality and asserts that dream is as authentic and present as any state of mind. In an excerpt from "Expounding a Dream Within a Dream," "Muchū setsumu" 夢中説夢, Dōgen clearly formulates his view of no distinction between a dream and waking state: "Study the present discourse of all Buddhas, thoroughly investigate the assembly of the Buddhas. This is no metaphor. Since the wondrous dharma of all Buddhas is [revealed] only between Buddha and Buddha, all dharmas of dreaming and waking [state] are equally true forms. In waking [state], there is aspiration for enlightenment, practice, awakening, and nirvāna. In dreaming [state], there is aspiration for enlightenment, practice, awakening, and nirvāna. Dreaming [state] and waking [state] are both true forms. Neither large or small, nor superior or inferior."[40] Dōgen's

---

[38] Kim, "'The Reason of Words and Letters,'" 71.
[39] T 08.236a.
[40] DZZ 1: 300.

accent on the nonduality of one's experience is apparent in his admonition "this is no metaphor," highlighting both states – and moments – of one's being as equally relevant, full-valued, and imbued with meaning and existence.

Dōgen is original in reading characters in an unconventionally creative sense, at times diverting from an accepted meaning of the word toward its either literal or figurative understanding. He takes words that have been in usage in contemporary Chinese and imbues them with a novel content and message. Some of these expressions can be taken as hallmarks of Dōgen's inventiveness, since they were also chosen as titles of his *Treasury* essays – for instance *kūge* or *mitsugo*. The word *kūge* 空華, which Dōgen uses in the sense of "flowers in the sky," in traditional Buddhist understanding denoted one's inability to see things clearly due to karmic conditions. Also, in everyday Chinese in the medieval times, *kūge* was a reference to eye cataract, a then-incurable condition that caused blurry or illusory visions. For Dōgen, however, *kūge* become "flowers in the sky," when read literally, or "flowers of emptiness," if read as a metaphor. In Dōgen's understanding and usage, *kūge* suggests an image of flowers blooming in space, referring to dharma "revealing itself to our senses, because it appears vague or unclear and is not recognized at first, but [what] eventually discloses its true significance."[41] Another example that can be illustrated under this heading is *mitsugo* 密語, which is usually translated as "hidden words" or "secret language." Dōgen once again opens up a way for an alternate meaning of the word *mitsu* and uses it to refer to something intimate – personal, direct, and innermost – that can be discovered and revealed through the creative use of language. Likewise, the word *dōtoku* counts among those that can be seen in a similar light. *Dōtoku* is generally translated as "expression" or "expression of the way," alternately as "expressing what one has realized." It comprises of characters for *dō* 道 standing for both "the way" and "to say," "to express," and *toku* 得 meaning "to receive," "to achieve," "to accomplish," or "to gain." Due to the combination of characters, *dōtoku* can indicate both the Buddhist way and words used for conveying the nuances of the way, indicating an underlying identity between the path and an expression – or enactment – of this path. In this manner, an ordinary word becomes extraordinary in Dōgen's usage, reflecting his understanding of language utilized as means for expressing the way and the truth of the dharma.

An intrinsic impartiality of one's views and experience is further evoked with the following compounds. *Zenki* 全機, which is similarly the title of one of the chapters in the *Treasury*, stands for "all activity" or "undivided activity." The character *ki* 機 is as multifaceted as the entire *Treasury* itself, and can be rendered quite diversely as "activity," "working," "dynamism," "function," or "pivot." In Dōgen's understanding and interpretation, *zenki* becomes a nondualistic and all-encompassing activity, a dynamism that defines and structures a practitioner's seemingly passive performance of just sitting combined with the execution of temple chores, as well as the underlying commonplace occurrences that are apparently unrelated to the monks' concrete enactments of everyday practice. A comparable example – also

---

[41] Heine, *Readings of Dōgen's Treasury*, 169.

used for a *Treasury* title of the chapter following "Zenki" – is the word *tsuki* 都機 that Dōgen employs for "the moon." Interestingly, he only writes the title of the fascicle in the aforementioned characters, and in the text itself uses *tsuki* in its single character 月 or in the native *kana* syllabary. Correspondingly to *zenki* standing for "all activity" or "all function," the word *tsuki* can, curiously enough, be also translated as "all activity." Since the first character 都 pertains to "all" or "everything," the core idea of "Tsuki" also relates the all-encompassing or all-inclusive message of the previous essay in the *Treasury*. Similar instances and underlying hermeneutic indications can be found in the words of "continuous practice," "flowers," "rice cakes," "old mirror," or "old Buddha mind." Dōgen's technique is concisely summarized by Heine who writes, "These expressions should not be taken as an analogy that represents the truth from a distance yet remains metaphorical. Rather, the sayings convey the 'true form of reality' just as it is,"[42] without the dual distinction of a mind untrained by continuous meditative practice.

(e) Tautology

The customary Buddhist tautology of absolute nonduality and identity of subject and object, form and emptiness, or practice and realization is prevalent in the *Treasury*. It is not only that Dōgen himself is drawn to such paradigmatic statements, he is also greatly inspired by the abundant instances of tautology in the writings of earlier Chan ancestors as well as Buddhist scriptures in general.

Perhaps the most famous of Dōgen's truth affirming pronouncements is found in the "Mountains and Waters Sūtra," "Sansuikyō" 山水経, where he repeats a saying by master Yunmen 雲門 (Jp. Unmon, 862–949): "Mountains are mountains, waters are waters."[43] Likewise in "The Moon," "Tsuki" 都機, Dōgen reaches for a poem that is attributed to the Sixth Ancestor Huineng 慧能 (Jp. Enō, 638–713) or alternately to the Tiantai scholar Zhiyi 智顗 (Jp. Chigi, 538–597). In it, Dōgen reiterates the master's saying before presenting his own formulation: "An ancient Buddha said: 'One mind is all things and all things are one mind.' Therefore, the mind is all things and all things are the mind."[44]

Concluding this group with an example of another quote by a Chinese teacher, in "The Point of Zazen," "Zazenshin" 坐禅箴, Dōgen chooses images and representations from the natural world, as he cites and offers his version of a poem composed by the Caodong master Hongzhi 宏智 (Jp. Wanshi, 1091–1157), a renowned proponent of the path of silent illumination:

Water, crystal clear all the way,
    Fish swim in it like fish.
    Sky, vast and transparent throughout,
    Birds fly through it like birds.[45]

---

[42] Ibid., 169.
[43] DZZ 1: 327.
[44] DZZ 1: 264.
[45] DZZ 1: 117.

Fish swimming like fish in water and birds flying through sky like birds seems to be stating the obvious, and therefore perhaps not worth the mention. This chapter, however, points to the heart-and-mind of meditation, as well as the meaning of zazen practice according to Buddha ancestors (*busso* 佛祖) or teachers of the ancestral school (*soshū* 祖宗). Clear water and limitless sky represent the boundless world of Buddha-dharma, while fish and birds refer to those grappling with the practice of seated meditation.[46] Water and sky is the habitat which enables the existence of fish and birds, yet these do not swim or fly against the current of the stream or the gush of air but use their surroundings to act out the movements that fulfil and give meaning to their existence. Entrusting their entire forms to their environment is what defines their being: fish swim in water as fish naturally do and birds fly in sky as birds instinctively do. Dōgen argues, without an intellectualization of the argument but rather by relying on plain natural imagery, that zazen is as inherent to people as swimming and flying are to fish and birds. The self-evident tautology thus becomes the vehicle for transmitting the teaching of the "great way of Buddha ancestors" (*busso no daidō*).

(f) Negative Tautology

In contrast to the previous category, Dōgen also employs the technique of negative tautology, whereby he seems to contradict his own earlier statement. One instance can be found in "The Moon," where it says, "Myriad forms are moonlight, not myriad forms."[47] The entire text deals with appearance, reflection, and observation, bringing into foreground issues of enlightenment and existence, individuality and diversity, as well as their presentation and perception within a constant flow of impermanence and changeability, for which Dōgen has found the ideal image in the symbol of the moon, *tsuki*. The myriad forms – which Dōgen asserts are moonlight, not myriad forms – are that which is enveloped, contained, and reflected in moonlight, assuming its own reflected light and its own inconstant shape, whereby they cease to exist on their own but are a result of the activity of the moon. As such, therefore, they are not their own countless forms but moonlight itself.[48]

Similarly ambiguous is Dōgen's statement in the already mentioned quote in the fascicle "Mountains and Waters Sūtra," where it says: "An ancient Buddha said, mountains are mountains, waters are waters. These words do not mean that mountains are mountains, but that mountains are mountains. If this is so, you should investigate mountains thoroughly. If you investigate mountains thoroughly, you will practice as mountains. Such mountains and waters themselves become wise, become sages."[49] Once again, it is a passage reoccurring in literature on Dōgen that characterizes his statements as idiosyncratic. I decided to quote the passage in full, not

---

[46] DZZ 1: 118.

[47] DZZ 1: 263.

[48] Tamaki Kōshirō 玉城康四郎, *Shōbōgenzō gendaigoyaku* 正法眼藏現代語訳 (Tōkyō: Daizō shuppan), vol. 3: 410.

[49] DZZ 1: 327–328.

merely the model sentence itself but also the subsequent lines that better explicate Dōgen's seemingly contrasting assertion. The point here is that Dōgen uses identical words to express diverse meanings; the forms are the same, yet their content varies. As Kawamura Kōdō, the main editor of *Master Dōgen's Collected Works* (*Dōgen Zenji Zenshū* 道元禅師全集) explains, mountains are the manifestation of the body and mind of Buddha ancestors. Therefore, Dōgen is being truthful when he says, "these words do not mean that mountains are mountains."[50] There is no ambivalence; mountains are not mountains as hills and peaks, but they are mountains as embodiments of Buddhas and ancestors. So, Dōgen reminds his disciples, they should investigate, study, and learn the body-and-mind and heart-and-soul of the teaching of ancient masters, they should embody and enact the dharma and practice it accordingly "as mountains," meaning as the masters themselves. Only then can students of "mountains and waters" become wise like the ancestors and sages before them.

(g) Turning Nouns into Verbs

The next category is of a grammatical nature and introduces the usage of nominative verbs (*dōmeishi* 動名詞) in Dōgen's works. These are nouns transformed into verbs by attaching the irregular verb -*su* to the original noun or noun compound. There are, for instance, many occasions when Dōgen urges his audience to study a matter in greater detail, to ponder an issue deeply and attentively. In such cases, he takes the noun "study" *shūgaku* 習学 and turns it into a verb, "to study," by adding the verb -*su* to the noun, thereby creating the nominative verb of *shūgaku-su* 習学す. Accordingly, the noun *kansō* 観想 ("contemplation") becomes nominative verb *kansō-su* 観想す ("to contemplate"), *ge'e* 解会 ("understanding") turns into *ge'e-su* 解会す ("to understand," "to comprehend"), and *choken* 覷見 ("seeing," "understanding") appears as *choken-su* 覷見す ("to see," "to understand"). Buddhist terms are, of course, treated correspondingly: *genjō* 現成 ("actualization") becomes *genjō-su* 現成す ("to actualize"), *jōdō* 成道 ("attainment of the Way") changes into *jōdō-su* 成道す ("to attain the Way") and *kyōryaku* 経歴 ("passing," "flowing") is turned into *kyōryaku-su* 経歴す ("to pass through," "to flow," "to flow through"). In his chapter on nominative verbs and their function in the history of Japanese language, Bjarke Frellesvig refers to their abundance in texts of Buddhist nature, yet he notes that they were "invariably taken in as nouns."[51] In Dōgen's rendition, however, and due to his inventiveness, the Sino-Japanese nouns are turned into Japanese nominative verbs of Chinese origins. Akin to the process of development of Japanese writing itself by means of adapting Chinese forms to the Japanese environment and its language, Dōgen shifts the customary usage of Chinese words of his own time to create a fresh wordplay for an original and intimate expression of Buddhist teaching.

---

[50] DZZ 1: 328.

[51] Bjarke Frellesvig, *A History of the Japanese Language* (Cambridge: Cambridge University Press, 2011), 287.

(h) Repeating the Same Expression as Noun and Verb

In this group I would like to present two examples, both from the fascicle "Being-Time" or "Existence-Time," "Uji" 有時, which is a fascinating accomplishment in its own right. Toward the end of the essay, Dōgen writes, "The flowing of spring, for example, always flows through spring,"[52] using the same expression for "flowing" and "to flow," *kyōryaku* 經歴 and its nominative verb of *kyōryaku-su* 經歴す. A few lines later, he continues, "Because of this principle, the morning star appears, Tathāgata appears, the eyeball appears, holding up a flower appears."[53] In its original classical Japanese, the sentence is a combination of nouns – morning star appearing, Tathāgata appearing, eyeball appearing, holding up of a flower appearing – that are appended with the verbal suffix of -*su*. In Dōgen's practice of nonduality, nouns and verbs are treated as equal vehicles of dharma.

In another example from "Being-Time," I wish to illustrate how Dōgen was truly unencumbered in his creativity. He writes: "To fully cover the entire world by fully covering the entire world is called fully experiencing. それ盡界をもて盡界を界盡するを、究盡するとはいふなり。"[54] Using the characters of the noun *jinkai* 尽界 ("entire world") in their reverse order *and* simultaneously as a verb, *kaijin-su* 界尽す ("to fully cover the world," "to cover the world entirely"), Dōgen seems to repeat what he has expressed previously, yet in fact he turns a term on its head and creates a novel expression with a radically original use comprised of the very same characters. In Dōgen's presentation, the nominative verb of "entire world" becomes "to fully cover the world" or "to actualize the entire world." Dōgen changes the word order, inverts the sequence of the characters, and in general breaks the established grammatical structure of the sentence, thereby creating new expressions and meanings. He uses Chinese formulations the significance of which would be straightforward if read as *kanbun*, yet he opts for an unconventional rendering that defies prevalent norms. He changes the form of certain expressions – from literary Chinese to classical Japanese – thereby transforming their content and message, and creates a fertile ground on which to expound not only his philosophy but philosophical linguistics. To Dōgen, language is not a means of just any kind of expression, but it is the means for expression and creation of Buddhist thought in its profoundness, fully covering the entire world.

(i) Experimenting with Homonymous Expressions

This category is Dōgen's version of a tongue twister, as well as an indication of a way to awakening granted by the master. For instance, in terms of Dōgen's usage of homonyms there is the concurrent usage of the word *busshi* in one sentence, where it assumes a diverse meaning depending on the characters it is written in. *Busshi* can mean either "Buddha heirs" 佛嗣 or "Buddha children" 佛子; or else, it now comes to my mind, *busshi* can also stand for "Buddhist teachers" 佛師. This

---

[52] DZZ 1: 244.

[53] DZZ 1: 245.

[54] DZZ 1: 243.

point can be illustrated by a selection from the fascicle "Transmission Documents," "Shisho" 嗣書, where it says: "Not knowing this principle means not understanding the Buddha way. Not understanding the Buddha way means one is not a Buddha heir. An heir of the Buddha (*busshi* 佛嗣) means a child of the Buddha (*busshi* 佛子)."[55]

At the risk of not strictly adhering to the homonymous rule within this category, I would like to present a few more examples that demonstrate how Dōgen's writings often feature an interchange of synonyms that are also similar sounding. The moon was already mentioned as a favorite symbol for Dōgen as well as the title of another of the *Treasury* texts. The opening sentences of "The Moon" feature the verbal form of the word *enjō* 圓成 meaning "becoming full," which is then replaced by *genjō* 現成, another frequent hallmark of Dōgen's vocabulary standing for "actualize," "realize" or "manifest." Several lines later, he reaches for another *genjō*, and albeit written diversely as 見成 also signifying "actualization, "appearance" or "manifestation." All of these expressions, *enjō* and the dual *genjō*, carry a slightly different meaning – their translation clearly varies – but they all directly relate to the moon as a representation for Dōgen's teaching in this particular chapter. Also, they highlight the contrast between a moon's presence and manifestation on the one hand and one's view and perception of it on the other. Thus, all these expressions pertaining to the activity and manifestation of the moon that are also incidentally related in sound create a sense of similarity and continuation threading through the entire fascicle serving as a sensorial reminder that operates as if in the background of one's attention. Like music coming from afar or a canvas underlying and connecting everything on the surface, the words, their written form as well as their sound intertwine into a constantly present notion adding another layer to the discourse.

Dōgen performs true lexical acrobatics when bringing to mind ancestors, their methods of teaching, transmitting the dharma, and relations to their disciples in "Entangling Vines." He writes: "There are ancestors whose entire body is skin, ancestors whose entire body is flesh, ancestors whose entire body is bones, and ancestors whose entire body is marrow. There are ancestors whose entire body is mind, ancestors whose entire body is body, and ancestors whose entire mind is mind. There are ancestors entirely ancestors, and ancestors whose entire body attains me, you, and so forth."[56] Even in translation, one needs to pay attention to carefully follow all relations and images in this passage, yet the words in the original Japanese necessitate an ultimate level of concentration. Especially the middle line which in Japanese reads: *Tsūshinjin no soshi ari, tsūshinshin no soshi ari, tsūshinshin no soshi ari.* 通身心の祖師あり、通身身の祖師あり、通心心の祖師あり。 Firstly, *tsūshinjin* 通身心 as "entire body-mind" varies from the double *tsūshinshin* following thereafter, but also *tsūshinshin* when merely pronounced can mean "entire body-body" 通身身 as well as "entire mind-mind" 通心心; they are written differently yet spoken identically. On the surface level, it is a playful tongue

---

[55] DZZ 1: 424.
[56] DZZ 1: 419.

twister; in its totality, however, it is a sum of the Chan/Zen discourse of mind-to-mind transmission and a prime example of Dōgen's inventiveness. Reading the line and concentrating on its pronunciation and meaning, as well as the teaching and message behind the words at the same time, one cannot help but think that Dōgen was probably both an enlightened master and a demanding teacher.

(j) Experimenting with Synonymous Expressions

Besides favoring homonymous expressions, Dōgen also explored the power of synonyms that he employed to illustrate the teaching with great attention to both detail and its overall message. To penetrate still more into Dōgen's thought, let me present a passage from "Buddha Nature," where he uses two words for a full moon, deliberately distinguishing between them on numerous occasions throughout the piece, only to then come to a conclusion of their nondual oneness. He portrays the moon as full, *mangetsu* 滿月, and round, *engetsu* 圓月. Even though the two words indicate a moon that is round, and therefore full – and being a full moon, it is evidently round – still Dōgen chooses to recognize the expressions in their different forms, to then settle on their eventual sameness. I have selected a few instances from the text relating to the moon where it becomes clear that Dōgen quite consciously differentiates between a full and a round moon, while using them as synonyms. It is apparent that, as was mentioned previously, the difference that the master aims to illustrate rests with words as forms, not with the content of the images and their significance, as they are equally used to support and supplement the meaning of Dōgen's message. Thus it says in "Buddha Nature:"

> Nāgārjuna's direct heir Kāṇadeva clearly understood the shape of a full moon, the shape of a round moon, the manifestation of his body, the nature of all Buddhas and the bodies of all Buddhas. [...]
>
> It is sad that neither laypeople nor monastics of the entire country of Song China, not one of them, have heard and understood Nāgārjuna's teaching or penetrated Kāṇadeva's words. How can they become intimate with the manifestation of Nāgārjuna's body? They dwell in darkness about the round moon, and they are separated from the full moon. [...]
>
> When you paint a moon of round shape, focus on the shape of a full moon, manifest the shape of a full moon. [...]
>
> The form of the manifested body is the body of a round moon, its shape is the shape of a full moon.[57]

A full moon and a round moon suggest the same moon that is round and full, yet Dōgen uses them as distinct phenomena that simultaneously contrast one another but are also mutually interrelated and complementary.

(k) Reflecting a Poetic Melodiousness in Successive Expressions

Adding to the previous grammatical, semantic, and rhetoric groupings, I would further like to present perhaps a somewhat unusual category of acoustic nature. Reading Dōgen's words aloud at times, I felt that even in the sound aspect of some of his sentences there is an intention behind the sequence and quality of the words

---

[57] DZZ 1: 28–31.

he uses. On a number of occasions when I felt besieged by the never-before-seen characters and grammatical structure that made my head spin, I would purpose-lessly repeat a sentence or its part aloud over and over again, in a mindless moment of inertia. Then suddenly, quite unintentionally, I would find myself listening to the words, catching the sound of how they float and drift away in a certain rhythmical pace, which reminded me of poetry recitation. As an illustration of this aspect of Dōgen's expressions in the *Treasury*, I will suggest two instances that caught my attention as melodious and poetic.

In "Being-Time," Dōgen writes: "The time of arriving at such a realm is no other than one shape and one form, understanding forms and beyond understanding forms, understanding shapes and beyond understanding shapes."[58] In classical Japanese, this reads as follows: *Tōinmo no denchi no toki, sunawachi issō ichizō nari* すなはち一草一象なり, *ezō fuezō nari* 會象不會象なり, *esō fuesō nari* 會草不會草なり. Here, the vocal playfulness rests in the tune of *issō ichizō... ezō fuezō... esō fuesō*, which evokes the rhythm of a poem.

Another example is from "All Activity," where it states: "There is abandoning life and death, and there is immersion in life and death. They are both the great way of thorough experience. There is relinquishing life and death and delivering life and death. They are both the great way of thorough experience."[59] The Japanese sound and flow of the passage reads as follows: "*Shusshōji ari, nisshōji ari. Tomoni gūjin no daidō nari. Shashōji ari, doshōji ari. Tomoni gūjin no daidō nari.* 出生死あり、入生死あり。ともに究盡の大道なり。捨生死あり、度生死あり。ともに究盡の大道なり。" This is a treasury (pun intended) of repetitive melodious allu-sions. Firstly, there is "abandoning life and death, *shusshōji* 出生死" and "immer-sion in life and death, *nisshōji* 入生死," followed by "relinquishing life and death, *shashōji* 捨生死" and "delivering life and death, *doshōji* 度生死." But also, these lines are linked with a resounding refrain, "They are both the great way of thorough experience, *tomoni gūjin no daidō nari*," reminding listeners of the innate nondual-ity of the sum of one's existence. In its original, it not only sounds as a poem but even resembles one:

出生死あり。　　*Shusshōji ari,*
入生死あり。　　*Nisshōji ari.*
ともに究盡の大道なり。　*Tomoni gūjin no daidō nari.*
捨生死あり。　　*Shashōji ari,*
度生死あり。　　*Doshōji ari.*
ともに究盡の大道なり 。　*Tomoni gūjin no daidō nari.*

Given the fact that essays in the *Treasury* were composed as informal *jishu* 示衆 sermons that were delivered orally and often in an impromptu manner at any loca-tion within the temple compound outside the dharma hall (*hattō* 法堂), it may easily be that Dōgen did attach a certain purpose to the sound of his sermons. In truth, due

_____

[58] DZZ 1: 241.
[59] DZZ 1: 259.

to his abundant lyrical legacy of both Chinese *kanshi* and Japanese *waka* verses, it is hard to imagine the master was inattentive to the rhythmical and poetic aspect of language in general. It is certain that Dōgen, who composed about 450 *kanshi* as well as approximately sixty *waka* poems, was aware of the rhyming and tonal patterns of verbal elocution. As a student of Rujing who excelled in poetry composition and a skilled versifier himself, Dōgen was much experienced in the Chinese poetic tradition and would therefore have had knowledge regarding the rules of Chinese prosody that he respected and preserved in his own creations. As a matter of fact, Dōgen was one of the first to introduce the poetic style of verse odes (*juko* 頌古) to Japan after his return from China, a four-line, seven-character poems approvingly reflecting on a *kōan* or some other remark of a master.[60] Consequently, it is safe to assume he mastered the intricacies of poetic theory and knew that "to be considered outstanding, the Chinese-style, or *kanbun*, poems must follow patterns for rhyming and rhythm that foster a cadenced approach to expressiveness influenced by local musical styles, such that the greatest poets were said to be singing or playing a 'fine tune,' 'keeping the beat,' or 'harmonizing with' their predecessors, peers, other interlocutors, and audience or readers."[61] Either consciously or unconsciously, Dōgen could have employed similar attitudes when composing the oral *jishu* sermons which comprise the *Treasury* in order to "harmonize with" his audience of disciples, and perhaps, figuratively speaking, also with the lineage of ancestors, which he asserts in "Entangling Vines," "Kattō." After all, sounds always played an essential role in the Chan lore, as the transmission of the light records prove with a number of narratives in which a teacher attained enlightenment upon unexpectedly hearing a sound that startled them. Master Xiangyan 香嚴 (Jp. Kōgan, ?–898) is famous for awakening when he heard a pebble hit a bamboo, the notoriously famous Muromachi-period Rinzai monk Ikkyū 一休 (1394–1481) experienced breakthrough upon the cry of a crow when meditating in a boat on lake Biwa, and Dōgen himself achieved enlightenment when hearing Rujing's admonition of "dropping of body and mind."

   This incident of Dōgen's own breakthrough, intriguingly, seems of utmost importance in the master's case, especially when exploring his understanding and stance toward the mutual relationship between language and enlightenment. It seems helpful to keep in mind that his experience of genuine awakening under Rujing occurred by means of an initial verbal and linguistic misunderstanding. Dōgen relates his enlightenment was triggered when his mentor was reproaching a fellow monk who had trouble staying awake during meditation and was reminded by the Chinese ancestor that "Studying Zen is dropping off body and mind."[62] However, the expression "dropping off body and mind," *shinjin datsuraku* 身心脱落 was not used by Rujing, despite being a phrase that he is, in retrospect, most famous for. Rather, the master is known for saying "casting off dust from the mind,"

---

[60] Heine, *Flowers Blooming*, 14.

[61] Heine, *Flowers Blooming*, 71.

[62] DZZ 7: 19.

心塵脱落. This is pronounced differently in classical Chinese but identically in Japanese, and it is therefore possible that it did, especially to Dōgen's ears of a foreigner, sound homophonous to "dropping off body and mind."[63] As Dōgen's own enlightenment occurred by means of a misconstrued verbal suggestion from his teacher, via the medium of sounds and language, it is not hard to imagine that, in effect, Dōgen had strong personal reasons to attach conscious importance not only to the form and content of the words he used but also to their sound and rhythm.

(l) Reduplicating Characters

The repetitive use of characters may be another aspect of Dōgen's writing that reflects his training in Chan poetic forms. Sometimes, the double use of characters is employed grammatically, as a noun in its plural instead of singular form, while on other occasions it serves as an embellishment placing emphasis on the semantic function of the respective expression. Among the first category, there are terms such as *butsu butsu* 佛佛 for "Buddhas," *soso* 祖祖 for "ancestors," and *teki* 嫡嫡 for "heirs" or "descendants." Remarkably, the word *jiji* 時時 can be rendered as multiple "times" or "moments," but also literally as "moment by moment" or "each and every moment," which presents one of the more subtle challenges when encountering the master's linguistic and verbal originality. Among the other group of literary adornments, one can mention the simple doubling of the character for "bright" and "shining," *myōmyō* 明明, which underscores the illuminating quality of the expression. Given the diverse possibilities for understanding of these words, it becomes apparent that even such unimaginative format as the doubling of characters can, in Dōgen's rendition, suggest either a simple lexical or a highly nuanced philosophical context that therefore needs to be approached with utmost attention.

(m) Negative Expressions

The last category introduced in this analysis relates to rhetorical and metaphysical implications in Dōgen's approach to words and letters. As a master of imbuing established notions with novel interpretations, Dōgen often targets conventional Zen or Buddhist utterances that may have become rigid as time passed. Even in the case of Zen locutions which may once have been expedient in communicating the message clearly and succinctly in a certain context, at a given place and time, they became increasingly stereotypical and stiff, thus losing the initial connection to the truth and eventually degrading into a fossilized shell of words.[64] Together with masters and ancestors, whom he respectfully and affectionately calls "old Buddhas," Dōgen was clearly aware of the danger of such ossification of expressions and attempted to constantly question phrases that have solidified over time to thereby radically reinterpret their established meaning. Under this heading belong Dōgen's frequent usage of negative, contrasting, and opposing expressions which fall under the general Zen category of *via negativa*. It is a means of conveying reality through

---

[63] Heine, *Readings of Dōgen's Treasury*, 16.

[64] Yorizumi, *Shōbōgenzō nyūmon*, 65.

negative terms such as "no mind" (*mushin* 無心) or "no thought" (*musō* 無想), where the latter is homonymous to "no form" (*musō* 無相) and synonymous to "beyond thought" (*munen* 無念). When mentioning homonyms, there is also *fudō* (不動) of "immovable," *fudō* (不道) of "beyond expression," and *fudō* (不同) of "uneven" or "dissimilar." "No-birth" (*fushō* 不生) and "no-death" (*fumetsu* 不滅) can also be rendered as "beyond birth" and "beyond death," while *fuchi* (不知) stands for "unknown" or "beyond knowledge," *mujin* (無盡) for "inexhaustible," *fukashigi* (不可思議) for "inconceivable," and so forth.

When referring to Dōgen's usage of negative phrases, it is obligatory to mention the highlight of his unorthodox usage of words, which can best be illustrated by his treatment of two synonyms of *fushiryō* 不思量 and *hishiryō* 非思量, referring to a negation of thought. In exemplifying this unique negation, Dōgen seems to have been inspired by the Chinese master Yaoshan 藥山 (Jp. Yakusan, 754–828), whose wordplay of "no thought" is especially elaborated on in the chapter "The Point of Zazen," yet referenced on a number of occasions throughout the *Treasury*. Both *fushiryō* and *hishiryō* employ a negative prefix and are thus synonymous, albeit with distinctive connotations. Although their translations are conceptually rather close and similar, the prefix *fu* 不 describes negation, while *hi* 非 relates to contrariety. *Fushiryō*, which translates as "not thinking," indicates a cessation of ordinary thought rooted in discrimination and conceptualization. *Hishiryō*, on the other hand, denotes "nonthinking," the fulfilment and result of the casting or dropping off of body-and-mind. While "not thinking" describes a difference in terms of thoughts that are either present or absent in one's mental processes, "nonthinking" refers to state of mind in meditation, transcending the "conventional boundaries of thought and thoughtlessness."[65]

As the plentiful contrary and opposing examples above attest, Dōgen was a master of innovation that he conveyed by means of verbal originality. Especially in reference to the examined topic, Kim outlines the master's stance as follows: "Dōgen was confident in what was yet to be expressed, in what had already been expressed, as well as in what had not yet been expressed or allegedly could not be expressed."[66] In case of negative formulations, however, Dōgen seems to have exercised a practice that had been abundantly present already in earlier Buddhist writings. The Heart Sūtra comes to mind as a suitable example of a popular Buddhist text that expounds: "There are no forms, no feelings, perceptions, mental formations, consciousness...," and continues to enumerate all that is not (無), closing the section with a reference to the Four Noble Truths, summarizing "There is no suffering, no causes [of suffering], no cessation [of suffering], and no path."[67] The lines of the sūtra do not, of course, describe the nonexistence of these concepts and phenomena, but rather their emptiness of an inherent nature (*svabhāva*, Jp. *jishō* 自性),

---

[65] Heine, *Readings of Dōgen's Treasury*, 21.

[66] Kim, *Eihei Dōgen*, 95.

[67] T 08.251.

since, as Williams notes, "it is because entities originate in dependence on causes and conditions that they lack intrinsic existence, they are empty."[68]

Dōgen illustrates his view on the essential quality of all things in the opening lines of "True Nature of All Things," "Shohō jisshō" 諸法實相, where he states:

> Actualization of Buddha ancestors is the true nature thoroughly experienced. True nature is all things. All things are thusness of form and thusness of nature. They are thusness of body, thusness of mind, thusness of the world and thusness of clouds and rain. Thusness of walking, abiding, sitting, and laying down, thusness of sadness and joy, motion and stillness, thusness of a monk's staff and abbot's whisk, thusness of Buddha's lifting up a flower and breaking into a smile, thusness of transmission of dharma and confirmation of enlightenment, thusness of study and endeavor of the way, thusness of pine roots and bamboo knots.[69]

One can clearly take notice of Dōgen's universal view on the intrinsic nature of phenomena, which is selfsame as true thusness (*tathatā*, *shinnyo* 眞如) or thusness (*nyo* 如), a point that Dōgen emphasizes by using their appellations interchangeably. Moreover, he finds their inherent character in all phenomena, whether they embody the teaching of the Buddha ("Buddha's lifting up a flower and breaking into a smile," "transmission of dharma and confirmation of enlightenment"), everyday monastic or even lay practice with its inner emotional experience and outward formal enactment ("walking, abiding, sitting, and laying down," "sadness and joy, motion and stillness") or whether they are reflected in the natural world ("clouds and rain," "pine roots and bamboo knots"). He weaves spontaneously between the various aspects of intrinsic quality of all phenomena, as a reminder that true nature is not limited to lay or monastic, inner or outer, personal or social, doctrinal or natural, as the "true nature is [indeed] all things," *shohō jissō*. In reference to negative expressions, and words and phrases as such, these too are "all things," neither positive nor negative, inside nor outside, dependent nor nondependent. To illustrate this with a statement from the essay "Dignified Conduct of Practicing Buddhas," "Gyōbutsu i'igi" 行佛威儀, here is the sum of his views, demonstrated upon the example of the purported goal of the Buddhist path, enlightenment: "Practicing Buddhas do not cherish neither original enlightenment, nor acquired enlightenment; we can neither say that they are unenlightened, nor enlightened. Indeed, this is the truth."[70]

6 Conclusion

On the pages above, I introduced several examples that illustrate some of Dōgen's innovative approaches to language and the techniques he used to formulate his teaching, displaying philosophical linguistics of unbounded creativity that lay at the

---

[68] Paul Williams, *Mahāyāna Buddhism: The Doctrinal Foundations* (Routledge: London, New York, 2009), 69.

[69] DZZ 1: 457.

[70] DZZ 1: 66.

basis of his teaching. Even though his language variations at times verges on conscious disregard for the existing lexical, semantic, and grammatical structure, they reflect an unbounded creativity of thought and expression. While I am aware of many other instances that could have been selected for either one or several other groups, I am also certain there are still others that I failed to mention or have not yet become aware of. And who knows, maybe under a detailed scrutiny Dōgen's inventiveness pertaining words and letters would amount to a list "fully covering" the entire alphabet.

As became clear during the compilation of the categories above, some of them are merely arbitrary to help separate (分) and understand (分) certain Dōgen's expressions, while others serve as representations of his approach to words but could also be joined into a single group. The suggested second, third, and fourth classifications – (b) Literal Reading of Characters, (c) Dissecting Expressions into Individual Characters, and (d) Attributing Novel Meanings to Conventional Expressions – could form an independent category of, for instance, "Devising Novel Meanings." Also, (e) Tautology and (f) Negative Tautology could create a common unit of "Rhetoric," which would then need to be supplemented with Dōgen's other figures of speech. By contrast, it is not entirely without complications to attempt to systematically label Dōgen's linguistic methods, as some of the featured cases can clearly be placed into several categories at once. The Japanese sentence of "*Tsūshinjin no soshi ari, tsūshinshin no soshi ari, tsūshinshin no soshi ari.* (There are ancestors whose entire body is mind, ancestors whose entire body is body, and ancestors whose entire mind is mind.)" that was illustrated as a homonymous example can also be placed within the first group of (a) Reshuffling of Characters, as Dōgen achieves his meaning here by freely and mutually combining the characters for "entire" 通, "body" 身, and "mind" 心. Likewise, as there is a certain rhythm and melody to the sentence, it could appear under the (k) heading that reflects a poetic melodiousness of Dōgen's sentences. The diversity of these groupings, ranging from lexical, grammatical, semantic, syntactic, rhetorical etc., demonstrates that Dōgen's inventiveness is limitless and beyond any kind of or attempt at classification; it is indeed impossible to thoroughly categorize such linguistic originality and put any definitive label on the creative genius to which his writings stand as testimony.

Tsunoda calls the *Treasury* a rare scripture and Dōgen a rare master who also "acknowledged the importance of language," claiming the significance Dōgen placed on language is one of the major characteristics of Dōgen's teaching in general.[71] Looking back at the phrases Zen attributes to Shākyamuni's pronouncement of a "teaching nondependent upon words and letters" and "transmitted outside scriptures" throughout the *Treasury* itself, it seems Dōgen was not a proponent of either of these expressions as they only appear on a few occasions in the entire work. This would suggest that Dōgen was not so much interested in a teaching independent of words and letters or outside the conventional sūtras and their established commentaries, as he was primarily concerned with spreading the "rightly

---

[71] Tsunoda, *Dōgen Shōbōgenzō wo yomu*, 31.

transmitted Buddha-dharma" (*shōden no buppō*) and the "great way of Buddha ancestors" (*busso no daidō*).

To Dōgen, language – similarly to zazen or any other monastic activity – is experiential. Just as it is certainly possible to convey the truth and essence of Buddhist practice through expressions, at the same time it is equally important to keep in mind that it is merely a device – as the motto of nondependency on words and letters suggests – and phrases can also fail in communicating and transmitting the teaching. In order to trigger awakening in his followers and practitioners, Dōgen establishes his own philosophical linguistics, where by means of rhetorical devices, verbal inventiveness, and wordplay he attempts to inspire, awaken, and guide those who come into contact with his teaching. The rhetorical devices, summarized in different categories in this paper, are also formulas and patterns that carry and convey, to an attentive and attuned mind, the underlying philosophical implications of Dōgen's thought. Consequently, similar to zazen being a vehicle of enlightenment in practical terms, words can serve as means to enlightenment in philosophical terms. Thus we return to Kim's initial understanding of Dōgen's attitude to teaching as seen through the two areas of activities (*gyōji*) and expressions (*dōtoku*), in which the goal "was not to be enfolded in, but was to unfold through."[72] While language is generally viewed as doctrinal and theoretical, and thus distant from or standing in opposition to the more practical seated meditation, for Dōgen it is highly experiential, just like the continuous monastic practice itself, as well as inseparable from it. Hence, similar to meditation or any other activity performed within the monastic context, even expressions can form a path of practice, *on par* with seated meditation.

Especially in relation to his own enlightenment, it seems Dōgen approached language consciously as a nondual issue and in the same light as any other occurrence, whether anyone else tends to label it as good or bad, agreeable or annoying, this or that. In "Being-Time," he writes: "Entering the mud and entering the water is equally time,"[73] thus equating all of human activity and experience that may be perceived contrastingly, underscoring the illusion of subjective perception and interpretation. Despite the necessary nondependence on language as a formal means of communication and the inherent tension between awakening and its expression, Dōgen's own experience showed an interdependence of language and enlightenment. Hand-in-hand with an awareness of the intricacies of language, Dōgen's choice of words suggest he was deeply conscious of the power of expression as well as its snares.

To return to Dōgen's *waka* poem relating to the "treasury of the true dharma eye" at the beginning of this paper and used as its title, just like with language "that is spoken beyond words [and] does not leave traces of the brush," throughout his written work Dōgen erases dualities between leaving traces and not leaving traces. Once dharma is transmitted "beyond words," *koto no ha no hoka*, and expresses "true form without form," *jissō musō*, it does not leave any traces that could be taken for obstructions on the way to enlightenment. On the path of language and expressions,

---

[72] Kim, *Eihei Dōgen*, 37.
[73] DZZ 1: 242.

overcoming the dichotomies of human mind that can be penetrated via the medium of words, Dōgen employs language as part of a practice of concentration and awareness. In the same way as he does not distinguish between meditation while sitting on a cushion and meditation while engaging in daily monastic chores that can equally present an opportunity for breakthrough, the practice of words and letters is, in Dōgen's rendition, likewise a moment constituting the opportunity for complete awareness of the present, instant after instant and expression after expression.

Bibliography

Primary Sources

Bukkyōgo daijiten 仏教語大辞典, Nakamura Hajime 中村元. Tōkyō: Tōkyō shoseki, 1981.
Dōgen Zenji zenshū 道元禅師全集 [Dōgen's Complete Works] , 7 volumes, edited by Kawamura Kōdō 河村孝道, Kagashima Genryū 鏡島元隆, Suzuki Kakuzen 鈴木格禅, Kosaka Kiyū 小坂機融 et al.Tōkyō: Shunjūsha, 1989–1995. [DZZ]
Shōbōgenzō gendaigoyaku 正法眼蔵現代語訳, 6 volumes, Tamaki Kōshirō 玉城康四郎. Tōkyō: Daizō shuppan, 1994–1998.
Shōbōgenzō yōgo sakuin 正法眼蔵用語索引, 2 volumes, edited by Katō Shūkō 加藤宗厚. Tōkyō: Risōsha, 1963.
Taishō shinshū daizōkyō Text Database 大正新脩大藏經タキストデータベース. https://21dzk.l.u-tokyo.ac.jp/SAT/. [T]
Zengaku daijiten 禅学大辞典, edited by Zengakudaijiten hensanjo. Tōkyō: Taishūkan shoten, 2020.

Secondary Sources

Frellesvig, Bjarke. *A History of the Japanese Language*. Cambridge: Cambridge University Press, 2011.
Heine, Steven. *Did Dōgen Go to China: What He Wrote and When He Wrote It*. New York: Oxford University Press, 2006.
Heine, Steven. *Readings of Dōgen's Treasury of the True Dharma Eye*. New York: Oxford University Press, 2020a.
Heine, Steven. *Flowers Blooming on a Withered Tree: Giun's Verse Comments on Dōgen's Treasury of the True Dharma Eye*. New York: Oxford University Press, 2020b.
LaFleur, William. "Dōgen in the Academy." In *Dōgen Studies*, edited by William LaFleur, 1–20. Honolulu: University of Hawai'i Press, 1985.
Kasulis, Thomas P. "The Incomparable Philosopher: Dōgen on How to Read the *Shōbōgenzō*." In *Dōgen Studies*, edited by William LaFleur, 83–98. Honolulu: University of Hawai'i Press, 1985.
Kim, Hee-Jin. *Eihei Dōgen: Mystical Realist*. Boston: Wisdom Publications, 2004.
Kim, Hee-Jin. "'The Reason of Words and Letters': Dōgen and the Kōan Literature." In *Dōgen Studies*, edited by William LaFleur, 54–82. Honolulu: University of Hawai'i Press, 1985.
Ōtani, Tetsuo 大谷哲夫, ed. *Dōgen yomi kaki jiten* 道元読み書き辞典. Tōkyō: Kashiwa shōbō, 2013.
Raud, Rein. "Inside the Concept: Rethinking Dōgen's Language." *Asian Philosophy* 21, no. 2 (2011): 123–137.

Tanahashi, Kazuaki. *Enlightenment Unfolds*. Boulder, CO: Shambhala, 2000.

Tanahashi, Kazuaki, ed. *Treasury of the True Dharma Eye: Zen Master Dogen's Shobo Genzo*. Boulder, CO: Shambhala, 2012.

Tsunoda, Tairyū 角田泰隆. *Zen no susume, Dōgen no kotoba* 禅のすすめ　道元のことば. Tōkyō: Kadokawa bunko, 2018.

Tsunoda, Tairyū 角田泰隆. *Dōgen Shōbōgenzō wo yomu* 道元『正法眼蔵』をよむ, 2 volumes. Tōkyō: NHK shuppan, 2021.

Williams, Paul. *Mahāyāna Buddhism: The Doctrinal Foundations*. Routledge: London, New York, 2009.

Yorizumi, Mitsuko 頼住光子. *Shōbōgenzō nyūmon* 正法眼蔵入門. Tōkyō: Kadokawa bunko, 2016.

Part II
Practice

Dōgen and the Buddhist Way

Aldo Tollini

1 The Buddha's Way

In this essay I intend to deal with an expression that Dōgen often uses in his writings, *butsudō* 仏道, the Buddha's Way.

Although at an early date in the texts of both Kūkai (774–835) and Saichō (767–822) we can find the term *butsudō*, that is, the path that a Buddhist school teaches to pursue enlightenment, it is, however, with Master Dōgen that the term *butsudō* began to be used in Japan in a consistent and specific way to mean that Buddhism is a path that leads, or can lead, whoever undertakes it, to spiritual realization, that is, to enlightenment or *satori*.

In *Shōbōgenzō* 正法眼蔵 ("Treasury of the eye of the true Law") the words *butsudō* and *bukkyō* 仏教 or "Buddha's Way" and "Buddha's teaching," or simply Buddhism, are used in different manners, with the second much less frequently used. In any case, the former is considered the realization of the latter and, therefore, its meaning involves the active participation of the practitioner with a view to spiritual perfection by way of implementing the teachings that the latter proposes. In fact, in the opening of the chapter "Bukkyō" 仏教 from the *Shōbōgenzō*, Dōgen writes that "the realization of the Way of all Buddhas is the Buddha's teaching."[1] Dōgen explains that the Buddha's teaching is not a theoretical set of doctrines, but their dynamic realization. So, it makes no sense to speak of the Buddha's teaching except as actualization of the Way of Realization. In other words, *bukkyō* is not

---

[1] 諸仏の道現成、これ仏教也. Etō, *op.cit.*, vol. 1, p. 363. All translations from the Japanese original are of the author.

A. Tollini (✉)
"Ca' Foscari" University of Venice, Venice, Italy
e-mail: tollini@unive.it

© The Author(s), under exclusive license to Springer Nature Switzerland AG 2023   111
R. Müller, G. Wrisley (eds.), *Dōgen's Texts*, Sophia Studies in Cross-cultural Philosophy of Traditions and Cultures 35,
https://doi.org/10.1007/978-3-031-42246-1_6

intended only as a subject of study and speculation, but as a guide to start a path following the example of the historical Buddha. In this context, *dō* is generally understood as a demanding Way that involves intense practice, study, and the realization of spiritual perfection, normally under the guidance of a master.

However, there is another important statement regarding the Buddha's Way: in the chapter "Hotsu bodai shin" of *Shōbōgenzō*, Dōgen says: "*Bodhi* is a term of the language of India and here it should be rendered with Way,"[2] meaning that the Sanskrit term *bodhi* should be rendered in the Sino-Japanese context as *dō* or Way, to which it corresponds. Therefore, for Dōgen, enlightenment is the Way itself, it is enlightenment itself in accordance with his conception of the identity relationship between practice and realization called *shushō ichinyo* 修証一如.[3] As a matter of fact, when we consider the identity of practice and realization, we should not forget that by practice 修 Dōgen intends a broader meaning than the practice par excellence, *zazen*. Rather, it refers to the pursuit and realization of the Way, that is, the commitment and dedication to follow the difficult path that leads to realization. Non self-centered commitment and tireless effort is both true practice and at the same time the path of the Way.

The topic of the Way relates the master to his time, the Kamakura period and its cultural environment, when the concept of *michi* 道 was gaining importance and started to be used widely in many fields of art and crafts, that largely took the Buddhist Way as their model.

For a better understanding of this topic, it is important to start considering the situation of Buddhism of that period and the cultural trends in which Dōgen's teaching developed. In the Kamakura period, with the coming to power of the *bushi*, culture, society and its ideals were transformed and took on completely new connotations compared to the previous period. It was in this cultural climate, and under its influence, that Dōgen matured and his teachings developed.

2 Traditional Buddhism and the New Trend

It is worth remembering that Buddhism in the traditional conception before the advent of the new schools of the Kamakura period had a dual aspect. On the one hand, it was at the service of the aristocracy and the state, and was intended to protect the imperial dynasty and the country from disasters by means of its salvific potential. In fact, in Japanese Buddhism until the great reformers of the Kamakura era, practice was limited to monastics, denying lay people the possibility of accessing enlightenment. Even in the temples, the actual practice, but also the observance of the precepts and generally the moral conduct in view of the pursuit of enlightenment, was rather poor.

[2] 菩提は天竺の音、ここには道という. Etō, *op.cit.*, vol. 2, p. 407.
[3] He also coined the expression *kyūdō* 求道, that is, "pursuit of the Way," which he also understood as corresponding to "pursuit of enlightenment," *tokudō* 得道, "obtaining the Way," or "obtaining enlightenment" and others.

In contrast to the priests of Old Buddhism who conducted the salvation of the emperor and nobility and prayed for the protection of the nation (*chingo kokka* 鎮護国家), the priests of Kamakura New Buddhism put their efforts into the salvation of the general population.[4]

The other type of medieval Japanese Buddhism was, instead, represented by people who were not part of formal structures, and consisted of independent monks, often itinerant, unattached to temples and organizations, who moved independently around the country with the aim of preaching, but also of exercising various esoteric practices and were called *hijiri* 聖.

Under these conditions, there was a strong discontent and critical attitude towards Buddhism and its institutions, which were considered too corrupt and inadequate to provide spiritual guidance. The institutions neglected the needs of the common people and the *hijiri* did not offer a coherent and structured message of salvation.

In this context, the Buddhism proposed by Dōgen – and in some ways also by other masters of his time – represented a radical innovation: he proposed a Buddhism in the form of a Way to be pursued individually, through a subjective spiritual experience open to anyone who had the will to pursue it. Dōgen taught the Buddha's Way as self-cultivation, that is, as a path to self-improvement and the attainment of wisdom.

The way in which the Mahāyāna tradition considered the nature of enlightenment also strongly conditioned the way it understood practice. On the one hand, the idea of original enlightenment called *hongaku* 本覚, pre-existing and all-pervading, already endowed *ab origine* by human nature, favoured in various ways a passive or even negationist conception of practice and of any activity positively oriented towards the acquisition of perfection.

In the tradition of Chinese Chán, from which Japanese Zen takes its origin, the idea was widely established that since enlightenment was already given, and the daily mind was considered to coincide with that of enlightenment (Mǎzǔ Dàoyī 馬祖道一), practice and any other form of purposeful striving for the acquisition of enlightenment was downgraded to a secondary, non-essential activity. However, the concept of practice and enlightenment in the Song period, when Dōgen was studying in China with his master Nyojō, had taken on different connotations: in principle, we are originally awakened but, in reality, that is in our ordinary life, we are deluded. Therefore, it is necessary to achieve enlightenment by means of practice. In this debate on the meaning of practice as related to enlightenment, Dōgen will give a very innovative vision, as explained later.

3   The Innovative Teaching of Dōgen

In the first half of the thirteenth century, Dōgen was the spiritual master who not only gave a new impulse to Japanese Buddhism, but also inaugurated a new vision of spirituality by placing the individual at the centre of religious activity and insisted

---

[4] Matsuo Kenji, "Official monks and reclusive monks: focusing on the salvation of women," in *Bulletin of the School of Oriental and African Studies* 64, no. 3 (2001), 369.

on the concept of personal effort, practice and the achievement of a goal, *satori*, or the so-called "enlightenment" open to all. The insistence on the need to search, to find a meaning beyond appearances, to give a new interpretation to the human dimension by rediscovering the great innate potential – the Buddha-nature – of which we are a part, are at the same time a new way of approaching the religious experience, and also a new vision of a more broadly spiritual dimension.

The universality of the salvific message through individual practice to which everyone could have access was not exclusive to Dōgen, but is also found among other religious reformers who were his contemporaries. However, Dōgen's original-ity lies in the fact that he proposes the above-mentioned themes applied to Buddhism of the great Chinese tradition, renewing its characteristics and applying it to the Japanese environment. In short, Dōgen radically renewed the Buddhist tradition of Chinese import. It was not his intention to create a new form of Buddhism, or even a new school, but to bring what he supposed to be the true form of Buddhism from China, or better from its birthplace India and refound Japanese Buddhism.

In this sense, Dōgen's teaching represents a fracture with the teachings of the previous schools in Japan, especially Tendai and Shingon, and inaugurates a new vision of the Buddha's Way. This new vision was both unprecedented and differed in important ways from the other new schools born in the same period.

Moreover, Dōgen's newly initiated conception of the Buddha's Way was to be pursued with unyielding commitment, dedication through the sublimation of one-self (*shinjin datsuraku*), and devotion of oneself completely to perfecting the Way. Again, in Dōgen's innovative vision, the Way is open to all those who are willing to devote themselves to it with seriousness and commitment – including the laity, at least until his transfer to Eiheiji.

There are two themes in the Master's teaching that I would like to focus on: (1) The universality of his message, and (2) The need to dedicate oneself to the Buddha's Way with commitment and dedication.

3.1 The Universality of his Message

For Dōgen, the social class no longer counts, nor does intellectual ability, but only the genuine aspiration to pursue a difficult path with all one's heart. No one before in Japanese Buddhism had posited the possibility of awakening for all only through effort, determination, and dedication to the Way and to practice, without distinction between intelligent or stupid, high or low status, in short for all, indiscriminately.

In *Zuimonki* Dōgen says:

> Even people who cannot understand a single sentence (of the scriptures), even stupid and ignorant people, if they devote themselves with determination to zazen, can be superior to those who are intelligent and have studied for many years.[5]

---

[5] Dōgen, *Shōbōgenzō Zuimonki*, ed. Mizuno Yaoko, Chōenji-bon 長円寺本 version (Chikuma shobō, 1992), 6–24, 405.

And:

> Buddha prepared precepts and teachings for everyone, even for people of low ability. All
> people have the possibility of attaining the Buddha-Dharma, and one should not think that
> one does not have the ability. If you rely on practice, you will surely attain (enlightenment).
>   If you practice the Buddha-Dharma, individual ability has nothing to do with it. One
> who is born as a human being has (innate) capacity (for enlightenment).[6]

3.2   The Need to Dedicate Oneself to the Buddhist Way with Commitment and Dedication

In Dōgen's vision, commitment to the Way implies first of all, a life of strict morality and respect for the precepts, on which he insists a great deal in his writings and
which he considers inviolable requirements.

In various texts such as the *Shōbōgenzō* and *Zuimonki*, Dōgen deals with the
subject of morality, the value of good and evil from the point of view of the Buddhist
law of cause-and-effect. However, this topic, dealt with extensively elsewhere, is
not the point here. Rather, I will focus on the emphasis given to the need of pursuing
the Buddhist Way by implementing virtuous behaviors in view of the practitioner's
spiritual improvement. Enlightenment is achieved by letting the self drop, abandoning the involvements and attachments, and opening up to a reality that is wider than
the individual one. This path requires a great capacity of perseverance, dedication,
and self-sacrifice. Without a demanding "asceticism," therefore without sacrifices,
it is impossible to get rid of one's self-centeredness.

Therefore, in the chapter *Shinjin gakudō* he says:

> By learning the Way in this manner, when there is personal effort, the reward comes by
> itself, but if there is only the reward without being accompanied by personal effort, [it's
> like] breathing in secretly borrowing the nostrils of the patriarchs.[7]

And a little after, "The Way is to be learned by walking barefoot."[8]

In Dōgen's view, enlightenment and the ideal of perfection in every sense, are
always conditioned by the acceptance of the privations that forge people's spirits
and enhance their morality and compassion toward others.

For him, moral demands are essential for the sphere of spirituality. Without dedication and effort, no Way can be attained and no improvement is achievable. The
spirit must be forged in difficulties, especially in the "renunciation" and "abandonment" of both material wealth in favor of poverty, and worldly comforts and plea-
sures are to be dropped in favor of solitude and "withdrawal from the world". The
abandonment and stripping of social superstructures is considered fundamental for
Dōgen and reaches its maximum expression in the renunciation of one's self

---

[6] Ibid., 316–317.

[7] Etō Sokuō (ed.), *Shōbōgenzō*, vol. 2, Iwanami shoten, Tokyo, 1961 (13° ed.), p. 122.

[8] Ibid.

(*shinjin datsuraku*), taking up the fundamental conception of Buddhism expressed with *anattā*.

Among the innovations introduced in Japanese Buddhism by his teaching, this is certainly one of the most radical, and one which had a strong consonance with the ideals proposed by the warrior class that had earned power by force and self-sacrifice. In the vision of the *bushi*, the importance of moral behaviour and effort in action become a consolidated concept in a path that envisages the goal of improvement to be pursued with mettle.

Pursuing the Way of Buddhism requires great effort and determination as it is distant and difficult, but we must not get discouraged, we must insist and bear the difficulties with courage and a resolute spirit.

Dōgen says (perhaps with the intention of criticizing the Pure Land school), "Simply strive hard on the Way."[9]

And:

> Those who love the easy things naturally understand that they are not fit for the Way. People who love the Way should not apply themselves to easy practices. In case they engage in easy practices, they will certainly not reach the True Earth and will not reach the place of the Treasure. Even the most skilled say that the practice is difficult. Realize how deep and great Buddhism is. If the Way of the Buddha were originally easy, people of ancient times with great abilities would not have said that the practice is difficult to implement and difficult to understand.[10]

Striving to maintain a pure conduct, which consists in adopting correct behavior, refraining from contaminating actions, remaining pure and vigilant, uncorrupted, in short, follow a path of moral improvement is the indispensable premise for accessing the supreme goal of enlightenment.

Dōgen's insistence on moral behavior reminds us of the moral virtues (Sanskrit: *śīla* Pāli: *sīla*) of the Noble Eightfold Path of original Buddhism and the *śīla pāramitā*; and indeed, the moral virtues of self-restraint and discipline of the Mahāyāna are indispensable in order to proceed on the path that leads to liberation. In this regard, it is possible to suppose that Dōgen, with the intention of radically renewing Japanese Buddhism, felt that an uncompromising stance toward behavior was the best way to give a decisive turn to Japanese Buddhism, which then suffered from decadence and laxity of morals. He felt himself like a pioneer bringing to his country the "true Buddhism" handed down through generations of patriarchs and masters.

It is interesting to note the striking contrast with Chinese Chán theories, especially from the Tang era, that proposed a Buddhism of a quietistic character, based on non-action, withdrawal from the world and acceptance of things as they are. In Dōgen's view, Mǎzǔ's famous affirmation that ordinary mind is already the Way 平常心是道, i.e., the doctrine that we are originally awakened, therefore everything we do is the manifestation of the Buddha's mind, hence practice is superfluous, is

---

[9] Dōgen, *Shōbōgenzō Zuimonki*, 1–10, 49.

[10] *Gakudō yōjinshū*. Itō Shūken, *Goroku. Genun taishō gendaigo yaku, Dōgen zenji zenshū, 14*, Shunjūsha, 2007, p. 62.

unacceptable. At the same time, also the Song stand according to which though we are originally awakened we should practice because we normally behave in a deluded manner, unconscious of our true nature, does not conform to his thinking. His innovative view is that: practice is essential not because we are not yet enlightened, but <u>because</u> we are already enlightened. This means that enlightenment is manifest in our meditation practice.

This is clearly expressed in a famous sentence of the chapter "Bendōwa," "Although this Dharma is inherently present in abundance in every person, it does not come to light until one practices it and if one does not become enlightened will not be attained."[11]

Effort and dedication in practice – a ceaseless practice not limited in time and space – is the indispensable requirement for having one's Buddha nature manifested. Dōgen's Zen based on the identity of practice and enlightenment is revealed in behaviour: though we are originally enlightened, we must strive to actualize our true nature by means of a continued effort in practice.

Since practice is the manifestation of one's Buddha-nature, practice and enlightenment coincide and are one. For the same reason – that is, because practice is not instrumental, namely, is not the accumulation of merits chronologically differentiated from enlightenment – practice is not separated from normal daily life: there is not a time of practice separate from a daily life of non-practice. True practice is continuous and unbroken: every moment and every place is the time of practice. Similarly, the manifestation of one's Buddha-nature is not intermittent, but can only be continuous. This implies always being in practice, that is, manifesting one's buddhahood at all times. Therefore, every action, (四威儀) must be the result of the ongoing perfection of one's buddhahood.

The word *igi* 威儀, which in standard Japanese has the meaning of "dignity," in the Buddhist environment has two different meanings: (1) The four main human physical behaviours: walking, standing, sitting and lying (行, 住, 坐, 臥), and (2) To behave in a correct (or dignified) manner, which, in particular, means that monastics should adhere to the precepts, follow the regulations, practice with commitment, and in all daily activities, whether religious or not, maintain impeccable behaviour. Dōgen deals with this topic in detail in chapter "Gyōbutsu igi" 行仏威儀 where he says, "All the Buddhas without exception fully actualize igi, this is the practicing Buddha."[12] And a little later, "What all the Buddhas strictly adhere to, is igi of the practicing Buddha (gyōbutsu igi)."[13]

This means that the behaviour characterised by *igi* is that of the Buddhas and that also human beings manifesting their buddha-nature, show *igi* in their behaviour.

Besides, he says that *saho* 作法 *is doctrine, obtaining the Way, is saho,*[14] where *saho* means "perform rituals correctly and behave according to the rules." Recently

---

[11] Etō Sokuō, *op.cit.*, vol. 1, p. 55.

[12] Ibid., 345.

[13] Ibid., 346–7. 威儀即仏法 作法是宗旨.

[14] Chapter "Senjō." Etō Sokuō, *op.cit.*, vol. 1, p. 107.

the Sōtō school has formulated the expression – not to be found in Dōgen's texts, but derived from his chapter "Senjō" – which says, "Correct behaviour is Buddhism, and correctly performing rituals is the doctrine."

Igi (correct behaviour) means to be free of attachments, free of any conditioning, dedicated, positive, unrestricted, selfless and attentive. In other words, uncontaminated by the stains, ties, and enticements of the world. It is a pure state of being, one that manifests and actualizes one's being as Buddha-nature.

Abandoning attachments and moving away from entanglements in worldliness is a concrete way of implementing what Dōgen considers the most important of the goals, the only one that allows access to enlightenment: abandoning one's body and mind or *shinjin datsuraku*. Only by committing relentlessly to dropping all involvements can one's self also be dropped. Abandoning attachments in every situation, both religious and mundane does not mean or require dropping all things one is involved in, but to behave unselfishly, or *muga* 無我.

The emphasis on respecting monastic precepts and rules, and to behave virtuously, is meant to both teach the importance of dropping one's self and foster the manifestation of *satori* (and of our original nature, which is Buddha-nature). Just as the practice of *zazen* (and any other kind of practice) is the way to manifest one's pristine Buddha-nature, in the same way, in everyday life, one must manifest a behavior of perfection. This is also the meaning of "oneness of practice and enlightenment" since practice is the purest manifestation of the enlightened reality.

Dōgen says:

> To make sure that daily practice and the Way are in harmony, how should one behave in everyday life? By having a mind that does not grasp and reject, a mind free from fame and profit. Do not practice thinking that it will benefit anyone.[15]

Igi in its most genuine and authentic meaning, means to act with purity, having dropped all the contamination that comes from attachments to worldly things. Therefore, *igi*, purity, strict morality, correct behaviour, and non-attachment are different ways of expressing the inner state of the seeker and practitioner of the Way.

Non-contamination is the behaviour of Buddha and patriarchs, "Non-contamination is 'this mind is itself the Buddha.' All the Buddhas are all the Buddhas of non-contamination."[16] Therefore, Dōgen says to practitioners, "Keeping the precepts, and pure conduct, are the standard of the Zen school and the usual behaviour of Buddhist patriarchs."[17]

An interesting indication of what Dōgen meant by "pure conduct" comes from the chapter "Senmen." The passage is related to physical purity that, however, includes and extends also to inner purity.

> Washing and cleaning one's body and mind, perfuming oneself and *removing all impurities is the priority of the Buddha-Dharma*. Wearing new, clean clothes is a way to cleanse yourself. By washing and purifying ourselves, removing impurities and applying perfumed oil

[15] *Gakudō yōjinshū*, https://dl.ndl.go.jp/info:ndljp/pid/1103265/2?tocOpened=1, pp. 5–6.
[16] Chapter "Sokushin zebustu." Etō Sokuō, *op.cit.*, vol. 1, p. 105.
[17] Chapter "Bendowa." Etō Sokuō, *op.cit.*, vol. 1, p. 70.

to the body, we become completely pure inside and outside. When the inside and outside are completely pure, the world outside us and ourselves are also pure.[18]

Purity of the body means purity of action and of intentions: if we act with pure intent, our *kokoro*[19] will also be pure. A correct behaviour makes the *kokoro* correct: *kokoro wo tadasu* 心を正す.

And (in the same chapter):

> Words of the Buddha: wash three times and perfume yourself three times. Cleanse the body and mind. In this way, the method to purify the body and purify the mind is definitely to take a bath once and perfume once …[20]
>
> …
>
> Although the Three poisons and the Four erroneous conceptions are not cast out, *the fact that the merits of purity present themselves to us immediately is the Buddha-Dharma.*[21]

Purity consists in abandoning all attachment, all worldliness and above all oneself, "Students of the Way, you must be very careful in abandoning worldly feelings. Leave the world, leave the family, leave the body, leave the mind."[22] Let go of all attachment to wealth and fame and to any advantage and throw your life into the arms of the Buddha-Dharma.

> Dropping your ego means throwing out your body-mind, and not practicing Buddha-Dharma for yourself. Just practice for the Way itself. If you throw your body-mind into the Buddha-Dharma, no matter how much suffering and frustration there is, you will practice following the Buddha-Dharma.[23]

But why is strict moral lifestyle important for Dōgen in order to reach enlightenment?

We find an answer in a sentence of *Zuimonki*, "… people who learn the Way: respecting the precepts and keeping yourselves pure and chaste, adopting the way of life of the Buddha and the Patriarchs and *regulating the body, the heart-mind will also follow*, regulating itself."[24] And, "Applying to learning the Way consists in the (intention to) abandon the original attachment; by improving the attitudes and *behaviours of the body, the mind will change accordingly. First, if we behave correctly by following the precepts, the mind will improve as a result.*"[25]

Dōgen does not think that enlightenment is an achievement and that the hardness of practice and asceticism is rewarded by the acquisition of enlightenment; rather, he holds that the enlightenment that always accompanies us manifests itself when we become aware of our original and ever-present enlightenment. Therefore,

---

[18] Etō Sokuō, *op.cit.*, vol. 2, p. 295.

[19] The term *kokoro* means, in the Sino-Japanese culture, the non-physical part of a person, that is: heart and mind together. This means that thought, rational capacity, sentiments, emotions are all included in the meaning of *kokoro*.

[20] Ibid., 298.

[21] Ibid.

[22] Dōgen, *Shōbōgenzō Zuimonki*, 2–18, 151.

[23] Ibid., 6–10, 358.

[24] Ibid., 1–3, 14–15.

[25] Ibid., 1–5, 24.

asceticism is not true asceticism: its meaning is not that of enduring privations and suffering in view of the accumulation of merits. Rather, its meaning is becoming aware of the distortion caused by attachments: they are the real cause of suffering, and the liberation from their yoke, although initially hard, is instead a path of liberation and joy.

The irreproachable moral conduct, the respect for the precepts and rules that Dōgen asks to follow in an almost maniacal way are, in his vision, the realization of buddhahood, having dropped all attachments and made oneself available to a severe and strict way of life of sacrifices. The acceptance of self-renunciation is the manifestation of one's Buddha-nature: only then is the "oneness of practice and enlightenment" made concrete. The meaning of this must be understood correctly. In Dōgen's thought, we can schematize the concept of *shushō ichinyo* in the following way: in enlightenment, practice is one with enlightenment → *shushō ichinyo*; in illusion, practice and enlightenment are two different and consequential stages → *shu* and then *shō*. This is the meaning of the opening sentence of "Genjō kōan" in which is written:

> When all dharmas are Buddha-Dharma, then there are illusion and awakening, practice, birth, death, all Buddhas and ordinary people.
> When the multitude of phenomena is not based on the ego, then there is no illusion or awakening, there are no Buddhas or ordinary people, there is no birth or extinction.[26]

For those who have reached enlightenment (*When the multitude of phenomena is not based on the ego*), the dualisms that were present in those who, relying on Buddhist doctrine, are still in the illusory state, no longer make sense: practice and enlightenment also cease to be two.

Also, it is clear from the following statement, "It should be known that one must practice having obtained enlightenment."[27]

In enlightenment, not only does the practice/enlightenment dualism lose its meaning, but what's more, also another dualism related to practice and enlightenment, that of "cause and effect" also loses meaning. The cause-and-effect relationship called *inga* 因果, which is none other than the law of *karma*, is understood as the postponed retribution of both positive and negative voluntary acts. Therefore, it relates directly to action, that is practice, i.e., daily action and behavior. It is an "accumulation" of merits or demerits that will bear fruit in the near or distant future. Therefore, practice and also moral behavior can be classified together in the same category of "accumulation" of merits that lead to enlightenment.

Dōgen supports the validity of the law of cause-and-effect without hesitation in a very evident way in *Shōbōgenzō*, for example in the chapters "Shinjin inga" and "Sanjigō." In the latter he says in no uncertain terms, "To begin with, negation of cause and effect, is insulting Buddha, Dharma, and Sangha and to negate the three periods (of effect) and liberation is an unorthodox view."[28]

---

[26] Chapter "Genjō kōan." Etō Sokuō, *op.cit.*, vol. 1, p. 83.
[27] Chapter "Bendōwa." Etō Sokuō, *op.cit.*, vol. 1, pp. 66–67.
[28] Etō Sokuō, *op.cit.*, vol. 3, p. 136.

In this chapter, Dōgen also refers to the Chinese Buddhist tradition by citing the case of the monk-fox, the subject of the second case of the *Mumonkan* which deals with the incorrect interpretation of the law of karma. The importance of *karma* for Dōgen is very clear and beyond any doubt, "In learning the Buddha-Dharma, the first priority is to clarify cause and effect."[29]

Dōgen instead of negating the dualism of cause/effect of the karmic law, gives it a new interpretation relating it to practice, "We should practice in good and evil, and in cause-and-effect, *without moving cause-and-effect and without producing cause-and-effect. Cause-and-effect, at times, causes us to practice.*"[30]

That is, one must practice knowing that the law of *karma* is omnipresent; therefore, one must practice in the context of *karma*, be aware of it, but without moving it, or without activating it. This means practicing without having the intention of accumulating merits and not using practice in an instrumental manner. Practicing in the context of *karma* without producing karmic traces means acting in a pure way, in other words according to the conception of *shushō ichinyo*.

How can this happen? He explains it to us in *Zuimonki*[31] where he says:

> One day, Ejō asked the Master: "(Among the sayings of Hyakujō) there is the principle according to which (a great practitioner) 'does not allow himself to be trapped by karma'. On this, what do you say?"
> The Master replied, "*He does not move karma.*"
> Ejō: "How can he drop it?"
> The Master: "*Clearly (cause and effect) manifest themselves simultaneously* (一時見)."

This important passage says that to those who have achieved enlightenment cause and its effect are simultaneous, so the cause is not accumulation and the effect is not retribution. For this reason, the enlightened person is free, without constraints and his actions are not karmic actions. Only the saints and the enlightened are free from *karma* and from the cycle of rebirth. Cause and effect do exist, but the enlightened person does not move them and is, therefore, free of their influence.

Simultaneity of cause and effect means the absence of accumulation of merits or demerits as in the case of *shushō ichinyo* practice.

This means that:

1. Like cause and effect, practice and enlightenment are simultaneous;
2. Moral behavior and manifestation of Buddha-nature are simultaneous.

Simultaneity is: not one, not two, or not one but not different 不一不二、不一不異: practice and enlightenment are not one, but not two, or, not one but not different. In simultaneity, though living in the midst of *karma*, one is free of it. It is within the law of cause and effect that *shushō ichinyo* is realized, "Students of the way do not try to dismiss cause and effect. If you discard cause and effect, you will ultimately turn your back on practice/realization."[32]

---

[29] Chapter "Shinjin inga." Etō Sokuō, *op.cit.*, vol. 3, p. 206.

[30] Chapter "Shoaku makusa." Etō Sokuō, *op.cit.*, vol. 1, p. 149.

[31] Dōgen, *Shōbōgenzō Zuimonki*, 2–4, 75.

[32] Dōgen, *Eihei kōroku*, ed. Watanabe Kenshū, Sozanbon (1989), vol. 2, 141, case 510.

The realization of buddhas and patriarchs, as well as that of all beings, is neither conditioned nor conditionable. It is not the result of efforts to accumulate merits or due to conditional causes or produced by intrinsic causes. Enlightenment is therefore not due to anything, so it is not a product of *karma* either, it is *a priori*. In other words, although enlightenment falls within the scope of the law of cause and effect, it is not a product of it. Only by becoming fully aware of the karmic law can one avoid activating it and avoid its consequences. Dōgen says:

> If all existent, all sentient beings depended on the accumulation of good circumstances or on conditioned causes or finally were the product of intrinsic causes, then the realization of all the saints and the enlightenment of all the buddhas and also the eyes of the buddhas and patriarchs would be due to the force of the accumulation of [good] circumstances, or due to conditioned causes or produced by intrinsic causes, *but this is not the case*.[33]

The identity between practice and enlightenment, as well as the independence from cause and effect proposed by Dōgen means conceiving action in the situation of here and now, without attachments for future retribution and without conditioning of past causes. Acting freely and without placing oneself at the center. Let's not forget that *karma*, in the original meaning refers to actions driven by <u>intention</u>,[34] a deed done deliberately through body, speech or mind, which leads to future consequences; therefore, *karma* is activated only when "intention" is present and there is a will that is driven by our ego, otherwise is not activated.

> The bearing of fruit is entrusted to you, and it is said to happen naturally. "Happen naturally" means "because of the practice comes the result". The *cause is impersonal and the result is impersonal*. By practicing impersonal cause and effect, impersonal cause and effect is produced.[35]

And also, "Cause and effect are clear, but they are not a personal matter."[36]

Any ego-free action, as it starts, at the same time should end without leaving any residue: it is pure, uncontaminated action, the action of the saint, *impersonal* and devoid of selfishness. An absolute and unconditional action, an action done only to be that action and nothing else. The Buddhist practice and also Buddhist moral behavior must also be like this: without expectations, made only to be done, in the present moment here and now.

"In any case, without intention and without discrimination, there is non-contamination."[37]

Here, then, we understand Dōgen's insistence on moral conduct and can answer the question formulated above: "But why is strict moral lifestyle important for Dōgen in order to reach enlightenment?"

---

[33] Chapter "Busshō." Etō Sokuō, *op.cit.*, vol. 1, pp. 315–316.

[34] Sanscrit *cetanā*, Sino-Japanese: 思.

[35] Chapter "Kūge." Etō Sokuō, *op.cit.*, vol. 2, p. 165. Here I translate 公界 as "impersonal," in the sense that it does not involve one's self.

[36] Dōgen, *Eihei kōroku*, ed. Watanabe Kenshū, Sozanbon (1989), vol. 1, p. 105, case 94. Here I translate 非己物 as "not a personal matter."

[37] Chapter "Yuibutsu yobutsu." Etō Sokuō, *op.cit.*, vol. 3, p. 228.

To strive to stick to moral rules is precisely the way to act in accordance with the principles of *shushō ichinyo* and independently of cause and effect. In some forms of Buddhist teaching one can find an opposite point of view: acting without rules and spontaneously is seen as sticking to the here and now and act without producing *karma*. This attitude is sometimes found in Tang-era Chinese Chan texts, for example. However, Dōgen does not agree with this view, and the reason is obvious: how can the deluded mind of the common person produce a "pure action" (practice or else)? Only the mind of people who have achieved the spiritual perfection of enlightenment can do this. Or, only having dropped one's self, does the karmic "accumulation of merits" lose its meaning – to whom would the merits stick? – and action is no longer the producer of karmic traces since there is no more "intention." In this case, moral behavior is no longer a personal ascesis but the impersonal manifestation of one's buddha-nature, or better the manifestation of the Buddha-nature that we ARE.

To strive for practice means to strive to behave as a Buddha and actualize the *kokoro* of a Buddha: in doing so, one can in time manifest one's true nature, that is Buddha-nature. Body and external perfection eventually will turn in the inner perfection of the *kokoro*.

For this reason, Dōgen's Buddhism is a Way: a path of self-improvement in order to manifest the Buddha-nature in all aspects, both external and internal, both physical and mental and moral. The ideal is that of the *bodhisattva* and his way of being in the world. Only perfection is pure, but the path to this goal is arduous and full of sacrifices aimed at letting the self be forgotten.

Further Readings

Brear, A. D. "The Nature and Status of Moral Behavior in Zen Buddhist Tradition." *Philosophy East and West* 24, no. 4 (1974): 429–441.

Cozort, Daniel and James M. Shields, eds. *The Oxford Handbook of Buddhist Ethics*. Oxford: Oxford University Press, 2021.

Etō, Sokuō, ed. *Shōbōgenzō*, 3 vols. Tokyo: Iwanami shoten, 1961.

Fox, A. Douglas. "Zen and Ethics: Dōgen's Synthesis." *Philosophy East and West* 21, no. 1 (1971): 33–41.

Kim, Hee-jin *Eihei Dōgen: Mystical Realist*. Somerville: Wisdom Publications, 2004.

LaFleur, William. "Dōgen in the Academy." In *Dōgen Studies*, edited by William LaFleur, 1–20. Honolulu: University of Hawai'i Press, 1985.

Leggett, Trevor. *Zen and the Ways*. London: Routledge, 1978.

Leighton, Taigen Dan. *Visions of Awakening Space and Time: Dōgen and the Lotus Sutra*. Oxford: Oxford University Press, 2007.

Loori, J. Daido. *The Heart of Being: Moral and Ethical Teachings of Zen Buddhism*. Boston: Charles E. Tuttle Co., 1996.

Ludwig, M. Theodore. "The Way of Tea: A Religio-Aesthetic Mode of Life," *History of Religions* 14, no. 1 (1974): 28–50.

Poceski, Mario. *Ordinary Mind as the Way. The Hongzhou School and the Growth of Chan Buddhism*. Oxford: Oxford University Press, 2007.

Steineck, Raji. "'Religion' and the Concept of the Buddha Way: Semantics of the Religious in Dōgen." *Asiatische Studien / Études Asiatiques* 72, no. 1 (2018):177–206.
Tollini, Aldo. L'ideale della Via. Samurai, monaci e poeti nel Giappone medievale, Torino: Einaudi, 2017.
Whitehill, James. "Is There a Zen Ethic?" *The Eastern Buddhist* 20, no. 1 (1987): 9–33.

Bibliography

Dōgen. *Shōbōgenzō Zuimonki*. Edited by Mizuno Yaoko. Chōenji-bon 長円寺本 version. Chikuma shobō, 1992.
Dōgen, *Eihei kōroku*, ed. Watanabe Kenshū, Sozanbon (1989), volumes 1 and 2.
Matsuo Kenji, "Official monks and reclusive monks: focusing on the salvation of women," in *Bulletin of the School of Oriental and African Studies* 64, no. 3 (2001), 369.

Do Not Lose the Rice: Dōgen Through the Eyes of Contemporary Western Zen Women

Laura Specker Sullivan

1 Introduction[1]

In *Bow First, Ask Questions Later*, Gesshin Claire Greenwood, a Soto Zen nun from the United States who ordained in Japan, describes an interaction with a Japanese nun that a fellow Australian nun later summarizes with the phrase, "just do your work, concentrate on that and nothing more, enlightenment is a male fantasy."[2]

Greenwood uses this interaction as an opportunity to reflect on Buddhist practice through sifting rice, an activity that Dōgen focuses on in the *Tenzo Kyōkun*, often translated as *Instructions to the Cook*. In the kitchen, Greenwood is assigned to separate the edible rice from the small stones and rice hulls intermixed with it. Bored with the practice, Greenwood begins thinking about a koan in which a monk, Xuefeng, is removing sand from rice, just as she is. Yet because Greenwood is in her head, and not focused on separating stones and hulls from rice, she does not accurately distinguish rice from hulls, and breakfast the next morning is ruined. When she then must re-do the work of separating hulls from rice, she ignores the koan, and focuses on the practice. She writes,

[1] Acknowledgments: This paper benefitted from helpful feedback from George Wrisley and Christopher Gowans, as well as participation in Upaya Zen Center's first Online Spring Practice Period: Honoring Women of the Way, in April 2020 and the Writing the Buddhist Essay online course at Barre Center for Buddhist Studies in early 2021.
[2] Gesshin Claire Greenwood, *Bow First, Ask Questions Later: Ordination, Love, and Monastic Zen in Japan*. Somerville (MA: Wisdom Publications, 2018), 74.

L. Specker Sullivan (✉)
Fordham University, Bronx, NY, USA
e-mail: lspeckersullivan@fordham.edu

125

I just tried to actually take the hulls out of the white rice. This is also my experience of zazen practice. In the beginning I wanted some sort of enlightenment experience or under-standing of Buddha. I didn't understand how a sitting practice could literally be *just sitting*. I sat, and I tried and tried to get enlightened, and this got in the way of actually sitting.

She continues, "Maybe I don't get koans, but at the end of the day, actually cooking rice is more important than answering a koan about rice, because a koan about rice is answered in cooking rice well."[3]

This passage in Greenwood's memoir illuminates two insights about how Western Zen women have interpreted Dōgen's ideas within Buddhist practice.[4] The first is that for Dōgen, zazen is fundamentally an embodied practice that is distorted when it is over-intellectualized. The second is that over-intellectualization, if it is a "male fantasy," is a problem to which feminist theorists and Dōgen scholars alike might offer a solution. These two insights are interconnected, for if alignment of Dōgen with feminism can offer a solution to over-intellectualization, then it can facilitate a return to embodied practice. This is a thought with some history. Philosopher Ann Pirruccello has compared Simone Weil's somatic practice with that of Dōgen,[5] while philosopher Erin McCarthy has found resonance between the form of non-dualism in Dōgen's writing and that of modern Western feminist philosophers such as Luce Irigiray, building from her earlier work on Watusji Tetsuro.[6] Similarly, Philosopher Ashby Butnor has highlighted the similarities between Dōgen's empha-sis on embodied practice and contemporary care ethics.[7] These philosophers under-score the interpretation of Dōgen as an ally in the use of feminist thought to encourage practitioners of all genders to *just sift the rice* - just do the practice, without pursuing an idea of enlightenment.

In this chapter, I describe how contemporary Western Zen women and their allies have begun to reexamine Dōgen's texts as tools of personal and social transforma-tion in line with feminist thought. In particular, I highlight the relationships between

---

[3] Ibid., 75.

[4] While I focus on interpretations of Dogen by women in the United States and Europe, this is not to disregard work on Dogen by Japanese women, such as in Paula Arai, *Bringing Zen Home: The Healing Heart of Japanese Women's Rituals* (Honolulu, HI: The University of Hawaii Press, 2011) and Paula Arai, *Women Living Zen: Japanese Soto Buddhist Nuns* (New York, NY: Oxford, 2012), and as referenced in Michiko Yusa, "Dōgen and the Feminine Presence: Taking a Fresh Look into His Sermons and Other Writings," *Religions* 9, no. 232 (2018). Rather, my aim is to highlight the intersection of feminism as a Western phenomenon and Zen women practitioners' interpretations of Dogen.

[5] Ann Pirruccello, "Making the World My Body: Simone Weil and Somatic Practice," *Philosophy East and West* 52, no. 4 (2002).

[6] See Erin McCarthy, *Ethics Embodied: Rethinking Selfhood through Continental, Japanese, and Feminist Philosophies* (Lanham, Maryland: Lexington Books, 2010) and Erin McCarthy, "Embodying Change: Buddhism and Feminist Philosophy," In *Buddhist Philosophy: A Comparative Approach*, ed. Steven Emmanuel. (Hoboken: John Wiley & Sons, Inc., 2018).

[7] Ashby Butnor, "Dōgen, Feminism, and the Embodied Practice of Care," in *Asian and Feminist Philosophies in Dialogue*, ed. Jennifer McWeeny and Ashby Butnor (New York: Columbia University Press, 2014).

Dōgen's *Tenzo Kyōkun*, his lesser-known *Raihai Tokuzui,* domesticity, and gender egalitarianism. This underscores the practical nature of Dōgen's thought, in contrast to self-centered preoccupation with individual enlightenment or spiritual attainment. This analysis reveals a new and relatively unappreciated role for Dōgen: as the women's Zen Buddhist theorist.

2   The Philosopher and the Cook

Alongside Kyoto School philosophers Nishida Kitaro and Watsuji Tetsuro, Eihei Dōgen may be the third most-studied individual within Japanese philosophy, at least as it is taught in the Western world. The reasons for the primacy of the Kyoto School are well-known, foremost of which is the fact that their engagement with Euro-American philosophers in the middle of the twentieth century brought Japanese philosophy to the world stage. Dōgen, on the other hand, writing six hundred years earlier, is studied in part due to his foundational role in Soto Zen in Japan, his rich yet enigmatic writing, and his influence on subsequent Japanese thinkers, including those in the Kyoto School. To study Dōgen as a philosopher is to acknowledge this influence and to validate the depth of his philosophical thought.[8]

Philosophical work on Dōgen largely focuses on the fascicles of the *Shobogenzo,* arguably his densest writing (historically, there is some variation in which fascicles count as the "*Shobogenzo*"). As a "deliberately systematic and rational exposition of his religious thought and experience" (according to one set of commentators) it is considered to be the heart of Dōgen's philosophical thought, his most important work and also his most voluminous, accounting for more than half of all the words he ever wrote.[9] This is not to say that the *Shobogenzo* is necessarily good for practice, at least for early practitioners. In Japan, a Zen priest conventionally refrains from teaching Dōgen until the age of 60, when their practice has matured.[10] The thought is that one ought to come to Dōgen with a bedrock of practice from which to draw; if this is the case, then the *Shobogenzo* may be the very worst place to start.

Nevertheless, in North America, philosophers often begin to study Dōgen by tackling the *Shobogenzo.* As a philosophical work, it allows for comparative studies

---

[8] See Thomas P. Kasulis, "The Zen Philosopher: A Review Article on Dōgen Scholarship in English," *Philosophy East and West* 28, no. 3 (1978).

[9] See Dōgen, *The Heart of Dōgen's Shobogenzo,* ed. and trans. Norman Waddell and Masao Abe (Albany, NY: State University of New York Press, 2002), xi-xii. It may come as a surprise that Waddell and Abe characterize the *Shobogenzo* as "deliberately systematic and rational." Arguably, this characterization depends on the point of comparison. Waddell and Abe's reference point is the literature of the Zen tradition, in the context of which Dogen's work certainly appears systematic and rational. This may not be the case if the reference point is changed to, e.g., Immanuel Kant.

[10] See Eido Frances Carney, ed. *Receiving the Marrow: Teachings on Dogen by Soto Zen Women Priests* (Olympia: Temple Ground Press, 2012), xi.

of, for example Dōgen and Heidegger,[11] Dōgen and Wittgenstein,[12] or Dōgen and Nietzsche.[13] In other words, the *Shobogenzo* is good material for *thinking* about Buddhism, and especially for the study of Buddhist metaphysics and epistemology. It contains ample material ripe for rumination and analysis.

The priority of the *Shobogenzo* in a philosophical context betrays a certain view of philosophy: philosophy as ideal or at the very least abstract thought, disengaged from practical experience and real life. This is the heritage of Western philosophy after Immanuel Kant: philosophy as the exercise of pure reason, of thinking purified of circumstance so as to permit logical analysis. Such a view of philosophy has been critiqued by a multitude of thinkers, of all genders and cultural backgrounds, who see philosophy not as abstract theorizing but as reflective practice.

One such critic is Annette Baier. In "Hume: The Women's Moral Theorist?" she argues that Humean ethics aligns with care ethics, in its thesis that "morality depends upon self-corrected sentiments, or passions, as much or more than it depends upon the reason that concurs with and serves those passions."[14] In contrast to Immanuel Kant, David Hume does not understand morality as conformity to general rules, and he emphasizes the interpersonal nature of the sentiments and the role of the family (biological and chosen) in moral development.

While the care ethicists to whom Baier refers have been criticized in recent years for a gender essentialist approach to moral thought, the crux of her argument need not rely on such points. Her thesis is that Kantian moral philosophy is just one type of philosophical thinking, which happens to be associated in the West with masculine character traits. Other types of philosophical thinking are equally rigorous and insightful, and Baier argues, may be even more practically useful. In another work, she proposes that moral reflection is a matter of "turning natural responses, not just on their natural target, but on responses, turning self-interest on the workings of self-interest, turning sentiments on sentiments"[15] not the "articulation of a system of moral laws vaguely anchored to intuitions."[16] In other words, Hume is the "women's moral theorist" because he focuses on the correction of the sentiments, which only happens through activity, not through detached thought, the latter of which has historically been the purview of men.

---

[11] See Joan Stambaugh, *Impermanence is Buddha-Nature: Dōgen's Understanding of Temporality* (Honolulu, HI: University of Hawaii Press, 1990).

[12] See Laura Specker Sullivan, "Dōgen and Wittgenstein: Transcending Language Through Ethical Practice," *Asian Philosophy* 23, no. 3 (2013).

[13] See George Wrisley, "The Nietzschean Bodhisattva—Passionately Navigating Indeterminacy," in *The Significance of Indeterminacy: Perspectives from Asian and Continental Philosophy*, Routledge Studies in Contemporary Philosophy, ed. Robert H. Scott and Gregory Moss (New York: Routledge, 2019).

[14] See Annette Baier, "Hume: The Women's Moral Theorist?" in *Women and Moral Theory*, ed. Eva Feder Kittay and Diana T. Meyers (Rowman and Littlefield, 1987), 45.

[15] See Annette Baier "Moral Theory and Reflective Practice," in *Postures of the Mind* (Minneapolis, MN: University of Minnesota Press, 1985), 225.

[16] Ibid., 223.

As with the philosophical focus on Kant to the exclusion of Hume, the focus on the *Shobogenzo* to the exclusion of Dōgen's other, more "practical" writings, betrays a bias in favor of abstract philosophical analysis, a form of thinking which is more concerned with the logical structure of conceptual space than with the relationship between being-time and doing the dishes. Yet from both a Buddhist practitioner and feminist perspective, such linkages are crucial and are central to Dōgen's philosophical project.

As it happens, among Zen Buddhist practitioners as compared with philosophers, the *Shobogenzo* is overshadowed by a different work: the *Tenzo Kyōkun*, or "Instructions to the Cook," initially translated into English by Thomas Wright and published alongside commentary by Kosho Uchiyama Roshi in 1983.[17]

If I had only learned of Dōgen through philosophy courses, I never would have heard of his *Tenzo Kyōkun*, despite the fact that it is written in a (slightly) more accessible style than the fascicles of the *Shobogenzo*. Buddhist practitioners, unsurprisingly, find great value in the *Tenzo Kyōkun* - especially American practitioners, ever practical and utilitarian. Bernie Glassman, founder of the Zen Peacemakers, a group dedicated to socially-engaged Buddhism, riffs off the *Tenzo Kyōkun* in his own *Instructions to the Cook*.[18] He attempts an explanation of the importance of the *Tenzo Kyōkun's* practical orientation in the prologue:

> As the Zen saying goes - 'you can't eat painted cakes.' This is true, as far as it goes, but like most truths, it is really only a half or perhaps three-quarter truth. Dōgen went deeper when he wrote in his greatest work the *Shobogenzo*, that 'painted cakes are real, too.' Maps, recipes, and instruction manuals are made up of real words and images that convey real information about our lives and the world we live in. A map can help us get from here to there; a recipe can help us bake a delicious loaf of bread; and words that come from experience and the heart can help us to live more fully and completely.[19]

The *Tenzo Kyōkun* is a metaphor, to a certain extent. As in the title of Kosho Uchiyama Roshi's commentary, it tells the reader "How to Cook Your Life." Glassman refers to personal development as a "supreme meal," requiring a menu, a clean kitchen to cook in, a set of ingredients, and people for whom to cook. Yet Glassman reminds us that the *Tenzo Kyōkun* is also a text about *how to cook*, quite literally. As Greenwood observes, a koan about rice might best be answered by cooking rice well.

In Kosho Uchiyama Roshi's commentary on the *Tenzo Kyōkun*, he relates a story about a university professor who came to visit his Zen monastery in Japan. This

---

[17] See Kōshō Uchiyama, *How to Cook Your Life: From the Zen Kitchen to Enlightenment: Dōgen's classic Instructions for the Zen Cook with commentary by Kōshō Uchiyama Rōshi*, trans. Thomas Wright (Boston: Shambhala, 2005). I am leaving out the *Eihei Koroku*, Dōgen's later work following the *Shobogenzo*, and the *Zuimonki*, another of Dōgen's more practical works, because they are overshadowed by the influence of the *Shobogenzo* among theorists and the *Tenzo Kyōkun* among lay practitioners.

[18] See Bernie Glassman and Rick Fields, *Instructions to the Cook: A Zen Master's Lessons in Living a Life That Matters* (Boulder, CO: Shambhala, 1996).

[19] Ibid., 10.

professor, he says, "refused to work alongside everyone else and when everyone was working in the garden or chopping wood he would be off reading a book somewhere. He claimed he was not any good at physical labor and said reading would be his work."[20] Uchiyama Roshi will have none of this - reading is not work, as growing an eggplant is work. The professor relents and chooses to do "the easiest task he could find," sweeping leaves into a pile to burn. When he lights the pile aflame, Uchiyama Roshi notices that the pile is underneath the camellia hedge and is scorching the flowers, and so must be put out and moved. "How can you assign work to a person like this?!" He asks. "Here was a fellow who, while the fire was burning right under his nose, could not even see where the heat and smoke were going."[21]

This passage reinforces the dichotomy I have been building in this section: between intellectual approaches to Dōgen on the one hand, and practical uses of his work, on the other. This tension can be seen in how Dōgen is studied by Western philosophers: through the abstract and inscrutable writing of the *Shobogenzo*, and how he is studied by Western Buddhist practitioners: through the practically oriented *Tenzo Kyōkun*. This dichotomy is just, of course, an interpretive lens: while my aim is to highlight certain features of the theory/practice distinction in interpretations of Dogen, this is not to undermine the relationship between theory and practice in Dogen's work or in legitimate appropriations of it by philosophers and practitioners alike.

In the next section, I introduce the *Tenzo Kyōkun* and explain how feminist reconstructions of Buddhism, and Dōgen in particular, can help to make sense of this interpretive divide, and I explore how they might begin to undermine it.

3 Dōgen and Domestic Life: The *Tenzo Kyōkun*

Philosophers might propose that, if practitioners are drawn to Dōgen's more practical writings such as the *Tenzo Kyōkun*, that is precisely because they are practitioners, and not theorists. Philosophers, they might offer, are primarily interested in conceptual understanding, not practical understanding. Yet as Annette Baier reminds us, this is only one view of what philosophy is and can be. Philosophizing need not be concerned only with conceptual reasoning purified of the residue of everyday life; it can examine the interface between our daily life and the concepts we use to describe and make sense of it. As Uchiyama Roshi understands Dōgen:

> The wonderful point about Dōgen Zenji's practice of zazen is that it is religion which must function concretely in one's daily life. He taught through the office of the tenzo [the cook], which he felt to be indispensable in a Buddhist community and which requires physical work, because he felt that zazen as religion must never be relegated only to those seeking to indulge in some rapturous state of mind.[22]

[20] See Uchiyama, *How to Cook your Life*, 52.
[21] Ibid.
[22] Ibid., 53.

It turns out that the care with which Dōgen approaches daily life in the *Tenzo Kyōkun* coheres with recent feminist interpretations of Buddhist thought. As Rita Gross notes about Buddhism more generally, "Both Buddhism and feminism begin with experience, stress experiential understanding enormously, and move from experience to theory, which becomes the expression of experience. Both share the approach that conventional views and dogmas are worthless if experience does not actually bear out theory."[23]

For Dōgen in particular, experiential activity is so central to Buddhism that practice *just is* enlightenment. Part of the revolution of Dōgen's thought was the idea that zazen is not a means to an end but is an expression of that end.[24] When practitioners meditate they aim to realize the truth of their enlightenment (or realization), not to attain it. To think about enlightenment in the hopes that, by knowing it intellectually one will attain it, is to misunderstand Dōgen's project.[25] From a certain philosophical perspective, it is an understandable mistake to make. But it is a mistake, nonetheless.

In her feminist reconstruction of Buddhism, Gross observes that "In Zen Buddhism, daily physical work has become a critical part of meditation training. Cooking, cleaning, gardening, building, and maintaining the monastery, are all done with precise mindfulness and are regarded as central to overall training... Monastics by no means spend all their time in study and meditation... In short, they engage in all sorts of mundane, everyday activities."[26] Domestic activities are central to monastic life - one cannot meditate all day. While cooking is a metaphor, it is also something that must be done and can be practiced mindfully or mindlessly.

Gross continues to explain that "The feminist reconceptualization calls for seeing 'ordinary' activities as sacred. This call is an important challenge to the conventional religions, especially to those, including Buddhism, that have a long tradition of seeing spiritual discipline as otherworldly and anti-worldly, as promoting freedom from the world. The feminist call is for nothing less than finding freedom within the world, within domestic concerns, within emotions, within sexuality, within parenthood, within career."[27] This argument lines up with feminist reconstructions of Dōgen which stress the centrality of embodiment to the Zen project, as in Ashby Butnor's analysis of Dōgen by way of Shigenori Nagatomo.[28] Butnor reminds us that "Dōgen is known for his advocacy of a nonrealistic achievement of bodymind and the 'oneness of practice-enlightenment' (*shusho ichinyo*). Given our

---

[23] See Rita Gross, *Buddhism After Patriarchy: A Feminist History, Analysis, and Reconstruction of Buddhism*, (Albany, NY: State University of New York Press, 1993), 130.

[24] See David Loy, "The Path of No-Path: Sankara and Dogen on the Paradox of Practice," *Philosophy East and West* 38, no. 2 (1988).

[25] This is not to say Dogen eschews thinking or writing about enlightenment completely: otherwise his prolific authorial output would be quite perplexing.

[26] See Gross, *Buddhism After Patriarchy*, 277.

[27] Ibid., 278.

[28] See Butnor, "Dōgen, Feminism, and the Embodied Practice of Care" and Shigenori Nagatomo, *Attunement Through the Body* (Albany, NY: State University of New York Press, 1992).

tendencies to 'live in our heads' and associate our senses of self with our ideas and beliefs, we often become disassociated from our bodies and the knowledge and habits that reside there... The trick, then, is to bring together, or 'harmonize,' body-and-mind."[29]

A central facet of contemporary feminist philosophical thought is the proposition that certain philosophical values, primary of which is theoretical detachment, privilege those in a position to theorize from an armchair, so to speak. It is more difficult for women to occupy this position, due both to social structures in which women are expected to be responsible for certain domestic tasks (cooking, cleaning, etc.) and due to unique features of female embodiment, in which female bodies carry, give birth to, and nurse new human life.[30]

Greenwood touches on this point, noting that in Japan, Zen nuns could not own temples and often either turned to crafts such as *chado* (tea ceremony) or *ikebana* (flower arrangement) to make a living, or they supported the practice of male monastics through cooking, cleaning, and organizing schedules.[31] Greenwood references Paula Arai's work, noting that "gratitude and full engagement with life become the main practice, instead of seeking an explicit kind of enlightenment on the cushion or a drastic overhaul of society."[32] Women's exclusion from the loftier realms of Buddhist practice led to their focus on the embodied practices they could control: cooking, cleaning, and so forth. This is not to say that domestic work is essentially feminine, just that in a patriarchal social structure men maintain positions of power and autonomous choice, while women are relegated to the supporting roles for those powerful positions. How many Zen men uncritically rely on the women in their lives for domestic support and emotional succor? I wonder.

If maintaining a dichotomy between detached monastic practice and domestic practice is a form of conditioned socialization, then there should be no reason, from a Buddhist perspective, why domestic practice does not fall under the umbrella of Buddhist practice.[33] Indeed, Zen Buddhism has historically paid special attention to the tasks of cooking, cleaning, and gardening (perhaps as compared with forms of Buddhism in other cultural contexts, where these tasks are not completed by monastics but are delegated to volunteers or paid staff). The elevation of domestic activity as a form of practice in Zen Buddhism is clearly seen in Dōgen's *Tenzo Kyōkun.*

Yet one need not engage in domestic activity in a monastic context for it to qualify as Zen practice. Michiko Yusa translates Dōgen in the *Shobogenzo Zuimonki* as making the point that, "Such a distinction as the one who renounces the world

[29] Ibid., 232.

[30] McCarthy, "Embodying Change."

[31] Arai, *Bringing Zen Home,* and Arai, *Women Living Zen.*

[32] Greenwood, *Bow First, Ask Questions Later,* 75.

[33] Paula Arai, "Soto Women's Zen Wisdom in Practice," in *The Theory and Practice of Zen Buddhism: A Festschrift in Honor of Steven Heine,* ed. Charles S. Prebish and On-Cho Ng (Singapore: Springer Nature, 2022).

and the one who remains at home is ultimately provisional."[34] Earlier in the passage, he writes:

> … it is not the Buddhist practice that chooses the person who will attain awakening, but rather it is the person who chooses whether or not to embrace the Buddhist path. The determination and motivation of those who take up religious life should be different from those who remain at home. Among those who remain at home, should there be a person who aspires to renounce the world, then, let her leave home. On the other hand, if the one who renounced the world still retains the mental attitude of someone who practices at home, then, such a person is committing double error. The very resolution to renounce the world should be something special.[35]

Dōgen seems to suggest that practice need not be zazen but can begin anywhere one is - with whatever type of life one chooses. If one feels called to be a Buddhist monastic, then one ought to do that wholeheartedly. The key is not the type of activity one is engaged in, but one's relationship with it - whether one is able to "just" do it, to embody the practice, while dropping body and mind. Dōgen thus gives considerable scope to individuals' agency in determining the appropriate path for themselves.

This is born out in Teijo Munnich's commentary on *Bendowa*, "Dancing the Dharma," where she describes her realization that being completely absorbed in the activity of dancing was an instance of *jijuyu zanmai*, or self-fulfillment, a form of "playing freely in Samadhi." She writes, "Samadhi is the kind of concentration in which you absolutely merge; there is no distinction between you and what you are doing."[36] Munnich underscores that dancing can be zazen, just as Greenwood found zazen in the sorting of rice.

In this section I have proposed that, paradoxically, it is the fact that women have often been confined to social roles that prevent their separation from the minutiae of everyday life that allows them to embody Dōgen's dictum to "forget the self and be actualized by myriad things." If one must begin where one is, without intellectualizing enlightenment or misconceiving reading as work, then the types of activities to which women have been relegated may be the most authentic Buddhist practice for non-monastics.

4   Dōgen and Gender Egalitarianism: The *Raihai Tokuzui*

Thus far, I have argued that practice is central to Dōgen's Zen Buddhist project, and that domestic activity is a notable yet philosophically underappreciated example of Zen practice. In this section, I will highlight resources in feminist thought for

---

[34] Yusa, "Dōgen and the Feminine Presence," 10.

[35] Ibid.

[36] See Teijo Munnich, "Dancing the Dharma: *Bendowa*," in *Receiving the Marrow: Teachings on Dogen by Soto Zen Women Priests*, ed. Eido Frances Carney (Olympia: Temple Ground Press, 2012), 7.

upholding the value of everyday practice in the face of tendencies towards detachment and abstraction found in philosophical analyses of Dōgen's work. I will show
how contemporary Western Zen Buddhist women have begun reappropriating
Dōgen's work in a uniquely American, but no less authentic, feminist Zen project.

That the project of valorizing Dōgen's gender egalitarianism has been carried out
by women perhaps comes as no surprise. Yet it is striking that, of numerous English-
language anthologies of Dōgen's work, including biographies, few highlight
Dōgen's gender egalitarianism or note the gender boundaries that existed at Dōgen's
time (or continue within Soto Zen Buddhism today), other than the work cited in
this chapter by Western Zen Women. This is despite a number of works that locate
Dōgen within other social and historical forces of his time. The fact that Dōgen was
a man writing within patriarchal social and institutional structures does not seem as
relevant to many authors as his economic class, family relations, or political associations. Yet surely, in a society that stratifies opportunity and choice by gender, the
fact that Dōgen is a male advocate of gender egalitarianism is relevant to his work.

Recently, Western Zen Buddhist women have begun to reevaluate Dōgen from a
feminist perspective. One of the most interesting "discoveries" is the *Raihai Tokuzui*,
translated by Kazuaki Tanahashi as "Receiving the Marrow by Bowing." In this
fascicle, written during Dōgen's Kosho monastery period from 1233–1243, Dōgen
advances a series of arguments for why women ought to be recognized as Buddhist
teachers and allowed to train as Buddhist nuns. Tanahashi's English translation was
published in 2010, and it is only in the past decade that English-speaking scholars
have realized the import of this particular fascicle.

In Grace Jill Schireson's commentary on *Raihai Tokuzui*, she explains the revo-
lutionary nature of Dōgen's argument in favor of women Zen teachers. She quotes
a passage in which Dōgen is unequivocal and direct:

> Why are men special? Emptiness is emptiness. Four great elements are four great elements.
> Five skandhas are five skandhas. Women are just like that. Both men and women attain the
> way. You should honor attainment of the way. Do not discriminate between men and
> women. This is the most wondrous principle of the buddha way.[37]

Schireson reads Dōgen as making eight arguments in favor of gender equality in
Zen practice. They are both theoretical and practical: (1) If all beings are buddha
nature, then the idea that women cannot be realized beings is a conventional attitude, (2) It can be very hard to find a realized Zen teacher; excluding women only
makes this harder, (3) Refusing to bow to a woman teacher is an exercise of ego,
which impedes realization, (4) Women Zen teachers do exist, and students have
been realized through them in China (this argument would have been influential in
early Japanese Zen, as it was based in the Chinese model), (5) Students who can be
realized by teachers despite social status and caste are especially humble, (6)
Women teachers is the way of Zen ancestors, (7) Zen practice requires dropping
both personal stereotypes and biases *and* cultural and social delusions, including the

---

[37] Dōgen, "Receiving the Marrow by Bowing," in *Treasury* of the *True Dharma Eye: Zen Master
Dogen's Shobo Genzo*, ed. by Kazuaki Tanahashi (Boston: Shambhala Publications, Inc., 2010), 77.

idea that gender relates to one's inner nature, and (8) There are numerous examples of Buddhist monks and sutras being distorted by negative cultural attitudes towards women, including the banning of women from sacred Buddhist sites in Japan such as Mt. Koya, Todaiji, and Mt. Hiei.

Schireson's commentary is part of *Receiving the Marrow: Teachings on Dōgen by Soto Zen Women Priests*, a collection of essays by eleven American Soto Zen women teachers. They draw inspiration from the fact that Dōgen himself advanced such clear and forceful arguments in favor of gender egalitarianism. Editor Eido Frances Carney describes Dōgen as a social reformer based on his more "enlightened" attitude towards women, inviting women students into his sangha and advocating for more egalitarian views of gender.[38]

In another passage of the *Raihai Tokuzui*, Dōgen writes:

Foolish people who have not heard buddha dharma call themselves great monks and would not bow to younger ones who have attained dharma. Those who have matured practice over a long period of time would not bow to latecomers who have attained dharma. Those who have certificates as masters would not bow to others who have not been certified. Those who are in charge of dharma matters would not bow to other monks who have attained dharma. Those who are bishops would not bow to laymen and laywomen who have attained dharma. Bodhisattvas of three classes and ten stages would not bow to nuns who have attained dharma. Those who are imperial descendants would not bow to retainers who have attained dharma. Such foolish people have neither seen nor heard the buddha way, just like the one who groundlessly left parents and wandered in another land.[39]

This passage highlights that Dōgen was remarkably attentive to the role of stereotype and bias in impeding Buddhist practice. Indeed, Dōgen is not just an ally in using feminism to enrich Buddhist practice by acknowledging the significance of domestic activity, but in bringing Buddhist practice in line with broader social equality.

Nevertheless, even now, Soto Zen temples in Japan maintain strict gender boundaries. Sally Tisdale, an American Zen teacher, nurse, and writer, describes a visit to *Eiheiji*, Dōgen's own temple, where she was told that women could not practice because they had not had time to build women's bathrooms in the eight-hundred-year history of the temple.[40] I visited Eiheiji in 2012 - somehow it seems fitting that the only souvenir I have is a pair of chopsticks. Luckily, I was able to use a bathroom.

Grace Schireson relates an experience similar to Tisdale's at the opening of her book *Zen Women: Beyond Tea Ladies, Iron Maidens, and Macho Masters*:

When a male teacher returned from an early North American conference of Zen teachers, one of his female students asked him, 'how many women teachers were included in this conference?' The male teacher answered, 'we were all women.' A long, confused silence followed... Do we as women not get it, or does this male teacher not get it? Fifteen years ago the women present looked uncomfortably at one another, perplexed at our bind, but

[38] Carney, *Receiving the Marrow*, xi.
[39] Dōgen, "Receiving the Marrow by Bowing," 74.
[40] Sallie Tisdale, *Women of the Way: Discovering 2500 Years of Buddhist Wisdom* (New York, NY: HarperCollins, 2006), 3.

didn't challenge his answer. Today I would cut through the confusion by asking him politely, 'how many of you women teachers used the ladies' room at this Zen conference?'[41]

Who uses which bathroom (as well as where that bathroom is, and in what condition it is kept) may seem to be a minor concern for those who can take it for granted, but it is an important marker of equality for those who have been socially marginalized.

In the *Raihai Tokuzui*, Dōgen argues that exclusion of women from the roles of students, monastics, and teachers is counter to Buddhist teaching. Essentially, gender discrimination is a conventional attitude, just like any other. A patriarchal structure, or at the very least one which separates out roles and possibilities for men and women practitioners, is not essential to Buddhism. In recognizing this, Dōgen is not just an ally in using feminist thought to bolster the Buddhist commitment to practice, but in using feminism to encourage Buddhism "be true to its own vision."[42] This means that, as Dōgen recognizes, working towards gender equality is a form of Buddhist practice, by working to see through concepts that buttress gender discrimination.

A number of scholars have gestured towards the "modern implications" and applications of Dōgen's Zen thought.[43] Yet arguably, gender egalitarianism is central to Dōgen's thought. If the core of Zen practice is learning to just sit free of conceptual intrusion, then acknowledging and dropping off negative stereotypes, be they gender, race, ethnicity, sexuality, and so on is central to Dōgen's project. Tackling a concrete issue like gender discrimination is not an *application* of Dōgen's work - it is inherent in it. It prevents the over-intellectualization of Zen by rooting practice in a delusion that many people struggle with on a day-to-day basis.

While it may seem more advanced to focus on the abstract themes in Dōgen's work such as being-time or buddha-nature, this is part of a culture of detachment with which Dōgen's work has been viewed, a culture fueled largely by contemporary academic philosophical norms but also by patriarchal structures that exist in Zen Buddhist institutions today. Reading Dōgen through the lens of Western Zen Buddhist women and their allies shows how contemporary practitioners of Zen are appropriating the elements of social transformation latent in his work.

This is quite clear in Bernie Glassman's *Instructions to the Cook: A Zen Master's Lessons in Living a Life that Matters*. Glassman, the founder of the Zen Peacemakers Order, proposes that there are five courses in the "supreme meal" that makes up a Buddhist life. The first three courses are oriented around the individual: spirituality, study, and livelihood. Practitioners must establish a firm foundation for themselves before they can begin to help others. The latter two courses are other-oriented: social action and community. While people focus on different courses at different stages of their life, ideally they come together in the last course, which is

---

[41] Grace Schireson, *Zen Women: Beyond Tea Ladies, Iron Maidens, and Macho Masters* (Boston, MA: Wisdom Publications, 2009), xii.

[42] Gross, *Buddhism After Patriarchy*, 153.

[43] Steven Heine, *Dōgen: Japan's Original Zen Teacher* (Boulder, CO: Shambhala, 2021), 271.

community, "the course that turns all the other courses - spirituality, livelihood, social action, and study - into a joyous feast."[44]

Glassman and others would argue that attention to gender discrimination - as well as discrimination on the basis of race, class, and so on - is a central aspect of Buddhist practice, not a particular application of it. Just as the university professor who visited Uchiyama Roshi's temple was unable to move beyond his self-centered focus on his own study, so Zen Buddhism urges practitioners and scholars alike to recognize the interconnection of theoretical understanding and practical action, especially as one moved through life's stages.

5   Dōgen: The Women's Zen Buddhist Theorist?

In the previous section, examination of the *Raihai Tokuzui* revealed Dōgen to be a theorist who not only had a keen sense of gender egalitarianism in practice, but who advanced theoretical and practical arguments in defense of the practice. This reading recalls Annette Baier's reading of David Hume as "the women's moral theorist," due to the resonance between his understanding of morality as a "correction of the sentiments through actual activity" and early work in feminist care ethics, such as that of Carol Gilligan.[45] While neither Dōgen's thought nor Hume's is essentially feminine, they accord with a set of virtues and values that have been conceptualized as feminine, and thus subordinate, to other virtues and values.

Acknowledging Dōgen's alignment with gender egalitarianism renders him as a special sort of thinker - one who is able to clearly see the relationship between theory and commonplace social practices. While this places him in the company of Baier's reading of Hume, it contrasts him with philosophers such as Immanuel Kant, whose work contains resources for a practical egalitarianism yet who was unable to think outside the social structures of his time.[46] Such a reading foregrounds the consonance or dissonance between a thinker's work and their way of life, and this type of reading remains controversial. Nevertheless, with Dōgen, it is striking that this type of analysis does not reveal dissonance between his abstract theory and his social understanding, but confluence - as well as the inherent resources in Buddhist thought for undermining discrimination based on gender, race, sexuality, class, and other forms of "conventional" thinking.

There is, however, a disconnect between Dōgen's thought and practice – a disconnect that existed for Hume, as well. Hume has been criticized for describing women as inferior to men in both bodily strength and intellect, such that Baier's contention that Hume was the "women's moral theorist" seems out of place. Likewise, Dōgen has been criticized for arguing in favor gender egalitarianism

[44] Glassman and Fields, *Instructions to the Cook*, 9.
[45] See Baier, "Hume," 37.
[46] Lucy Allais, "Kant's Racism." *Philosophical Papers* 45, no. 1–2 (2016).

while ultimately caving to patriarchal social pressures in restricting women's access to elements of Zen Buddhist training within Japan.[47] As Heine notes, Dōgen reinforced the traditional hierarchy of monks over nuns and monastics over non-monastics in his activities at Eiheiji.[48] Others have suggested that Dōgen changed his views about women later in his career, although Paula Arai argues convincingly that this is a misreading and that "the case for Dōgen reversing his views on women is not well-supported."[49]

If Dōgen did limit women's participation in Zen training in Japan, Carney suggests that Dōgen "may simply have chosen his battles,"[50] while Yusa argues that the fact that Dōgen had female students and disciples underscores his willingness to act outside of social convention. Baier's defense of Hume is also helpful here. She observes that Hume was a product of his time, such that his observation of women's inferiority states a social fact: women in Hume's society did have less power than men. Yet on Baier's reading, Hume did not essentialize this inferiority, but understood it to be a contingent social reality, not a necessary truth. Indeed, his work speculates on the possibilities for women should they avoid "servile dependence" on men and attain independence.[51]

As with Hume, Dōgen was also a product of his time, and Carney is likely right that Dōgen chose his battles. Yet the fact that his thinking ran up against social norms in practice need not negate his gender egalitarianism. Dōgen recognized the problems with gender discrimination, even if he could not change such practices wholesale. This is, again, in contrast to someone like Kant, whose intellectual achievements did not prevent him from embracing discriminatory views *and* practices.

6   Theory and Practice

It may be tempting to set up a dichotomous lens through which to view Dōgen. Either he is a religious practitioner or he is a philosopher. Either his words are studied as a form of scholarship, or as a form of practical inspiration. Feminist analysis of Dōgen helps to collapse this dichotomy.

Michiko Yusa highlights the following poem, which Dōgen wrote for a student:

'The mind is Buddha'—this is hard to practice but easy to preach.
  'It is no mind, no Buddha'—this is hard to preach but easy to practice.[52]

---

[47] Carney, *Receiving the Marrow*, xi and Yusa, "Dōgen and the Feminine Presence," 3.
[48] Heine, *Dōgen*, 25.
[49] Arai, "Soto Women's Zen Wisdom in Practice," 259.
[50] Carney, *Receiving the Marrow*, xi.
[51] See Baier, "Hume," 54.
[52] Yusa, "Dōgen and the Feminine Presence," 7.

Dōgen was uniquely sensitive to the dichotomy of words versus action. Analysis of Dōgen by Western Zen women highlights the resources in his form of Zen Buddhism for collapsing this dichotomy - in which language aids practice, and practice inspires linguistic expression.

I have posited that over-intellectualization of Dōgen's work misses the signifi-cance of daily, domestic life for his understanding of Zen practice. Further, I argued that Western feminist analyses of Dōgen undermine this intellectualization by focusing attention on his arguments in favor of gender egalitarianism. Is this a "re-appropriation" of Dōgen as a women's Buddhist theorist?

In one sense, yes. As contemporary Western Zen women have increasingly rec-ognized, Dōgen is a powerful ally in attempts to make Zen Buddhist institutions more equitable: he not only sees the world through a woman's lens when he valo-rizes practice in everyday life, but he argues directly for gender egalitarianism in Buddhist practice. As Michiko Yusa observes, "the picture of 'Dōgen the feminist' (if I may) emerges more convincingly, who stood by his original conviction of the equality of male and female in attaining awakening in the practice of zazen. The study also shows the fundamental importance of compassion that was at the heart of his practice. This nicely balances the image of Dōgen that tends to put stress on the philosophical and wisdom-oriented side."[53]

It likely comes as no surprise that these calls are coming from the Western world. As Sally Tisdale (optimistically) observes,

> Part of the American character is to push at boundaries. We are used to differences, and most Americans are fairly tolerant, I think. We are open enough as a culture to question our own cultural conditioning - not only about gender but about race, ethnicity, nation, age, class, and sexual orientation. It also happens that Buddhist practice requires us to question our assumptions - all the dear and deeply held beliefs by which we conduct our lives. One of the privileges of being an American Buddhist is the opportunity to speak openly about such things and try new things. American Buddhism can justly claim to have given women a far more equal share than that given in any other culture. We have to be careful not to think that talking about it means we are free from cultural conditioning.[54]

Tisdale cautions that this is not to say that Western Buddhists are more "enlight-ened," to use another meaning of the word. As Sebine Selassie has recently written, "An American Buddhist teacher, Joseph Goldstein, tells a story of his Indian teacher, Munindra-ji, who described his Western students as extremely diligent practitioners who were like people fiercely rowing boats, not realizing they were still tied to the dock."[55]

Western Buddhists have inherited their own cultural conventions - one of which is an alignment of patriarchal, colonialist values with elite scholarship. To return to Selassie: "In line with its elevation of rational intellectualism, the colonization

---

[53] Ibid., 20.

[54] Tisdale, *Women of the Way*, 14.

[55] Sebene Selassie, "Turning Toward Myself," in *Black and Buddhist: What Buddhism Can Teach Us About Race, Resilience, Transformation, and Freedom.*, ed. Pamela Ayo Yetunde and Cheryle Giles (Boulder, CO: Shambhala, 2020), 75.

project privileged written languages (associated with elite 'classes') over oral traditions. In South Asia, the project of translating ancient texts fed into the colonialist process of domination. Scholarly interpretations of texts produced Orientalist (often simplified) versions of what was in fact a complex interplay of lived practices."[56] While Western feminists work to simultaneously reinforce the relevance of Zen practice in everyday domestic life *and* to advocate for gender equity such that women are not confined to domestic work, it is crucial to remember that many of these texts grew out of a very different set of day-to-day experiences in Asian societies.

In the *Raihai Tokuzui*, Dōgen does not stop at gender egalitarianism, but is powerfully egalitarian in a broader sense. He writes, "In encountering teachers who expound unsurpassable enlightenment, do not consider their caste or facial appearance; do not dislike their shortcomings or judge their activities."[57] In the United States, while we have a come long way towards addressing gender discrimination, we still have a long way to go towards recognizing teachers as teachers, without regard to race, class, ability, and so on.

In another sense, it is not a re-appropriation to call Dōgen a "women's Buddhist theorist." Dōgen, as Michiko Yusa reminds us, "in his anti-denominationalist and a-sectarian stance, was adamantly opposed to calling the practice centered in zazen 'Zen school,' let alone calling his teaching 'Soto Zen'."[58] As I have emphasized throughout this chapter, social and institutional gender discrimination is an enshrinement of a deluded conventional attitude that Dōgen would have - and did - object to. If it benefits sentient beings to call Dōgen a feminist thinker, then so be it.

Finally, as Thomas Kasulis notes in the foreward to Erin McCarthy's *Ethics Embodied,* "Philosophy is, after all, the 'love of wisdom,' not knowledge. The knowledgeable person tells us something we did not know; the wise person reminds us of something important that we have forgotten, repressed, or ignored."[59]

Until recently, it seems that scholarship on Dōgen has, generously, "forgotten" the extent of Dōgen's gender egalitarianism and the significance he accorded to the work of daily life. It is easy to ignore these features of his thought in the context of philosophical scholarship that reveres abstraction and detachment. Yet as feminist theorists remind us, wisdom is often found in the particular and contingent nature of everyday life. Indeed, in their introduction to *Asian and Feminist Philosophies in Dialogue*, Ashby Butnor and Jennifer McWeeny propose that "we could characterize feminist comparative methodology in terms of the idea that philosophical insight and the personal, intellectual transformations that it entails occur when a philosopher: 1. Endeavors to acknowledge and embody, rather than ignore and transcend,

---

[56] Selassie, "Turning Toward Myself," 73–74.
[57] Dōgen, "Receiving the Marrow by Bowing," 73.
[58] Yusa, "Dōgen and the Feminine Presence," 2.
[59] See Kasulis in McCarthy, *Ethics Embodied*, xiv.

her own subjectivity and 2. Makes genuine, authentic contact with another philosophical perspective."[60] In this sense, Dōgen and contemporary Western feminist thought is a good match.

7 Conclusion

In this chapter, I have proposed that, by viewing Dōgen through the eyes of contemporary Western Zen women, Dōgen can be thought of as the "women's Buddhist theorist." I have described a gap between his reception by philosophy scholars in the United States, who focus on his more abstract writings such as the *Shobogenzo*, and contemporary American practitioners, who often refer to the *Tenzo Kyōkun*. I have posited that this gap reveals an under-explored role for domestic activity in Dōgen's philosophical project, one which is supported by feminist analysis and bolstered by Dōgen's own arguments in favor of gender egalitarianism in the *Raihai Tokuzui*. I have argued that, contrary to suggestions that Dōgen's philosophical project can be fruitfully *applied* to contemporary issues of discrimination and inequity, Dōgen himself makes such issues integral to his project and, in some sense, a test of the successful interpretation of his work. This reading of Dōgen underscores that the work of *jijiyu zammai* or *shikantaza* begins at home: with our relationships to family and friends, with how we maintain our space, and with our role in our community. This is especially relevant for practitioners who do not become monastics and remain in lay practice, and who have not made the intentional choice to leave home. As Dōgen himself notes, what matters is not the choice that one makes, but whether one wholeheartedly practices in line with it.

Bibliography

Allais, Lucy. "Kant's Racism." *Philosophical Papers* 45, no. 1–2 (2016): 1–36.
Arai, Paula. *Bringing Zen Home: The Healing Heart of Japanese Women's Rituals.* Honolulu, HI: The University of Hawaii Press, 2011.
———. *Women Living Zen: Japanese Soto Buddhist Nuns.* New York, NY: Oxford University Press, 2012.
———. "Soto Women's Zen Wisdom in Practice." In *The Theory and Practice of Zen Buddhism: A Festschrift in Honor of Steven Heine*, edited by Charles S. Prebish and On-Cho Ng, 255–274. Singapore: Springer Nature, 2022.
Baier, Annette. "Moral Theory and Reflective Practice." In *Postures of the Mind*. Minneapolis, MN: University of Minnesota Press, 1985.
———. "Hume: The Women's Moral Theorist?" In *Women and Moral Theory*. Edited by Eva Feder Kittay and Diana T. Meyers. Rowman and Littlefield, 1987.

---

[60] Ashby Butnor and Jennifer McWeeny, "Feminist Comparative Philosophy: Performing Philosophy Differently," in *Asian and Feminist Philosophies in Dialogue*, ed. Jennifer McWeeny and Ashby Butnor (New York: Columbia University Press, 2014), 12.

Butnor, Ashby. "Dōgen, Feminism, and the Embodied Practice of Care." In *Asian and Feminist Philosophies in Dialogue,* edited by Jennifer McWeeny and Ashby Butnor, 223–243. New York: Columbia University Press, 2014.

Butnor, Ashby and Jennifer McWeeny. "Feminist Comparative Philosophy: Performing Philosophy Differently." In *Asian and Feminist Philosophies in Dialogue,* edited by Jennifer McWeeny and Ashby Butnor, 1–33. New York: Columbia University Press, 2014.

Carney, Eido Frances, ed. *Receiving the Marrow: Teachings on Dogen by Soto Zen Women Priests.* Olympia: Temple Ground Press, 2012.

Dōgen. *The Heart of Dōgen's Shobogenzo.* Edited and translated by Norman Waddell and Masao Abe. Albany, NY: State University of New York Press, 2002.

———. "Receiving the Marrow by Bowing." In *Treasury* of the *True Dharma Eye: Zen Master Dogen's Shobo Genzo.* Edited by Kazuaki Tanahashi. Boston: Shambhala Publications, Inc., 2010.

———. *How to Cook Your Life: From the Zen Kitchen to Enlightenment.* Translated by Thomas Wright. Boston, MA: Shambhala, 1983.

Glassman, Bernie and Rick Fields. *Instructions to the Cook: A Zen Master's Lessons in Living a Life That Matters.* Boulder, CO: Shambhala, 1996.

Greenwood, Gesshin Claire. *Bow First, Ask Questions Later: Ordination, Love, and Monastic Zen in Japan.* Somerville, MA: Wisdom Publications, 2018.

Gross, Rita. *Buddhism After Patriarchy: A Feminist History, Analysis, and Reconstruction of Buddhism.* Albany, NY: State University of New York Press, 1993.

Heine, Steven. *Dōgen: Japan's Original Zen Teacher.* Boulder, CO: Shambhala, 2021.

Kasulis Thomas P. "The Zen Philosopher: A Review Article on Dōgen Scholarship in English." *Philosophy East and West* 28, no. 3 (1978): 353–373.

Loy, David. "The Path of No-Path: Sankara and Dogen on the Paradox of Practice." *Philosophy East and West* 38, no. 2 (1988): 127–146.

McCarthy, Erin. *Ethics Embodied: Rethinking Selfhood through Continental, Japanese, and Feminist Philosophies.* Lanham, Maryland: Lexington Books, 2010.

———. "Embodying Change: Buddhism and Feminist Philosophy." In *Buddhist Philosophy: A Comparative Approach.* S. Emmanuel, Ed. Wiley. 2017

McWeeny, Jennifer and Ashby Butnor, eds. *Asian and Feminist Philosophies in Dialogue: Liberating Traditions.* New York, NY: Columbia University Press, 2014.

Munnich, Teijo. "Dancing the Dharma: *Bendowa.*" In *Receiving the Marrow: Teachings on Dogen by Soto Zen Women Priests,* edited by Eido Frances Carney, 1–14. Olympia: Temple Ground Press, 2012.

Nagatomo, Shigenori. *Attunement Through the Body.* Albany, NY: State University of New York Press, 1992.

Pirruccello, Ann. "Making the World My Body: Simone Weil and Somatic Practice." *Philosophy East and West* 52, no. 4 (2002): 479–497.

Schireson, Grace. *Zen Women: Beyond Tea Ladies, Iron Maidens, and Macho Masters.* Boston, MA: Wisdom Publications, 2009.

Selassie, Sebene. "Turning Toward Myself," in *Black and Buddhist: What Buddhism Can Teach Us About Race, Resilience, Transformation, and Freedom,* ed. Pamela Ayo Yetunde and Cheryle Giles, 65–81. Boulder, CO: Shambhala, 2020.

Specker Sullivan, Laura. "Dogen and Wittgenstein: Transcending Language Through Ethical Practice." *Asian Philosophy* 23, no. 3 (2013): 221–235.

Stambaugh, Joan. *Impermanence is Buddha-Nature: Dōgen's Understanding of Temporality.* Honolulu, HI: University of Hawaii Press, 1990.

Tisdale, Sallie. *Women of the Way: Discovering 2,500 Years of Buddhist Wisdom.* New York, NY: HarperCollins, 2006.

Uchiyama, Kōshō. *How to Cook Your Life: From the Zen Kitchen to Enlightenment: Dōgen's classic Instructions for the Zen Cook with commentary by Kōshō Uchiyama Rōshi.* Translated by Thomas Wright. Boston: Shambhala, 2005.

Wrisley, George. "The Nietzschean Bodhisattva—Passionately Navigating Indeterminacy." In *The Significance of Indeterminacy: Perspectives from Asian and Continental Philosophy.* Routledge Studies in Contemporary Philosophy. Edited by Robert H. Scott and Gregory Moss, 309–329. New York: Routledge, 2019.

Yetunde, Pamela Ayo. and Cheryle Giles, eds. *Black and Buddhist: What Buddhism Can Teach Us About Race, Resilience, Transformation, and Freedom.* Boulder, CO: Shambhala, 2020.

Yusa, Michiko. "Dōgen and the Feminine Presence: Taking a Fresh Look into His Sermons and Other Writings." *Religions* 9, no. 232 (2018): https://doi.org/10.3390/rel9080232

Philosophy, Not-Philosophy, *Non-Philosophy*: Dōgen's *Religio-Philosophical* Zen

George Wrisley

What kind of philosopher was Dōgen? What forms did philosophy take in his normative conception of Zen?[1] To answer these questions, I will lay out and discuss how the central form of practice in Dōgen's Zen is zazen-only, a continuous activity that occurs both on and off the cushion. One of zazen's central philosophical activities is transforming apparent dualities, e.g., practice and realization, self and other, sentient and insentient, etc., through the application or enactment of emptiness (Skt. *śūnyatā*), into what I am identifying as "non-dual dualities." However, in doing this transformation of apparent dualities, one must also *jump off*[2] of and *express*[3] both sides of the enacted non-duality, since the non-dual duality remains a duality, *just* one that is non-dual. This jumping off and expressing both sides means that while each side is expressed, neither is clung to nor pushed away in aversion; but rather, each side is "taken up" and for- and backgrounded as needed. In this soteriological context, two further loci of philosophical activity in Dōgen's Zen are the way in which in enacting non-dual dualities and jumping off of and expressing both sides

---

[1] In answering these questions, I will not be directly arguing for the legitimacy of viewing Dōgen's Zen and his texts as philosophical or Dōgen as a philosopher. I assume the legitimacy of these later views and focus instead on several central loci of philosophical activity in Dōgen's normative vision of Zen, his own practice and the expounding it, and the practice of his Zen by monks and lay persons.

[2] See Nishiari Bokusan, "Commentary by Nishiari Bokusan" in *Dogen's Genjo Koan: three commentaries* (Berkeley: Counterpoint, 2011), 33–34.

[3] See Shohaku Okumura, *Realizing Genjokoan: The Key to Dogen's Shobogenzo* (Boston: Wisdom Publications, 2010), 18.

G. Wrisley (✉)
History, Anthropology, & Philosophy, University of North Georgia, Gainesville, GA, USA
e-mail: George.Wrisley@ung.edu

© The Author(s), under exclusive license to Springer Nature Switzerland AG 2023   145
R. Müller, G. Wrisley (eds.), *Dōgen's Texts*, Sophia Studies in Cross-cultural Philosophy of Traditions and Cultures 35,
https://doi.org/10.1007/978-3-031-42246-1_8

of them, one must engage in *weighing emptiness*[4] and *non-thinking*. Weighing emptiness acknowledges and grapples with the need for nondiscriminating discrimination so as to achieve harmony and fairness—emptiness does not wash out all distinctions relevant to assessing situations and courses of action. Non-thinking is the non-dual duality of thinking and not-thinking, a mode of consciousness that neither tries to stop thought nor pursue it, but which is marked by a radical, non-judgmental awareness central to zazen on and off the cushion—off the cushion the dynamicity of non-thinking is foregrounded.

Aside from the importance of better understanding the central philosophical aspects of Dōgen's Zen, focusing on the transformation of apparent dualities into non-dual dualities, and the concomitant activities of weighing emptiness and non-thinking, in the way this chapter does, further addresses the problem Hee-Jin Kim emphasizes when he notes that, "equality is all too often privileged over differentiation (*shabetsu*)—despite their nonduality (*byōdō soku shabetsu*)—so much so that differentiation is rendered all but ineffectual, and even drastically neutralized at worse."[5] Kim claims that, "This has been the congenital disease in Mahāyāna in general and Zen in particular."[6] It is not my aim to adjudicate this last claim, but one can imagine that insofar as it is true, it is due in part to the skillful means (*upāya*) and the need to counter deeply entrenched beliefs and habits of differentiation.

However, in addition, Kim would attribute this equality-privileging conception of Zen to what he calls, "the most prevalent conception of Zen—largely attributed to D.T. Suzuki—[where] the essence of Zen consists in the unmediated enlightenment experience (or state of consciousness), totally untainted by ideational and valuational mediations as well as by historical and social conditions." It is not that the religio-philosophical nature of Dōgen's Zen means that to practice Zen is to adopt the position of the *thinker*; rather, it is the position of the *non-thinker*, who, off the cushion and negotiating the world, belies the picture of the sage who, rooted in an unmediated grasp of the ineffable ground of existence, spontaneously and perfectly responds to any situation they are confronted with.

In what follows, I will methodically explore each of the points outlined above concerning non-dual dualities, weighing emptiness, and non-thinking. I begin with a discussion of the nature of "zazen-only," emphasizing that we can read it as meaning *only do zazen throughout the day*. This means that there is both a paradigmatic

---

[4] I take this phrase, "weighing emptiness," from Hee-Jin Kim's discussion of it but also from Kim's translation of "Muchū-setsumu," where Dōgen writes, "[The steelyard] weighs emptiness and things; whether emptiness or form, expounding a dream in a dream is invariably in accord with equality." See Hee-Jin Kim, *Dōgen on meditation and thinking: a reflection on his view of Zen* (Albany: State University of New York Press, 2007), 42. And see Hee-Jin Kim, *Flowers of Emptiness: Selections from Dōgen's Shōbōgenzō*, Studies in Asian Thought and Religion, Vol 2. (Edwin Mellen Pr, 1985), 282.

[5] Kim, *Dōgen on meditation and thinking*, 46.

[6] Kim, *Dōgen on meditation and thinking*, 46.

seated form and a "figurative"[7] form off the cushion. Drawing attention to the more "passive" and more dynamic forms of zazen is needed to do justice to the religio-philosophical complexities of Dōgen's form of zazen, or "just sitting" (*shikantaza*) . I next elaborate on the *religio-philosophical* nature and functioning of non-dual dualities in Dōgen's approach to Zen, emphasizing the centrality of the transformational process for practice-realization, the non-dual duality, the "oneness," of practice/zazen and realization/enlightenment. The heart of the paper is the discussion of the religio-philosophical nature and functioning of both weighing emptiness and non-thinking in Dōgen's *philosophical* Zen. Indeed, weighing emptiness and non-thinking off the cushion, especially, both constitute, at various times, in various ways, central loci of philosophical activity in Dōgen's Zen.

1 Zazen-Only: On and Off the Cushion

Dōgen's Zen is often described as *zazen-only*, with the usual interpretation of this as meaning that, as with other Kamakura Buddhist leaders who centered practice on a singular method, he viewed the practice of zazen in the form of *shikantaza* or "just sitting" as the *only* activity needed for enacting enlightenment. This disregard for the other practices associated with Zen, including reading sutras, chanting, burning incense, etc., can be seen in various places in the *Shōbōgenzō Zuimonki* and in the *Kana Shōbōgenzō*. However, in neither text is this issue so straightforward. Importantly, given the aims of this chapter, and given the oft found understanding of seated meditation's goal as being to quiet the mind, or enter into deep states of concentration that effectively embody a retreat from the everyday world, or to reach a state of no thought, or even Dōgen's idea of non-thinking, one might be concerned that Dōgen's zazen-only negates or diminishes the possibility of a religio-philosophical Zen practice. Thus, in order to consider Dōgen's practice to be philosophical, one must grant that zazen-only is not confined to the seated posture alone. The cushion should not be mistaken for an armchair, so to speak. So, we now turn to look at these issues in more detail.

Dōgen is clear about the necessity of zazen for practice-enlightenment. A typical passage is, "The practice of Zen (*sanzen*) is zazen." And a line that indicates both the oneness of practice and realization (enlightenment), and the sufficiency and necessity of zazen, reads: "…sitting in the meditation posture is itself the king of samadhis. It is itself entering realization. All other samadhis serve the king of samadhis."[8] Fitting well this last line is, "…zazen is the decorous activity of practice after realization. Realization is simply just sitting zazen."[9]

---

[7] I take "figurative" from Steven Heine. See Steven Heine *Readings of Dōgen's Treasury of the True Dharma Eye* (New York: Columbia University press, 2020), 186–187.

[8] See Dōgen, *Treasury* of the *True Dharma Eye: Zen Master Dogen's Shobo Genzo*, ed.by Kazuaki Tanahashi (Boston: Shambhala Publications, Inc., 2010a), 669.

[9] See Dōgen, *Dōgen's Extensive Record: A Translation of the Eihei Kōroku*, ed. Taigen Dan Leighton, trans. Taigen Dan Leighton and Shohaku Okumura (Boston: Wisdom Publications, 2010b), 292, §319.

In addition to the idea that seated zazen is the only form of practice needed, there is another possible meaning of *zazen-only*. Dōgen is adamant that there is no final state of liberation where practice-realization is no longer necessary, meaning that a practitioner should not expect zazen to consist of a series of special experiences, culminating one day in a final enlightenment, after which these experiences and the transformation they have purportedly effected are then applied to times off the cushion. Therefore, if enlightenment for Dōgen is practice (zazen), then *zazen-only* should mean continuously practicing zazen *on and off the cushion throughout the whole day, each day*.

Dōgen clearly advocates for the necessity of *seated* zazen for enacting practice-realization throughout the *Shōbōgenzō* and his other texts. So, what evidence is there for thinking Dōgen advocated for the *figurative* zazen needed for zazen-only in our second sense of doing only zazen throughout the day? There are two main sources of reasons to think that he does. First, what we might call *conceptual reasons*; second, and connected to the conceptual, direct *textual evidence* that clearly indicates, explicitly or implicitly, that there is a *figurative* sense of zazen for practice-realization off the cushion.

First, *conceptually*, since for Dōgen there is no final point of enlightenment but rather the work of continuous practice and eventual realization of "going beyond Buddha," then if *literal* zazen were the only way to actualize enlightenment, then a good deal of a practitioner's life would be unenlightened activity, especially if they are a monk who has cycled out of the monastery and into the *marketplace*. Thus, in Dōgen's own case, his writing the fascicles for the *Shōbōgenzō* and preparing Dharma talks, as those in *Eihei Kōroku*, would not themselves be moments of enacting practice-realization. Further, teaching/expounding the Dharma would not enact practice-realization either. Nor would more mundane daily activities such as eating, going to the bathroom, cleaning oneself, grooming oneself, going for a walk, talking with a stranger or friend, etc.

Second, as a version of the *conceptual evidence turning into textual*, if practice-realization can only be enacted in literal seated *just sitting*, then it would be difficult to understand how Dōgen's Zen could be an instance of the more general Mahayana Bodhisattva Ideal. For if zazen-only has only a literal "seated" meaning, then doing seated zazen would be the only possible form of engaging the Bodhisattva ideal of bringing all other beings to liberation before oneself.

Third, from the *Tenzo Kyōkun*, we need to bring to mind that throughout it he exhorts the tenzo, for example, to diligently pay attention while working with ingredients, to be attentive when washing, cutting ingredients, etc. That is, the tenzo is supposed to make their managing the kitchen and food their practice, their zazen off the cushion.

Lastly, in the fascicle, "The Point of Zazen," Dōgen comments on a dialogue between Nanyue and Mazu. A key moment of which is:

> Nanyue continued: "If you practice sitting Zen, [you will know that] Zen is not about sitting or lying down."
>   What Nanyue meant is that zazen is zazen, and it is not limited to sitting or lying down. … When you reflect on your life activities, are they intimate with zazen or remote

from it? Is there enlightenment in zazen, or is there delusion? Is there one whose wisdom penetrates zazen?[10]

In this section of the fascicle, Dōgen considers the question of zazen's "identity" again and again, each time from a different angle. When we combine the idea above that zazen is not limited to sitting or lying down with the next lines, the open identity of zazen blossoms: "Nanyue said further: 'In the practice of sitting buddha, the buddha has no fixed form.'… The reason why sitting buddha is neither singular nor plural is that sitting buddha is adorned with no fixed form."[11] Since zazen has no singular form, and since zazen is sitting buddha, the latter cannot be identified as singular or plural; thus, it cannot be said to be singularly sitting zazen. Lastly, Dōgen quotes Nanyue's saying, "If you are identified with [confined by] the sitting form, you have not reached the heart of the matter."[12]

Thus, because of both the conceptual reasons and what we have seen from Dōgen's writings, there is good reason to hold, as many do, that Dōgen endorses the possibility—if not *necessity*—of "sitting buddha" in all activities. So, we do not need to automatically reject the possibility of Dōgen's zazen being a religio-philosophical activity, especially off the cushion. Now the question is in what way zazen, on the cushion or off, involves (at least the possibility of) philosophy.

2 Dual, Not-Dual: Non-Dual

A main locus of Dōgen's personal philosophical activity is his relentless application of emptiness so as to remove all traces of duality as he transmits tradition—creatively misreading canonical texts, for example, so as to be able to express his understanding of the authentic Dharma. By applying emptiness to "remove" all traces of duality he is transforming apparent dualities into non-dual dualities. I will elaborate on this idea shortly, but for now it is important to note that, in addition to the transforming of apparent dualities being central to Dōgen's philosophical expounding of the authentic Dharma, it is also central to the Zen practice he teaches. It is therefore a religio-philosophical aspect of Zen practice itself. That said, the *degree* to which transforming apparent dualities is philosophical may vary. Let us unpack these ideas, situating duality and non-duality in the basic soteriological aims of Dōgen's Zen, before going into detail about Dōgen's understanding of non-duality. In doing so, we will be able to see how philosophically complex Dōgen's writings and practice are.

Dōgen's Sōtō Zen, as a form of Buddhism, is centered on the end or transformation of suffering/dissatisfaction/dukkha (Skt.) through Buddhist practice. One of the key differences between forms of Buddhism are their specific details regarding the

---

[10] See Dōgen, *Treasury*, 307. Interpolation in the original.

[11] Ibid., 308.

[12] Ibid., 308. Interpolation in the original.

nature of awakening and the correct method of practice. In Zen, generally, *enlightened* and *delusive* are not predicates for two different, divided realities or "sets" of experiences; rather, the (delusive) world of suffering is the same/"same" world as the (awakened) world of enlightenment, which is free from suffering. Further, in Zen there is a focus on zazen as the main form of practice. Practice needs to overcome delusion so as to achieve enlightenment: an awakening to the world as it "really is." It is this last part regarding the *dualistic, means-ends,* "escape" from the delusive into the enlightened that often preoccupies Dōgen's expounding and writing about the authentic Dharma. Thus, he focuses much of his attention on spelling out the nature of the non-dual duality of practice and realization (enlightenment) so often understood to be two distinct things. As we will see, he takes them to be non-dually one.

Thus, generally, if we are to penetrate "the abysmal depths" of Dōgen's Zen practice, then we must come to grasp the nature of dualities such as delusion and enlightenment, zazen and enlightenment, and the more general practice and realization. What this means is that these and other apparent dualities (see below) must be transformed into non-dualities, or, better, non-dual dualities, through one's practice. However, what is necessary to realize from the outset is that in actualizing, non-duality *one does so through duality itself.*

How might we clarify this point further? Consider a substance dualism such as Descartes conception of the mental and physical. The former's essence is thinking, the latter's is extension. *Each can exist independently of the other.* A denial of such a dualism is usually understood in terms of monism. For example, one might claim that monism is true of mind and body, since everything that appears mental is really just physical. However, that is not the idea of non-duality. Non-duality, unlike *not-duality*, does not deny that there is a duality, it "just" denies that that duality is of the nature of the above example of substance dualism. Moving from duality to non-dual duality is partially an epistemic movement, we might say. That is, the "actual" nature of the non-dual duality has not so much changed, as one's way of *seeing* it has—where "seeing" is embedded in *doing.* That is what is transformed.

Now, let us apply the basic idea of a duality transformed into non-duality to a fundamental idea of Dōgen's: the oneness of practice and enlightenment. First, Dōgen challenges the conventional understanding of practice/zazen as a *means* for achieving the state of enlightenment, which is to make practice and enlightenment into a genuine duality. Dōgen, by contrast, does not view zazen as means to achieve some different, future end, such that once that end is achieved, the means can be discarded. Yet this is the image to which we often default: the idea of the Buddha's teachings being a raft that we use to get to the other shore; once there, we don't need the raft and so we put it down and move on. For Dōgen's conception of practice, practice and enlightenment (realization) are not separate in this way. As he says in *The Buddha's Teachings*: "Do not think that practice leads to the other shore. Because there is practice on the other shore, when you practice, the other shore arrives."[13] Practice awaits one on the other shore, and what sounds at first paradoxi-

---

[13] Dōgen, *Treasury,* 282.

cal, as soon as one practices, one has reached the other shore (enlightenment), which "only" means more practice. In other words, for Dōgen, zazen enacts realization, it is not a means to it.

Returning now to the question of how the duality becomes non-dual, consider, as with Descartes' substance dualism, that a property of a genuine duality is that each side is what it is on its own so to speak. Cognitively, this position cashes out to "practice has *these* characteristics and enlightenment has *those* characteristics." Afterall, it is by way of practice having certain characteristics that one cultivates the right state of mind for enlightenment, but the former is something genuinely separate as a means. Just as money is the means to buy an item—the money is one thing, the boat something else—practice is not enlightenment itself.

By contrast, part of what it is for an apparent duality to become, or be actualized as, non-dual is for each of the parts to be seen not to be genuinely separate but rather causally and conditionally dependent upon each other for their nature and identity. *Practice* this moment constitutes *realization* since they are not a true duality. This makes realization into an ongoing activity, as above with the shore being reached at the moment of practice and practice waiting for one on the other shore. As we saw earlier, "We should know that zazen is the decorous activity of practice after realization. Realization is simply just sitting zazen."[14] The practice of zazen continues after realization, but realization is just zazen itself, in the context of enacting them non-dually.

However, we must be careful. Even though Dōgen insists again and again on the oneness of practice and realization, if a duality is non-dual, the duality is not erased. Rather, we have the idea of the non-dual duality constituting a "not one, not two." We cannot say that the apparent duality is a straight duality of two, nor a fusion into a whole possessing a singular identity. While just sitting is just sitting in radical presence and openness to what comes, without trying to make a Buddha, it is nevertheless true that, as Dōgen is recorded as saying in *Shōbōgenzō Zuimonki*, "With zazen…, if you do it for a long time, naturally the time will come when you suddenly clarify the great matter, and you will know that zazen is the true gate [to the Buddhadharma]."[15] Yet, despite this, zazen is not a means to clarifying anything. It is realization itself. If it were not, then you would have a duality of times, present and not present (future), on top of the duality of practice and realization, and the being of a person and time itself. As we'll see again below when we take up Dōgen's understanding of *non-thinking*, by comporting oneself to each moment as though it were an end in itself (realization itself, not a means to it), one enacts a minimal condition for practice-realization, where the other conditions for non-duality concern the way the apparent duality is to be negotiated so its non-dual duality manifests.

With the above in mind, we can better understand Steven Heine's point that, as soon as one arouses the aspiration for enlightenment/realization and engages in

---

[14] Dōgen, *Dōgen's Extensive Record*, 292, §319.

[15] Dōgen, *Dōgen's Shōbōgenzō Zuimonki: The New Annotated Edition*, ed. and trans. Shohaku Okumura (Somerville: Wisdom Publications, 2022), 195, 5–3. Interpolation in the original.

zazen, "enlightenment at that very moment is already being realized, *at least in a partial sense*, yet with the notable caveat that for Dōgen *partiality encompasses entirety*."[16] This "at least in a partial sense" acknowledges that while there is a sense in which engaging in authentic practice is sufficient for enacting realization, yet there is still a difference between the realization of just sitting (itself) and the realization that may be triggered at any moment of zazen. Yet, again, any apparent duality has to be realized as a non-duality. And this includes *this* moment of practice and *that* moment of realization two years later.

Thus, let's consider the "four main stages of training"; Heine summarizes them thus: there is, "...(a) arousing the longing and resolve for enlightenment (*hosshin*), (b) practicing with determination (*shugyō*) to attain nirvāṇa, (c) realizing the awakening of wisdom (*bodai*, Skr. *bodhi*), and (d) cultivating the body-mind after realization (*gyōji*)"[17] These might seem to each be separate aspects or stages that one progresses through over time. However, given Dōgen's transformation of the apparent temporal duality of present-not-present into a non-dual unity, which is much of the point of *Uji*, any given present moment is non-dual with any and all not-present moment(s). Part of Dōgen's firewood-ash analogy reads, "Understand that firewood abides in its condition[18] as firewood, which fully includes before and after, while it is independent of before and after."[19] The firewood and ash are not two, but not one, for they are non-dual. Thus, each of (a)-(d) might have a distinct temporal location; however, as with the firewood-ash non-duality, each of (a)-(d) is non-dual with each and all of the others. And, as Heine points out, their distinctly appearing as genuine dualities is merely on the surface and is itself a form of delusion.

Before turning to the full range of the kinds of dualities that Dōgen is most interested in transforming into non-dual dualities, let's foreground an essential aspect of Dōgen's practice-realization. Some dualities in the general Zen context, such as form and emptiness, delusion and enlightenment, language and silence, thinking and not thinking, and grasping and letting go, may appear to concern a movement from the left one to the right one. Thus, one might think that enlightenment means grasping emptiness and letting go of form, enacting enlightenment and letting go of delusion, enacting silence and letting go of (delusive) language, enter into the calm mind of not thinking about anything during zazen, and learning to continuously let go, never grasping. The problem with this view is that it ends up denying the full non-dual nature of the duality and the dynamicity of life.

Again, non-duality is realized, actualized, through duality; as before, this is a main locus of both Dōgen's own religio-philosophical practice and the practice of the Zen he teaches and writes about. One can gain skill at recognizing non-dualities

---

[16] Heine, *Readings*, 97. My emphases.

[17] Ibid., 97.

[18] The word translated as "condition" here is *hōi*, which literally means "dharma stage" or "dharma position" and is, "The unique, nonrepeatable stage of a thing's existence at a given moment." See Kazuaki Tanahashi, *Moon in a Dewdrop: Writings of Zen Master Dōgen* (San Francisco: North Point Press, 1985), 318.

[19] Dōgen, *Treasury*, 30.

that appear as straight dualities, though this does not diminish the philosophical nature of enacting practice-realization, which also has a very real lived component, since a genuine apprehension of non-duality, and its subsequent enactment, implicates one's thinking, valuing, speaking, and acting more generally.

3 *Jumping off of* and *Expressing* Both Sides of Duality

Each part/side of a duality is what it is because of the other; to give preference to one side over the other ignores this but also can quickly lead to a form of delusive clinging, which entails suffering when the preferred part is not found or achieved. Shohaku Okumura helpfully emphasizes the way in which, for Dōgen, we are the intersection of equality (unity) and inequality (difference). In his commentary on Dōgen's "Genjōkōan" fascicle he writes that the foundational position of Mahayana Buddhism and Zen is seeing the same reality from these two sides: sameness/difference, unity/separation, equality/inequality.[20] However, he points out that for Dōgen, "...to see one reality from two sides is not enough; he said we should also *express* these two sides in one action."[21] Similarly, also commenting on "Genjōkōan," Nishiari Bokusan comments, "The Buddha Way does not fall into form, and does not fall into emptiness. There is a point at which you jump off both form and emptiness, and do not abide there. You must see through this. That is practice."[22] This "jumping off" can be understood as letting go of both, not trying to control them, but living with them "as they are," while also being able to skillfully engage and work with one *now* and another *then*. Moreover, Bokusan emphasizes, "Form-and-emptiness are necessary. But if we abide in either, it is not 'the Buddha Way.' The Buddha Way does not stay on the side of form or emptiness, being or non-being. For that reason, we say, 'transcendence.' So in transcendence, there is definitely form and emptiness."[23] Transcendence is not leaving behind form and emptiness; it is actualizing their non-dual duality through practice.

A central example of this non-moving "movement" between form, emptiness, and nondual form-emptiness, which is itself transcended, is at the very beginning of Dōgen's important and well-known fascicle "Genjōkōan." For ease of understanding, I have broken the paragraph up into each "moment" of "the movement" and provided commentary.[24]

---

[20] See Shohaku Okumura, *Realizing Genjokoan: The Key to Dogen's Shobogenzo* (Boston: Wisdom Publications, 2010), 18.

[21] Ibid.

[22] Nishiari, "Commentary," 33–34.

[23] Ibid., 33.

[24] I put *moment* in quotation marks to signal that these are not intended to be sequential moments in time.

As all things are buddha dharma, there is delusion, realization, practice, birth [life] and death, buddhas and sentient beings.

As Dōgen puts it in "Great Manifestation of Prajna," "Form is form. Emptiness is emptiness."[25] Since there is form/particularity (buddha dharma), there are the particulars/forms of delusion, realization, etc. However, since form is emptiness and emptiness is form:

As myriad things are without an abiding self, there is no delusion, no realization, no buddha, no sentient being, no birth and death.

Because of all form being emptiness, there is no self that is numerically identical over time or self-existent, there is no delusion, no realization, etc., because there is no genuinely separate entity/form that is self, delusion, etc. However, we cannot penetrate delusion if we believe it is removed by moving from grasping forms to grasping emptiness. Thus:

The buddha way, in essence, is leaping clear of abundance and lack; thus there is birth and death, delusion and realization, sentient beings and buddhas. Yet in attachment blossoms fall, and in aversion weeds spread.[26]

We must leap clear of form and emptiness, which means, in part, letting go of/transcending both while simultaneously navigating their often-complex, non-dual dualities so that we are able to express both sides in one action. In this fully engaged transcendence there are the newly understood non-dual particulars of birth and death, delusion and realization, etc. However, despite the non-dual dualities, if we form attachments to some things and are averse to others, blossoms fall and weeds spread. In other words, through attachments we affirm straight dualities and thus there seem to be the unchanging and independent occurrences of blossoms falling and weeds spreading.

It should be emphasized that the transcendence described in these passages does not deny Hee-Jin Kim's important point that for Dōgen non-duality, "...did not signify the transcendence of duality so much as the realization of it."[27] Further, "Nonduality was always embedded and active within duality itself—as the guider, purifier, and empowerer of duality. The two were appropriated soteriologically, not theoretically or as explanatory concepts...."[28] Here we see Kim doing what he does so well, namely, foregrounding not the image of the person seated facing the wall in zazen, but the practitioner who, without choice, must engage the world and all its delusive glory and complexity.

To be clear, by "emptiness," I understand not a "thing," but the denial of any persisting, independently existing entity because all "entities" are impermanent moment to moment and are what they are only because of the reciprocal relationships they stand in with everything else being what it is. However, because

[25] Dōgen, *Treasury*, 25.
[26] Ibid., 29.
[27] Kim, *Dōgen on meditation and thinking*, X.
[28] Ibid.

emptiness is dependent upon form and is continuously unfolding in new and unforeseen ways, emptiness is empty. And it is (empty) emptiness that is *utilized* in practice to transform apparent dualities into non-dual dualities. Present (moment) and not present (moment) are apparently separate, but each is what it is only because of various causes and conditions entangling their existence—while each is/has its unique "Dharma Position" (*hoi*).[29] Dōgen's firewood-ash analogy is relevant here; he writes in part: "Understand that firewood abides in its condition[30] as firewood, which fully includes before and after, while it is independent of before and after."[31]

What we have to do, even if we have achieved the realization of wisdom (*bodai*, Skr. *bodhi*), is to continue with practice (zazen), *always*, for this is practice-realization. The reason for this continuous practice of expressing both sides of reality, of jumping off of form and emptiness, is that there is not simply one thing that is *expressing or jumping off of both sides.* Moreover, since conditions are always changing, each duality must be negotiated, or at least examined, anew so as to properly actualize its non-duality. This is one way to set up an interpretation of Dōgen's, "Accordingly, endeavors in practice-realization of the way are not limited to one or two kinds. The thoroughly actualized realm has one thousand kinds and ten thousand ways."[32]

We might see this manifold of kinds and ways as due to all the different apparent yet delusive dualities that we need to penetrate and actualize non-dually in the continuous activity of practice-realization. For example, including ones from earlier, there is delusion and enlightenment, form and emptiness, practice and realization, self and other, other and other, present moment and not-present moment, language and silence, birth (life) and death, good and evil, means and ends, thinking and not-thinking, grasping and letting go, beginning of practice and great realization, time flowing and time ever present, obstruction and not-obstruction, mind and body, skillful means and absolute truth, time and being, and so on. And, again, these manifold kinds and ways are due in part to the variable and various ways in which any given duality manifests and is interpreted and enacted non-dually. For example, the self-other non-duality that exists between me and my wife would be enacted differently than that between me and my father, especially since his death.

I have taken us through the above discussion of Buddhist practice generally, and the more specific details of the relationship between delusion and enlightenment in Dōgen's Zen, and the necessity of continuously probing and penetrating experience for *any trace of affirmation* of genuine duality, whether in perception, thought, feeling, speech, or action. One goal has been that we might begin to see more clearly how the enacting of a non-dual duality, expressing and jumping off both sides of reality, is not a mechanical activity. We don't learn how it goes one time, with one

---

[29] Again, the word translated as "Dharma position" here is *hōi*, which is, "The unique, nonrepeatable stage of a thing's existence at a given moment." Tanahashi, *Moon*, 318.

[30] The word translated as "condition" here is *hōi*, op cit.

[31] Dōgen, *Treasury*, 30.

[32] Ibid., 159.

thing, and thereby learn a mechanical procedure for knowing exactly how enacting, expressing, and jumping off will always go, what it will demand of us and others, all of us non-dual with each other and the world, and our past and future "selves." No. The "messy," temporal nature of life requires ongoing judgment and refinement, mistake after mistake.[33] What is needed for properly expressing both sides of reality, form and emptiness, and both sides of practice and realization, is the so-called weighing of emptiness and enacting non-thinking through thinking not-thinking. Both weighing emptiness and non-thinking have philosophical aspects, which will be brought out the more skillful one is with them.

4   *Weighing Emptiness*: The Deconstructive and Reconstructive Functions of Emptiness

It is not difficult to find passages from Dōgen where he is utilizing or drawing attention to a non-dual duality. For example:

(a) "*For the time-being* here means time itself is being, and all being is time."[34]
(b) "The way the self arrays itself is the form of the entire world. See each thing in this entire world as a moment in time."[35]
(c) "Understand that firewood abides in its condition as firewood, which fully includes before and after, while it is independent of before and after."[36]
(d) "Water is not sentient or insentient. The body is not sentient or insentient. All things are like this."[37]

Being "told" that "all being is time," "the form of the self is the form of the world," "the moment of firewood (before burning to ash) the firewood 'includes' and does not, both before and after," "Water, the body, all things, are neither sentient nor not sentient" can make it seem like these are black and white non-dual dualities. However, that *all being is time* and that *firewood does and does not include before and after*, do not always come out to the same insofar as what we should do to enact their non-duality. That is, while they may *qua* non-duality be the same, how that non-dual duality should be negotiated and fully enacted is not always the same. Hence, the need to "weigh emptiness."

Earlier in *Dōgen on Meditation and Thinking*, before Kim discusses what he calls the *weighing of emptiness*, Kim illustrates the distinction between what he

---

[33] Cf. Dōgen, "Two thousand years ago, he was our ancestral father. He is muddy and wet from following and chasing after the waves.184 It can be described like this, but also there is the principle of the way [that we must] make one mistake after another." See Dōgen, *Dōgen's Extensive Record*, 132, §88.

[34] Dōgen, *Treasury*, 104.

[35] Ibid., 105.

[36] Ibid., 30.

[37] Ibid., 49.

calls the *deconstructive* and *reconstructive* aspects of emptiness. Discussing Dōgen's position on light and darkness, and how the light does not remove the darkness but penetrates it (in non-duality), Kim writes:

> ...the notions of light and darkness must be first deconstructed by emptiness; only then can they function effectively, now reconstituted (or reconstructed) as salvific foci, through emptiness. ... Dōgen's contributions primarily lie in the latter [reconstructive] aspect of this dual role of emptiness, or in the treatment of duality in the pair of duality and nonduality.[38]

I take both these functions of emptiness, the deconstructive and reconstructive, to be challenging in many cases to carry out, and impossible to do through passive actions, observation alone, or by trying "simply" to let go of everything moment to moment. As above, one must "negotiate the way" in the two senses of *working with/discussing compromise* and *finding a way through obstacles and impediments*. One such obstacle Kim discusses is that when one begins to grasp the deconstructive aspect of emptiness, this can leave the practitioner feeling as though they are hanging in the empty air with nothing solid to grasp or cling to. Emptiness "...deconstructs our conventional worldviews so relentlessly that nothing is left to rely on and feel certain of. And yet, this is precisely what practitioners must grapple with—a complete collapse of the reificational way of thinking and its implications."[39] Yet, the reconstructive function of emptiness does not leave the practitioner simply flailing in midair. This is because through (reconstructive) emptiness, practitioners are enabled "...to discern that the existential and spiritual predicament of hanging in empty space, however abysmal, frightening, and uncertain, is none other than the liberating occasion of 'right this moment' (*shōtō immoji*), with an inclusive sense of efficacy."[40]

Let us clarify the reconstructive function of emptiness further. According to Kim, the deconstructive part by itself is not sufficient, since, "...as ultimate truth [it] lacks a dynamic, dialectical relationship with worldly truth. Consequently, its soteriological scope, hitherto unnecessarily constrained, should be expanded to include the reconstructive function of emptiness with respect to worldly truth...."[41] Worldly truth (form) needs to be both *deconstructed* and *reconstructed* in light of that which it is nondual (emptiness, and the emptiness of emptiness); to leave worldly truth deconstructed into some undifferentiated wholeness and momentariness is to neglect to fulfill emptiness's full salvific functionality.

According to Kim, the *reconstructive aspect* is: "Emptiness cares about differences in worldly truth so as to bring about fairness."[42] In fleshing this out, Kim makes much of Dōgen's use of the analogy of a steelyard in the fascicle "Expounding a Dream in a Dream" (*Muchū Setsumu*). The steelyard is a scale one can hold up (in

---

[38] See Kim, *Dōgen on meditation and thinking*, 14. Interpolation mine.
[39] Ibid., 44.
[40] Ibid., 45.
[41] Ibid., 52.
[42] Ibid., 43.

the air, i.e., emptiness) that has uneven arms. On one side is placed that which is to be weighed; on the other, there's a moveable weight and scale. By adjusting the moveable weight, one attains balance/equilibrium with the weight of the object. Dōgen writes, "Study a steelyard in equilibrium. When we study it, our power to discern minute differences in weight manifests itself without fail, and thus puts forth the expounding of a dream within a dream."[43] Following Kim here,[44] the point is that we do not *realize* and *actualize* the non-dual duality of form and emptiness appropriately if we do not take note of differences, if we do not take the focal point of form (delusion) seriously: Emptiness is not the obliteration of distinctions. Kim writes elsewhere that, "Dōgen...brings up the...analogy of a steelyard as a way to...bring out the nondual relationship between emptiness and form."[45] Abe and Waddell write: "As long as one remains within realization after transcending the realm of differentiation, complete liberation is unachieved. Complete liberation requires transcending realization as well and reentering the realm of differentiation in order to work for the salvation of others."[46] Just as the tenzo must count the rice[47] discriminating in nondiscrimination to bring about fairness in what is served, so, too, our negotiating the world requires weighing emptiness in the sense of appropriately balancing/equalizing form and emptiness in the context of nonduality with the concomitant actualization of *fairness*; and it is fairness that serves as "the great principle of the steelyard."[48]

Kim in the same vein as above: "By analogy, 'equality' is the point of equilibrium of emptiness and form, of original enlightenment and acquired enlightenment, etc."[49] With this we can better understand Dōgen's writing, "[By virtue of this principle of fairness] we weigh emptiness and things; whether it be emptiness or form, [we weigh it to] meet fairness. This is the expounding of a dream within a dream as well. In no case is there liberation that does not expound a dream within a dream."[50] For Dōgen, even when we express both sides of reality in one action or jump off of both form and emptiness, neither clinging to, nor lingering in either, we do not enter into a different world in terms of ontology. In other words, there is not the world of delusion and a different world that is the world of clear insight; hence, for Dōgen, it

---

[43] Ibid., 42.

[44] Kim notes that in regard to the steelyard passage, "commentarial works in the Sōtō tradition have conveniently muted and trivialized its true significance to the extent that they have virtually buried it, instead favoring the static, uncritical, transcendentalistic meaning of emptiness in the name of equality." See Kim, *Dōgen on meditation and thinking*, 43.

[45] See Kim, *Flowers of Emptiness*, En. 10, 285–86.

[46] See Dōgen, *The Heart of Dōgen's Shobogenzo*, ed. and trans. Norman Waddell and Masao Abe (Albany, NY: State University of New York Press, 2002), 9.

[47] See Dōgen, *Dōgen's Pure Standards for the Zen Community*, ed. Taigen Daniel Leighton, trans. Taigen Daniel Leighton and Shohaku Okumura (Albany, NY: State University of New York Press, 1996), 38–39.

[48] See Kim, *Dōgen on meditation and thinking*, 42.

[49] Kim, *Flowers of Emptiness*, En. 11, 286.

[50] See Kim, *Dōgen on meditation and thinking*, 42.

would be a mistake to describe practice in terms of waking up from a dream. Rather, everything is "dreamy"; hence, we are to "expound a dream within a dream," thereby fully appropriating and acknowledging form in relation to emptiness and vice versa. But, as Dōgen says, we must "weigh" emptiness so as to bring about equality and fairness in this expressing of a dream within a dream. And we can add, *in this expressing of both sides of reality*, form and emptiness, and by implication, all non-dual dualities.

We see a version of weighing emptiness along with the deconstructive and reconstructive functions of it in the *Tenzo Kyōkun*, where Dōgen writes, "Being harmonious and pure like this, do not lose either *the eye of oneness* or *the eye that discerns differences*."[51] This is an instance of the steelyard balance scale where balance/harmony comes from weighing emptiness, noting differences while also embracing wholeness. And this is how we should read Kim's translation of Dōgen's claim about "negotiating the way" being a matter of "discerning all things in view of enlightenment, and putting such a unitive awareness (*ichinyo*) into practice *in the midst of the revaluated world (shutsuro*)."[52] The world is revaluated through the deconstructive and reconstructive functions of emptiness working together in everything we say, do, think, and feel.

Hence, we can readily agree with Kim's way of emphasizing these points:

> ...in the mundane situation, the balancing efforts of weighing, measuring, and calibrating (and by extension, *reasoning, reflection, and deliberation*) must go on incessantly—consciously and unconsciously, intrapersonally and interpersonally, locally and globally, and beyond—in order to generate fairness as the conditions of that situation change.[53]

This continuously taking up the scale, "weighing, measuring, and calibrating," and carrying out the deconstructive and reconstructive functions of emptiness, Dōgen tells us, as above, is the expressing of a dream within a dream. And "In no case is there liberation that does not expound a dream within a dream."[54] Thus, practice-realization is, among much else, the continuous (unceasing) practice of weighing emptiness, of carrying out the complicated task of deconstructing and reconstructing all aspects of, and perspectives on, reality. And this practice of weighing emptiness is one of the central ways in which duality is actively transformed into a non-dual duality and both sides of reality are expressed in a single action.

Given the complexities of the weighing task in the "nitty-gritty" delusive reality we find ourselves in day to day, we can see how complex the two functions of emptiness, deconstructive and reconstructive, are, as they will require various kinds and instances of penetrating a concept, idea, or problem through and through, i.e., doing philosophy, whether in a more theoretical or practical mode, or both. And to nuance this, we can and do rely on past instances of figuring out, all while staying vigilant for signs of inadequacy as we go forward relying on them. Moreover, as emphasized

---

[51] My emphasis.

[52] Quoted in Kim, *Dōgen on meditation and thinking*, 21. Emphasis mine.

[53] Ibid., 46–47. My emphasis.

[54] Ibid., 42.

earlier, whether or not a particular instance of figuring out is philosophical may depend on who's doing it, why exactly (teaching, living, learning, etc.), what the topic is, and just how much penetration of an issue requires reflection. However, if this weighing emptiness is genuinely a part of practice-realization, then it must be done through non-thinking.

5   Thinking, Not-Thinking: Non-Thinking

The other philosophical aspect of practice that we will focus on, and which is needed for actualizing dualities as non-dual dualities, is thinking (*shiryō* 思量) not-thinking (*fushiryō* 不思量) through non-thinking (*hishiryō* 非思量). The kōan Dōgen cites from is one that he returns to repeatedly in his writings and talks. Here is the version at the beginning of "The Point of Zazen":

> Yaoshan, Great Master Hongdao, was sitting. A monk asked him, "In steadfast sitting, what do you think?"
> Yaoshan said, "Think not-thinking."
> "How do you think not-thinking?" Yaoshan replied, "Non-thinking."[55]

This "sitting" is, of course, zazen, and the question at issue is what exactly is the mind doing, since it should avoid falling into the many dualisms of ordinary thinking, but should also not fall into the "monism" of a static or thoughtless mental state, thereby obliterating duality. As we have seen, dualities need to be affirmed and transformed into non-dual dualities. Thus, thinking and not-thinking as a duality must be transformed into a non-dual duality, namely, non-thinking. For Dōgen, zazen is not the negation of (normal) thinking nor the affirmation of (normal) thinking. The former is too close to negating cogitation altogether and the latter is too dualistic.

We need to come to understand that both thinking and not-thinking are what they are because of each other, and, thus, they are a non-dual duality. For example, to think thought X, one must be not-thinking thoughts that are not-X; and to be not-thinking (of anything), there must be something that can be thought, such as X, Y, Z, etc. To see blackness when one's eyes are closed requires seeing non-black when one's eyes are open; the person blind from birth does not see black or anything when their eyes are closed.

In line with the above, Leighton and Okumura describe non-thinking as "a state of active awareness that includes both thinking and not-thinking, but does not grasp, or get caught by, either thinking or not thinking."[56] Again, as always, not grasping and not pushing away are key to practice-realization. They go on to say that both thinking and not-thinking are let go of and the mind does what it does, the world

---

[55] See Dōgen, *Treasury*, 303. Modified so that the last line reads as it does instead of "Beyond thinking."

[56] See Dōgen, *Dōgen's Pure Standards*, 81.

around does what it does, and all are allowed to simply be, being unjudged as to whether they should be there or not. All is allowed come and go like clouds in the sky. However, this last part of what they say seems better suited to literal seated zazen, because it is too passive of a position for practicing zazen off the cushion.

However, there are other ways of looking at zazen off the cushion where non-thinking is more dynamic. Compare Heine, "As Dōgen explains, nonthinking does not indicate a deficiency of thought but is a matter of keeping free from the coveting and grasping that tends to accompany ordinary cogitation, *while staying fully involved in creative modes of deliberation and discourse*."[57] With a similar emphasis on the dynamic, lived aspects of non-thinking, Kim notes, first, that from one angle nonthinking is like the "mediator" or "custodian" between thinking and not-thinking. Second, that it is because of this coordinating function of non-thinking that, "…the meditator's thinking (as well as not-thinking) is guarded against the pitfalls and dangers of a reifying, referential mindset. *It is freed cognitively, affectively, and conatively to negotiate the Way, by wisely and compassionately dealing with the mundane matters in everyday life*."[58]

Non-thinking has the "passive" side described above, which we can further see in Dōgen's basic method of just sitting (*shikantaza*), which aims not for the achievement of any particular mental state, much less enlightenment, but rather is "simply" radically open, focused and unfocused together, in full presence while accepting of whatever comes. We should note, as mentioned earlier, that part of the way that Dōgen transforms the apparent duality of practice and enlightenment is to insist that practice is enlightenment, i.e., when we practice, we don't seek something outside of that moment. Thus, each moment is an end in itself. Nevertheless, this does not negate that we also are *doing something* each moment, and whatever we're doing, there is an end that the activity stretches toward, so to speak.

The dynamicity of practice, again, is more apparent off the cushion, where non-thinking would mean, in part, bringing full attention and awareness to what one does and what comes, engaging the world each moment as an end in itself, while also engaging in a nondiscriminating discrimination in the sense Okumura and Leighton describe: "Zazen practice usually emphasizes nondiscrimination. But this nondiscrimination also does not discriminate against the careful calculations and consideration necessary for attentive practice amid the diversity of ordinary everyday life."[59] Heine elaborates further on this idea of nondiscriminating discrimination, writing:

> Sometimes referred to as an ability to carefully discern distinctions while recognizing the basic unity underlying all apparent differences or a paradoxical nondiscriminative discrimination, the state of nonthinking, or thinking-as-not thinking, reflects the continuing circulation of constructive reflections. This is achieved without lapsing into an attachment to any particular standpoint since all ideas are innately relative and constantly shifting.[60]

---

[57] Heine, *Readings*, 188. My emphasis.

[58] Kim, *Dōgen on meditation and thinking*, 92. My emphasis.

[59] Ibid., 52–53.

[60] Heine, *Readings*, 188.

One form of these "constructive reflections" is, as we've seen, weighing emptiness.

As discussed at length in the foregoing, with weighing emptiness, the "enormous range of activities" that constitute the "critical, constructive negotiation between weighing and fairness" requires the appropriate kind of discrimination. If Kim is right, then in weighing emptiness in the context of non-thinking, we must make judgments of good and bad, right and wrong, etc., in their moral and nonmoral forms. This is one of the ways that we might see seated zazen as different in detail from figurative zazen off the cushion. That is, in seated meditation, one's posture is seated and still, only breathing with a profoundly alert and capacious nondiscriminating consciousness. In this context, one can practice letting go of everything, all that comes, "good" or "bad," and doing so will not leave one ineffectual and quietistic in life.

However, off the cushion, engaging the world through an emptiness-weighing non-thinking in the "nitty-gritty reality of our flesh-and-blood existence from which we cannot escape for a moment when it comes to the pressing matters of truth and meaning, right and wrong, good and bad, just and unjust, and so forth."[61] We cannot *not* think of good or bad, right or wrong. In this situation, even within the framework of practicing Zen, within practice-realization, expressing both sides of reality, weighing emptiness and non-thinking, "...our 'vast and giddy karmic consciousness' must still operate in full capacity to choose, decide, and act, not only for mere survival but for authentic living.[62]

Making choices means committing to some act with some end in mind, which means endorsing some set of values over others. However, the nondiscrimination nevertheless involved in non-thinking does not make such values, commitments, and choices impossible. It means, rather, that none of them are held on or clung to. As Dōgen writes in a different context with a different set of "objects" in mind: [All these] are expounding a dream in a dream as [ways of] 'holding fast' and 'letting go.' ... Whether holding fast or letting go, we should learn from a balanced steelyard."[63] Recall that for Dōgen, "...whether it be emptiness or form, [we weigh it to] meet fairness. This is the expounding of a dream within a dream as well. In no case is there liberation that does not expound a dream within a dream."[64]

For us, it is vital to see that non-thinking is not the simple negation of thinking, nor the simple affirmation of not-thinking. Non-thinking is the *thinking* of *not-thinking*, it is the actualization of their non-duality, and that actualization is central, along with weighing emptiness, to authentically actualizing the non-duality of practice-realization, which itself is constituted by non-thinking, weighing emptiness in the enacting of the non-dual duality of form and emptiness, and all this in such a way that one expresses both sides of reality in every action, utilizing them unincumbered and unattached.

---

[61] Kim, *Dōgen on meditation and thinking*, 49.

[62] Ibid., 49.

[63] Kim, *Flowers of Emptiness*, 281–82.

[64] Kim, *Dōgen on meditation and thinking*, 42.

6 Conclusions: Dōgen as *Philosopher*, Dōgen's *Religio-Philosophical* Zen

In this chapter I have articulated those aspects of Dōgen's conception of Zen practice that are themselves religio-*philosophical*, specifically, his use of emptiness for transforming apparent dualities into non-dual dualities and his own relentlessness in doing this, both requiring as they do various philosophical work to properly penetrate the more complex of the apparent dualities such as practice and realization, time as static and time as flowing, being/existence and time, and many others. However, properly enacting non-dual dualities means simultaneously expressing and jumping off both sides of the apparent duality reconstructed non-dually. In order to properly do this expressing and jumping off, the practitioner must engage in further activities that have philosophical aspects, namely, weighing emptiness and non-thinking. But at no point is the duality negated in the name of equality or the like. Non-dual dualities are expressed through the transformation and affirmation of dualities.

In creating the normative vision of Zen that he did, and in expounding it and writing it, Dōgen engaged in these forms of practice, and as so much of the *Shōbōgenzō*, for example, shows, he did all these things with great philosophical insight and rigor. Further, as we've seen, his conception of Zen practice invites and even requires some level of philosophical engagement. The level of philosophical engagement one brings to practice will vary in relation to the practitioner's abilities, interests, and those of their teacher. However, the more skilled one is at, and the more one is open to, the philosophical aspects, the greater one's ultimate understanding, grasp, and ability to practice authentically will be. Dōgen is not an elitist *per se*; rather, his own understanding goes so deep and his ability to express what he took to be the authentic Dharma was so skilled, that he could not help but envision and expound a philosophical Zen, one that makes frequent philosophical demands on practitioners, even if not everyone can fulfill them to the same degree.

All this said, we should not lose sight that Dōgen's ends are soteriological; so, what he writes will perforce be understood differently and evaluated epistemically very differently whether one is attempting to practice Dōgen's Zen, philosophy, both, or neither. Either way, given Dōgen's own relentless application of emptiness, it is not a matter of *philosophy* or *not philosophy*; thus, we might say that Dōgen's *religio-philosophical* Zen is rather an example of *non-philosophy*.

Bibliography

Bokusan, Nishiari. 'Commentary by Nishiari Bokusan'. in *Dogen's Genjo Koan: three commentaries*. Berkeley: Counterpoint. 2011. 5–90.

Dōgen, *Dōgen's Pure Standards for the Zen Community*. Edited by Taigen Daniel Leighton, translated by Taigen Daniel Leighton and Shohaku Okumura. Albany, NY: State University of New York Press, 1996.

_____.*The Heart of Dōgen's Shobogenzo*. Edited and translated by Norman Waddell and Masao Abe. Albany, NY: State University of New York Press, 2002.

_____. *Treasury* of the *True Dharma Eye: Zen Master Dogen's Shobo Genzo*. Edited by Kazuaki Tanahashi. Boston: Shambhala Publications, Inc, 2010a.

_____. *Dōgen's Extensive Record: A Translation of the Eihei Kōroku*. Edited by Taigen Dan Leighton. Translated by Taigen Dan Leighton and Shohaku Okumura. Boston: Wisdom Publications, 2010b.

_____. *Dōgen's Shōbōgenzō Zuimonki: The New Annotated Edition*. Edited and translated by Shohaku Okumura. Somerville: Wisdom Publications, 2022.

Heine, Steven. *Readings of Dōgen's Treasury of the True Dharma Eye*. New York: Columbia University press, 2020.

Kim, Hee-Jin. *Flowers of Emptiness: Selections from Dogen's Shobogenzo*, Studies in Asian Thought and Religion, Vol 2. Edwin Mellen Pr, 1985.

_____. *Eihei Dōgen: Mystical Realist*. Somerville: Wisdom Publications, 2004.

_____. *Dōgen on meditation and thinking: a reflection on his view of Zen*, Albany: State University of New York Press, 2007.

Okumura, Shohaku. *Realizing Genjokoan: The Key to Dogen's Shobogenzo*. Boston: Wisdom Publications, 2010.

Flowers of Dim-Sightedness: Dōgen's Mystical 'Negative Ocularcentrism'

Adam Loughnane

In addition to the significance of vision intimated by the title of Dōgen's collected writings, "Treasury of the True Dharma Eye" (*Shōbōgenzō* 正法眼蔵),[1] metaphor and metaphysics inspired by the sense of sight pervade his works. Although, he does thematize other perceptual modalities, it is within the realm of vision that Dōgen embarks on some of his most expansive and profound explorations. Yet, the importance of vision in his philosophy is also decisive where it goes un-mentioned. Dōgen's philosophy might be described as "ocularcentric" not merely because of the quantity or the inventive nature of his insights regarding vision, but because even where explicit reference is absent, the structure of the visual subtly informs the architecture of his philosophy and soteriology. In this paper, I distinguish the centrality of vision in Dōgen's philosophy from Western ocularcentrism, and critiques thereof, by casting his philosophy as a "negative ocularcentrism" and propose this as an alternative to Hee-Jin Kim's notion of realist mysticism.

The ocularcentric privileging of the visual to the neglect of other perceptual modalities has come under increased scrutiny in recent scholarship that surveys both Eastern and Western philosophies. Scholars have identified a tendency in the history of both Greek and Asian thought towards philosophical structures whose goals are construed according to the aim of gaining a better, clearer visual grasp of the world,

---

[1] Dōgen's use of the title was not the first occurrence in Buddhist history but a re-invocation of a classical story of Śākyamuni bestowing the "treasury of the eye of the true Dharma" on Mahākāśyapa.

A. Loughnane (✉)
University College Cork, Cork, Ireland

© The Author(s), under exclusive license to Springer Nature Switzerland AG 2023
R. Müller, G. Wrisley (eds.), *Dōgen's Texts*, Sophia Studies in Cross-cultural Philosophy of Traditions and Cultures 35,
https://doi.org/10.1007/978-3-031-42246-1_9

which typically demands proceeding from darkness into light.[2] This privileging of
the visual has been associated with many destructive tendencies, primary among
those being the position of detached and disinterested spectatorial distance associated with positivist and representational theories of vision. Although I claim that
Dōgen's philosophy is "ocularcentric", I seek to distinguish his version from prevailing critiques, East and West. My claim is that the centrality of the visual in Dōgen's
thought evades the perils of both Greek and Mahāyāna Buddhist ocularcentrism.

Despite legitimate concerns some have articulated regarding the "hegemony of
the visual," the argument I would like to advance is that the liabilities of ocularcentrism reside not in the philosophical prioritization of sight to the neglect of other
senses, but specifically in the latent *positivism* visual metaphor tends towards. To
distance Dōgen from this critique, I cast his philosophy as a "negative ocularcentrism". Dōgen, I argue, ontologizes vision according to the Mahāyāna notion of
emptiness (*śūnyatā*), and thus discloses how seeing is inflected by non-seeing, by
the visually negative, including: blindness, illusion, invisibility, darkness, and other
forms of visual obstructions.

To distinguish Dōgen's appeal to vision from positivist approaches, I follow
Hee-Jin Kim's proposal to interpret his philosophy according to his central concepts, "activity" (行持 *gyōji*) and "expression" (道得 *dōtoku*).[3] This reading drastically expands the visual and establishes a negative ocularcentrism evading the perils
of positivist, representational visual models and philosophies structured thereupon.

I follow Kim's interpretation with the goal of questioning another proposition he
puts forth; that is, the claim that Dōgen's philosophy is a form of "mystical realism".[4]
I seek to extend several of Kim's insights regarding mysticism by applying them to
Dōgen's thinking on vision. More specifically, I consider how his interpretations of
Dōgen's notions of obstruction (罣礙 *keige*),[5] "activity" and "expression" further

---

[2]D.M. Levin, *Sites of Vision: The Discursive Construction of Sight in the History of Philosophy*
(MIT Press, 1999); D.M. Levin, *Modernity and the Hegemony of Vision* (University of California
Press, 1993); Martin Jay, *Downcast Eyes: The Denigration of Vision in Twentieth-century French
Thought* (University of California Press, 1994); David McMahan, *Empty Vision: Metaphor and
Visionary Imagery in Mahayana Buddhism* (Taylor & Francis, 2013).

[3]Hee-Jin Kim, *Eihei Dōgen: Mystical Realist* (Boston: Wisdom Publications, 2004).

[4]Ibid.

[5]The question of emptiness and obstruction has a long history in Buddhist philosophy. Dōgen's use
of the concept "obstruction" invokes the Huayan notion of "nonobstruction of all phenomena" (c.
shishi-wuai, 事事無礙; j. *jiji-muge*), based on the principle of "mutual identity and mutual penetration" (*sōsoku-sōnyo*). While Huayan is regarded as putting forth the notion of "non-obstruction"
(c. *wuai* 無礙; j. *muge*), which might seem to go against Dōgen's notion of obstruction, this does
not capture the complexity of Dōgen's position nor the multitude of competing positions within
Huayan itself. While there is non-obstruction of phenomena, there are also three other levels where
non-obstruction obtains. Huayan resolved earlier doctrinal disputes by focusing specifically on the
fourth (non-obstruction of phenomena and phenomena) where the fourth patriarch Chengguan in
particular posited the presence of ineliminable obstructions. (*See Thomas F. Cleary, Entry into the
Inconceivable: An Introduction to Hua-Yen Buddhism and Jin Y. Park, Buddhism*, and
Postmodernity: Zen, Huayan, and the Possibility of Buddhist Postmodern Ethics). When Kim
writes "Dōgen maintained that the concrete particularities of dharmas, radically discrete spatially
and temporally, are interpenetrated and unobstructed," his notion of "unobstruction," misses this
particularity of Huayan and also the crucial reflexivity of Dōgen's notion as "obstruction obstructing obstruction".

support the account of negative ocularcentrism I seek to establish. The outcome is a mysticism, shaped by Dōgen's negative ocularcentrism, which escapes realism by virtue of a creative visual engagement in/as the world that mysticism demands.

1   Ocularcentrism in Mahāyāna Buddhism

To begin, I would like to consider Dōgen's challenge to a latent positivism discernible within Mahāyāna's ocularcentrist tendencies. Let us reflect upon some of the ways visual thinking developed in that tradition. Early Indian Buddhism leans heavily on vision and light-based metaphor and symbolism.[6] While there are exceptions where other perceptual modalities are employed, we find near inexhaustible examples of elaborate visual scenography, sophisticated visual rituals, and endless visual tropes offering meaning as well as structure to Buddhist writings, practice, and soteriology. Vision served as metaphor for knowledge, wisdom, awakening, enlightenment, as well as the buddha's actions and insights. We find appeals to light, luminosity, fire, mirrors, and lamps to describe realization of the Buddhist way, as well as eye diseases and sleep to invoke the poisons of suffering, craving, hatred, jealousy, attachment, and ignorance. Visual practices also abound. Meditative techniques often aim at holding and controlling images of the Buddha and Buddha realms in one's mind. Mandala visualizations, tantric visual practice (*sādhanas*), Deity visualization, Vipaśyanā ("discerning vision") meditation were all structured according to the processes of visual realization. Bodhisattvas were distinguished as visionary beings, as "lights and leaders of the world" as opposed to the orthodox "hearers" (*srāvakas)*, who maintained the Hinayana by way of the oral. As McMahon writes, "the six perfections are a bodhisattva's light, torch, and illumination; the bodhisattva's compassionate work is an abundant light that purifies the eyes of all beings, freeing them from *samsāra* and a light to the blind."[7] The mind and the Buddha's dharma are said to be transparently luminous (*prabhdsvara*). The body of the Buddha is often depicted as radiant and emitting light, which pervades all realms. Meeting eyes with a Buddha was thought to impart enlightenment or disclose the Buddha's visual field to an onlooker.

More specifically regarding Mahāyāna as it developed throughout East Asia, with Chan and eventually Zen, there are deployments of the visual particular to these schools, most prominently in the vision-based notion of enlightenment as *kenshō* (見性), which refers to "seeing rightly," or "seeing into one's true nature".

---

[6] Indian Buddhist terms associate vision and wisdom, including "mirror-like knowledge" (*ādarśajñāna), "pristine wisdom that is mirror-like", (*ādarśajñāna), "right view" (*samyak-dṛuṣṭi*), "the knowledge and vision (*jñāna-dar-sana*) of the Buddha," the "divine eye" (*divyacakṣus*), the "wisdom eye" (*jñāna-cakṣus*), the "Buddha eye" (*Buddha-cakṣus*), and the "Dharma eye" (*Dharma-cakṣus*), as well as "having limitless vision" (*Samantadarśin*) and being "one with the universal eye" (*Samantacakṣus*). See McMahon (2013).

[7] McMahan, *Empty Vision*, 72.

Throughout the Zen tradition there are continuous appeals to the notion of mirroring, transmission associated with the lamp, and silent illumination. Lastly, Chan meditative practices are uniquely visual in that they generally dictate that one's eyes remain open during practice.

1.1   From Hinayana to Mahāyāna: from Aural- to Ocular-Centrism

What explains the overwhelming dominance of the visual in Mahāyāna? After all, Indian philosophy was not always oriented so strongly according to the sense of sight. The key here is the early establishment of Mahāyāna and its efforts to counter the orthodox Hinayana lineage around the beginning of the common era. As McMahon details in his study *Empty Vision*: *Metaphor and Visionary Imagery in Mahāyāna Buddhism*, a major aspect of the establishment of Mahāyāna Buddhism and its eventual supplanting of Hinayana lies in a momentous cultural shift in South Asia away from oral towards visual culture. At this time there was an explosion of visionary literature, rituals, visual arts, vision-inspired philosophical and religious writing, teaching and practices.

Mahāyāna gained a great deal of its legitimacy from having both capitalized on and also inspired this broad shift towards a visual culture. The older Hinayana Buddhist tradition, on the other hand, had developed within a culture that was predominantly oral. Practice was oriented not towards "seeing rightly" but in favor of hearing the teachings of the Buddha. Emphasis was on recitation, memorization, reading and hearing sutras, and thus the modalities of voice, sound and language were central. Hinayana leaders were venerated as "hearers" (*srāvakas)* not seers. As Mahāyāna began to gain adherents it moved away from the Hinayana emphasis on *hearing* the Buddha's teachings and away from language towards vision. The newly developing body of Mahāyāna sutras depicted the Buddha's visual experience with extravagant imagery and sophisticated portrayals of his visual fields and ocular powers. Practices and rituals followed this shift towards seeing and often aimed at visualizing, controlling, and manipulating images of the Buddha. While this movement towards the visual animated the early Mahāyāna corpus with spectacular new sensorial dimensions, it was here that we can find the emergence of a latent positivism that accompanied the denigration of language and attendant critique of Hinayana. As we advance to consider Zen Buddhism, we see this denigration persisting as one of its most abiding dictums; "not relying on words and phrases, a separate transmission outside the scriptures," (*furyū monji, kyōge betsuden* 不立文字, 教外別伝). The disparagement of language, as well as the implicit division enforced between language and vision, abide as core features of Mahāyāna to this day, with Dōgen's Sōtō Zen being a significant exception. This study will explore how reading Dōgen according to Kim's interpretation can overcome the Mahāyāna denigration of language and attendant positivism, and thus uncover new and expansive relations between vision and language.

1.2   Traces of Positivism in Mahāyāna: Language and Vision

How might there be a vestige of positivism within Mahāyāna, the very school of Buddhism that sought a "middle way" between the positive and negative? While the dangers of ocularcentrism have been well articulated in recent scholarship, we must be careful to distinguish any element of positivism from those, which are characteristic of Western philosophy. What we do not find in Mahāyāna ocularcentrism are subject–object metaphysics, representational epistemologies, disengaged spectatorship and, most crucially for this dialogue, Mahāyāna was not positivist in the sense of reifying light or upholding a strict light-darkness binary. Yet, to enforce a division between vision and language involves a reification, which installs aspects of positivism within Mahāyāna ocularcentrism. Let us dig deeper into the above discussion regarding the Mahāyāna denigration of language exploring how this relates to the visual.

One of the main reasons why seeing came to be prioritized over the oral was based on the belief that vision was a passive reception of sensory data, un-mediated by language and thus not denigrated by language's reificationary or conceptual tendencies. There was a danger thought to attend language that vision was free from. Vision was thought to be pure. Seeing was seeing. It did not add anything to or distort experience the way language was thought to. Thus, vision provided a model for associated practices and conceptions of enlightenment, which were aimed at attaining awareness of oneself and the world un-mediated by the conceptual apparatus associated with language. Hearing was also thought to be mediated, and did not enjoy the purity of vision. Hearing was too closely associated with language and language led to conceptual attachment, grasping (*grha*) and clinging (*upādāna*). Further, hearing was decidedly not passive, not un-mediated as vision was thought to be. Hearing was not *only* hearing. As a perceptual modality it was defined by its relation to language, conceptual thought, and the binary logic that leads to craving, attachment, grasping, and hypostatization.

The Mahāyāna conception of vision as *just vision not language* leads to a reification of the perceptual modality and thus to a positivist element inherent to its ocularcentrism. In construing seeing as passive and non-expressive receptivity, vision is grasped, at least in this one way, as *non-relational*. Vision is not dependently originated with hearing and language. In this framework, one can strive towards a pure form of visual grasp, which would not accrue anything from language because vision's purity depends on a separation from the features of language that impede realization. Two of those features of language are *activity* and *expression*. This denigration of language and sequestration of vision is, I claim, deeply at odds with Mahāyāna ontology. To be more precise, this conception is positivist in that it takes vision merely as a faculty *to see emptiness*, yet as an action, vision is not *construed as empty itself*. To use Dōgen's language, we might say that vision is not "cast off" (*datsuraku* 脱落) or "undefiled" (*fuzenna* 不染汚). Through Kim's interpretation, we will see how Dōgen challenges Mahāyāna orthodoxy regarding language, and in treating vision ontologically—and thus according to the structures of emptiness,—he challenges the ocularcentric positivity of Mahāyāna and discloses deep relationality between vision and language, neither of which is pure or unmediated. By following Kim in reading Dōgen's account of vision according to his concepts of "activity" (*gyōji* 行持) and "expression" (*dōtoku* 道得), we can see how the Sōtō Zen Buddhist overcomes the division of the visual and the linguistic by not only conceiving of them as faculties *for seeing and speaking of emptiness*, but as faculties *that are themselves empty*.

2   Vision and Light in Dōgen's *Shōbōgenzō*

Let us now consider Dōgen's appeals to the sense of sight to understand how vision is not merely a faculty *to see emptiness*, but *an empty sensory faculty*. In the following section, I develop an argument that his negative ocularcentrism brings vision fully within the realm of emptiness, as vision "cast off" (*datsuraku* 脱落), where seeing is deeply related to language, accruing its dangers while also expanding according to its structure as an expression.

Dōgen is no exception to the Mahāyāna prioritization of the ocular. Throughout his many fascicles, we find countless appeals to the visual, including: moonlight, mirroring, reflection, "eye of practice" (*genjō* 現成), "radiant light" (*komyō* 光明), "dim-sightedness" (*gen'ei* 眼翳), "flowers of vision," "dharma Eye" (*hōgen* 法眼), "luminous pearl" (*myōju* 明珠), "primordial mirror" (*kokyō* 古鏡), "opening up and illumining" (*kaimei* 開明) among many others. And, of course, in line with Zen more generally, in his manuals on monastic and meditative practice, Dōgen advocates keeping one's eyes open while sitting.[8]

Where do we find Dōgen challenging the positivism of the Mahāyāna denigration of language and forced separation from vision? The central claim of this paper is that to take vision beyond positivist tendencies it should be fully ontologized based on emptiness, not just in what it sees, but in what it is. To do so, vision should be ontologized in relation to the visually negative, in relation to non-vision.[9] When considering Dōgen's deployment of visual structures to inform his philosophy, we see that he too thinks the visual as inflected by the visually negative (darkness, opacity and illusion) and constituted by its relation with the non-visual, including language.

---

[8] In his *Dōgen's Manuals of Zen Meditation* Carl Bielefeldt compares passages from Dogen's various writings on Zen meditation with eleventh-century Chan Buddhist Ch'ang-lu Tsung-tse's manuals to illustrate the influence of earlier Chan Buddhism on Dōgen's rules for meditative practice. His *Bendō hō*, *Fukan zazen gi* and *Shōbōgenzō* all quote almost verbatim from Ch'ang-lu's *Principles of Zazen* (坐禅仪*Tso-ch'an i*): "The eyes should remain slightly open, in order to prevent drowsiness. If you attain samādhi [with the eyes open], it will be the most powerful. More recently, the Ch'an master fa-yün Yüan-t'ung criticized those who sit in meditation with their eyes closed likening [their practice] to the ghost cave of the Black Mountain." Carl Bielefeldt, *Dogen's Manuals of Zen Meditation* (University of California Press, 1990).

[9] Despite the ostensible positivism I seek to exhibit, early Mahāyāna did consider vision within a non-dual framework of seeing (*adṛśa*) and non-seeing (*adarśana*).

2.1 Dōgen's Negative Ocularcentrism: Vision "Cast off"

2.1.1 Darkness and Dim-Sightedness

The negativity of Dōgen's philosophy of vision is most conspicuous in the place he makes for what would otherwise be taken as deficient modes of seeing or simply ignored as non-visual. Dōgen thinks vision according to emptiness by including the visually negative as intertwined with the visual. Thus, there is a constitutive role for darkness, opacity, obscurity, blindness etc., alongside notions associated with the visually positive, such as light, clarity, illumination, and transparency. As opposed to a conception of enlightenment where the world would be fully illumined and one's seeing entirely un-obstructed, in his view, darkness remains as a counterpart to illumination. We see this in his "Genjōkōan" where one of Dōgen's central Mahāyāna innovations involves making room for the visually negative in his understanding of enlightenment.

> It is not like a reflection dwelling in the mirror, nor is it like the moon and the water. As one side is illumined, the other is darkened.[10]

Kim claims that this statement epitomizes Dōgen's mystical realism insofar as dualities are realized rather than overcome.[11] Binaries typically enforced within a positive ocularcentrism such as light vs. darkness, clear vs. obscured vision, and associated notions of delusion vs. enlightenment are realised within Dōgen's philosophy. He reflects earlier Chinese Buddhist and Daoist tendencies by casting vision as the realization of light *and* darkness, not the overcoming of one or the other. *As Heine writes* "vision is dependent on dimness, which is the main feature enabling us to see".[12] Kim further reinforces this point. He writes,

> the picture Dōgen offers here is neither that of light's conquest of darkness nor that of light's eternal struggle against darkness. Just as when enlightenment breaks through delusion, it is never outside that delusion, so light, however brilliant and dazzling, works always in and through darkness.[13]

What is vision if it remains wed to darkness as one pursues illumination? One might wonder if we *see less* because the visual is inflected by the negative. Is this a deflationary account of vision and thus of enlightenment based thereupon? In his "Flowers of Emptiness" fascicle Dōgen writes, "[All the buddhas] let their visions (*gen*) realize through dimsightedness (*ei*). They realize the flowers of emptiness in their visions, and their visions in the flowers of emptiness."[14]

---

[10] Kim, *Eihei Dōgen: Mystical Realist*, 105.

[11] Ibid.

[12] Steven Heine, *Readings of Dōgen's "Treasury of the True Dharma Eye"* (Columbia University Press, 2020).

[13] Hee-Jin Kim, *Dōgen on Meditation And Thinking: A Reflection on His View of Zen* (State University of New York Press, 2006), 15.

[14] Kim, *Dōgen on Meditation And Thinking*, 18.

Deficiencies of vision and diseases of the eye have been invoked throughout the Buddhist cannon to symbolize ignorance, attachment, and impediments to enlightenment, which disallow one from "seeing things as they are" (*kenshō*). Thus, when we consider Dōgen's notion of "dim sightedness" (*gen'ei* 眼翳) within this tradition, it would be easy to misconstrue it by counting it as yet another deficiency of seeing. It might seem to be a deflationary account to construe vision as "dim"; as though it is *less than* fully illumined seeing. This is a valid assumption that would follow from a positivist ocular framework, yet as we continue following Dōgen's thinking on the visual, his negative ocularcentrism allows us to appreciate how "dim sightedness" is in fact a highly inflationary account of vision.

Another way that ocular deficiencies have been referred to in the Buddhist tradition is with the trope "the flowers of emptiness" (*kūge* 空華). This term, traditionally employed to refer to illusions hindering one's vision is creatively re-rendered by Dōgen. As he writes, "[Some unenlightened scholars] only think that the flowers seen in the sky (*kūge*) are due to faulty eyesight (*gen'ei*)". Yet, Dōgen realizes the traditional duality that would bifurcate vision from illusion: "When and where one supreme vision is, there are the flowers of emptiness and the flowers of vision. The flowers of vision are called the flowers of emptiness."[15] This playful re-reading has deep significance for Dōgen's thought beyond his theory of vision. Because his philosophy is ocularcentric, his implicit notion of vision informs how he understands the structure of realization. In this case, it implies a quite profound critique of orthodox notions, which describe enlightenment as overcoming illusion and manifesting clear, un-obstructed vision. Rather than eliminating illusion, Dōgen sees "flowers" as essential to realization. "Dim sightedness (*gen'ei*) is what it is" he writes, "by virtue of the flowers of emptiness (*kūge*)"[16] and thus, enlightenment is what it is not by eliminating but by realizing its relation with illusion i.e., non-vision. This realization of duality is what Kim takes to be one of the characteristic aspects of a realist form of mysticism.

We find another approach to describing the realization of delusion and enlightenment in a common Mahāyāna visual trope, the Chan story of the tile polishing Ma-tsu and his teacher Nan-yüeh.[17] In Dōgen's creative re-appropriation, no longer does polishing a tile in hopes of making it a mirror symbolize the futility of meditation. The one-ness of delusion and enlightenment entails a one-ness of tile and mirror. It is not through one's own polishing/meditating efforts that one is transformed into an enlightened being, from a being with limited vision of oneself (tile) to one with unlimited vision (mirror); tile and mirror, delusion and enlightenment are co-implicated, or in Dōgen's words , "un-defiled" (*fuzenna* 不染汚). As Kim writes, "while the tile is the mirror, the self is buddha in zazen; this undefiledness occurs always at the confluence of tile and mirror, of self and buddha. It is an event, not a

---

[15] Kim, *Eihei Dōgen: Mystical Realist*, 92.

[16] Kim, *Dōgen on Meditation And Thinking*, 18.

[17] Heinrich Dumoulin, *A History of Zen Buddhism*, p. 124.

state."[18] Thus, we can see how Dōgen's reappropriations of Mahāyāna ocular metaphor and allegory disclose an underlying negative ocularcentric structure, which does away with any latent positivity or reification of vision or light as separate from blindness or darkness.

2.1.2 Vision Ontologized: Empty Seeing

Insofar as visual metaphor occupies a central role in Dōgen's philosophy, we can see negativity within his invocations of vision but also in the structure of his ontology and soteriology. Vision is indeed central to his thinking as evinced by the plethora of visual metaphor in his writings. Yet, with the inclusion of the visually negative as part of vision, the aspect of seeing that Dōgen highlights goes beyond metaphor to ontology. Thus, Dōgen revises Mahāyāna ocular positivism by reading vision more deeply according to the notion of emptiness as *śūnyatā* (and related notions of non-obstruction (ch. *Wuai*, jp. *muge* 無礙)), which we discuss in a coming section.

Returning to Kim's interpretation, we can see that he also remarks on Dōgen's theory of vision making the leap from metaphor to ontology, i.e., he understands his philosophy as ocularcentric. Kim points to what he describes as Dōgen's alternative approach to the Chan notion of *kenshō* (見性) as it was construed in visual terms by Huineng as "seeing into one's nature" or "seeing things as they are". The representational implications of this dictum should be clear: Vision is a tool *to see emptiness*. Yet, my reading of Kim is that he suggests that any latent positivity is overcome by Dōgen because for him *Kenshō* is not simply "seeing *into* one's nature", but most crucially for this discussion, "from Dōgen's standpoint, the activity of seeing *was one's own nature*."[19] Here we find the suggestion that Dōgen goes beyond construing vision as a *tool to see emptiness* and suggests that vision itself as a perceptual faculty *is empty*. Kim is pointing out that vision is not treated simply as a human faculty but is a valence of all phenomenal reality itself.

And, to foreshadow the concluding section, Kim goes even farther to characterize this aspect of Dōgen's philosophy, not simply as "seeing things as they are" but seeing as "*making things as they are*". Let us examine more of Dōgen's own depictions of the visual to test whether Kim's interpretation holds.

2.1.3 Expanding Ocularcentrism: Synaesthesia and Visual Ontology

To interpret vision ontologically—in the case of Mahāyāna, to interpret it as empty—involves putting the visual in relation to the visually negative. Doing so should have two implications. Firstly, there should be a blurring of boundaries

---

[18] Kim, *Dōgen on Meditation And Thinking*, 28.
[19] Kim, *Eihei Dōgen: Mystical Realist*, 57. (italics added).

between the visual and non-visual. This will disclose further relations between seeing and other perceptual faculties, bodily capacities, time and of course, language. Secondly, there should also be a breakdown of boundaries between sentient visual beings and what would have been taken as insentient *non*-visual entities. We find both of these positions in Dōgen's negative ocularcentrism, and in such a way that can further challenge the Mahāyāna separation between vision and language.

Regarding the first point, we can discern wider relations articulated between vision and the non-visual in Dōgen's several appeals to synaesthetic experience. He comments on Chinese master Dongshan's references to synaesthesia where he speaks of "the voice heard by the eyes"[20] and also claims that time itself has a visual aspect, where "various times have such colors as blue, yellow, red, white".[21] In his "Daigo" fascicle, Dōgen writes, "at times, the eyeballs might be regarded as the present time".[22] If all of one's senses were discrete and reified perceptual modalities—that is, aesthetic not *syn*aesthetic—then the visual would only *achieve* a relation to the non-visual as the result of one's acts, but the visual and non-visual would not be originally co-constitutive. Yet, read according to the relationality of emptiness, vision is *originally* related to and constituted by the other non-visual sense faculties, not as a result of one's deliberate actions aiming to bring them together, but as a result of their being empty. Thus, synaesthesia is not the achievement of a volitional self but is a baseline quality of perceptual relationality, which encompasses seeing, speaking, touching, bodily motion,[23] and even time. Synaesthesia is simply the internal relation of each perceptual modality to what it is not, e.g., seeing to non-seeing; seeing to touch, hearing, taste, etc. While the above fragments of Dōgen's writings can be read as merely poetic or suggestive renderings of visual experience, interpreted in the context of the visually negative, we can appreciate these sayings as poetic precisely because this is the idiom that is appropriate for describing vision itself when it is understood as an empty perceptual faculty— vision with an ontological relation to the non-visual.

Regarding the second point, if seeing is ontologized and construed according to emptiness, we should also expect that the indexing of sentient and insentient beings to the visual and non-visual would be problematized; that is, we should expect a de-anthropization of vision. Such a position is already well noted regarding Dōgen's understanding of language. One aspect of his de-anthropization of language involves challenging the parallelism between the linguistic/non-linguistic and sentient/

---

[20] Heine, *Readings of Dōgen's "Treasury of the True Dharma Eye"*. Dōgen inverts the saying "because the voice is heard by the eyes must be the same as the voice heard by the ears" to "the voice heard by the eyes is not the same as the voice heard by the ears" and further explains that "we should not take Dongshan's remark to mean that there is an ear functioning in our eye, or that the eye becomes the ear, or that there are voices occurring within the eyes."

[21] Kim, *Eihei Dōgen: Mystical Realist*, 150.

[22] Ibid., 153.

[23] In a similar vein, vision is expanded beyond the perceptual to the motor body. "the entire body itself is the arms and eyes" and "if the arms reaching behind are wondrously working, there should also be the wondrous working of the eyes reaching behind." (Kim (2004) p. 206).

insentient binaries. In Dōgen's view, all the world, not just sentient beings, are constantly expressing themselves just as humans are. Thus, it is not just a Buddha, but a broken ladle, a fly whisk, mountains, oceans, earth, sun, moon, and stars that all proclaim the sutras and the dharma.[24]

Moving from language to vision, we find a similar de-anthropization, which expands the visual beyond the sentient/insentient binary. Objects too, insofar as they are visual, have their existence expanded through vision and light. Here, we see how Dōgen's understanding of vision is anything but deflationary. Seeing is not limited to simply *representing* a world or objects whose existence is indifferent to the visual. Thus, the moon is not merely a celestial body that reflects light, which then appears in other bodies of water, in a puddle, or in the drop of water on a crane's bill, which is then represented by, and only by, sentient visual beings. This form of representational fragmentation is broken. No longer is one object reflected in another ontologically distinct object: The moon itself exists there in the puddle or the drop of water. It is not a copy of the moon represented in some other non-visual body, but instead a "water-moon" (*sui-getsu* 水月), a moon whose existence expands throughout the visual world by way of light, reflections, other bodies, and all the world's seers. Insofar as moonlight is meant to symbolize the enlightened mind, Dōgen's negatively ocularcentric re-rendering of this visual metaphor informs his soteriology where the phenomenal world of objects is inseparable from one's realization. Thus, by including the complexities of the visually negative, Dōgen's ocularcentrism evades the perils of positivism at the level of ontology and soteriology.

When seeing is construed as synaesthetic (and enlightenment is understood thereupon) the result is a drastically expanded context for understanding vision since seeing obtains in and through all sentient and insentient beings in the phenomenal world. Thus, to have "dim vision" is not to see less. The flowers of emptiness do not limit the visual, but greatly expand it. It is a type of vision that gives up on pure, positivist visual apprehension (or a type of knowledge or realization based on metaphor that assumes such purity) and in so doing vision obtains everywhere, not only limited to the visual apparatus of sentient beings, but throughout the body, in one's language, in objects, other humans, non-humans, and as time itself. This is one step towards expanding Kim's notion of mysticism in the direction of the visual, that is, as a realization of the visual/non-visual binary.

---

[24] "It is a broken ladle, all dharmas, and the three worlds, i.e., mountains, oceans, earth, sun, moon, and stars. The Buddhist teaching is all the phenomenal world before us. "outside" means "inside" and "coming inside" (Kim Zenji, Dōgen. Flowers of Emptiness; Selections from Dōgen's Shōbōgenzō, p. 22.); "It is impossible, [N]ot to proclaim those sutras-that is how they are proclaimed. "Proclaimed" means the entire universe, and the entire universe proclaims…This world and other worlds also proclaim those sutras. . .We must know that the vast and unlimited Buddhist teaching is not separate from the shippei or fly whisk. The vastness of the Buddhist teaching is revealed in a staff and fist. (p. 28); "The mouth," Dōgen writes, "is hanging on all the walls-every mouth is on all the walls."(p. 80); "Like the rice, hemp, bamboo, and reeds of this world, it is easy to acquire the body-mind, but it is rare to meet the Dharma…therefore, we should beseech the trees and rocks to expound the Dharma, and ask the fields and villages to interpret the Dharma. Similarly, we may put a question to the pillars, and learn from walls and partitions". (p. 288).

In being grasped according to its emptiness, vision is liberated from the confines of the anthropocentric (and thus from representational positivism). This form of vision does not achieve illumination as the clarity of un-obstructed universal light, which would reveal discrete objects, but in a dimness instituted because vision sees things that are themselves without circumscribable boundaries, that is, vision sees things in and through emptiness. Vision is not dim because it is *less than* it is within a positivist ocularcentric philosophy, it is dim because everything we see is much more vast than we imagined; vision is not just a *way to see* being and nothingness, but is part of our adherence therein. Thus, we can read the below quote not as a poetic indulgence, but as an appropriate description of the expansive nature of vision when conceived between positivity and negativity, where one's vision is much more than one's own vision:

> seeing by the Buddha's eyesight and seeing by the ancestor's eyesight; seeing by the Way's eyesight and seeing by the blind's eyesight; seeing in terms of three thousand years and seeing in terms of eight hundred years; seeing from the perspective of a hundred kalpas and seeing from the perspective of immeasurable kalpas. Although these ways all see the "flowers of emptiness," the "emptiness" is ever variegated, and the "flowers" ever manifold.[25]

While including darkness within light, and delusion within realization could be read as a deflationary account of vision and enlightenment, we must grasp this realization as highly expansive. If vision were only vision, it would not multiply through its relation to language, through the moving body, through the perspectives of other beings, objects, time, or through the perspective of other Buddhas. If vision were only vision, if it were only a passive reception of un-mediated sensory data, as the positivist tendencies in early Mahāyāna cast it, it would take additional deliberate acts of a subject to bring it into relation with language. But, when properly elevated to the ontological and grasped not just as a *faculty to see emptiness* but as a *faculty that is empty*, vision is inherently mediated but drastically expanded such that it cannot be conceived as separate from any human faculty, or as ultimately separate from anything, especially not language.

3 Hee-Jin Kim: Dōgen's "Activity" and "Expression"

I would like to now engage more closely with Hee-Jin Kim's interpretation and attempt to transpose a number of his insights regarding language to the visual realm. Kim suggests that Dōgen's concepts "activity" (*gyōji* 行持) and "expression" (*dōtoku* 道得) are central concepts through which the entirety of his philosophy should be read. As he writes, "The prototype of zazen-only has two aspects: activities (*gyōji*) and expressions (*dōtoku*)."[26] In the remaining sections of this study, we

---

[25] Kim, *Dōgen on Meditation And Thinking*, 69.
[26] Kim, *Eihei Dōgen: Mystical Realist*, 67.

will follow Kim in reading Dōgen's understanding of the ocular as such, to test his predication of realism to Dōgen's mysticism.

Recall that one of the main reasons for Mahāyāna prioritizing the visual and denigrating language was that the former was thought to be a passive reception of sensory data not mixed up with forms of reification, conceptual grasping, and hypostatization, which were associated with language. Thus, vision was decisively *not* understood as expression or activity: Mahāyāna prioritized the visual over the linguistic precisely because vision was thought to be passive and *non-expressive*. We do find confirmation that Dōgen is also thinking of vision in relation to expression. In "Dōtoku", he writes;

> Because you regard seeing-then (*kano toki no kentoku*) as true, you do not doubt that expression-now (*ima no dōtoku*) is true as well. Accordingly, expression-now is provided with seeing-then, and seeing-then is prepared with expression-now. Thus, expression exists now, seeing exists now. Expression-now and seeing-then are ever one in their perpetuation. Our efforts now are being sustained by expression and seeing.[27]

Reading vision in relation to expression brings the sense of sight into the realm of Dōgen's interpretation of language since a great deal of his elaboration of "expression" is articulated specifically regarding language. If we can interpret vision as both *active* and *expressive*, we counter one aspect of Mahāyāna visual positivism precisely by allowing for a continuity and interplay between vision and language. Let us dwell on the notion of expression in relation to Dōgen's de-anthropocized conception of language and from there take the further step to test whether this understanding of expression and activity can be carried over to describe vision.

3.1   From Language to Vision: Reflexivity

Dōgen is well-known for his radical innovations and interventions in classical Buddhist language and expressions. He takes a strong stand against the Chan orthodox "no dependence upon words and letters (*furyū monji*)" and thus counter to the original departure that initiated the Mahāyāna movement. He does so not merely by employing his own innovative linguistic expressions but by reversing the denigration of language and deploying it as a soteriological tool.

Let us consider one of his unorthodox expressions for what it says about both the visual and the linguistic. In his "Sansuikyō" he writes that "water sees water". The reflexive structure of this short saying—a structure we read throughout the *Shōbōgenzō*[28]—implies a radical position regarding both language and vision. We

---

[27] Ibid., 96.

[28] Some examples include; "obstruction obstructs obstruction", "water speaks of water", "vines entangling vines," "mountains hidden in hiddenness". For a different perspective on reflexivity as "self-relational structure", which invites the reader into the text, see Ralf Müller, "Philosophy and the Practice of Reflexivity: On Dōgen's discourse about Buddha-nature," in *Concepts of Philosophy in Asia and the Islamic World. 2 Vols*, ed. R.C. Steineck (Koninklijke Brill NV, 2018).

can expose this position by examining features of Dōgen's notion of language, and as a second step, attempt to transpose those features onto the visual.

The de-anthropocentric expansion of language is particularly prominent in Dōgen's revision of Kukai's "*hosshin-seppō*" (法身説法) which attributes the language of the Buddha only to sentient beings. Dōgen proposes his "*mujō-seppō*" (無情説法) to enlarge the linguistic by attributing the speaking of the Buddha's dharma to all phenomenal reality.

> What we mean by the sūtras is the entire universe itself. There is no space nor time which is not the sūtras. They use the words and letters of the ultimate truth as well as the words and letters of the worldly truth. They adopt the symbols of heavenly beings as well as those of human beings. They use the words and letters of beasts and asuras as well as those of hundreds of grasses and thousands of trees. For this reason, the long and short, the square and round, the blue and yellow, the red and white—marshalling solemnly in the ten directions of the universe—are undeniably the sūtras' words and letters and faces. They are the instruments of the great Way and the scriptures for a Buddhist.[29]

Thus, we find throughout the *Shōbōgenzō* instances of language being attributed to the non-sentient world of objects. "Boundless words and letters (*kōdai no monji*) permeate the universe with overflowing abundance,"[30] writes Dōgen in his "Bendōwa".

In de-anthropizing language, expression is thus not a strictly human activity it does not abide the cleaving of the sentient from the insentient. One's expressivity is a way of being deeply connected to the world, a continuity not a discontinuity. When the sentient/insentient binary is realized, linguistic expressivity cannot be described as a one-way verbal projection of human beings directed at an objective non-verbal world. All the world and the 10,000 things are expressive. Language is not a uni-directional projection, but a reflexive relation between all beings in a world conceived of as linguistic and expressive. Thus, to speak is not simply to insert language into a non-linguistic world. In what might be a precursor to hermeneutic philosophy, Dōgen's ontological notion of language suggests that the way we speak of the world impacts how that world is and how it expresses itself back to us. This explains why Dōgen is so adamant about the soteriological importance of language. When he deconstructs previous Buddhist expressions, he is not merely searching for new ways to *represent* a non-linguistic world, he is striving for giving that world new life as an expressive world.

To take the next step and consider seeing in the context of this structure of expression, we should consider whether a similar reflexive expressive structure is tenable with Dōgen's theory of vision. If we carry his thinking over to the visual domain, and if we realize the binaries dividing the sentient from the insentient, and the visual from non-visual, then we should find a similar expressive *visual* reflexivity like the one that is explicit regarding language. On this point, we can return to Dōgen's dictum "water sees water" and see how it supports this interpretation. In this short

---

[29] Kim, *Eihei Dōgen: Mystical Realist*, 77.

[30] Ibid., 78.

phrase, we find the first aspect discussed above regarding linguistic expression. That is, a de-anthropocentric framework, now applied to seeing. It is water that sees. Moreover, Dōgen clearly admonishes us to see water beyond our own limited view and to behold it as dragons or fish do, as a palace, and as flowing not just on the earth but in the sky, upward and downward.[31] Accordingly, we should not reduce all the different views to one, and in attributing vision to water itself the sentient/insentient binary is realized regarding the visual. Further, and regarding the second point articulated above, we also find a similar reflexive structure within Dōgen's view of language. If it were simply the case that water sees other things or sees us, this would not account for the most important subtlety of the reflexivity Dōgen intends. It is not simply that *I see* and that *water also sees*, but that water's seeing is a *self-seeing*. Seeing is seeing-seen, and while this might sound like an imposition of recent western phenomenological conceptions onto Dōgen's thought, it might actually be that the Sōtō Buddhist monk anticipated these ideas by many centuries.[32] Vision is thus not simply a uni-directional representational phenomena moving in vectors between entities; there is a reflexivity, which drastically expands the event of seeing and being seen by realizing the polarity between the two. Vision is not simply a circumscribable event *within a world*: "there is a world in water" writes Dōgen in his "Sansuikyō". As such, vision is woven into the very fabric of emptiness itself.

Following Kim, we can see that Dōgen's de-anthropocized, perspectival, and ontological notion of vision is an *expressive* worldly event. And thus, we find a strong connection between the structures Dōgen attributes to language and also vision. If such an extension were tenable, we can then ask about further possible relations between the visual and linguistic. Regarding the latter, Dōgen is well known for a soteriology based on his poetic form of creative/destructive linguistic appropriation. Can we say the same for the visual? If seeing the world has a similar seeing-seen, expressing-expressed reflexivity, in seeing the world actively and expressively is there the possibility of a creative *visual* re-making of the world? And if so, how might we think of vision in relation to the poetic act in the sense Dōgen intends for activity (行持 *gyōji*).

3.2 Impossible to Act (gyōfutokutei), Impossible to Express (setsufutokutei)

If we understand language and vision as related by way of their expressive and active elements, as faculties not just to *see and speak of emptiness* but as *themselves empty*, what soteriological implications follow for visual activity? Is it possible to

---

[31] Graham Parkes, "Dōgen's 'Mountains and Waters as Sūtras'," in *Buddhist Philosophy: Essential Readings*, ed. William Edelglass (Oxford: Oxford University Press, 2009).

[32] Merleau-Ponty is well-known for having instituted this form of visual reflexivity as "seeing-seen", most notably in his *The Visible and the Invisible* (1979) and earlier in his 1950s Course Notes transcribed in *Nature* (1995).

exert one's seeing *actively* to re-make the visual world the same way Dōgen seeks
to make the world linguistically through his poetic interventions? If so, this would
counter Mahāyāna's main recourse to vision as a passive sensory reception.

Of course, in Dōgen's philosophy "activity" (*gyōji*) is not anthropocentric. It is
not the activity of a reified self over against a passive world of matter. One does not
exert oneself as an individual circumscribed subject, but as "total exertion" (*gūjin*
究盡), which includes the agency of the entire world and the 10,000 things. As he
writes "the now of activity (*gyōji no ima*) is not the self's primordial being, eternal
and immutable, nor is it something that enters and leaves the self."[33] Dōgen further
elaborates in his "Gyōji" fascicle:

> This is the perpetuation of the Way through activity (*gyōji-dōkan*). Consequently, supreme
> activity is neither a contrivance of the self nor that of others; it is activity undefiled. The
> power of such an activity sustains my self and others. Its import is such that all the heavens
> and the entire earth in the ten directions enjoy the merit of my activity.[34]

This expanded form of activity does not arise from one definable locus but is rather
a diffuse agency accruing the activity of all beings and the world as a whole. This
idea is reinforced throughout Dōgen's writing. We find it when he casts Buddhist
practice not as "carry[ing] yourself forward and experience myriad things" but as
"myriad things com[ing] forth and experience themselves."[35] Similar ideas can also
be found in Dōgen's conception of dependent origination itself. As he writes,
"dependent origination (*engi* 縁起) is activity, because activity does not originate
dependently".[36] Thus, "activity" (*gyōji*) is not human activity, instead

> the sun, the moon, and the stars exist by virtue of such creative activities. The earth and the
> empty sky exist because of activities. Our body mind and its environment are dependent on
> activities; so are the four elements and the five skandhas.[37]

Returning to the question of visual activity, how do we understand the type of cre-
ative/destructive linguistic activity but now in the visual domain?[38] Before focusing
on what will be a greatly expansive interpretation of vision, let us consider limitations that arise: Limitations that will initially appear deflationary yet turn out to
deliver a highly expanded account of expression. One such *expansive limitation*

---

[33] Kim, *Eihei Dōgen: Mystical Realist*, 164.

[34] Ibid., 76.

[35] Dōgen, *Moon in a Dewdrop: Writings of Zen Master Dōgen*, trans. K. Tanahashi (North Point Press, 1985, 1985), 69.

[36] Kim, *Eihei Dōgen: Mystical Realist*, 164.

[37] Ibid.

[38] We should note that in his "Gyōji" Dōgen does invoke the relation between activity and expression: "In these ongoing endeavors, activity and expression are such that when activity is totally
exerted, there is nothing but activity, and similarly, when expression is totally exerted, there is
nothing but expression. Thus, "while activity (*gyō*) fathoms the way to be in unison with expression (*setsu*), expression has the path to be attuned with activity." After all, humanity "enacts that
which is impossible to enact" (*gyōfutokutei*) and "expresses that which is impossible to express"
(*setsufutokutei*). (Kim (2004), p. 76).

arises when we consider the impossibility of expression or "the inexpressible". As Kim writes:

> Dōgen also employs another word *fudōtoku*, which means "that expression which is not or beyond expression" or "the inexpressible." Note that what is not/beyond expression is itself ultimately an expression, not an extra expressive substratum or reality. For Dōgen, the inexpressible is never reified as the opposite of expression.[39]

If expression and non-expression were reified, that which is impossible to express would be a straightforward limit of what one can say. But, within an ontology of emptiness, non-expression is part of expression. The inexpressible, that which is impossible to express is then not strictly speaking impossible, it is merely impossible for a self to express, but here we are speaking of the expression of the non-self. As Dōgen writes in his "Gyōji", humanity "enacts that which is impossible to enact (*gyōfutokutei*)"[40] The inexpressible would be straightforwardly impossible within positivist and anthropocentric notions of expression and selfhood. Yet, when expression and the self are grasped within the relationality of emptiness, one can "express that which is impossible to express (*setsufutokutei*)."[41]

Thus, we can now frame the conception of activity underlying Dōgen's efforts as creative/destructive linguistic expression, as a structure which vision shares. When that expressive activity is grasped as the activity of emptiness, it is not the individual positive self but the expressive world, which can express the inexpressible. The linguistic and visual self as empty and "undefiled" is only one focus within the field of reflexive expression and activity.

3.3 *"Radiant Light" and Reflexive Visual Obstructions*

In this section, I would like to dig deeper into Kim's conception of mystical realism, by considering his understanding of obstruction in more detail. He writes that "Dōgen-like mystical realism, [w]as epitomized in Dōgen's statement: 'Obstruction hinders obstruction, thereby obstruction realizes itself'"[42]. We see in this quote that Dōgen's construal of obstruction has a similar structure as discussed earlier where realisation includes that which hinders it; that is, revealing includes concealing. In

---

[39] Kim, *Dōgen on Meditation And Thinking*, 64. In their Volume two of their translation of the *Shōbōgenzō* (2008), Nishijima and Cross write: "*Fudōtoku* can be interpreted literally as "beyond-expression attainment," i.e., attainment that is beyond verbal expression. At the same time, *dōtoku* as a compound has evolved the meaning of "expressing the truth," independently of its component characters. *Fudōtoku*, "not expressing the truth," may therefore simply be seen as the dialectical opposite of *dōtoku*, "expressing the truth." In other words, the two expressions describe the same state." G. W. Nishijima and C. Cross, *Shōbōgenzō: The True Dharma-Eye Treasury: Volume 2*, 4 vols., vol. 2 (*Numata Center for Buddhist Translation and Research*, 2008).

[40] Kim, *Eihei Dōgen: Mystical Realist*, 76.

[41] Ibid.

[42] Ibid., 157.

his *Eihei Dōgen: Mystical Realist*, Kim explains how obstruction is not an unambiguous constraint, but is a source of freedom.

> Dōgen explained immediately after this passage, "obstruction" (*ge*, a shortened expression of *keige*) was not used in the ordinary sense of the word, but in the sense of "self-obstruction" while abiding in a Dharma-position. A thing was obstructed by itself and nothing else; that is, it exerted itself in perfect freedom.[43]

By way of contrast, if we turn to Greek ocularcentric metaphysics and epistemology, what we find is that they were structured in analogy with a type of vision thought to be universal, abstract, and un-situated. The latent positivism came by way of conceiving of vision strictly as revealing, and successful visual apprehension (and by extension, knowing-as-seeing) as entirely *un*-obstructed. The body was, of course, one of the main obstructions to the mind's way of knowing-as-seeing, and thus the task of the philosopher was to overcome the bodily form of seeing. Light was thought to be uninflected by the visually negative and thus could, in theory, fully eliminate darkness and reveal the object in its non-perspectival generality. These positivist applications of visual metaphor to metaphysics and epistemology pave the way to the myth of the un-situated and un-obstructed "view from nowhere", and motivate the idea that the philosopher's task is to exit the darkness of the cave entirely and ascend into the pure light of reason. The view from nowhere is precisely the positivist dream of a type of vision not limited by any obstructions. The tragic mistake of positivist ocularcentrism is that it mistakes obstruction minimisation for visual/epistemic maximisation. Dōgen, on the other hand, saw that vision and light are involved in a much more complex relation and thus our engagement with the world is augmented *because of* obstructions and concealing. As Kim writes,

> radiant light for Dōgen is not a diffuse, universalized light so much as it is a confocal (with respect to light and darkness as binary foci), differentiated light, invariably local and temporal as a specific thing, being or phenomenon.[44]

For Dōgen, "radiant light" (*komyō* 光明) is *this* light, in *this* moment and *this* locus, it is the light of one's own embodied and situated specificity. As such, it is always a view *from somewhere*. Situated vision, by definition, cannot be a view from nowhere. As situated and particular, radiant light must be partially obstructed. Firstly, because illumination is always attenuated (and augmented) by darkness. Thus, when a type of vision, which includes the negative is expanded to inform and structure ontology and soteriology, we should not be surprised that we have an account of enlightenment, which realizes rather than overcomes the obstructions of delusion and concealment. Vision for Dōgen is not what we would arrive at if we could discard all bodily particularities and manifest an abstract view of the world, or universal definitions of objects applicable in all times, all places, and to all humans. Thus, Kim writes that Dōgen's notion of radiant light

---

[43] *Ibid.*

[44] Kim, *Dōgen on Meditation And Thinking*, 15.

becomes potent and efficacious only when localized and temporalized in concrete beings and situations. Only in that context can light not only break darkness but, more importantly for our purpose, penetrate darkness with the heightened awareness of its abysmal depths.[45]

Just as dimming vision could easily be taken as a deflationary, as *less than* a universal, fully clarified way of seeing, likewise, we could construe obstructed vision as *less than* un-obstructed vision, less than the un-situated view from nowhere of Greek ocularcentrism. Less is less, it is thought. However, this is a further conceit of the positivist model of vision and positivist visual metaphor, which is crucial to overturn. If vision is conceived of in positivist terms as simply visual, with no ontological relation to the non-visual, no relation to language, movement, darkness, etc., we might be inspired by this idea of un-obstructed vision, we might think it is *more than* obstructed vision but, the problem is that there is no such vision. Conceiving the ocular within its full positive and negative valences means acknowledging obstructions, delusions, darkness, etc., and those *obstructions do not render vision 'less than'*: Obstructions arise because vision is construed in the most expansive way possible, beyond the anthropocentric conception and thus, obstructions are instituted precisely because vision embraces the entirety of the phenomenal world, sentient and insentient alike. When vision is grasped according to the negative vision is now everything, part of the fabric of emptiness itself. Vision is an element of the phenomenal, radically expanded beyond the positivist view which construed it strictly as a human faculty with no relation to the non-visual, the negative. Vision in the positivist framework is only vision. In Dōgen's negative ocularcentrism, vision is empty, and thus related to and expanded through the non-visual, i.e., all things, all beings, and all the world at all times. De-anthropocized as such, seeing is a reflexive expressive relation, is it now a worldly event at once obstructed and drastically expanded.

Moving now to the next section, I would like to discuss how the expansive limitations within Dōgen's negative ocularcentrism allow for a deeper participation of the seer within the visual. Rather than a subject representing a pre-existent visual object, we are *active* and *expressive* in creating the visual world we are part of.

4   Visual "Hermeneutics of Intrusion"

To move towards concluding, I would like to return to the goal I began with, to extend and also challenge Kim's ascription of realism to Dōgen's mysticism. I would like to undertake that work now by following his own thinking on the linguistic in Dōgen and extending this to the visual in Dōgen. In terms of language, it is well noted that Dōgen sees great soteriological value in a poetic idiom, which he enacted as a linguistic creative-destruction of the Buddhist tradition. He is constantly re-working the language, famous stories and expressions of classical sutras

---

[45] Ibid.

to subvert and also invent meaning with the aim of opening new soteriological possibilities. Moving from language to vision, I would like to inquire into how we
might transpose this creative-destruction Dōgen explicitly endorses in the linguistic
realm onto the visual world. How does one achieve realization not simply as *seeing
the world as it is* but as *making the world how it appears*? If Dōgen's creative reappropriations of the Buddhist cannon are what Steven Heine calls a "hermeneutics
of intrusion", can we find a *visual* hermeneutics of intrusion implicit within Dōgen's
negative ocularcentrism, and what might this say about his version of mysticism?

Dōgen's linguistic interventions could be understood as a heightening of his own
expressive activity yet, to read his innovations according to his own notion of
expression (*dōtoku*), we must challenge the positivist reading that would consider
expression as an activity of an individuated self. Following his own theories of
activity" (行持 *gyōji*) and "expression" (道得 *dōtoku*), his creative relation to the
language of the Buddhist cannon should be seen as a negation of the expressive self,
an active subordination of his individual expressive desires, which allows him to
participate as one node in a larger linguistic-expressive world. To express oneself as
Dōgen did is not to be a self in control of language, but is to forget the self, as he
did, and to allow the 10,000 things to come forth and express the inexpressible.

If Dōgen's conception of vision has a similar active and expressive reflexivity as
language does, what would that visual expression of the inexpressible look like?
How do we follow Dōgen's creative re-appropriation of the linguistic in terms of a
creative re-appropriation of the visual? If *Dōtoku* is achieved by Dōgen through
"inversions, repetitions, or reversals based on wordplay and other resourceful rhetorical devices" can one achieve similar in the visual sphere? If so, this would constitute a soteriology of a negatively ocularcentric mysticism. Kim himself suggests
the movement from a linguistic to a visual hermeneutics when he asks what a cre-
ative/destructive visual hermeneutics would look like in his further commentary on
Dōgen's re-reading of Hui-Neng's "seeing into one's own nature". Kim says that
"Dōgen's Zen thus deepens the meaning of 'seeing things as they are' by construing
it as 'changing/making things as they are'."[46] With this we find what we might consider a *linguistic* hermeneutics elevated to a *visual* hermeneutics of intrusion. In a
footnote, Kim is even more incisive:

> "things" seen as they are are transformable. Every practitioner's task is to *change* them by
> seeing through them. From Dōgen's perspective, this is the fundamental difference between
> contemplation (*dhyana*) and zazen-only. To him, seeing was changing and making.[47]

We can now return to the two elements of Mahāyāna positivism articulated in the
beginning of this analysis and see how Dōgen's negative ocularcentrism overcomes
both. First, in his writings, vision is construed not just as a tool to see emptiness but
as an empty perceptual faculty. Secondly, as empty, vision is not passive reception
but has the same reflexive structure of "activity" and "expression" as language does
in Dōgen's philosophy. As opposed to the vestige of visual positivity in early

---

[46] Ibid., 52.
[47] Kim, *Dōgen on Meditation And Thinking*, 38.

Mahāyāna, which separated seeing from speaking, in Dōgen's philosophy they are deeply related on the ontological level as activities and expressions, which embrace the negative. Thus, Dōgen's mystical negative ocularcentrism, in realizing duality on the plane of both language and vision, offers a greatly expanded soteriology where an expressive-expressed reflexivity enables a creative-destructive re-making of the linguistic as well as the visual world.

5   Conclusion: Mysticism as Impossible Expression

To conclude, I would like to now return to Kim's predication of realism to Dōgen's mysticism. We should begin by being clear that he does not intend "realism" in the typical Western sense of a stable mind-independent reality. He employs the term to refer to a realization of duality enabling a special kind of action and then the emptying of that very action. As he explains,

> Dōgen's non-dualistic mystical thinking had an especially realistic thrust, which permeated all aspects of his religion and philosophy. That is to say, nonduality did not primarily signify the transcendence of duality so much as it signified the realization of duality. When one chose and committed oneself to a special course of action, one did so in such a manner that the action was not an action among others, but the action—there was nothing but that particular action in the universe so that the whole universe was created in and through that action. Yet even this action was eventually cast off, leaving no trace of the Way whatsoever. This was indeed far from being a kind of mysticism that attempted to attain an undifferentiated state of consciousness. On the contrary, Dōgen's thought was entirely committed to the realm of duality—including its empirical and rational aspects.[48]

As Kim develops his interpretation, he refers to a form of realization that agrees with Dōgen's emphasis on "activity" (行持 *gyōji*) and "expression" (道得 *dōtoku*). To extend this structure of realization and associated activity to encapsulate Dōgen's philosophy offers an innovative means of characterizing an original mystical structure in his soteriology while evading the standard dismissals of mysticism within philosophy. In this sense, Kim's is an important interpretation of Dōgen's thought, as well as a worthwhile means for redeeming his Buddhist philosophy *as philosophy*. Where I will seek to take issue is not with the predication of realism itself but with its compatibility with other aspects of Kim's Dōgen interpretation.

To begin, we must first distinguish Dōgen's mysticism from other versions. While there are far too many instances to discuss in their particularity, whether Eastern or Western forms, mystical philosophies typically posit some element of reality as inaccessible to human knowledge, thought, or language. Kim rightly points to "obstructions" (*ge* 礙) as the element in Dōgen's philosophy representing such limitations, and I believe he quite aptly characterizes the radicality of his

---

[48] Kim, *Eihei Dōgen: Mystical Realist,* 105.

mysticism when invoking Dōgen's "obstructions obstructing obstructions".[49] Kim writes that "Dōgen-like mystical realism, [w]as epitomized in Dōgen's statement: "Obstruction hinders obstruction, thereby obstruction realizes itself".[50] Kim reveals how Dōgen's construal of obstruction has a similar structure discussed earlier where realization involves revealing and concealing, enlightenment includes delusion. Accordingly, Kim explains how obstructions are not ontologically deflationary, or even soteriologically limiting, but our source of freedom.

> Dōgen explained immediately after this passage, "obstruction" (*ge*, a shortened expression of *keige*) was not used in the ordinary sense of the word, but in the sense of "self-obstruction" while abiding in a Dharma-position. A thing was obstructed by itself and nothing else; that is, it exerted itself in perfect freedom.[51]

How can we characterize the reflexive self-obstructive aspect of Dōgen's mysticism? His version must be further distinguished from others in that there is not simply some circumscribed part of the world or creation that is invisible to our eyes, unknowable, or un-expressible in language. It is not that there is some part of creation that is out of bounds for expression, and other parts that we can refer to. Just as we have uncovered a dynamic reflexivity of linguistic and visual expression in Dōgen's philosophy, likewise there is a reflexivity in his notion of obstruction. That obstructions obstruct obstructions adds a layer of elusiveness, a complexity to the negative. Obstructions cannot be a static limitation, which would be characteristic of most negative theology. If an obstruction were static, if it did not also self-obstruct, if we knew that only certain things were obstructed, such as God or nature, and we knew other things were not obstructed, then this conception of obstruction would be circumscribed in its negativity, and an element of positivity would be reinscribed. Emptiness would not itself be empty. In such a case, and this might be the typical case, obstructions could be properly acknowledged by one's restraint, by being silent, i.e., the cessation of activity and expression. One is simply silent and that would suffice for properly acknowledging mystical limitations. But, Kim insist that for Dōgen, activity and expression must be maintained. Silence for Dōgen is not the end of expression or activity. Dōgen's mysticism is not apophaticism. Not only is darkness part of illumination and delusion part of enlightenment, likewise obstruction is not an impediment to realization, but one of its conditions. As Steven Heine writes, "Getting there is obstructed by getting there, but not by not getting there. Not getting there is obstructed by not getting there, but not by getting there… Obstruction obstructs obstruction and thus realizes obstruction." [52]

---

[49] Ibid., 157.
    We see further that Dōgen himself sanctions our proceeding from this notion of obstruction to expression when he writes "Expression obstructs expression, and thereby sees expression."
[50] Ibid.
[51] Ibid.
[52] Steven Heine, *Readings of Dōgen's "Treasury of the True Dharma Eye"* (Columbia University Press, 2020).

What is unique of Dōgen's mysticism, is that obstructions that limit (but also make possible) expression are dynamic and non-reifiable i.e., they must not be an exception to obstruction. In this sense, he is deploying the Mahāyāna logic of the emptiness of emptiness (śūnyatāyāh śūnyatā). To avoid reification, emptiness itself cannot be an exception to its own emptying dynamic, likewise obstruction is not free of obstruction.

What though could be problematic about predicating realism to this particular form of mysticism? My claim is that, to qualify Dōgen's mysticism with any binary-invoking term undermines the type of realization, which Kim himself otherwise insists on maintaining. Since Kim's realism is not the typical Western version, it is not clear what the other pole of that opposition would be, but if realism is "A", then we do not need to know exactly what the not-A is, only that A implies a not-A, realism implies a type of mysticism that would not be realist. Thus, the problem is with predication itself. To predicate any binary of Dōgen's form of mysticism is to leave that binary un-realized and, therefore, ignoring something crucial that Kim otherwise, and rightly, insists on to define Dōgen's mysticism. What *can* we say about Dōgen's mysticism? My claim is that the nature of that mysticism demands that we not predicate anything at all. The radicality of his mysticism is that it evades any static predication by its very nature, but crucially, disallows apophatic silence. We cannot abdicate saying anything, we cannot abdicate "activity" (行持 *gyōji*) or "expression" (道得 *dōtoku*), but predication is also problematic.

Prior to qualifying Dōgen's mysticism as realist, perhaps the best or only way to follow the radicality of that mysticism is to re-invoke the dynamic and reflexive obstruction we find as an aspect of linguistic and, I argue, visual, activity and expression. Thus, we should assume that there is a reflexive obstruction in ascribing any qualities to Dōgen's mysticism, a constitutive inexpressibility, but importantly, this is itself the condition that enables expression. The obstruction does not simply hinder our characterization, but it does demand a particular kind of active expression, which realizes speech and silence. And, in this sense, we find an answer in Dōgen's writing for what this entails. The tightwire between speech and silence is the creative-destructive expressive activity Dōgen employs to interpret the Buddhist tradition, and also the fabric of linguistic phenomenal reality itself. What does this mean for characterising his mysticism? Simply that once we have established the form of dynamic self-obstruction always in play, we then must realize our characterizations of that mysticism. Here, we face Dōgen's impossibility of expression (*setsufutokutei*), but as Kim states, "for Dōgen, the inexpressible is never reified as the opposite of expression." In the face of such inexpressibility that we must nevertheless remain engaged in expression and activity. It is impossible to predicate anything of mysticism but, nevertheless, we must remain engaged in expressive activity, not lose the word in apophatic silence. My claim is that when we recognize the limitations of propositional language for qualifying Dōgen's mysticism, (and perhaps all phenomenal reality) that he does provide a way through the expressible and inexpressible. That is, we must follow him beyond predication and engage in the same kind of "hermeneutics of intrusion" he aims at the Buddhist tradition. His mysticism empties its own emptiness and we must acknowledge that it can never be expressed but constantly demands expression. This might be one way of understanding the kind of poetic idiom Dōgen favours, rather than propositional language or un-realized binary terminology.

Allow me to finish by applying this meagre hesitation regarding Kim's "mystical realism" to the notion of negative ocularcentrism I am attempting to develop from within his own project. If Dōgen can be considered ocularcentrist, his is a variety that avoids the dangers of Mahāyāna visual positivism and does so by a thoroughgoing submission of vision to emptiness where it can be seen in a continuity with language and all phenomenal reality. Thus, obstructed dim-sightedness is not less than universal, un-obstructed sightedness would be. Dim-sightedness is a radically expanded form of vision that does not simply see emptiness, but is itself empty, and thus demands activity and expression as a condition of being woven into the fabric of visual phenomenal reality, and perhaps even as a condition of our authentically deploying the concept in our own experience. It is here, empty without any grounds, that all phenomena visual reality reflexively obstructing itself as a condition of its expansive revealing that we arrive at a groundlessness which is another way of characterizing the ocularcentrism in Dōgen's philosophy in line with his mysticism. This is not to claim the visual world is realist or otherwise, but by following Dōgen, we can put aside predication for participation, and in the creative hermeneutics of intrusion into the visual world not describe that world but participate in its genesis through visual activity and expression.

Bibliography

Bielefeldt, Carl. *Dōgen's Manuals of Zen Meditation*. University of California Press, 1990.
Dōgen. *Moon in a Dewdrop: Writings of Zen Master Dōgen*. Translated by K. Tanahashi. North Point Press, 1985.
Heine, Steven. *Readings of Dōgen's "Treasury of the True Dharma Eye"*. Columbia University Press, 2020.
Jay, Martin. *Downcast Eyes: The Denigration of Vision in Twentieth-Century French Thought*. University of California Press, 1994.
Kim, Hee-Jin. *Dōgen on Meditation and Thinking: A Reflection on His View of Zen*. State University of New York Press, 2006.
———. *Eihei Dōgen: Mystical Realist*. Boston: Wisdom Publications, 2004, 2004.
Levin, D.M. *Modernity and the Hegemony of Vision*. University of California Press, 1993.
———. *Sites of Vision: The Discursive Construction of Sight in the History of Philosophy*. MIT Press, 1999.
McMahan, David. *Empty Vision: Metaphor and Visionary Imagery in Mahayana Buddhism*. Taylor & Francis, 2013.
Müller, Ralf. "Philosophy and the Practice of Reflexivity: On Dōgen's Discourse About Buddha-Nature." In *Concepts of Philosophy in Asia and the Islamic World. 2 Vols*, edited by R.C. Steineck: Koninklijke Brill NV, 2018.
Nishijima, G. W., and C. Cross. *Shōbōgenzō: The True Dharma-Eye Treasury: Volume 2*. 4 vols. Vol. 2: Numata Center for Buddhist Translation and Research, 2008.
Parkes, Graham. "Dōgen's 'Mountains and Waters as Sūtras'." In *Buddhist Philosophy: Essential Readings*, edited by William Edelglass. Oxford: Oxford University Press, 2009.

Dōgen as Philosopher, Metaphysician, and Metaethicist

Audrey Guilbault

1 Introduction: Dōgen's Place in the Buddhist Philosophical Tradition

For decades, Dōgen's work has captured the interest of scholars interested in the doctrinal and philosophical aspects of Buddhism, thanks to its linguistic complexity and doctrinal sophistication.[1] Recently, however, the philosophical reception of Dōgen has come in for criticism on two fronts.

One line of critique—pursued most notably by Raji Steineck[2]—suggests that, in reading Dōgen with an eye to philosophical content, we may be imposing presuppositions and methodology that Dōgen actively opposed and rejected. If we understand 'philosophy' as the field of inquiry that addresses fundamental concerns of human life by means of argument and persuasion, proceeding by means of "disputation among a community of equals," avoiding recourse to any "absolutely authoritative source,"[3] then it may be a poor fit. Dōgen's approach to the same fundamental questions is characterized more by bare assertion of doctrines, coupled by the

---

[1] I am grateful to Nic Bommarito, Tanya Kostochka, Natalie Nitsch, George Wrisley, and Brook Ziporyn for helpful feedback, as well as to the online audience at the workshop that generated this volume, and to Ralf Müller for the invitation to participate.

[2] Raji C. Steineck, "A Zen Philosopher?—Notes on the Philosophical Reading of Dōgen's *Shōbōgenzō*," in *Concepts of Philosophy in Asia and the Islamic World*, vol. 1, ed. Raji C. Steineck, Ralph Weber, Robert Gassmann, and Elena Lange (Leiden: Brill, 2018a). See also his paper in this volume.

[3] Ibid., 582.

A. Guilbault (✉)
University of Chicago, Chicago, IL, USA
e-mail: audreyrg@uchicago.edu

injunction "to *study it in practice (sangaku su* 参学す)."[4] His epistemic reliance on meditation is also indicated by the use of the term 證 *shō* ("certification", "proof") to characterize meditative practice. Where meditative verification leaves off, appeal to religious authority and precedent take over. Perhaps, then, Dōgen's value lies not in his philosophy, but in what Steineck calls his challenge to philosophy.

Dōgen's use of language offers another reason to doubt the soundness of the philosophical approach to reading Dōgen. For one, literary allusion and analogy, as well as contradictory or paradoxical language, serve as the principal vehicles Dōgen uses to assert his philosophical and doctrinal views. It is thus left to the audience to draw out the adumbrated conclusion.[5] Other Dōgen scholars emphasize the fact that Dōgen views language itself as "coextensive" with enlightenment, such that the use of language becomes a self-sufficient activity, independent of any semantic content or communicative function.[6] Both of these make trouble for the methodological claim that we can draw out well-defined views that admit of philosophical assessment. Thus, we have two formidable challenges to the philosophical reception of Dōgen's thought.

In what follows, I will respond to this twin challenge. I will attempt to vindicate the scholarly practice of reading Dōgen primarily for the philosophical content of his writings, and I will argue that we can mostly penetrate through the haze of allusion, wordplay, and other mischief to identify some clearly demarcated philosophical views articulated in Dōgen's work. I will not, however, go so far as to disagree with Steineck that Dōgen does not make much use of philosophy as a methodology, as Steineck defines it. Rather than engaging in debate with non-Buddhist opponents or marshaling arguments to support his claims, Dōgen does indeed rely on appeals to authority and meditative experience.[7] In what sense, then, is Dōgen philosophically significant at all?

---

[4] Ibid. 585.

[5] Chung-Ying Cheng, "On Zen (Ch'an) Language and Zen Paradoxes," *Journal of Chinese Philosophy* 1 (1973); John Spackman, "The Tiantai Roots of Dōgen's Philosophy of Language and Thought," *Philosophy East and West* 56, no. 3 (2006); Laura Specker Sullivan, "Dōgen and Wittgenstein: Transcending Language Through Ethical Practice," *Asian Philosophy* 23, no. 3 (2013): 223–4.

[6] Hee-jin Kim, "'The Reason of Words and Letters': Dōgen and Kōan Language," in *Dōgen Studies*, ed. William LaFleur (Honolulu: University of Hawai'i Press, 1985), 56–60; David R. Loy, "Language Against Its Own Mystifications: Deconstruction in Nāgārjuna and Dōgen." *Philosophy East and West* 49, no. 3 (1999); Steven Heine, "Dōgen on the Language of Creative Textual Hermeneutics," in *The Oxford Handbook of Japanese Philosophy*, ed. Bret W. Davis, (Oxford University Press, 2015).

[7] At the same time, it is important not to take this point too broadly, for Dōgen does offer arguments for positions. For instance, at *Bukkyō* 佛教 107b20–c9, Dōgen, *Shōbōgenzō: The True Dharma-Eye Treasury*, 4 vols., trans. Gudo Wafu Nishijima and Chodo Cross Moraga (CA: BDK America, 2007–8), Dōgen offers an argument (acknowledged by Raji Steineck, "'Religion' and the Concept of the Buddha Way: Semantics of the Religious in Dōgen," *Asiatische Studien/Études Asiatiques* 72, no. 1 (2018b): 195–6) against the then-ascendant notion of Chan as a "separate transmission outside the teachings" (教外別伝), better calibrated than scriptural transmission for the attainment of "the one mind" or "Buddha-mind" (一心, 佛心, *i.e.*, Buddha-nature). Since the Buddhist teach-

My proposal is that we can best understand the philosophical significance of Dōgen's work by reading him with an eye to the fact that he is but one participant in a larger tradition. Dōgen confronts and offers novel solutions to various philosophical problems that are internal to Buddhist doctrine, while outsourcing the task of demonstrating the validity of Buddhist doctrine from the ground up. That work has already been done by Dōgen's forebears, and is demonstrated implicitly, for him, by the continued vitality of the Buddhist community across great physical and temporal distances.[8] By reading Dōgen with attention to his intellectual-historical context, then, we can fruitfully understand him as offering a straightforwardly descriptive, representational account of the ultimate nature of reality—that is, we can read him not only as a philosopher, but specifically a metaphysician. I pursue this line of thought in §2, focusing on the doctrine of Buddha-nature (佛性 busshō) and its metaphysical implications.

In §3, I then consider a metaethical problem raised by Dōgen's version of the Buddha-nature doctrine. In brief, Dōgen's account of the Buddhist metaphysical picture precludes any fundamental distinction between good and bad, valuable and disvaluable acts or states of affairs. Why, then, should anyone bother to engage in Buddhist practices of self-cultivation, or uphold its highly demanding ethical principles? Dōgen's answer, I argue, is to take the *modus ponens* and accept that there is no ultimate distinction between good and bad states of affairs, while maintaining that adherence to ethical precepts is built into the conventions willingly accepted by Buddhist practitioners.

Having rehearsed all of this, I then draw out the implications of this reading for Dōgen's reception as a philosopher. The problem addressed by Dōgen is known to his Tendai compatriots at the time of his writing, but Dōgen's solution is a novel one. It also links Dōgen to the Indian Mādhyamika philosophers, who offer a similarly sparse metaphysics and thus face an analogous metaethical concern. Contemporary philosophers attempting to respond to this problem, on behalf of the Mādhyamikas, develop a solution strikingly similar to Dōgen's. Dōgen thus helps underwrite what would otherwise be a purely speculative and contemporary philosophical innovation. This episode also points to the value of including East Asian Buddhist figures in philosophical conversations currently dominated by Indo-Tibetan philosophers. That the former do not often adhere to conventions familiar to readers of Indian *śāstra* is no barrier to their making substantial advances on the same philosophical problems.

---

ings are themselves identical to Buddha-nature, Dōgen points out, there can be no "separate transmission outside the teachings" except one that leads *away* from Buddha-nature (if the notion is even coherent at all). On the origins of 教外別伝, see Griffith T. Foulk, "Sung Controversies Concerning the 'Separate Transmission' of Ch'an," n *Buddhism in the Sung*, eds. Peter N. Gregory and Daniel A. Getz, Jr. (Honolulu: University of Hawai'i Press, 1999). On its reception among Dōgen's Japanese contemporaries, see Stephan Kigensan Licha, "Separate Teaching and Separate Transmission: Kokan Shiren's Zen Polemics," *Japanese Journal of Religious Studies* 45, no.1 (2018). Still, I acknowledge that Dōgen's core metaphysical position, as I explain it in §2, is not defended by means of argument in this way.

[8] Steineck, "'Religion'," 188–92, 196–201.

Having thus offered a proof of concept for the philosophical use of Dōgen, I close, in §4, by considering Steineck's claim that Dōgen puts forward a "challenge to philosophy" as a methodology for answering fundamental questions about human life. I try to sharpen Dōgen's purported challenge, arguing that it must lie in Dōgen's epistemological reliance on religious authority, precedent, and meditative experience. I conclude by urging that philosophical inquiry itself has purchase with respect to these issues, as is abundantly clear from Indo-Tibetan sources. The debate over the sources of justification available to Buddhist philosophers will have to proceed with attention to both Indo-Tibetan and East Asian sources.

2   The Metaphysics of Buddha-Nature

First, I will try to demonstrate that Dōgen's use of language, however abstruse and allusory it may be, nonetheless conveys assertions about the nature and structure of reality.[9] In other words, I will show that Dōgen makes metaphysical claims.[10]

An obvious and well-known source for such claims is the *Busshō* 佛性 fascicle.[11] Before continuing, I will note that one of Steineck's criticisms of the philosophical literature on Dōgen is that it focuses overwhelmingly on a few of the *Shōbōgenzō*'s fascicles, like *Busshō* and *Uji*.[12] Steineck's contention is that this handful of chapters is really where the action is, philosophically speaking, and that the bulk of the *Shōbōgenzō* is more given to non-assertoric or mystical language—language that resists philosophical interpretation.[13] I will try to push back against this claim by citing from the more obscure fascicles, to show how the Buddha-nature metaphysic is a major driving force unifying most of the *Shōbōgenzō*.

The key to the reading of the *Busshō* fascicle as containing metaphysical claims lies in Dōgen's repeated emphasis on the fact that *every* entity and state of affairs, according to Dōgen, is *identical* to the Buddha-nature itself. For instance:

> 91c16–21: What is the purpose of the World-Honored One's "All living beings totally have Buddha-nature?"... In short, [it is that] "total existence" is "Buddha-nature."[14]

---

[9] Some of the material in this section is drawn from my "Emptiness And Metaethics: Dōgen's Anti-Realist Solution," *Philosophy East and West* 70, no. 4 (2020): 958–962.

[10] Kevin Schilbrack, "Metaphysics in Dōgen," *Philosophy East and West* 50, no. 1 (2000).

[11] Translations are either my own, with reference to Nishijima and Cross' translation in Dōgen, *Shōbōgenzō*, vol. 2, 3–42, or are modifications of Nishijima and Cross. I cite from the Taisho edition of the *Shōbōgenzō*, *T* 82, no. 2582.

[12] *Cf.* Ralf Müller, "Philosophy and the Practice of Reflexivity: On Dōgen's Discourse about Buddha-Nature" in *Concepts of Philosophy in Asia and the Islamic World*, vol. 1, ed. Raji C. Steineck, Ralph Weber, Robert Gassmann, and Elena Lange (Leiden: Brill, 2016), 545.

[13] Steineck, "A Zen Philosopher?" *passim*.

[14] *cf.* Dōgen, *Shōbōgenzō*, vol. 2, 4.

93a26–7: Looking at mountains and rivers is looking at Buddha-nature.

97c16–8: Grasses, trees, and national lands are mind itself… [as are] the sun, the moon, and the stars.[15]

101a14–5: To express Buddha-nature further… It is fences, walls, tiles, and pebbles.[16]

Importantly, this theme—that everything is identical to, or is a manifestation of, Buddha-nature—is not negated or contradicted anywhere in the fascicle, and is reinforced consistently throughout most of the other fascicles as well.[17] This provides support for rejecting or tempering the claim that Dōgen's self-contradiction in the *Shōbōgenzō* is so extensive as to threaten the retrieval of assertoric philosophical content.[18]

In addition to its status as the ground of all manifest phenomena, Dōgen adds that Buddha-nature is equivalent to both emptiness (空 *kū*) and impermanence (無常 *mujō*).[19] He approvingly quotes Huineng as having explicitly identified Buddha-nature and emptiness (94a7). As for Buddha-nature's identity with impermanence, Dōgen again quotes Huineng: "The impermanent just is the Buddha-nature. The permanent just is the mind that divides all *dharma*s into good and bad."[20] Notably, Huineng's statement here also contrasts Buddha-nature with the division or differentiation of experienced phenomena (法 *hō*, *dharma*). Dōgen comments:

> In sum, the impermanence of grass, trees, and forests is just Buddha-nature. And the impermanence of the body and mind of a human being is Buddha-nature itself. The impermanence of national lands and mountains and rivers is because they are Buddha-nature. The truth of *anuttarā samyak saṃbodhi*, because it is Buddha-nature, is impermanent. The great state of *parinirvāṇa*, because it is impermanent, is Buddha-nature. [Adherents of] the various small views of the two vehicles, as well as scholars of the Tripiṭaka who teach sutras and commentaries and so on, might be astonished, doubting, and afraid at these words of

---

[15] *cf.* Ibid., 21.

[16] *cf.* ibid., 30. 91c16–21: 世尊道の一切衆生悉有佛性は、その宗旨いかん… すなはち悉有は佛性なり. 93a26–7: 山河をみりは、佛性をみるなり. 97c16–8: 草木國土これ心なり… 日月星辰これ心なり (*cf. Bukkyo* 佛教 107b20–29 and *Kobusshin* 古佛心 173b18–19). 101a14–5: 佛性を道取すれに… 牆壁瓦礫なり (*cf. Shin fukatoku (ka)* 心不可得 (下) 81b9–10).

[17] See, for instance, *Sangai yuishin* 三界唯心 and *Shohō jissō* 諸法實相, as well as the passage in *Tsuki* 月 discussing the "true Dharma body" (眞法身) of the Buddha (starting at 168a15).

[18] Steineck, "A Zen Philosopher?" 589; Ralf Müller, "Philosophy and the Practice of Reflexivity," 577–8.

[19] See also *Kūge* 空華 170b19–20, where Dōgen equates various trappings of spiritual accomplishment (*nirvāṇa*, enlightenment, *etc.*) with "flowers in space" (*kūge*), a canonical symbol of things empty of independent existence. Later in the fascicle, Dōgen endorses the expansion of the extension of 'empty' to include all entities or phenomena: "Those who study [according to the idea] that flowers in space are not real, whereas other flowers are real, are people who have not seen or heard the Buddha's teaching" (空華は實にあらす、餘華はこれ實なりと學すれは、佛教を見聞せさるものなり, 171b19–22; *cf.* Dōgen, *Shōbōgenzō*, vol. 3, 18).

[20] 無常は者、即ち佛性なり也. 有常は者、即ち善惡一切諸法分別の心なり也 (95a7–8). *cf.* Dōgen, *Shōbōgenzō*, vol. 2, 14.

the Sixth Patriarch. If they are astonished or doubting, they are demons and heretics (*cf.* Dōgen 2007, vol. 2, p. 14).[21]

The claim that Buddha-nature *is* emptiness, or that it *is* impermanence, raises the question of just what kind of thing Buddha-nature is. Here Dōgen is consciously wading into a protracted controversy over the metaphysical status of Buddha-nature (which I will explore in greater detail below), and his anticipation of the "astonished, doubting, and afraid" reactions of his opponents makes clear that he takes himself to be stating a controversial thesis. Various remarks clarify the identity of Dōgen's primary target: interpretations of Buddha-nature as an enduring substance, of which experienced phenomena are proper parts. For instance:

91c24–6: As for the 'existence' just now [spoken of as being] 'totally possessed' by Buddha-nature, it is other than the "existence" of existence and nonexistence.[22]

92a13–4: 'The entire universe is my possession' is the wrong view of heretics.[23]

92a22–3: Hearing the word "Buddha-nature", many students falsely equate it to the 'self' of the Senika heresy.[24]

94c21–4: People today, hearing of Buddha-nature, do not ask further about what kind of Buddha-nature this is. They seem only to discuss the meaning of Buddha-nature's existence, nonexistence, and so on. This is too hasty.[25]

100a2–4: Zhaozhou says [of Buddha-nature], "It exists." This kind of 'existence' is beyond the 'existence' of scholastic commentary teachers and the like, and beyond the 'existence' of the Existence [Sarvāstivāda] school.[26]

---

[21]95a25–b4: すなはち佛性なり。人物身心の無常なるこれ佛性なり。國土山河の無常なる。これ佛性なるによりてなり。阿耨多羅三藐三菩提、これ佛性なるかゆゑに無常なり。大般涅槃これ無常なるかゆゑに佛性なり。もろもろの二乘ノ小見、および經論師の三藏等は、これ六祖の道を驚疑怖畏すへし。もし驚疑せんことは、魔外の類なり。

[22]*cf.* Dōgen, *Shōbōgenzō*, vol. 2, 4.

[23]*cf.* ibid., 4–5.

[24]Śreṇika or Senika, and his eponymous doctrinal error, appears in the *Saṃyuktāgama* 雜阿含經, *juan* 卷 5, no. 105 (*T* 99, 31–2), the *Mahāparinirvāṇa Sūtra* 大般涅槃經, *juan* 卷 39 (*T* 374, 594–7), and the *Da zhidu lun* 大智度論, *juan* 卷 42 (*T* 1509, 368–9). See Robert E. Buswell, Jr. and David S. Lopez, Jr., eds. *The Princeton Dictionary of Buddhism* (Princeton NJ: Princeton University Press, 2013), *s.v.* "Śreṇika heresy," as well as Bernard Faure, *A Cultural Critique of Chan/Zen Buddhism* (Princeton, NJ: Princeton University Press, 1991), 59–65. Dōgen offers his own more extensive account of, and reply to, the Senika heresy in the *Sokushin zebutsu* 即心是佛 fascicle.

[25]*cf.* ibid., 13.

[26]Much more should be said about the role of the Sarvāstivāda school of Buddhist Abhidharma, which flourished in North India between the third century BCE and the sixth century CE or later, in Chinese and Japanese Tiantai/Tendai and Chan/Zen thinkers' conceptions of their own place in the doctrinal history and development of Buddhism. For now, it should suffice to note that 'Sarvāstivāda' here seems to function as a stand-in for the whole sweep of Buddhist philosophy that seeks to identify which entities exist in an ontologically fundamental way, which Dōgen would identify using terms like 'self' (我) or 'permanence' (常). The predominance of Sarvāstivāda texts among the translated sources of Abhidharma thought available to the Chinese, and Kumārajīva's education therein, are undoubtedly part of the story of how the term 'Sarvāstivāda' came to function in this way. See Erik Zürcher, "Buddhism Across Boundaries: The Foreign Input," *Sino-Platonic Papers* 222 (2012): 16–17.

101a12–3: Many stupid people think of Buddha-nature as consciousness of spirit, as the original person. One could die laughing![27]

In reference to Yanguan Qi'an's declaration, "All living beings have Buddha-nature!", he writes:

> We should study in practice (參學) that he does not say "All living beings just are Buddha-nature," but says "All living beings have Buddha-nature." He should certainly discard the "have" in "have Buddha-nature."[28]

He also approvingly quotes Baizhang: "To preach that living beings have Buddha-nature is to insult Buddha, Dharma, and Sangha. And to preach that living beings are without Buddha-nature is also to insult Buddha, Dharma, and Sangha."[29]

Dōgen thus clearly and forcefully rejects any understanding of Buddha-nature on which it exists in the same way as ordinary objects do, such that it could be held or possessed. He also emphatically refutes the interpretation of Buddha-nature as a hidden, underlying substance unifying manifest phenomena (an *ātman* or *Brāhman*).[30]

How, then, should we interpret the philosophical intuition underlying Dōgen's intervention in the Buddha-nature debate? For a positive account of the metaphysics of Buddha-nature in Dōgen, I am partial to the reading first advanced by Kevin Schilbrack.[31] On this reading, Dōgen is setting out two transcendental conditions on the very possibility of experience or existence, grouping them under the heading of 'Buddha-nature'. Anything we might encounter in experience will exist dependently on everything else and will be impermanent. This fits with his identification of Buddha-nature with emptiness and impermanence; both of these seem to be metaphysical descriptions of states of affairs, rather than states of affairs themselves. It also fits with the fact that experienced phenomena seem to necessarily, not contingently, participate in Buddha-nature.

Dōgen's claim can also be expressed in terms of *fundamentality*, an important and recently ascendant focus of metaphysicians' attention. Buddha-nature, for its

---

[27] 91c24–6: しるへしいま佛性に悉有せらるる有は、有無の有にあらす。92a13–4: 遍界我有は、外道の邪見なり。92a22–3: 佛性の言をききて、學者多く先尼外道の我のごとく邪計せり。94c21–4: いまの人も、佛性とききぬれは、さらにいかなるかこれ佛性と間取せす。佛性も有無等の義をいふかことし。これ倉卒なり。100a2–4: 趙州いはく、有。これ有の様子は、教家の論師等の有にあらす。有部の論有にあらさるなり。101a12–3: 癡人多く識神を認して、佛性とせり。本來人とせり。笑殺人なり。

[28] 一切衆生即佛性といはす、一切衆生有佛性といふと參學すへし。有佛性の有、まさに脱落すへし (97c27–98a1). *cf.* ibid., 21.

[29] 説くも衆生に有佛性と、亦謗するなり佛法僧を。説くも衆生に無佛性と、亦謗するなり佛法僧を (98b14–5). *cf.* ibid., 23.

[30] There is broad consensus among interpreters on this point. See Faure, *The Rhetoric of Immediacy*, 192; David R. Loy, "The Path of No-Path: Śankara and Dōgen on the Paradox of Practice," *Philosophy East and West* 38, no. 2 (1988): 128; Joan Stambaugh, *Impermanence Is Buddha-Nature: Dōgen's Understanding of Temporality* (Honolulu: University of Hawai'i Press, 1990), ch. 2.

[31] Schilbrack, "Metaphysics in Dōgen."

substantialist proponents, is the only fundamental entity, the only entity occupying the lowest level of their ontology, the ground of everything that exists. Dōgen holds that any entity can be felicitously equated with Buddha-nature. This statement trades on the canonically fundamental status of Buddha-nature to deny fundamentality to the distinctions between entities or states of affairs.[32] However, Dōgen also rejects the substantialist view of Buddha-nature, instead using the term to designate transcendental conditions applying to any entity that exists. Thus, for Dōgen, there is *no* entity that enjoys fundamentality; everything is metaphysically dependent.[33]

Situating Dōgen within the broader history of *tathāgatagarbha* and Buddha-nature thought can also facilitate the recognition of the pointed philosophical insight underlying his characterization of Buddha-nature. Of the earliest Mahāyāna texts that make reference to a *tathāgatagarbha*, most (including the *Ratnagotravibhāga*, the *Mahāparinirvāṇa Sūtra*, and the *Śrīmālādevī Sūtra*) characterize it as immune to impermanence and emptiness. The *Ratnagotra*, for instance, describes the *tathāgatagarbha* as being characterized by bliss (*sukha*), permanence (*nitya*), and selfhood (*ātma*), striking a self-conscious contrast with the historical Buddha's description of all phenomena as characterized by dissatisfaction (*duḥkha*), impermanence (*anitya*), and non-self (*anātman*).[34] The *Ratnagotra* and *Mahāparinirvāṇa* both also explicitly set themselves up as rebuking, or correcting, the Prajñāpāramitā (and, by extrapolation, Madhyamaka) emphasis on universal emptiness.[35] This way of thinking about Buddha-nature was profoundly influential in China.[36] On the other hand, there is also a robust tradition of viewing *tathāgatagarbha* or Buddha-nature as simply an effective way to reveal or explicate universal emptiness, as in the

---

[32] *cf.* Jacqueline I. Stone, *Original Enlightenment and the Transformation of Medieval Japanese Buddhism* (Honolulu: University of Hawai'i Press, 1999), 50.

[33] On the notions of fundamentality, grounding, and levels, see Kit Fine, "The Question of Realism," *Philosophers' Imprint* 1, no. 2 (2001); Gideon Rosen, "Metaphysical Dependence: Grounding and Reduction," in *Modality: Metaphysics, Logic, and Epistemology*, ed. Bob Hale and Aviv Hoffman (Oxford University Press, 2010); Jonathan Schaffer, "On What Grounds What" in *Metametaphysics: New Essays on the Foundations of Ontology*, ed. David J. Chalmers, David Manley, and Ryan Wasserman (Oxford University Press, 2009). For an application of these conceptual resources in an Indian Buddhist context, see Allison Aitken, "No Unity, No Problem: Madhyamaka Metaphysical Indefinitism," *Philosophers' Imprint* 21, no. 31 (2021).

[34] Jikido Takasaki, *A Study on the* Ratnagotravibhaga (Uttaratantra)*: Being a Treatise on the Tathagatagarbha Theory of Mahayana Buddhism* (Rome: Italian Institute for the Middle and Far East, 1966), 56, 218ff.

[35] Ibid., 54–7. Takasaki 2014c, pp. 302–7.

[36] Jungnok Park, *How Buddhism Acquired a Soul on the Way to China*, ed. Richard Gombrich (Oxford: Equinox Publishing, 2012), esp. ch. 7; Sangyop Lee, "The Soteriology of the Soul: The *Shen bumie* 神不滅 Discourse in Early Medieval Chinese Buddhism," Ph.D. dissertation (Stanford University, 2021).

Laṅkāvatāra Sūtra or the *Foxing lun* 佛性論.[37] This latter strand of Buddha-nature thought is the one taken up by Tiantai thinkers.[38] Still, a number of factors would have motivated and justified Dōgen's reiteration of the claim that endorsement of Buddha-nature is consistent with thinking that all things are empty: the continued vitality of the more *ātman*-friendly strand in both China and Japan[39]; the wide currency of the language of permanence and self to describe Buddha-nature, sourced from the *Mahāparinirvāṇa* and elsewhere; and the importance of the point for Dōgen's metaethical claims (to be examined in the next section).

Before continuing, I will pause here to draw two interpretive lessons from the preceding discussion. First, the vocabulary of contemporary metaphysics is not at all out of place in an analysis of Dōgen's work. There is clear overlap between the questions salient to those steeped in contemporary metaphysics and those salient to Dōgen. Far from imposing alien concerns and goals on Dōgen, the philosophical reading of him reveals (at least a significant part of) the logic underlying the decisions he makes in the text.

Second, taking stock of Dōgen's context in Buddhist intellectual history—the doctrinal and philosophical issues in the air at the time of his writing—allows us to see him as straightforwardly conversing with his contemporaries on metaphysical issues. His difficult turns of phrase, seen in this light, become simple rhetorical strategies: creative and compelling ways of expressing content which would nevertheless also have admitted of expression in a more plain and assertoric fashion.

---

[37] On the *Mahāparinirvāṇa*, see Ming-Wood Liu, "The Doctrine of the Buddha-Nature in the Mahāyāna *Mahāparinirvāṇa-Sūtra*," *Journal of the International Association of Buddhist Studies* 5, no. 2 (1982). On the *Laṅkāvatāra*, see Florin Giripescu Sutton, *Existence and Enlightenment in the Laṅkāvatāra-sūtra: A Study in the Ontology and the Epistemology of the Yogācāra School of Mahāyāna Buddhism* (Albany, NY: State University of New York Press, 1991), 51–78. On the *Foxing lun*, see Sallie B. King, *Buddha Nature* (Albany, NY: State University of New York Press, 1991). It should be noted, however, that the *Laṅkāvatāra*—despite its heavier emphasis on emptiness—also describes the *tathāgatagarbha* as pure, eternal, undestroyed, and so on. The text was received and initially transmitted along with the *Ratnagotra* in China. See Jikido Takasaki, "Sources of the *Laṅkāvatāra* and Its Position in Mahāyāna Buddhism," in *Collected Papers on Tathāgatagarbha Doctrine* (Delhi: Motilal Banarsidass, 2014b).

[38] Paul L Swanson, "T'ien-t'ai Chih-i's Concept of Threefold Buddha Nature—A Synergy of Reality, Wisdom, and Practice," in *Buddha Nature: A Festschrift in Honor of Minoru Kiyota*, eds. Paul J. Griffiths and John P. Keenan (Reno, NV: Buddhist Books International, 1990); Brook Ziporyn, "Tiantai Buddhist Conceptions of 'The Nature' (*Xing*) and its Relation to the Mind," *Journal of Chinese Philosophy* 37, no. 3 (2010).

[39] See also *The Nirvana Sutra (Mahāparinirvāṇa-Sūtra): Volume I*, ed. and trans. Mark Blum (Moraga, CA: BDK America, 2013), xix. Kūkai was probably responsible for the introduction of *tathāgatagarbha* thought to Japanese Buddhist thought in general, and to Tendai in particular. His works describe an eternal, substantial Buddha-nature very much in line with that attacked by Dōgen. See Jikido Takasaki, "Kōbō Daishi (Kūkai) and Tathāgatagarbha Thought," in *Collected Papers on Tathāgatagarbha Doctrine* (Delhi: Motilal Banarsidass, 2014a).

3 Dogen's Metaethical Innovation

When one considers the metaphysical status specifically of moral properties of
actions or states of affairs, Dōgen's emphasis on the fundamental non-distinctness
of all phenomena or entities raises a problem.[40] If the point is that any difference in
properties between two entities is merely apparent and illusory, then there is no
metaphysically fundamental way to morally distinguish some actions or states of
affairs from others. But, one might think, we need such a distinction in order for
moral claims to be well-founded. In short, Dōgen's view of Buddha-nature puts him
in metaethical trouble; the situation in which he finds himself is analogous to that of
contemporary metaethicists concerned with the question, "Why be moral?"[41]

Dōgen himself acknowledges the consequences of his Buddha-nature metaphysic for the possibility of moral distinctions, as can be seen in several key passages throughout the *Shōbōgenzō*:

> *Uji*, 46b18–22: [E]ven half-perfectly-realized existence-time is the perfect realization of
> half-existence-time. Even those phases in which we seem to go wrong are also existence.

> *Shōaku makusa*, 42b7–9: Right and wrong are time; in time there is no right or wrong.
> Right and wrong are the Dharma; in the Dharma there is no right or wrong.

> *Hokke-ten-hokke*, 73b13–26: This expression, "the dharma-flower is turning", means
> "deluded mind"; the mind being deluded is just the dharma-flower turning. Therefore, when
> the mind is in delusion, we are being turned by the Flower of Dharma. This means that even
> when delusion is myriad phenomena, "form as it is" is still being turned by the Flower
> of Dharma…
>
> So do not worry about the mind being deluded. Your actions are the bodhisattva way
> itself…[42]

Dōgen's solution, as previously stated, is to simply bite the bullet: Buddhists' first-
order normative claims are devoid of any fundamental justificatory basis. Instead,
their force derives from mere conventions, the acceptance of which is constitutive
of being a Buddhist. It is insofar as we are already committed to following the
Buddhist path, Dōgen argues, that adherence to Buddhist moral precepts is obligatory, since it is only by means of such observance that the accomplishment of
Buddhist soteriological aims is possible. This reading is amply supported by

---

[40] Some of the material in this section is drawn from my "Emptiness And Metaethics," 962–70.

[41] Christine M. Korsgaard, *The Sources of Normativity* (Cambridge, MA: Harvard University Press,
1996), 7–18.

[42] *Uji*, 46b18–22: たとひ半究盡の有時も、半有時の究盡なり。たとひ蹉過とみゆる形段
も、有なり。*Shōaku makusa*, 42b7–9: 善惡は時なり。時は善惡にあらす。善惡は法な
り。法は善惡にあらす。*Hokke-ten-hokke*, 73b13–26: いはゆる法華轉といふは、心迷な
り。心迷はすなはち法華轉なり。しかあれはすなはち心迷は、法華に轉せらるるなり。
その宗趣は、心迷たとひ萬象なりとも。如是相は法華に轉せらるるなり。[...] しかあれ
は心迷をうらむることなかれ。汝等か所行、是れ菩薩道なり。

Dōgen's statements in the *Shōbōgenzō zuimonki*, consisting of more accessible statements on practical matters by Dōgen to his students.[43] For instance:

> To enjoy doing evil deeds, saying that a Zen monk does not cultivate good and need not be virtuous, is extremely wrong. In the customs before us (*sengi* 先規), such enjoyment of doing evil deeds has never been heard of.[44]

> While you should maintain the precepts and eating regulations, to emphasize them as essential, establish them as a practice, and think you can gain the way through them is indeed wrong. It is only because they are the path of robed monks, the family style of the Buddha's children that we follow them. You should accomplish them, but definitely not take them as essential. Thus, I am not saying that you can violate the precepts and become self-indulgent. Clinging to such an attitude is an evil view, and heterodox. Only because they are the rules of the Buddha's family, the family style of the [Buddhist] monastery, do we follow them.[45]

Furthermore, while the problem is a familiar one within the Tiantai/Tendai sphere, the solution is due entirely to Dōgen.[46]

It is noteworthy that Dōgen's solution to the tension between Buddha-nature and morality converges with developments in recent work on Indian Mādhyamaka philosophy. Bronwyn Finnigan and Koji Tanaka (2010) have observed that Mādhyamikas, like Dōgen, cannot "appeal to actual properties or states of affairs in the world to function as truthmakers," since "there are no actual properties or states of affairs in the world that could function in this way"[47] What is sought after is something enjoying metaphysical fundamentality. Both Mādhyamikas and Dōgen

---

[43] Similar statements can occasionally be found in the *Shōbōgenzō* itself, notably at *Bukkyō* 107c20–25: "[E]very individual who studies the true reality of the Buddha-dharma, when deciding upon teaching and learning that has come from the past, inevitably investigates it under the Buddhist patriarchs… If we hope to determine whether the teachings we rely upon are right or not, we should determine it under the Buddhist patriarchs." 佛法の眞實を學する箇箇、ともにみな從來の教學を決擇するには、かならず佛祖に參究するなり。[...] 依教の正不をを決せんとおもはんは、佛祖に決すへきなり。

[44] Dōgen, *Dōgen zenji zenshū: genbun taishō gendaigoyaku* 道元禅師全集:原文対象現代語役, ed. Kagamishima Genryū 鏡島元隆, et al. 17 vols (Tokyo: Shunjūsha, 1999): vol. 16, 130: 禅僧は、不修善、不要功德と云って、好惡行きはめて、僻事也。先規、未聞如是好惡行事。

[45] Ibid., 217: 戒行持齋を、守護すべければとて、強て宗として是を修行に立て、是によりて得道すべしと思ふも、亦これ非なり。只是れ衲僧の行履、佛子の家風なれば隨ひ行ふなり。是れを能事と云へばとて、必ずしも宗とする事なかれ。然あればとて、破戒放逸なれと云には非ず。若亦かの如く執せば邪見なり、外道なり。只佛家の儀式、叢林の家風なれば、隨順しゆくなり。

[46] For extensive discussion of an earlier Tiantai solution to the problem, see Brook Ziporyn, *Evil and/or/as the Good: Omnicentrism, Intersubjectivity, and Value Paradox in Tiantai Buddhist Thought* (Cambridge, MA: Harvard University Press, 2000). David R. Loy, "Evil as the Good? A Reply to Brook Ziporyn," *Philosophy East and West* 55, no. 2 (2005) offers a helpful and concise articulation of why that solution may not be of much help in guiding action, much less so in guiding action that turns out according to recognizably Buddhist moral intuitions. Dōgen's view is much more successful on that score, though of course it brings along what may be thought a high cost: the abandonment of a philosophically deep answer as to *why* these particular first-order moral claims turn out to be the right ones.

[47] Bronwyn Finnigan and Koji Tanaka, "Ethics for Mādhyamikas," in *Moonshadows: Conventional Truth in Buddhist Philosophy*, ed. the Cowherds (Oxford: Oxford University Press, 2011), 223.

deny that any such things exist; for both, then, moral claims are left without meta-physical underwriting.

Finnigan and Tanaka suggest that Mādhyamikas can nonetheless establish conventions distinguishing morally right and wrong actions. Among those adhering to a given convention (or system of conventions), moral reasons for and against courses of action can be traded; such reasons do not, however, have any justificatory force for agents who reject the convention altogether.[48] Categorical, universally-binding moral normativity is simply not on offer given a Buddhist metaphysic.

That Dōgen offers an analogous view is significant. Finnigan and Tanaka's view is reconstructive: it addresses a philosophical problem with the Madhyamaka view that is apparent from our own contemporary vantage point, and not necessarily from the Mādhyamikas'. Including Dōgen in the conversation thus allows us to point to a tradition-internal source for this philosophical innovation, supporting the intuition that the problem is a serious one and that Buddhists owe a response. Conversely, contextualizing Dōgen's work with Indic sources in view allows us to see the ways in which Dōgen is operating in the same problem-space.

As an aside, there is good reason to think that the continuity here is potentially historical rather than simply thematic. Dōgen frequently discusses the Madhyamaka philosopher Nāgārjuna, often in ways intended to support Dōgen's anti-foundationalist ontology and his emphasis on the significance of impermanence.[49] Nāgārjuna is known to the Chinese tradition primarily (at least among the literate, educated, philosophically-inclined part of that audience) for his (purported) author-ship of the *Da zhidu lun* 大智度論.[50] Yoshitaka Nagai has shown that Dōgen quotes extensively from the *Da zhidu lun*, and was clearly very familiar with its contents.[51] This lead, which calls for further pursuit, offers yet more support for the approach that draws Indo-Tibetan and East Asian philosophical figures together in conversation.

4 Dōgen's Challenge to Philosophy, and Philosophy's Challenge to Dōgen

Steineck argues that, instead of understanding Dōgen as a philosopher, we should understand him as issuing a challenge to those of us who adopt a philosophical methodology to addressing ethical and metaphysical questions. He writes:

---

[48] Ibid., 223–4.

[49] See, for instance, the first section of the *Gakudō yōjinshū* 学道用心集, discussed in Steineck, "'Religion'," 15.

[50] See Young (2015) for an account of the many *non*-philosophical ways in which Madhyamaka philosophers like Nāgārjuna and Āryadeva were characterized in the Chinese Buddhist imagination.

[51] Yoshitaka Nagai 永井賢隆, "*Dōgen Zenji to* Dai chido ron,"「道元禅師と『大智度論』」, *Indogaku Bukkyōgaku Kenkyū* 印度学仏教学研究 60, no. 1 (2011).

One of the *challenges to philosophy* that is constituted by Dōgen's texts, if taken on their own grounds, is the need to explain why we should be dealing with fundamental questions of human life by way of philosophy and not by other ways, such as the one that Dōgen proposes.[52]

Insofar as philosophy is understood strictly as open disputation among equals, conforming to agreed-upon rules of inference, it is entirely reasonable to ask whether philosophy is the most effective or accurate method for resolving such questions. What, though, is Dōgen's proposed alternative method? It is clear that Dōgen is not strictly an anti-philosopher in the sense of wanting to give up on addressing philosophical concerns altogether. As we have seen, though Dōgen's language can suggest such an attitude, his work nonetheless yields a number of straightforwardly assertoric position statements on ethical and metaphysical matters. Dōgen is also himself critical of the idea that rationality has no place in deliberation on issues of fundamental human significance. Addressing the view that *kōan*s are merely "irrational conversations... [which] do not involve deliberation",[53] he says:

> Those fellows who talk in this way have never seen a true teacher, and do not have the eye of studying in practice (参学). They are little idiots who don't bear talking about... they are more foolish than heretics... What [you] baldies call 'irrational conversations' are irrational only to you. Not so for the Buddhist patriarchs.[54]

Instead, Dōgen quite intentionally trains his focus on problems that would generally be expected to fall under the provenance of philosophers, staking out determinate positions in response. Dōgen's rebellion against philosophy, then, must be purely methodological, consisting in his reliance on religious authority and appeals to meditative experience, rather than argument conceived as "disputation among equals".

Which of these methods is best suited to addressing the sorts of fundamental questions, those linked most closely to "the overall horizon of human interaction with the world?[55] I would like to suggest that, in the absence of any given means for adjudicating this dispute, philosophy is precisely what suggests itself. The philosopher, unlike her opponent, can ask this question; she can demand reasons supporting the reliance on authority and meditation rather than argument. If someone of the opposing methodological persuasion cannot give us cogent reasons for that choice, then he has effectively given up on making his project one that speaks to universal human concerns. I think this kind of solution is sufficiently out of step with Dōgen's own soteriological goals, and those that show up with great consistency in the

---

[52] Steineck, "A Zen Philosopher?" 583.

[53] *Sansuikyō* 山水経, 63c21–6: 無理會話なり... 念慮にかかわれす...

[54] 63c29–64a10: かくのことくいふやから。かつていたまた正師をみす。參學眼なし。 いふ にたらさる小獸子なり... 外道よりもおろかなり... 禿子かいふ無理會話。なんちのみ無理 會なり。*Cf.* Dōgen, *Shōbōgenzō*, vol. 1, 220. 佛祖はしかあらす。 Kim, "'The Reason of Words and Letters'," 56–7 and Heine, "Dōgen on the Language," 4, both make the same point about the significance of this passage.

[55] Steineck, "A Zen Philosopher?" 582.

broader Buddhist tradition, that we should be extremely cautious about attributing it to Buddhist figures.

Dōgen does not offer us much in the way of argument supporting the authority-and-meditation approach. As I have said, he "outsources" this task to his predecessors, taking the efficacy and epistemic value of Buddhist meditative practices to have been thoroughly established. So, we must have the debate on his behalf. Fortunately, such a debate need not be purely reconstructive, but can draw on ample conceptual resources and arguments from within the tradition. Dōgen's Indo-Tibetan predecessors, in particular, have thoroughly worked over the issue of how philosophical reasoning, scriptural authority, and meditative cultivation (Skt. *yukti*, *āgama*, and *bhāvanā*, respectively) interact, and it is often precisely the epistemic value of meditation as opposed to reasoning that is at issue. The way forward, then, involves taking a historically broad and proleptic view of the Buddhist philosophical tradition as a whole, conversing with sources where philosophical argumentation is foregrounded, as well as those whose argumentative and assertoric features are not readily apparent. Doing so will allow us to draw our own conclusions about the epistemic and transformative value of the meditative practices in which Dōgen rests his faith.

Bibliography

Abe, Masao. "The Oneness of Practice and Attainment: Implications for the Relation between Means and Ends." *Dōgen Studies*, edited by William LaFleur, 99–111. Honolulu: University of Hawai'i Press, 1985.

Aitken, Allison. "No Unity, No Problem: Madhyamaka Metaphysical Indefinitism." *Philosophers' Imprint* 21, no. 31 (2021): 1–24.

Buswell, Jr., Robert E. and David S. Lopez, Jr., eds. *The Princeton Dictionary of Buddhism*. Princeton, NJ: Princeton University Press, 2013.

Cheng, Chung-Ying. "On Zen (Ch'an) Language and Zen Paradoxes." *Journal of Chinese Philosophy* 1 (1973): 77–102.

Dōgen 道元. *Dōgen zenji zenshū: genbun taishō gendaigoyaku* 道元禅師全集:原文対象現代 語 役. Edited by Kagamishima Genryū 鏡島元隆, et al. 17 vols. Tokyo: Shunjūsha, 1999.

———. *Shōbōgenzō: The True Dharma-Eye Treasury*. Translated by Gudo Wafu Nishijima and Chodo Cross. Taishō edition. 4 vols. Moraga, CA: BDK America, 2007–2008.

Faure, Bernard. *The Rhetoric of Immediacy: A Cultural Critique of Chan/Zen Buddhism*. Princeton, NJ: Princeton University Press, 1991.

Fine, Kit. "The Question of Realism." *Philosophers' Imprint* 1, no. 2 (2001): 1–30.

Finnigan, Bronwyn and Koji Tanaka. "Ethics for Mādhyamikas." In *Moonshadows: Conventional Truth in Buddhist Philosophy*. Edited by the Cowherds, 221–231. Oxford: Oxford University Press, 2011.

Foulk, T. Griffith. "Sung Controversies Concerning the 'Separate Transmission' of Ch'an." In *Buddhism in the Sung*, eds. Peter N. Gregory and Daniel A. Getz, Jr., 220–94. Honolulu: University of Hawai'i Press, 1999.

Guilbault, Audrey. "Emptiness And Metaethics: Dōgen's Anti-Realist Solution." *Philosophy East and West* 70, no. 4 (2020): 957–976.

Heine, Steven. "Dōgen on the Language of Creative Textual Hermeneutics." In *The Oxford Handbook of Japanese Philosophy*, ed. Bret W. Davis, 215–229. Oxford University Press, 2015.

Kasulis, T. P. *Zen Action/Zen Person*. Honolulu: University of Hawaiʻi Press, 1981.

Kim, Hee-Jin. "'The Reason of Words and Letters': Dōgen and Kōan Language." In *Dōgen Studies*, ed. William LaFleur, 54–82. Honolulu: University of Hawaiʻi Press, 1985.

King, Sallie B. *Buddha Nature*. Albany, NY: State University of New York Press, 1991.

Korsgaard, Christine M. *The Sources of Normativity*. Cambridge, MA: Harvard University Press, 1996.

Lee, Sangyop. "The Soteriology of the Soul: The *Shen bumie* 神不滅 Discourse in Early Medieval Chinese Buddhism." Ph.D. dissertation. Stanford University, 2021.

Licha, Stephan Kigensan. "Separate Teaching and Separate Transmission: Kokan Shiren's Zen Polemics." *Japanese Journal of Religious Studies* 45, no.1 (2018): 87–124.

Liu, Ming-Wood. "The Doctrine of the Buddha-Nature in the Mahāyāna *Mahāparinirvāṇa-Sūtra*." *Journal of the International Association of Buddhist Studies* 5, no.2 (1982): 63–94.

Loy, David R. "The Path of No-Path: Śankara and Dōgen on the Paradox of Practice." *Philosophy East and West* 38, no. 2 (1988): 127–46.

———. "Language Against Its Own Mystifications: Deconstruction in Nāgārjuna and Dōgen." *Philosophy East and West* 49, no. 3 (1999): 245–60.

———. "Evil as the Good? A Reply to Brook Ziporyn." *Philosophy East and West* 55, no. 2 (2005): 348–52.

Müller, Ralf. "Philosophy and the Practice of Reflexivity: On Dōgen's Discourse about Buddha-Nature." In *Concepts of Philosophy in Asia and the Islamic World*, vol. 1, edited by Raji C. Steineck, Ralph Weber, Robert Gassmann, and Elena Lange, 545–76. Leiden: Brill, 2016.

Nagai, Yoshitaka 永井賢隆. "*Dōgen Zenji to* Dai chido ron." 「道元禅師と『大智度論』」. *Indogaku Bukkyōgaku Kenkyū* 印度学仏教学研究 60, no. 1 (2011): 211–4.

The Nirvana Sutra (Mahāparinirvāṇa-Sūtra): Volume I. Edited and translated by Mark Blum. Moraga, CA: BDK America, 2013.

Park, Jungnok. *How Buddhism Acquired a Soul on the Way to China*. Edited by Richard Gombrich. Oxford: Equinox Publishing, 2012.

Rosen, Gideon. "Metaphysical Dependence: Grounding and Reduction." In *Modality: Metaphysics, Logic, and Epistemology*, eds. Bob Hale and Aviv Hoffman, 109–36. Oxford University Press, 2010.

Schaffer, Jonathan. "On What Grounds What." In *Metametaphysics: New Essays on the Foundations of Ontology*, eds. David J. Chalmers, David Manley, and Ryan Wasserman, 347–83. Oxford University Press, 2009.

Schilbrack, Kevin. "Metaphysics in Dōgen." *Philosophy East and West* 50, no. 1 (2000): 34–55.

Spackman, John. "The Tiantai Roots of Dōgen's Philosophy of Language and Thought." *Philosophy East and West* 56, no. 3 (2006): 428–50.

Specker Sullivan, Laura. "Dōgen and Wittgenstein: Transcending Language Through Ethical Practice." *Asian Philosophy* 23, no. 3 (2013): 221–35.

Stambaugh, Joan. *Impermanence Is Buddha-Nature: Dōgen's Understanding of Temporality*. Honolulu: University of Hawaiʻi Press, 1990.

Steineck, Raji C. "A Zen Philosopher?—Notes on the Philosophical Reading of Dōgen's *Shōbōgenzō*." In *Concepts of Philosophy in Asia and the Islamic World*, vol. 1, eds. Raji C. Steineck, Ralph Weber, Robert Gassmann, and Elena Lange, 577–606. Leiden: Brill, 2018a.

———. "'Religion' and the Concept of the Buddha Way: Semantics of the Religious in Dōgen." *Asiatische Studien/Études Asiatiques* 72, no. 1 (2018b): 177–206.

Stone, Jacqueline I. *Original Enlightenment and the Transformation of Medieval Japanese Buddhism*. Honolulu: University of Hawaiʻi Press, 1999.

Sutton, Florin Giripescu. *Existence and Enlightenment in the Laṅkāvatāra-sūtra: A Study in the Ontology and the Epistemology of the Yogācāra School of Mahāyāna Buddhism*. Albany, NY: State University of New York Press, 1991.

Swanson, Paul L. "T'ien-t'ai Chih-i's Concept of Threefold Buddha Nature—A Synergy of Reality, Wisdom, and Practice." In *Buddha Nature: A Festschrift in Honor of Minoru Kiyota*, eds. Paul J. Griffiths and John P. Keenan, 171–80. Reno, NV: Buddhist Books International, 1990.

Takasaki, Jikido. *A Study on the* Ratnagotravibhaga *(*Uttaratantra*): Being a Treatise on the Tathagatagarbha Theory of Mahayana Buddhism.* Rome: Italian Institute for the Middle and Far East, 1966.

———. "Kōbō Daishi (Kūkai) and Tathāgatagarbha Thought." In *Collected Papers on Tathāgatagarbha Doctrine*, 451–79. Delhi: Motilal Banarsidass, 2014a.

———. "Sources of the *Laṅkāvatāra* and Its Position in Mahāyāna Buddhism." In *Collected Papers on Tathāgatagarbha Doctrine*, 128–55. Delhi: Motilal Banarsidass, 2014b.

Young, Stuart H. 2015. *Conceiving the Indian Buddhist Patriarchs in China.* Honolulu: University of Hawai'i Press.

Ziporyn, Brook. *Evil and/or/as the Good: Omnicentrism, Intersubjectivity, and Value Paradox in Tiantai Buddhist Thought.* Cambridge, MA: Harvard University Press, 2000.

———. "Tiantai Buddhist Conceptions of 'The Nature' (*Xing*) and its Relation to the Mind." *Journal of Chinese Philosophy* 37, no. 3 (2010): 493–512.

Zürcher, Erik. "Buddhism Across Boundaries: The Foreign Input." *Sino-Platonic Papers* 222 (2012): 1–25.

Part III
Time

From Uji to Being-Time (and Back): Translating Dōgen into Philosophy

Raji C. Steineck (ORCID)

1 Dōgen and Philosophy: A Case for Cautious Appropriation

Philosophical reception of Dōgen has to start from the premise that his project was different from philosophy as we understand it today and as it is practised in this book. The dominant understanding of philosophy that, to repeat, is in operation in all contributions to this book, is defined by the critical and open-ended exploration of questions of fundamental human concern[1] – even if some contributions may

---

[1] For extensive discussions of this concept of philosophy in the context of a global perspective on philosophy and its history, and in application to Japanese philosophical traditions see *Begriff und Bild der modernen japanischen Philosophie*, edited by Steineck, Lange and Kaufmann (Stuttgart-Bad Cannstatt: Frommann-Holzboog, 2014); *Concepts of Philosophy in Asia and the Islamic World, Vol. 1: China and Japan*, edited by Steineck, Weber, Gassmann, and Lange (Leiden & Boston: Brill, 2018); Kaufmann and Steineck, 'Another Discourse on the Method: Understanding Philosophy through Rhetorical Analysis'. *European Journal of Japanese Philosophy* 3 (2018): 59–86.

Research for this paper was supported by an ERC Advanced Grant (No. 741166 – TIMEJ) and presented at the Annual Conference of the European Network of Japanese Philosophy in Hildesheim in 2018 and at the online Dōgen symposium in January 2021. I am grateful to the European Research Council for their generous support and to discussants at ENOJP and all attendees at the 2021 online Dōgen symposium for their helpful comments.

R. C. Steineck (✉)
University of Zurich, Zürich, Switzerland
e-mail: raji.steineck@aoi.uzh.ch

R. Müller, G. Wrisley (eds.), *Dōgen's Texts*, Sophia Studies in Cross-cultural Philosophy of Traditions and Cultures 35,
https://doi.org/10.1007/978-3-031-42246-1_11

207

thematically argue for a re-formulation of the project of philosophy. Dōgen was not participating in such an open-ended discourse, and expressly rejected such participation. His declared aim was to instruct his addressees about the correct understanding of the Buddha's teaching.[2] From his first doctrinal exposition, he claimed to do so from a position of equal insight with all Buddhas and enlightened beings.[3] Acknowledging the difference of Dōgen's project to that of philosophy as it is practiced today has important consequences for the reading of his work, and for his philosophical reception. When Dōgen's texts are read in a straightforward manner as expressions of philosophy, they are transposed inadvertently from one field of discourse (authoritative instruction about the Buddha's teaching) into another (philosophy). Such transposition is not illegitimate, but it needs to be made in a conscious manner to preserve the full meaning of the ideas that Dōgen's texts might offer to philosophy. As this paper shall illustrate, the theory of translation can help to understand what the consequences of such a transposition are; and this goes a long way in enabling a better-informed use of Dōgen's work for philosophy.

Two clarifications are in order. First, the general notion of philosophy on which my argument is based does not exclude *praxis* as an important element of philosophy, as Laurentiu Andrei insinuates in his contribution to this volume. Indeed, I would argue that spending time to argue about theoretical issues is also a form of *praxis*. Furthermore, if philosophy is to be conducted as an open-ended exploration of issues of fundamental human concern, this requires a readiness to consider opposing standpoints, which is, once more, a *practical* and *ethical* attitude. Last but not least, I am fully aware that philosophers of earlier times have often argued that a certain way of life is essential in order to be able to think in this manner, and, as Andrei aptly demonstrates, have created institutions that would train their members accordingly. Such claims and endeavors may no longer be a part of academic philosophy today. Still, I do not argue that taking such a position and following up on it in life should exclude anyone from being called a philosopher. The point of distinction relevant for my argument is therefore not that Dōgen emphasized religious practice and especially, seated meditation. The point is that he repudiated engagement in theory and open-ended arguments and that he instructed his disciples about the necessity to do the same, in other words, to dissociate themselves from philosophical theorizing and reflection. One may argue, in philosophy, about the relative weight to be given to critical argument and whatever praxis is deemed necessary to sustain it. Academic philosophy today is based on the premise that no specific practice beyond that of philosophical argumentation is necessary in order to do philosophy. That has, as I will demonstrate below, strongly influenced contemporary philosophical readings of Dōgen as well. One may want to dispute this premise and

---

[2] Steineck, 'A Zen Philosopher? – Notes on the Philosophical Reading of Dōgen's Shōbōgenzō', *Concepts of Philosophy in Asia and the Islamic World, Vol. 1: China and Japan* (Leiden & Boston: Brill, 2018), 577–606.

[3] Steineck, 'Enlightened Authorship: The Case of Dōgen Kigen'. In *That Wonderful Composite Called Author*, edited by Schwermann and Steineck (Leiden: Brill, 2014), 195–219.

change the course of philosophy. But that is different from refusing, as Dōgen did, to engage in open-ended dispute altogether and requiring others to do the same.

Second, I do not want to argue that philosophers should not read Dōgen, or that his thought is irrelevant to philosophy. What I do want to argue is that philosophers, at least as far as they consider themselves to be scholars, should be aware of what they are doing in the process, namely, that they are transposing his texts into a different genre, or, to speak with Cassirer, a different symbolic form altogether. Symbolic forms determine to some degree expectations as to the content that is communicated, the aim of the communication, the form of communication, and the relation between addresser and addressees involved.[4] A change of symbolic form therefore of necessity entails a high degree of semantic, syntactic, and pragmatic *productivity*. Reading Dōgen's texts *as philosophy* involves their transposition from the symbolic form of religion to that of theory or knowledge. This entails productive investments on the side of the philosophical recipients, whether they be authors or a readers. The theory of translation provides the means to become aware of these investments, the dimensions of the texts they affect, and the consequences they may have for the interpretation of Dōgen.

In the main part of the ensuing argument, I will first demonstrate to what extent different philosophical readings of Dōgen's seminal text on time, *Uji*, have made creative investments in its meaning. I will then briefly summarize a paradigm of translational equivalences that can be used to analyze and calibrate the transformations made when reading Dōgen as a philosopher. But before going into these topics, some words are in place to explain why I believe that we should better not speak of Dōgen as a philosopher, as I myself have done previously.[5]

The detailed analysis of the rhetorical structure of Dōgen's *Shōbō genzō*, plus a conceptual analysis of his use of all the terms that might represent "philosophy" in his writings, such as *dō* 道 ("the way"; "sayings"), *kyō* 教 ("teachings"), or *ken* 見 ("doctrines", "views") has convinced me otherwise.[6] To summarize, in terms of conceptual analysis, a survey of the semantic fields and usages of *dō* 道 ("way", also translation of skt. *marga*), *kyō* 教 and *ken* 見 in 15 fascicles of the *Shōbō genzō* that have been received as philosophical texts showed that Dōgen consistently uses these terms in a strongly evaluative fashion. That is, none of them functions as a neutral hyperonym, as a general name identifying all reasoned reflection on fundamental

---

[4] Cassirer, 'Das Symbolproblem und seine Stellung im System der Philosophie' *Gesammelte Werke*, Bd. 17: *Aufsätze und kleine Schriften (1927–1931)* (Hamburg: Meiner, 2004, 257–58.

[5] Steineck, 'Kommentar: Philosophische Perspektiven von Dōgen: Genjōkōan und Busshō'. In *Dōgen als Philosoph*, edited by Steineck, Rappe, and Arifuku (Studies in Oriental Religions 51. Wiesbaden: Harrassowitz, 2002), 119–51.

[6] See Steineck, 'Das Bendōwa von Dogen: Narratologische Analyse eines doktrinären Textes'. Asiatische Studien, 63 (3) (2009): 571; idem.,'Zen in der Kunst der Persuasion: Zur Rhetorik einer mittelalterlichen Lehrschrift', *Rhetorik im Vormodernen Japan*, edited by Buck-Albulet (München: Iudicium, 2015), 127–49; 'A Zen Philosopher? – Notes on the Philosophical Reading of Dōgen's *Shōbōgenzō*', in *Concepts of Philosophy in Asia and the Islamic World, Vol. 1: China and Japan*, 577–606; idem.,'"Religion" and the Concept of the Buddha Way: Semantics of the Religious in Dōgen'. *Asiatische Studien* 72 (1) (2018): 177–206.

questions of human life. To the contrary, the "way" and "teaching" are either Buddhist, then they are appreciated as correct and true, or they are "extraneous" (*gedō* 外道). The critical issue here is that texts and ideas considered as "extraneous" are judged by Dōgen to be not even worthy of consideration; not once does attempt to appreciate arguments in their favor. *Ken,* which is also the translation term for Sanskrit *darshana,* a word that comes very close to what we call "philosophy", is almost always combined with derogatory qualifications. To sum up, in Dōgen's view, should one happen to be engaged in something like "philosophy", the one thing to do is to cease that engagement immediately. What one should do instead is enter the Buddhist path and model one's life and thoughts after that of the Buddhas and patriarchs – without ever considering any alternatives. Dōgen's rhetoric matches this conceptual outlook: Throughout, he speaks as the enlightened master, whose aim is to convey the correct teaching and insight to his disciples. There is no room for open-ended argumentation – to the contrary, that would defy the whole purpose of communication, which is to lead the addressees on the correct path of the Buddhist teaching.

So what, one may argue, still, his thought is complex and consistent enough to be philosophically interesting. Why not read him as a philosopher?

Indeed, why not. We, as philosophers, may want to read Dōgen. My point is not that we shouldn't do that. My point is that if we do it thinking Dōgen was a philosopher himself, we will probably not be fully aware of the productive investments we make in your readings. These investments may have their rewards. But all production is also, as Marx once observed, a form of creative destruction. As philosophers and scholars, we should be aware of what we produce and what we destroy.

In the following paragraph, I will therefore analyse four prominent examples of straightforward philosophical readings of Dōgen to see what is created and what is lost by this mode of interpretation.

2 Translating Dōgen into Philosophy: Semantic Shifts in Prominent Examples

All four readings relate to the following famous passage from Uji:

> いはゆる有時は、時すでにこれ有なり、有はみな時なり。丈六金身これ時なり、時なるがゆゑに時の莊嚴光明あり。いまの十二時に學すべし。三頭八臂これ時なり、時なるがゆゑにいまの十二時に一如なるべし。十二時の長遠短促、いまだ度量せずといへども、これを十二時といふ。去來の方跡あきらかなるによりて、人これを疑著せず、疑著せざれどもしれるにあらず。衆生もとよりしらざる毎物毎事を疑著すること一定せざるがゆゑに、疑著する前程、かならずしもいまの疑著に符合することなし。ただ疑著しばらく時なるのみなり。[7]

[7] Ōkubo, ed. 'Uji 有時', in Dōgen Zenji Zenshū I (Tōkyō: Chikuma shobō, 1969), 189.

The following is a tentative translation[8] that leaves open as much as necessary and warranted:

> Said [word] *uji* means that time is already what is real, and that whatever is real is [also] time. The golden body of one *jō* six is time, and because it is time, there is the sublime light of time. One can[or: should] study this in[or: with respect to the occasion of] the present twelve [zodiacal] hours. The three heads and eight arms [either a demon (*asura*) or a guardian deity (*myōō*)] are time, and because they are time, they are one and the same with the twelve hours. Even without having measured the length and shortness of the twelve hours, we call this the twelve hours. Since the traces of passing and coming are obvious, people don't doubt them, but even though they don't doubt them, that doesn't mean that they know them. Since doubting what the various living beings originally don't know is not well-defined, the earlier instances of doubting do not necessarily match with the present one. For the time being, doubting is simply [a] time."

To briefly name some points of contention in the literature, the *u* of *uji* is often translated as "being". Based on Rolf Elberfeld's discussion of the passage,[9] I have opted here for "what is real" to match the original meaning of Chinese *you*, which designates the facticity (Kant's "Dasein") of something that has specific properties (Kant's "reality"), as visible in the conventional usage of the term *uji* or *aru toki*: "there was/is a time when". The quoted passage accords with this understanding, because *u* here clearly refers to specific objects or states of affairs, not to abstract *being* as such. It is further an open question whether in *Uji, u* was meant to denote the abstract notion of *being* at all.

Ji or *toki* in Japanese is indefinite in terms of number, so it might refer to "time", "a time" or "many times". The phrase *ji wa mina*, "every time", "all times", in the passage quoted above is a clear case of usage indicating a plural sense of the term.[10]

"*Jūniji ni gaku su beshi*" can be "one can[or: should] study this <u>within</u> the twelve zodiacal hours" or "<u>according to/on</u> the occasion of the twelve hours". Two things are important about this passage: first, in terms of pragmatics, it indicates that Dōgen wants to incite his recipients to do something – namely study and practice. *Uji* is a conative text, a text that is intended to impact the practical actions of its recipients. Second, whatever is meant with *uji* is apparently not detached from or opposed to quantified time, although time's quantification clearly should, in Dōgen's eyes, not be taken for granted.

That said, let us take a look at what can happen when *Uji* is read in a straightforward manner as a philosophical text. My first example is somewhat extreme in that it is taken from a philosopher who does not intend to deeply engage with Dōgen, but merely adduces him as an authority to connect his own thought to Japanese tradition. Ōmori Shōzō is known as one of the most eminent Japanese philosophers in

---

[8] Here and in the following, all translations without references are mine.

[9] Elberfeld, *Phänomenologie der Zeit im Buddhismus: Methoden interkulturellen Philosophierens* (Stuttgart-Bad Cannstatt: Frommann-Holzboog, 2004), 230–33.

[10] See Elberfeld on why to read *ji*, not *toki*: Elberfeld, *Phänomenologie der Zeit im Buddhismus* (Stuttgart-Bad Cannstatt: Frommann-Holzboog, 2004), 231–32

the ordinary language approach of the analytical tradition.[11] As such, he is certainly
not the most likely candidate to reference Dōgen, but he does so in his explication
of *tokimeki* 時めき – the quick of time. The following paragraph is a good example
for the transformations that can occur when Dōgen's texts are transposed from the
symbolic form of religion to that of theory.

> 身のまわりにある何でもない平凡な事物、例えば机や椅子、台所用品がそれぞれ
> の場所に「存在する」のを見るときにその存在とは持続的存在をいみしているこ
> とは確かである。机でも鍋でもそこに「ずーっと存在し続けている」といういみ
> でそこに在る。その鍋は突然そこに出現したのではなくしばらく前から存在し続
> けている。ここで「しばらく前から」とは当然「過去」を意味しているのだか
> ら、鍋の存在の意味が過去の意味が含まれていることは明白にある。…こうして
> 平凡な日用品の存在の中に、すでに過去現在未来という時間の三様態が意味的に
> 含まれているのである。多少の誇張と強弁を加えれば、存在とは既に時間であ
> り、時間は既に存在に含まれている、と言えよう。…この含まれている意味をあ
> らわにとり出すことを「存在の時めき」と呼びたい。この「存在の時めき」は道
> 元がその『正法眼蔵』第二十『有時』で「有時」と読んだものに他ならないと
> 私には思われる。

> いはゆる有事は、時すでにこれ有なり、有はみな時なり。丈六金身これ時なり、
> 時なるがゆへに時の荘厳光明あり。…三頭八臂これ時なり。

> 道元はその生活環境からして鍋などの代わりに丈六その他の仏像を例にとっては
> いるが、それらの物体の存在の時めきを説いている、と見て差支
> えないだろう。[12]

When we see ordinary, inconspicuous things that surround us, like a desk, a chair,
or kitchen tools, "being" at their place, it is certain that this being means a durational
being. It means that a desk or a pot "continues to be there all the while". This pot
hasn't suddenly appeared, but has continued to exist for a while. Because this "continued all the while" evidently refers to the past, the meaning of the being of the pot
clearly comprises that of past [existence]. ... In this manner, the being of ordinary
everyday tools already comprises the three temporal dimensions of past, present,
and future. Taking this slightly further, one may go as far as to say that being is
already time and that time is inherent in being. ... To make this inherent meaning
explicit, I choose to call it "being's quick of time". I believe that this "being's quick
of time" is what Dōgen called *uji* in the 20th chapter *Uji* of the *Shōbō genzō*: "The
expression *uji* means that time is already being, and every being is time. The golden
body of one *jō* six is time, and because it is time, there is the sublime light of time.
... The three heads and eight arms are time." In accord with his own environment,
Dōgen takes Buddha statues of one *jō* six instead of a pot as an example, but it is still
safe to say that he teaches the quick of time in material being.

Ōmori appropriates Dōgen's words for an analysis of the temporal implications
of ordinary language. In the process, Dōgen's discourse is thoroughly normalized in

---

[11] Kobayashi, 'The Komaba Quartet', *The Oxford Handbook of Japanese Philosophy* (Online edition 2019).
[12] Ōmori, *Jikan to sonzai* 時間と存在 (Tōkyō: Seidosha, 1994), 19–21.

terms of modern philosophy. The transformation is evident: the more exotic constituents of his speech, such as references to the golden body of the Buddha, or the figure of a non-human being with three heads and eight arms, are reduced to "ordinary, inconspicuous" human artifacts on a par with kitchen tools. Their sacral aspects and soteriological meanings vanish in the process, as do the specifics of religious behaviour and attitudes. This includes the temporal implications of such behaviour and attitudes. One wouldn't normally bow to a pot in hope of receiving its support on a spiritual path – but making obeisances is exactly the expected form of behaviour to the sacred figures in Dōgen's monasteries, as evident from his guidelines for behaviour in the monks' hall.

Ōmori's Dōgen is perfectly accessible to the contemporary secularized reader. He doesn't challenge one to change one's behaviour in accord with a vision of salvation.

Another transformation is less conspicuous, but equally important in the conceptual interpretation of Dōgen: in Ōmori's quote the *u* of *uji* has, without much ado, become "being", an abstract noun indicating a universal. Dōgen's *uji* has been integrated into the philosophical discourse of ontology, of theoretical reflection on the concept of being as such. I do not want to argue that one cannot relate Dōgen's propositions on *uji* to ontological discourse. My point is that one should be more careful when doing so. As I said earlier, the context of the source passage indicates that *u* does not refer to abstract universal "being", but to something real with distinct properties. To equate *u* with being is in danger of conceptually misreading Dōgen, to say the least. Such a reading therefore needs to be argued for and reconciled with conflicting evidence. It cannot be simply taken for granted.

Before I leave Ōmori Shōzō let me state that, even if his use of Dōgen is spurious, his philosophy deserves more attention than he has been getting in the West so far. The text that entails the above-quoted paragraph, for example, convincingly argues against the idea of a moment without duration[13] – an idea that has been identified with Dōgen's thought by Rein Raud in an interpretation to be discussed below. Furthermore, his way of appropriating Dōgen is certainly not without precedent. At least the second, conceptual transition evident in his quotation of Dōgen is pervasive in the literature that reads Dōgen as a philosopher.

We find it already in Akiyama Hanji's seminal *Study of Dōgen*, published in 1935. Akiyama paraphrases 「時すでにこれ有なり、有はみな時なり」 much like Ōmori to say that "Time is identical with being, and being is immediately time." 「時間とは存在のこと、存在は直ちに時間である」.[14] He is careful to acknowledge that in the context of our passage from *Uji* the term refers to individual objects and their respective times. But to him, this is only one side of the term's meaning. The other side relates to Buddha nature as "absolute nothingness" (絶対

---

[13] Ōmori, *Jikan to sonzai* 時間と存在 (Tōkyō: Seidosha, 1994), 27–46; idem., 'Die Produktion der linearen Zeit' *European Journal of Japanese Philosophy* 6 (2021): 125–36.

[14] Akiyama, *Dōgen no Kenkyū* 道元の研究 (Tōkyō: Iwanami Shoten, 1935), 127.

無), and this "nothingness", he says, limits or determines itself into these individual *uji* "without reason and in an irrational fashion."[15]

Uji thus indicates the self-determination of nothingness into discrete, individual, temporal instances of what he nevertheless calls "absolute being" (絶対の存在).[16] It is no mere coincidence that this sounds conspicuously like Nishida Kitarō's "self-aware determination of nothingness" (無の自覚的限定),[17] because we know that Akiyama had studied with Nishida in the late 1920s.[18]

Again, my point here is primarily that this interpretation with all its investments into speculative dialectics is introduced by Akiyama without further discussion, as a mere paraphrase of what Dōgen is saying. Yet, I don't see any talk of "self-determination" or "irrationality" in the passages quoted from *Uji*. Moreover, to say that objects and situations occur "without reason" is an interpolation that needs to be reconciled with Dōgen's, or indeed Buddhism's, insistence on conditioned occurence. Akiyama is aware of this latter problem. He attempts to solve it with another interpolation, by way of an analogy to Husserl's distinction between the "natural" stance and that of phenomenological reduction[19]: The "natural stance", he says, is immersed in the world of consciousness, where events are connected by causal chains. Enlightened insight is aware that each conscious instant, however, occurs spontaneously and without reason. In Akiyama's words, which take their key terms from Husserl (or, perhaps, Nishida's reading of Husserl):

不昧因果とは勝義に於いては正に此のノエシス的に非連続的なる現前の一瞬中に摂せられたるノエマ的に過去未来共にわたて連続的なる因果の認識をいふのである。[20]

Not obscuring cause and effect in the higher sense actually refers to the noematic knowledge of continuous causation that spans the eternal past, present, and future, which is contained in the noetic, discontinuous present moment.

This attempt to reconcile the idea of an absolute, discontinuous reality with that of dependent origination is certainly worthy of consideration – but its relation to Dōgen's texts is far from self-evident. To distinguish both sides as belonging to "noematic" and "noetic" reality, respectively, remains an interpolation for which Akiyama fails to adduce direct supporting evidence.

A similar "phenomenological turn" can also be found in another seminal philosophical reading of Dōgen, Tanabe Hajime's "My view on the philosophy of the

[15] Ibid.,   131:   無の自己限定の起るはただ忽然として起るのみ、無理由にして非合理的である。

[16] Ibid., 133.

[17] Nishida, *Mu no Jikakuteki Gentei* 無の自覚的限定, Nishida Kitarō Zenshū 西田幾多郎全集 6 (Tōkyō: Iwanamishoten, 1965).

[18] Wakatsuki, Zenki ni okeru Shūgaku Kenkyū no "Shūhen" (1): Akiyama Hanji Cho "Dōgen No Kenkyū" ni tsuite 昭和前期における宗学研究の「周辺」*Komazawa University Journal of Buddhist Studies* 8 (October 1977): 130. [Do you mean p. 30? Or is that another source?]

[19] Akiyama, *Dōgen no Kenkyū* 道元の研究 (Tōkyō: Iwanami Shoten, 1935), 172.

[20] Ibid., 176.

Shōbō genzō", 田邊元『正法眼蔵の哲學私觀』.[21] Tanabe again refers to the quoted passage from *Uji,* saying:

> 彼（道元）はもと單に「時間有つて」即ち「有る時」「ある時」從つて「或時」の
> 意味を有するに過ぎないと思はれる有時の語を解釋して、「いはゆる有事は、時
> すでにこれ有なり、有はみな時なり」と說いて、今日ハイデッガーの說く如きい
> はゆる存在即時間の時間的存在論を主張する。而しも人此の如き存在即時間を「
> 疑着せざれども之をしれるにあらず、…疑着しばらく時なるのみなり」といつ
> て、人間の直接的日常現存在と其自覺存在との相關を示して居る。 [22]

> In interpreting the word *uji,* which originally is taken to simply mean "there is a time", therefore "at a given time", therefore "some time", he [Dōgen] explains, "what is called *uji* means that time is already being, and beings are all time", positing like today Heidegger a temporal ontology that states the identity of being and time. In further saying about this identity of being and time that "while not being doubted, it is not known as such, … doubting is none other than time", he points to the relation of people's immediate, everyday Dasein and its self-aware being.

(Just to be clear about what I have done in my own translation of Tanabe's: First, I have translated his quotes from Dōgen in the way that his own interpretation suggests. Second, I have turned what is in the Japanese original a nominalized phrase, i.e., 存在即時間, "being is time", into the compound nominal expression "the identity of being and time".)

Independent of translation problems, at first sight the passage looks innocent enough in its dense use of citations from the original. Note, however, that Tanabe takes the second quotation out of its immediate context, where it refers to clock time, and relates it to time in general. Further, Tanabe turns Dōgen into an existential philosopher *avant la lettre* – a Japanese medieval Heidegger. As stated in the preface to his book, part of his project is to reaffirm the value of pre-modern Japanese thought vis-à-vis what he considers to be the questions of contemporary avantgarde Western philosophy.[23] By reading Dōgen as an existentialist philosopher, Tanabe demonstrates that what was most worthwhile in the modern Western mind had already been there in Japan at a much earlier time – a figure of thought that was already present in Watsuji's *Shamon Dōgen.*[24]

Leaving the political aspect aside, Dōgen's topic is arguably the relation between the views of the unenlightened (*shujō* 衆生), who are bound to transmigration in the cycle of existences, and the liberating insight and practice of the Buddhas and Patriarchs. Tanabe turns this into the difference between "immediate, everyday Dasein" and "self-aware being": it is awareness of the structure of existence that distinguishes the one from the other, not realization of the Buddha Way. The

---

[21] Tanabe, *Shōbō Genzō no Tetsugaku Shikan* 正法眼蔵の哲学私観 (Tōkyō: Iwanami Shoten, 1939); see also Müller, ' Getting Back to Premodern Japan: Tanabe's Reading of Dōgen' (*Frontiers in Japanese Philosophy* Vol. 1. Nanzan Institute for Religion and Culture 2006).

[22] Tanabe, *Shōbō Genzō no Tetsugaku Shikan* 正法眼蔵の哲学私観 (Tōkyō: Iwanami Shoten, 1939), 62–63.

[23] Ibid., 1.

[24] Watsuji, *Nihon Seishinshi Kenkyū* 日本精神史研究 (Tōkyō: Iwanami shoten, 1992).

productive element lies in this universalistic, but also scholastic turn. It allows Tanabe to read Dōgen as an analyst of the structure of human existence, and to create links to contemporary philosophical issues. What gets lost is the specifics of Dōgen's own questioning of time, which is inextricably linked to Buddhist soteriology. If this were a painting, you might still recognize a similarity of structure, and a shared theme, but the atmosphere, the appeal, and the message would have decidedly changed.

To finally turn to a recent and thorough engagement with Dōgen, the 2012 article by Rein Raud on "The existential moment" intends to "reinterpret the concept of time in Dōgen's theory from a different position, with stress on the momentary rather than the durational, and to offer an alternative reading of the *Uji* fascicle as well as certain other key passages in Dōgen's work that, … will enable a less complicated and more lucid understanding of his ideas."[25]

In the course of the article, Raud gives the following translation of the above-quoted passage from *Uji*:

> The so-called 'existential moment' means that each moment is in itself an existence and that all existences are momentary. The 'golden body of the Buddha' is a moment, and because it is momentary it has its moment of ethereal glow. You should study this in the context of the twelve hours of the present. The 'three heads and eight shoulders of an asura' are just a moment and because of this momentariness, they are such during the twelve hours of the present. The twelve hours have length and distance, shortness and proximity, and even if you are not conscious of their measure, you still call this system 'the twelve hours'. Because the marks of their going and coming are clear, people do not doubt them, but even if they do not doubt them, it is not the same as understanding them. Even if sentient beings do not make it a general principle to doubt every thing and every event that they do not initially understand, it does not follow that they necessarily agree with everything before they start doubting it. Their doubts are no more than fleeting moments as well.[26]

He continues to explain:

> The first difference in reading between the momentary and durational modes emerges in establishing the relation of *uji* with the measurable time-system. The durational translations allow it to be merged with the 'twelve hours of the present' …; the momentary version separates them because time has duration, but moments do not.[27]

As is evident from the passages quoted, Raud's project is to read Dōgen as the proponent of a theory of momentariness and *Uji* as an exposition of that theory, and his contribution to the current volume further develops that interpretation.[28] In this sense, he is following up on one side of Akiyama's interpretation, without, however,

---

[25] Raud, 'The Existential Moment: Rereading Dōgen's Theory of Time'. *Philosophy East and West* 62 (2) (2012): 153.

[26] Ibid., 159–60.

[27] Ibid., 160.

[28] See Raud, in this volume, where he states that *Uji* "leads them [the readers] through the 'holistic' understanding of the phenomenological present to the ontological understanding of existence as essentially momentary."

mentioning Akiyama. His above translation may be seen as an experiment in that regard.

To briefly assess the gains and losses of this approach in the passage in question, the translation has a high degree of terminological and conceptual consistency. It reads like a fairly straightforward argument about the relation of the "existential moment" – which is Raud's translation of *uji* – and measurable time, the time of the "twelve hours". Raud's argument is based on the idea that Dōgen is a momentarist who holds that immeasurable moments are true and real but measurable time is secondary at best. He therefore wants us to separate *uji* and the *twelve hours* and gives "The 'three heads and eight shoulders of an asura' are just a moment and because of this momentariness, they are such during the twelve hours of the present." for what is in the original 「三頭八臂これ時なり、時なるがゆゑにいまの十二時に一如なるべし。」 – more literally: "Three heads, eight arms are *ji,* and because they are *ji* they have to/should be (*narubeshi*) the same (*ichinyo*) as the twelve hours now."

Raud has managed to give his translated sentence a meaning that is consistent with his fundamental idea, but this came with several creative investments into the text. His identification of the "three heads, eight arms" with an asura is in line with part of the tradition.[29] But other than Arifuku Kōgaku, for example, he takes the expression out of its soteriological context, which is about the relation between different phases of realization on the Buddha Way, such as bringing forth the bodhi-mind, practicing, achieving highest insight or enlightenment, and returning to the world to save sentient beings. Arifuku, in contrast, explicitly connects the expression to the passage in the Kannon chapter of the Lotus sutra, where Kannon promises to appear in this shape to convert sentient beings, if necessary.[30]

Semantically, Raud has created an abstractive translation for the second instance of *ji* ("momentariness"), and has severed the link between *ji* and the "twelve hours" that Dōgen ties both with his injunctions to study and understand *uji* within present measured time and his statement that the three heads and eight arms are "one with the twelve hours".

All of this, or so I would argue, hinges on Raud's interpretation of *ji* as *moment in an Aristotelian sense:*

> *Time* thus has, by definition, measurements and is analogous to a *line* in space, as opposed to *the now (to nyn),* which relates to *time* as a point relates to a *line* – it is in/on it, but not a part of it. ... Analogically, a *moment* appears to us in a different register of being than *time.* Moments are without duration, just as points are without measurements.[31]

I beg to differ on two points. First, it is debatable whether the *ji* in Dōgen's *uji* is really designating "moments" at all. Since he relates the term to meta-stable states

---

[29] Others, such as Yorizumi Mitsuko, identify it with the guardian deity Fudō myōō. See Yorizumi, *Dōgen: Jiko, Jikan, Sekai wa dono yōni Seiritsu suru no ka* 道元: 自己・時間・世界はどのように成立するのか (Tōkyō: Nihon Hōsō Shuppan Kyōkai, 2009), 87.

[30] Arifuku, *Dōgen no Sekai* 道元の世界 (Ōsaka: Ōsaka Shoseki, 1985), 233; Kato and Soothill, *The Threefold Lotus Sutra.* New York: Weatherhill, 1975), 322.

[31] Raud, 'The Existential Moment: Rereading Dōgen's Theory of Time'. *Philosophy East and West* 62 (2) (2012): 153.

such as bamboos, pine trees, Buddhas, and Wisdom kings, and uses the image of the season to elucidate his notion of *kyōryaku*, I tend to follow Kawamura Kōdō, who equated *ji* with *jisetsu* 時節 (a limited phase or period of time). In this reading, which was continued by Ishii Kiyozumi, *ji* is less about moments without duration and more about phenomena of limited duration without underlying substance.[32]

That said, as Akiyama and others have pointed out, there is clear evidence that Dōgen works from an underlying ontology of momentariness. However – and that would be my second point of contention – the "moments" in question are not "points", but, if we need an analogy from modern science, temporal "quanta", that is, discrete units of minimal temporal duration. This is evident in passages where Dōgen talks about instantaneous arising and cessation. Here is a pertinent passage from *Shōbō genzō Shukke kudoku*:

> しるべし、今生の人身は、四大五蘊、因和合してかりになせり、八苦つねにあり。いはんや刹那刹那に生滅してさらにとどまらず、いはんや一弾指のあひだに六十五の刹那生滅すといへども、みづからくらきによりて、いまだしらざるなり。すべて一日夜があひだに、六十四億九万九千九百八十の刹那ありて五蘊生滅すといへども、しらざるなり。あはれむべし、われ生滅すといへども、みづからしらざること。この刹那生滅の量、ただ佛世尊ならびに舍利弗とのみしらせたまふ。[33]

> You should know that the human body of this life has provisionally come to be by the meeting of the four elements and five skandha as well as of causes and conditions, and it is continually beset by the eight forms of suffering. Not to mention that even though it ceaselessly arises and perishes from instant to instant, it is blind to this fact and therefore does not know it. In the course of one day and night, there are 6 billion 400 million 99 thousand 980 instants, and the five skandhas arise and perish on that rate without knowing. It is deplorable that we arise and perish without being aware of it ourselves. The rate of this arising and perishing something we know only from the Buddha, the World-Honored One and Shaributsu.

In other words, the *setsuna* or "moment" that Dōgen talks about here does have a measure (*ryō* 量) which one can easily calculate using his words – it comes down to 0.0000135 modern seconds. The *setsuna*-moment comprises arising and perishing, and it is part and parcel of larger units of time, such as "one day and night". I would therefore concur with Rein Raud that Dōgen's view on time in *Shōbō genzō* included a momentarist element, but deny that in Dōgen's own idea, the moments are somehow separate from larger aggregates of measured time, or that any aggregation of moments to the meta-stable state of "something", be it bamboo or Buddha, is "illusory by definition".[34]

---

[32] Kawamura, '*Shōbōgenzō* "Uji" ni tsuite –Busshō no Mondai to no Kanren ni oite', *Journal of Soto Zen Studies*, no. 3 (March 1961), 117–118; Ishii "'Zengo saidan' ni tsuite", *Journal of Soto Zen studies*, no. 40 (March 1998), 47.

[33] Ōkubo, 'Shukke Kudoku', *Dōgen Zenji Zenshū* I, 603–18. (Tōkyō: Chikuma shobō, 1969), 607.

[34] Raud, in this volume; note, by the way, that Raud on the other hand posits that the ordinary view, which allows for temporal measurement and duration, forms an indispensable part of the complementary duality of "provisional" and "holistic" truth, each of which is incomplete and "neither of them self-sufficient".

Now, the relation between *Shukke kudoku,* which belongs to the new, 12 fascicle *Shōbō genzō,* and the *Uji* fascicle has been a topic of much debate. So, I am not going here into the question of whether and, if yes, how, we can construe a consistent theory of time from the sum total of Dōgen's writings. It may still be that the *ji* of *Uji* points to a dimension beyond measured time. What that "beyond" means, and how it relates to measured time, is a topic for further discussion.[35]

3 Transposition: The Problem of Equivalence

In this paper, my topic is the transformations that are taking place when Dōgen's texts are transposed into philosophy. I hope I have been able to show by way of my four examples that reading and translating Dōgen as a philosopher tends to create certain shifts in the mode and style of discourse, the reading of his syntax, the semantic of key terms, and in the pragmatics, the constellation of addresser and addressees that is envisaged in the text.

Let me be clear. I do not believe that such shifts are entirely illegitimate. My argument is in favour of making *conscious* shifts. I also believe that the reading of texts such as the *Shōbō genzō,* much as the reading of, say, *The Critique of Pure Reason,* becomes more relevant when we follow the original as far as we can – because, to use a thought exposed by Dōgen in *Kattō* and *Dōtoku,* it is by running into obstacles and falling into traps that we are made to move beyond our current understanding. In the following, I therefore want to propose a model from translation studies as a kind of checklist to prevent *inadvertent shifting.*

A useful template in this regard are the "frames of equivalence" (*Bezugsrahmen der Äquivalenz*) proposed by Werner Koller.[36]

Koller identifies five such frames:

1. denotative equivalence: relating to extralinguistic facts and issues
2. connotative equivalence: relating to the way a meaning is verbalized, associations, expectations of style etc.
3. text-normative equivalence: relating to normative expectations concerning content, organization, style, lexis, syntax
4. formal-aesthetic equivalence: relating to the level of *elocutio,* the individual choices made by an author in expressing his message
5. pragmatic equivalence: relating to the addressees of a source text and the translation/transposition, the relation between addresser/addressee, as well as the agency of the text.[37]

---

[35] This question is discussed extensively in my forthcoming book on Dōgen and time: Steineck, *Zen Time: Dōgen in Context.*

[36] Koller, *Einführung in die Übersetzungswissenschaft* (Heidelberg: UTB Quelle & Meyer, 1979), 214–72.

[37] Ibid., 216.

The translation of a text into another language may involve shifts in any and several of these frames. A scholarly translation of a *Shōbō genzō* text into a European language, for example, may preserve a high degree of equivalence in the denotative frame, but will not achieve the same degree in the connotative frame, because of differences in the lexicon of the target language and the cognitive repertoire associated with it. By way of being a scholarly translation, it will of necessity fail to achieve pragmatic equivalence, as it involves an attitude of the translator towards the recipients of the translation and vice versa that is different from those at play between Dōgen and the addressees of his *Shōbō genzō* texts. Translations that aim at pragmatic equivalence, on the other hand, may sacrifice certain denotative equivalences (typically, for example, in references to the hours of the clock or the dates of the calendar) in order to not burden the reading of the text with obstacles to understanding that have only a quaint relation to its central message.

Readings that transpose a *Shōbō genzō* text into philosophy inevitably involve even greater shifts, most of all concerning the frames of the pragmatic and of text normativity. In the following, I will briefly elaborate on these shifts and how they relate to shifts within the dimension of the semantic (frames 1 and 2). Within the frame of pragmatic relations, philosophy comes with the expectation of free reasoned discourse, in which the addresser is expected to convince the addressee by way of argument and reason. Conversely, the addressee is allowed to challenge the addresser as well as their sources on the same grounds. In philosophy, it is a legitimate endeavor to prove Kant, Heidegger, Nishida, or Dōgen wrong, although it is more valuable if you do so by also appreciating where they were right. In Dōgen's Buddha Way, one cannot prove the Buddha-patriarchs wrong, and one may not try to do so, even if one is allowed to move "beyond" them, whatever that means. As far as addresser and addressees are concerned, most of the *Shōbō genzō* texts were initially *jishū*, informal teachings to the inner circle of monastic disciples. They were intended to guide a group of dedicated adepts on a shared path. In terms of pragmatics, this implied the superior authority of the addresser ("master Dōgen") and the inferior status of his recipients ("the assembly"). Instead of offering propositions for critical scrutiny, the texts are presented as expressions of enlightened insight; recipients are exhorted to contemplate these expressions in order to deepen their own appreciation of the Buddha Way. This has important implications for the denotative and connotative frames. In the context of the *Shōbō genzō*, and of *kōan* literature in general, apparent contradictions for example do not present logical conundrums to be resolved in order to achieve a theoretical synthesis. They provide opportunities to consider aspects of the authoritative sayings in different perspectives. Validity is not a problem, as it is considered a given – and, as T.G. Foulk has insightfully pointed out, much of *kōan* literature would be meaningless if it were not accepted as such.[38]

For centuries, the texts were treated as secret teachings; access was proof of belonging to the inner circle. That of course changed with the integration of the

---

[38] Foulk, '1: The Form and Function of Koan Literature', The Koan: Texts and Contexts in Zen Buddhism, ed. by St. Heine and D. S. Wright, 15–45 (New York: Oxford University Press, 2000).

Shōbō genzō into the canons of "Japanese thought" and "Japanese literature". Dōgen's texts are today presented in modern editions, readily available for purchase by individuals and public or academic libraries, and often supplemented with explanatory notes that would, in the more distant past, have been provided orally by a competent teacher, ideally one standing in the direct line of transmission. Such notes, obviously, impact on the connotational and denotational levels of meaning. One should therefore keep in mind that even the "original" texts we are reading today are, on the level of pragmatics, far removed from what they were at the time of their writing, and that this impacts also on their semantics.

Modern editing also engenders changes within the frame of formal-aesthetic equivalence. Characters are often standardized, and many editions use the modern instead of the older form. Some editions also collate texts from various manuscripts. A further formal-aesthetic change that has direct impact on the connotational and denotational levels is the insertion of line breaks to create paragraphs where there are none in the manuscripts.[39] On the recipient side, modern editions are for a large part used for individual silent reading, which then may translate in public discussion. Access rules for such discussion are academic rather than religious. The fact that in this book, non-clerical professional scholars present arguments on Dōgen to readers who are also for the most part neither monastics nor formally members of the Zen School or any other Buddhist denomination is a pragmatic sea change. Its implications still need to be accounted for in interpretation. And even where Dōgen is translated and explained for use in Zen Training (as in the Sōtō School Translation Project, or in the translations edited by Kazuaki Tanahashi), the social organization, the environment, and the conditions of training have changed to a large degree in comparison to Dōgen's own time. Furthermore, to secure "pragmatic equivalence", one has to account for the cognitive repertoire of the audience, which is very different between a contemporary European or American Zen community and the assembly in Dōgen's monasteries. Again, changes concerning the pragmatic dimension of necessity reflect on the semantic dimension of what is being said, and how it is being understood.

As for the frame of text-normative expectations, philosophical texts – the texts of this book, for example – are expected to proffer and possibly discuss concepts and theories. Different textual traditions have their respective conventional text forms catering to this end, and these have changed over time. Still, all of them are meant to clarify and elucidate certain ideas pertaining to questions of fundamental importance to all humankind. Only very few texts from the *Shōbō genzō* conform to these expectations, if measured against indigenous Japanese or East Asian formats such as *ron* or *gi*. This is clear from direct comparison between Dōgen and other Japanese Buddhist authors such as Kūkai.[40]

---

[39] Bodiford has recently published an insightful article outlining the scope of changes that have been made to Dōgen's texts due to modern editorial demands and decisions. See Bodiford, 'Rewriting Dōgen', *Kokusai Zen Kenkyū* 国際禅研究 4 (2019): 219–302.

[40] Kaufmann and Steineck, 'Another Discourse on the Method: Understanding Philosophy through Rhetorical Analysis', *European Journal of Japanese Philosophy* 3 (2018): 59–86.

4 Conclusion

The point to keep in mind is that, as already stated by Kawamura some decades ago, and recently reiterated by Tsujiguchi Yōichirō, *Uji* was not intended as a philosophical treatise on the concept of time,[41] and *mutatis mutandis* the same is true for other *Shōbō genzō* texts that have been received into modern philosophical discourse. These texts provide guidance on how to deal with certain terms and concepts when negotiating the Way of the Buddhas and Patriarchs. To transform them into expositions of theory means to transpose them into a different kind of text altogether. As the examples given above have shown, this has important consequences for the meaning attributed to them. One needs, in other words, to keep track of how the said transposition affects Koller's frames of equivalence 1 and 2 – the levels of denotation and connotation, or, generally, the dimension of the semantic. As I have demonstrated above, there is a tendency to make inadvertent denotative and connotative changes. Dōgen's *u* is not Heidegger's *Sein/Being,* and his *ji* is not an Aristotelian *nyn,* an infinitesimally small point in time. The "golden body of a Buddha" is a soteriological figure and an object of reverence, not an "inconspicuous, ordinary thing" like a kitchen pot. Such shifts have consequences for the conceptual interpretation of Dōgen's texts. They may be productive, but the danger is to lose precisely what makes Dōgen's thought special and poses a challenge to our own preconceptions. If we read Dōgen as Hegel, Heidegger, or Nishida avant la lettre, why read him anyway, if we are not committed to the extra-philosophical project of upping the value of historic Japanese culture for whatever political ends? We are free to enter into a philosophical dialogue with his writings – let us make sure to let him state his points in his own way and according to his own agenda.

References

Akiyama, Hanji 秋山範二. *Dōgen no Kenkyū* 道元の研究. Tōkyō: Iwanami Shoten, 1935.
Arifuku, Kōgaku 有福孝岳 *Dōgen no Sekai* 道元の世界. Ōsaka: Ōsaka Shoseki, 1985.
Bodiford, William. 'Rewriting Dōgen'. *Kokusai Zen Kenkyū* 国際禅研究 4 (2019): 219–302.
Cassirer, Ernst. 'Das Symbolproblem und seine Stellung im System der Philosophie (1927)'. In *Gesammelte Werke*, Bd. 17: *Aufsätze und kleine Schriften* (1927–1931), 253–82. Hamburg: Meiner, 2004.
Elberfeld, Rolf. *Phänomenologie der Zeit im Buddhismus : Methoden interkulturellen Philosophierens.* Philosophie interkulturell 1. Stuttgart-Bad Cannstatt: Frommann-Holzboog, 2004.
Foulk, Theodore Griffith. '1: The Form and Function of Koan Literature'. In *The Koan: Texts and Contexts in Zen Buddhism,* edited by Steven Heine and Dale S. Wright, 15–45. New York: Oxford University Press, 2000.

---

[41] Kawamura, '*Shōbōgenzō* "Uji" ni tsuite –Busshō no Mondai to no Kanren ni oite. *Journal of Soto Zen Studies*, no. 3 (March 1961): 119; and Tsujiguchi, *Shōbōgenzō No Shisōteki Kenkyū* (Tōkyō: Hokuju shuppan, 2012), 172.

Gassmann, Robert H., Elena L. Lange, Angelika Malinar, Ulrich Rudolph, Raji C. Steineck, and Ralph Weber. 'Introduction: The Concept of Philosophy in Asia and the Islamic World'. In *Concepts of Philosophy in Asia and the Islamic World, Vol. 1: China and Japan*, edited by Raji C. Steineck, Ralph Weber, Robert H. Gassmann, and Elena L. Lange, 1–52. Leiden & Boston: Brill, 2018. Online: http://www.zora.uzh.ch/id/eprint/151593/

Ishii, Kiyozumi 石井清純. 'Zengo saidan' ni tsuite 「前後際断」について. Tōkyō: Sōtōshū sōgō kenkyū sentā: *Shūgaku kenkyū/Journal of Soto Zen studies*, no. 40 (1998): 43–48.

Kato, Bunno, and William Edward Soothill. *The Threefold Lotus Sutra*. New York: Weatherhill, 1975.

Kaufmann, Paulus, and Raji C. Steineck. 'Another Discourse on the Method: Understanding Philosophy through Rhetorical Analysis'. *European Journal of Japanese Philosophy* 3 (2018): 59–86.

Kawamura, Kōdō 河村孝道. 'Shōbōgenzō "Uji" ni tsuite –Busshō no Mondai to no Kanren ni oite 正法眼蔵「有時」について–仏性の問題との関連に於いて'. *Journal of Soto Zen Studies* 宗学研究, no. 3 (1961): 117–25.

Kobayashi, Yasuo. 'The Komaba Quartet'. *The Oxford Handbook of Japanese Philosophy*, 2019. Online: https://doi.org/10.1093/oxfordhb/9780199945726.013.31.

Koller, Werner. *Einführung in die Übersetzungswissenschaft*. Heidelberg: UTB Quelle & Meyer, 1979.

Müller, Ralf. 'Getting Back to Premodern Japan: Tanabe's Reading of Dōgen.' In *Frontiers of Japanese Philosophy Vol. 1*, 164-183. Nanzan Institute for Religion and Culture Nanzan, 2006.

Nishida, Kitarō 西田幾多郎. *Mu no Jikakuteki Gentei* 無の自覚的限定. Nishida Kitarō Zenshū 西田幾多郎全集 6. Tōkyō: Iwanami shoten 1965.

Ōkubo, Dōshu 大久保道舟, ed. 'Shukke Kudoku 出家功徳'. In *Dōgen Zenji Zenshū I* 道元禅師全集 I, 603–18. Tōkyō: Chikuma shobō 1969.

———. 'Uji 有時'. In *Dōgen Zenji Zenshū I* 道元禅師全集 I, 189–94. Tōkyō: Chikuma shobō 1969.

Ōmori, Shōzō 大森荘蔵. *Jikan to sonzai* 時間と存在. Tōkyō: Seidosha 1994.

———. 'Die Produktion der linearen Zeit'. Translated by Raji C. Steineck. *European Journal of Japanese Philosophy* 6 (2021): 113–36.

Raud, Rein. 'The Existential Moment: Rereading Dōgen's Theory of Time'. *Philosophy East and West* 62 (2) (2012): 153–73.

Steineck, Christian. 'Kommentar: Philosophische Perspektiven von Dōgen: Genjōkōan und Busshō'. In *Dōgen als Philosoph*, edited by Christian Steineck, Guido Rappe, and Kōgaku Arifuku, 119–51. Wiesbaden: Studies in Oriental Religions 51. Harrassowitz, 2002.

———. 'Das Bendōwa von Dogen: Narratologische Analyse eines doktrinären Textes'. *Asiatische Studien : Zeitschrift der Schweizerischen Gesellschaft für Asienkunde = Études Asiatiques : Revue de la Société Suisse d'études Asiatiques* 63 (3) (2009): 571.

Steineck, Raji C. 'Der Begriff der Philosophie und seine taxonomische Funktion bei Nishi Amane'. In *Begriff und Bild der modernen japanischen Philosophie*, edited by Raji Steineck, Lange, Elena Louisa and Kaufmann, Paulus, 41–62. Stuttgart-Bad Cannstatt: Frommann-Holzboog, 2014.

———. 'Enlightened Authorship: The Case of Dōgen Kigen'. In *That Wonderful Composite Called Author*, edited by Christian Schwermann and Raji C. Steineck, 195–219. Leiden: Brill, 2014.

———. 'Zen in der Kunst der Persuasion: Zur Rhetorik einer mittelalterlichen Lehrschrift'. In *Rhetorik im Vormodernen Japan*, edited by Heidi Buck-Albulet, 127–49. München: Iudicium, 2015.

———. A Zen Philosopher? – Notes on the Philosophical Reading of Dōgen's *Shōbōgenzō*. In *Concepts of Philosophy in Asia and the Islamic World*, Vol. 1: China and Japan, edited by Raji C. Steineck, Elena L. Lange, Ralph Weber, and Robert H. Gassmann, 577–606. Leiden & Boston: Brill, 2018. Online: http://www.zora.uzh.ch/id/eprint/151550/

———. '"Religion" and the Concept of the Buddha Way: Semantics of the Religious in Dōgen'. *Asiatische Studien – Études Asiatiques* 72 (1) (2018): 177–206.

———. *Zen Time: Dōgen in Context*. Forthcoming.

Steineck, Raji, Lange, Elena Louisa, Kaufmann, Paulus. 'Moderne japanische Philosophie – historiographische Ansätze und Probleme'. In *Begriff und Bild der modernen japanischen Philosophie*, 1–37. Philosophie Interkulturell 2. Stuttgart-Bad Cannstatt: Frommann-Holzboog, 2014.

Tanabe, Hajime 田邊元. *Shōbō Genzō no Tetsugaku Shikan* 正法眼蔵の哲学私観. Tōkyō: Iwanami shoten, 1939.

Tsujiguchi, Yuichirō 辻口雄一郎. *Shōbōgenzō no Shisōteki Kenkyū* 正法眼蔵の思想的研究. Tōkyō: Hokuju shuppan, 2012.

Wakatsuki, Shōgo 若月正吾. 1977. 'Shōwa Zenki ni okeru Shūgaku Kenkyū no "Shūhen" (1): Akiyama Hanji Cho "Dōgen No Kenkyū" ni tsuite 昭和前期における宗学研究の「周辺」(1) -秋山範二著「道元の研究」について- *Komazawa University Journal of Buddhist Studies* 駒澤大学仏教学部論集 8 (1977): 29–41.

Watsuji, Tetsurō 和辻哲郎. *Nihon Seishinshi Kenkyū* 日本精神史研究. Tōkyō: Iwanami shoten, 1992.

Yorizumi, Mitsuko 頼住光子. *Dōgen: Jiko, Jikan, Sekai wa dono yōni Seiritsu suru no ka* 道元：自己・時間・世界はどのように成立するのか. Shirīzu tetsugaku no essensu. Tōkyō: Nihon hōsō shuppan kyōkai, 2009.

Thinking the Now: Binary and Holistic Concepts in Dōgen's Philosophy of Time

Rein Raud

The aim of this article is to present an interpretational framework for Dōgen's thought, based on a close philosophical reading, and to apply this framework to his time-vocabulary. Elsewhere I have argued at length why a philosophical reading of texts such as Dōgen's is both possible and necessary[1]; here, I would just like to point out that on a philosophical reading, our goal should not be the most accurate possible reproduction of what went on in the consciousness of the historical Dōgen – which is, in any case, impossible –, but a productive engagement with what has been expressed in his text. An interpretation is a necessary prerequisite both for a text staying alive within its own tradition, as well as for its transposition to other timespaces, that is, translation, which gives a new and different life to the text in a different cultural, historical, institutional, intellectual setting – and only the meaning of an unread text can ever remain the same, as the interpretative environment is in constant change.

1 Concepts in Dōgen's Text

While Dōgen's own primary strategy for the production of new meaning is his notorious and often-discussed manipulation of the syntax of his source quotes, he also thinks creatively on the level of single concepts. To see this, it is useful to

---

[1] Raud, 'Thinking with Dōgen: Reading Philosophically into and beyond the Textual Surface', in *Philosophizing in Asia* (Tōkyō: UTCP, 2013), 27–46.

R. Raud (✉)
School of Humanities, Tallinn University, Tallinn, Estonia
e-mail: rraud@tlu.ee

R. Müller, G. Wrisley (eds.), *Dōgen's Texts*, Sophia Studies in Cross-cultural Philosophy of Traditions and Cultures 35,
https://doi.org/10.1007/978-3-031-42246-1_12

distinguish between three ways in which words behave in a philosophical text. They can be (1) *fixed terms*, which always have the same definition in the entire corpus of a philosopher's *oeuvre*, so whenever a passage seems vague, we only need to evoke that definition in order to make it clear again; (2) *floating*, that is, they can legitimately have multiple meanings and which of these is intended should ideally be clear from the context (to select the appropriate one is the task of the interpreter); finally, there are (3) *multi-level signifiers*, which also have different meanings, but all of these are relevant for a particular context. A multi-level signifier behaves a bit like a poetic image would in a different type of text, but while a poetic image can be vague on purpose, a multi-level signifier refers clearly, even if ambiguously. Multi-level signifiers have an important role to perform in philosophical texts, where they convey both a surface meaning and an idiosyncratic meaning intended by the author (think of the vocabulary of Hegel's logic). Texts can employ various strategies to make the reader aware of the multi-level nature of a particular term.

As usual, fixed terms (*immo* 恁麼 "suchness", *nikon* 而今 "the very now" etc) form the background for conceptual innovations also in Dōgen's thought. There are also quite a few floating terms in it, many of these inherited from general Buddhist usage, such as *hō* 法 "dharma" that can mean both the minimal, momentarily existing carrier of being and the Buddhist teaching (and it is not always clear which is meant), or *sō* 相, which can refer both to mutuality or interdependence and *lakṣaṇa*, the characteristic mark of a momentary instance of being by which it can be known. Floating terms can occasionally be converted into multi-level signifiers, when a term should refer to one of its meanings according to its immediate surroundings, but the broader context makes it clear that the other meaning is also relevant. This is something that happens, for example, in phrases like, "the time when all dharmas become Buddha-dharma" (*Genjōkōan*)[2]: while the immediate context of both occurrences of the term *hō* suggest different relevant meanings ("being-instance" for the first and "teaching" for the second occurrence), the sentence is constructed so that the two necessarily conflate and produce a meaning of an elementary particle of existence simultaneously embodying the teaching, thus generating the idea that the universe is, by itself, significant.

The production of multi-level signifiers is one of the most characteristic meaning-generation strategies deployed in Dōgen's text. This is why we have to note another thing when we approach his lexicon: the meaning of a word can be seldom established only with the help of dictionaries, including special dictionaries of Buddhist terms. What is needed is reference to other occurrences of the same word in Dōgen's work. Even that may occasionally present problems. Dōgen's views changed over time and the way in which a term is used in the *Bendōwa*, for example, does not necessarily correspond to its behaviour in the 12-fascicle *Shōbōgenzō*. Secondly, certain terms are sometimes foregrounded and scrutinized in detail in one particular

---

[2] 諸法の佛法なる時節。Unfortunately, there exists no equivalent of "Bekker numbers" for Dōgen's work and many editions are concurrently in use, which is why I am not referring to any of them, but providing the original for all quotations. The reader can locate the context in an online edition such as http://www.shomonji.or.jp/soroku/genzou.htm.

fascicle, but mostly dropped thereafter, so that we do not have a much broader context for them. These difficulties aside, however, Dōgen's textual corpus should still remain our primary source for determining the meaning of any particular item of his vocabulary.

2   Two Attitudes Towards Reality

Dōgen's thought is on the whole grounded in two epistemological attitudes, which are to a certain extent opposed to each other, but neither is sufficient to provide an adequate picture of reality by itself. Therefore, they should be viewed as complementary. In broad strokes, the framework outlined below develops certain crucial insights of Yorizumi Mitsuko[3] and Tsujiguchi Yūichirō[4] who both posit a bifurcation of lived reality into "element-based reality-1" (Yorizumi) or "interference" (Tsujiguchi) on the one hand, and "relation-based reality-2" (Yorizumi) and "non-interference" (Tsujiguchi) on the other, with a third level of "emptiness" (Yorizumi) or "the boundless" (Tsujiguchi) underlying/transcending them both. I agree with them wholeheartedly that a tripartite scheme of this type is vital for the understanding of Dōgen's work, although the account I propose differs somewhat from both of them. For example, in Yorizumi's scheme of things reality-2 opens up after a transformative experience, an encounter with emptiness and the intuitive grasping of the world as the absolute Other, or senselessness itself[5] placing the three in a hierarchical or sequential order, while it seems to me that Dōgen considers an alternation between the two epistemological attitudes possible and does not allocate the first completely to the naïve state of mind. Provisional reification of reality becomes a distortion of it only if the attitude ceases to be heuristic. Tsujiguchi, on the other hand, has somewhat surprisingly equated the "non-interference" with the presence, not absence of particular perspectives in his discussion of his tripartite division in the context of time,[6] which seems to me unwarranted: it is the presence of multiple perspectives and the clinging of the particulars to them, letting themselves be determined by them that leads to their mutual interference. It therefore seems that "interference" is more suited to correlate with the "conceptual, binary, perspectival" point of view and "non-interference" with the absence of the determining perspective.

We are thus to distinguish between two epistemological attitudes, both of which rely on the axiomatic distinction between reality as it is and reality as it is accessible to us in perception. For Indian philosophy, of course, the Western way of distinguishing between ontology and epistemology has been a misguided affair from the beginning. A variant of what is called the Kantian "Copernican revolution", or the

---

[3] Yorizumi, *Shōbōgenzō Nyūmon* (Tōkyō: Kadokawa, 2014), 120–29.

[4] Tsujiguchi, *Shōbōgenzō No Shisōteki Kenkyū* (Tōkyō: Hokuju Shuppan, 2012), 60ff. and 164–68.

[5] Yorizumi, *Shōbōgenzō Nyūmon* (Tōkyō: Kadokawa, 2014), 124–25.

[6] Tsujiguchi, *Shōbōgenzō No Shisōteki Kenkyū* (Tōkyō: Hokuju Shuppan, 2012), 164.

acknowledgment that only representations of the world are accessible to us, and not the "things in themselves", which are covered by "the veil of *māyā*", has been one of its premises all along. This attitude has been inherited, although in a different form, also by Buddhism, which considers empirical reality illusory and "ultimate truth" (*paramārthasatya*) to be something beyond ordinary human reach (although possibly accessible for the enlightened mind). This, however, as Nāgārjuna pointed out in MMK 24.8-10., does not make the category of truth in its "ordinary", day-to-day sense irrelevant, but only makes it provisional, as truth and falsehood can also be distinguished in the shared epistemological realm of social experience. This two-truth dichotomy was developed further by the Tiantai school, which added to it the "third" or "middle" truth, or the assertion that ultimate and provisional truths are true equally, thereby completely flattening the underlying ontology: there is no "higher", second-tier reality beyond the one that is accessible to us – so the only reality there is is the one we are engaged in as human beings. However, and crucially, we are by definition engaged with it precisely in our capacity of human beings, embedded, specific creatures who embody a certain limited perspective. Tiantai goes on to teach that all perspectives are also contained within each other so that the result is a multiverse consisting of 3000 worlds – each of them not existing separately, but as versions of the one reality we sentient creatures all share –, and this multiverse is, in principle, accessible through every single minuscule part of it and can be contained in a single, indivisibly short moment of thought.

Dōgen took this scheme one step further by adding to it the logical conclusion that, if the two original truths are not overlapping, but true equally, then neither of them necessarily covers the entire reality – "when one side is illuminated, the other one is dark".[7] On the one hand, the idea of the ultimate truth neglects the necessary perspectivality of any actual take on reality, on the other, however, that same perspectivality does not let the particular to apprehend the entire reality while remaining determined by its embeddedness. The distinction is similiar to the wave and corpuscular theory of light, both correct but, what is stressed less often, neither of them is complete. Or, adopting a more mundane metaphor, we can liken this to the choices a photographer has between different apertures and shutter speeds when taking a photo of a fountain: it is necessarily one photo that they are taking, and they may increase shutter speed until single drops of water become visible, or reduce it to show a smooth flow. Both are, in their particular ways, accurate images of the fountain, but neither of them is "ultimately" true in the sense of covering all its aspects – and yet only one of them is accessible to the lens (or mind) at any given moment.

The choice we face, as a result, is between two epistemic attitudes. But, as neither side provides the complete solution, we once again need a third position, corresponding to the third, middle truth of Tiantai, or the non-choice.

Famously, the three options are outlined at the beginning of the *Genjōkōan* fascicle:

---

[7] 一方を證するときは一方はくらし。

(1) At the moment when all dharmas are the teaching of the Buddha, there is [opposition between] delusions and enlightenment, there is practice, there is birth, there is death, there are all the Buddhas, there are sentient beings.

At the moment when the myriad dharmas are without self, there is no delusion, there is no enlightenment, there are no Buddhas and no sentient beings, there is no birth, no extinction.

The Buddhist way has from the very beginning transcenced such proliferation and parsimony, therefore there are [the binaries of] birth and extinction, delusions and enlightenment, beings and Buddhas.

While we say that this is how it is, flowers fall regardless of our regret, and weeds just continue to grow despite our aversion.[8]

Commentators have evaluated these statements variously: there is a tradition of stressing that all three positions are equal,[9] and there are also quite a few ways of explaining them in a hierarchical order. Okumura Shōhaku, for example, says that the first position is that of the historical Buddha, the second corresponds to the mainstream Mahāyāna view and the third presents Dōgen's own viewpoint,[10] while Heine suggests this parallels Qingyuan's dictum about "mountains are mountains" being replaced by "mountains are not mountains" after 20 years of practice, just to be restored again to "mountains are mountains" at the end of his life,[11] thus signifying different stages along the axis of spiritual development. A more promising approach is suggested by Yasutani Hakuun, who, even though subscribing in broader strokes to the "sequential" view of the three stages,[12] characterizes the first position as "relative in the midst of the absolute" or "affirmation with negation as its ground" and the second as "absolute in the midst of the relative" or "negation with affirmation as its ground".[13]

Neither of these are thus, strictly speaking, positions, but rather vectors or movements within an epistemic space or between the levels of a multi-level signifier. "Relative" might here be understood as a term including also such nuances of meaning as "binary, conceptual, perspectival, particular" and "absolute" to mean

---

[8] 諸法の佛法なる時節、すなはち迷悟あり、修行あり、生あり、死あり、諸佛あり、衆生あり。

萬法ともにわれにあらざる時節、まどひなくさとりなく、諸佛なく衆生なく、生なく滅なし。

佛道もとより豐儉より跳出せるゆゑに、生滅あり、迷悟あり、生佛あり。

しかもかくのごとくなりといへども、花は愛惜にちり、草は棄嫌におふるのみなり。

[9] Nishiari, 'Commentary by Nishiari Bokusan' in *Dogen's Genjo Koan: three commentaries* (Berkeley: Counterpoint, 2011), 20.

[10] Okumura, *Realizing Genjokoan: The Key to Dogen's Shobogenzo* (Boston: Wisdom Publications, 2010), 24.

[11] Heine, 'What Is on the Other Side? Delusion and Realization in Dōgen's "Genjōkōan"', in *Dōgen: Textual and Historical Studies*, ed. by Heine (Oxford: Oxford University Press, 2012), 49.

[12] Yasutani, *Flowers Fall: A Commentary on Dōgen's Genjōkōan* (Boston: Shambhala. 1996), 14.

[13] Ibid., 13–14.

"holistic, non-discriminative" and so on; it might therefore be tempting to read the first as expressing the "unenlightened", the other the "enlightened" view. On the whole, the text indeed shows a preference for the holistic view, but admitting this would invalidate that very same view, which consists precisely in not making such binary and hierarchical discriminations.

Another term which the conceptual/binary position is readily identified with is *shiryō* 思量 or *shiryō-bumbetsu* 思量分別, analytical thinking. As it might be expected of Buddhist texts, Dōgen readily recognizes the limitations of this faculty, but this does not at all mean that he would neglect or demean it – often *shiryō* is mentioned in the same row with sight, knowledge and other basic cognitive and intellectual faculties, which characterize the perspective of a person. At times he identifies one topic or another that his reader should analyse precisely with the help of this faculty. As expected, however, there are important domains out of its reach as well, accessible to a person in the state of without-self, where the corresponding faculty is *hishiryō* 非思量, "non-thinking". This is not to be confused with *fushiryō* 不思量, "not thinking": as Dōgen makes clear in the *Zazenshin* fascicle, non-thinking is not the absence of intellectual activity, but a different kind of it, and in *praxis*, all three are entangled in mutual interdependence.[14]

Before we move on to the third component, another layer needs to be added to this complementarity, one directly related to the preceding. In the *Sammai ōzammai* fascicle, Dōgen distinguishes between "*zazen* of the body" and "*zazen* of the mind" emphasizing the two are not the same[15]: the first, translated here as "practice", involves actual meditation exercises (or other actions qualifying as Zen practice), while "*zazen* of the mind", or *praxis*, places no restriction on what is actually performed and pertains only to the mental state ideally arising from such action. It is possible to practice without actually doing *praxis*, for example, to sit in a meditation posture being constantly torn between aching legs and worries about undone chores, and, conversely, it is also possible to be in the state of *praxis* without doing the exercises at the moment. When Dōgen says in the *Bendōwa* that "in Buddhism, practice and enlightenment are identical",[16] it is this state of *praxis* that he means.

It might thus seem that when the state of *praxis* is reached, this is the final destination of the spiritual journey, but that is not the case, because of two reasons. First of all, the thought of any stopping point would contradict the idea of radical impermanence and fundamental dynamism that characterizes all reality ontologically, secondly, it would imply the possibility of separating the actions of the mind and the body from each other. The aim of Dōgen's teaching is not to propagate some kind of aimless, indifferent drifting through our lifeworld, but a meaningful relationship with it. Thus, while we may, I think, assume that "practice" corresponds to the "binary" position in the complementarity and *praxis* to the "holistic", we need to

---

[14] "In order to think no-thoughts, it is necessary to revert to non-thinking" 不思量底を思量する には、かならず非思量をもちゐるるなり。

[15] 心の打坐あり、身の打坐とおなじからず。身の打坐あり、心の打坐とおなじからず。

[16] 佛法には修證これ一等なり。

remember Dōgen's cautionary words in the *Genjōkōan* that "when the teaching has completely overtaken the bodymind, it seems that one side of it is still missing".[17] This, I would argue, is why Dōgen speaks about "going beyond the Buddha" (*bukkōjō* 佛向上), and "the traces of enlightenment are put on hold, and these paused traces of enlightenment are cast out to grow longer and longer".[18] These refer to the third option where even the difference between binary and holistic (or duality and non-duality) is no longer relevant and we therefore also cannot make any distinction between practice and *praxis*, or, for that matter, the binary and the holistic takes on reality as outlined above.

And this is precisely what characterizes the third component in this complementarity. The thing uncapturable by either of the two approaches to reality is, of course, reality-as-such itself, in its entirety. But as soon as we try to conceptualize it, we have slid back to the conceptual approach again, and something inevitably remains unreached. There are also other dangers. When Dōgen writes, as he often does, about something that "it is not encapsulated by the dichotomy of being and nothing" (*u-mu ni arazu* 有無にあらず), this statement implicitly posits a new dichotomy between imaginables that are and are not encapsulated in this lower-level dichotomy. This could easily turn into an infinite regress. Therefore, the third option in Dōgen's complementarity can neither reassert nor deny either of the former two positions, but has to transcend them. The binary approach, moving out of experience towards conceptual distinctions, produces new and new concepts as it seeks precision; the holistic approach, moving out of the conceptual plane towards the core of experience, seeks to deconstruct them; the third constituent, as Dōgen says, "originally transcends the opposition between such [conceptual] proliferation and parsimony"[19]; metaphorically speaking, it is precisely that something that can be neither swallowed nor spat out (*Uji*).[20]

When we reread the first two positions in this light, it might help to add quotation marks to the concepts listed therein:

(2) At the moment when all dharmas are the teaching of the Buddha, there is [opposition between] "delusions" and "enlightenment", there is "practice", there is "birth", there is "death", there are "all the Buddhas", there are "sentient beings".

At the moment when the myriad dharmas are without self, there is no "delusion", there is no "enlightenment", there are no "Buddhas" and no "sentient beings", there is no "birth", no "extinction".

As opposed to these two complementary views, the third position is not concerned with concepts, but with the dynamism of reality.

---

[17] 法もし身心に充足すれば、ひとかたはたらずとおぼゆるなり

[18] 悟迹の休歇なるあり、休歇なる悟迹を長長出ならしむ。

[19] もとより豊倹より跳出せる. For a similar reading of this phrase, see Kasulis, 'Meaning and Context: Dōgen's Genjōkōan', in *Japanese Philosophy: A Sourcebook*, ed. by Heisig, Kasulis, and Maraldo (Honolulu: University of Hawaii Press, 2011), 144.

[20] 呑却せざらんや、吐却せざらんや。

In this "third" state, there is no firm connection between what happens and what is perceived, as Dōgen points out: "flowers still fall regardless of our regret, and weeds just continue to grow despite our aversion".[21] In modern terms, a break is articulated here between the epistemic and the ontological, that is, the third position attempts to say the world as it is, not as it appears to us. Characteristically, Dōgen does not try to explain in spefific detail how the world is (by itself) – given that the two avenues that are available to us for the purpose are, by definition, both incomplete. All in all, the topic of this third statement is what Dōgen refers to with the term *mubusshō*, "nothing-as-Buddha-nature".[22] It can perhaps be argued that Dōgen's view of reality as significant may seem to contradict this, but, as I have argued elsewhere,[23] this claim does not go beyond stating that the way reality is consists in its constant becoming-itself-for-another, which is equated to being meaningful, and this meaningfulness "pertains primarily to the very concrete level of navigating our immediate environment"[24] thus, unlike Western metaphysical theories, making no overarching structural claims about reality as such – except for its radical impermanence. Nothing endures, except "nothing", and even that "nothing" is not self-identical, but fundamentally dynamic.

To sum up, the view of ontological reality upheld in the *Core Transmission* sees it as radically impermanent, centreless, groundless and dynamic; no individual thing endures beyond the absolute present, thus any existence is momentary. There is no privileged, godlike "view from nowhere" to capture this reality, because it discloses itself (to use a term favoured by feminist philosophy of science) always and exclusively to embedded particular perspectives. This is fully in accord with the teaching of all major Buddhist philosophical schools since the emergence of Gandhāran abhidharma[25] and, in particular, corresponds to the views of the Sautrāntika school that have informed Vasubandhu's *Abhidharmakośabhāsya*. Quotations and references throughout the *Core Transmission* indicate that Dōgen was at least generally familiar with these doctrines. Later developments, such as the Mahāyāna schools Dōgen also occasionally refers to, critique this view as *too* reificationist rather than not object-centred enough. Any claim contradicting this and claiming that Dōgen's ontology grants a stronger status to things or minds as enduring in time should be backed up with textual evidence.

There are two complementary ways to engage with this reality, neither of them self-sufficient. One involves binary oppositions, conceptual thought and practice (in the sense of commitment to particular actions), the other is holistic, focussed on the nondual, and embodied in *praxis* (in the sense of a particular state of mind that can,

---

[21] 花は愛惜にちり、草は棄嫌におふるのみなり

[22] For a more detailed discussion see Raud, 'Dōgen's Idea of Buddha-Nature: Dynamism and Non-Referentiality', *Asian Philosophy* 25(1) (2015): 1–14.

[23] Raud, 'Dōgen and the Linguistics of Reality', *Religions* 12(5)(2021): 331.

[24] Raud, 'Dōgen's Idea of Buddha-Nature: Dynamism and Non-Referentiality', Asian Philosophy 25(1) (2015): 1–14, p.10.

[25] See Bronkhorst 'Abhidharma and Indian Thinking', in *Text, History, and Philosophy: Abhidharma across Buddhist Scholastic Traditions*, edited by Dessein and Teng (Leiden: Brill, 2016), 30–32.

in principle, accompany any action whatsoever). However, the ontological "absolute now" always slips out of the individual's grasp, which means that *praxis* has no final goal and, if authentic, goes on endlessly – because it is nothing else than the actual fusion of reality and mind. This also highlights the nature of existence as relational, relations here occurring not between independent relata, but, on the contrary, formative of the situations from which such particulars can spring forth. A personal, fully experienced realization of this reality as the state of mind, the absolute present not captured by the phenomenological present of the self, will always remain in the moment that is constantly slipping away from one's grasp – but a moment is everything there is. Therefore, the incorporation of the dynamism of existence into one's own *praxis*, the gearing of one's mind towards this realization is what proper practice entails and the fundamental unattainability of an enduring, personalized enlightenment is what enlightenment actually is.

3   Dōgen's Time-Theoretical Vocabulary

When we now approach the concepts Dōgen uses for discussing time and temporality, we note immediately that one large part of often-recurring concepts clearly belongs to the binary, another to the holistic register. Among the first we see, of course, *jūniji* 十二時 "the (system of) twelve hours", but also *kagen(tō)rai* 過現(當)來 "past, present and (relevant) futures" and *zengo* 前後 "the before-after opposition", while the second is prominently represented by expressions such as *shōtōimmoji* 正當恁麼時 "the immediately present moment of suchness" and *nikon* 而今 "the very now". With other terms, the situation is not immediately clear. For example *jisetsu* 時節, the word used in the *Genjōkōan* fascicle to refer to the different moments on which the binary and the holistic mode of understanding are at work, also takes on the role of a philosophical term in its discussion in the *Busshō* fascicle. What is of particular interest here is Dōgen's treatment of the phrase *jisetsu nyakushi* 時節若至, taken from a quotation, which should conventionally be translated as "as the time arrives". But not for Dōgen (which is why I will leave *jisetsu* untranslated for the moment):

> The phrase "as the *jisetsu* is reached" means that the *jisetsu* has already reached us... The phrase "as the *jisetsu* is reached" means that the twelve hours of the day are without empty intervals. "As is reached" is similar to saying "has been reached". If we would understand it as "when the *jisetsu* is reached [i.e., will be reached]", Buddha-nature would never arrive. For this reason, the *jisetsu* has already been reached and this is also why Buddha-nature is directly available to us..[26]

---

[26] 時節若至といふは、すでに時節いたれり [...] 時節若至は、十二時中不空過なり。若至は、既至といはんがごとし。時節若至すれば、佛性不至なり。しかあればすなはち、時節すでにいたれば、これ佛性の現前なり。

The word that seems to create a sort of a *non sequitur* here is "already" (*sude ni*). But, as Yorizumi has noted,[27] this word, when used in Dōgen's text, does not denote a *temporal*, but a *logical* order of precedence: when we say [B], we have already postulated [A], if this particular [B] does not make sense without it. When we say, "x is a reflection in the mirror", we have postulated a figure it is the reflection of; when we say, "m is the endpoint", we have postulated a line it is the endpoint of. This clarification helps to make sense of quite a few passages that seem cryptic or logically inconsistent, and *jisetsu nyakushi* is a case in point. When Dōgen asserts that "the phrase "as the moment arrives" means that the moment has already arrived", what he is saying is that by speculating about the moment we have already postulated it, so it is already logically present, even though its predicted arrival may not have occurred in observed reality.

The text thus clearly asserts that a *jisetsu* cannot be placed on the past-present-future axis, but is always necessarily present, already-arrived – at least for the state of *praxis*. During the "twelve hours of the day", there is never an empty interval, empty (durational) passing, which would place itself between the moment of the present and a moment in the future. There is thus reason to view *jisetsu* in its role of a term as the temporal condition for the experience of *praxis*, the "time" of "riding the moment", which is no longer the immediately available epistemic time, but also (by virtue of its being experienced) not a part of some mind-independently ontological time. In that sense, Heine's suggestion to translate *jisetsu* as "existential occasion"[28] is very much to the point, as is Orimo's definition of *jisetsu* as the articulation of dynamic time at every particular instant.[29] When we look at some other seemingly innocuous occurrences of the term, we can see that this interpretation adds a level of lucid sense to those passages, as for example in this passage of the *Genjōkōan* fascicle:

> The way in which enlightenment and a person do not interfere with each other is similar to the way how the [reflecting] dewdrop and the moon in the sky do not interfere with each other. The depth of the one measures the height of the other. As to whether a *jisetsu* is long or short, you might just as well find out whether "water" is big or small or reach a decision on whether the sky and the moon are broad or narrow.[30]

Jisetsu here refers to the moment of *praxis*, which is not a measurable amount of time, just as what is shared between the reflexion of the moon in a dewdrop and the moon itself in the sky cannot be expressed in terms of measurement.[31] It is therefore

---

[27] Yorizumi, *Shōbōgenzō Nyūmon* (Tōkyō: Kadokawa. 2014), 133–34.

[28] Heine, *Existential and Ontological Dimensions of Time in Heidegger and Dōgen* (Albany: State University of New York Press, 1985), 22.

[29] Maître Dôgen, *La vraie Loi, Trésor de l'Oeil: Textes choisis de Shôbôgenzô* (Paris: Seuil. 2004), 46.

[30] 人のさとりを罣礙せざること、滴露の天月を罣礙せざるがごとし。ふかきことはたか き分量なるべし。時節の長短は、大水小水を點し、天月の廣狹を辨取すべし。

[31] For reasons of space, I will not be touching here on the wider context of *jisetsu* in relation to causal linkages, which the *Busshō* fascicle also discusses.

misleading to interpret *jisetsu* as duration or interval, although this is what the word means in ordinary language.

When we now turn to the concept of *uji*, I would like to start by suggesting is that it is a multi-level signifier *par excellence*, which first makes the readers uncomfortable with the limits of the "binary" register of time-talk, where it is approached, then leads them through the "holistic" understanding of the phenomenological present to the ontological understanding of existence as essentially momentary. The term thus has legitimate meanings in all three registers, resounding with each other.

As it is well known, the concept is created by the arbitrary insertion of a predicative relation between its two components: *u* = *ji*. As Tsujiguchi emphasizes,[32] the question of what the *ji* of *uji* means here depends completely on how we understand the *u*. While it is sometimes suggested that the word signifies abstract Being, there is simply no textual evidence for such a reading, nor would it be compatible with the rest of Dōgen's thought. Therefore, it is fundamentally incorrect to translate *uji* as "being-time", although this is the most widespread way in which this concept is interpreted. And what does it even meant to state that "being is time"? Both terms of this phrase are floating, so without further specification this sentence is meaningless.

It seems possible, however, to take *u* to refer to particular phenomena. First of all, *u* is regularly referred to as a multitude, which alone makes it impossible to read it as an underlying level of Being. Secondly, the text contains multiple assertions of the type "x is *ji*", where x can be Qingyuan, Huangbo, a pine or a bamboo plant. The x here should be collectively designated as *u*. These x are, of course, epistemologically available phenomena, not ontologically real entities with self-natures of their own. If so, the phrase *ji sude ni kore u nari* 時すでにこれ有なり can be taken to mean "whenever *ji* occurs, it presupposes a phenomenon". In other words, there are just as many *uji*'s as there are *u*'s. In that case, *uji* would refer to individual time-regimes of the myriad particular phenomena and belong to the "binary" register of engaging with reality. This is a legitimate interpretation, but it comes at a price: on this view, the *u* can no longer have anything to do with the ontological base level of "being" or "existence", but only with what Dōgen has described as "dharma-configurations" (*hō'i* 法位 or *i* 位 for short) or "patterns" (*gōsei* 合成).[33] Such phenomena are illusory by definition, mere ways of organization of the dharmas as disclosed to a particular perspective, and if the concept of *uji* is only about them, it no longer says anything about the ontological, "true" level of reality.

---

[32] Tsujiguchi, *Shōbōgenzō No Shisōteki Kenkyū* (Tōkyō: Hokuju Shuppan, 2012), 161.
[33] 薪は薪の法位に住して、さき　ありのちあり。前後ありといへども、前後際断せり。 "Firewood abides in the dharma-configuration of firewood, and it has a before and after. But although we can say that the before and the after exist, it is [as itself] cut off from the before-after axis" (*Genjōkōan*). 水は衆法を合成して水なり、雲は衆法を合成して雲なり。雲を合成して雲なり、水を合成して水なり。鉢盂は但以衆法、合成鉢盂なり。但以鉢盂、合成衆法なり。 "Water becomes water through the patterning of the multitude of dharmas. A cloud becomes a cloud through the patterning of the multitude of dharmas. A cloud becomes a cloud as the pattern, water becomes water as a pattern. An eating bowl, too, is only a patterning of the multitude of dharmas as an eating bowl." (*Hou*).

Another, more promising approach is suggested by Tsujiguchi Yūichirō, who emphasizes that the *u* are not to be thought of as self-identical objects, but *actions*, *occurrences* or *events*, such as "the instance of skyflying" Dōgen describes in the *Zazenshin* fascicle.[34] Bret Davis has aptly termed such an elementary constituent of reality "a singular event of interconnection" and to adequately know a segment of reality is to "participate in the perspectival opening of a singular event of interconnection".[35] On this view, the concept of *uji* does not refer to the time-regimes of particular things, because there are no particular things outside these singular events of interconnection, and fits better with the other terms in the "holistic" conceptual register.

But this is not the end of the story. In order to proceed, I would like to take a closer look on a concept mentioned as a commonsensical characteristic of time, namely *korai* 去來 "going-coming". This concept is introduced at the start of the fascicle as the aspect of time that is not habitually problematized by people ("the direction and trace of the going-coming [of time] being clear, people do not have doubts about it"[36]), but this is unacceptable for Dōgen, who later brings the concept up again and considers it in its relation to "time" from two sides, both of which yield different interpretations of what *uji* is. This is an extremely dense passage[37] and I will start the analysis with its structural layout with its main concepts untranslated.

> (1) If *ji* is not in the *sō* of the *korai*, then the *ji* of "climbing the mountain" is the *nikon* of the *uji*. If *ji* is carrying the *sō* of the *korai*, then the *nikon* of the *uji* is in the *ware*. This is what *uji* means.

"Climbing the mountain" here refers to the preceding passage in the fascicle, where a distinction is made between climbing a mountain and residing in a palace on its top. Moriyama and Sakon correctly identify these with goal-oriented practice and enlightenment.[38] I suggest we provisionally substitute "self" for *ware* and "the very now" for *nikon* so that we get

> (2) If *ji* is not in the *sō* of the *korai*, then the *ji* of "climbing the mountain" is the "very now" of the *uji*. If *ji* is carrying the *sō* of the *korai*, then the "very now" of the *uji* is in the self. This is what *uji* means.

To proceed, we need to address the *sō* 相. Many translators, myself included, have previously rendered it here in its terminological meaning of "aspect, characteristic feature, mark", which is indeed the meaning in which it is met most frequently on its own. However, the usage of the expression *no sō ni arazu* elsewhere in the *Core Transmission* suggests something else. We find it in "it does not consist in the

---

[34] Ibid., 162.

[35] Davis, 'Zen's Nonegocentric Perspectivism'. in *Buddhist Philosophy: a Comparative Approach*, ed. by S. M. Emmanuel (Hoboken: Wiley-Blackwell. 2017), 135.

[36] 去來の方跡あきらかなるによりて、人これを疑著せず

[37] 時もし去來の相にあらずは、上山の時は有時の而今なり。時もし去來の相を保任せば、われに有時の而今ある、これ有時なり。

[38] Moriyama and Sakon, 'Dōgen on Time and the Self'. *Tetsugaku* 4 (2020), 142.

opposition of the old and the young" in the *Gabyō* fascicle,[39] "it does not consist in the opposition of men and women" in the *Raihai tokuzui* fascicle[40] and "it does not consist in the opposition of going and coming, the measurement of big and small, or the debate between the old and the young" in the *Sangai yuishin* fascicle.[41] In other words, in the expression *no sō ni arazu* what is meant by *sō* is "a binary opposition" rather than "a characteristic mark". We thus have

> (3) If *ji* does not consist in the binary opposition of the *ko-rai*, then the *ji* of "climbing the mountain" is the "very now" of the *uji*. If *ji* is carrying the *sō* of the *korai*, then the "very now" of the *uji* is in the self. This is what *uji* means.

On its second use, however, the word *sō* is on its own, the meaning of "binary opposition" therefore no longer relevant, and the habitual meaning of "characteristic mark" is more appropriate – and yet the previous meaning seems to linger, making the term another multi-level signifier, in which the nature of the "characteristic mark" is precisely its encapsulation of the "binary opposition":

> (4) If *ji* does not consist in the binary opposition of the *ko-rai*, then the *ji* of "climbing the mountain" is the "very now" of the *uji*. If *ji* is characteristically marked by the binary opposition of the *ko-rai*, then the "very now" of the *uji* is in the self. This is what *uji* means.

The context now leads us to look at the concept of the *korai* not as referring to the "going" and the "coming" of time as its attributes or modes of taking place, but as the fact that the one is binarily opposed to the other. Dōgen often employs such binary concepts, f.ex. *meigo* 迷悟 (*Genjōkōan*) does not refer to "illusions" and "enlightenment" together, but to a situation where illusions are opposed to enlightenment. This view corresponds well to what the text is saying: the practice of *zazen* ("climbing the mountain") is directed at the elimination of such binaries, while the temporal experience of the self is grounded in change. We proceed to

> (5) If *ji* does not consist in the binary opposition of [temporal] "going" to "coming", then the *ji* of "climbing the mountain" is the "very now" of the *uji*. If *ji* is characteristically marked by the binary opposing of [temporal] "going" to "coming", then the "very now" of the *uji* is in the self. This is what *uji* means.

At this point we should look more carefully at the notion of "self", which is here connected to one aspect of the *uji*, making the individual subject its carrier (as the time-regime reading indeed implies). But given Dōgen's frequent attacks on what he calls the "Śreṇika heresy", or the idea that an enduring subjective consciousness really exists, this does not make sense. Some commentators on Dōgen's time theory, both denominational[42] and academic[43] have tried to escape this difficulty by postulating a twofold concept of self, distinguishing between an egocentric self in the

---

[39] 老少の相にあらず

[40] 男女等の相にあらず

[41] 去來の相にあらず、大小の量にあらず、老少の論にあらず

[42] Uchiyama *Deepest Practice, Deepest Wisdom: Three Fascicles from Shōbōgenzō with Commentaries* (Somerville: Wisdom Publications. 2018), 189; 210–11.

[43] Moriyama and Sakon, 'Dōgen on Time and the Self'. *Tetsugaku* 4 (2020), 139.

ordinary sense of the word and another, cosmic one (which Moriyama and Sakon refer to as SELF, in capital letters), at one with all things, a particular manifestation of the Buddha-nature.[44] This reading is problematic, however, as it turns Dōgen into a crypto-Brahmanist, because the SELF is dangerously similar to *ātman*, essentially identical to the world-soul of *brahman*. There is also virtually no textual evidence in support of this distinction – according to the theory, Dōgen uses all of his self-vocabulary (*ware*, *jiko*) indiscriminately to refer to both types of selves, so it gives the reader a considerable *carte blanche* to decide which side of selfhood is meant in each particular case. It seems much more plausible that if Dōgen had indeed made that distinction, he would have spelled it out explicitly and used a separate word for both self-concepts. However, what he does is just the opposite, denying the relation between truth and selfhood in no uncertain terms.[45]

The *locus classicus* for the understanding of "self" is, of course, the famous statement in the *Genjōkōan*:

> To study the way is to study the self. To study the self is to forget the self. To forget the self is to be witnessed by the multitude of existents. To be witnessed by the the multitude of existents is to let go of the body-mind of the self and the body-minds of others. The traces of enlightenment are momentarily paused, and these momentarily paused traces of enlightenment will continue endlessly.[46]

But "forgetting the self" is not the same as "undoing the self" or "destroying the self" – it is letting the "self" fade out of the determining position in which it only admits interaction with the world if the world is arranged according to its will. This includes both the conceptual structures that the "self" is likely to impose on reality, the speeds and scales of the things around us, and also all the possible ways to classify those things into the desirable, the abject and the irrelevant, resulting in ideas about their "use-value" and so on. These particular views of things obviously always result from our perspectival embeddedness as well as the specific setup of our cognitive apparatus. As Dōgen is quick to observe, what we see as a body of water may seem like a magnificent palace from the point of view of fish and like jewels from a celestial orbit (*Sansuikyō*),[47] and it is not that these other perspectives, or even all of them, are mistaken – on the contrary, they are all true, but only from these specific points of view.

It is also clear that "forgetting the self" or "letting go of the bodymind" (*shinjin datsuraku* 身心脱落) does not imply leaving the bodymind behind and moving on

---

[44]Tsujiguchi notes this interpretation is debated from both sides already in the first commentaries on the Core Transmission. See Tsujiguchi, *Shōbōgenzō No Shisōteki Kenkyū* (Tōkyō: Hokuju Shuppan, 2012), 174–75.

[45]"Even though we say there is a truth out there, it is not to be fixated to any kind of idea about the self" たとひまことありといふとも、吾我のほとりにとどこほるものにあらず。(*Immo*)

[46]佛道をならふといふは、自己をならふ也。自己をならふといふは、自己をわするるなり。自己をわするるといふは、萬法に證せらるるなり。萬法に證せらるるといふは、自己の身心および他己の身心をして脱落せしむるなり。悟迹の休歇なるあり、休歇なる悟迹を長長出ならしむ。

[47]いはゆる水をみるに瓔珞とみるものあり。。。龍魚は宮殿とみる、樓臺とみる。

in some other, unembodied form – it is merely the authority of defining the world and the capacity to determine our actions that the "self" is no longer credited with. As I have suggested elsewhere,[48] Dōgen's idea of *shinjin datsuraku* relies on the ability of the human being to stray from the karmically (psychophysically) determined trajectory of expected actions and thereby to rise above one's destiny, so to say, which implies the uncoupling of oneself as a creature from a rigidly determined/determining perspective in the sense described here.

Now it seems no longer even warranted to translate the terms *jiko* and *ware* literally as "self", because the use of this term brings with it a host of connotations that may not be completely applicable to the meaning these words have in Dōgen's text. When we acknowledge, on the one hand, that there is a certain role for *ware* to play in the journey toward authentic being, and on the other note that Dōgen is very strict in his denial of an enduring self as suggested by the Śrenika heresy, then – taking a cue from Davis, who characterizes Dōgen's thought as "egoless perspectivism"[49]– it begins to seem that the most appropriate equivalent for *ware* and *jiko* is "particular perspective". The reader is indeed encouraged to try out "particular, embedded perspective" as the equivalent of *ware* and *jiko* in different contexts, and to see for themself that many a cryptic passage will thereby find a lucid intepretation.

In particular, this helps at one of the hardest knots of Dōgen's *ware*-theory, the discussion of a sentence from the *Vimalakīrti sūtra* in the *Kaiin zammai* fascicle. The original quote reads, in habitual interpretation, as "at the moment of arising [of dharmas], only dharmas arise; at the moment of extinction, only dharmas are extinguished; at this moment of arising, it is not said that an "I" arises; at this moment of extinction, it is not said that an "I" is extinguished",[50] but Dōgen manipulates the syntactic connections between the characters as usual and ends up with a legitimate, albeit fully unexpectable reading, "at this moment of arising, the unsaid (unsaying, unsayable) *ware* also arises, at this moment of extinction, the unsaid *ware* is also extinguished". If we read *ga* (*ware*) here as "self", we end up positing a self-identical subject, however short-living. No such problem emerges, however, when we translate this sentence as "at this moment of arising, a tacit perspective also arises, at this moment of extinction, a tacit perspective is also extinguished". A tacit perspective is a position from which a sentient being could potentially engage with the world, but nothing has been said about such a creature actually emerging. On the contrary: as Dōgen goes on to say, "arising does not consist in reflection or perception. This is why we call it the arising of the tacit perspective. There is no separate person who

---

[48] Raud, '*Shinjin-Datsuraku*, or "Dropping off the Bodymind" in Dōgen's Philosophy', in *Key Concepts in World Philosophies: Everything You Need to Know About Doing Cross-Cultural Philosophy*, ed. by S. Flavel and C. Robbiano (London: Bloomsbury Academic, 2022).

[49] Davis 'The Philosophy of Zen Master Dōgen: Egoless Perspectivism', in *The Oxford Handbook of World Philosophy* (Oxford: Oxford University Press, 2011).

[50] 起時唯法起、滅時唯法滅。此法起時、不言我起。此法滅時、不言我滅。

would see, hear, reflect upon, know or rationally analyse together with this arising of dharmas".[51]

Therefore, we have reason to wonder whether the two theses expressed in the *korai* passage do really express equally valid statements. "Climbing the mountain," as said, refers to the state of practice (as opposed to *praxis*) and we also know that the self is something that should be forgotten in order to attain that state of *praxis*. So perhaps this is another case of Dōgen's famous "while one side is illuminated, the other retreats into darkness" – in other words, that both statements are equally insufficient? Both the rejection and the endorsement of the binary opposition between "going" and "coming" express a part of the matter, but are untrue on their own. The situation is analogous to the discussion of *zengo*, "before and after" in the *Genjōkōan* fascicle: "Firewood abides in the dharma-configuration of firewood, where it has a before and an after – but while we can say there is a before-after to it, it [the configuration] is cut off from the before-after axis".[52] On the one hand, there is a going-coming to the absolute present of the *uji*, but on the other it has been cut off from the going-coming axis.

That this is the case is also suggested by the sentence immediately following this passage: "This *ji* of climbing the mountain and passing the river, this *ji* of residing in the vermillion tower – is it possible to swallow it? is it possible to spit it out?"[53] Swallowing and spitting out are mutually exclusive reactions to a disturbing object in one's mouth, and so are the incompatible endorsement and rejection of the binary between temporal going and coming – both move away from what is meant by *uji*. To express this, we will have to diverge slightly from the structural pattern of the text:

(6) The rejection of the binary opposition between temporal "going" and "coming" ties the very now of the *uji* to the temporal regime of practice. The endorsement of the binary opposition between temporal "going" and "coming" ties the very now of the *uji* to the particular perspective. What *uji* is emerges between these two views.

One final step still needs to be taken, and this is the determination of the relationship between *uji* and *nikon* in this passage. Are they separate in the sense that there is an *uji* without *nikon*, and a *nikon* without *uji*? Or are they aspects of the same thing? Neither of these options works if we take *uji* to signify an individual temporality. A particular person can have (an experience of the) absolute present, but an individual temporality cannot – because this temporality needs to contain the entire time of the individual by definition. An absolute present cannot *belong* to an individual temporality, be contained by it – because an absolute present is simultaneous for every individual in it (or consituted by it). But similarly, it cannot be an *aspect* of an individual temporality. Try as we might, inserting "individual time-regime" where *uji* is in this passage does not yield meaningful sentences.

---

[51] 起は知覺にあらず、知見にあらず、これを不言我起といふ。我起を不言するに、別人は此法起と見聞覺知し、思量分別するにはあらず。

[52] 薪は薪の法位に住して、さきありのちあり。前後ありといへども、前後際斷せり

[53] かの上山渡河の時、この玉殿朱樓の時を呑却せざらんや、吐却せざらんや。

However, the problem disappears when we take *uji* to mean "the existential moment":

> (7) The rejection of the binary opposition between temporal "going" and "coming" ties the absolute present of the existential moment to the temporal regime of practice. The endorsement of the binary opposition between temporal "going" and "coming" ties the absolute present of the existential moment to the particular perspective. What the existential moment is emerges between these two views.

Both phrases refer to the effort of the practicing self to reach the state where it is in alignment with *uji*. While the self and the practice are two, this will not happen. Only in their fusion is the fabric of the epistemological, "self"-dependent reality torn to the extent that the self becomes one with its practice, or enters the state of *praxis*, and the ontological reality of momentary existence becomes its own.

4 Conclusion

In this article, I have introduced the idea of multi-level signifiers as concepts which acquire additional levels of meaning during the reading of the text, forcing the reader to actively participate in the production of, or movement towards the ideas expressed. Further, developing similar schemes proposed by Yorizumi Mitsuko and Tsujiguchi Yūichirō, I have suggested a complementarity of binary and holistic conceptual registers as the framework in which to interpret Dōgen's thought, and tried to apply this approach to his time-vocabulary in particular. As a result, I have suggested that Dōgen's presentation of his views on time takes the reader from the binary and perspectival view of individual time-regimes to a holistic and perspective-transcending view of momentary existences, which fuses the idea of perspectival self with the present moment of *praxis*, or enacted alignment with the groundless dynamism of reality. What I have proposed is a reading of *uji* as a multi-dimensional signifier that contains, but transcends its first-level interpretation as individual time-regimes, pertaining to the binary conceptual register, and then leads the reader through the tackling of *(shōtō)immoji*, "the immediately present moment of suchness" and *nikon*, "the very now", to a rupture in the fabric of perceived reality, a disclosure of the momentary nature of all existence, the *uji no nikon*, aptly characterized by Tsujiguchi as "the *now* that does not pass".[54] Although the former reading remains legitimate as a point of entry into the discourse, there are many occasions in the text where it does not work, and regrettably many translations have chosen to simply glide over the problematic spots, creating an impression that this reading is sufficient.

For reasons of space, I have not been able here to discuss certain other central concepts of Dōgen's time-theory, such as *dōji* 同時 "simultaneity", *hairetsu* 排列

---

[54] Tsujiguchi as "the *now* that does not pass". See Tsujiguchi, *Shōbōgenzō No Shisōteki Kenkyū* (Tōkyō: Hokuju Shuppan, 2012), 176.

"rearrangement", *kenkyaku* 間隙 "intervals" or *kyōryaku* 經歷 "shifting", which, in my view, all fit in very well with the present reading. Nonetheless I hope to have shown that a philosophical close reading of the densest passages, taking them to be fully rational, if not necessarily in the most habitual sense of the word, can account for many elements of Dōgen's text that religiously oriented interpretations often leave untouched as examples of unfathomable paradoxicality. This should be reason enough to prefer philosophical reading to other interpretational regimes that are happy to halt before whatever they take to be a stop-sign. But, just as Dōgen urges us "to go beyond the Buddha", we, too, should never stop the search for legitimate, productive and coherent interpretations of thinkers like him.

References

Bronkhorst, Johannes. 'Abhidharma and Indian Thinking'. In *Text, History, and Philosophy: Abhidharma Across Buddhist Scholastic Traditions*, edited by B. Dessein and W. Teng. 29–46. Leiden: Brill. 2016.

Davis, Bret W. 'The Philosophy of Zen Master Dōgen: Egoless Perspectivism'. in *The Oxford Handbook of World Philosophy*. Oxford: Oxford University Press. 2011.

———. 'Zen's Nonegocentric Perspectivism'. in *Buddhist Philosophy: a Comparative Approach*, edited by S. M. Emmanuel. Hoboken: Wiley-Blackwell. 2017.

Heine, Steven. *Existential and Ontological Dimensions of Time in Heidegger and Dōgen*. Albany: State University of New York Press. 1985.

———. 'What Is on the Other Side? Delusion and Realization in Dōgen's "Genjōkōan"'. In *Dōgen: Textual and Historical Studies*, edited by S. Heine. Oxford: Oxford University Press. 2012.

Kasulis, Thomas P. 'Meaning and Context: Dōgen's Genjōkōan'. In *Japanese Philosophy: A Sourcebook*, edited by J. W. Heisig, T. P. Kasulis, and J. C. Maraldo. 144–47. Honolulu: University of Hawaii Press. 2011.

Maître Dôgen. *La vraie Loi, Trésor de l'Oeil: Textes choisis de Shôbôgenzô*. Paris: Seuil. 2004.

Moriyama, Shin'ya, and Takeshi Sakon. 'Dōgen on Time and the Self'. Tetsugaku 4 (2020): 135–50.

Nishiari, Bokusan. 'Commentary by Nishiari Bokusan. in *Dogen's Genjo Koan: three Commentaries*. Berkeley: Counterpoint. 2011.

Okumura, Shohaku. *Realizing Genjokoan: The Key to Dogen's Shobogenzo*. Boston: Wisdom Publications Inc. 2010.

Raud, Rein. 'Thinking with Dōgen: Reading Philosophically into and Beyond the Textual Surface'. In *Philosophizing in Asia*. 27–46. Tōkyō: UTCP. 2013.

———. 'Dōgen's Idea of Buddha-Nature: Dynamism and Non-Referentiality'. *Asian Philosophy* 25(1) (2015.): 1–14.

———. 'Dōgen and the Linguistics of Reality'. *Religions* 12(5) (2021): 331.

———. 'Shinjin-Datsuraku, or "Dropping Off the Bodymind" in Dōgen's Philosophy'. In *Key Concepts in World Philosophies: Everything You Need to Know About Doing Cross-Cultural Philosophy*, edited by S. Flavel and C. Robbiano. London: Bloomsbury Academic. 2022.

Tsujiguchi, Yūichirō. *Shōbōgenzō No Shisōteki Kenkyū*. Tōkyō: Hokuju Shuppan. 2012.

Uchiyama, Kōshō. *Deepest Practice, Deepest Wisdom: Three Fascicles from Shōbōgenzō with Commentaries*. Somerville: Wisdom Publications. 2018.

Yasutani, Hakuun. *Flowers Fall: A Commentary on Dōgen's Genjōkōan*. Boston: Shambhala. 1996.

Yorizumi, Mitsuko. *Shōbōgenzō Nyūmon*. Tōkyō: Kadokawa. 2014.

On Flowing While Being: The (Mereo) Logical Structure of Dōgen's Conception of Time

Felipe Cuervo Restrepo

1 Introduction[1]

Quite often, the hermeneutical challenges associated with reading Dōgen in the West are summarized in one question: should we read him as a philosopher? The purpose of this chapter is to argue for a more precise position: instead of merely arguing that reading Dōgen's texts philosophically (whatever that might mean) is productive, I will try to demonstrate that reading him through the lens of contemporary logic can help dispel obscurities and solve interpretative dilemmas. This, though, does not mean I intend to formalize Dōgen for the sake of formalization; instead, in a vaguely Wittgensteinian fashion, I plan to use logic therapeutically, in order to prove that what many have considered worrisome (more precisely, worrisome in so far as it is paradoxical) should not worry us at all. I hope to argue in favor of the hermeneutic technique performatively, if you will, by showing its advantages when faced with one of the most difficult sides of Dōgen's writings, his ideas on time, mostly, though not limited to, the manner in which they are expressed in the *Uji* fascicle.

---

[1]A somewhat different version of this chapter appeared as chapter IV of my thesis, "Perception of Events", which I defended at the Universidad de los Andes (Bogotá, Colombia) in December, 2022.

F. Cuervo Restrepo (✉)
Universidad de los Andes, Bogotá, Colombia
e-mail: f.cuervo126@uniandes.edu.co

© The Author(s), under exclusive license to Springer Nature Switzerland AG 2023
R. Müller, G. Wrisley (eds.), *Dōgen's Texts*, Sophia Studies in Cross-cultural Philosophy of Traditions and Cultures 35,
https://doi.org/10.1007/978-3-031-42246-1_13

In English, there are now several attempts to explain the *Uji* fascicle,[2] but, except for those that have tried to dispel the appearance of paradox by searching for openly metaphysical conceptions of time,[3] I will not be discussing them explicitly, despite how much I have learned from them. Instead, I will follow the lead of those who, though they have not concentrated on Dōgen's writings,[4] have approached Buddhist philosophy in general by making use of tools belonging to the tradition of analytical philosophy and formal logic.[5]

2   The Paradox of Time in Dōgen

Given how often the problem of time in Dōgen is discussed, one would expect there to be clarity as to what exactly the problem is; unfortunately, even at this earliest of stages in the discussion, there is no clear consensus beyond the fact that Dōgen's conception of time seems to be paradoxical, and most (though not all) scholars believe it is due to his explicitly endorsing two opposing accounts of temporality. This paradox manifests itself in two different aspects, which I will, for now, label sets 1 and 2 (in Sect. 4, I will offer a unified account of these two aspects). The

[2]Among which some, such as Masao Abe, "The Oneness of Practice and Attainment: Implications for the Relation between Means and Ends," in *Dōgen Studies*, ed. William LaFleur (Honolulu: University of Hawai'i Press, 1985a), "Dōgen on Buddha-Nature," in *Zen and Western Thought*, ed. Masao Abe and William R. LaFleur (London: Macmillan, 1985b), "Dōgen's View of Time and Space," *The Eastern Buddhist* 21, no. 2 (1988); Steven Heine, "Temporality of Hermeneutics in Dōgen's *Shōbōgenzō*." *Philosophy East and West* 33, no. 2 (1983): 139–147, *Existential and Ontological Dimensions of Time in Heidegger and Dōgen* (Albany: SUNY Press, 1985); Joan Stambaugh, *Impermanence Is Buddha-Nature: Dōgen's Understanding of Temporality* (Honolulu: University of Hawai'i Press, 1990); Rein Raud, "'Place' and 'Being-Time': Spatiotemporal Concepts in the Thought of Nishida Kitarō and Dōgen Kigen," *Philosophy East and West* 54, no. 1 (2004), have become canonical.

[3]Dirck Vorenkamp, "B-Series Temporal Order in Dōgen's Theory of Time," *Philosophy East and West* 45, no. 3 (1995); Rein Raud, "The Existential Moment: Rereading Dōgen's Theory of Time." *Philosophy East and West* 62, no. 2 (2012).

[4]Exceptions to this include (Garfield & Priest 2003; Priest 2018), which discuss a few specific passages as part of a more general discussion on Buddhism and paraconsistency, and the detailed discussion of paradoxes in Dōgen that can be found in (Tanaka 2013; Deguchi et al. 2013).

[5]Good examples of which are Jay L. Garfield and Graham Priest, "Nāgārjuna and the Limits of Thought," *Philosophy East and West* 53, no. 1 (2003), "Mountains are Just Mountains," in *Pointing at the Moon. Buddhism, Logic, Analytic Philosophy*, eds. Mario D'Amato, Jay L. Garfield, and Tom J. Tillemans (Oxford: Oxford University Press, 2009); Yasuo Deguchi, Jay L. Garfield, and Graham Priest, "The Way of the Dialetheist: Contradiction in Buddhism," *Philosophy East and West* 58, no. 3 (2003); Yasuo Deguchi, "Constructing a Logic of Emptiness: Nishitani, Jízāng, and Paraconsistency," in *The Moon Points Back*, ed. Koji Tanaka, Yasuo Deguchi, Jay L. Garfield, and Graham Priest (Oxford: Oxford University Press, 2015); Aaron J. Cotnoir, "Nāgārjuna's Logic," in *The Moon Points Back*, ed. Koji Tanaka, Yasuo Deguchi, Jay L. Garfield, and Graham Priest (Oxford: Oxford University Press 2015); Graham Priest, *The Fifth Corner of Four: An Essay on Buddhist Metaphysics and the Catuṣkoṭi* (Oxford: Oxford University Press, 2018).

following passages are the most frequently discussed concerning set 1; I will quote them in full, so that the reader can form her own opinion of the paradox, before discussing the texts in some detail.

1.1) The three heads and eight arms were time yesterday; the sixteen-foot or eight-foot [golden body][6] is time today. Even so, this Buddhist principle of yesterday and today is just about moments in which we go directly into the mountains and look out across a thousand or ten thousand peaks; it is not about what has passed. The three heads and eight arms pass instantly as my existence-time [有時]; though they seem to be in the distance, they are [moments of] the present. (I: 145/46a)[7]

1.2) The triple world is not original existence, the triple world is not present existence [今有], the triple world is not fresh realization, the triple world does not arise from causes and conditions, and the triple world is beyond beginning, middle, and end. [...] The triple world seen here and now [今此] is the object seen as the triple world, and this object seen is [the agent's] "seeing it as the triple world". (III: 62/ 178b)

1.3) Because this triple world here and now [今此] is the Tathāgata's "own possession", the whole universe is the triple world. Because the triple world is the whole universe, "here and now" is the past, present, and future. The reality of past, present, and future does not obstruct "the here and now". (III: 63/ 178b)

1.4) Because [real existence] is only this exact moment, all moments of existence-time [有時] are the whole of time, and all existent things and all existent phenomena are time. The whole of existence, the whole universe, exists in individual moments of time. (I: 144/ 45c)

The three quotes belonging to series 1 obliterate one aspect of our usual conception of time: the essential separation between past, present, and future. At first glance, the general idea seems to be that past, present, and future are not ontologically exclusive: quite on the contrary, one single present, the 今此, encompasses them all. There is, though, some doubt as to exactly how this occurs: in the two quotes discussing the nature of the triple world, it would seem as though there is a single point of view, an absolute present, from which all moments of time can be simultaneously grasped, as if *sub specie aeternitati*[8]; such is, for example, the most intuitive reading of the metaphor that opposes the "progressive" perception of time as what we see while ascending the mountain to the simultaneous perception gained by us upon reaching the summit: the thousand peaks we walked through one by one are now

---

[6] English interpolations in square brackets, if unaccompanied by a note, are due to Nishijima and Cross. Interpolations in Japanese, as well as those accompanied by a note reading, "inserted by the author," are my own.

[7] Given it is the most accessible (it can now be downloaded for free from the site of BDK America: https://bdkamerica.org/?s=dogen&post_type=product), all translations from Dōgen are taken from Dōgen. *Shōbōgenzō: The True Dharma-Eye Treasury*. Translated by Gudo Wafu Nishijima and Chodo Cross. Taishō edition. 4 vols. Moraga, CA: BDK America, 2007–8. References have the following structure: (Volume: Page/Canonical reference).

[8] A parallel view is expressed by Boethius in *De consolatione philosophiae*, Book V, Prosa VI: 10–11: "Aliud est enim per interminabilem duci vitam [..], aliud interminabilis uitae totam pariter complexum esse praesentiam, quod diuinae mentis proprium esse manifestum est. Neque deus conditis rebus antiquior uideri debet temporis quantitate sed simplicis potius proprietate naturae."

given to us in a single act of perception. Given it has been endorsed by several interpreters (including Vorenkamp), this reading deserves a name: let us call it the "absolute present reading".

Nevertheless, several parts of *Uji*, including the ones quoted in 1.1 and 1.4, suggest a very different picture: instead of there being one location outside of time from
which all times are grasped as one, each temporal instant contains the whole of
time. Thus, every past and every future exist at the same time as the present, given
they are all somehow contained within it: let us call this the "temporal monad
reading".[9] The difference is substantial: the "absolute present view" seems to imply
an ontological hierarchy, with there being a "divine" (the Tāthagata's) point of view
from which time as a stream loses its defining characteristic, while nothing is said
about the relations between each particular instant. The "temporal monad reading",
on the other hand, implies no such hierarchy: quite on the contrary, the ontology
accompanying this view includes a perhaps infinite number of "ultimate" temporal
components, each of which somehow encompasses all the others. In other words,
while the "absolute present reading" implies the existence of a point of view outside
time, from which time as a whole can be known, the "temporal monadology view"
posits nothing beyond temporality. Given such radically different metaphysical
structures, we seem forced to choose between one of the two interpretations, and the
fact that passages such as 1.2 and 1.3 can be explained as exemplifying one instance
of a "temporal monad", while 1.1 and 1.4 are incomprehensible from the "absolute
present reading", the "temporal monad reading" seems the more coherent approach.
Proper philosophical reasons for choosing the "temporal monad reading" will have
to wait until Sect. 4, at which point we will have the necessary technical resources;
right now, we need to understand the paradoxical nature of what they both share: the
levelling of differences among the three temporal aspects.

To better grasp the issue, it might be best if we state it in terms of truth attributions: given the two propositions $\exists xFx$ and $\neg \exists xFx$ in non-paraconsistent contexts,
we would conclude there is a contradiction and assume one of the two propositions
must actually be false, despite initial appearances. But if we add a temporal quantifier, the problem disappears: if, for example, we are told that (t_1) $(\exists xFx)$ and (t_2) $(\neg
\exists xFx)$, the contradiction no longer arises. But both the interpretations given above
seem to deny this: regardless of whether it is the absolute present or each individual
present, Dōgen would be claiming that there is a present at which contradictory
propositions would be true simultaneously. Now, it might be objected that this is a
false paradox, since we can always claim, following Frege's lead, that it is forever
true that, at t_1, $\exists xFx$, and forever true that, at t_2, $\neg \exists xFx$; this perspective from logical
eternity, though, does not fit with Dōgen's text, which insists on there being a time
at which they are true (notice, for example, that, diverse as they might seem, all
expressions translated as "present", including the here and now of the Tathāgata,
make use of the individuating indexical 今). Attempting to combine this with

---

[9] In reference, of course, to Leibniz's *La monadologie*, §56: "[C]haque substance simple a des rap-
ports qui expriment toutes les autres, et qu'elle est par conséquent un miroir vivant perpétuel de
l'univers".

Frege's logical eternity would give us a formalization in the manner of (t_R) (t_1) $(\exists xFx) \land (t_2) (\neg \exists xFx)$, where t_R is to be read as "reference time" and considered neutral on the question of whether it is a unique reference time or if each present serves as a reference time for all possible temporal propositions. Now, the truth conditions of the conjunction just mentioned, at least in the most obvious reading of the double temporal quantification, are indifferent to the t_R; to put it informally, if we say that "on the 8th of September 2021 there was no essay on Dōgen, mereology, and time, and on the 10th of September 2021 there was an essay on Dōgen, mereology, and time", the information we need in order to determine the truth of the conjunction is which entities existed on the 8th of September, and which on the 10th of September, and the result will not be affected by what existed (or not) on the 7th of September. This, though, would be to weaken Dōgen's philosophy of time to the point of making it identical to our usual notions, and, perhaps more importantly, would provide expressions affirming the presence of one time in another at best a misleadingly metaphorical reading.

Of course, there is another way of reading the double quantification (which would need, though, important alterations to the usual formal systems of quantified logic), such that the truth values of the conjunction depend on the reference time in so far as there is, in some sense, a t_1 and a t_2 within t_R, which would have to be logically distinct from t_1 and t_2 in themselves (otherwise, once again, we would be able to determine the truth value of the conjunction without considering the reference time at all). But this proves to be even more troublesome: if these times within a reference time are logically independent of those times in themselves (or in a different reference time), why then are we entitled to consider them the same times? If we add to this that having different times within a time would do little beyond reproducing our initial problem at the level of individual times (given those two times would have to be distinct to prevent a contradiction), the only evident paths to explaining Dōgen's conception of time turn out to be inconsistent. We are left, then, with our first paradox:

(P1) How can all times be identical to, or contained within, a single reference time?

Now let us consider a different set of quotes, the 2 series:

2.1) We should not understand only that time flies. We should not learn that "flying" is the only ability of time. [...] To grasp the pivot and express it: all that exists throughout the whole universe is lined up in a series and at the same time is individual moments of time. If we just left time to fly away, some gaps in it might appear. (I: 145/46a)

2.2) Existence-time [有時] has the virtue of passing in a series of moments [経歴]. That is to say, from today it passes through a series of moments to tomorrow; from today it passes through a series of moments to yesterday; from yesterday it passes through a series of moments to today; from today it passes through a series of moments to today; and from tomorrow it passes through a series of moments to tomorrow. Because passage through separate moments is a virtue of time, moments of the past and the present are neither piled up one on top of the other nor lined up in a row. (I: 145/46a)

2.3) If time does not have the form of leaving and coming, the [past][10] time of climbing a mountain is the present [而今] as existence-time [有時]. If time does retain the form of leaving and coming, I have this present moment [而今] of existence-time[有時], which is just existence-time itself. (I: 145/45c)

2.4) When a man is sailing along in a boat and he moves his eyes to the shore, he misapprehends that the shore is moving. If he keeps his eyes fixed on the boat, he knows that it is the boat that is moving forwards. Similarly, when we try to understand the myriad dharmas on the basis of confused assumptions about body and mind, we misapprehend that our own mind or our own essence may be permanent. If we become familiar with action and come back to this concrete place, the truth is evident that the myriad dharmas are not self. Firewood becomes ash; it can never go back to being firewood. Nevertheless, we should not take the view that ash is its future and firewood its past. Remember, firewood abides in the place of firewood in Dharma [法位]. It has a past and a future. Although it has a past and a future, the past and the future are cut off. (I: 42/ 23c-24a)[11]

These selections show a rather different problem: the question here is not how different times are related to one another, as in series 1, but what the nature of time is, whether it is essentially a flow or flight, or is fundamentally constituted by separate moments. In more contemporary terms, the question here seems to be the much-discussed debate on whether instants are ontologically independent entities the combination of which, somehow, produces the phenomenological impression of flowing (as when numerous still photographs are quickly passed by to create the sense of movement), or whether the flow is metaphysically prior to the instants. Though Dōgen is not very explicit, the point of rejecting the "piling up" and "lining up" metaphors used in 2.2 would seem to be that the flow of time is not guaranteed merely by there being times designated as past, present, and future relative to each other, but that, somehow, that relation is anchored in, perhaps justified by, the distinctive nature of the flow. In other words, not just any times can be the past and the future for a certain present (this would be simply piling up independent times); somehow, the nature of the flow imposes a structure that determines the relationship between distinct moments. In Sect. 4, I will attempt to fill up some of the details that are missing, but so that this does not sound stranger than it should, I would like to point out to the reader that our intuitive grasp of time assumes that it flows in one and only one direction, and thus imposes an asymmetry between past and future.[12] All times are connected, but they are not connected haphazardly: this is the reason we can understand the notion of necessary and sufficient causality without mistaking cause and effect. So as to not forget Dōgen's worries concerning the origin of time's structure, let us introduce a certain terminological shorthand: whenever a time is thought of from the point of view of its connection to other times, I will call it a stage; when, on the contrary, it is considered in itself, I will call it a moment. We could then say that the problem these

[10] Inserted by the author.

[11] Dōgen, Shōbōgenzō.

[12] I owe this realization to the remarkably beautiful, Antony Galton, "Time flies but space does not: Limits to the spatialization of time," Journal of Pragmatics 43 (2011), which I'd recommend to all philosophers studying time.

quotes create is that they alternate between defending a "moment priority" theory of time, in which moments are ontologically primary, and the flow of time is constituted by the union of various moments, and a "stream priority" theory of time, in which the flow is ontologically prior, and specific stages exist only as dependent on the flow. Although not quite precise, it might be useful to think of this debate as that between an atomistic conception of time ("moment priority"), and a holistic conception of time ("stream priority"). The difficulty is, of course, compounded once we realize that, although grasped from a different perspective, stages and moments seem to refer to the same entities: points in time.

The reader might, at first glance, feel 2.4 should be placed in a different category, given it discusses stages in an object's existence instead of the nature of time; at this point, I cannot provide too detailed an explanation (we will need some of the ideas developed in Sect. 4), but it can be argued that this captures a parallel debate[13] at a different ontological level: the question here is the ontological independence of object-stages from the whole history of the object, just as in the other quotes the problem is whether moments are independent from the stream of time of which they are moments. If, as I do, the reader believes Dōgen defends a radical ontology of tropes, in which time is the substrate of which all characteristics are predicated,[14] there is not even the need to postulate a different ontological level: it is simply the same argument, but with "tropes" included. But, since I would rather state the problem without relying on a specific interpretation, I shall offer the following elaboration in lieu of an argument: (a) If we accept the "moment priority" theory, then moments are ontologically independent, and the flow of time is the result of grouping distinct moments; if, instead, we accept the "stream priority" of time, then the flow of time is ontologically primary, and stages are dependent on their position in the flow to acquire their ontological determinations. (b) If we accept the "moment priority" theory of objects, moments in an object's history are ontologically independent, meaning that an instant can be a firewood-stage regardless of whether its future includes its transformation into ashes or not, and that the life history of an object is the result of grouping distinct moments. If, instead, we accept the "stream priority" of objects, then an object's history is ontologically primary, and its stages are dependent on it in order to acquire their ontological determinations.

We can now state our second problem:

(P2) How can the "moment priority" theory and the "stream priority" theory be simultaneously true? I.e., how can our ontology of time be both atomistic and holistic?

Before proceeding any further, I believe a small comment is in order in case the reader feels any doubt about the difference between the two problems: although it might be natural to assume that the reference time(s) discussed in the first problem are moments, and thus that, regardless of how we broach that problem, the solution

---

[13] Actually, one of the two positions in the debate.

[14] For the specific case of Dōgen, I know Yasuo Deguchi has defended this interpretation in at least one conference on Dōgen. For a more general defense of Buddhist ontology as trope theoretical, see Jonardon Ganeri, *Attention, Not Self* (Oxford: Oxford University Press, 2017) and the references there mentioned.

to the moment/stream paradox must give priority to moments, this is not the case: there is no reason to assume that the present is a moment, a durationless point in time. Many philosophers, among whom the best known, at least in the English-speaking world, is William James, have argued that we live in the specious present, a minimum duration of time smaller than which we cannot perceive[15]; it is not my intention to discuss the details of this proposal, but suffice it to say that it is not inherently impossible and that, without further argumentation, there is no reason to assume the reference time must have the nature of a durationless instant instead of a specious present.

3 Two Contemporary Attempts to Solve the Paradoxes

As I mentioned in the introduction, the two best known metaphysical approxima-tions to the problem of time in Dōgen are Vorenkamp[16] and Raud,[17] and I believe it might be instructive to take a quick look at both.

Vorenkamp's article is constructed around the belief the Dōgen's conception of time is essentially that of a defender of McTaggart's B-series, and much of his time is dedicated both to explaining in detail the differences between the A-series and the B-series, and to correlating certain passages in Dōgen to the latter. Without going into too much detail, the difference between both series can be distilled into the question of whether temporal relations are essentially changing or static. In the A-series, moments are classified as past, present, or future in relation to an ever-changing perspective: time, in other words, is assumed to flow essentially. In the B-series, moments are arranged as prior, simultaneous, or posterior to each other, and these relations are never altered. Time, in other words, is conceived as a com-pletely determined ordering, without there being a privileged position from which all other times are ordered. Changing perspectives, we might say the A-series assumes there is a privileged ontological position, the present, which is not an inter-nal characteristic of moments (in as far as they progressively acquire and lose it); what exactly the present is depends on the specific defender of the A-series, but, in general, the present might be said to be what is real, as opposed to the future and, according to some, the past. A B-series theorist, on the other hand, assumes no such privileged position: in terms of reality, all moments are equally real, the only differ-ence from the point of view of reality being between things that have, are, or will happen and those that never come to be. The present, in their view, is not an onto-logical fact, but, similar to the case of "here" with regards to space, a matter of perspective: "now" is whichever moment a subject is at, but this does not mean that

---

[15] For a well-regarded contemporary account, see Barry Dainton, "The Experience of Time and Change." *Philosophy Compass* 3, no. 4 (2008a), and "Sensing Change." *Philosophical Issues* 18 (2008b).

[16] Vorenkamp, "B-Series."

[17] Raud, "The Existential Moment."

moment is any more real than any of the other moments at which the subject might be (in the same way my being "here" does not make "there" unreal).

Most of Vorenkamp's arguments for considering Dōgen a B-series theorist come from series 1. Thus, discussing 1.1, Vorenkamp concludes:

> Dōgen is clearly making a statement concerning the relativity of time and passage to the individual subject. In the case of B-theorists, their contention is clear: in stating that temporal becoming is subjective, B-theorists mean that it is relative to, a product of, the individual mind and is not an objective feature of the cosmos.[18]

In isolation, it might be open to discussion whether Dōgen is affirming that the past is now because it is still present in the now, or because the past is a separate but equally real now, but what then are we to do with 1.3 and 1.4? 1.3 quite explicitly states that all times are united in a single present, and, even if we adopt the "absolute present reading" discussed in Sect. 2, we are still required to account, on the one hand, for the existence of a present, absolute as it may be, and for the unity of all times in one. Perhaps it might be argued that the supposed absolute present is Dōgen's metaphorical attempt to capture ultimate reality, which is not a present in the strict sense, but then we are faced with the same problem 1.3 and 1.4 posed to the "absolute present reading": Dōgen quite openly and unambiguously states that all times are the totality of time, meaning there is more than one present, and each of these contains them all. Not only is nothing in the B-series theory capable of capturing the interpenetration of distinct moments in a single present, but there is also an important difference between saying that all moments are real because the present is subjective and saying that all presents are real: the first is a reductionist approach to the present, while the second is closer to what we may describe as temporal pluralism.

Aside from the difficulties faced by trying to equate (P1) with the B-series theories, Vorenkamp faces an additional difficulty: as I mentioned a couple of paragraphs back, the B-series is essentially static, and Dōgen, as we discussed earlier, is quite insistent when it comes to recognizing that time flows. Vorenkamp himself confesses that "Since Dōgen clearly considers A-series passage as essential to his view of time, the A-theory phrases [...] would seem to mitigate against the B-theory views we have also found,"[19] and, after casting about for a solution, ends up by concluding in what can almost be read as a recognition of (P2):

> In light of the problems with each of the three alternatives above, we must be open to a fourth option: the real problem on this issue may simply lie with our assumption of consistency. Simply put, Western philosophical views concerning the incompatibility of the A- and B theories may be correct even within the context of traditional Buddhist philosophy, and Dōgen is therefore offering us an inconsistent philosophy of time.'[20]

This is, of course, a rather unsatisfactory position, specially concerning a philosopher, such as Dōgen, who openly criticized those who attempted to portray Buddhist

---

[18] Vorenkamp, "B-Series," 392.

[19] Ibid., 398.

[20] Ibid., 400.

philosophy as irrational; thus, the need to search for an alternative explanation such as the one I will offer in Sect. 4.

Raud's approach is almost completely the opposite of Vorenkamp's; whereas Vorenkamp's interpretation was dependent mostly on set 1, Raud's emphasis is on set 2, which, he believes, is mysterious only because we have forced our own conception of moments of time as durations, instead of attempting to adapt our own notion to Dōgen's. Raud suggests that we read Dōgen's *uji* not as durations, but as dimensionless moments. Since, on the one hand, the best arguments for his positions are his capacity to make sense of otherwise obscure passages, and, on the other, this would mean that my reading of set 2 as defending that time is primarily both moments and a stream is false, I shall discuss some of his interpretations in detail. For example, Raud interprets 2.2 as:

> [T]he existential moment shifts from so-called "today" into "tomorrow," because at the time that we now call tomorrow we will experience the existential moment just as we do now: we take it with us. However, the now-present existential moment, the way things are just now, will also shift away from us into what we will start to call "yesterday," when "tomorrow" has arrived. [...] Seen thus, kyōryaku [author's insertion: this is the term Nishijima and Cross translate as passage: 経歴] is not a deep and metaphysically loaded concept, but simply the capacity of the momentary existences that allows us to relate our experience of reality to our conceptualization of time in the linguistic model where deictically defined time-designations exist and can be opposed to each other. What it requires is dismissing the notions of "today," "yesterday," and "tomorrow" from among the categories of our direct experience, and assigning them the role of merely linguistic devices that help us to approach reality but are never able to completely and fully refer to it.[21]

Let us begin with a general remark on the notion of "dimensionless": what lacks dimensions must also, by necessity, lack the possibility of overlapping something else, given overlap is the coexistence of parts, one each (at least) belonging to the overlapping entities, along one and the same dimension. Thus, if time is essentially constituted by dimensionless moments, the passage of time can only be conceived as jumps from one moment to the next, giving us an image of time as an ordered set of discrete entities. This, though, seems to correspond to the conception of moments as piled up or lined up that Dōgen explicitly rejects in the last sentence of 2.2. In fact, if we start with this sentence and read backwards, Dōgen's point seems to be that the relations of "yesterday", "tomorrow", and "today" are not merely ways of indicating a stage's relative position (which is one of the implications of considering them mere deictic devices), but imply some sort of ontological dependence: today flows from yesterday not because yesterday came before today (the "piling up" metaphor), but because today is what it is, has the ontological determinations it has, because yesterday was what it was and had the ontological determinations it had. Under Raud's reading, this distinction is lost and no sense can be made of Dōgen's remarks on the peculiarity of the flow of time.

A similar problem shows up when Raud interprets the risk of gaps showing up in the flow of time with which 1.1 closes:

---

[21] Raud, "The Existential Moment," 164–65.

But the problem is solved if we assume that what are seen to fly by are moments: if we would, indeed, against the text's admonition, presume that moments fly past, one after another, like the stages of the movement of Zeno's arrow, it would be very logical to ask what is present during the almost imperceptible interval when one moment has already passed and another one is still not yet here. However, this is not the case: the moments follow each other as an unbreakable, continuous chain that makes "me" up in the process, leaving no position from where the gaps could actually be observed.[22]

Raud's solution is ingenious: even if time is granular, we would not notice the fact, given that noticing the gap would mean the gap is a moment during which we are conscious, which would mean, of course, it is not truly a gap. Nevertheless, he misses an important point: his account gives us a discrete set of momentary consciousnesses, but not a consciousness of distinct moments. In other words, to use the classical formulation, the problem with gaps in temporal consciousness is the result of the difference between the succession of perceptions and the perception of succession, for which Raud's account offers no explanation. The fact that Dōgen states the point in terms of something missing in the "flying" conception of time might, at first glance, be taken as a demand for stability within the flow, or perhaps a perspective that, being outside the flow, manages to grasp several moments in one unique act of perception, but this is not the only possibility. If we recognize that Dōgen is defending that the flow of time is not a mere sequence, but a structure in which the ontological determinations of a moment are inextricably bound up with those before and after it, a new interpretation surfaces: since the present contains the past and the future in its ontological weave, grasping the one is grasping the others. The demand, then, might be better read as one for a stronger sense of time as a stream, instead of one in which the stream breaks up into independent moments.

Probably none of the above criticisms are knock-down arguments, but I hope they do leave the reader with the impression that many of the problems we noticed in Sect. 2 are left unaccounted for, and thus that there are good reasons to search for a new reading of the texts.

4   The Origin of the Paradoxes

Before facing the paradoxes and attempting to extract a coherent philosophy of time from them, I believe we should ask ourselves a question which, so far as I can see, has received little attention: what led Dōgen to the theses included in (P1) and (P2)?

Much of the strangeness behind Dōgen's conception of time as flowing disappears if we tie it to the idea of co-dependent origination, especially as formulated by Nāgārjuna.[23] Perhaps the first thesis one thinks of when Nāgārjuna is discussed is

---

[22] Ibid., 164.

[23] All quotes from Nāgārjuna's *Mūlamadhyamakakārikā* will come from Jay L. Garfield, *The Fundamental Wisdom of the Middle Way. Nāgārjuna's* Mūlamadhyamakakārikā (Oxford: Oxford University Press, 1995), and will be quoted, for ease of comparison with other translations, according to the following convention: (Chapter-Verse: Page number in Garfield's edition).

the Doctrine of the Two Truths, most clearly expounded in Chapter XXIV of the *Mūlamadhyamakakārikā*, according to which one can know the world either by means of conventional truths,[24] which captures, among others, everyday objects,[25] or by means of the ultimate truth, which teaches that all objects captured by means of conventional knowledge are co-dependently arisen and thus essentially empty.[26] To make proper sense of this thesis, we need a couple of definitions: co-dependently arisen entities are those the existence of which somehow depends on the existence of another entity, usually by means of causal relations, though many of Nāgārjuna's arguments might be read (more profitably, in my opinion) as demonstrating that the nature of an entity is captured by means of concepts that can only be understood by reference to a whole conceptual scheme.[27] In Nāgārjuna's terms, a thing can only have an essence in so far as the logical possibility of its existence is absolutely independent of any other entity or proposition.[28] Since entities that are co-dependently arisen lack an essence, when we attempt to capture them in themselves, without reference to other entities or propositions, they turn out to be empty.

The connection with Dōgen first shows up when we realize that Nāgārjuna tied the notion of co-dependent origination with temporality: "Whatever comes into being dependent on another/Is not identical to that thing. / Nor is it different from it. / Therefore it is neither nonexistent in time nor permanent."[29] I believe the best way to make sense of this is to argue that since Nāgārjuna understands permanent entities as those whose existence is independent (meaning it is true that they exist at any time whatsoever and thus regardless of whether any other proposition is true or not), and, since co-dependently arisen entities are, by definition, those which are not independent, their existence must be temporally bounded.[30] This, by itself, is

---

[24] Ibid., XXIV-8: 296.

[25] Ibid., XXIV-18; 304.

[26] Ibid., XXIV-19: 304. The Doctrine of the Two Truths is among the most widely debated issues in Buddhist Philosophy; what I present here is but a general outline with which, I am sure, many will find reasons for disagreeing. Unfortunately, trying to argue for my interpretation would take too much time and space, so I can but hope that the causes of disagreement do not affect the chapter's general outline. The interested reader can gain a good overview of where the contemporary debate lies, at least among analytically leaning philosophers, from the many essays in The Cowherds, *Moonshadows: Conventional Truth in Buddhist Philosophy* (Oxford: Oxford University Press, 2010).

[27] This, of course, might be better phrased as: reading Nāgārjuna with the help of both Quine and Davidson's work on the interrelation of beliefs can, I would argue, both make his arguments stronger and provide us with a more coherent interpretation of his ideas as a whole.

[28] "Essence arising from / causes and conditions makes no sense. / If essence came from causes and conditions, / Then it would be fabricated." Garfield, *The Fundamental Wisdom*, XV-1: 220.

[29] Ibid., XVIII-10: 252.

[30] It would seem this argument fails given the possibility of interrelated necessary truths; I would argue that part of Nāgārjuna's works should be read as arguing that there can be no such a thing as necessary truths, but that would take us too far. Since all we need is to understand Nāgārjuna's ideas, regardless of whether they are cogent or not, I believe this discussion can wait for a different occasion.

illuminating, but Nāgārjuna takes it a step further, and argues that distinct moments are also co-dependently originated:

> If the present and the future / Depend on the past, / Then the present and the future / Would have existed in the past. // If the present and the future / did not exist there, / How could the present and the future / Be dependent upon it? // If they are not dependent upon the past, / Neither of the two would be established. / Therefore neither the present / Nor the future would exist.[31]

At first sight, the argument might seem circular, but this is quickly dispelled if we read it as pressing a point similar to Dōgen's in 2.2: if we are to theoretically capture the flow of time from past to present to future, we cannot conceive of them as absolutely distinct moments, but must assume they are somehow ontologically imbricated. In other words, the mere fact that first there was one moment and then another is insufficient to describe one as the past and the other as the present, for example. They would simply be distinct moments and nothing else. The past is the past of the present not because it belongs to a different point in the temporal timeline, but because it holds a distinctive relation to it, a relation which, as I mentioned before, can best be captured as asymmetrical: the past is that which can come before the present but not after it. Following his usual style of argumentation, Nāgārjuna interprets this as proof that any proposition that incorporates temporality can only be true, can only be understood, in fact, if there are other propositions that make use of a whole set of temporal concepts, which means that whatever is captured by means of temporal concepts is co-dependently originated. In other words, time, as a succession of stages related to one another as past, present, and future, is metaphysically prior to any particular moment of time; thus, time cannot be conceived as constituted by the mere sum of its moments. If we add to this that all co-dependently arisen entities are temporal, we can conclude that, in Nāgārjuna's metaphysics, all conventional truths are temporally bounded and, thus, are inextricably tied to a set of stages to which it relates as its past, present, and future.

Hopefully, the reader is by now aware (and convinced, I would like to think) of the connection between Dōgen's philosophy of time and Nāgārjuna's metaphysics. Nevertheless, before continuing with Dōgen, there is one other lesson to be learned from the *Mūlamadhyamakakārikā* concerning the soteriological significance of the Doctrine of the Two Truths, which leads us to another of Nāgārjuna's famous theses, the identity of saṃsāra and nirvāṇa:

> There is not the slightest difference / Between cyclic existence and nirvāṇa. / There is not the slightest difference / Between nirvāṇa and cyclic existence. // Whatever is the limit of nirvāṇa, / That is the limit of cyclic existence. / There is not even the slightest difference between them, / or even the subtlest thing.[32]

This comes after a long and detailed demonstration that, were any distinctive concept predicated of nirvāṇa, it would become yet another co-dependently arisen entity, which would make it nothing but part of saṃsāra. Nāgārjuna's still beautiful

---

[31] Ibid., XIX-1-3: 254–255.

[32] Ibid. XXV-19-20: 331.

insight, both by its philosophical audacity and its religious profundity, is to recognize that nirvāṇa cannot count as one of the existents (or non-existents, for that matter), cannot be a separate entity or place, but can only be the grasping[33] of reality from the perspective of ultimate truth: understanding that everything that supposedly is, is empty. In other words, ultimate reality is not ontologically distinct from conventional reality; it is, rather, conventional reality seen through the prism of enlightenment. Once this perspective is achieved, in accordance with the teachings of the Four Noble Truths, we should be freed from attachment and the world of co-dependent origination to which it belongs. For our purposes, this is the lesson we should take: reality is not constituted, as many traditions assume, by two distinct worlds, one human and one divine, but by two different perspectives, one showing us co-dependently arisen temporal entities, and the other, well, I guess I have to say emptiness, though it must be kept in mind that emptiness should not here be understood as a particular entity, since this would mean falling once more into the perspective of saṃsāra.

Before returning to Dōgen, it is worthwhile to elaborate the preceding paragraph's last phrase: when told that conventional truths are, in a sense, illusions (given they are not truly independent), and that there is a different level of reality that is ultimate, there is a tendency, perhaps informed by atomism, to assume that the illusions are somehow constituted by whatever belongs to ultimate reality. This, though, is a tendency we must oppose: the relation of constitution is among those Nāgārjuna characterizes as giving us reason to believe that both the constituting parts and the constituted whole are co-dependently arisen.[34] More generally, entities belonging to the world of conventional truth can in no way be constituted, caused, or explained by ultimate reality; believing otherwise would drag ultimate reality back into conventionality.

"The mountains are time, and the seas are time. Without time, the mountains and the seas could not exist: we should not deny that time exists in the mountains and the seas here and now."[35] This is Dōgen, once again, but what would have otherwise sounded mysterious is now, I believe, a clear demonstration of Dōgen's endorsement of the essential temporality of the objects of conventional truths. If to this we add the fact that time, from the perspective of saṃsāra, must be understood primarily as a flow and only derivatively as composed of moments, we have a clearer picture of why Dōgen insisted on "stream priority" in (P2): without it, he would have no way of characterizing temporality in the realm of conventionality, in the world of everyday lived experience. The question, then, is: why does he simultaneously insist on the ontological primacy of moments? A few quotes should give us the answer:

---

[33] I deliberately chose an ambiguous verb to indicate that the debate on what exactly this consists in is still open. Quite evidently, Nāgārjuna believed that at least part of this was intellectual, but since, sadly, most of those who read and, presumably, understand his works are unenlightened and may as well remain so, this cannot be the whole story.

[34] See, for example, ibid., chapters I, IV, V, and XIII.

[35] Dōgen, *Shōbōgenzō*, I:48/47a.

People in many ages from the ancient past to the present have thought that the words "when the time has come..." are about waiting for a time in the future when the buddha-nature might be manifest before us. [...] [But] there has never been a time that was not time having come, nor any buddha-nature that was not the buddha-nature manifesting itself before us.[36]

Remember the manifestations, the coming into the present of the various stages of samādhi, is in the same state of "all relying on the buddha-nature". The "dependence upon this", and the nondependence upon this, of all six powers, are both in the state of "all relying on the buddha-nature."[37]

These two quotes, which can be replaced by nearly any passages from the *Busshō* fascicle, state that any single moment in the existence of any of the temporal entities belonging to the world of conventionality "has"[38] the buddha-nature it needs to achieve liberation from saṃsāra. Now, it may be tempting to interpret this Buddhist tenet as affirming that the experiencing mind is, at any moment, endowed with the conditions necessary to liberate itself and reach nirvāṇa. Dōgen, though, is clearly antagonistic to this interpretation, which he labels the Senika Heresy and characterizes as non-Buddhist thought, the reason being that this implies the mind is not a conventional entity, but belongs instead to ultimate reality; true Buddhist thought, instead, at least according to Dōgen, includes the belief that the mind is yet another co-dependently arisen conventional entity attachment to which must be broken before enlightenment comes about.[39] In other words, it is the moment itself that, from a certain perspective, "has" buddha-nature, while the mind arises only when different moments are grasped as co-dependently arisen in terms of mental causality.[40] But why the need to insist so much on this point? The reason is, as with Nāgārjuna, soteriological: if enlightenment depended on the satisfaction of certain conditions, if the buddha-nature were temporally bounded or conditioned by a past, present, or future occurrence, we would no longer be dealing with ultimate reality and liberation, but with an illusion of paradise in a world of painful attachments. From a slightly different perspective, the argument can be stated as the contrapositive of Nāgārjuna's demonstration of the temporal boundedness of co-dependently arisen entities: given buddha-nature is not co-dependently arisen, it must be

---

[36] Dōgen, *Shōbōgenzō*, II: 7/92c-93a.

[37] Ibid., II: 8/93a-93b.

[38] As we mentioned when discussing Nāgārjuna, the relation between entities and the ultimate reality is not one of constitution or any variety of quality possessed. If we were looking for precision, we might say something like: any stage in the existence of a conventional entity can be grasped as the ultimate reality. For the sake of readability, I'll use "have" instead, though the reader is advised to keep in mind this is an analogical and slightly misleading use of the verb.

[39] *cf.* ibid., I: 65-67/28a-28b; I: 68/29b.

[40] This, I take it, is the lesson behind the following affirmation: "Mind as mountains, rivers, and the earth is nothing other than mountains, rivers, and the earth. There are no additional waves or surf, no wind or smoke" (Ibid., 64/29b), as well as of the famous discussion on whether the bell, the wind or the mind rings (*cf.* ibid., II: 154/125b).

permanent, temporally unbounded, indifferent to temporal quantifiers. It "is"[41] at any and every moment.[42] The "moment priority" thesis of (P2) turns out to be motivated by the belief that all moments "have" buddha-nature, and thus, from the perspective of ultimate reality, are independent of all others.

Before reformulating (P2) with our newly acquired insights, it will only take us a minute to extricate the explanation of (P1) from the last paragraph's conclusion, the paradoxical nature of which, we might say, is the result of interbreeding two distinct conceptions of time: as we mentioned when discussing Vorenkamp's text, A-theories share a belief in the ontological uniqueness of the present: among times, only it can wear the crown of reality. But this accords poorly with Dōgen's soteriological democracy, which recognizes equal importance (and, hence, reality) for all times: otherwise, Dōgen would be forced to concede that past and future enlightenment are, in some sense or another, less real than present enlightenment, and this, following the *reductio* scheme we have encountered several times, implies enlightenment is among the facts of conventional reality.[43] All times, then, must be equally real, given they all "have" buddha-nature. The reader, I assume, already guesses the explanation behind the identity of times: it is nothing but Dōgen's elaboration of Nāgārjuna's thesis of the ontological imbrications of temporality. (P1), in other words, turns out to be not a distinct thesis or problem, but a synthetical account of the two positions included in (P2).

This, though, only makes it more paradoxical than we originally believed it to be: we now know that Dōgen is trying to formulate a metaphysics of time in which, on the one hand, all moments are equally real and, in so far as they "have" buddha-nature, ontologically independent, and in which, on the other hand, time as flow, which imposes a tight ontological interdependence among moments, is conceived as primary. Both problems, then, reduce to one question: how can moments be ontologically independent and "have" their own buddha-nature when they occur in a flow of time that is primary regarding its stages?

Before turning to my proposed solution, there is one possible reaction against which I believe we must guard ourselves: attempting to eliminate the paradox by arguing that each account of time applies for only one of the two realms in Nāgārjuna's philosophy. First, this approach falls afoul of the timelessness of ultimate reality: distinct independent moments cannot be distinct entities in ultimate reality, given ultimate reality holds no distinctions. Each moment is equally real not because it exists on its own in ultimate reality, but because ultimate reality can be grasped from any moment whatsoever, independent of what counts as its past or future; all moments, in other words, have an equal potential for liberation (at least from an ontological perspective), which means they all exist as equals in the plane

---

[41] "To be", when within quotation marks, is to be understood by analogy with "to have" in quotation marks.

[42] "Per æternitatem intelligo ipsam existentiam, quatenus ex sola rei æternæ definitione necessario sequi concipitur." (Spinoza: *Ethica I.Def.VIII*).

[43] An intrepid philosopher might say that this philosophical principle is the explanation behind the eternal, in Spinoza's sense, existence of past and future Buddhas in Buddhist cosmology.

from which one is to be liberated. And yet this does not imply they either exist in or are correlated to moments in the plane towards which one is liberated. More succinctly, it seems impossible to formulate this solution without introducing a wedge in the identity of saṃsāra and nirvāṇa. Second, it ignores part of what I will call the existential import of Dōgen's thesis: individuals that live in the flow of time are enlightened at moments that belong to that same flow of time. This is the whole point of Dōgen's comments on "when the time comes...": individuals do not have to wait for the moment or occasion for liberation, do not have to search for it in foreign lands or eras; every moment in an individual's lifetime, a fragment of the stream of time, is a moment endowed with the possibility of enlightenment.

5   A Mereological Solution

At first glance, the dual nature of time in Dōgen's metaphysics might be considered but a slight step away from a clear-cut paradox, but this, I would argue, is not the result of an actual *contradictio in terminis*; the contradiction is only reached if we assume an additional premise, which I believe to be a philosophical prejudice. But let us take it one step at a time.

Towards the end of the previous section, we discovered Dōgen holds the following two theses regarding the nature of time: (1) moments are ontologically independent; (2) the stream of time is primary regarding its stages. To conclude that this is a contradiction, we must assume that the moments of (1) are identical to the stages of (2), and thus that they are both ontologically independent and ontologically dependent. This seems like an evident step: the stream of time has stages as its parts, and those parts are moments, in the same way an extended area or volume of space has lesser area or volumes, or perhaps points, as its parts. Attempting to deny the validity of this step, at least according to what many philosophers consider commonsense, is a breach of rationality, given moments and stretches of time are "evidently" related as parts and whole, and one can either assume an atomistic position, according to which the parts are ontologically prior and constitute the whole, or a holistic position, and argue that the parts exist only in so far as they are parts of the whole. Denying this implicit premise would be equivalent to being a holistic atomist, which is a contradiction, and hence the fountain from which the paradoxical nature of Dōgen's conception of time flows.

And yet denying the premise is what I plan on doing, by arguing that it depends on assuming a mereological isomorphism between time as a flow and moments, an isomorphism that, regardless of appearance, our folk metaphysics already denies. Since my purpose here is not to argue for the truth of Dōgen's ideas, but to prove they are not inconsistent, I will begin by pointing out a few cases in which we have no problem denying the mereological isomorphism between occupier and occupied, and then proceed to formalize a few of the concepts involved.

Most of us are willing to agree that the great majority, if not all, of what we usually call things, such as people, poplars, and pens, have an existence that somehow or other occupies extensions of both space and time, but we are not often consciously aware of the fact that we understand "occupation" in different ways. An example might be the best way of proving the point: if we are shown a mound of sand that occupies space x, we have no problem understanding the idea that, if there is a space y that is a part of space x, then there will be a part of the mound of sand that occupies space y; if we are also told that the mound in question exists from time t_0 to time t_4, we will accept that there is a stretch of time t_2-t_3, which is part of t_0-t_4, but will most surely feel mystified if told that there is a part of the mound of sand that occupies t_2-t_3.[44] In case the reader still has doubts, another example might be of use: if shown a certain jigsaw puzzle at a certain time and told that, at that same time, only part of the jigsaw puzzle exists, the affirmation will seem comprehensible given we can assume it means that the jigsaw puzzle we see is incomplete and there are other pieces that are either being manufactured or will be so in the future. But what would happen if the jigsaw puzzle manufacturer replied that our interpretation is mistaken, and that, from the perspective of its total number of pieces, the jigsaw puzzle in front of us is complete, and yet is still only a part of the jigsaw puzzle? I believe we would assume the manufacturer is either slightly unhinged or does not fully understand the meaning of the word "part".

Both examples prove we can, without metaphysical discomfort, understand the idea of things having spatial parts, but can, at least when uncontaminated by excessive philosophy, make no sense of their having temporal parts (which does not mean we cannot understand the concept "temporal part" at all; the problem is limited to its meaning in the context of a certain kind of entity), and yet both understand and accept that things are extended in both time and space. If to this we add the apparently unproblematic belief that time has parts (as in "a minute is part of an hour"), we can conclude that folk metaphysics can make use of the idea that occupiers can occupy what they occupy in two different manners, the one allowing for the inference that, for every part of the occupied, there is a part of the occupier (the case of space), but not the other (the case of time). Since we will now proceed to formalize these ideas, we might as well introduce the technical terms for both cases: the former is extensive occupation and the latter, intensive occupation.[45]

---

[44] I am well aware that every thesis I have here mentioned is an object of controversy for some group of philosophers, be it those that deny the existence of arbitrary parts, be it those that believe that objects are four-dimensional worms, among many others. My purpose, though, is not to endorse them, but to point out to the reader that she already makes use of certain concepts that, if presented from an abstract perspective, she might reject as nonsensical.

[45] These terms, as well as much of what follows, are based mainly on Peter Simons, "Extended Simples: A Third Way between Atoms and Gunk," *The Monist* 87, (2004) and "Where It's At: Modes of Occupation and Kinds of Occupant," in *Mereology and Location*, ed. Shieva Kleinschmidt (London: Oxford University Press, 2014); an elaborate argumentation proving the concept is not logically contradictory can be found in Raul Saucedo, "Parthood and Location," in *Oxford Studies in Metaphysics, Vol. 6*, ed. Karen Bennett and Dean W. Zimmerman (Oxford: Oxford University Press, 2011). Still other authors that work on the concept and attempt to use it in order to account for different problems are Daniel Nolan, "Balls and All," in *Mereology and Location*, ed. Shieva Kleinschmidt (London: Oxford University Press, 2014); Kris McDaniel, "Extended simples,"

Using the following two basic definitions:

(D1) Pxy = $_{def}$ x is part of y^{46}
(D2) Lxy = $_{def}$ x is located at y

and reading the second variable of Lxy as being replaceable by a set of points in the occupied, we can formalize both kinds of occupation as follows[47]:

(Extensive occupation) $L_e$xy = $_{def}$ Lxy → ∀z(Pzy → ∃w(Lwz ∧ Pwx))
(Intensive occupation) $L_i$xy = $_{def}$ Lxy → ∀z(Pzy → ¬ ∃w(Lwz ∧ Pwx))

The reader can easily check that the second definition is a well-formed formula with no internal contradictions; she might, though, worry that the existence of an entity that complies with this definition will end up causing inconsistencies in whichever logical system it occurs. Given both its extension and technical difficulty, I cannot offer a proof to the contrary here, but the interested reader can find a detailed argumentation in (Saucedo 2011), where he examines an impressive array of such misalignments between the mereological structures of occupiers and what they occupy, and argues that they are all logically sound.

Hopefully, having seen that the concept of intensive occupation is certified both by everyday use and can be stated using formal logic, the reader will be willing to rely on it when attempting to make sense of Dōgen's notion of temporality. Nevertheless, we are faced with a rather evident difficulty: is there a difference between occupier and occupied in the paradox as I formulated it at the end of the previous section? Not really, but then we can do without it, given the concept of location. Making sense of this requires that we take a second look at what we have been calling stages, which are defined in terms of their ontological imbrication with a set of pasts and futures. Thus, the present of a certain bud is ontologically determined by its imbrication with its having been a certain seed in its past and its going to be (let us hope) a flower in the future, but not by the present being this or that specific moment; stages, I mean to say, are not determined as occurring at a specific

---

Philosophical Studies 133 (2007a) and "Brutal Simples," in *Oxford Studies in Metaphysics, Vol. 3*, ed. Dean W. Zimmerman (Oxford: Oxford University Press, 2007b); Josh Parsons, "Theories of Location," in *Oxford Studies in Metaphysics, Vol. 3*, ed. by Dean W. Zimmerman (Oxford: Oxford University Press, 2007); Hud Hudson, "Simples and Gunk," *Philosophy Compass* 2, no. 2 (2007), "Multiple Location and Single Location Resurrection," in *Personal Identity and Resurrection. How Do We Survive Our Death?* ed. Georg Gasser (London: Routledge, 2010), and "Transhypertime Identity," in *Mereology and Location*, ed. Shieva Kleinschmidt (London: Oxford University Press, 2014).

[46] For our purposes, we do not need to specify whether the whole is part of itself or not.

[47] These definitions are rather simplistic, both because they assume the question of extensive and intensive occupation is not subject to degrees, and because they assume occupation varies only along the extensive/intensive axis. For more complex definitions that include other varieties of occupation, I cannot recommend enough a careful perusal of Simons, "Where It's At." Although the extensive/intensive axis is not considered in their work, the mereotopology of Roberto Casati and Achille C. Varzi, *Parts and Places. The Structures of Spatial Representation* (Cambridge: The MIT Press, 1999) includes quite useful ideas on the nature of location.

moment, but in relation to other specific stages, regardless of when those specific relations occur, while moments are ontologically independent from whatever stages occur at them. Strange as it may sound, this is nothing but a recapitulation of Dōgen's theses on time: the flow of time is extended over moments, but the flow is determined by its internal relations, while moments are not. This does not mean that there are two "times"; there are, certainly, two levels of temporality, one at which temporality is conceived as relations, the other as the location of those relations, but no new ontological category is introduced. This would be the same as saying that, for one point in space to be to the left of another, there would have to be two spaces, one being the space of relations and the other the space where those relations are located. Of course, in folk metaphysics, this argument does nothing other than prove the evident: spatial relations are spatial facts. But if we add the stream of time's ontological independence to the mixture, we reach our intended result: time as a flow is extended over the moments of time (i.e., is located at a set of moments), but there is no part of the flow corresponding to the moments.

The reader is probably weary of wondering what all the fuss is about, so I will state my main conclusion and add a few more details later: if the flow of time is to be constituted by moments, then moments must be, at least in a very wide sense, its parts; given we tend to assume a mereological isomorphism between what is extended and the points over which it extends, it is almost natural to conclude that the flow of time does have moments as parts. If, though, we assume that the stream of time is intensively extended over moments (i.e., if it is true that for any segment S of the stream and any set M such that, for every moment m at which it is true to say that S occurs, L_iSM), then moments cannot be its parts, and thus cannot constitute the stream of time, which does not mean that there are two distinct times, such that moments belong to one and the stream to the other. The stream of time occurs at moments without being reducible to it. And the whole point of the formal explorations of the last few paragraphs is to prove this is neither contradictory nor as alien to commonsense as one might think.

It is high time I pay a debt I owe since almost the beginning of the chapter: what, then, is a stage if not a part of the stream of time? I see two possible solutions: we can either accept that stages are parts, but assume a strong holism, such that the parts do not constitute the whole but are ontologically grounded upon it,[48] or deny that stages are parts. I will opt for the second and define stages as truth-makers for propositions stating the occurrence of the stream of time at a moment. Truth-makers wear their definition on their sleeves, but, just in case, I should say that a truth-maker is whatever makes a certain proposition true. Thus, rather intuitively, we would say that the truth-maker for "Dōgen is laughing" is Dōgen's laughter, be that

---

[48] It is rather easy to adapt the tools of Jonathan Schaffer, "Monism: The Priority of the Whole," *Philosophical Review* 119, no. 1 (2010) on monism to this specific case. Retaining Pxy as the parthood relation, and adding Dxy = $_{def}$ x (ontologically) depends on y, s = "the stream of time", a predicate for stagehood Hx = $_{def}$Pxs, as well as the predicate "being basic", formalized as Bx = $_{def}$Hx∧¬ ∃y(Hy∧Dxy), then holism is expressed as a specifically temporal variety of monism: (∃!x)(Bx∧Bs).

an Aristotelian accident, a fact, a transient entity, or whatever pleases the reader's ontological palate. The point to notice is that, tempting as it may be (and philosophical theories that haven fallen to this temptation and, with it, into fallacy are not as scarce as one might wish), there is no reason to assume truth-makers are independent entities: we do not need to assume Dōgen's laughter can exist without Dōgen for it to make it true that Dōgen is laughing. Thus, stages can be truth-makers for propositions such as "a certain segment x of the stream of time occurs at moment y" without there having to exist an independent entity endowed with the property stagehood: stages are nothing but the occurrence of the stream of time at a moment, which does not mean the whole stream must then occur. Stages, if you will, are to time what perspectives are to space, and in the same way (*pace* Russell) that perspectives cannot exist without something of which they are perspectives, stages occur only in so far as the stream of time to which they belong occurs. Thus, Dōgen's ontological imbrication is preserved.[49]

This discussion leads the way to the last of our logical asides: Dōgen's insistence on the identity of particular times and the whole of time. As we discussed a while back, misunderstanding this idea can easily result in contradictions, but the problem can be solved without much effort if we take two things into account. The first is the manner in which what are technically called occurrents (processes, events, actions, changes, and, of course, the flow of time) occur: baking a cake, for example, includes mixing ingredients in the proper order, prepping the mold, pouring the batter into the mold, baking the batter, taking the baked cake out of the oven, and feeling quite happy at the end. And yet, when only the very first stage is occurring, it is nevertheless true that the baking is occurring, which does not mean that all the other stages are occurring simultaneously. In fact, for an occurrent to occur, it must be the case that only one if its stages is occurring at a certain moment, while the others are not. Were all of them to occur simultaneously (assuming it possible), we would have a very different entity in our hands. In other words, it is true that a certain occurrent is occurring because only some of its stages are occurring.

Before making use of this, let us introduce our technical concept: relative identity. I will not attempt to argue for its validity, but merely mention that, although we tend to think identity is an "absolute" predicate, a system in which identity is relative to times can be consistently developed.[50] Introducing the concept by means of an everyday example might be helpful: if, for example, I was elected the chairman of a certain committee from 2010 to 2012, and there were other chairmen both

---

[49] The ideas in this paragraph are heavily indebted to Kevin Mulligan, Peter Simons, and Barry Smith, "Truth-Makers," *Philosophy and Phenomenological Research* 44, no. 3 (1984) without pretending to reflect that article's theses.

[50] The *locus classicus* for relative identity is Peter T. Geach, "Identity," *Review of Metaphysics* 21 (1967). A well-developed logical system, from which the formulation in the next footnote is adapted, can be found in George Myro, "Identity and Time," in *Philosophical Grounds of Rationality. Intentions, Categories, Ends*, ed. Richard E. Grandy and Richard Warner (Oxford: Oxford University Press, 1986a) and "Time and Essence," *Midwest Studies in Philosophy* XI (1986b).

before and after me, then it is true to say that, during those two years, the chairman
and I had the relation of identity, despite the fact that, at other times, we did not.
This, of course, implies a modification of Leibniz's law: we can no longer say that
two identical entities share all possible predicates, but only those which apply to
them during the time they were identical. Thus, if the chairman after me had a
healthy and abundant mane, while I stubbornly hold on to what should in all honesty
be called the memory of hair, a traditional account of identity would lead us straight
into a contradiction, since the chairman would both have a full head of hair and
border on absolute baldness. Instead, if we grant that identity is relative to times, we
would be forced to preface each proposition with a quantifier determining the time
range within it was true (or a specific time within that range), and, as long as those
temporal quantifiers are different, no contradiction arises.[51] Returning to Dōgen,
given whatever is true of a stage at a moment is true of the stretch of the stream of
time that occurs at that moment, and that whatever is true of the stretch at that
moment is true of the stage, then, by the inverse of Leibniz's law, we can conclude
that the stretch of the stream and the stage are identical at that moment, without
having to attribute to the stage whatever is true of the stream at other moments. If
we assume that the stream of time is unique, then, for every moment, there is a stage
occurring at that moment such that it is then identical to the whole stream of time.

6 Conclusions

So far, I have argued that a first look at Dōgen's texts implies the existence of at least
two philosophical issues: (P1) how can all times be identical to, or contained within,
a single reference time?; and (P2) how can the "moment priority" theory and the
"stream priority" theory be simultaneously true? After considering Nāgārjuna's
ideas on temporal stages as co-dependently originated, as well as the identity of
nirvāṇa and saṃsāra, we concluded that both problems stem from an attempt to
combine two insights: on the one hand, given entities belonging to the world of
conventional truths are necessarily temporal, and given the co-dependent origination of temporal stages means that the existence of any stage presupposes its specific relations to others (which means the existence of one stage implies the existence
of time as a whole), Dōgen was led to believe that time as it manifests itself in the
realm of conventionality must be understood holistically; on the other hand, given
enlightenment cannot depend on external entities or times (otherwise, it would be
co-dependently arisen), and thus that each moment has to possess its own buddha-
nature, Dōgen was forced to accept that all moments are equally real and contain at
least the possibility of freedom from co-dependent arising. Since none of these

---

[51] Formally, we would say that a well-formed formula including identity must have the form (t)
$(x = y)$, were t is a temporal quantifier and $x = y$ is a place holder for any well-formed formula the
highest ranked operator of which is =. Leibniz's law could then be formulated as the following rule
of deduction: $(t) (x = y), (t) (Fx) \vdash (t) (Fy)$.

truths can be reduced to the other, Dōgen had no option but to argue that both conceptions of time are true. Hence the origin of what we assume is a paradox. At this point, I argued that the paradox only arises if we assume there is, from a mereological perspective, a structural isomorphism between occupiers and what they occupy. Given we can consistently deny this isomorphism, we can conclude that, without contradictions, we can make sense of the stream of time as extended over moments of time without being dependent on them (or constituted by them). Since this implies a distinction between moments and stages, this means we can also consistently affirm stages are dependent on time as a whole while they occur at moments that are ontologically independent. If all this is correct, I have both offered an interpretation of Dōgen's ideas on time that is neither inconsistent nor passes over certain problematic aspects of the text and, having done so by means of analytical and formal tools, proven this specific approach to Dōgen is worthwhile.

Before finishing, I would like to make a brief remark concerning the existential import of my interpretation. As opposed to much of Western religious thinking, Buddhism is often taken to affirm that "paradise" is not a location or plane different from the one we inhabit, but a certain way of being in the world, a way which brings us closer to fundamental reality; in other words, it is often believed that the Buddhist path does not lead to the "other side of reality", but "even closer to this side."[52] In a similar vein, it might be said that traditional Western conceptions of temporality imply that freeing oneself from the pains of mortality implies jumping out of the stream of time into frictionless eternity. If my interpretation of Dōgen is correct, his position is quite the opposite: the buddha-nature is not beyond the reaches of time, but in the moments over which it extends: it is not by all together abandoning the stream of this world that we attain liberation, but by diving ever deeper into time.

Bibliography

Abe, Masao. "The Oneness of Practice and Attainment: Implications for the Relation Between Means and Ends." In *Dōgen Studies*, edited by William LaFleur, 99–111. Honolulu: University of Hawai'i Press, 1985a.

———. "Dōgen on Buddha-Nature." In *Zen and Western Thought*, edited by Masao Abe and William R. LaFleur: 25–68. London: Macmillan, 1985b.

———. "Dōgen's View of Time and Space." *The Eastern Buddhist* 21, no. 2 (1988): 1–35.

———. "God, Emptiness, and the True Self." In *The Buddha Eye. An Anthology of the Kyoto School and Its Contemporaries*, edited by Frederick Franck, 55–68. Bloomington: World Wisdom, 2004.

Casati, Roberto and Achille C. Varzi. *Parts and Places. The Structures of Spatial Representation.* Cambridge: The MIT Press, 1999.

Cotnoir, Aaron J. "Nāgārjuna's Logic." In *The Moon Points Back*, edited by Koji Tanaka, Yasuo Deguchi, Jay L. Garfield, and Graham Priest, 176–88. Oxford: Oxford University Press 2015).

---

[52] *Cf.* Masao Abe, "God, Emptiness, and the True Self," in *The Buddha Eye. An Anthology of the Kyoto School and Its Contemporaries*, ed. Frederick Franck (Bloomington: World Wisdom, 2004).

D'Amato, Mario, Jay L. Garfield, and Tom J. Tillemans, eds. *Pointing at the Moon. Buddhism, Logic, Analytic Philosophy*. Oxford: Oxford University Press, 2009.

Dainton, Barry. "The Experience of Time and Change." *Philosophy Compass* 3, no. 4 (2008a): 619–638.

———. "Sensing Change." *Philosophical Issues* 18 (2008b): 362–384.

Deguchi, Yasuo. "A Mountain by Any Other Name: A Response to Koji Tanaka." *Philosophy East and West* 63, no. 3 (2013): 335–343.

———. "Constructing a Logic of Emptiness: Nishitani, Jízāng, and Paraconsistency." In *The Moon Points Back*, edited by Koji Tanaka, Yasuo Deguchi, Jay L. Garfield, and Graham Priest, 150–75. Oxford: Oxford University Press, 2015.

Deguchi, Yasuo, Jay L. Garfield, and Graham Priest. "The Way of the Dialetheist: Contradiction in Buddhism." *Philosophy East and West* 58, no. 3 (2003): 395–402.

Dōgen. n.d. *Shōbōgenzō: The True Dharma-Eye Treasury*. Translated by Gudo Wafu Nishijima and Chodo Cross. Taishō edition. 4 vols. Moraga: BDK America.

Galton, Antony. "Time Flies But Space Does Not: Limits to the Spatialization of Time." *Journal of Pragmatics* 43 (2011): 695–703.

Ganeri, Jonardon. *Attention, Not Self*. Oxford: Oxford University Press, 2017.

Garfield, Jay L. *The Fundamental Wisdom of the Middle Way. Nāgārjuna's Mūlamadhyamakakārikā*. Oxford: Oxford University Press, 1995.

Garfield, Jay L. and Graham Priest. "Nāgārjuna and the Limits of Thought." *Philosophy East and West* 53, no. 1 (2003): 1–21.

———. "Mountains are Just Mountains." In *Pointing at the Moon. Buddhism, Logic, Analytic Philosophy*, edited by Mario D'Amato, Jay L. Garfield, and Tom J. Tillemans, 71–82. Oxford: Oxford University Press, 2009.

Geach, Peter T. "Identity." *Review of Metaphysics* 21 (1967): 3–12.

Heine, Steven. "Temporality of Hermeneutics in Dōgen's *Shōbōgenzō*." *Philosophy East and West* 33, no. 2 (1983): 139–147.

———. *Existential and Ontological Dimensions of Time in Heidegger and Dōgen*. Albany: SUNY Press, 1985.

Hudson, Hud. "Simples and Gunk." Philosophy Compass 2, no. 2 (2007): 291–302.

———. "Multiple Location and Single Location Resurrection." In *Personal Identity and Resurrection. How Do We Survive Our Death?* Edited by Georg Gasser, 87–102. London: Routledge, 2010.

———. "Transhypertime Identity." In *Mereology and Location*. Edited by Shieva Kleinschmidt, 135–155. London: Oxford University Press, 2014.

McDaniel, Kris. "Extended Simples." *Philosophical Studies* 133 (2007a):131–141.

———. "Brutal Simples." In *Oxford Studies in Metaphysics*, 3, edited by Dean W. Zimmerman, 233–266. Oxford: Oxford University Press, 2007b.

Mulligan, Kevin, Peter Simons, and Barry Smith. "Truth-Makers." *Philosophy and Phenomenological Research* 44, no. 3 (1984): 287–321.

Myro, George. "Identity and Time." In *Philosophical Grounds of Rationality. Intentions, Categories, Ends*, edited by Richard E. Grandy and Richard Warner, 383–410. Oxford: Oxford University Press, 1986a.

———. "Time and Essence." *Midwest Studies in Philosophy* XI (1986b): 331–341.

Nolan, Daniel. "Balls and All." In *Mereology and Location*, edited by Shieva Kleinschmidt, 69–90. London: Oxford University Press, 2014.

Parsons, Josh. "Theories of Location." In *Oxford Studies in Metaphysics*, 3, edited by Dean W. Zimmerman, 201–232. Oxford: Oxford University Press, 2007.

Priest, Graham. *The Fifth Corner of Four: An Essay on Buddhist Metaphysics and the Catuṣkoṭi*. Oxford: Oxford University Press, 2018.

Raud, Rein. "'Place' and 'Being-Time': Spatiotemporal Concepts in the Thought of Nishida Kitarō and Dōgen Kigen." *Philosophy East and West* 54, no. 1 (2004): 29–51.

————. "The Existential Moment: Rereading Dōgen's Theory of Time." *Philosophy East and West* 62, no. 2 (2012): 153–173.

Saucedo, Raul. "Parthood and Location." In *Oxford Studies in Metaphysics,* 6, Karen Bennett and Dean W. Zimmerman, 225–284. Oxford: Oxford University Press, 2011.

Schaffer, Jonathan. "Monism: The Priority of the Whole." *Philosophical Review* 119, no. 1 (2010): 31–76.

Simons, Peter. "Extended Simples: A Third Way Between Atoms and Gunk." *The Monist* 87, (2004): 371–384.

————. "Where It's At: Modes of Occupation and Kinds of Occupant." In *Mereology and Location*, edited by Shieva Kleinschmidt, 59–68. London: Oxford University Press, 2014.

Stambaugh, Joan. *Impermanence Is Buddha-Nature: Dōgen's Understanding of Temporality.* Honolulu: University of Hawai'i Press, 1990.

Tanaka, Koji. "Contradictions in Dōgen." *Philosophy East and West* 63, no. 2 (2013): 322–334.

The Cowherds. *Moonshadows: Conventional Truth in Buddhist Philosophy.* Oxford: Oxford University Press, 2010.

Vorenkamp, Dirck. "B-Series Temporal Order in Dōgen's Theory of Time." *Philosophy East and West* 45, no. 3 (1995): 387–408.

A Philosophical Endeavour: The Practice of Time in Dōgen and Marcus Aurelius

Laurentiu Andrei

1 Introduction

One of the major religious figures of the Japanese Sōtō School of Zen, the Buddhist monk Dōgen 道元 (1200–1253) has also been described as one of the most important premodern Japanese philosophers. The first philosophical approach to Dōgen's writings was that of Watsuji Tetsurō 和辻哲郎 (1889–1960) in his seminal article *Shamon Dōgen* (沙門道元), *The monk Dōgen*.[1] It was Watsuji that took Dōgen's writings out of the exclusive reach of the sectarians and highlighted their philosophical character. Soon after, Tanabe Hajime 田辺元 (1885–1962), who closely followed the footsteps of Watsuji, advocated for a philosophical approach to Dōgen's texts and drew the attention of philosophers and historians of ideas.[2] A question was inevitably raised: could Dōgen be approached as a philosopher or should he rather be considered as a leading figure in the history of Japanese Buddhism? This question was the topic of a crucial collection of articles published in 1985.[3] Among the authors, some have sought to highlight the value of a historical approach to Dōgen's texts describing him as an important religious figure but also

---

[1] Watsuji, *Shamon Dōgen*, in *Nihon seishinshi kenkyū*, 9th ed. Tōkyō: Iwanami Shoten, 1998.

[2] Tanabe, *Shōbōgenzō no tetsugaku shikan* (正法眼蔵の哲学私観) (Tōkyō: Iwanami Shoten, 1939). On this point see Müller (2006, 2009).

[3] LaFleur, ed. *Dōgen Studies* (Honolulu: University of Hawaii Press, 1985).

L. Andrei (✉)
Philosophies et Rationalités – Université Clermont-Auvergne, Clermont-Ferrand, France
e-mail: laurentiu.andrei@inventati.org

as a failed politician.[4] Others, while recognizing the relevance of a philosophical reading of Dōgen and describing him as "the incomparable philosopher", tried to show the inadequacy of the comparative method to account for Dōgen's writings in a way that could make sense to a Western philosopher.[5] More recently, however, studies have argued in favour of a comparative and philosophical approach.[6] Nonetheless, the question of how to read his texts is still in place[7] and testifies to the difficulty of a philosophical approach to Dōgen's writings.

In order to address this question, I propose to consider Dōgen's case as part of a larger issue that appeared in Buddhist Studies concerning the question of whether certain texts pertaining to the Buddhist canon are to be qualified as philosophical or not. In an attempt to deal with this problem, several comparisons were made between texts of the Buddhist tradition and texts belonging to the Hellenistic period, notably those of the Stoic sect.[8] My argument is consistent with this kind of comparative approach and entails a *technical conception of philosophy*[9], i.e., philosophy understood as an art/skill/technique (τέχνη). It will probe a paradigmatic example of "spiritual exercise"[10] – that I call the *practice of time* – focused on the idea of impermanence (*mujō* 無常) and change (μεταβολή) that appears in some of Dōgen's writings and in the *Meditations* of the Roman emperor Marcus Aurelius (121–180) in order to show that they are both engaged in a similar philosophical endeavour.

2   Philosophy: A Technical Conception

The question of how to read Dōgen's texts can be seen as pertaining to a larger issue concerning the way to approach Buddhist texts. Inside Buddhist Studies a tenacious tendency has been noted: the refusal to qualify as "philosophical" certain literature from the Buddhist canon.[11] Among the main reasons invoked, the idea that philoso-

---

[4] Bielefeldt, "Recarving the Dragon: History and Dogma in the Study of Dōgen", *Dōgen Studies* (Honolulu: University of Hawaii Press. 1985), 49.

[5] Kasulis, "The Incomparable Philosopher: Dōgen on How to Read the Shōbōgenzō", *Dōgen Studies* (Honolulu: University of Hawaii Press, 1985), 83.

[6] Kopf, "'When All Dharmas Are the Buddha-Dharma' Dōgen as Comparative Philosopher", *Dōgen and Sōtō Zen*, ed. Heine (Oxford, New York: Oxford University Press; 2015).

[7] (Steineck 2018).

[8] Kapstein, "'Spiritual Exercise' and Buddhist Epistemologists in India and Tibet". In *A Companion to Buddhist Philosophy*, 2013a) 270–89; and idem., "Stoics and Bodhisattvas: Spiritual Exercise and Faith in Two Philosophical Traditions". In *Ancients and Moderns: Essays in Honor of Pierre Hadot*, 2013b), 99–115.

[9] I borrow this expression from John Sellars, *The Art of Living: The Stoics on the Nature and Function of Philosophy*. 2nd ed. (London: Bristol Classical Press, 2009).

[10] An expression that Pierre Hadot takes from the Jesuit father Ignatius of Loyola and re-actualises in a specific way. See Hadot, *Exercices spirituels et philosophie antique* (Paris: Albin Michel. 2002).

[11] Eltschinger, "Pierre Hadot et les 'exercices spirituels': Quel modèle pour la philosophie bouddhique tardive?", *Asiatische Studien / Études Asiatiques*, 62(2) (2008), 485–544.

phy, from its Greek origins, is to be understood as a truth seeking activity taking place primarily in argumentative (or systematic) writings and/or debates concerned with giving rigorous rational arguments and solving problems. Accordingly, leaving aside all practical considerations, one should only consider as philosophical those texts that imply a theoretical endeavour and an argumentative rigour.

In a similar vein, Raji C. Steineck writes in his contribution to the present volume that "philosophy comes with the expectation of free reasoned discourse, in which the addresser is expected to convince the addressee by way of argument and reason".[12] Steineck doubts that a philosophical approach is the most appropriate one to engage Buddhist texts such as Dōgen's. In a previous paper, he argued that Dōgen's endeavour is not a philosophical one. To his view, among other criteria, the "philosophical style of communication (…) is one of disputation among a community of equals".[13] Insofar as Dōgen occupies an authoritative position (the master) from which he transmits the indisputably right path to his community of disciples, considering him as a philosopher would conceal the fact that he was rather committed to an "extra-philosophical project"[14] that is to transmit the way of life of the Enlightened, the Buddha Way (butsudō 仏道). Steineck opposes this to philosophy: "to practice the Buddha Way (as proposed by Dōgen) is not to do philosophy, and to do philosophy is not to practice the Buddha Way",[15] considering that "philosophy is above all an intellectual enterprise with a strong theoretical bent".[16] Therefore, understanding any of the Shōbōgenzō's (正法眼蔵) fascicles as philosophical could be misleading. Indeed, as Tanabe, many have read Dōgen as "an existential philosopher avant la lettre – a Japanese medieval Heidegger".[17] On this point, I entirely agree with him. However, if Steineck's argument has the considerable merit of preventing superficial or careless readings of, and hasty comparisons between, Dōgen's writings and those of some representatives of philosophy in vogue during Meiji Japan, it is a conception that has also the disadvantage of putting outside the philosophical field what is there from the outset: an ascetic, theological/cosmological and ethical dimension oriented towards the injunction of a constant re-evaluation of the relationship with oneself and the world that entails self-control and self-transformation.

Indeed, if such purely theoretical criteria were strictly to be applied to texts belonging to the Hellenistic period, such as those of Epicurus, or those of the Stoic tradition, such as the writings of Arrien reporting the teaching of his master Epictetus, etc., it would be difficult to understand their place in the ancient philosophical schools, and thus to properly interpret them. According to Pierre Hadot, in

---

[12] Steineck present volume, 222.
[13] Steineck, "A Zen Philosopher? – Notes on the Philosophical Reading of Dōgen's Shōbōgenzō " (2018), 582.
[14] Steineck present volume, 224.
[15] Steineck, "A Zen Philosopher? – Notes on the Philosophical Reading of Dōgen's Shōbōgenzō " (2018), 597.
[16] Steineck, "A Zen Philosopher? – Notes on the Philosophical Reading of Dōgen's Shōbōgenzō " (2018), 580.
[17] Steineck present volume, 217.

the ancient Greek world, philosophy implied adopting a certain way of life, often in a community where the disciples lived with a master. The master helps his disciples to achieve moral progress through theoretical teaching, but this only makes sense if it can bring serenity, in other words, if it has a therapeutic or soteriological dimension.[18] In this context, there is no separation between philosophical discourse and philosophy as a way of life. Thus, one cannot understand and interpret these discourses by simply analysing their structure independently of the life of the philosopher who deployed them.[19] The idea of a close relationship between philosophy and biography is, I will argue, relevant in the case of Dōgen who, as a Zen master, used pedagogical, rhetorical and psychological strategies in his written and spoken discourses aimed at transforming his disciples in accordance with the Buddha Way. While argumentation is part of his strategies, it is not an end in itself, but one of several means to enable spiritual progress on the path to enlightenment.

Following this line of thought, I consider that in order to judge the philosophical status of a text pertaining to an ancient tradition (and beyond), a strictly theoretical conception of philosophy remains highly debatable. I will thus argue that the whole issue of determining what is or is not to be considered as philosophical is related precisely to this debatable aspect inside the history of philosophy that Meiji-era (明治時代) intellectuals seem to have generally omitted[20]. So, in my view, the issue is not, as Steineck claims, to decide whether it is better to read and translate Dōgen as a philosopher or not, but rather to determine what conception of philosophy allows one to approach his writings (and by the same token of other Buddhist texts) without distorting the soteriological and paideutical dimension of those texts. As pointed out by Kapstein, from a more general perspective, the difficulty is obviously a definitional one: "we cannot ask ourselves what Buddhist philosophy might be without at the same time asking what it is that we mean by 'philosophy'"[21]. In order to deal with this problem, several attempts were made to parallel Buddhist texts and philosophical texts from the Hellenistic period, notably those of the Stoic tradition[22]. When it comes to Japan, my argument is to say that if the question concerning the

---

[18] Hadot, *Pierre Hadot: L'enseignement des antiques, l'enseignement des modernes.* ed. A. I. Davidson and F. Worms, (Paris: Rue d'Ulm. 2010b), 21.

[19] Hadot, *Qu'est-ce que la philosophie antique?* (Paris, Folio, Essais. 1995), 21.

[20] On this point see below.

[21] Kapstein, *Reason's Traces: Identity and Interpretation in Indian and Tibetan Buddhist Thought* (Boston: Wisdom Publications, 2001), 4. This question is addressed *in extenso* by Wrisley in his "Dōgen as Philosopher, Dōgen's Philosophical Zen" presented at the workshop, "Dōgen's texts: Manifesting philosophy and/as/of religion?" January 21–23, 2021. Available at: https://www.georgewrisley.com/Do%CC%84gen%20as%20Philosopher,%20Do%CC%84gen%E2%80%99s%20Philosophical%20Zen-Wrisley.pdf

[22] See for instance Bouquet, "Stoics and Buddhists", *Philosophical Quarterly*, n° 33 (1961), 205-21; Gowans, "Medical Analogies in Buddhist and Hellenistic Thought: Tranquillity and Anger", *Roy. Inst. Philos. Suppl. Royal Institute of Philosophy Supplement* 66 (2010), 11–33; and Kapstein, "'Spiritual Exercise' and Buddhist Epistemologists in India and Tibet". In *A Companion to Buddhist Philosophy*, 2013) 270–89; and idem., "Stoics and Bodhisattvas: Spiritual Exercise and Faith in Two Philosophical Traditions". In *Ancients and Moderns: Essays in Honor of Pierre Hadot*, 2013b), 99–115.

nature and definition of philosophy, as it arose among Meiji intellectuals, faced a rejection of the idea that there was any such thing as philosophy in Japan before that time,[23] it is in all likelihood because of an oversight or rather an omission with regard to the above-mentioned debate inside the Western history of philosophy. This debate, which will be outlined here briefly, concerns mainly the opposition between a theoretical conception of philosophy (concerned with argument and knowledge) and a technical/ascetic one (that emphasises a way of life based on a specific philosophical training/skill and not only knowledge). While the latter places the philosopher's life at the centre of his or her activity, the former relates rather to a disembodied and impersonal endeavour.

The issue emerged in relation to Socrates in Hegel's *Vorlesungen über die Geschichte der Philosophie*. Indeed, the German philosopher faced the problem of how to discuss the case of Socrates. Hegel thought philosophy was to be understood "as a matter of universal thought directed towards truth"[24] and thus he considered it to be detached from the life of an individual, from his or her biography[25]. This problem relates to a definition of philosophy that goes back to Aristotle. According to the Stagirite, philosophy was to be understood as a matter of λόγος: a way to give a rational account of the world's principles and causes[26]. The resulting knowledge (ἐπιστήμη) being of theoretical or intellectual nature cannot be considered to have any impact on the life of someone who possesses this knowledge[27]. However, as it has been pointed out by John Sellars, Aristotle forged this definition in opposition to the Socratic conception of philosophy as an art/technique (τέχνη) concerning one's way of life (βίος).[28] Following the work of predecessors such as Pierre Hadot and Michel Foucault, Sellars argues that this conception of philosophy as an art of living (τέχνη περὶ τὸν βίον) of Socratic origin takes root in Stoic school.[29] According to the Stoics, philosophy is a technical activity based on a close association of theory (λόγος) and exercises (ἄσκησις) to be carried out in accordance with the theory.[30] As Sellars further explains, a "(…) technical conception of philosophy conceives philosophical knowledge (ἐπιστήμη) as technical knowledge, its paradigm being the kind of knowledge found in an art or craft (τέχνη). This is clearly

---

[23] Maraldo *Japanese Philosophy in the Making 1: Crossing Paths with Nishida* (Nagoya: CreateSpace, 2017), 29.

[24] Sellars, *The Art of Living: The Stoics on the Nature and Function of Philosophy*. 2nd ed. (London: Bristol Classical Press, 2009), 1.

[25] From the Greek word βίος which primally means 'manner of life'. See Sellars, *The Art of Living: The Stoics on the Nature and Function of Philosophy*. 2nd ed. (London: Bristol Classical Press. 2009), 1, n. 6.

[26] Sellars refers to Aristotle, *Metaphysics* 981b5–6.

[27] This does not mean however that Aristotle neglected philosophical training. On the contrary he also insisted on the importance of cultivating the virtues in order to lead a good life.

[28] Sellars, *The Art of Living: The Stoics on the Nature and Function of Philosophy*. 2nd ed. (London: Bristol Classical Press, 2009), 50 sqq.

[29] Ibid., 54.

[30] Ibid., 9.

very different from an account of philosophy in which knowledge (ἐπιστήμη) is conceived as rational explanation or intellectual analysis (λόγος). It is particularly important to be precise here. In attempts to draw a distinction between philosophy primarily concerned with theoretical knowledge and philosophy primarily concerned with practical wisdom, an implicitly Aristotelian distinction is sometimes drawn between ἐπιστήμη and φρόνησις. While the former is said to focus upon a rational understanding of the world, the latter is said to focus upon how one should act. For the Stoics, there is no conceptual distinction between knowledge (ἐπιστήμη) and wisdom (φρόνησις, σοφία). Presenting philosophy as something concerned with one's life does not involve a rejection or devaluation of theoretical or scientific knowledge (ἐπιστήμη) but rather a different conception of such a knowledge" – a technical knowledge that can be acquired by exercise (ἄσκησις) and can be transposed into one's actions (ἔργα) as prosaic as they might be.[31] Insofar as Dōgen placed great emphasis on the study and practice (sangaku 参学) of the Buddhist teachings, I believe that such a technical conception of philosophy allows us to approach him as a philosopher while including religious and even political aspects of his life[32].

As generally acknowledged by historians, Dōgen was a Buddhist monk of the Kamakura period (鎌倉時代), considered to be the founder of the Zen Sōtō sect (曹洞宗) in Japan. The traditional sectarian narrative relates that he was born into a family of the Kyōto aristocracy and lost his parents at a very young age.[33] A tragic event that may have made him aware of the impermanence of all things that later led him to recommend meditation on impermanence to strengthen the commitment to pursue the Buddhist path. A commitment that seems to have led Dōgen to undertake a spiritual journey to China where he experienced enlightenment under his master Tiāntóng Rújìng (天童如淨) (1163–1228) and to assume the mission to transmit the Buddhist teachings on his return to Japan. Regardless of their historical accuracy, these few biographical details that appear in some of his writings (or attributed to him)[34] show that (way of) life and teaching ought not to be seen as separated in his case. In the same vein, it is not insignificant to recall for the sake of the present argument that Dōgen's major writing, the Shōbōgenzō (正法眼蔵), may have been seen in Japanese culture as a precursor to a literary form of expression known as watakushi-shōsetsu or shi-shōsetsu (私小説), namely "novel of the I", because of Dōgen's idiosyncratic and prominent use of the first-person pronoun.[35] Far from being a simple detail, this usage of the first-person narrative present in Dōgen's writings is an important point to keep in mind when considering the important connection between an individual's philosophy and his or her way of living (βίος) that

---

[31] Ibid., 171.

[32] Regarding the way of considering philosophy from an Aristotelian perspective in relation to Dōgen's approach, cf. Wrisley, "Dōgen as Philosopher."

[33] Bowring, "Biography of Dōgen", Brill Encyclopedia of Buddhism II (2019), 933–40.

[34] See for instance Hōkyōki (寶慶記) and Bendōwa (辨道話).

[35] Faure, Chan Insights and Oversights: an Epistemological Critique of the Chan Tradition (Princeton: Princeton UP, 1996), 248, n. 4.

existed in the world of Greco-Roman antiquity.[36] In fact, when it comes to the more general question of how to read ancient texts or even to discuss ancient figures that have not produced any writings, and in Dōgen's particular case as well, it can be most useful to relate way of life (biography) and philosophy.

Considering Marcus Aurelius case, it is acknowledged that he wrote a series of notes reassembled and preserved in the *editio princeps* titled *Ta eis heauton*, meaning *To himself*[37]. These notes do not have any particular order, and they concern various personal reflections on a wide range of topics such as the importance of having good masters, the dangers of erudition, the importance of meditating on the perpetual change of all things, what is it that we call a self, etc. It worth noting that all these topics can be found in the writings Dōgen addressed to his religious community. In the case of Marcus Aurelius, nothing can lead us to believe that these unstructured notes, which have nothing to do with a philosophical treatise, were destined for anything other than private usage. So, how are we to read these private notes of a statesman who seems to have a special acquaintance with the philosophy of the Stoic school? Is Marcus to be considered as a Stoic philosopher or just as a powerful emperor who had an interest in Stoic philosophy? This kind of questions has been raised mostly by historians, for it has been noted that the general tendency to situate the Roman emperor in the ranks of the philosophers of the Stoic sect stemmed precisely from a philosophical reading of these texts.[38] Some argued that the writings of the Roman emperor are not really philosophical but rather represent a certain ethical usage of the *logoi philosophoi* peculiar to the Stoic doctrine, considered from the point of view of their effectiveness and not of their truth. For Pierre Versperini, this resembles the case of a modern European who would make use of Chinese medicine without recognizing oneself as a disciple of Lao Zi.[39] In any event, this is interesting precisely because the question of whether Marcus' writings are philosophical has been raised. I thus argue that a comparison with Dōgen's case may prove to be a very relevant tool in order to account for a philosophical approach to their respective writings.

One might wonder however what justifies a comparison between the writings of a Buddhist monk at the head of a religious community and those of a Roman emperor? Their scope appears indeed to be different: if the latter writes for himself in order to lead a philosophical life according to the principles of the Stoic sect, the former has more of a religious and soteriological aim, as he writes in order to teach

---

[36] Sellars, *The Art of Living: The Stoics on the Nature and Function of Philosophy*, 2nd ed. (London: Bristol Classical Press. 2009).

[37] On this point see Sellars, "Marcus Aurelius and the Tradition of Spiritual Exercises". Forthcoming in Garani, Konstan, and Reydams-Schils, eds. *The Oxford Handbook of Roman Philosophy* (New York: Oxford UP, 2021).

[38] See Vesperini, *Droiture et mélancolie : Sur les écrits de Marc Aurèle* (Lagrasse: Editions Verdier, 2016).

[39] Vesperini assertion that Chinese medicine is peculiar to Taoist philosophy remains however highly problematic. See Vesperini, *Droiture et mélancolie : Sur les écrits de Marc Aurèle* (Lagrasse: Editions Verdier, 2016), 23.

the Buddhist doctrine to his community[40]. Despite this difference between a personal level discourse and a community addressed one, it is worth mentioning that the soteriological dimension is in no way lacking in the writings of the Roman emperor. Indeed, as a true follower of Stoicism, Marcus never ceases to refer in his writings to the constant relationship one should cultivate with the divine nature of all there is in order to lead a good life, freed from trouble and suffering. In this respect he refers to the philosophical discourses of the Stoic doctrine where theological and soteriological aspects are strongly embedded[41]. Therefore, the difference here between a religious and philosophical scope of a discourse is to be handled *cum grano salis*[42].

Two more arguments account for the interest of this comparison. The first is that the two authors insist on a special kind of spiritual training that consists of becoming aware of the impermanence of all things. The second argument concerns the idiosyncratic way in which Dōgen and Marcus reiterate and re-appropriate theoretical principles of their respective doctrinal traditions within an ascetic perspective. Not surprisingly, this kind of comparison has already been suggested by the French scholar Pierre Hadot – despite the reticence he may previously have had towards comparative philosophy – in the preface to one of the French translations of *Shōbōgenzō*[43]. According to Hadot, in Marcus and Dōgen's writings, we can detect an important link between the practice of philosophy in the form of written discourse (that echoes and reinterprets doctrinal elements) and the possibility of a transformation of life in accordance with the principles conveyed by the doctrinal tradition in question. In other words, in both cases we are dealing with a strong relationship between philosophy and way of life. Steineck is right then when he writes that what matters for Dōgen is to "enter the Buddhist path and model one's life and thoughts after that of the Buddhas and patriarchs",[44] but from the perspective of a technical conception of philosophy, this is rather an argument in favour of

---

[40] In this respect, Epictetus would appear to be a better candidate for such a comparative analysis between Buddhism and Stoicism. Indeed, though he never wrote any philosophical texts, he taught Stoic philosophy to a community of disciples. But, as I have no knowledge of any contestation in the history of Western philosophy of his statute of representative of Stoic philosophy, I think that for the sake of the present argument the case of Marcus is a better choice, as doubt was raised when it came to the question whether to count him among the Stoic philosophers or not. See infra.

[41] However, this aspect will not be insisted upon in the present paper.

[42] On this point cf. Wrisley, "Dōgen as Philosopher."

[43] There he writes: "Yoko Orimo a étudié avec une grande finesse et une grande subtilité la manière d'écrire de Dôgen. Elle dit notamment: '*L'écrit, l'action transformatrice de l'écriture, n'a pas pour Dôgen une valeur simplement descriptive, prescriptive ou doctrinale – il s'agit d'un acte performatif ou plus simplement d'une pratique qui est aussi un geste d'actualisation par lequel la tradition appartient au présent...*' Nous pouvons comprendre cela, si nous nous rappelons qu'une telle action formatrice et transformatrice de l'écriture se trouve par exemple dans l'écrit de l'empereur Marc Aurèle adressé à lui-même. Lui aussi reprend parfois les dits des philosophes qui l'ont précédé, mais aussi et surtout le dogmes traditionnels du stoïcisme, pour créer en lui la disposition intérieure qui l'entraînera à vivre selon la Raison." See Hadot in Orimo, *Le Shōbōgenzō de maître Dōgen* (Vannes: Sully. 2004), 15.

[44] Steineck present volume, 212.

a philosophical approach to Dōgen and not the other way around. My argument is to say that if a technical conception of philosophy opens up the possibility of counting Marcus among the Stoic philosophers, it should, for the same reasons, lead us to consider Dōgen as an eminent representative of Buddhist philosophy, understood as way of life shaped by the theoretical principles transmitted within Buddhist teaching.

3 A Paradigmatic Example: Meditation on Impermanence and Change

3.1 The Practice of Time

What I call the "practice of time" is a spiritual exercise common to both Stoic and Buddhist traditions that consists in meditating on impermanence and change. It is indeed an important philosophical training insofar as Stoic and Buddhist literature converge upon the idea that there is nothing in the world whose existence is not transitory, reality as a whole is characterised by change and impermanence.

From the Buddhist perspective all forms of existence (*issai hō* 一切法) emerge only in the dynamics of a universal causal interdependence called dependent arising (*engi* 縁起) and for that very reason each and every form of existence bears the following marks or characteristics: impermanence (*mujō* 無常), suffering (*ku* 苦) and absence of self (*muga* 無我). This is how the perpetual change of all things and phenomena is described by the doctrine of dependent arising[45]: as things and phenomena occur momentarily through the conjunction of causes and conditions, they lack any substantial core. Their so-called existence is thus regarded as empty, without self (non-self), and as such they are evanescent, impermanent. The idea of emptiness joins here that of causality[46]. All is empty and nothing lasts. Not grasping the sense of impermanence leads inevitably to suffering. However, impermanence is not itself considered as a cause of suffering. This cause is to be found in ignorance (*mumyō* 無明)[47] of the impermanent character of things and phenomena, given their interdependent existence and thus their emptiness. Suffering appears precisely where there is confusion between permanent and impermanent. Because of this confusion, one longs for permanence and becomes attached to oneself. Meditating on impermanence becomes thus crucial in order to overcome this attachment that stems from a lack of discernment on the true nature of things. Grasping the truth of

---

[45] The Buddhist *credo* is to believe that the one who becomes Buddha is able to realise the dependent arising of all things under the form of a chain of twelve causes (*jūni innen* 十二因縁).

[46] Dependent arising is equated to emptiness especially in the Mādhyamika school (Nāgārjuna, *Mk.* 24.18).

[47] According to *Saṃyutta-nikāya* (II, 94–95), one of the oldest texts, the causal sequence begins with ignorance (*mumyō* 無明)

impermanence is nothing less than to reach the very nature of enlightenment (*busshō*仏性). Such goes in sum the Buddhist doctrine (*buppō*仏法).[48]

Dōgen acknowledges these doctrinal principles in the fascicle *Busshō* (仏性), following the example of Huìnéng (慧能) (638–713):

> The Sixth Ancestor addressed his follower Xing Chang, saying, "'Impermanence' means the Buddha-nature. 'Permanence' means the mind that discriminates all the dharmas, good and bad." The "impermanence" spoken of by the Sixth Ancestor is not what is calculated by the likes of the alien paths and two vehicles. The two vehicles and the alien paths, from first founder to final follower, may say it is impermanent, but they do not exhaust it. Therefore, impermanence itself preaching, practising, and verifying impermanence – they are all impermanent.[49]

Beyond the polemical and sectarian aspect of this passage, it can be noted that, in interpreting Huìnéng's words, Dōgen takes on a bias that could be called psychological, inasmuch as it is a question of relating the problem to the capacities of the mind. The untrained mind tends to oppose things and to consider them as having a permanent nature. On the contrary, according to the Buddhist teachings, only a trained mind can be purged of simplistic discrimination: long/short, noble/commoner, etc. Through training, the mind can be liberated from illusions and became able to access reality as it is, as it appears in the light of the Buddha-nature (*busshō*仏性), i.e., impermanent:

> Therefore, grasses, trees, thickets and groves are impermanent and this is Buddha-nature; humans and things, body and mind are impermanent – because they are Buddha-nature. Lands, mountains, and rivers are impermanent – this is Buddha-nature. *Annuttara-samyak-saṃbodhi*, because it is Buddha-nature, is impermanent; the great *parinirvāṇa*, because it is impermanent, is Buddha-nature.[50]

For Dōgen, only a trained mind can grasp the equation between impermanence (*mujō* 無常) and Buddha-nature (*busshō* 仏性), knowledge of the Buddha's true teachings (*shōbō*正法):

> When learning the Buddhist path, what is difficult to see and to hear is the skill/technique of the mind according to the right dharma.[51]

In the example here under discussion the Buddhist training clearly concerns a spiritual exercise, a skill/technique of the mind (*shinjutsu* 心術). In order to give an account, Dōgen refers to the Indian Buddhist Patriarch Nāgārjuna who taught that

[48]Yorizumi, *Dōgen: jiko, jikan, sekai wa dono yōni seiritsu suru no ka* (Tōkyō: Nihon Hōsō Shuppan Kyōkai. 2005), 48, 71.

[49]Kawamura (ed.), *Dōgen zenji zenshū* (here after DZZ) I, 24 sqq (Tōkyō: Shunjūsha. 1988). Translation: Bielefeldt, Sōtō Zen Text Project 2010.

[50]DZZ 1, 25. Translation modified.

[51]DZZ 1, 280. All the other translations of DZZ are mine.

meditating on impermanence is equivalent to adopting the mind of enlightenment (*hotsu-bodaishin* 発菩提心)[52]:

> The mind of enlightenment receives many names, but this mind is one mind. The Patriarch Nāgārjuna said: "The mind that meditates on the perpetual arising and decaying of things and thus sees the impermanence of the world is also called the mind of enlightenment". Therefore, should we rely on this mind for a while and call it the mind of enlightenment? When we truly meditate on impermanence, the mind of me and mine does not occur, nor do thoughts of fame and profit arise. Frightened by the speed of time, it matters to train according to the Way as if a fire were burning on your head.[53]

Recalling the words of an important figure of the Buddhist tradition is a way to highlight the importance of this specific training of the mind in order to overcome the fear of death and the suffering that it generates. This training consists precisely in a meditation on impermanence, on arising and decaying (life and death) of all there is (*sekan no shōmetsu mujō wo kanzuru shin*世間の生滅無常を観ずる心). Elsewhere, Dōgen explains that mind is under control (*jōshin* 調心) when it easily grasps the meaning of impermanence[54]. This unobstructed mind (*shin jizai* 心自在)[55] is the mind of enlightenment (*hotsu-bodaishin* 発菩提心), a firm resolution to renounce all thoughts of fame and interest which precedes the practice of the Buddha Way (*butsudō* 仏道), the intention to attain the state of the Buddha. Meditation on impermanence is thus the first step on the path to liberation from suffering, and as such it has an important soteriological dimension. We can read this essential step on the Buddhist path as a practice of time implying self-detachment, that is detachment (*datsuraku* 脱落) from the wrong conception of me and mine (*waga* 吾我), from body and mind (*shinjin* 身心). In sum, for Dōgen, the Buddhist path is about self-transformation through learning and practising (*sangaku* 参学す) doctrinal principles leading to the liberated state of the Buddha. The urgent character of this endeavour, expressed by the image of a fire on the head (*zunen* 頭燃), is an aspect that will be analysed later on.

Let's turn now to the Stoic doctrine according to which all things are in perpetual change (μεταβολή). This is due to the activity of the divine breath through matter, an activity that animates the world such that living organisms are constantly transforming. There is here a significant cosmological difference between Stoic and Buddhist doctrines. Indeed, if in the Stoic case we are dealing with a cosmology in which the constitution and functioning of the world are based on divine activity that causally determines the whole world movement, from the Buddhist perspective this

---

[52] This notion which translates the Sanskrit *bodhicitta* and refers to the thought/intention of enlightenment (*cittotpāda*) that the future *bodhisattva* formulates when taking his vows and which consists above all in the tenacious will to attain enlightenment for the benefit of all. This state of mind translates the primary aspiration to bring about and develop a profoundly altruistic attitude towards all living beings. But only through the practice of virtues and constant training, the thought/intention of enlightenment matures and the *bodhisattva* can attain perfect enlightenment (*anuttarā-samyak-saṃbodhi*) (Cornu 2006).

[53] DZZ 5, 15.

[54] DZZ 3, 263.

[55] DZZ 2, 403.

can absolutely not be the case because there is nothing in the whole world determined by divine causation. As mentioned above, Buddhists hold in contrast to the Stoics that all comes from an impersonal causal law of dependent arising. Nevertheless, in spite of this major difference at the doctrinal/theoretical level, Stoic training is tantamount to the Buddhist one insofar as it concerns an exercise of meditation on the ephemeral character of things. One of the most important examples of this spiritual exercise is to be found in the writings of Marcus Aurelius. In order to live a good life, which from the Stoic perspective means tuning into the changing course of the world determined by the causality of fate as manifestation of divine will, one needs to observe and acknowledge how things never cease to change. In order to realise this genuine character of things, Marcus often insists on the importance to meditate on the perpetual change (μεταβολή) of all there is.

> All things are changing: and thou thyself art in continuous mutation and in a manner in continuous destruction, and the whole universe too.[56]

> Soon will the earth cover us all: then the earth, too, will change, and the things also which result from change will continue to change forever, and these again forever. For if a man reflects on the changes and transformations which follow one another like wave after wave and their rapidity, he will despise everything which is perishable.[57]

> The universal cause is like a winter torrent: it carries everything along with it.[58]

> Look at everything that exists, and observe that it is already in dissolution and in change, and as it were putrefaction or dispersion, or that everything is so constituted by nature as to die.[59]

To further illustrate the transitory nature of the human condition, Marcus recalls the words of the *Iliad*:

> "Leaves, some the wind scatters on the ground – So is the race of men." Leaves, also, are thy children; and leaves, too, are they who cry out as if they were worthy of credit and bestow their praise, or on the contrary curse, or secretly blame and sneer; and leaves, in like manner, are those who shall receive and transmit a man's fame to after-times. For all such things as these "are produced in the season of spring," as the poet says; then the wind casts them down; then the forest produces other leaves in their places.[60]

As humans, we tend to forget that we belong to this perpetual movement of things and no longer know what truly is self and what is not (or, from a Buddhist perspective, is non-self). Therefore, we become attached to our bodies and souls, to our assets or even to ephemeral glory. Marcus insists on the importance to take the measure of time in human life. The following passages can be read as describing a

---

[56] MS. IX, 19. All the translations of the *Meditations* (here after MS) of Marcus Aurelius are from Long, tr., *The Thoughts of the Emperor Marcus Aurelius Antoninus* (Boston: Little Brown, and Company, 1889).
[57] MS. IX, 28.
[58] MS. IX, 29.
[59] MS. X, 18.
[60] MS. X, 34.

practice of time that consists in observing the change of all things (πάντα ἐν μεταβολῇ) and realising the evanescent or impermanent character of all there is.

> Of human life the time is a point, and the substance is in a flux, and the perception dull, and the composition of the whole body subject to putrefaction, and the soul a whirl, and fortune hard to divine, and fame a thing devoid of judgment. And, to say all in a word, everything which belongs to the body is a stream, and what belongs to the soul is a dream and vapor, and life is a warfare and a stranger's sojourn, and after fame is oblivion. What then is that which is able to conduct a man? One thing, and only one, philosophy.[61]

> Acquire the contemplative way of seeing how all things change into one another, and constantly attend to it, and exercise thyself about this part [of philosophy]. For nothing is so much adapted to produce magnanimity. Such a man has put off the body, and as he sees that he must, no one knows how soon, go away from among men and leave everything here, he gives himself up entirely to just doing in all his actions, and in everything else that happens he resigns himself to the universal nature. But as to what any man shall say or think about him or do against him, he never even thinks of it, being himself contented with these two things – with acting justly in what he now does, and being satisfied with what is now assigned to him; and he lays aside all distracting and busy pursuits, and desires nothing else than to accomplish the straight course through the law and by accomplishing the straight course to follow God.[62]

> (…) But thou, in what a brief space of time is thy existence? And why art thou not content to pass through this short time in an orderly way? What matter and opportunity [for thy activity] art thou avoiding? For what else are all these things, except exercises for the reason, when it has viewed carefully and by examination into their nature the things which happen in life? Persevere then until thou shalt have made these things thy own, as the stomach which is strengthened makes all things its own, as the blazing fire makes flame and brightness out of everything that is thrown into it.[63]

These are just some samples among many of how the Roman emperor intended to lead a philosophical life. He understands philosophy as a "contemplative way (θεωρητικὴν μέθοδον)", but this theoretical way is paved by "exercises for the reason (γυμνάσματα λόγου)", and thus has the ascetic dimension of the hadotian "spiritual exercises"[64] echoing in some way Dōgen's skill/technique of the mind (*shinjutsu* 心術)[65]. What Marcus means by philosophy is obviously more than the ability to give rational arguments: a special training according to the doctrinal precepts that ought to be most intimately assimilated in order to lead a life according to nature or divine will.

For Marcus, the practice of time that consists in a meditation on the perpetual change of things opens the way to self-examination that leads to self-detachment and ultimately to self-mastery (ἐγκράτεια). In this respect, he followed the Socratic philosophical stance according to which an unexamined life it not worth living[66].

---

[61] MS. II, 17.

[62] MS. X, 11.

[63] MS. X, 31.

[64] Hadot, *La philosophie comme manière de* vivre (Paris: Albin Michel), 2001.

[65] See above.

[66] See Plato, *Apology of Socrates* (Harvard University Press. 2005), 38a.

> Whatever this is that I am, it is a little flesh and breath, and the ruling part. Throw away thy books; no longer distract thyself: it is not allowed; but as if thou wast now dying, despise the flesh; it is blood and bones and network, a contexture of nerves, veins, and arteries. See the breath also, what kind of a thing it is; air, and not always the same, but every moment sent out and again sucked in. The third, then, is the ruling part; consider thus: Thou art an old man; no longer let this be a slave, no longer be pulled by the strings like a puppet to unsocial movements, no longer be either dissatisfied with thy present lot, or shrink from the future.[67]

Observing the ephemeral character of the psycho-physical aspects of oneself and of others leads to an abandonment of pride, personal glory, one's body, soul and possessions. This detachment rhymes with a profound transformation of one's way of life (βίος), which corresponds in a sense with a thorough rewriting of one's biography, i.e., making a work of art of one's life. For Marcus, the practice of Stoic philosophy was reflected in his biography (in the primary sense of the term), and this reason only would suffice, according to the ancient standard, to place him in the ranks of the philosophers. Marcus' account of the way to reach awareness of one's ephemeral condition, leading to a genuine detachment from oneself bears a strong similarity to Dōgen's expression "casting off body-mind" (*shinjin datsuraku* 身心脱落).[68]

In a nutshell, even though in Stoic and Buddhist traditions important differences are at stake concerning the causal explanation of the impermanent or changing character of all things, we can recognise in both Marcus and Dōgen's writings a sort of practice of time understood as meditation on change and impermanence leading to self-detachment and attuning to nature (φύσις) / Buddha-nature (*busshō* 仏性)[69]. In the following, I will show how the practice of time involves a reflection on the time of practice.

3.2   The Time of Practice

Aware of the evanescent nature of things, the wise constantly seek to harmonise their will with that of nature, teaches the Stoic doctrine. Each here and now should become a favourable occasion (καιρός) to put this attuning in place through philosophical training. Marcus writes:

> How plain does it appear that there is not another condition of life so well suited for philosophizing as this in which thou now happenest to be.[70]

The path of Stoic wisdom begins in the present, because this is the only time that has a certain tenure. In fact, the present is "the only mode of time that is given to us"[71]

---

[67] MS. II, 2.

[68] DZZ 7, 19.

[69] By putting these notions together, I do not suggest a collusion between them. The question of their similarities and differences will be however set aside in this study.

[70] MS. XI, 7.

[71] Goldschmidt, *Le système stoïcien et l'idée de temps* (Paris: J. Vrin. 1998), 168.

and thus we must seize it as opportune moment (καιρός). In his description of the Stoic theory of time, Victor Goldschmidt explains that for the Stoics, "the instant is the only time we have, it is also (…) the only time of salvation (…)".[72] It is therefore only in the present that one can deploy all the efforts in order to act in harmony with nature. A true follower of the Stoics must therefore pay attention to the present of every action and use every moment as a favourable occasion to practise virtue. A point that Marcus acknowledges in these terms:

> That is for the good of each thing, which the universal nature brings to each. And it is for its good at the time when nature brings it.[73]

> About what am I now employing my own soul? On every occasion I must ask myself this question, and inquire, What have I now in this part of me which they call the ruling principle? and whose soul have I now, – that of a child, or of a young man, or of a feeble woman, or of a

tyrant, or of a domestic animal, or of a wild beast?[74]

In order to better grasp the meaning of what we call "self", Marcus questions here what has been given to us by nature. By doing so, he is actually practising in accordance with the Stoic philosophical *logoi*, i.e. theoretical principles concerning the divine nature of the ruling part of one's soul that is common to that of the whole world. Obviously, inside Marcus' writings related to the topic of time, cosmological and psychological theoretical aspects are intertwined with practical ones concerning the best use one can make of one's soul on every occasion. From the perspective of a technical conception of philosophy, his writings are enacting theoretical principles of the Stoic doctrine and as such they count as Stoic philosophy.

If the philosophical *logoi* are recalled, it is not for a purely theoretical purpose, but in order to persuade himself that the most adequate way to pursue the path of virtue is the one that nature brings, in this very moment. There is no better time for acting appropriately, according to nature (i.e., divine will manifested in the form of the causal chain of fate), than the present moment. One can even "eat one's soup 'so as to please the gods'".[75] For the Stoics, the most prosaic matters are occasions to do good by focusing attention on what is happening now as an effort to accept events as they happen[76]. Meditation on change is thus a philosophical training that requires one to seize every opportunity as the right one in order to follow the ideal of harmony with nature (universal reason).

---

[72] Ibid., 169.

[73] MS. X, 20.

[74] MS. V, 11.

[75] Goldschmidt, *Le système stoïcien et l'idée de temps* (Paris: J. Vrin. 1998), 169.

[76] As pointed out by P. Hadot: "La philosophie était pour eux un acte unique, qu'il fallait pratiquer à chaque instant, dans une attention (*prosoché*) sans cesse renouvelée à soi-même et au moment présent. L'attitude fondamentale du stoïcien, c'est cette attention continuelle, qui est une tension constante, une conscience, une vigilance de chaque instant. Grâce à cette attention, le philosophe est sans cesse parfaitement conscient, non seulement de ce qu'il fait, mais de ce qu'il pense – c'est la logique vécue – et de ce qu'il est, c'est-à-dire de sa place dans le cosmos – c'est la physique vécue." See Hadot, *Qu'est-ce que la philosophie antique?* (Paris, Folio, Essais. 1995. 215).

> The man to whom that only is good which comes in due season, and to whom it is the same thing whether he has done more or fewer acts conformable to right reason, and to whom it makes no difference whether he contemplates the world for a longer or a shorter time – for this man neither is death a terrible thing.[77]

From the Stoic perspective, the path to salvation consist precisely in taking every occasion as the right one, as a favourable moment, "which comes in due season" (εὔκαιρον), to engage life philosophically. Marcus recalls that the practice of time is destined to transform oneself in order to make the best use of the present moment. But as the time-lapse of life is terribly short, exercising in this way is of the utmost urgency:

> Thou canst remove out of the way many useless things among those which disturb thee, for they lie entirely in thy opinion; and thou wilt then gain for thyself ample space by comprehending the whole universe in thy mind, and by contemplating the eternity of time, and observing the rapid change of every several thing, how short is the time from birth to dissolution, and the illimitable time before birth as well as the equally boundless time after dissolution![78]

Marcus further explains that this philosophical training is of urgent matter not only because death is approaching every day, but also because the capacities needed for leading a good life perish first:

> (…) the power of making use of ourselves, and filling up the measure of our duty, and clearly separating all appearances, and considering whether a man should now depart from life, and whatever else of the kind absolutely requires a disciplined reason, – all this is already extinguished. We must make haste, then, not only because we are daily nearer to death, but also because the conception of things and the understanding of them cease first.[79]

It thus becomes imperative:

> (…) never to desert philosophy in any events that may befall us, nor to hold trifling talks either with an ignorant man or with one unacquainted with nature, is a principle of all schools of philosophy; but to be intent only on that which thou art now doing and on the instrument by which thou doest it.[80]

Marcus clearly sees philosophy as an activity of self-transformation that needs to constantly take place in every here and now of daily life. This amounts to never postponing the practice of philosophy or sparing one's efforts in the pursuit of virtue to which we naturally inclined. This natural tendency implies that philosophical training is not reserved to a certain category of people or to a particular moment in life. As the possibility of developing ethically belongs to everyone, independently of social origin or context, this ethical development can intervene and transform the

---

[77] MS. XII, 35.
[78] MS. IX, 32. Cf. MS. X, 15.
[79] MS. III, 1.
[80] MS. IX, 41.

entire personality at every moment of one's existence.[81] So, the most appropriate time of practice is the present occasion of each and every action.

From a Buddhist perspective, Dōgen reiterates a similar understanding of the commitment to the path of enlightenment.

> (...) the Buddhist Way does not deny old age or great age, youth or middle age. Thus, Jōshū, who did not begin to use Zen until he was over sixty, was nonetheless an eminent figure on the hierarchical headquarters of the patriarchs. Similarly, the young girl Teijō, who by the age of twelve had already completed a long study of Buddhism, was able to become an important person in the community.[82]

In a similar vein as the Roman emperor, Dōgen considers that there is no time in life more or less favourable to devote oneself to the practice of the Buddhist path. It is necessary to commit oneself to it as soon as possible. The brevity of life means that there is no time to lose, because time does not wait and does not spare humans.[83] As death is near, Dōgen constantly reminds us of the urgency of the practice:

> Don't wait in vain, but put out the fire burning on your head immediately and energetically. Apply yourself diligently with courage. At this very moment, how are you practising?[84]

> Impermanence is swift – [without appeal] –, life and death are matters of great importance. As life is short, if there is any good to practice and learn something, we must practice the Buddhist way and learn its teachings.[85]

> Students [of the way], it is necessary to reflect on the fact that death is inevitable. The principle of the way naturally stipulates this fact. Even if we do not think about it, we should not waste time unnecessarily, nor indulge in futile things. On the contrary, we should do what is worthwhile. What is really worthwhile is the constant activity of the Buddhas and patriarchs, apart from which, everything is unimportant.[86]

> As soon as we find a master, we must set aside the countless commitments and, without wasting a moment, we must strive to continue on the path. To train with the mind, without the mind and with half-mind. Thus, to extinguish the fire on our head, we must learn to stand on tiptoe.[87]

As for Marcus, spiritual training appears to be an urgent task. The sense of urgency is expressed by the image of a fire on the head (*zunen* 頭燃), meaning that continuous assiduity (*shōjin* 精進) is required from the one who resolves himself on the Buddhist path. The spiritual practice referred to is sitting meditation (*zazen* 座禅), as the quintessence of Zen, but it is a practice that entails mind training and must be

---

[81] Gill, "Le moi et la thérapie philosophique dans la pensée hellénistique et romaine", *Le moi et l'intériorité* (Paris: J. Vrin. 2008), 92.
[82] DZZ 5, 29.
[83] DZZ 3, 11.
[84] DZZ 4, 81
[85] DZZ 7, 72.
[86] DZZ 7, 97.
[87] DZZ 1, 302.

prolonged as a continuous endeavour (*anri* 行履) in all daily activities.[88] The most common activities as sitting, eating, thinking, walking, etc., offer as many favourable moments or occasions (*jisetsu*時節) to achieve enlightenment. It is obvious that in Dōgen's case too we are dealing with a valorisation of the present moment. Indeed, Dōgen subscribes without any difficulty to the idea that what matters is to act and manifest Buddha-nature (*busshō* 仏性) in the reality of the present moment (*uji* 有時).[89] Dōgen teaches indeed that Buddha-nature is nothing else than the causes and conditions of the opportune moment (*jisetsu no innen* 時節の因縁) and thus every moment is an occasion to realise it.[90] This echoes the words of Mǎzǔ Dàoyī (馬祖道一): "This [present] mind is the Buddha (*sokushin ze butsu* 即心是仏)".[91] There is nothing to wait in order to achieve Buddhahood, for Buddhahood is nothing outside this very moment (*nikon* 而今). There is no better time of practice. As in Marcus' case, for Dōgen, too, the practice of time is a kind of "science of the moment"[92] that needs to be reflected throughout the actions of daily life.

4 Conclusion

In spite of the important difference concerning the fact that Dōgen's texts mentioned here contain mostly teachings addressed to the members of his religious community on how to train oneself according to the Buddhist doctrine (*buppō*仏法), while those of Marcus Aurelius are exercises addressed to himself based on the Stoic *logoi philosophoi*, it is possible to say that both share the idea that one must deploy a skilful knowledge (a know-how) of the present moment, so that the most prosaic daily activity can become a favourable occasion for attunement with nature or Buddha-nature, such that one is liberated from suffering in the present life. When comparatively probed, their writings have in common an idiosyncratic way to reiterate and re-appropriate the principles of Buddhist and respectively Stoic doctrinal discourses with a paraenetic aim: the exhortation to re-evaluate one's relationship to oneself and to the whole world by the same token. These writings can be described either as spiritual exercises *per se* or as containing injunctions pointing to ways of practising these exercises. As far as one is willing to adopt the standpoint of a technical conception of philosophy, it appears that the spiritual training here comparatively addressed, and thus the texts containing it, have definitely a philosophical dimension that ought not to be overseen.

---

[88] Leighton, "Dōgen Approach to Training in Eihei ko-roku", *Dōgen: Textual and Historical Studies*, ed. St. Heine (Oxford, New York: Oxford University Press, 2012), 124.
[89] Nakimovitch, *Dōgen et les paradoxes de la bouddhéité* (Genève-Paris: Droz, 1999), 103.
[90] DZZ 1, 18.
[91] DZZ 1, 155.
[92] Nakimovitch, *Dōgen et les paradoxes de la bouddhéité* (Genève-Paris: Droz, 1999), 128.

If this comparison aims to show that a philosophical reading of the writings of both Marcus and Dōgen is possible, it goes without saying that by no means are other possible readings to be disregarded. However, this approach based on a technical conception of philosophy presents the significant advantage of not dismissing the historical, religious and social aspects that have shaped the cultural context in which philosophers have lived their lives, as a purely theoretical conception of philosophy would tend to do.

References

Bielefeldt, Carl. "Recarving the Dragon: History and Dogma in the Study of Dōgen". In *Dōgen Studies*. Honolulu: University of Hawaii Press. 1985.
_____. Tr. Sōtō Zen Text Project: <https://web.stanford.edu/group/scbs/sztp3/about_sztp/project.html>. 2010a.
Bouquet, A.C. "Stoics and Buddhists". In *Philosophical Quarterly*, no 33 (1961): 205–21.
Bowring, Richard. "Biography of Dōgen". In *Brill Encyclopedia of Buddhism* II : 933–40. 2019
Cornu, Philippe. *Dictionnaire encyclopédique du bouddhisme*. Paris: Seuil. 2006.
Eltschinger, Vincent. "Pierre Hadot et les 'exercices spirituels': Quel modèle pour la philosophie bouddhique tardive?". In *Asiatische Studien / Études Asiatique*s, 62(2) (2008): 485–544.
Faure, Bernard. *Chan Insights and Oversights: an Epistemological Critique of the Chan Tradition*. Princeton, Princeton University Press. 1996.
Gill, Christopher. "Le moi et la thérapie philosophique dans la pensée hellénistique et romaine". *Le moi et l'intériorité*. 83–105. Paris: J. Vrin. 2008.
Goldschmidt, Victor. *Le système stoïcien et l'idée de temps*. Paris: J. Vrin. 1998.
Gowans, Christopher W. "Medical Analogies in Buddhist and Hellenistic Thought: Tranquillity and Anger". In *Roy. Inst. Philos. Suppl. Royal Institute of Philosophy Supplement* 66 (2010): 11–33.
Hadot, Pierre. *Qu'est-ce que la philosophie antique ?* Paris, Folio, Essais. 1995.
_____. *La philosophie comme manière de vivre : entretiens avec Jeannie Carlier et Arnold I. Davidson*. Itinéraires du savoir. Paris: Albin Michel. 2001.
_____. *Exercices spirituels et philosophie antique*. L'Évolution de l'humanité. Paris: Albin Michel. 2002.
_____. *Pierre Hadot: L'enseignement des antiques, l'enseignement des modernes*. ed. A. I. Davidson and F. Worms, Paris, Rue d'Ulm. 2010b.
Kapstein, Matthew T. *Reason's Traces: Identity and Interpretation in Indian and Tibetan Buddhist Thought*. Boston: Wisdom Publications. 2001.
_____. "'Spiritual Exercise' and Buddhist Epistemologists in India and Tibet". In *A Companion to Buddhist Philosophy*, 270–89. 2013a.
_____. "Stoics and Bodhisattvas: Spiritual Exercise and Faith in Two Philosophical Traditions". In *Ancients and Moderns: Essays in Honor of Pierre Hadot*, 99–115. 2013b.
Kasulis, Thomas P. "The Incomparable Philosopher: Dōgen on How to Read the Shōbōgenzō". In *Dōgen Studies*. 83–98. Honolulu: University of Hawaii Press. 1985.
Kawamura 河村, Kōdō 孝道. ed. *Dōgen Zenji Zenshū* (道元禅師全集). 7 vol. Tōkyō: Shunjūsha. 1988.
Kopf, Gereon "'When All Dharmas Are the Buddha-Dharma' Dōgen as Comparative Philosopher". In *Dōgen and Sōtō Zen*, ed. Steven Heine, Oxford, New York: Oxford University Press. 2015.
LaFleur, William R. ed. *Dōgen Studies*. Honolulu: University of Hawaii Press. 1985.
Leighton, Taigen D. "Dōgen Approach to Training in Eihei ko-roku". In *Dōgen: Textual and Historical Studies*, ed. St. Heine, Oxford, New York: Oxford University Press. 2012.
Long, George. Tr. *The Thoughts of the Emperor Marcus Aurelius Antoninus*. Boston: Little Brown, and Company. 1889.

Maraldo, John C. *Japanese Philosophy in the Making 1: Crossing Paths with Nishida*. Nagoya, Japan: CreateSpace Independent Publishing Platform. 2017.

Müller, Ralf. "Getting Back to Premodern Japan: Tanabe's Reading of Dōgen". In *Frontiers of Japanese Philosophy 1*, Ed. J. W. Heisig, 164–183. 2006.

_____. "Watsuji's Reading of Dōgen's Shōbōgenzō". In *Frontiers of Japanese Philosophy 6*, Ed. J. W. Heisig and R. Bouso, 109–125. 2009.

Nāgārjuna, *Madhyamaka-kārikās, Stances du milieu par excellence*, tr. Guy Bugault. Paris: Nrf Gallimard. 2002.

Nakimovitch, Pierre. *Dōgen et les paradoxes de la bouddhéité*. Genève-Paris: Droz. 1999.

Orimo 折茂, Yoko 洋子. *Le Shōbōgenzō de maître Dōgen*. Vannes: Sully. 2004.

Plato. *Euthyphro, Apology, Crito, Phaedo*. Loeb Classical Library. Harvard University Press. 2005.

Sellars, John. *The Art of Living: The Stoics on the Nature and Function of Philosophy*. 2nd ed. London: Bristol Classical Press. 2009.

_____. "Marcus Aurelius and the Tradition of Spiritual Exercises". Forthcoming in M. Garani, D. Konstan, and G. Reydams-Schils, eds. *The Oxford Handbook of Roman Philosophy*. New York: Oxford University Press. 2021.

Steineck, Raji J. "A Zen Philosopher? – Notes on the Philosophical Reading of Dōgen's Shōbōgenzō ." In *Concepts of Philosophy in Asia and the Islamic World, Vol. 1: China and Japan*, eds., Raji C. Steineck, Elena L. Lange, Ralph Weber, and Robert H. Gassmann. Leiden Boston: Brill. 577–606. 2018.

Tanabe 田邊, Hajime元. *Shōbōgenzō no tetsugaku shikan* (正法眼蔵の哲学私観) Tōkyō: Iwanami Shoten. 1939.

Vesperini, Pierre. *Droiture et mélancolie : Sur les écrits de Marc Aurèle*. Lagrasse: Editions Verdier. 2016.

Watsuji 和辻, Tetsurō 哲郎. *Shamon Dōgen* (沙門道元) in *Nihon seishinshi kenkyū* (日本精神史研究) 9th ed. Tōkyō: Iwanami Shoten. 1998.

Yorizumi 頼住, Mitsuko 光子. *Dōgen: jiko, jikan, sekai wa dono yōni seiritsu suru no ka* (道元 : 自己・時間・世界はどのように成立するのか) Tōkyō: Nihon Hōsō Shuppan Kyōkai. 2005.

Appendix: Two Types of Language in Dōgen's Shōbōgenzō

Ralf Müller

The aim of the following pages is to demonstrate Dōgen's usage of language, as well as his reflexive approach to language, within the *Shōbōgenzō*. I will thereby underscore the fact that Dōgen does not, more broadly speaking, "devalue" language, but rather engages with language as the medium, expression and realisation of the Buddhist path. Included is my translation of the crucial fascicle of the *Shōbōgenzō* on *dōtoku* (see below at the end of this article).

Mapping the Theoretical Grounds of Dōgen's Texts

To achieve the above aim, I will first address and analyse the *Shōbōgenzō*, based on two kinds of language that can be mapped onto the two concepts of truth; i.e., finite and infinite language: *monji* and *dōtoku* (1. Language and the Two Truths). Explicating these notions of language helps to determine the levels which enable a philosophical appropriation of the *Shōbōgenzō*. Next, I will treat the conceptualisation of *dōtoku* in the fascicle of the same title (2. A Concept and Theory of Language based on "Dōtoku"), and then discuss the broader theorisation in various parts of the *Shōbōgenzō* (3. Ramifications of the Conceptualisation of "Dōtoku"). Finally, I will examine the critique of tradition (4. A Linguistic Critique of Tradition) and conclude by adopting a meta-perspective to review Dōgen's thinking on language (5. A Meta-perspective on "Dōtoku").

As explained in the volume's introduction, it is crucial to review Dōgen's thinking about language from within his religious horizon: language has always been said to manifest more than just human workings. Despite not needing to suppose that Dōgen assumes magical powers, it is still vital to distinguish two types of language, or a narrower and a broader concept. To deepen our understanding of these two types and to follow further the ramifications of this conceptual discernment, I will move on from the broader spectrum of Dōgen's writings to the *Shōbōgenzō* and lay out the ground for what I suggest to be a quasi-terminological coinage. On the one hand, there is the traditional expression for language (*monji*) and, on the other, the new coinage (*dōtoku*). As a pair, they can be considered isomorphic to what we can call first and second language. This differentiation allows us to reconstruct Dōgen's *Shōbōgenzō* philosophically, according to his thinking on language (g. *Sprachdenken*).

Language and the Two Truths

In the Buddhist tradition, ordinary human language is often seen as antithetical to Buddhist teaching. Yet sometimes, though rarely, it is regarded as also being complementary; and as we read Dōgen, ordinary language, even vernacular Japanese not only complements the teachings but is interwoven with them, over, under, and throughout. The relationship between the "two truths," secular and sacred, is analogous.

The usefulness of ordinary language is questioned at an early stage in Buddhism, in that sound and writing are first and foremost regarded as particular and finite. Although they are recognised as necessary for communication, and thus as having a limited functionality, at the same time they warn against the substantialisation of language in its signifying function and, as a consequence, confusing the sign with the signified in their relationship to each other. In this respect, the tradition holds that ordinary language radically fails in relation to sacred truth. In short, language in Buddhism is understood primarily as *human* language, and, thus, poses a specific challenge for human beings in *samsara*. As such, ordinary thinking is predominantly criticised as a thinking that substantialises language or conceives of it according to a Wittgensteinian-like picture theory of language (g. *Abbildtheorie der Sprache*).

This view is particularly evident in the criticism against Hindu grammarians raised by Mahāyāna Buddhists such as Nagarjuna. At the same time, however, it can be argued that in unfolding his critique of the grammarians in the play of negations, Nagarjuna does not simply want to go beyond language. He seeks to draw attention to and foreground a second layer of language, thereby identifying a productive potential in language itself.[1] One consequence of this doubling of language is that no critique of language can be totalising. While language is a link in the chain of causes of human life and suffering, it is also the means of naming and resolving this connection. Recognising that language can function differently, however, is only a first step, for this does not give language validity in itself. Language still seems ultimately deficient and incapable of articulating Buddhist truth, because it is conceived solely from the human point of view.

On the Etymology and Meaning of "Words and Letters"
Nevertheless, following Nagarjuna, we can take up and further elaborate this double perspective on language. In other words, we ascribe a second layer to language, and this second layer is inherent or intrinsic to human language itself. Parallel to the

---

[1] Nagarjuna.

distinction between secular and sacred truth, there are corresponding expressions for the two types of language, which are now introduced from a philological perspective: "words and letters" for human language in a narrow sense and "perfect expression" for the broader concept of language that permeates all of human language but extends beyond its means of expression. The following Sino-Japanese words can be used as equivalents for the first of the two expressions. Human language, in terms of communication can be referred to using various Japanese words: j. *monji* for "words and letters," j. *myōji, myōsō, myōshiki* for "name and form" and j. *gengo* for "language."[2]

In early Buddhist texts, various metaphorical expressions for language are known in the sense of "name and form." The above three expressions *myōji, myōsō* and *myōshiki* can be rendered in this sense according to their basic meaning. onsidering the direction of translation into the Sino-Japanese vocabulary, these terms are preceded by a large number of Sanskrit equivalents.[3] In the first place, *myōji* means "name" or "designation" (s. *nirukti, nāman*). But in Buddhist literature it also means "term" and "word." The word *myōsō* (s. *nāma-samsthāna*) can be more accurately translated as "name and appearance." This expression means that which is seen with the eyes and heard with the ears. What is seen or heard is considered to be unreal or empty and, therefore, a source of delusion. However, if language is recognised as "name and appearance" in its provisional nature, it can also serve positively in communication as a provisional means on the Buddha's path.

Better known and also documented in canonical sources is s. *nāma-rūpa*, j. *myōshiki*: literally "name and colour," usually translated as "name and form." While in the early Upanishads this term denotes all the physical phenomena of the universe, in early Buddhism it means mind or heart and body, i.e., the psycho-physical existence of the human being, which, despite its impermanence, is the only means to the path of awakening.[4] However, language also gains an existential dimension from its reference to this psycho-physical unity of the human being. This existential dimension becomes tangible above all at the level of the use of, and practical

---

[2] The corresponding sinograms are 文字 for the reading *monji* (with the variant *moji*), 名字 for *myōji*, 名相 for *myōsō*, 名色 for *myōshiki* and 言語 for *gengo* (with the variant *gongo*).

[3] For *myōji* alone, s. *aksara, abhidhā, nāma-kāya, nāma-dheya, nāma-pada, nāma-samketa, nāmâdhisthāna, nāmâpadeśa, nirvacana, pratirūpaka, samketa, samjñā, sammata* are found in relevant lexicons.

[4] According to this understanding, the human being consists of the five aggregates (j. *un*, s. *skandha*): Body, sensation, perception, volition and consciousness (the latter constituting the "name" and *rūpa* the "form"). The first four characteristics are mental, and the last characterisation is material. Dictionaries describe *rūpa* as the smallest particle of matter. An embryonic body is something that can be designated (s. *kāya*) (*nāma-rūpa*). On *nāma-rūpa* see also Schlieter *Versprachlichung – Entsprachlichung: Untersuchungen zum philosophischen Stellenwert der Sprache im europäischen und buddhistischen Denken* (Köln: edition chōra, 2000), 155–156; on the pre-Buddhist meaning ibid. 206–209. In the three cases mentioned, one uses language throughout as a term to be critically elucidated. Finally, following the word for speech and the contemporary expression for language, we must mention j. *gengo* (s. *vāc*). In dictionaries, one translates *gengo* as "to discuss," "to express in words" (s. *abhidhāna, abhidhātarya*).

engagement with, language, thus opening up a productive aspect of language. This dimension, connoted in early Buddhist expression, is still reflected in Zen when, for example, the patriarchs such as Jōshū[5] or Rinzai speak of the living words and the turning words (j. *tengo*) as both means and expression of the Buddha Way. Finally, it is also the verbal dialogue that can be considered paradigmatic for an authentic tradition in Zen. In written form, it loses some of its significance, but it can claim to be valid as an actualisation of a more original dialogue situation.

This ambivalent – but already partially affirmative – attitude to language in Zen comes to fruition in Dōgen. In his writings, we find above all the expressions *monji* and *myōsō*, in a neutral sense, alongside *gengo* (more rarely *myōshiki* and *myōji*). As indicated, in particular *monji* refers to the deficient concept of human language in Zen Buddhism.[6] In a figurative sense, *monji* also refers to the sacred texts, the sutras and commentaries. As collections of Buddhist scholarship and scholasticism, these become the object of Zen Buddhist attacks against the ossifications of tradition, insofar as religious truth is reduced to its written expression and is elevated to the exclusive object of worship (cf. Nakamura 1995: 801). But in Dōgen, *monji* undergoes a comprehensive re-evaluation.

Such re-evaluation is already evident on the philological side. Drawing on various evidence from Dōgen's writings, the ZGDJ gives for *monji* firstly the literal meaning of "signs written on paper" (ZGDJ 1230d). Yet beyond that, the expression is positively turned towards another language when "all the different appearances point to the manifestation of the infinite and absolute reality" (ibid.).[7] In the composition of "essence-lessness of words and letters" (ibid.), the positive function is again critically relativised insofar as "truth transcends the interpretation of words and letters [of the sacred writings]" (ibid.). Once again, however, as a reference to the "transcendent origin" of human language, *monji* can be understood as a translation for s. *vyañjana* or s. *akṣára*, i.e., in the sense of the "written word" as the breath and life of the body of the Buddha manifesting the truth.[8] Meaning is in constant flux, and thus an ambiguity already appears in this first expression, when the language of the Enlightened One is different from that of man and yet refers to it.

---

[5] The Tang period Chan master Zhaozhou Congshen 趙州從諗 (778–897).

[6] Apart from the translation used below as "words and letters," *monji* also means "writing" as well as "word," "letter" or "phoneme" according to the basic Sino-Japanese meaning of "sentence" and "sign." It is translated in many different ways in Buddhist literature. In the broadest sense it means "words," but in the context of Buddhist linguistics it means, in particular, the sound and the meaning of a word, as well as the smallest element in the theory of signs "syllable," going back to Skt. *vyañjana*. Cf. Nakamura, *Iwanami bukkyō jiten* [Iwanami Dictionary of Buddhism] (Tokyo: Iwanami, 1995), 801. According to Buddhist terminology, several syllables form a designation, name or title (j. *myōshō* 名称, also j. *myō* 名), while several names form a sentence j. *shoku* 章句 (j. *bunshō-ku* 文章・句). We can find these differentiations already in the texts of the Buddhist Kusha and Yuishiki schools. They formulate the essence-lessness of the characters (j. *shin fusō ōgyō hō* 心不相応行法).

[7] ZGDJ 1230d, evidenced by a quotation from the *Bendōwa* fascicle.

[8] Cf. the meaning of the syllable *ro* in the sinogram 嚕.

"Words and Letters" as Human Language in Dōgen's Texts

Dōgen's relationship with language shifts from a practical means of communication to its affirmative theorisation, when he formulates the idea of an all-encompassing articulation of the world through language. In doing so, he removes the distinction between first (*monji* – the traditional expression) and second (*dōtoku* or "perfect expression" – the new coinage) language. Dōgen's affirmative reconceptualisation allows for the first language to be approached anew through the lens of the second, resulting in a sharpened critique of the Zen Buddhist tradition. Dōgen dismantles the conventional meaning of certain Zen expressions and idioms from the perspective of the second language, leading to a greater understanding of their implications.

Thus, Dōgen's awareness of the danger of "obfuscation" by ordinary language, along with the intrinsic valorisation of language, finds expression in later writings, as well in his comparison and contrasting of the sayings and commentaries of the patriarchs of the tradition. At times, Dōgen claims that the abilities of certain masters surpassed those of other scribes in India and China. At the same time, he claims that of these superior ones, one or the other "failed to say the essentials to define [an expression]" (DZZ 1: 297). Therefore, the person in question was "only someone who studied the [common] language" (DZZ 1: 297) and remained attached to it. Elsewhere he comments on a saying from ancient times, stating that it is understood by "stupid people" only as "words of exhortation" (DZZ 1: 298), and not appreciated in its deeper meaning. Finally, Dōgen also speaks of the "silly words" (DZZ 1: 311) of monks who were only concerned about their own salvation, or he opposes the name "Zen" and considers such designations to be "nonsensical words" and emphasises that "descendants of the Buddhas and patriarchs should not [use] such words" (DZZ 1: 478).

When language is spoken of in neutral form (j. *gongo*) in most of the passages quoted above, it is specifically marked for devaluation. For human language as "name and form" (j. *myōsō*) has consistently negative connotations, as was already made clear above in the quotation from notes from the Hōkyō era.[9] Thus, in answer to the question of whether the practice of *zazen* loses its salvific effect in times of the decline of the Buddha's teaching, Dōgen states elsewhere that the expression of the "last [epoch] of the teaching" (j. *mappō*) as such is causally ineffective and thus meaningless as a word:

> While the scribes make a big deal about name and form [*myōsō*], in the true teaching of the Mahāyāna there is no division into the three epochs of the teaching. [The teaching] says that all attain the way of the Buddha when they practise. (DZZ 2: 476)

---

[9] Thus, with reference to Hōyū (chin. Farong), who had the reputation of being familiar with the entire canon already at the age of 19. At the same time, Dōgen criticises him (in *Butsu kōjō ji*, DZZ 1: 294).

Dōgen is even more explicit in the speaking of *monji*. In *Bendōwa*,[10] which follows *Fukan zazen gi*, the importance of bodily practice, even of sitting exclusively, is once again justified over reading the sutras, burning incense, etc. The text which formulates the practice in this way is relativised in its importance with reference to the practice of *zazen*. It states, for example, that one should seek out true masters, but "not scholars who count out words and letters (j. *monji*)". Such scholars are "like the blind leading the blind" (DZZ 2: 467–468). Conversely, he encourages his listeners to devote themselves to practice, which will soon enable them to recognise the true path of the Buddha: "How can those who are caught in the traps and snares of words and letters (j. *monji*) compete with you" (DZZ 2: 468)? In these sentences, Dōgen turns against the one-sidedness of the scholastics but soon afterwards also against the belief in an independent tradition of "Zen," as already noted. He even considers this linguistic designation and delimitation to be a deviation from the Buddha's path, as the latter is indivisible in simplicity and uniqueness. Seen in this way, "Zen" is no more than "name and form" and thus also misses something seemingly ineffable.

On the Etymology and Meaning of "Perfect Expression"

However, the apparently prevailing ambiguity of Dōgen's criticisms of "word and name" dissolves when one considers his other uses of it. The fact that Dōgen reflects on the double relation of language in his own way is evident not only in the rethinking of ordinary linguistic expression in the sense of *monji*, but already in the quasi-terminological version of another, further concept of language, i.e., *dōtoku* or "perfect expression." Before interpreting this new coinage in the context of the "Dōtoku" fascicle, and in the broader context of the *Shōbōgenzō*, it will be helpful to examine the etymology of *dōtoku*, as well as its Buddhist and Zen Buddhist contexts.

Dōgen's quasi-conceptual version of the broader concept of language is *dōtoku* 道得 and is translated here as "expression," or more precisely as "perfect expression of truth." This is a "quasi" concept, since Dōgen does not build up a complete terminological system in a strict sense. Nevertheless, he holds on to this expression for several years and, at least in his usage, develops the meaning of *dōtoku* in connection with other expressions, which together produce a stabilising yet open, even *creatively* open, network of expressions rich in philosophical meanings and connotations. It is already clear from the dedication of a separate fascicle in the *Shōbōgenzō* mentioned above, and the frequency of its use that the expression dōtoku occupies a central position in his writings. The expression is found about 130 times in the entire *Shōbōgenzō* in more than a fifth of the 95-fascicle edition, especially in fascicles from the period 1240–1243. Of these, about 33 passages are in the fascicle of the same name.

---

[10]The text *Bendōwa* 辨道話, meaning *Discourse on the Practice of the Way* or *Dialogue on the Way of Commitment*, sometimes also translated as *Negotiating the Way*, *On the Endeavor of the Way*, or *A Talk about Pursuing the Truth*, is an influential essay written by Dōgen, the founder of Zen Buddhism's Sōtō school in Japan.

The number of occurrences increases if variants in the form of compounds or negations are included.[11] However, the extent of the reflection on language in the *Shōbōgenzō* can only be grasped if one also includes sense-related expressions. These include close variants such as *iū* ("say"), *dōha*, *dōshu* and *dōjaku* ("utter"), which share the first part of the binomial *dōtoku* with *dō*.[12] Finally, it quickly becomes clear that the theme of language (with its focus on the "perfect expression of truth") is a central issue when more distant expressions are added, such as *setsu* ("to set forth") or *sesshu* ("to preach")[13] and correlative terms such as *gongo* (language) or *monji* ("letters and signs").[14]

Philologically, we can explain *dōtoku* as follows. The expression literally means "to be able to speak" and consists of two components. The first part *dō* is mainly translated as "way," "principle," "truth" or "reason."[15] Dōgen, however, uses the character here in the rarer, philologically secondary meaning of "word," "language" or "speech." The double meaning of the sinogram finds its way into the Chinese translation of the Bible with: "In the beginning was the word [*dō*]".[16] The second sinogram of the binomial *dōtoku* in the nominal reading *toku* means "profit," "gain," "benefit" or "advantage." In the Japanese reading *eru/uru* as a verb, it correspondingly denotes "gain," "acquire," "get," and in verbal compounds also to "be able" and "be capable." Dōgen uses the compound expression both as a noun and as a verb: thus, we can translate it as "to be able to speak," "to be able to talk," or nominally as "speech" or "speaking ability".

The existing European-language translations of the *Shōbōgenzō* render the expression in the fascicle's title as "expression parfait," "voicing the way" or even "gelingendes Sprechen." Thus, they single out different nuances as the primary meaning, but also seem to vary according to context. The expression *dōtoku*, with "speaking ability" as its centre, encompasses a circle of meaning of "principle," "truth" or "reason," and from the Buddhist context also "path," "awakening" and "wisdom." Hence, language becomes the mediating moment of theoretical, as well as practical, understanding and ability. Dōgen writes and asserts, for example, that the awakened sages, the Buddhas, literally translated, "can speak," or that, terminologically, they are "able to give perfect expression to truth."

"Expression" here means symbolic articulation as a manifold structuring of reality; be it discursive or expressive. The articulation is always symbolic. Nevertheless, "perfect" does not mean completed, i.e., finished and absolute, but "perfect" in the sense of the structuring of a situation in its wholeness, which is held for a moment

---

[11] Cf. as examples *dōtokujin* 道得尽, *dōtokutei* 道得底, *dōdōtoku* 同道得 and *midōtoku* 未道得, *dōfutoku* 道不得, *fudōtoku* 不道得 respectively.

[12] Cf. for example *iu* 道ゔ, *dōha* 道破, *dōshu* 道取, *dōja* 道著.

[13] Here *setsu* 説 and *sesshu* 説取.

[14] For further relevant entries see Katō Shūkō (ed.), *Shōbōgenzō yōgo sakuin* (2 vols., 1987).

[15] We can derive these meanings from the basic meaning "path," which one can see in the kanji components: 「首」, a long neck/tubular neck leading from the head to the torso → pass through, and 「辵」, movement → path or road leading through a settlement.

[16] For these other entries see Ricci.

and yet dissolves again. It is not the expression of "truth" in the sense of the representation of a state of affairs, but rather the expression of wholeness as a reference to the continuous interrelatedness of all that exists. The perfect expression as an utterance of a Zen master and awakened person is spontaneous, dynamic and open. Its manifestation is not restricted to verbal language, but encompasses it, time and again.

Finally, let us note two related expressions: If *dōtoku* refers to perfect expression in general or the corresponding faculty, *dōshu* means the concrete instance; accordingly, it is translated as far as possible as "to utter" or as "utterance"; the same applies to *dōjaku*. The two words *dōjaku* and *dōshu* refer to the act and activity of utterance. The term *dō* alone, on the other hand, means a traditional saying, expression or word. Of course, it would also be necessary to examine how it is interwoven with, and differs from, other linguistic expressions such as "to preach" or "to expound." Nevertheless, with *dōtoku* and the direct and indirect reference of all synonyms for *dōtoku*, we can make the general claim that Dōgen obtains the presentational nature for his concept of language to prove true the authenticity of his texts in the "liveliness" of all forms of articulation.

On "Dōtoku" in Buddhist Literature Until Dōgen

Although Dōgen's use of the term *dōtoku* is unique, it is based on Buddhist literature. This is especially evident as there is no indication of *dōtoku* being used in a comparable manner outside of Dōgen's work, in Chinese or Japanese texts. Explicit proof of *dōtoku* as a "faculty of speech" is infrequent. Additionally, there is no verifiable link with the translation of Indian Buddhist texts into Chinese or Japanese, which could indicate an etymology rooted in Sanskrit or Pali.[17] In terms of meaning, *dōtoku* probably comes closest to s. *vāc* for "speech," "verbal expression," "utterance."[18] The word *vāc*, in turn, is rendered into Sino-Japanese by *setsu*, *gongo*, *gonsetsu* and similar expressions. Within Japanese literature, *dōtoku* is only present in Dōgen's works and in the commentaries written on his texts. The sole passage concerning Zen Buddhism in Chinese sources is located in the anthology of the layman P'ang (740?–808). It is transcribed from a dialogue the was recorded in the early Ninth century.[19]

Furthermore, *dōtoku* is also closely tied to tradition in terms of content. On an etymological level, some have discussed the double meaning of *dō* as path/enlightenment and language/speech. Therefore, even though Dōgen himself does not present the connection, it can be referred back to another term composed of the same sinograms as *dōtoku* only in reverse order: *tokudō* – "attainment of the Way" in the sense of "attainment of enlightenment" through following the precepts, practising meditation, and cultivating wisdom. If one interprets Dōgen's quasi-conceptual

---

[17] Further research revealed sites in the *Yogācārabhūmi-śāstra*.

[18] Corresponding passages are found in the Chinese text of the *Yogācārabhūmi-śāstra* (j. *Yugaron*) and the *Saddharma Puṇḍarīka Sūtra* (j. *Hokkekyō*).

[19] See Sasaki, Iriya, and Fraser, The Recorded Sayings of Layman Pang: A Ninth-Century Zen Classic (Tokyo: Weatherhill, 1971).

reinterpretation as a reversal of the common expression *tokudō*, then the attainment of awakening lies even and precisely in the ability to speak.

In the relevant Buddhological resources, the term *dōtoku* is explained mainly in monastic and soteriological contexts, which in my opinion are conducive to a philosophical interpretation. In ZGDJ, the only reference before Dōgen is the aforementioned quotation from the layman P'ang, translated as "interpreting the truth of the Buddhadharma without rest" (ZGDJ 937b). The word *dōtoku* is explained there as "right speech" in the context of a Buddhist's authentic way of life. Furthermore, according to the ZGDJ, it means the activity of the whole body and heart of the Buddhas and patriarchs, and at the same time, it refers to they themselves. Finally, in a cosmological dimension, it means a saying as an expression of universal truth.

In the commentaries of the various editions of Dōgen's works and modern translations of them, the quasi-term *dōtoku* is given a strongly associated with religion. The proper way to enter the status of Buddha is to strictly adhere to the Buddha's precepts and to accept the robe as a symbol of transmission. In upholding and continuing the life of the Buddhas and patriarchs, *dōtoku* then refers to the act of practising with great effort and demonstrating the way in which the truth of the Buddha is fully expressed in all moments and aspects of life. This principle is achieved not only through verbal communication (linguistic expression of right speech) but also through the cultivation, discernment, and exposition of the Buddhas and patriarchs, encompassing the entirety of existence and reality. This is demonstrated both in literal speech and in wordless gestures and, more generally, in nonverbal actions.

Additionally, the *Dōgen Jiten* (*Dōgen Dictionary*) draws attention to another aspect. With regard to the speaker, it states (paraphrasing the beginning of the fascicle "Dōtoku" translated below) that the patriarch has an experience, and must then also be able to express it. The experienced pertains to the "reality of the Buddha Law" which, when viewed externally, denotes the spiritual moment of awakening.[20]

The "Dōtoku" Fascicle
Dōgen dedicates the eponymous fascicle "Dōtoku" (see translation below) to "perfect expression," having already used the new coinage in various sections of the *Shōbōgenzō*. In the edition used, the text "Dōtoku" consists of 19 paragraphs, which can be divided into three parts. The first of these three parts is characterised by a rather high degree of abstraction and theorisation. In the discursive medium of language, the content of the expression *dōtoku* is determined in the form of conclusion-like statements. In contrast, the two subsequent parts are based on the interpretation of *kōan*-like events of tradition. They thus each begin with figurative moments to illustrate the content of the expression *dōtoku*.

Insofar as the *kōan* cases are not self-evidently comprehensible to the practitioner, Dōgen unfolds the content through other images and theoretical considerations, even though he remains committed to the non-discursive character of the *kōans*. With a view to their content, he repeatedly challenges his readers to study them closely. This is, in part, because doing so will help open up both the *kōans*, and the

---

[20] Cf. the introductory headnote explaining the title in DZZ 1: 374.

typical contexts of their practical exercise, to a discursive space not unlike what Wilfrid Sellars calls "the logical space of reasons."[21] Thus, Dōgen also broadens the understanding of *study* vis-à-vis the practice of *zazen*, as he seeks to cultivate a philosophically and soteriologically penetrative and productive understanding of the *kōan* case at hand in the context of studying (practicing) the path, the Buddha Way.

As we can see in the following sections, in the "Dōtoku" fascicle, Dōgen deploys a concept of language that forms the basis for the productive appropriation of a theory of language. To bring to light the quantity and quality of Dōgen's quasi-theorising about language, we will first focus on the one fascicle on language and then make our way through various other fascicles.

A Concept and Theory of Language Based on "Dōtoku"

The translated fascicle (see below) begins with a quasi-definition of awakened masters of Buddhism: "All Buddhas and patriarchs are able to express [the truth] perfectly." The definition of Buddhas and patriarchs by "perfect expression" turns on its head an idea of the Zen Buddhist tradition, according to which there is a unique, speechless tradition outside scholasticism.

Buddha's Name of Wisdom and Writing

There are several reasons for positing that the fundamental tenets of Zen teachings are transmitted silently through unmediated intuition. Thus, even the earlier schools of Buddhism portrayed the historical Buddha Shakyamuni, the sage (s. *muni*) of the Shakya (s. *Śākya*) lineage, as the great silent One. Shakyamuni is believed to have maintained silence during and after his enlightenment, at least as far as the experience of this supreme religious experience is concerned. He was equally sparse on essential metaphysical questions of the tradition.[22] In later texts of Mahāyāna Buddhism, it is stated that the Buddha did not speak a single word

---

[21] "The essential point is that in characterising an episode or a state as that of knowing, we are not giving an empirical description of that episode or state; we are placing it in the logical space of reasons, of justifying and being able to justify what one says." See Sellars, *Empiricism and the Philosophy of Mind* (Cambridge: Harvard University Press, 1997), §36. As Dōgen admonishes in "Sansui Kyō" or "The Mountains and Waters Sutra," only "illiterate shavepates" think the *kōan* cases are illogical, irrational, or incomprehensible. From the perspective of at least some twentieth century philosophers – Sellars, Donald Davidson, John McDowell, Hilary Putnam, et al. – there would be a stark choice: either *kōans* are illogical or not. If they are illogical, then they have no connection with the logical/comprehensible, aside from denying it; thus, insofar as *kōans* are illogical, they have nothing to do with our experience, assuming the latter is logical. That may seem to be the point of *kōan* study, i.e., to help break us out of some logical yet delusive prison of concepts and conceptions. Still, for Dōgen, the power of *kōans* to conduce to awakening is not due to their illogicality.

[22] We could distinguish different aspects of silence: The silence in the practice of meditative immersion, the silence about what Buddha experienced at the moment of enlightenment, and the silence about the questions about the whence and whither of human life and metaphysics as a whole.

during his entire life.[23] This belief is adopted by the Zen tradition, which views sitting in silence as the original form of Buddha's teaching.

Nevertheless, the transliteration of the name Shakyamuni offers arguments in favour of Dōgen's interpretation. Translated from Sanskrit into Sino-Japanese as *shakamon*,[24] the name demonstrates a connection between wisdom and writing. This is due to *mon*, as the Sino-Japanese form of *muni*, denoting a letter or writing. The honorific term *shakuson* refers to the hermeneutic aspect of wisdom, as the character for *shaku* connotes "explanation" or "interpretation."[25] Dōgen's reinterpretation of the Zen tradition aligns with this understanding, as he posits that even awakened ones and masters of Buddhism employed diverse modes of language to articulate themselves accurately convey the truth of Buddha's teaching.

As advised by the philosopher and historian of culture Watsuji Tetsurō,[26] the initial sentence can be read literally as an assertion of identity: "All the Buddhas and patriarchs are the faculty of speaking." Furthermore, to read this passage in a more limited sense of "speak" or "talk," i.e., to start, like Watsuji, from verbal language, finds its philological justification in the binomial *dōtoku* coined by Dōgen after the first part *dō* (when read as *iu*). Yet a radical reinterpretation of the tradition must also commence here in regards of its content. Verbal language, in particular, is regarded as the greatest hazard on the path to enlightenment.

The Interpretation of the Fascicle "Perfect Expression"
Dōgen recognizes the significant function of verbal language. That is why he not only focuses on verbal expression but also other forms of articulation in his reconstruction of the transmission between master and student. He interprets the relationship between the awakened individual and practitioner as a dialogical confrontation, a specific form of communication in which parties strive towards an adequate articulation of the path and the truth. Verbal language undoubtedly plays a vital role in the relationship between the enlightened master and the diligent student, however, other means of expression must not be overlooked. A Buddha has the freedom of expression and is not limited to mere spoken words:

> [1.] All the Buddhas and patriarchs are able to express [the truth] perfectly. Therefore, Buddhas and patriarchs, in order to choose Buddhas and patriarchs, certainly ask whether [they] have already expressed [the truth] or not. [They] enquire into this with the heart or with the body; [they] enquire into this with [everyday things such as] the stick and the flyswatter or with pillars and lanterns [and whatever else is at hand]. If [the enquirer and the enquired] are not Buddhas or patriarchs, there is no enquiry, there is no expression; for [without them], there is no ground for it.

---

[23] See Suzuki, *The Lankavatara Sutra: a Mahayana text* (London: Kegan Paul, 1999). However, a complex reflection on language and sign criticism can already be discerned here, which fits into the horizon of the proposed interpretation.

[24] j. *shakamon* 釋迦文.

[25] j. *shakuson* 釈尊. Cf. also the references given by Pörtner, "Zu Kūkais Sprachphilosophie. Notizen zu 'Shō-ji-jissō-gi'" (1988), 263.

[26] That is also the argument of Watsuji, see Müller, *Dōgens Sprachdenken* (Freiburg: Alber 2013), 123.

The significance of the subjectivity of experience and the investment of one's own understanding are demonstrated by the fact that the examination is not on the inwardness and purity of enlightenment (whatever that may entail), but rather on genuine expression through dialogue. This expression and its examination are universal, insofar as they occur – on the subject-related plane – both spiritually and physically ("heart" and "body"); and they do not remain limited – on the object related plane – to the clerical or secular world ("stick" and "flyswatter" or "pillars" and "lanterns"). The methods and means of expression used are ubiquitous. Due to the "traps and snares" of human language, the discourse on doctrinal issues takes a secondary role at present. Nevertheless, even these issues are not fundamental obstacles to achieving enlightenment and could potentially convey truth. Moreover, language should not be entirely excluded. It is crucial to recognize that the unrestrained and unscripted dialogue of the Zen masters themselves is the vital prerequisite for expression, as the final sentence puts it.

The Dynamics of Perfect Expression

If we assume that Dōgen links (perfect) expression to Buddhahood in the initial paragraph, it thereby establishes the standard for Buddhahood in the confirmation dialogue. In contrast, the second paragraph exhibits that expression, in addition to its usage in conversation, has not only an intersubjective but also a transsubjective dimension. However, this does not signify a transcendent dimension. Even though it is not an inherent or an acquired ability, neither mimesis nor talent are necessary for perfect expression. Rather, it is connected to a continuous effort to comprehend the Buddha Way correctly. The focal point is the active actualisation and autonomous demonstration of expression. Exploring the teachings or the essence of the Buddhas and patriarchs is, in reality, to explore oneself since every being is always already Buddha. Thus, the perfect expression is based on the "thorough enquiry" of oneself alone, as Buddha and patriarch. Dōgen goes on:

> [2.] Such an ability to express is not attained by following someone else, and it is not within the capacity of one's own power; only when one really thoroughly investigates the [teachings of the] Buddhas and patriarchs is there the perfect expression of the Buddhas and patriarchs. In this ability to express, one formerly practised and got to the bottom of enlightenment, and also now, one applies oneself to understanding the Way. When Buddhas and patriarchs apply themselves to [the teachings of] Buddhas and patriarchs and affirm what they express, this expression becomes by itself the applying of oneself for three, eight, thirty, or forty years, and it expresses [the truth] expanding all powers. [On the back of the sheet, it is written:] Thirty or twenty years is the period of time it takes to realise the ability to express. This period of time gathers the powers and brings about the perfect expression [of truth].

Each expression has a temporal horizon that extends towards the past and future, in addition to being instantaneous. This is achieved through the present act of "applying oneself to" and "affirmation": As stated in the beginning regarding the tradition of the Buddhas' mutual examination, the exercise of expression gains a dynamism and detachment from the respective actors, perpetuating its longevity. For the expression is not only a process that is relational (between the Buddhas and patriarchs) and dynamic (in enquiry and response), but also quasi-autonomous, as "these months and years unite the powers and bring about the perfect expression." This also means that in the fundamentally continuous exercise and enquiry of striving for enlightenment, the moments of "affirmation" and "confirmation" of expression as punctual aspects constitute an overarching dynamic of expression, despite their singularity. A relational structure is created through the continuity of "thorough research" and "endeavour" on the one hand and "affirmation" on the other. This leads to the expression of truth becoming an independent and dynamic entity, beyond the scope of any individual practitioner. Temporally, this processual form of expression extends to an indefinite duration.

The Experience of Perfect Expression

[3.] Up to this point in time, there has been no lack of ability, may the expression even stretch out into many decades. Thus, the perfect experience when getting to the bottom of enlightenment must be authentic. Since the past experience is authentic, the expression of truth now is unquestionable. Therefore, the expression now carries within it the past experience. [And] the past experience carries within it the expression now. For this reason, there is now perfect expression, and there is now perfect experience. The expression now and the past experience are [continuous and inseparable as] one *Jō* and are [extended as] ten thousand *Ri*. Applying oneself now to [the truth] is, in other words, sustained through perfect expression and perfect experience.

The autonomy of the expression is reasserted in this section by plaching the word "expression" in the grammatical subject position repeatedly. In addition, the continuity of expression is clarified. The ongoing pursuit of perfect expression in the past and present, and its uninterrupted attainment, are justified by the complementary nature of experience and expression. Dōgen's theoretical grasp of this concept brings us closest to the aspect of enlightenment's inwardness. Insight into the experience of enlightenment is intimately linked with its articulation, creating a cohesive unity between the two. The foundation of expression lies in the experience and its authenticity ensures the expression's truthfulness. This relationship is not only complementary but reciprocal, with temporal reversibility as the "experience of that time carries the expression of the present."[27] The unity and continuity between expression and experience validate the emphasis on teaching mentioned at the beginning. For at no point is expression conceived as something passively mimetic. Here, on the contrary, the effort of concentration that is related to the experiencing subject is connected to a fundamental dynamic of expression itself.

The Manifestation of Perfect Expression
While the third paragraph emphasises the longevity of the expression and the effort involved in its articulation, the fourth paragraph links the processual dynamics of the salvation event with the momentary event. The continuity of effort enables the expression of truth to endure but this Endeavour must be continuously renewed. The effort itself manifests the whole truth in each fleeting instant as it condenses in

---

[27] Sakamoto points to the student-master relationship: "A buddha-patriarch's voicing of the Way emerges from his discernment of the Way". See Sakamoto "The Voicing of the Way: Dōgen's Shōbōgenzō Dōtoku" in *The Eastern Buddhist* 16 (1), (1983): 94. From this, the disciple feels spurred to understand the meaning of the expression himself and to attempt an utterance of his own. Until he is really able to do so.

time to a unifying moment. Effort as an instantaneous expression rises from duration into pure presence, as the years and months of concentration "are cast off".
With "casting off," Dōgen coins a term that can be comprehended as going back to
a pre-dualistic wholeness that does not negate the multiplicity and singularity of
moments. Dōgen states:

> [4.] This applying oneself is relentless and accumulates over many months and long years,
> and in turn casts off the applying of previous years and months. When you get to where it
> casts it off, it affirms that it likewise casts off skin, flesh, bones, and marrow and also affirms
> that it casts off lands, earth, mountains, and rivers. This time, when one aims at reaching the
> casting-off as the ultimate treasure [of *nirvana*], this aim is as such [its] emergence, which
> is why at the very moment of this casting-off, the expression [of truth] immediately mani-
> fests. It is neither a power of the heart nor a power of the body, but the perfect expression
> occurs [through heart and body]. Once the truth has been perfectly expressed, one does not
> consider it surprising or strange.

We can identify a regression to the pre-dualistic level formulated in the fact that the
expression in casting off is confirmed by "skin, flesh, bones and marrow" as the
quasi-subjective dimension and by "earth, mountains and rivers" as the quasi-
objective dimension. These quotations signify that there is no differentiation
between inside and outside in the wholeness of articulation. If one objectifies this
moment and intends to awaken and achieve redemption in *nirvana*, then, according
to existentialist language, they are already "beyond [themselves]" and no longer
present in the moment. However, *nirvana*, as a universal reality, grasps existence
precisely from the blind spot of its directedness towards this goal. The striving for
nirvana is no less a moment of reality than the casting off of all intentionality and
the experience of enlightenment itself. That is why it is ultimately "natural." The
expression of awakening does not stand out in its ordinariness, as it says at the end.

The Unexpressed of Perfect Expression

The final section focuses on the contrastive aspect of expression, particularly its
visibility or lack thereof. It examines the connection between expression and what
is unexpressed, insofar as every (visible) expression stands out against the unexpressed. The latter can be interpreted in two ways, either as indirectly or directly
unexpressed. The concept of the indirectly unexpressed refers to that which is connoted, while that of the directly unexpressed is that which is neither connoted nor
denoted within the realm of what is expressed.[28] The latter, viewed as a radical
other, is excluded under the premise that the whole world and everything that exists
is considered articulated. There is only an outside of what is articulated in human
language. In the sense of the connoted, moreover, every articulated thing is always
already related to everything else: there is no particular referentiality but the radical
referentiality to the world as a whole, which, however, cannot be represented holistically in a single expression. And as long as one does not penetrate this "negative"

---

[28] Here Sakamoto gives the reference to Tōzan Ryōkai in a footnote: "Grasp through voicing that
which cannot be grasped through practice; grasp through practice that which cannot be grasped
through voicing." See Sakamoto, "The Voicing of the Way: Dōgen's Shōbōgenzō Dōtoku" in *The
Eastern Buddhist* 16 (1), (1983): 95.

moment of articulation, one has not grasped articulation in its positivity. Therefore, Dōgen notes:

> [5.] However, when one succeeds in uttering this perfect expression, one keeps quiet about what cannot be expressed. Even if one fully realises what one is able to express – as long as one does not, in an enlightened manner, fathom the inexpressible as that which cannot be expressed, [the expression] is not yet the true face of the Buddhas and patriarchs, nor is it the "bone and marrow" of the Buddhas and patriarchs. Therefore, how can one compare [the wordless] expression [of the Second Patriarch Taiso Eka] [classified as] the marrow [of the truth] when bowing three times [to the First Patriarch Bodhidharma] and remaining in place with the expressions of the [other three] disciples who are classified [as] the skin, flesh and bones [of the truth]? The expressions of the latter do not come the least bit close to the expression of the former and have no part in it. That I and others move in different worlds and yet meet is that he and others move in different worlds and yet meet.

Dōgen distinguishes between different forms of articulation and qualifies as the highest expression of truth only the one that also articulates the unsaid. And so it seems that his attitude fits into the traditional interpretation of the transmission of the Dharma to the next disciple of Bodhidharma: among the four disciples up for election, it is only one who renounces verbal articulation and thus expresses that and what the others have not said or were unable to say. It is suggested that Eka's non-verbal articulation surpasses the three previous attempts, which differ only in degree but can still be compared. In contrast, the fourth answer appears as radically different. Hence, it is noted that the expressions neither touch nor include each other.

The incommensurability between Eka and the other disciples is restated in the following sentence from a different perspective but in a generalised form. In the distinction that relates to the salvific history between two worlds of the sacred and the profane; i.e., the enlightened world of nirvana and the dark world of *samsara*, the question arises as to how the practitioner, here in the perspective of the first person, can be part of one world and the other at the same time. But the dichotomy itself proves to be only a provisional distinction from the perspective of the enlightened one, i.e., the Buddha. Thus, Eka's competitive situation vis-à-vis his comrades-in-arms is also only an apparent one. Therefore, Dōgen writes in summary:

> In me, there is the expressed as well as the unexpressed. In him, there is the expressed as well as the unexpressed. In the said, there is the self and the other, just as in the unsaid, there is the self and the other.

In reality, every practitioner appears as someone who has spoken but conveys something else beyond. This holds true both for the first- and third-person perspectives. Conversely, every statement made or all that remains unspoken has an inner and outer perspective, referring to the sign-like nature of the expression itself at the moment of articulation. Ultimately, a Buddha is itself a sign beyond its completed articulation.

Ramifications of the Conceptualisation of "Dōtoku"

The preceding presentation of the expression *dōtoku* is based on a self-contained text that is predominantly discursive, but is also theoretical in that it aims directly and explicitly at determining the perfect expression. In contrast, the following discussion collects references from various fascicles that are useful for further defining *dōtoku* but are interpreted only within the horizon of the expression itself, rather than that of the original textual context. Since these passages are less explicative and explicit, the interpretation relies more on the use of *dōtoku*. At the same time, it becomes clear that Dōgen uses linguistic expressions in a conceptual way. This is true even when there are no clear distinctions and terminology remains vague. Dōgen does not systematically unfold words in a conceptual network. In terms of content, the following compilation serves, on the one hand, to deepen the provisions on *dōtoku* and, on the other hand, to prove that *dōtoku* is a central expression for Dōgen in the multitude of passages found throughout the *Shōbōgenzō*.

"Buddha Nature": The Need for Articulation of Perfect Expression

Numerous mentions of *dōtoku* are present in "Buddha nature" (*Busshō*), a fascicles of the *Shōbōgenzō*, that provides a thorough and comprehensive discussion of a canonical term. Originally, *busshō* referred to the essence and characteristics of an enlightened being. However, in the course of the give-and-take within the context of what can be considered the metaphysics of "Buddha nature," the term *busshō* represents the conceptual framework to encompass the entirety of existence. The most comprehensive interpretation of *busshō*, however, is only carried out by Dōgen himself in his analysis of the traditional versions. Dōgen significantly enhances language. This primarily involves its methodological significance, as Dōgen extensively examines the true definition of "Buddha nature" without providing a resolution in referene:

> In sum, since they have not awakened from viewing Buddha nature as [activities of everyday mind] such as their momentary thinking, knowing, recollecting or perceiving, it is like they lose the access point [from which to penetrate] the saying "being-Buddha nature" and also the saying "nothing-Buddha nature," and they hardly ever learn that they must utter [Buddha nature]. [...] In all directions [of the compass] there are chief priests who end their lives without once having uttered a perfect expression that says Buddha nature. Or they say, "Someone who listens to the teachings of the sutras talks about Buddha nature, but monks who practice *zazen* shouldn't speak of it." Such people are really nothing but animals. (DZZ 1: 32–33)

The appreciation of language is accompanied by the critique of its everyday understanding, as Dōgen disapproves the linking words and subjective workings of the mind or heart ("thinking, knowing, recollecting or perceiving") in the opening sentence. However, he stresses that every Buddhist must strive for the right understanding, and by this he means both the practical and intellectual dimensions of understanding, manifested here in an adequate articulation of Buddha nature. Dōgen advocates for rearticulating words in an innovative manner rather than refraining from using them. He sees verbal language as a tool for creatively and productively adopting tradition. The aim of overcoming the discursive use of language is to break free from dogmatic favouritism and exclusion of such means. The possibilities of articulation go beyond verbal language and ultimately lie in a specific attitude towards life:

> Even if the national master did not assign his understanding to a perfect expression [dōtoku] for the time being, this does not mean that there will not be the opportunity for doing so. Likewise, the present expression [of truth] [dōtoku] is not in vain and without meaning. [...] Thus, for the utterance [dōshu] of a [perfect] expression [dōshu] [of truth], it takes a whole life, and several lives may also be attached to that utterance [dōshu]. (DZZ 1: 34)

The success of a perfect expression is dependent on the proper situation and timing which is why the understanding gained and its articulation can fall apart in time. The reverse case may also exist: "Just as little is today's expression in vain and without meaning." The perfect expression always has a moment of originality that arises contextually. An expression, especially when spoken, can detach itself from its historical context and continue to have an effect in the present as part of tradition, without therefore "being in vain and without meaning." This is based not least on the fact that the respective expression may be indebted to a specific occasion, but at the same time grows on the ground of lifelong learning and practice. Furthermore, a perfect expression can only find its appropriate context in later times. This contextuality of all expressing ultimately confirms that even the historical Buddha was not privileged in his expressions. There is no one true articulation that conveys and asserts everything. Taking the expression "Buddha nature" as an example, Dōgen revisits the interpretation of a word without concluding or defining it as a concept. Consequently, Dōgen notes the following:

> Shakyamuni explained the way: "Altogether, all living beings have Buddha nature." And Dai'i[29] explained the way: "All living beings do not have Buddha nature." The words "have" and "have not" must be different in meaning, so one can doubt which expression [dōtoku] is correct and which is wrong. Therefore, Hyakujō[30] says: "To expound that all living beings have Buddha nature is to denigrate the Buddha [...]. To expound that all living beings do not have Buddha nature is to denigrate the Buddha [...]." So that means that whether you say there is Buddha nature or there is not, both become a denigration. Even if it becomes a denigration, one cannot help but utter something [dōshu]. Now listen to me, Dai'i and Hyakujō, I want to ask you something: it is now impossible without denigration. Have you sufficiently explained Buddha nature or not? Assuming you have sufficiently explained it, this will limit the explaining. If there is an explanation, it has to be interrogated in unison with it. And to Dai'i I must say that although you express perfectly [dōtoku] that all living beings have no Buddha nature, you do not say "all Buddha nature has no living being," nor "all Buddha nature has no Buddha nature," and of this, that all entire Buddhas have no Buddha nature, you have not seen anything even in a dream. (DZZ 1: 34–35)

The main focus of Dōgen's remarks is the commitment to actively express one's understanding, obtained through practicing on the Buddha's path or conveying it through attainment. Regardless of whether language is used or not, it is crucial to articulate oneself, however partial or situational the statement made may be. In this

---

[29] Dawei 大潙, an alternate name for Lingyu 靈祐 (771–853). He was one of the two founders of the Weiyang school 潙仰宗 of Chan, posthumously named Dayuan Dashi 大圓禪師.

[30] Baizhang Huaihai 百丈懷海 (720–814), a highly influential Chan monk of the Tang dynasty.

respect, every articulation is always already a "denigration." Even in the subsequent turn towards expounding and the expounding of "something," there is a limitation that cuts through to the universality of Buddha nature. By sharply delimiting and opposing the act of explaining on the one hand, and the object of explanation on the other, it is sometimes overlooked that explaining itself is in turn a manifestation of Buddha nature. Thus, even in their most generic form, corresponding statements remain particular.

Based on Dōgen's interpretation of Buddha nature, which expands the term "all living beings" to encompass "all that exists," including the inanimate – the negation that "all living beings have no Buddha nature" is still particular and can be further "permuted" to "all Buddha nature has no living being" and "all Buddha nature has no Buddha nature" (DZZ 1:35). Strictly logically, these turns cannot be adequately interpreted. However, if viewed as a linguistic game, these statements can be analysed through various rhetorical figures. To reach what is perhaps the most controversial statement, "all entire Buddhas have no Buddha nature," Dōgen suggests a complete suspension of meaning, which can at best be anticipated in dreams; which can only be understood ironically if one disregards the fact that even the reality of fantasy is itself an expression of universal reality.[31]

"A Shining Pearl": The Perfect Expression Behind the Name

We discover an early reference to *dōtoku* in "A Shining Pearl" ("Ikka myōshu"), a fascicle in which Dōgen presents a shift between first and second language. A name belonging to a specific discursive order becomes the true expression of the whole universe. In response to the saying of a Zen master quoted by Dōgen, "She, the world in all ten directions, is a shining pearl" (DZZ 1: 77), one would expect an interpretation of this sentence as either a metaphorical expression or an ontological statement in line with the doctrine of salvation in Buddhism. Dōgen brackets the expression and states: "This one shining pearl is still not a name, but it is a perfect expression [*dōtoku*]. As such, one recognises it as a name" (DZZ 1: 78).

Dōgen thus establishes a connection and rationalises the use of everyday language through the perfect mode of articulation. What appears to be an ordinary name refers to a more primal articulation that enables nameability in the first place. Consequently, he challenges the popular belief that linguistic expression is solely a matter of convention. Alternatively, he points to a superordinate context of reference from which everything that exists is structured by a double structure of sign and being. This leads to detaching the expression from a purely referential context of meaning and criticising a naïve conflation of semantics and ontology. Dōgen associates perfect expression with its practical application when he states:

> To utter the said expression [of truth], Gensha[32] speaks, "The world in all ten directions is a shining pearl, what is there to understand?" This utterance is a perfect expression in which the Buddha inherits the Buddha, the patriarch inherits the patriarch, and Gensha inherits

---

[31] See also the "Muchū setsumu" fascicle.

[32] Xuansha Shibei 玄沙師備 (835–908), a monk of the Qingyuan 青原/清源 branch of the Southern school of Chinese Chan.

> Gensha. If you wanted to escape succession, you would probably not be without refuges, but even if you escaped succession for a while, the fact of bearing the utterance is the unobstructed opportunity of [the shining pearl's] manifestation. (DZZ 1: 79)

The first sentence posits that the perfect expression (*dōtoku*) encompasses both the potential and the actual execution of the utterance, whereas j. *dōshu* denotes its realisation. Gensha, his rhetorical query of "what is there to understand," references the originality and comprehensiveness of the statement, which cannot be viewed objectively as it precludes the isolation of both the interpreting subject and the statement to be interpreted. Furthermore, the qualification as all-pervading truth as well as all-encompassing being expresses the non-dualistic idea of a salvific-historical approach to language.

Language is considered crucial to achieving enlightenment. However, language is also decentred to make room for a wider view of the world. For an expression is metaphorical and, at the same time, perfect: It refers to the totality of the world, so to speak, or makes a universal statement. However, on an ontological level, it is denied in the sense that it exists in the world and is therefore particular and distinct. Ultimately, the connection between ordinary language and enlightened language usage becomes a theme. The succession's self-referentiality indicates everything that exists, as well as language itself. Therefore, the articulating subject can always only conditionally escape the position it occupies within the play of referential contexts.

"The Heart of the Ancient Buddhas": The Question as Perfect Expression

The fascicle "The Heart of the Ancient Buddhas" ("Kobusshin") begins by demonstrating that perfect expression always denotes the potential of a single, traditional saying. Thus, it is said:

> Once a monk asked the National Teacher, "What is this heart of the ancient Buddhas?" The Teacher said, "Hedge, walls, bricks and pebbles." The monk's question states, this [heart] is here, this [heart] is there. [The monk] cites this perfect expression [of truth] [*dōtoku*] and makes it a question. This question becomes a perfect expression [*dōtoku*] of past and present far and wide. Therefore, the ten thousand trees and a hundred grasses in their blossoming are the expression [*dōtoku*] of the ancient Buddhas and the questions of the ancient Buddhas. (DZZ 1: 89)

The traditional understanding of the original quote (j. *ikanaru ka kore kobutsu shin*) means "What is the heart of the ancient Buddhas?" In contrast, Dōgen's interpretation (based on the opposite reading j. *ikanaru (mono) mo kore kobutsu shin*) suggests that "Everything is the heart of the ancient Buddhas." As a result, he argues that the monk is questioning whether "Everything is the heart of the ancient Buddhas?" Furthermore, the query is, in fact, actually itself already a declaration, a perfect expression, which at the same time contains the openness of an unanswerable question. As a result, the master can freely refer to the plurality of all that exists by means of individual things. Dōgen adds inanimate objects of nature to the list of things made or used by human hands, whereby the (opening) flowers denote the articulatedness of the articulation of Buddha nature.

"Instructions for Zazen": Writing down the Perfect Expression

Perfect expression is not only manifested in a single word or sentence. It is also manifested in the detailed instructions for the right posture of "body and heart" (j. *shinjin*) in the practice of *zazen*. These instructions already pronounce the entire reality and are as such its perfect expression. Precisely insofar as articulation includes both the mediated form of verbal representation and the immediacy of sign-like presence, there is a relationship of correlative identity between the practice of posture and the posture's representation in written form. This is why Dōgen, in valuing the instructions for doing *zazen* and their transmission, can write in "Instructions for Zazen" ("Zazenshin") "the one written by Zen master Wanshi[33] [...] alone is [that of] a Buddha and patriarch" and thus "a [real] instruction for *zazen*, which as such is the perfect expression [of truth]" (DZZ 1: 113).

"Samadhi of the Sea Inscription": Inner Collection as Perfect Expression

In "Samadhi of the Sea Inscription" ("Kaiin sanmai"), Dōgen considers further aspects of the practical exercise of *zazen*. It has an essentially correlative relationship to its expression and thus approaches the image of the shining pearl quoted above. It represents a unity which, as in the text about the shining of the pearl, at the same time transcends itself. In *zazen*, it is the posture of the practitioner who gathers herself in seated meditation. This is why Dōgen writes:

> Samadhi is full manifestation [of reality] and perfect expression [of truth] [*dōtoku*], it is like blindly reaching out for the pillow at night. (DZZ 1: 123)

In the practice of *zazen*, the profound gathering of self (j. *jiko* 自己) in the state of "inner contemplation" (s. *samadhi*), both in the outer sitting posture and in the inner stance, is a kind of articulation. One can even interpret the title of the fascicle accordingly: If the sea symbolises the state of deep immersion in meditation, at the same time, an inscription is realised in it. Something is inscribed within the practitioner, which is then expressed outwardly in the sitting posture.

The addition "it is like blindly reaching out for the pillow at night" is reminiscent of a dialogue between the patriarchs Ungan[34] and Dōgo[35] (cf. the corresponding passages in the fascicle "Kannon") and in its metaphor speaks of the fact that both hands and eyes reach aimlessly into the void or into an infinite fullness, but are unable to grasp anything definitively: be it theoretically or practically. For, in union with meditative immersion, reality manifests itself both in its particularity and in its momentariness, and is thus always singular in its infinite fullness. Similarly, perfect expression is always open and infinite. At the same time, it is bound to momentary articulation, not only outwardly but also inwardly, inasmuch as a

---

[33] Hongzhi 宏智 (1091–1157), the Buddhist heir of Daxia Zizhun.

[34] Yunyan Tansheng 雲巖曇晟 (782–841), a monk in the lineage of Qingyuan Xingsi 青原行思 (?–740).

[35] Daowu Yuanzhi 道悟圓智 (769–835), Tang-period Chan monk. Daowu was a student of Baizhang 百丈, then became dharma heir of Yaoshan Weiyen 藥山惟儼, along with Daowu's biological and dharma brother Yunyan 雲巖, the teacher of Dongshan, founder of the Caodong 曹洞 Lineage.

separation of inside and outside is relative. With regard to this inwardness, Dōgen also argues against verbal articulation:

> "Without words" is not to say nothing; for a perfect expression is not [identical with] putting something into words. (DZZ 1: 121)

"The Uninterrupted Practice": Body and Heart of the Perfect Expression

The fascicle "The Uninterrupted Practice" deals with more than just – literally – the adherence to and continuous practice of *zazen* or other principles of Buddhist life. It is concerned with the dynamism and being of the entire universe, which Dōgen suggests precedes the principle of the interdependence and relationality of everything that is generally taken to be fundamental to Buddhism as a whole. Accordingly, Dōgen writes of the circularity of the Buddha path, which is based on activity:

> Treading on the path of the Buddhas and patriarchs involves without fail the highest practice, [forms] a circular wheel and [continues] uninterruptedly. [The Way] is the evocation of the heart, the practice, the awakening and nirvana without the slightest pause; it is the circular wheel of uninterrupted practice. [...] The arising in dependence is the uninterrupted practice because the uninterrupted practice is not conditioned by dependent arising. This is what needs to be cultivated and studied carefully. The uninterrupted practice that fully manifests this practice is, as such, our momentary practice. (DZZ 1: 145, 146)

The dynamics of the universe are not detached from the practitioners. Suppose that what is happening in the universe cannot be based on a privileged position of the subject. In this case, it is at the same time no more than the dynamism manifesting itself in the world, for there is no other-worldly potentiality that fuels finitude. In the participation and realisation of "uninterrupted practice," the practitioner simultaneously realises – in the sense of giving reality to – the perfect expression of the Buddhist truth, which does not manifest itself in something extraordinary, but already finds an appropriate form in the still and silent sitting in the practice of *zazen*. As Dōgen notes:

> Quietly realise the uninterrupted practice without leaving the monastery. Do not follow the east and west winds to the east and west. When for ten or five years the spring wind [blows] and the autumn moon [passes], there is an utterance [of truth] [*dō*] free from voice and sound, even if it remains unrecognised. Such a perfect expression of truth [*dōtoku*] is unknown to me [until now], and I have not heard it [in the present time]. It is necessary to understand that every moment of uninterrupted practice is precious. Do not doubt whether the wordless [*fugo*] is empty. Entering [monkhood] is a monastery, leaving [it] is a monastery, the way of the birds is a monastery, the whole world is a monastery. (DZZ 1: 155)

Just as the monastery is a place of practice, and participation in, or realisation of practice, is extended to all spheres and forms of life, so the articulation of truth can be extended to the whole world. And yet it only manifests where it is accomplished: be it in a single utterance, or be it in the right form of life, which – though wordless – is by no means speechless. This other way of speaking may be wordless because it is free of sound and form. It may even remain unreciprocated because it is unrecognised. After all, such expression is not commonplace but a special event, as even Dōgen notes from his perspective. A perfect expression is self-sufficient, so that the intentionality of the articulation is also undermined:

> While the Zen master Shikan of Kyōgen[36] was practising the Way under Dai'i, he tried several times to express a verse in a perfect way [*ikku wo dōtoku sen to suru*], but in the end, he could not. Disappointed, he burnt his books and spent years and months as a monk serving meals. Later, he visited [Zen master] Daishō[37] on Mount Butō [c. Wu-tang]. He built a hut there and lived a solitary and quiet life. Then one day, just as he began to sweep the path, a pebble jumped away and hit a bamboo stalk: through the sound, he experienced enlightenment all at once. (DZZ 1: 165)

Of course, on the path of the Buddhas and patriarchs, if we are to speak of the success or failure of perfect expression, the one who wants to achieve it, must exert him- or herself in intentional effort. But in the end, even an unmotivated sound or a sudden noise can articulate the truth. In the horizon of the awakening, they take on their proper significance and meaning. And yet it is precisely the disengagement and radical freedom of articulation that, in relation to artistic expression (in the poetic language of a learned Zen monk, for example), is to be located here at the other end of the scale, so to speak, in a quasi-naturalistic form:

> It is reported that there are ponds and rivers on Mount Isan (c. Weishan), where ice and mist accumulate. It was a life of seclusion beyond human endurance; yet both the Buddha Way and the deep solitude have been transformed in novel ways. Thus, we recognise [here] the perfect expression [of truth] [*dōtoku*] [that Dai'i] practised unceasingly. […] Later, Kyōzan[38] came and served [Dai'i]. Kyōzan was – originally in the community of the past master Hyakujo – a Sariputra with a hundred answers to ten questions, but he remained on Mount Isan and cultivated the path for three years, watching over the ox. This is the uninterrupted practice that has gone out in more recent times and is neither seen nor heard of. Watching over the ox for three years made it completely unnecessary for him to ask anyone for a perfect expression. (DZZ 1: 190)

It appears that Kyōzan is caught between two extreme choices of lifestyle: that of a reclusive hermit and that of Sariputra, a figure in Zen who is treated with conflicting attitudes, yet widely regarded as omniscient and the wisest of Shakyamuni Buddha's ten primary disciples. However, similar to the ox as an animal (metaphorically representing the manifestation of Buddha nature) that gives off its largely unmotivated forms of articulation, perfect expression can also be heard in silence. Here, Dōgen redirects his focus from active expression to its passive reception. Thus, it is possible to read about Dai'i and his practice at the mountain hermitage where he expresses something in his own way, although he has never heard it before, it can still be heard in silence, even if unperceived. He does not require direct instruction from anyone regarding the proper form of articulation. Nonetheless, Dōgen further clarifies the particular connection between verbal expression and silent communication in *zazen*:

> Think in silence how short life is; to perfectly express [*dōtoku*] even two or three words and sayings [*goku*] of the Buddhas and patriarchs is to perfectly express [*dōtoku*] the Buddhas

---

[36] Xiangyan Zhixian 香嚴智閑 (?–898). A Nanyue Huairang 南嶽懷讓 (677–744) lineage monk who joined the monkhood under Baizhang Huaihai 百丈懷海 (720–814) before later going on to study under Weishan Lingyou 溈山靈祐 (771–853).
[37] Nanyang Huizhong 南陽慧忠 (d. 775), a disciple of Huineng 慧能.
[38] Jiashan 夾山, the name of a monk and monastery in Lizhou 澧州 during the Tang.

and patriarchs. Why is this so? Because for Buddhas and patriarchs, body and heart are one, so all of them, one saying and the other saying, are the warm body and heart of the Buddhas and patriarchs. Their body and heart come forth and give perfect expression [*dōtoku*] to our body and heart. At the very moment of utterance, the perfect expression [*dōtoku*] comes forth and utters [*dōshu*] our body and heart. Let it be so that this life expresses [*dōshu*] the earthly body, which is enriched with past lives. Therefore, when we become a Buddha or patriarch, we transcend the Buddha or the patriarch. For sayings, [uttered] through uninterrupted practice, be they but three or two, are of such a nature. Do not chase sounds and forms of fame and gain in vain. (DZZ 1: 202)

In the realm of expression, practice is a moment of expression in and of itself, establishing a connection between verbal expression and the actual practice and embodiment of expression. Proper verbal expression serves to articulate the Buddhas and patriarchs. However, this unity of body and mind is expressed as part of the world in the present moment, and extends beyond time and generations. In contrast, there are indeed forms of expression in the transient world that do not relate to the comprehensive articulatedness of this world.

"This-Ness": The Perfection of Expression

Clearly, there is no "absolute" expression. Every perfect expression must be placed in a relation, even if it's suitable for a specific context. Expressions, like everything else, exist in a relationship dispersed across all times and spaces. This is why "saying nothing" is also taken up emphatically, as it is said in "This-ness" ("Inmo"): The "perfect expression" always omits something that, hence, remains unsaid – unless one comprehends this, one does't understand it. This is relevant to dualistic-sounding statements from tradition:

> These perfect expressions [*dōtoku*] are from [the regions] above and below heaven, from the heaven of the west [from India] and the eastern land [from China]. They are perfect expressions [*dōtoku*] of the past and the present times, of the old and the new Buddhas. These expressions leave nothing unsaid [*dōmijin*] and speak nothing false [*dōkiketsu*]. However, to have only this understanding and to be without incomprehension is like not exploring these words. In fact, the expressions [*dōtoku*] of the ancient Buddhas were transmitted in this way, but again, when one hears the words of an ancient Buddha as an ancient Buddha, it should be a supreme listening. (DZZ 1: 205)

Dōgen highlights the situatedness of all perfect expression and its limitations, which in no way detract from its perfection. He also acknowledges that every articulation entails a corresponding listening that may or may not be suitable for what is being articulated. It is not solely a matter of speech wherein something may remain unsaid, but it also encompasses "listening to" what is not being spoken.[39]

"Bodhisattva Avalokitesvara": The Incompleteness of Perfect Expression

The topic of incomplete articulation is dealt with in more detail elsewhere: Thus, the various fascicles initially depict the circumstances and levels of perfect expression, such as everyday life, body, nature, practice, intention, failure, or enlightenment. It

---

[39] Kim, "The Reason of Words and Letters" in *Dōgen Studies.*, ed. by W.R. LaFleur. (Honolulu: University of Hawaii Press, 1985), 212–213.

is crucial to examine the extent to which linguistic expression truly extends and what is ommunicated through it: what is uttered, what remains unsaid? The fascicle "Bodhisattva Avalokitesvara" ("Kannon") elaborates on this:

> Great Master Ungan Muju asked Great Master Shu-itsu of Mount Dōgo: "What does the Bodhisattva of Great Compassion do with so many hands and eyes?" Tao-wu said, "It is just like someone reaching backwards for his pillow at night." "I understand, I understand." "What do you understand?" "Hands and eyes are on the whole body [of the Bodhisattva Avalokitesvara]." "What you say is very well said, but it is only able to express eight or nine parts." "I am just like this, how about you, revered brother?" "The whole body is hands and eyes." (DZZ 1: 213)

Dōgen analyses the dialogue's various statements and aspects but ultimately addresses what is actually left unsaid and the significance of leaving things unsaid. In doing so, he brackets the concrete statements and analyses the functioning of language itself. According to his analysis, perfect expression does not necessarily require many words, but the choice of the appropriate expression, which initially may also appear imperfect. Yet Dōgen insists that it is precisely in this imperfection where perfection lies:

> Dōgo says, "What you say is very well said, but it can only express eight or nine parts [dōtoku]." The meaning of this utterance is that the perfect expression [dōtoku] says it very well. "To say it very well" means to say it accurately, to express it, that there is no such thing as an imperfect expression that leaves something unsaid. If one utters a still imperfect expression, something ultimately inexpressible and impermanent, then one is only able to express eight or nine parts. Even if one [expresses] ten parts, a study of the meaning of what is said would not be a penetrating exploration unless one has the skill to say something imperfectly. It will be a perfect expression whether one speaks eight or nine parts, whether one speaks ten parts of what one has to utter. At that moment, he should express himself in a hundred, a thousand, and ten thousand expressions, but his skill being miraculous, he expended little effort and just expressed it in one expression of eight or nine parts. In other words, commenting in a hundred, a thousand, and ten thousand words in all ten directions of the world is superior to saying nothing. But to comment on it in a single expression is no ordinary skill of this world. That is the meaning of [saying] something [only in] eight or nine parts. (DZZ 1: 217–218)

The text highlights that silence alone is far from being a perfect form of expression. However, what about using numerous words or being succinct? Dōgen argues that a solitary expression cannot convey everything. Nevertheless, this issue cannot be resolved by using a multitude of words, as this does not cancel out the expression's specificity and concreteness. Even general statements, such as quotes about living beings and Buddha nature, can be consistently negated. However, individuals may become trapped in a nihilistic state or pursue additional articulation if they fail to adhere to a positive, rather than negative approach. For it is precisely not a *via negativa* that Dōgen is aiming at. His objective it not to relinquish the moment of expression, but to maintain a constructive albeit constrained discourse that manifests as verbal and non-verbal forms of expression.

The Linguistic Critique of Tradition

Dōgen employs language creatively, without attempting to exceed or leave its confines. He identifies language in various ways by using language itself. He employs the quotation device to comment on other patriarchs' sayings. A well-known example is Dōgen's exposition of a quote from the *Nirvana Sutra* in the "Busshō" fascicle which was discussed above.

Let us focus on the opening sentences of this fascicle. All statements are based on quotations and operate at the level of intertextuality, removed from direct references to the real world and situated within commentary literature. The initial source is itself nothing but a quotation: the *Nirvana Sutra* cited by Dōgen quotes a speech by Shakyamuni Buddha that was allegedly transcribed into text by a disciple from memory. It says: "All living beings, all being is Buddha nature. The Tathagata is eternal, he is without change." Dōgen undertakes an interpretation of this quote by commenting on it through a series of quotations. For instance, a first "interpretation" states that the meaning of the Buddha's saying lies in the phrase "What is that which comes to me thus?"

Furthermore, it should be noted that Dōgen incorporates language extensively in his reflections at a philological level. For instance, when recalling the Buddha's speeches or the dialogues of the patriarchs with their disciples as spoken words, he presents them as spoken words. Buddha Shakyamuni "spoke" (j. *iu* or *notamau*), a monk "asked," and the patriarch's "word" and "saying" was thus and thus. Additionally, in "Busshō" as in other texts, Dōgen repeatedly asks about the meaning of a word, expression, or sentence. He points to conventional names or clarifies the meaning and connotation of a word or phrase. As he notes in "Busshō," one "calls" the Buddha nature "living being" or "sentient being." Or, using the equivalent of the copula, the text states:

> The word "all being" is (j. *shitsuu no gon*, *sarani… ni arazu*) neither "newly arisen being" nor "original being" or "wondrous being." (DZZ 1: 15)

Dōgen's approach shifts the consideration of traditionally factual questions from an ontological to a semantic level. In the present fascicle's discussion of the "being" and "nothingness" of Buddha nature, he highlights his opposition to hypostasising these expressions. Thus, Dōgen first revisits the level of meaning. Returning to this level does not imply that Dōgen simplifies the factual context to a semantic, quasi-linguistic inquiry. However, the web of language is not dispensed with in favour of an actual reality, but interrogated for its portrayal of reality. As Dōgen notes at one juncture:

> The words "whoever wishes to realise the meaning of Buddha nature…" refers not only to that kind of knowledge, but also to "whoever wishes to practise it [Buddha nature]," "whoever wishes to realise it," "whoever wishes to explain it," and even "whoever wishes to forget it." (DZZ 1: 17)

It is noteworthy that the statements enclosed in inverted commas are treated as quotations, despite Dōgen establishing a causal connection between their content within his remarks. However, the "bracketing" of the statements and their use as quotations is clarified later by Dōgen, when he expounds on the temporal causal structure of the Buddhist principle of karma in terms of semantic determinations.

Dōgen acknowledges the relationship between language and the world. He also examines the process of verbal expression and other subject-related aspects, such as cognition and knowledge, in a manner that does not favor either the objectivity of the world or a mystical standpoint. The world is not given directly but mediated in many ways, including mediation through language and concepts. To reiterate, Dōgen values language not just for its analytical capabilities, but also as a genuine means of expression.

In the subsequent sections, we will expand on these points by revisiting previously discussed fascicles and exploring new ones concerning language overall. The term *dōtoku* remains the conceptual centerpiece, while also providing insight into a more comprehensive topic and its discourse.

"Buddha Nature": Language, Names, and Beings

Dōgen addresses language from a broader perspective as he explores the correlation between "name" and "being." He begins scrutinising a Wittgensteinian picture theory-like comprehension of language. Dōgen challenges this idea in "Busshō" through the following story: before the fifth patriarch becomes the fifth patriarch, he meets – according to tradition – the fourth patriarch as an old monk. The latter asks him to come to him as a younger person; reincarnated as a child. The future fifth patriarch again asks the fourth patriarch for instruction. Dōgen presents the account and then offers his interpretation as follows:

> When the [Fourth] patriarch saw the master [as a young child], he asked him: "You, what is your name?" The master replied, "I have a name, but it is not an ordinary name." The patriarch said, "What name is this?" The master replied, "It is this, the Buddha nature." The patriarch said, "You have nothing of Buddha nature." The master replied, "Since the Buddha nature is empty, you call it nothing [j. *mu to iu*]." The patriarch realised that [this child] was a vessel of the Dharma and made him his servant. [...] Later, he shared with him the *Storehouse of the Eye of Right Teaching*. He lived on the eastern mountain of Ōbai [c. Huangmei] and made the wind of his wisdom blow great. [Dōgen continues:] For the fathoming of the utterances [j. *dōshu*] of the patriarch and the master, [the sentence] "The Fourth patriarch said, 'What is your name?'" contains an important teaching. Once upon a time, someone had said, "I am from What-land. I have the name What." That is, [the patriarch] is teaching here: "You have the name What." This is the same as uttering [j. *dōshu*], "I am just like this, you are just like this." The Fifth patriarch said, "My name is being, which is not an ordinary name." What has been said [j. *iwayuru*] means that the identity of name and being does not exist in ordinary names. Ordinary names are not this, identical with being. The Fourth patriarch said, "This-is is what kind of name?" That means, What is it-is-this; It-is-this is made into "what." That is the "name." The "what" comes into being because of the "It-is-this." It is the function of the "what" that gives rise to the "It-is-this." The "name" is both "It-is-this" and "what." It is found in the herbal decoction, in the tea water, in everyday eating and drinking. (DZZ 1: 20)

The fourth patriarch's initial inquiry regarding the name of the younger one is, on the discursive level, the question of family affiliation and origin. However, it also connotes the query of his true essence. This is signified by the external resemblance of the Chinese characters (姓 for name and 性 for nature/essence) and their reading (for both characters c. *xing* and j. *shō*). The fifth patriarch's response confirms that the initial inquiry deals with the essence of the fifth patriarch. The fourth patriarch's reply to the younger patriarch's answer is only seemingly a denial of this fact. It is a provocation to which the fifth patriarch delivers a fitting response with his final statement: "Because Buddha nature is empty, you call it nothing [j. *mu to iu*]." With this statement, the fifth patriarch simultaneously provides a foundation for critically examining any "philosophy of nothingness" that defines itself through a naïve opposition to ontology: He cautions against oversimplifying the world into mere dualities. Describing it as "empty" does not negate its determination or determinability.

However, Dōgen states that the opening query does not entail a dualistic comprehension of self and world due to its non-interrogative nature. Rather, he interprets it as an allusion to a conventional narrative: The well-known statement "I am from What-land" rejects a referential answer to the question of identity if the person's essence is to be determined by origin. It eludes conclusive determination and warrants a "tangible openness" that is contingent upon context, time, and location. Therefore, to explain the name "what," Dōgen recounts the dialogue between Nangaku[40] and Enō[41] (Chinese: Nanyue and Huineng), in which it is said: "I am the same, you are the same." This saying does not challenge individual existence but rather highlights the uniqueness of each and every thing. This uniqueness is, therefore, universal and requires us to broaden our perception of existence's plurality.

To correctly interpret the Chinese text, Dōgen prioritises an alternative reading to the conventional one, which translates j. *shō sunawachi ari* (姓即有) as "there is a name" or "I have a name": Instead, Dōgen reads j. *shō soku u*, meaning "name is being." "Ordinary names" may not be identical with the signified being, however, "unusual" names connote the this-ness of the signified, unlike abstract general terms. Consequently, Dōgen derives the "unusual" name from the relationship between question and indicative determination: "'This-is is what kind of name?' That means: what is 'it-is-this'; 'it-is-this' is made into 'what.' This is the 'name.'" In concrete beings, the intersection of universal reality and particularity reflects the plurality of being. This is why Dōgen refers to the "emptiness" of Buddha nature, as follows:

> The Fifth patriarch said, "Because Buddha nature is empty, you call it nothing." What he is obviously uttering [j. *dōshu*] is: "Empty" is not "nothing." When he utters [the expression] "Buddha nature is empty" [j. *dōshu*], he does not say anything about a pound or five hundred grams [of hemp], but literally conceives it as "nothing" [j. *mu to gonshu suru*]. He does not say "empty" because it is empty, or "nothing" because it is nothing, but because Buddha nature is empty, he says "nothing." Thus, every single "nothing" is a mark that utters "empty" [j. *dōshu*], and "empty" is the power that utters "nothing" [j. *dōshu*]. What is called "empty" is not the "empty" of the phrase "form is empty." Nor does "form is empty" mean

---

[40] Nanyue 南嶽, a name of the Tang Chan monk Huairang 懷讓 (677–744) who lived at Nanyue mountain at Bore temple 般若寺 of Hengyue 衡嶽.

[41] Huineng 慧能 (638–713), a Chinese Chan monk who is one of the most important figures in the tradition.

to overwhelm form and make it empty, or to divide the empty and produce forms from it. It must be the "empty" of "The empty is empty." The empty of "The empty is empty" is like in the words "a single stone in space." So it is with the questions and answers of the Fourth and Fifth patriarchs about "Buddha nature is nothing," "Buddha nature is empty" and "Buddha nature is being." (DZZ 1: 21–22)

Dōgen provides an interpretation of the fifth patriarch's saying that surpasses mere caution against a dichotomous worldview. He "literally conceives [Buddha nature] as 'nothing' [j. *mu to gonjū*]," since only its self-identity abides for its conceptual determination. Logically, it can only be conveyed by a tautology or a paradox; Buddha nature is empty because it is empty. Language plays a crucial role in this regard. Only through linguistic discourse and the division of the world into signs and meanings can the self-identity and individuality of existence be articulated in its mode of being present. From this viewpoint, Dōgen challenges the established interpretation of a concise passage in the *Heart Sutra,* explaining that the genuine self-identity of existence can only be revealed amidst the diversity of beings. From the self-identity of existing beings, all linguistic expressions then also have a character of being, whether it is "Buddha nature is nothing," "Buddha nature is empty" or "Buddha nature is being."

Dōgen's explanations, along with all additional explanations offered in the "Busshō" fascicle, challenge various efforts to resolve the connection between "being," "nothing," and "empty" through formal-logical or dialectical means. From the perspective of his language thinking, the passages appear to focus on exploring the many potentialities of semantic expression in order to critique an ontological dualism of being and nothingness. Language, too, would ultimately only acquire a deviant status. However, the meaning of linguistically mediated understanding becomes clear later on when – from a soteriological point of view – becoming Buddha is linked to language and, particularly, to dialogue about Buddha nature. Firstly, it is important to hear, listen and comprehend the contexts. Beyond this, the path of the Buddha is grounded in independent articulation, going beyond passivity. Thus, Dōgen writes:

When one first hears the Buddha and sees the Dharma, what is difficult to grasp and hear is that "living beings are nothing-Buddha nature." Whether you learn it from a good master or by reading the sutras, these are the very words to rejoice in when you hear them: "Living beings are nothing-Buddha nature." If you are not yet fully absorbed in seeing, hearing and recognising "All living beings, nothing-Buddha nature," then you do not yet see, hear or know anything about Buddha nature. When the Sixth patriarch asked to become a Buddha, the Fifth patriarch did not say anything else and did not use any other artifice to make him become a Buddha. He only said [j. *iu*], "People of Lingnan, nothing-Buddha nature." You must realise that the uttering and questioning [j. *dōshu monshu*] of the nothing-Buddha nature is the direct speaking [j. *jikidō*] to bring forth the Buddha. Accordingly, at the very time [of uttering] "nothing-Buddha nature" is becoming Buddha. When nothing-Buddha nature is not yet perceived and uttered, one has not yet become Buddha. (DZZ 1: 23)

It has become evident from the discussion of the traditional terminology "Buddha nature," that there is no solitary word that accurately conveys the truth within the Buddha-way. Substituting or designating it as "empty," "nothing" or "being" fails to eliminate all provisionality since all articulation is contingent on situation and context. The proper form of an expression is only confirmed through examples when

Dōgen recollects, dissects, or clarifies the one dialogue through the other. It becomes evident that this text does not solely concentrate on human verbal communication, as seen in a later example where the context of expression is rephrased in a quasi-natural manner. A comparison is made between a monk's reply, which must abide by cultural standards of modesty and humility, and the innate vocalisation of a water buffalo:

> Ōbaku said, "Not at all." He says this because in the Song realm, when you are asked if you possess an ability, you say "not at all," even if you mean to say that you possess it. That is, saying [j. *dō*] "not at all" does not mean "not at all." One should not think that this perfect expression [j. *dōtoku*] is identical with its [literal] utterance [j. *dōshu*]. When a superior old man expresses his insight, he must say "not at all," however much of a superior old man or Ōbaku may be. "When a water buffalo comes, he can only say 'moo-moo' [j. *dō*]." To utter [j. *dōshu*] in this way is an utterance [j. *dōshu*]. Think about an utterance, which in turn is an utterance of the uttered meaning, and try to utter it. (DZZ 1: 37–38)

Dōgen urges practitioners to articulate themselves appropriately without relying on subjective evaluations. Although there is no absolute criterion for perfect expression, it is important to adhere to naturalness in free and original expression. Ultimately, the enlightened ones will evaluate the expression's meaning, which transcends the discursive order, based on their perspective and understanding of Buddha's teachings. Only from the non-ordinary order of the world do mundane phrases attain their new meaning. Therefore, depending on the speaker or listener, one can attribute a profoundness to language:

> Therefore, sayings [j. *dōshu*] and questions [j. *monshu*] about Buddha nature are the everyday life and tea-drinking in the house of the Buddhas and patriarchs. (DZZ 1: 40)

This can lead to the misconception, for those without expertise, that a specific sentence lacks importance beyond its individual meaning:

> These words [j. *go*] have long been in circulation even among ordinary people; here, however, it is a perfect expression [j. *dōtoku*] of Jōshū. (DZZ 1: 41)

"The Uninterrupted Practice": Language Between Zen Theory and Practice

The issue of how to apply practice in particular exercises is explored in several places, including in "Uninterrupted Practice" ("Gyōji"), a fascicle in which Dōgen emphasises on the connection between verbal instruction and practice. Surprisingly, verbal instruction is prioritised over practice, as the text suggests that it is crucial to practice what cannot be explained and to explain what cannot be practised. Language serves a crucial and irreducible role. There is a correlative relation that, which, for the sake of its irreducibility, also grants language a necessary and definite place. There can be no real value in an ordinary, merely discursive expression since practice remains superior to it. But when meaning is raised to the level of perfect expression in the form of a Zen master's utterance, the boundaries dissolve. Then, as in Seppō's case, every expression can become practice and, conversely, sitting silently and practising in the monastery can become an authentic expression. Thus, the Zen Master Kanchū[42] says of the relationship between speech and practice the following:

> A *shaku* [about 30cm] of practice is more than a *jō* [about 1.2m] of expounding [j. *settoku*], a *sun* [about 3cm] of practice is more than a *shaku* of expounding.

Dōgen explains in response:

> It may seem that he is warning his contemporaries against neglecting uninterrupted practice and forgetting the realisation of the Way. Yet, his words do not say it is wrong to expound a *jō,* only that a *shaku* of practice is of greater merit than a *jō* of expounding. However, it is not just a question of the quantity of *jō* and *shaku* [...] The perfect expression [quoted] here does not mean that Kanchū speaks by itself, but it is by itself Kanchū's saying [j. *ima no dōtoku wa, Kanchū no jiidō ni arazu, Kanchū no jiidō nari*]. The grand master Gohon of the Tōzan said, "I expound something that I am not able to practise and practise something that I am not able to expound." This is the saying of a High patriarch. Its meaning is that practice illuminates the path that leads to expounding, and that there are ways in which expounding leads to practice. Therefore, to expound from morning till night is to practise the whole day. The meaning of this is to practise something that cannot be practised and to explain something that cannot be explained. [...] The grand master Kokaku of Mount Ungo,[43] having fully penetrated the saying [of Gohon of the Tōzan[44]], says: "For the time of expounding, there is no trace of practice, for the time of practice there is no trace of expounding." This perfect expression [*dōtoku*] does not say there is neither practice nor expounding. The time of expounding means not leaving the monastery for a whole lifetime. The time of practice means washing one's head and going before Seppō. (DZZ 1: 161–162)

Perfect expression effectively unites practice and theoretical instruction, erasing a causal and functional divide between the two. "Expounding" in this context refers to theoretical instruction, typically disregarded in Zen practice. Dōgen aims to counteract the overemphasising of practice in Zen tradition, so the balanced correlation of practice and theory allows each to reciprocally contribute to the other.

"The Task of Ascending Beyond the Buddhas": Language as Path and Practice

A Dōgen never diminishes language to a mere and superfluous aspect of practice as evidenced by the fascicle "Ascending Beyond the Buddhas" ("Bukkōjōji"). The practice of *zazen* that is never viewed as complete. Even after attaining enlightenment and ascending to the Buddhas, one must continue to transcend and go beyond them through ongoing practice. This process of ascent and transcendence is also achieved through the use of language. Thus, Dōgen elaborates on the saying of a patriarch, "If you succeed physically in ascending beyond the Buddhas, then you will indeed also have a small share in the conversation [of the Buddhas]" (DZZ 1: 285), as follows:

---

[42] Huanzhong 寰中 (780–862). A Tang period Chan 禪宗 monk from Puban 蒲坂 in Hedong 河東 (present day Puzhou 蒲州 in Shanxi 山西) who was a Dharma heir of Baizhang 百丈 in the Nanyue 南嶽 school.
[43] Yunju 雲居 (929–997). The Chan monk Yunju Daoqi Chanshi 雲居道齊禪師.
[44] Wuben 悟本, posthumous name of Dongshan Liangjie 洞山良价.

> If there is no conversation, one does not succeed bodily in ascending beyond the Buddhas. [Conversation] is not a reciprocal revealing or concealing, a reciprocal giving or taking. For this reason, it is precisely in the moment when conversation manifests where the ascent beyond the Buddhas lies. (DZZ 1: 286)

The focus here is on engaging in dialogue along the path of the Buddhas and patriarchs, while remaining aware of the connection between ascension and physical practice. The conversations referred to are not intended for instructing one another, showcasing something or proving superiority over one another. A successful conversation can result in an ascension beyond the Buddhas. Genuine conversation does not allow for mere passive listening. As per the opening quotation, this has already been stated:

> Then a monk asks, "What kind of talk is this?" The grand master says, "When you speak, [...] you do not listen." The monk replies, "Does the master listen to himself [while speaking] or not?" The grand master says: "When I do not speak, I listen." (DZZ 1: 285)

Dōgen comments: "We can experience [enlightenment] when we succeed bodily in not listening for the time of the conversation" (DZZ 1: 285). If one assumes that speaking and listening are mutually dependent, Dōgen elevates the moment of this single activity in verbal dialogue. Dōgen also emphasises elsewhere that "the manifestation of 'only listening' must at the same time be a 'not speaking'" (DZZ 1: 287). Similarly, someone who ascends to the Buddhas through conversation remains unchanged in their "purity" of activity. Dōgen initially cites the following sayings:

> A monk asks, "What is a person who ascends beyond the Buddhas?" The grand master says, "A non-Buddha." Unmon[45] says, "We cannot name it, and we cannot describe it. So we call it 'not'." Hofuku[46] says, "Buddha is a 'not'." Hōgen[47] says, "As a means [of instruction on the Way], we call it 'Buddha'." (DZZ 1: 287)

Every practising being already possesses Buddha nature and is therefore a Buddha. So there is a touch of irony when Hōgen refers to "Buddha" only as a provisional means of instruction. It is justified, however, in that in the ascent and transcendence of the Buddhas, Dōgen warns, on the one hand, against fixating on the goal of becoming a Buddha; while on the other hand, one overcomes this fixation by urging the transcending of the Buddhas. "Buddha," "non," as well as "non-Buddha," are always only provisional designations, which is why Dōgen explains the words "non-Buddha" as follows:

> If we doubt what a "non-Buddha" is, it is necessary to consider: One does not call [anyone] a "non-Buddha" because he is not yet a Buddha or because he is no longer a Buddha; nor because he transcends the Buddhas; merely because he ascends beyond the Buddhas, one calls him a "non-Buddha". He is called a "non-Buddha" because the face and eyes as well as the body and heart of a Buddha have been cast off. (DZZ 1: 288)

---

[45] Yunmen 雲門 (d. 949), the popular name of Wenyan 文偃, a major Tang period master of the Chan 禪 movement.
[46] Baofu Congzhan 保福從展 (−928).
[47] Fayan 法眼 (885–958), an important Chan monk of the Five Dynasties period.

Dōgen adds his own coinage as a further explanation: "casting off" – here of face, eyes, body and heart. Even the word "Buddha" is understood here only as a means on the path to Buddhahood and, at the same time, explained in relation to the non-Buddha. But one can still wonder if something is lacking in this questioning of the highest being in the Buddhist cosmos. There is also the negation of the Buddha here, at least in name. Language then becomes a means of the path of salvation. Indeed, not merely a means, but also its positive affirmation and attainment.

"Mountains and Waters Sutra": The Many Names of Water

In the "Mountains and Waters Sutra" ("Sansuikyō"), Dōgen again criticises against the one-sided anti-language attitude in Zen, before moving on to his own reflections on language. He states: "Mountains and waters present now are the manifestation of the words of the ancient Buddhas" (DZZ 1: 316). Dōgen further writes:

> To see the heart and to see the nature of being is an occupation outside the Way; to persist in words and sayings is not an utterance of liberation. [But] there are such [words] as to penetrate and resolve from [*samsaric*] conditions, such as "The blue mountains advance continually" or "The eastern mountains run over the water." They must be studied carefully. (DZZ 1: 318)

Dōgen here takes up the conventional demand of the Zen tradition to explain enlightenment as the act of seeing: observing the all-encompassing heart and one's own inner nature of being. Dōgen diverges from being fixated on the sense of sight or on what is called intuition, akin to perception as inner seeing. It is worth noting that he does not consider solely studying the words and compositions of former masters as the authentic option. Nevertheless, the author notes that some sayings whose meaning needs to be studied more closely because they "penetrate and resolve from [*samsaric*] conditions," i.e., contribute significantly to understanding the path towards enlightenment:

> These [people] say the following: Speaking of the East Mountain walking on water or speaking of Nansen's[48] sickle are nonsensical (j. *muri ewa*). By this is meant that speech that involves all kinds of thinking is not Zen speech (j. *zen wa*) in the sense of the Buddhist masters. [But] nonsensical discourses are these: the enunciations of the Buddhas and patriarchs. Therefore, Ōbaku's use of the stick and Rinzai's thundering are difficult to understand and have nothing to do with reflection. They are thought to be the great awakening that still precedes the arising of any sign. [But actually] the devices of the earlier masters, i.e., the use of verses that cut off everything entangled [j. *kattō danku*], are incomprehensible. (DZZ 1: 319)

Dōgen opposes those who view the irrational and senseless actions in the Zen tradition as the true and appropriate methods for teaching disciples. Dōgen utilises rationality in all his work and writing to facilitate the transmission and dissemination of the Buddha Way. Additionally, he encourages his readers to employ their thinking and writing skills:

---

[48] Nanquan Puyuan 南泉普願 (748–835), major Chan teacher of the Tang, one of the most cited figures in the *kōan* literature.

How pathetic! These [unteachables] do not know that reflection is words and sayings, and words and sayings pervade and liberate reflection. When I was in the Song realm, I laughed at them, to which they could not reply and only fell silent. They only utter the erroneous view of the meaninglessness [of the sayings] they had just expressed. (DZZ 1: 320)

For Dōgen, however, insight into the perspectivity of language is part of the practitioner's true understanding. Thus, with regard to the comprehensiveness of language in transcending its human use and arriving at a quasi-naturalistic context, one reads:

It is not only a matter of fervently learning how man and heaven see water, […] it happens that water [itself] fervently expresses "water." (DZZ 1: 321)

But it is ultimately the word itself that can simply be used in different ways:

There is the one who, looking at what is called water, sees a string of pearls. […] What he thinks is a string of pearls, I see as water. There is the one who sees water as a wondrous flower. Yet the water is not to be used as a flower. The hungry spirit sees water as wild fire and as festering blood. Dragons and fish see it as a palace and as a pavilion. (DZZ 1: 321)

"The Teachings of Buddha": The Transmission within the Scriptures

The critique of the Zen notion of wordless transmission, expressed in "Hidden Words", is explored in several contexts with further elaborations. In "The Teachings of Buddha" ("Bukkyō"), the depiction of Vulture Peak is protected against dualistic beliefs, not regarding the use of word and gesture, but respects to form and content. There is no separate meaning that exists beyond words. Therefore, it is important to note that the significance of the Buddha is not only limited to his "mind", but also extends to his teachings: "The manifestation of the words of all the Buddhas themselves are the Buddha teachings" (DZZ 1: 380). Furthermore, it is important to emphasise that there is no room for dualistic notions, as the teaching content is not transmitted separately from the words. Similarly, the counterpart is not outside the teaching, and the event as a whole is the manifestation of a reflexive structure: the text communicates itself.

"Buddha teaching" means the ten thousand appearances lined up. "Outside" [of the scriptures] means "here" or "coming to this place." Since it is transmitted from self to self, "right transmission" means a self is in that transmission. It is the transmission from heart to heart; in right transmission there is one heart. (DZZ 1: 382)

The Buddhist doctrine reveals a quasi-monistic dimension that provides excellent self-explication of a pluralistic text. This is supported by an argument that dismantles the notion of separating the doctrine into inside and outside, instead revealing a unity of language and meaning in the tradition:

However, those who speak of a special tradition outside of scholasticism do not yet know this meaning. Therefore, one must not trust the false presentation of a special tradition and err in the teaching of the Buddha. If it were as you say, you would also have to speak of the teaching as a special tradition outside the heart. If you speak of a special tradition outside the heart, no sentence and no half verse should have been handed down; without speaking of a special tradition outside the heart, you need not speak of a tradition outside scholasticism. (DZZ 1: 382)

If there is no tradition beyond the teaching, then the three schools and twelve kinds of sutras known to tradition are also the perfect embodiment of the Buddha. They may be called provisional means, each meeting different needs. Yet, Dōgen asserts the perfect unity of reading "I" and the "this-ness" of the teaching, as Dōgen interprets the Buddha's teaching through a saying of the ancient masters.

"Entanglements": The Snares of Language

The positive aspect of language is exemplified in Dōgen's reinterpretation of the Zen-specific critique of language in the master-student relationship, where he interprets the common expression *kattō* in the fascicle of the same name. This expression literally translates to arrowroot and wisteria vines and typically serves as a metaphor for conflict, strife and difficulty. In Zen practice, however, it primarily indicates ongoing discussion and fixation on "words and letters." So, There is also the pejorative expression *kattō zen*. Dōgen transforms its meaning into a positive one when he states:

> Although the saints mostly aim at a study that cuts off the root cause of entanglements, they do not learn that "cutting off" means cutting off entanglements by means of entangled discussions. Nor do they know that discussions are entwined by discussions. How could they have the slightest idea that discussions are followed by discussions? Little known is that the Dharma succession is this entwined discussion. No one has heard this. Nor has [anyone] uttered [this] [*dōjaku*]. How could there be many who understand this? My former master, the Old Buddha, said, "The gourd entwines." This exposition before the assembled monks has never been seen nor heard before in any direction past or present; first my former master alone said and pointed this out. That gourd vines entwine gourd vines means that Buddhas and patriarchs explore Buddhas and patriarchs, that Buddhas and patriarchs prove and equal Buddhas and patriarchs. In other words, they transmit [the teaching] from heart to heart [*isshin denshin*]. (DZZ 1: 416–417)

In the same fascicle, Dōgen clarifies that there is no hierarchy among the schools in the tradition or in "individual" transmission between the masters and disciples, regardless of the respective verbal or non-verbal expression of the teaching. According to a story, Bodhidharma instructed his disciple Eka to succeed him with the expression: "You have my mark." According to the conventional interpretation, unlike his rivals, Eka had testified to the most profound understanding of the teaching by responding with a non-verbal gesture. Yet, according to Dōgen, the entire "corpus" of the teaching is always transmitted: encompassing more than just skin, flesh, bone or marrow. This justifies the infinite plurality and reveals the radical sameness in expressing the truth.

"Hidden Words": Names and Words

In this context, all texts have a place, even the "words and letters" used by the sometimes-reviled scribes in their commentaries on the interpretation of the sutras remain valid, although they may no longer hold *universal* validity. Discursive language can also be significant and provide an "actual" expression alongside the non-discursive form. As Dōgen writes in *Hidden Words* ("Mitsugo"):

> If one were to assume that the words (j. *gon*) of the Exalted One [Shakyamuni Buddha] are shallow, so must be his blinking with the eye while holding up the flower [in transmitting the teaching to his next disciple]. Those who take his words as names and forms [j. *myōsō*]

are not disciples who study the Buddha's truth. Although they may be said to know that the words are names and forms, they do not yet know that the Exalted One is [indeed words but] not names and forms. (DZZ 1: 492)

By extending human language to encompass the linguistic richness of things, Dōgen explores the workings of human language itself. Thus, in "name and form," he uncovers a dimension of language that imbues the early Buddhist expression of *myōsō* with a positive connotation and expands the concept of language itself. The historical Buddha uses discursive language without reducing it in its nominal organisation to its designative and representational function. He subverts the pitfalls of attachment and hypostasis in the form of names, thus placing them in their own right alongside present tense expression. Ultimately, there is "nothing hidden" and the relationship between "name and form" and the "declared" presents itself in a relationship of "being familiar with each other" (DZZ 1: 490–491).

"Buddhist Sutras": The Plurality of Languages

Dōgen's critique of the patriarchs surpasses the refusal of a separate name to distinguish the Zen school from other traditions. In essence, it leads to the renunciation of the foundation myth accredited to the first patriarch, Bodhidharma. The claim codified in the founding myth of *furyū monji* to subvert the use of signs in the transmission of the teaching is turned by Dōgen into a plurality of "words and letters," as he writes in "Buddhist Sutras" ("Bukkyō"):

The so-called sutra scrolls are the world itself in all ten directions. There is neither time nor place without sutras. They use the words and letters [j. *monji*] of the supreme truth and the words and letters of everyday truth. The words and letters of heaven and men, as well as the words and letters of animals and spirits. They use the words and letters of the hundred grasses and the thousand woods. (DZZ 2: 15)

In the dualistic view of ordinary and higher truth, the sacred scriptures of Buddhism are first of all the texts written in human "words and letters," from which the "actual" truth nevertheless remains divorced since human language, at best, refers to rather than manifests or actualises the Buddhist truth. Human language, however, is viewed sceptically in the Zen tradition if it is to serve as an instance and preservation of truth. Dōgen turns the scepticism of language around by expanding the meaning of "words and letters" and associating them with the whole world in an all-encompassing way. "Words and letters" do not function solely as human expression; in this way, human language loses its privileged position as a means of expression and is placed in a higher arrangement of the world. There is an infinite variety of languages, just as there is an endless variety of things in the world. Thus, not least, the question arises of the identity and difference of sutras and the world, which can no longer be radically distinguished from a cosmic perspective (cf. DZZ 2: 18).

A Metaperspective on "Dōtoku"

Dōgen does not rely on the "omnipotence" of language, particularly not on the ability of discursive language to represent the world universally and wholistically. Notwithstanding, there is no hint that the Zen Buddhist is opposed to language or, in a positive sense, that language is merely a means of *via negativa*. The absence of a transcendent instance, in the sense of an otherworldly absolute that could be the objective of a – consistently ineffective – attribution, contradicts this in principle. On the contrary, the Buddhist perspective highlights that no external connection can ensure a positive meaning of the world. Instead, the worldliness of Eastern "theology" provides the rationale for a *via positiva*, which has become visible in the preceding. Adhering to the grammar of the subject-object relation, it is impossible to depict the world in its entirety. However, one can articulate it adequately – either verbally or in other forms of expression.

The Unexpressed and the Inexpressible

Thus, for a Zen master, it is without fail possible to find an expression in a cosmological perspective; an expression that is appropriate to the articulateness of the world. In the face of this articulateness, it is precisely his task to give his wisdom and truth an expression, however particular it may be. Kim has already drawn attention to this point when, in his interpretation of Dōgen, he translates the linguistic negation of perfect expression (j. *fudōtoku*) not as the fundamentally inexpressible but as the still unexpressed.[49] In extending the expression to the infinity of all that exists as that which is articulated in each case, the cosmological perspective becomes clear once again. The transcending of individual and momentary attempts at expression towards an articulation of the world also stands out from a temporal perspective. As Dōgen states in the "Dōtoku" fascicle, it stands out when the "then" and the "now" of expression are connected and transcended in opposite directions. In quasi-naturalistic diction, Dōgen invites all practitioners to express themselves spontaneously, but to actually let the Buddha nature itself "have its say" in this.[50]

Meanwhile, this radical positivity of perfect expression is inconceivable from the perspective of Tanabe Hajime earlier. For Tanabe the relationship between expression and non-expression forms an antinomic figure: the tension cannot be resolved or decided in one direction. For him, it is essential to conceive of expression and non-expression as a logical form of opposition. This dualistic conception, however, does not do justice to the diversity of possibilities of expression. In contrast to this logical reduction, Watsuji comes closer to the openness and incompleteness of the forms of expression, since he does not interpret the opposition in the same radically pronounced way. In Watsuji's view, the quasi-contradictory structure between different statements about tradition cannot be fully rationalized.[51] As the dialectical

---

[49] Kim, *Eihei Dōgen: Mystical Realist* (Boston: Wisdom Publications, 2004), 95.

[50] Ibid., 96.

[51] Cf. Müller, "Watsuji's Reading of Dōgen's *Shōbōgenzō*" in Frontiers of Japanese Philosophy, ed. by James W. Heisig and Raquel Bouso (2009), 174–191.

moments of affirmation and negation do not completely cancel each other out either, an irrational residue remains.

Thus, following Watsuji,[52] one can say that Dōgen conceives the perfect expression in a non-dualistic conception of opposites. This conception is by no means merely mediating. Instead, Dōgen aims at a plurality of articulation that also overcomes the formal structure of logic. As a plural dynamic of articulation, the expression spans between the singular manifestation of the Buddha, who is himself interpreted as a sign, and the universal Buddha nature to which the respective individual instantiation of the articulation in its plural constitution points. From the practitioner's perspective, a Buddhist's whole form of life becomes an articulation that has to be performed and thus articulated anew at every moment. Finally, from a linguistic point of view, the expression of the Buddhas and patriarchs is appropriate to what is being expressed. It is a perfect utterance of the attained awakening, yet the latter manifests itself only at the moment of enunciation. Even if the expression is incomplete or perfected, the speaking remains holistic in each instance.

The Breadth of Human Self-Explanation

We can think of what is at stake in Buddhism as something practical, as a path to and of salvation. The corresponding term *dō* for way or path is prominent, but it is more often translated, specifically in the context of Dōgen's reflections, as "principle."[53] Eventually, he claims exclusivity for his account, which certainly justifies speaking of "truth" in the philosophical sense. The Buddhas and patriarchs speak the truth emphatically; their speaking is an authentic expression of truth. Thereby, their expression co-originates with their own being. The content of what is said cannot be separated from the way in which it is said. Moreover, content and form refer to each other. The openness and spontaneity of expression go very far. Through gesture, silence, question or lyrical formulation, they go so far as to push the statement of a discursive dialogue to the level of the expressive, as an expression of, or reference to, the diversity of all that exists itself or the way of life as a whole.[54] In the sense of the second language, it means that the Buddhas and patriarchs do not make use of verbal language alone. Still, it can make use of all forms of articulation – always situationally bound and yet complementary to verbal language as the first language.

Consequently, Dōgen adopts a broad conception of language when, starting from human speech, he also refers to other forms of articulation as *dōtoku*. The word is therefore best translated as "expression." Moreover, insofar as Dōgen starts from an enlightened use of language, the meaning and form of language itself, from a Zen Buddhist perspective, expands into a cosmic dimension. From the perspective of the awakened, everything that exists, animate and inanimate, is imbued with Buddha

---

[52] Ibid.

[53] J. *dōri* 道理.

[54] In the complete edition arranged by Kagamishima, reference is made to the holistic nature of the expression of truth in a comprehensive way of life. Translations into modern Japanese vary considerably.

nature. In other words, the entire world presents itself as an expression of itself. The tradition of silent meditation thus becomes a universal articulation of the world, in which everything that exists relates to each other in universal resonance. An "objectivist" interpretation, in which *dōtoku* is nominally translated as expression and not also grasped verbally, overrides the dynamici of articulation in the inertia suggested by the grammar. However, the world is not trapped in a state of expression, but is subject to constant change. In this, the expression refers to the articulating subject and always remains bound to the perspective of the subject.[55]

This broad concept of language, in turn, permits us to explore first and second language at a meta-level. It also allows us to contrast the expressed and the unexpressed as follows: The unexpressed means that which is non-discursively symbolised. Suppose that what is designated by the expression refers to existence as a whole. In this case, the unexpressed means the sensual-visual dimension of every articulation of life, which is not limited to the intended representation of certain ideas and ideals, but is always intended in its sign-like dimension as well. Ultimately, however, the verbally unexpressed refers to an overarching context of reference from which the literally articulated is to be interpreted as a pre-subjective form of expression.

One can then apply the reference context in the last quoted sentence to the articulating Buddhas and patriarchs themselves, insofar as the plurality of subjects is always already and still present in verbalisation.[56] The plurality of subjects, however, refers once again to the diversity of forms of articulation. Articulation itself is to be seen as an ongoing process of infinite possibilities in the horizon of the still unexpressed. In this process, it is not the absolutely inexpressible as something beyond, but the infinity of this-worldly possibilities. In the world of finite subjects, every articulation remains particular, and no single expression can present the whole, even if it remains related to the multiplicity of being. There remains a final

---

[55] The moment of perspectivity is also central insofar as one can never give an ultimate expression of Buddhist truth. Articulation is processual, albeit undirected and spontaneous. Finally, perfect expression integrates various temporal aspects: the world is always already articulated, but the practitioner is also concerned with generating a present actualisation. Manifestation also encompasses the aspect of the future in the orientation towards the moment of enlightenment and a perpetual transcending of it. Modal aspects of possibility, reality and necessity of articulation can be formulated in relation to temporal aspects.

[56] However, not everything that can be articulated discursively can be articulated non-discursively in a presentational mode and vice versa. A picture says more than a thousand words – a fact that is in turn difficult to express in pictures. What is unique about language is that it unites both structures when used in the form of metaphors and other rhetorical figures which emerge from discursively organised grammatical structures. From the point of view of the articulated world, there is no non-articulation. From the point of view of the subject, there is actualising articulation, which is always only partial. What remains is the inarticulate. In particular, there is the actualising articulation in the form of discursive language that simultaneously says and does not say what is not said. Thus, there are two forms of non-articulation: the discursively inarticulate and the inarticulate in the presenative mode. The contradictory mode of expression forces us to understand *dōtoku* in a broad sense. As a perfect expression, it encompasses the unverbalised as well as the moment of the unsaid.

difference inherent in each expression itself, insofar as it is itself part of the world. There is no outside and zero point from which the context of designation and reference could neutrally begin.

The Limits of Language
Let us return to the initial question of the relationship between speech and silence from the opposite perspective. In this case, the silence of enlightenment can also be made the object of an infinite interpretation, which at the same time points to the performative dimension of all articulation – verbal as well as non-verbal. The supposed self-contradiction in the interpretation of silence as a speechless tradition comes up against the differential identity of statement and action. Still, it does not offer a transcendental zero point of the outside.

Seen from within the Buddhist transmission, Dōgen's *Shōbōgenzō* is the carrying forward of the real, and at the same time, fictitious, text of tradition. And we ought to interpret it as such without discounting the dynamic structure of Dōgen's work and neutralising it hermeneutically. This shows that language in Zen is a complex subject. It is not a mere language-negating attitude that is the basic condition of *kōan* use but rather sophisticated rhetoric that structures the text collections. Even if one integrates this rhetoric into religious practice, basic philosophical ideas can be extracted that are more or less in line with the tradition of Mahāyāna, especially Kegon and Tendai Buddhism, which Dōgen develops further.

While we cannot claim that the second language tradition in Dōgen's coinage is unique and specific to him as a perfect expression within the Zen tradition, his appropriation of the tradition is at least unique in the field of *kōan* literature. It has a double structure: Generally speaking, *kōans* serve as a limitation of discourse since no consequential response in dialogue is possible. In his texts, however, Dōgen pursues, on the one hand, an analytical-hermeneutical strategy that reintegrates *kōans* into discourse. On the other hand, he does not ultimately resolve the *kōans'* opaqueness and elucidate their intrinsic meaning. He retains *kōans* as a means of leading beyond the boundaries of the theoretical text, pointing to symbolisations outside of language.[57]

Based on the use of *kōans*, reflexivity can be introduced into language, allowing for the identification and experience of language's fundamental properties without the need to elaborate theory or terminology. Above all, this sets the Zen tradition apart from the second (or sacred) language that can be detected in various cultures as a whole: as a language practice that can be defined more precisely in terms of rhetoric.[58] Dōgen is positioned within the Zen tradition and intensifies this language practice in two directions. As has been pointed out from the beginning, Dōgen criticises attempts to overcome language based on the notion of a special transmission outside the scriptures. This critique manifests in his texts as a sort meta-level reflecting on tradition in theoretical and philosophical terms. The quasi concept *dōtoku* is

---

[57] See the commentary by Nakimovitch, *Dōgen et les paradoxes de la Bouddhéité* (Genève: Droz, 1999).

[58] Cf. Müller, *Dōgen Sprachdenken* (Freiburg: Karl-Alber, 2013), 347–351.

integral to this reflection and serves to reintegrate *kōans* into the discourse. Further elaboration on Dōgen's reintroduction of *kōans* through rhetoric is also possible.[59]

The objective nature and finiteness of each perspective, which can also be discerned with the shifting between first and second language,[60] are fundamental to the revelation of the uniqueness of all that exists, whether in transcending human language or in reconnecting it to alternative modes of speaking. This fundamental relationality, as highlighted by Dōgen, is inherently linked to the agency of the individual subject. At the same time, it is not possible to exclude this subjectivity in favour of a divine standpoint to cancel out and semantically secure the multiplicity of modes of expression. This is precisely why there is no way out of language, that is, here, out of symbolic articulation.

Silence and the Unspeakable

We have already answered the initial question about the location of the unsaid in silence. We can grasp it from the relationship between first and second language; that is, from the organisation of the forms of the discursive and non-discursive symbols. Silence is not so much a reference to something fundamentally unspeakable as to the fact that one cannot utter the totality of the world in a single sentence. With a view to the first language, it can simultaneously be interpreted as a dismissal of a picture-theory like conception of language. Statements always consist of differences: separating the signified from the signifying. In the horizon of the second language, the essential break away from the conventionalist conception of language consists precisely in not taking a transcendental standpoint; i.e., Dōgen is not taking a step backwards. Rather one needs to interpret the world as a whole as articulated and structured. This is the case even if, from a finite point of view, it can only ever be brought to form in a partial way.

This extension of articulation to the totality of the world is only an apparent contrast to the use of language, since it also encompasses all non-linguistic means of expression such as the withdrawal of expression in silence. Silence, too, can be nothing other than a kind of articulation which, in the worst case, seeks to deprive a previously used expression of its signifying function. Finally, articulation is significant because it encompasses both expressive and interpretative dimensions. In this perspective, it becomes possible to theoretically link discursive and non-discursive moments in a comprehensive concept of experience.

As a final outlook, we ought to note that with the phenomena described we have only taken a first step into another tradition. We can very well rationally describe the dimensions of the second language in the horizon of the first and vice versa in terms of what lies outside Europe or outside what analytical philosophy conventionally interprets. Dōgen, in particular, offers a multi-faceted view in this relationship of languages. Hon the one hand, he presents a specific language practice, yet simultaneously incorporates his own theory, which we can interpret in rudimentary ways, within the horizon of Buddhist ontology. Yet it is precisely the language

---

[59] Cf. the importance of metonymic structure, which can be described using the concept of parallax.
[60] More precisely, the parallactic structure in the relationship between first and second language.

practice – even at the textual level – that, from a Western perspective, presents itself via a theory of rhetoric as an object that reveals the critical and, at the same time, the speculative potential for a comprehensive theory of symbols.

Translation

Perfect Expression

[A: 1.] All the Buddhas and patriarchs are able to express [the truth] perfectly. Therefore, Buddhas and patriarchs, in order to choose Buddhas and patriarchs, certainly ask whether [they] have already expressed [the truth] or not. [They] enquire into this with the heart or with the body; [they] enquire into this with [everyday things such as] the stick and the flyswatter or with pillars and lanterns [and whatever else is at hand]. If [the enquirer and the enquired] are not Buddhas or patriarchs, there is no enquiry, there is no expression; for [without them], there is no ground for it.

[2.] Such an ability to express is not attained by following someone else, and it is not within the capacity of one's own power; only when one really thoroughly investigates the [teachings of the] Buddhas and patriarchs is there the perfect expression of the Buddhas and patriarchs. In this ability to express, one formerly practised and got to the bottom of enlightenment, and also now, one applies one-self to understanding the Way. When Buddhas and patriarchs apply themselves to [the teachings of] Buddhas and patriarchs and affirm what they express, this expression becomes by itself the applying of oneself for three, eight, thirty, or forty years, and it expresses [the truth] expanding all powers. [On the back of the sheet, it is written:] Thirty or twenty years is the period of time it takes to realise the ability to express. This period of time gathers the powers and brings about the perfect expression [of truth].

[3.] Up to this point in time, there has been no lack of ability, may the expression even stretch out into many decades. Thus, the perfect experience when getting to the bottom of enlightenment must be authentic. Since the past experience is authentic, the expression of truth now is unquestionable. Therefore, the expression now carries within it the past experience. [And] the past experience carries within it the expression now. For this reason, there is now perfect expression, and there is now perfect experience. The expression now and the past experience are [continuous and inseparable as] one *Jō* and are [extended as] ten thousand *Ri*. Applying oneself now to [the truth] is, in other words, sustained through perfect expression and perfect experience.

[4.] This applying oneself is relentless and accumulates over many months and long years, and in turn casts off the applying of previous years and months. When you get to where it casts it off, it affirms that it likewise casts off skin, flesh, bones, and marrow and also affirms that it casts off lands, earth, mountains, and rivers. This time, when one aims at reaching the casting-off as the ultimate treasure [of nirvana], this aim is as such [its] emergence, which is why at the very moment of this casting-off, the expression [of truth] immediately manifests. It is neither a power of the heart nor a power of the body, but the perfect expression occurs [through heart and body]. Once the truth has been perfectly expressed, one does not consider it surprising or strange.

[5.] However, when one succeeds in uttering this perfect expression, one keeps quiet about what cannot be expressed. Even if one fully realises what one is able to express – as long as one does not, in an enlightened manner, fathom the inexpressible as that which cannot be expressed, [the expression] is not yet the true face of the Buddhas and patriarchs, nor is it the "bone and marrow" of the Buddhas and patriarchs. Therefore, how can one compare [the wordless] expression [of the Second Patriarch Taiso Eka[61]] [classified as] the marrow [of the truth] when bowing three times [to the First Patriarch Bodhidharma] and remaining in place with the expressions of the [other three] disciples who are classified [as] skin, flesh and bone [of the truth]? The expressions of the latter do not come the least bit close to the expression of the former and have no part in it. That I and others move in different worlds and yet meet is that he and others move in different worlds and yet meet. In me, there is the expressed as well as the unexpressed. In him, there is the expressed as well as the unexpressed. In the said, there is the self and the other, just as in the unsaid, there is the self and the other.

[B: 6.] The Grand Master Shinsai from Jōshū[62] addressed the assembly of monks and said: "If, without leaving the monastery throughout your life, you sit motionless and silent, be it ten or five years, no one will call you a mute. Subsequently, not even all the Buddhas will come close to you!"

[7.] Hence, as one stays in a monastery for ten or five years and repeatedly goes through the frost and the blossoms, considering the applying of oneself to understanding the Way, sitting motionless without leaving the monastery for a whole lifetime constitutes multiple expressions [of the truth]. Without leaving the monastery, [everyday monastic life such as] practising meditative walking, sitting meditation, and lying down, is really so that no one treats you like a mute. Even though you don't know where one's life comes from, it will not leave the monastery if you let it become a monastic life. So, what paths through the sky connect life and monastery? Intensive sitting alone is to be affirmed and do not call it not speaking. Not speaking is the beginning and end of the perfect expression of [truth].

[8.] The motionless sitting is a lifetime or two, not a moment or two. If you sit intensely for ten or five years and do not speak, not even one Buddha should look down on you. In truth, this motionless sitting and non-speaking is what even the Buddha-eye does not see, though it sees [everything]; it is what even the Buddha-power does not attain, though it moves [everything]. For no Buddha does what it is for you to do.

---

[61] Dazu Huike 大祖慧可 (487–593).

[62] The Tang period Chan master Zhaozhou Congshen 趙州從諗 (778–897).

[9.] What Jōshū is saying with his statement about sitting silently motionless is that even all the Buddhas are unable to call someone mute, but neither are they able to call someone not mute. If that is so, then not leaving the monastery for a lifetime means not leaving the perfect expression [of truth] for a lifetime. To sit silently motionless for five or ten years is to express oneself perfectly for five or ten years. [It is] not to leave not expressing oneself for a lifetime; [it is] not to express oneself for five or ten years. [You] sit [yourself] beyond the hundred and thousand Buddhas, the hundred and thousand Buddhas sit beyond you.

[10.] Consequently, the perfect expression of the Buddhas and patriarchs is not to leave the monastery for a lifetime. Even if someone is mute, there will be an expression [of the truth]; do not think that the mute cannot give expression [to the truth]. It is not that one in possession of perfect expression is by any means mute. Even the mute is able to give expression to truth. The voice of the mute is audible, hear the words of the mute. How can one associate and confer with a mute without being mute? [We] are already mutes, how do [we] associate and consult [ourselves]? It is necessary to study in this way and to fathom the mute.

[C: 11.] In the assembly of the Grand Master Shinkaku of Peak Seppō,[63] there had been a monk who went into the mountains and made a hut for himself out of grass tied together. Although years passed, he did not have his hair shorn. Who could know about the life in the hermitage, the signs of life from the mountains were sparse. He fashioned a ladle from a branch and went to the area of a river to draw water to quench his thirst. He was truly of the kind that drinks from rivers. Spending the days and months thus, his secretive way of life became known to the outside world, one day a monk came and asked the hermit, "What is the reason that the founder of the school [Bodhidharma] came from the West?" The hermit said, "The river is deep and the ladle is long." Without saying anything in reply, bowing to him or asking for more, the enquiring monk walked away. He descended the mountain and reported [the hermit's answer] to Seppō. When Seppō heard this report, he said, "[The answer] is most unusual, nevertheless the old monk [Seppō] himself will go and test him; only then does the [hermit], [learn the meaning of the question]."

[12.] Seppō actually said that [the hermit's] answer was so good that it seemed suspicious; therefore, the old monk went himself to test his understanding. So it happened that one day Seppō set off abruptly with an assistant, whom he had made carry the razor. He soon reached the hut. As soon as he saw the hermit, he asked, "If you are able to express [the truth] perfectly, I will leave your skull unshorn."

[13.] This question must be understood! "If you are able to express [the truth] perfectly, I will leave your skull unshaven" sounds as if not shaving expresses [the truth] perfectly. Is that so? If this expression is also a perfect expression, then [the hermit] would remain unshorn in the end. It is valid, if one has the strength,

---

[63] Chan master Xuefeng Yicun 雪峰義存 (822–908), known by the name of Mt. Xuefeng 雪峰山.

to ask for such an expression of truth. And it is necessary to explain [it] for those who have the strength to ask for it.

[14.] At that moment, the hermit stood before Seppō with his head washed. Again, the question is whether he stepped forth because he expressed the truth perfectly or not. So Seppō sheared the hermit's hair.

[15.] This story is as true as the appearance of the Udumbara flower. It is not only rare to encounter it, but also rare to hear of it. It does not occur in the realm of the seven or ten degrees of sacredness, nor is it glimpsed in the three or seven degrees of wisdom. Still less is [the appearance] to be gauged by people like the masters of the sutras and commentaries, or by people who deceive one by virtue of their magic. To witness the Buddha's entry into this world is like hearing such a story.

[16.] Now what about Seppō's statement "If you express [the truth] perfectly, I will leave your skull unscathed"? Those hearers who have not yet given expression [to the truth], but have the strength to do so, will be astonished and doubtful; those who have no strength to do so will be stunned. [Seppō] does not ask what the Buddha is, does not talk about the Way, does not ask what *samadhi* is, and does not talk about *dharani*; to ask in the way [Seppō] does seems like a question, but it is rather like a statement. This should be studied very carefully.

[17.] Meanwhile, the hermit, being authentic, was not stunned when spurred on by [Seppō's] perfect expression. Without denying his way of life, he came forward with his head washed. This is exemplary behaviour that the Buddha's wisdom cannot approach. It must be the appearance of [his] body, [his] exposition of the teaching, the saving of existing beings; it must be stepping forward with a washed head.

[18.] If Seppō had not been that person at that moment, he would have laughed out loud, "Haha!" and dropped the razor. But since Seppō had the strength and was that person [who he was,] he shaved off the hermit's hair. Indeed, had it not been for Seppō and the hermit, and had they not [communicated] from Buddha to Buddha, it [would not] have [happened] like that. Without the first and the second Buddha, it would not have [happened] like this. Without [the encounter between] the dragon and the dragon, it [would not have happened] like this. Although it is said that the black dragon relentlessly protects the gemstone, it is in the hand of the one who can empower himself.

[19.] One must realise: Seppō examines the hermit, the hermit sees Seppō. [One] expresses [the truth] perfectly, [the other] leaves it unsaid: hair is shorn, [someone] shears hair. In other words, there was, contrary to expectation, a way for a good friend who expresses [the truth] perfectly to seek out and question [the hermit]. [And] though he did not expect it, there was a moment of being understood for the companion who left the truth unsaid. When there is a study of [mutual] understanding, there is a manifestation of expression.

This was written on the 5th of October 1242 in the Kannondōri-Kōshōhonrinji. Transcribed on the 2nd of November of that same year by Ejō.

References

DZZ = *Dōgen Zenji zenshū* [Zen Master Dōgen's Complete Works]. 7 vols. Ed. by Sasaki Kakuzen et al., Shunjūsha, 1988–1993.

ZGDJ = *Zengaku daijiten* [Great Dictionary of Zen Studies]. Daishūkan Shoten, 1985.

RICCI = *Grand dictionnaire Ricci de la langue chinoise*. 8 vols. Paris: Desclée de Brouwer.

Katō Shūkō (ed.). *Shōbōgenzō yōgo sakuin* (Index of *Shōbōgenzō* Terms). 2 vols., 1987.

Kim, Hee-Jin. "The Reason of Words and Letters." In *Dōgen Studies*. Ed. by W.R. LaFleur. 54–82. Honolulu: University of Hawaii Press, 1985.

Kim, Hee-Jin. *Eihei Dōgen: Mystical Realist*. Boston: Wisdom Publications, 2004.

Müller, Ralf. *Dōgens Sprachdenken*. Karl-Alber Verlag, 2013.

Nakamura Hajime. *Iwanami bukkyō jiten* [Iwanami Dictionary of Buddhism], Iwanami, 1995.

Nakimovitch, Pierre. *Dōgen et les paradoxes de la Bouddhéité*, Genève: Droz, 1999.

Pörtner, Peter. "Zu Kūkais Sprachphilosophie. Notizen zu 'Shō-ji-jissō-gi.'" In K. Antoni et al. (eds.), *Referate des VII. Deutschen Japanologentages in Hamburg, 11. - 13. Juni 1987*. 261–271. Hamburg: MOAG 1988.

Sakamoto, Hiroshi. "The Voicing of the Way: Dōgen's Shōbōgenzō Dōtoku". In *The Eastern Buddhist* 16 (1), (1983): 90–105.

Schlieter, Jens-Uwe. *Versprachlichung – Entsprachlichung: Untersuchungen zum philosophischen Stellenwert der Sprache im europäischen und buddhistischen Denken*, Köln: edition chōra, 2000.

Sellars, Wilfried. *Empiricism and the Philosophy of Mind*. Cambridge: Harvard University Press, 1997.

Suzuki Daisetz Teitarō. *The Lankavatara Sutra: a Mahayana text*, London: Kegan Paul, 1999.

Index

Printed in the USA
CPSIA information can be obtained
at www.ICGtesting.com
LVHW021821101223
766125LV00006B/485